A HISTORY OF
PRIVATE LIFE

Philippe Ariès and Georges Duby
General Editors

II · Revelations of the
Medieval World

A HISTORY OF PRIVATE LIFE

II · Revelations of the Medieval World

Georges Duby, Editor
Arthur Goldhammer, Translator

The Belknap Press of
Harvard University Press
CAMBRIDGE, MASSACHUSETTS
AND LONDON, ENGLAND

Originally published as Histoire de la vie Privée, vol. 2,
De l'Europe féodale à la Renaissance, © Editions du Seuil,
1985.

Library of Congress Cataloging-in-Publication Data
(Revised for vol. 2)

A history of private life.

   Translation of: Histoire de la vie privée.
   Bibliography: v. 1, p. 647–655; v. 2, p.
   Includes indexes.
   Contents: 1. From pagan Rome to Byzantium /
Paul Veyne, editor—2. Revelations of the medieval
world / Georges Duby, editor; Arthur Goldhammer,
translator.
   1. Manners and customs—Collected works. 2. Family
—History—Collected works. 3. Civilizations—History
—Collected works. 4. Europe—Social conditions
—Collected works. I. Ariès, Philippe. II. Duby,
Georges.
GT2400.H5713   1987   390'.009   86-18286
ISBN 0-674-39976-5 (alk. paper) (cloth)
ISBN 0-674-40001-1 (pbk.)

Contents

Overleaf: Hall and chamber.
Renaud de Montauban, 15th century.
(Paris, Arsenal Library, ms 8073.)

Preface

Georges Duby

IN *Montaillou,* Emmanuel Le Roy Ladurie depicts women, on abundant evidence, as much given to gossip and even more to curiosity, their eyes glued to keyholes, spying out what goes on inside other people's houses so they can tell the neighbors about it. He concludes: "Not until our own day and the advent of more bourgeois societies enamoured of private life did this female espionage diminish or at any rate decline somewhat in the face of repression."

This is a clear statement about a question that this book hopes to answer in part. Is it legitimate (not merely pertinent) to speak of private life in the Middle Ages, to transfer to such a remote era the idea of *privacy,* which first emerged in the nineteenth century in England, at that time the society that had progressed furthest in the establishment of a "bourgeois" culture? All things considered, I believe the question can be answered in the affirmative. It was no more legitimate for historians to apply, say, the concept of class struggle to the feudal era, yet it has proved undeniably useful that they have done so. The exercise not only showed how the concept needed to be refined but, more important, clarified the nature of power relations in an archaic social system, in particular those relations that had nothing to do with class conflict. Hence we have not hesitated to use the concept of private life, anachronistic as it may be. We have attempted to identify the dividing line between what people in medieval society considered private and what they did not, and to isolate that sphere of social relations corresponding to what we nowadays call "private life."

The exploratory, tentative nature of our investigation cannot be overemphasized. The text you are about to read has many question marks. Like archaeologists beginning work on a village abandoned after the Great Plague of the fourteenth century, we have made some initial soundings; like them we expect to discover only a few rich sites—elsewhere coming up empty-handed. The results of our venture depend on the density and quality of the remains: not only written sources but also artifacts, as well as sculpted and painted images that can tell us something about how people lived.

We begin around A.D. 1000, when the documentary record suddenly becomes richer. Another turning point, no less dramatic, occurred some time between 1300 and 1350. After this, everything takes on a new coloration. The change was in part accidental (precipitated, most notably, by the Black Plague of 1348–1350), yet within a few decades it profoundly altered the way people lived throughout the Western world. A related phenomenon is the shift that occurred in the focus of European development, which moved from northern France to Italy primarily but also to Spain and northern Germany. Other changes affect our sources of information, enabling us to see more clearly the realities of what we are calling private life. During the first half of the fourteenth century a large piece of the veil that previously masked those realities was suddenly torn away.

Profound developments led men of that age to study material things with greater lucidity and attention than ever before. As the *contemptus mundi,* the attitude of contempt for the world, that had dominated the high culture of the Middle Ages began to wane, appearances, deceptive and sinful as they may have been thought to be, no longer seemed quite so reprehensible as in the past. Consequently, around 1300, art—the art of representing aspects of life by means of line and volume, the art of painters and sculptors—took a turn toward what we now call realism. The scales fell away from men's eyes. Artists began to transcribe exactly what they saw, using all the techniques of illusion at their disposal. Because painting enjoyed the fullest arsenal of such techniques, it became preeminent among the arts, and the first painted images of intimate scenes began to appear. Through the eyes of the painter we can penetrate the interior of the home, of private space, after 1350, much as the curious women of Montaillou had done a few decades earlier. For the first time the historian has the means to play the voyeur, to observe without indiscretion what went on in this closed world where Van der Weyden, for example, placed the Virgin of the Annunciation and the Angel.

And that is not all. Physical artifacts of private life, of great use to the historian, become much less scarce after the middle of the fourteenth century. Archaeology has recovered vestiges of everyday life that throw light on the last two centuries of the Middle Ages. Most of the excavations have been carried out on the sites of deserted villages—and large numbers of villages were deserted after the Black Plague. Of the castles, urban dwellings, and village houses still extant, the oldest, with few exceptions, date from the fourteenth century, no doubt as a consequence of the rise in the overall standard of living that followed the period of depopulation initiated by the pandemic. This is also true of what remains of furnishings and finery. Look at any museum. At the Cluny, for example, there is an extraordinary disproportion between exhibits of items from after 1300 and those from before; if we look only at those items that concern private life, the disproportion is even greater.

As realism made its influence felt in literature, the texts begin to reveal things that had previously appeared only in brief snatches. The romances ceased to be quite so lost in the mists of reverie. The documents that survive in ever greater numbers in the archives as one moves toward the end of the Middle Ages are more loquacious and inquisitive than earlier sources. Like the new painting, they enable us to glimpse what went on inside the home, to look behind the screens, to insinuate ourselves into domestic interiors and spy on their inhabitants.

Among these new sources are numerous official documents, for by the fourteenth or fifteenth century the state, stronger and more powerful than in the past, had conceived the ambition of total control, of exploiting its citizens to the full. To that end it had to know what went on in people's minds, the better to extort from them their belongings and repress their rebellious tendencies. Public authorities conducted investigations, required declarations, and in various other ways penetrated the secrets of private life. The record book of Jacques Fournier, inquisitor and future pope, from which Emmanuel Le Roy Ladurie learned all he knows about the private life of the peasantry, dates from the beginning of the fourteenth century. Fournier's was but one of many similar investigations, the record of which somehow miraculously escaped the ravages of time.

Because the struggle between rival institutions for control of the lives of private individuals was intensifying during this period, in their efforts to resist, people attempted to construct a "wall" around private life. By the fourteenth century we know a great deal more about what went on behind that wall, because private individuals began to write more than before, because they began to employ notaries for private business, and because we begin to see the first in that unbroken chain of eloquent documents that have proved so useful to historians: estate inventories, marriage contracts, and wills. Soon the archives would begin to collect even more instructive intimate writings: letters, memoirs, and family record books.

As the fourteenth century dawns, we catch sight of a vast panorama that had previously lain almost entirely shrouded in shadow. What people commonly take to be the Middle Ages, the period that serves as backdrop to historical novels, of which we dream along with Victor Hugo and Jules Michelet, is not the period around the year

1000, nor is it the time of Philip Augustus. It is—in terms of feelings, ways of loving, table manners, rules of etiquette, the inner life, and piety—the Middle Ages of Joan of Arc and Charles the Bold. The structure of this book is dictated in large part by the major change that occurs in the first half of the fourteenth century. What comes before is far more problematic and, for our purposes, lacking in substance.

The mists that obscure our view begin to lift around A.D. 1000 and continue to evaporate right down to the dawn of the fourteenth century, thanks to steady material progress and its effects on spiritual life. Three centuries of uninterrupted economic growth is a fact to be reckoned with. What concerns us here, however, is the direct impact of economic growth on the nature of private life. The increasingly common use of money was not without consequence for the concept of personal property, for the very idea of what belongs to one person and not to others. Another consequence of progress was a gradual transition from a gregarious to a more individualistic existence, which led to greater introspection; within the privacy of the house there developed an even more intimate preserve, an inner privacy of the self. This period of general relaxation and constant renaissance saw a greater openness to remote or forgotten cultures: Islam, Byzantium, ancient Rome. People discovered, in the exotic behavior of others, structures in which the relation of public to private was different from what they were used to, and the discovery gradually changed the way they behaved. The steady rise in the standard of living, the unequal distribution of the fruits of the expanding seigneurial mode of production, and the growing differentiation of social roles heightened the contrasts between city and countryside, wealthy and poor households, and men and women. At the same time, the increasingly rapid circulation of men, ideas, and fashions tended to diminish regional distinctions and spread uniform standards of behavior throughout the West.

In a work of this kind all observations must be dated as precisely as possible. Yet we begin at so rudimentary a level that it is not always possible to organize our scant knowledge in strictly chronological fashion. We therefore decided that it would be more appropriate and useful to structure the work differently. Because we do not wish to conceal how fragmentary our understanding is, we have divided the book into various sections. The first of these consists of two parts. One is concerned with private life from 1000 to 1220, focusing primarily on the period 1150–1220 (when the pace of progress apparently quickened, the gap between generations probably was wider than it has ever been until recent times, and the sources for the first time begin to disclose the attitudes of people outside the ambit of the Church). Another deals with a period, region, and social stratum for which we possess especially abundant source materials: the notables of Tuscany in the fourteenth and fifteenth centuries. The last major sections of the book are more adventurous. In them we examine two aspects of the overall evolution of western European society during an extended period of time—the transformation of domestic space and the flourishing of the individual—concentrating on religious and artistic expressions of individuality. Separating these major sections is one dealing with the imagination; it is based on literature from northern France composed between the twelfth and fifteenth centuries. Fiction, though it must be interpreted with a delicate touch, yields irreplaceable information about how private life was actually experienced.

This book is a joint project, and in the early stages we dreamed of working together so closely that it would be impossible to detect what each person had contributed. It quickly turned out that this was too ambitious. We did cooperate quite effectively (especially in the Sénanque colloquia, where we collectively profited from hearing reports of the work of our invited guests). Each of us complemented and corrected the work of the others. Yet in the end it seemed less artificial and more equitable to assign primary responsibility for each part or section to one individual.

A HISTORY OF
PRIVATE LIFE

Revelations of the
Medieval World

A troop of knights. Illustration from Vincent of Beauvais, *Miroir historial*, 13th century. (Boulogne Library, ms 130.)

1

Introduction

Georges Duby

A private gift of public power. Scene of investiture, fresco in Ferrande Tower, Pernes-les-Fontaines, ca. 1270.

✣ Private Power, Public Power

WHAT was private life like in the feudal age? To answer this question requires a sound method, and there is none better, I think, than to begin with words, to explore the terrain of semantics and ferret out the niche in which the concept of privacy lies hidden. In choosing this approach I feel that I am being faithful to the spirit of the learned men of the time, whose function was similar to mine and who, being first of all grammarians, attempted to fathom the unknown by studying vocabulary, by proceeding from what they knew well to what they knew less well.

In nineteenth-century French dictionaries, compiled at a time when the notion of private life first took on its full importance, one finds the verb *priver*, meaning to tame or domesticate. The example in Littré's dictionary, *oiseau privé* (domesticated bird), reveals the meaning of the word: to pluck a creature from the wild and move it into the familiar surroundings of the home. We also find the adjective *privé*, which in a more general way also suggests the family, the home, the domestic interior. Among the examples cited by Littré is an expression just then coming into current use: "Private life should be lived behind walls." He proposes the following, highly revealing gloss: "It is not permissible to inquire or talk about what goes on in the home of a private individual [*particulier*]." As the word *particulier* in its primary, direct, and most common meaning indicates, private is here opposed to public.

In order to understand the meaning of private, we must refer to the word *public*. Here is Littré's definition: "That which belongs to an entire people, that which concerns an entire people, that which emanates from the people." In other words, authority and the institutions that support it, the state. This primary meaning shades into another: we call public that which is shared in common or available for the use of all, which is not subject to private appropriation but accessible or widely distributed. This derivation leads to the noun *the public*, designating the group to which public goods are available or distributed. The shift in meaning does not end here: public also refers to that which is openly visible, manifest. Thus the word came to signify the opposite of private in the sense of private property, that which belongs to a particular individual, as well as the opposite of *hidden, secret,* or *reserved* (what is removed from public view).

In classical Latin a similar constellation of meanings clustered about the antonym *publicus/privatus*. In Cicero's vocabulary, to act *privatim* (the adverb whose opposite is *publice*) is to act not as a *magistratus* invested with a power emanating from the people but as a simple private individual, in a different juridical realm; the private act was one committed not in the open, in the forum, before the eyes of all, but inside one's own house, in isolation, hidden from the view of others. The noun *privatum* refers to a person's own resources, property for his own use; and, again, to the home (*in privato, ex privato*: inside or outside the home). *Privus* denotes both the singular and the personal. Thus the two systems of meanings, that of nineteenth-century French and that of classical Latin, are the same: the root meaning of *public* is that of common possession by all the people; in opposition to this we have two derivative senses of *private*, one conveying the idea of exemption or departure from common usage, the other conveying a sense of domesticity—the private individual surrounded by those who are close to him. The legal concept embraces that which escapes the jurisdiction of the "public power," the power of the people, as well as that which is protected against intrusion by the mob. The *res publica* encompassed whatever belonged to the community as a whole and which was therefore *extra commercium*, immune from being bartered on the marketplace. The *res privata*, on the other hand, was *in commercio* and *in patrimonio*, in other words, subject to a different power, that of the *pater familias*, primarily exercised within the walls of the *domus*, or house.

If we turn to the Middle Ages and consult the glossaries of Du Cange or Niermeyer or Godefroy, we find—not surprisingly, since the semantic structure is the same in the nineteenth century as in classical Rome—that it remained

essentially unchanged in the interim. The Latin of the chronicles and charters characterizes as *publicus* that which falls to
the sovereign, which is part of his regalian rights or which
falls within the jurisdiction of the magistrates charged with
preserving peace and justice (as in the expressions *via publica,
functio publica, villa publica,* or in Marculf's Merovingian formula, *publica judiciaria potestas*). The *publicus* was the agent of
sovereign power, the *persona publica*, responsible for acting
on behalf of the people to defend the rights of the community.
As for the verb *publicare*, its meaning was to confiscate, seize,
remove from private use or ownership. In a bequest, for
example, we read: *Si absque herede obirent* (If the donors die
without heirs) *ad monasterium publicatur praedia vel quid haberent
hereditario jure* (all that they held under the laws of inheritance
shall be withdrawn and assigned to the monastery). Or consider this, from Ordericus Vitalis' *History*: *Si facultates inimi-
corum publicarentur paupertas egenorum temperaretur* (If the
possessions of the enemies were confiscated, the poverty of
the indigent would be diminished).

In opposition to *publicus* and related words, *privatus* and
its derivatives take on their various meanings, suggesting the
familial and nonfestive. (In the Rule of Saint Benedict, for
example, *privatis diebus* means non-holy days.) The notion of
the festival will prove to be important in what follows. We
shall be looking at ceremonies and staged spectacles, at the
gestures that people made, the words they spoke, and the way
they presented themselves to others. Words associated with
privacy were not applied to this kind of festive behavior but
reserved for more homely activities, especially those prescribed by rule for monks. Thus, in one document in the
archives of the abbey of Saint-Gall, a donor stipulates: *Filius
meus privitatem habeat inter illis fratribus* (My son will have this
privitas among the brothers of the monastery), that is, he will
enjoy the privileges collectively belonging to the members of
the closed, isolated monastic community, separated by the
walls of the monastery from public society. The word *privatus*
also came to mean "in retreat." In a genealogy composed by
Lambert of Saint-Omer early in the twelfth century, *privata* is
used to describe the life that Robert le Frison, count of Flanders, led for a time at the monastery of Saint-Bertin. This was
indeed a "private" life, for this prince, this *persona publica*
invested with the power of governing his people, made a
retreat during the Lent prior to his death, temporarily abandoning his sovereign role. By choosing to live inside the

cloister, as a simple private individual, and by abandoning his arms, symbols of his power, he entered another realm of law, another *ordo*, that of penitence. Culminating this line of etymological evolution, the word *privatae* in the written Latin of the monasteries denoted latrines.

In the Romanesque vernaculars the word "private" meant almost the same thing as in Latin. *Privé, privance,* and *priveté* refer, in courtly French, to the people and things included within the family circle (familiars and not strangers, *estrayns o privats,* as it is phrased in a chanson by William of Aquitaine), to the domestic, to that over which the master of the house exercised his power ("his men led by twelve of his *privés,*" says Wace). The attachment remains even when this group is drawn into the outside world ("wherever I am, I am your *privé,*" we read in the Chanson d'Aspremont). We also find a shift in meaning toward the intimate and secret, the same as in Latin and modern French. The *Quest for the Holy Grail* speaks of "great secrets and *privetés* of Our Lord," and when Wace, in the *Roman de Rou,* based on Dudo of Saint-Quentin, shows the notables of Normandy gathered in secret assembly to search for ways to avoid the exactions imposed on their land by the Franks, he says that they have met *privément,* in other words, not as in those meetings held in the open where people spoke their minds and deliberated upon matters of common concern. Here, although the meeting is concerned with the common interests of the community, it is carried on in secret, behind closed doors. This shows how the meaning of the word changed from affectionate intimacy to clandestine, hence suspect, activities—suspect, that is, in the eyes of oppressive outside authorities. It was therefore the duty of the authorities to uncover and ferret out such private conspiracies. Thus the relation between public and private came to be one of conflict, and the private was seen as contained within an enclosure, a protected zone, much like a fortress under siege.

This much we learn from a preliminary look at the vocabulary. Let me call attention to the solidity of the meaning of privacy. The concept remained constant over the ages. Quite obviously the idea embodied in the Latin word *privatus* was still quite clear in the feudal age: namely, that there are acts, individuals, and objects by law not subject to public authority; for that reason they are situated in a precisely delineated sphere designed to thwart any attempt at intrusion. Now, since my purpose is not to define privacy in general but private life as opposed to public life, the first point to note is that this opposition hinges on place. The zone of private life is apparently that of domestic space, circumscribed by walls, like those of the cloister to which Count Robert of Flanders retired so as to exclude from his mind all thoughts but those of his soul; the tenor of his existence changed the moment he crossed the threshold. Note, however, that there are degrees of seclusion and that the notion of private life is relative, since one moves gradually from the most external to the most internal, from the forum, highway (*strada, estrade*), or stage to the ultimate redoubt where the individual locks away his most precious riches or thoughts, where he closets himself away in positions that it would be indecent to exhibit publicly. Consequently, it must be acknowledged that the opposition between private life and public life is a matter not so much of place as of power.

But the contrast is not between power and nonpower; it is between two different kinds of power. Think of two realms in which peace and order were maintained in the name of different principles. In both the individual was disciplined, supervised, corrected, and punished, but correction and punishment were administered by different authorities. In one the purpose was to govern the *res publica*, the *populus*, the group of men (women had no place here) who, assembled, constituted the state, administered communal property, and shared responsibility for the common good. This is the realm of collective, hence inalienable goods; as the Romans said, the public good is *extra commercium*. The *res populi* is *res nullius*, and its administration is the responsibility of the magistrate, of *rex* and *lex*, the king and the law, the latter being the voice of the people. Between the *res publica* and what twelfth-century texts explicitly designate as the *res familiaris* stands a fundamental legal barrier. One of the cartularies of the Cluny abbey contains a document entitled *dispositio rei familiaris*. It is a plan of management drawn up in 1148 at the behest of the father of the Cluniac fraternity, Abbot Peter the Venerable, and concerned with improving the domestic economy, as it was within his duty and power as *pater familias* to do. The *res familiaris* was clearly a cornerstone of family life, where family here refers to a community distinct from the community of all the people, defined by its natural meeting place, or perhaps I should say its natural place of confinement, the house. This private community was governed not by law but by "custom." Certain members of the community were also members of the larger community and therefore fell under the jurisdiction of the law, but only as long as they remained outside the private community and participated in public life.

Private life is therefore family life, not individual but convivial and founded on mutual trust. Associated with the various words for privacy was a constellation of other terms. One of them, *commendatio*, merits further comment. It is a key word because it defined the initiation into the harmonious private community. How should it be translated? Commendatio was an act whereby an individual pledged himself, his very person, to the leader of the group and through the leader to all the group's members. The relation between member and leader, a very powerful emotional bond, was called "friendship" in both Latin and the vernacular; it was the cement that held the group together. These friendships formed a bulwark against the "law," which insinuated itself wherever it could, manifesting its power when successful through a symbolism of penetration.

Privacy in Early Medieval Law

Before beginning to study the place of private life in what has been called feudal society, we must locate the boundary between two rival powers, one of which was considered "public." The nature of feudal society was dramatically disclosed when, in the last two decades of the tenth and the first two decades of the eleventh century, the rotten facade of the state, which had long obscured the underlying social structure, finally collapsed. What occurred then may seem an invasion of the state by private powers. In fact, however, the power structure now exposed to public view was not new; it had existed for a long time. Previously the documents had scarcely mentioned it, and then always inadvertently; suddenly they begin to talk about it openly. This is the essence of a change that has been called the "feudal revolution." Official documents never mentioned these existing power relations because they were still evolving, still taking shape gradually, out of the public eye, in a realm of which we usually know nothing. They were *private* relations that were now thrust into the foreground and made paramount over all others. Historians generally agree that feudalization represents a privatization of power. We read, for example, in J.-F. Lemarignier's *France médiévale* (p. 119), that "public laws ultimately took on a patrimonial character, and customs, considered in this light public laws, became the object of transactions." Patrimony and transaction: these were precisely the features which, in classical law, distinguished the *res privatae* (which were *in commercio, in patrimonio*) from the *res publicae*. To put it rather dramatically, as society became feudal, the public sphere shrank steadily until ultimately everything was private, and private life was everywhere.

Nevertheless, feudalization should also—and, I think, primarily—be seen as a fragmentation of public power. In Lemarignier's words: "Public authority was dismembered and at times reduced to little more than crumbs." This crumbling of authority ultimately resulted in a broad dissemination of the prerogatives of government; each great household became a sovereign state unto itself, where the power exercised by the master, though limited in scope, nevertheless preserved its original nature, which was public. So we might equally well say that in feudal society everything became public. What happened in reality was that aspects of power perceived to be public diminished in importance up to the beginning of the twelfth century; then, as states began to reconstitute themselves, the extent of public authority again began to increase. At no time, however, not even at the nadir of public authority—around 1100—did people lose sight of the idea that there is a specifically public way to rule. They continued to believe in the existence of distinctly public rights such as the regalia, to which the emperor laid claim in Italy in the twelfth century. (His claim was based on Roman law, newly rediscovered in this period of renaissance, of return to classical juridical forms that had been swept away by the great feudal wave.) Study of the political vocabulary has shown that the private-public distinction survived. How did the social significance of the distinction change in this time of upheaval?

What obstacles did public power encounter? At the base of society stood what was called, in Latin, the *populus*: a community of adult males, distinguished by their free status. In the late tenth century, when the feudal revolution began, to be free meant to partake of both rights and duties, fixed by law. The free man enjoyed the right and duty to work with his fellows to maintain the *res publica*. (Admittedly the notion of the *res publica* was clearly formulated only in the minds of the highly educated; still, it was familiar to most literate people, for whom the ideal of peace and justice on earth simply mirrored the perfect order already prevailing, by God's will, in heaven.) It was the free man's right and duty to defend the community, as well as the country in which it was located, the *patria*. (Like the *res publica*, the notion of *patria* had survived from antiquity and was still current, as is proven by numerous allusions in the twelfth-century chronicles; the concept of public activity was very closely associated with a sentiment that can only be called patriotism.) Free men were supposed to defend their community against aggression by participating in military expeditions—expeditions referred to in early-eleventh-century Catalan documents as "public." They were also supposed to defend it against internal dissension, or "peace-breaking," by avenging "public" crimes serious enough to sully the reputation of an entire people; in assemblies called "public" they helped reconcile other free men who through some misfortune found themselves in conflict.

These activities were carried out under the direction of magistrates invested with coercive powers. Magistrates were authorized to convoke the army, to lead it into battle, to preside over assemblies of justice, and to carry out the judgments of those assemblies. In compensation for these services they received a portion of the fines levied on free men who broke the peace. Their power varied. It was greatest when in the field with troops outside the "fatherland." Inside the borders the power of magistrates was most oppressive and invasive in what were called "dangerous" times (the word *danger* being a derivative of the Latin *dominiura*, denoting a need to exercise greater powers of domination and more strict discipline). Night was one such time: at Valenciennes, for example, peace ordinances adopted in 1114 refer to a curfew bell that signaled when fires were to be extinguished in all hearths and everyone was to return home. Evacuating public space ensured that no one would remain abroad except the enemies of peace, who would thereby reveal themselves and become easier to eliminate.

Part of the territory of the fatherland fell under the jurisdiction of the public authorities. The *Usages of Barcelonne* from the second half of the twelfth century state that "the highways and public roads, running water and fountains, meadows, pastures, forests, and garrigues" are public. Thus public territory included primarily roads and other places of passage, but by extension also places where any errant (meaning stranger to the community, hence suspect) creature or person was likely to be found. Such places were kept under surveillance. They were by their very nature "dangerous," because they were visited by people who came from other places and were unknown locally (like the communities of aubains, or resident aliens) or people whose beliefs and rites excluded them from the community (like the Jews). Also included in public territory were areas of wilderness, or *saltus*, uncultivated or uncultivatable land, grazing areas, hunting grounds, places for gathering the fruits of nature. All these were the collective property of the people. In the Mâconnais in 1000, this public territory was referred to as the "land of the Franks," meaning that it belonged not to any one individual but to the entire community.

Public law tells us about times, places, ways of acting, and social categories. It also defines the boundaries of a sphere over which the magistrates had no power, a sphere whose independence was indicated by obvious signs. Medieval culture had little use for writing but made a great deal of emblems. Because private property legitimately existed in the private sphere, the signs designating that sphere expressed first of all a right of ownership. Wooden poles (about which so much is said in the so-called barbarian laws composed in Frankish Gaul) were stuck in parcels of land to indicate that the land belonged to a particular individual. They were planted in meadows when the grass began to grow and in fields when the wheat first sprouted—in other words, at the season when the cultivated plot ceased to be indistinguishable from common grazing land. I have no hesitation in drawing an analogy between these poles and the pickets with banners that troops planted in conquered lands to distinguish between private booty and collective spoils. Such pickets are mentioned by the chronicler Galbert of Bruges in his account of the troubles that followed the murder of Charles the Good, count of Flanders, in 1127. Various groups of assailants hastened to attach their insignia to the tower of the murdered count as well as that of the provost of the chapter accused of leading the assassins. These properties were ripe for the taking, for the crime that had just been committed rendered them vulnerable to public vengeance. The first marauders to seize the now public prey withdrew it from collective ownership and incorporated it into their own patrimony; enclosures went up around the booty, like those that surrounded fields and meadows prior to cultivation.

The most important sign of appropriation and privacy was not the banner, however, but the barrier, the enclosure, the hedge—a sign of the utmost legal importance of which there is much discussion in the regulations governing social life. Consider Salic Law 34,1 concerning "those who break enclosures (*saepes*)," or Burgundian Laws 55, 2 and 5, which state that "when a boundary marker is removed or broken, if it is done by a free man he shall have his hand cut off, and if it is done by a slave he shall be killed." The reason for this severity is that the nature of the peace is not the same on both sides of the boundary: outside it is public, inside private. The Frankish texts distinguish between the *clausum*, within which vinestocks were planted, and the hedge (*haia*) surrounding the park (*foresta*), uncultivated but enclosed land; both, however, were private territory, not subject to public law. The distinction is sharpest, however, with respect to the "court."

The word *court* comes from the Latin *curtis*, which in its primary meaning is synonymous with *saepes*, enclosure (as in the Law of the Bavarians 10,15), but it designates a particular kind of enclosure, that which is erected around the house. Court and house are in essence one, together constituting the *casa*. This much is clear from a document found at the abbey of Saint-Gall and dating from 771: *casa curte circumclosa cum domibus edificiis* (the casa [or territory governed by private law in which the family resides] enclosed by the court, with houses, buildings). Or again, consider the capitulary *De villis*, an edict containing rules of administration for the royal estates issued in the time of Charlemagne: *ut edificia intra curtes nostras vel saepes in circuitu bene sint custodire* (keep a close watch on things built inside our courts and our fences). The enclosure circumscribed the protected zone to which men retired to sleep, where they kept their most precious belongings, and where they were required to stay after curfew. Perhaps the best analogy is from biology: the court was like a cell, with the house as nucleus and the enclosing fence or wall as membrane, together forming a unified whole to which texts from the Carolingian era refer as the *mansus*, the place where a man lives.

Some houses were not surrounded by enclosures. A peace edict promulgated in Allemania in the early twelfth century proclaims: "Let them have peace within houses and courts as well as within those legitimate areas [that is, recognized by public law, to which such enclaves posed an obstacle] known in the vulgar tongue as *Hofstatten*, whether surrounded by an enclosure or not." Either the absence of a wall was accidental or, more commonly, dwellings were grouped within a common enclosure that served the entire village. Normally no house was without a surrounding enclosure. When attempts were made to create new villages for colonists to settle, it was carefully stated that the lots for building were "courts" and that the first thing to be done was to erect an enclosure (*Liber traditionum* of Freising, 813). The purpose of the enclosure was to ward off violence, to drive it away from the place where people were most vulnerable, and the law—public law—was at pains to guarantee the safety of the *atrium*, "vulgarly referred to as the court" (says Hariulf's chronicle), by threatening with severe punishment anyone who dared to violate the taboo and cross the threshold, especially at night. Theft, arson, and murder committed by an intruder inside the enclosure were subject to twice the usual penalty, for the crime was doubled: besides the offense itself the criminal committed the further felony of breaking and entering. On the other hand, if the criminal happened to be a person who normally resided within the walls, the magistrate could not intervene, could not enter the courtyard, unless invited by the head of household. In the early Middle Ages, courts were like islets dotting the territory, exempt from public law, refuges within which the "people" asserted collective rights and acted as a community. Anyone who decided to venture outside had to take along another, more visible protective shield, another emblem of protection. For free men this meant bearing arms, signs of their freedom. Women were required to cover their heads with a veil.

Within the walls were kept all the *res privatae* or *res familiares*: private, movable property including reserves of food and clothing and livestock as well as those human beings not counted as part of the *populus*, such as males too young to bear arms, take part in military expeditions, or sit in assemblies of justice; women; minors; and the nonfree of both sexes and all ages. These people were under the jurisdiction not of public law but of the authority of the head of household, the *domus* or *dominus* (as the Latin sources put it). They were said to be "in his hand," or, to use the Latinized German of the scribes, in his *mundeburnium*, pieces of property like the livestock in his stables; they comprised the *familia, mesnage, maisnie,* or *masnade*. These people came into another "hand," that of the public authorities, in only three circumstances: (1) if they ventured outside the enclosure onto public territory, roads, or places and were not accompanied by either the head of the household or other free men of the family; in such cases they were classed with aliens, and it was up to the magistrate, as surrogate for paternal authority, to oversee their "conduct" and maintain discipline; (2) when the head of household was absent and no free adult male capable of protecting the minors of the "family" was available; it was the original function of the king, which he delegated to his agents, to take care of widows and orphans; and (3) the authority of the magistrate could be expressly invoked by an appeal, a complaint, known as the *clamor* or "hue and cry"; the grievance was thus made public, and the guilty parties turned over to communal authorities.

The truth of the matter is that the dividing line between public and private, although still referred to in official tenth-century documents, had long been obscured by private encroachment. This was not a consequence of Germanic influences overwhelming Roman, of barbarism driving out civilization; the change had already begun to take place before the destruction of the classical culture of the ancient world. It was connected with ruralization: the city, which had been conceived as a stage for the exhibition of public power, was slowly invaded by the countryside, while the power of the magistrate was increasingly scattered among rustic households. Imperceptibly the "court" supplanted the city as the primary model of social life. Of course the idea persisted, at least in the minds of cultivated men, that the function of the king was to preserve peace and justice in a community of free men, that it was the king's duty to be the agent of what Jonas of Orléans in the early tenth century called "peace in its plenitude" and to bring about the "unanimity of the people." Nevertheless, as a consequence first of all of the Christianization of kingship, the king, looked upon as the representative of God, to be sure, but God the Father, slowly came to be perceived as a father himself, invested with a power analogous to that of the fathers who governed in every household. Furthermore, his kingly powers came to be seen more and more as his private, personal, and hereditary property. This private appropriation of public power began at the top of the political hierarchy. As Fustel de Coulanges remarked long ago, *publicus* in ancient Rome meant that which belonged to the people; in Frankish Gaul, that which belonged to the king. The regalian power had become family property transmissible through copulation, through the blood, to one's offspring; at each inheritance it was either divided among the children "of the blood" or held undivided by a group of brothers, like a house. Slowly the *palatium* or palace in which the sovereign rendered justice came to be seen as a dwelling place, affecting the meaning of certain words such as the Latin *curia*.

Originally that term referred to the assembly of the Roman people; later it came to mean the Senate. In surviving documents the meaning of *curia* begins to shift in the eighth century toward *curtis*, designating the enclosure from which public power is legitimately excluded. Conversely, even the best of scribes use *curtis* in speaking of the royal palace. In the most solemn documents they place the words *in curte nostra* in the mouth of Charlemagne. Clear evidence of this interpenetration can be seen in the structure of the imperial palace at Aix, the prototype of all princely residences in the Middle Ages. Some elements of this ungainly building were constructed of fine stone like that used in the public edifices of ancient Rome, harking back to the urban civic tradition: the monumental gate; the gallery and the two buildings at either of its extremities; the basilica to the north where the sovereign pronounced the law and gave orders to enforce it; and the oratory to the south, preceded by an atrium where the people gathered to look upon their sovereign standing above them or to listen to him speak from a loggia. Here, however, the throne faced inward, which gave the sanctuary something of the look of an enclosed room in which the members of the household sat at the feet of the master, the terrestrial image of the heavenly Father. And did not the facade look like a *curtis*, a barricade between the outside world and the place where the king lived with his familiars, bathed, slept in wooden buildings, and fed his men? The palace at Aix and palaces subsequently erected elsewhere by other Carolingian princes (like one recently excavated at Fécamp, built on orders of Duke Richard of Normandy) actually resembled a Roman *villa rustica*, housing huge staffs divided into two major departments, the chapel and the chamber, which had somehow invaded buildings that appeared to be public. In the chapel the ecclesiastics of the "family" flanked the master whenever he prayed in public, but they served him even more frequently on "private" days, when he withdrew to pray in seclusion. In the chamber was kept the strongbox, which was no longer regarded, except by linguistic habit, as the public treasury, the *arca publica*; now it contained the most precious items of the *res familiaris*. For Carolingian kings, according to a biographer of Louis the Pious, these included "royal ornaments [emblems of power, now regarded as private objects], weapons, vases, books, and priestly vestments." For the Monk of Saint-Gall, the chamber was a cloakroom where all kinds of clothing were kept, and we know from a diploma of Charles the Bald dated 867 that flax and wool garments woven by peasant dependents were collected there each year, along with gifts received from the most powerful men in the empire. All such gifts, products of an obligatory but private generosity, together with fees levied on slaves taken into the royal household—everything except for beverages and fodder for the horses—were placed, according to the domestic rules of the Carolingian palace, under the supervision of the king's wife, who, being a woman, was excluded from the *populus* and confined to the palace: a powerful symbol of the ineluctable transfer of power from the public to the private sphere.

Another clear sign was the nature of the bond between the king and the members of his entourage. This was a nomadic group, which ventured forth each spring on military adventures and at other times on hunting parties into the wilderness. What bound its members together, in the palace and at temporary campsites, was at first the fact that they took meals together, eating with the master, whom they viewed as a source of nourishment; these were the "king's guests" mentioned in Salic Law. Meals thus played a preeminent symbolic role in the rites of power. Devotion to the sovereign, expressed by the word *obsequium* (deference), and the free gift of their services made the royal dinner companions dependent on the king's patronage. The bond was sealed by a gesture of the hands: the master clasped within his two hands the joined hands of the man who, by thus submitting his body, placed himself in the posture of a child before his father. Owing to the growing importance attached in the eighth, ninth, and tenth centuries to the gestures associated with the distribution of food and the establishment of pseudo-filial trust, *functio*, or public service, became increasingly identified with attitudes of friendship, gratitude for food received, and deference of client toward patron. In springtime, when everyone of importance in the Carolingian state assembled in the presence of the king, the atmosphere resembled that of a family reunion, with an exchange of gifts and banqueting. This royal ostentation was not a luxury but a necessity. Public and private mingled freely. If the palace increasingly resembled a private house, the house of every man who possessed a fraction of the regalian power had to be made to look like a palace. It had to be open, its interior on display; even more important, the master's meal had to be a ceremonial occasion. The very high aristocracy, the counts, turned their homes into palaces as early as the ninth century. Counts stood in for the absent king in palaces erected in the cities of the kingdom. Like the sovereign they were simultaneously public figures and generous fathers; to demonstrate their generosity they exhibited their *privance*. The process of feudalization began with this diffusion of the royal household model.

In the decades preceding A.D. 1000 the pace of change accelerated. The chain of authority broke in numerous places, leaving isolated pockets of power. In the past, kings in their incessant peregrinations had visited innumerable scattered palaces, which between royal visits were occupied by counts; these now became autonomous. For some time the counts in France had considered the public power delegated to their ancestors by the king a part of their own patrimony. The roots of dynasties were planted in cemeteries, and the kin of the counts were organized in lineages, just like those of the king. Claiming the emblems and virtues of royalty for themselves, the counts little by little ceased to make regular calls upon the sovereign; their withdrawal, along with that of the bishops, dimmed what memories remained in the royal court of the days when power was a public good. By 1050–1060 the Capetian monarch's only remaining allies were his close relatives, a few hunting companions and comrades-in-arms, and the heads of his household departments. The powers of peace and justice were exercised locally by independent princes, who from time to time met where their respective territories touched, on neutral ground, to declare their friendship. At these meetings each prince comported himself as a monarch, treating the portion of the kingdom subject to his power as an annex of his household.

So sudden was the ascendancy of images and customs formed by, and long associated with, private life that people soon began to conceive of the state as a kind of family. Consider two examples. That excellent historian Landolf the Old described, some fifty years after the fact, what the principality of Milan had been like around A.D. 1000. He speaks of Milan, the city and its rural surroundings, as though he were describing a household—in this case the household of Saint Ambrose, since the regalian power now belonged to the saint's successor, the archbishop of Milan. It was a well-ordered household, with the various domestic functions in its immense court divided among ten offices, or "orders," as Landolf calls them. These were hierarchically ordered, each run by a "master." Highest in rank and most numerous were the departments

Feudalism and Private Power

charged with administration of the sacred. At the bottom of the hierarchy, however, were two departments concerned with secular matters. One comprised the archbishop's household staff. The other was run by the viscount, heir to the magistrates of old but now considered a private officer. Under its head were included, for the purpose of enforcing the laws or waging war outside the *domus*, all the people of Milan, the entire community of free men, or "citizens" as they are called here, although Landolf sees them as domestics of the prince, whom all are supposed to serve. In return the citizens claim the prince as their patron and expect Saint Ambrose to defend them as would their own father. On occasion they expect to be fed by the saint; indeed Archbishop Ariberto is shown in time of famine distributing coins and clothing and ordering the master of the bakery to prepare eight thousand loaves each night and the master of the kitchen to boil eight large measures of broad beans to feed the hungry. The effect of this image is to incorporate all the people thus fed into the prince's private household.

A second example, also Italian but from a later period, is taken from a document celebrating the victorious expedition of the Pisans against Majorca in 1113. This epic admittedly distorts the symbolism somewhat, but the distortion makes the meaning only more apparent. The camp of the Pisan army, that is, of the public community convoked for the purpose of military adventure, is again compared to a house, or, rather, to a large hall decked out for one of the feasts the master is obliged to offer his commensals. The tent of the archbishop, who takes the place of Christ, occupies the center; it is surrounded by the tents of the twelve "great men" who, taking the place of the apostles, lead troops of combatants. These leaders are bound to the prelate by kinship, their duty as vassals, and the fiefs they hold of him, that is, by private bonds. Each is the patron of a "company" (from the Latin *cum-panis*, with bread, again suggesting the idea of shared nourishment) drawn from the populace, whose tents form a large circle ringing the smaller circle of the nobility. Patronage upon patronage: that is the image of princely power in this time. Each prince thought of his house as sheltering under its wings a number of subordinate households, each directed by a grandee exercising power, analogous to that of the prince, over a portion of the population.

In the eleventh century these satellite houses were castles, edifices combining symbols of public and private power: on the one hand the tower, looming and erect emblem of the power of coercion; on the other hand the enclosure (the castle wall or *chemise* as it was called in Old French), emblem of domestic exemption. Actually autonomous, these houses were always pictured in imagination as though surrounded by the house of some patron. Nor was the patron's house considered totally isolated from the palace of the king. By custom the heads of subordinate families were obliged temporarily to ally themselves with the master of the family above them in the hierarchy. When the latter, emulating the Carolingian kings of old, invited his friends to gather on major holidays in his court (which the scribes cannot make up their minds whether to call *curtis* or *curia*), they spent several days ostensibly playing the role of servants.

Listen to Thietmar of Merseburg describing the court presided over by the king of Germany at the beginning of the eleventh century. Four dukes serve their prince. (Thietmar uses the word *ministrare*; in this reconstruction of the scene, these great personages play the role of *ministeriales*, each heading up a domestic department.) One is in charge of food, of the king's table; this is the highest position in the hierarchy. Another is in charge of the bedchamber, a third of the wine cellar, a fourth of the stables. These convivial, almost cousinly relations were experienced for much longer periods by the sons of patrons of the second rank, who commonly spent their adolescence in the next-higher-ranking court, eating with the master, sleeping and hunting in his company, educated by him, vying with one another to please him, receiving from him clothing and pleasure and eventually arms and possibly even a wife. Weapons and a woman; these were the essentials that every vassal needed to set up a household of his own, independent yet closely linked to the prince's succouring household by reminiscences of shared youth. The fundamental point is that it was in the forms of private life that public power "disintegrated" in the feudal era. Friendship had its source in private life, as did pledges of mutual service and hence that devolution of the right to command, which was held to be legitimate only where there was mutual devotion, of protector toward protégés and of protégés toward protector. The image that ultimately emerged was a hierarchy of four degrees: the royal household, the princely households, the castles, and the people, living in groups around each castle tower.

With the advent of what we call feudalism, two distinct

classes of people emerged. Only some adult males were fully entitled to perform the paramount civic office, that of bearing arms, furnished with the finest equipment. In the Latin texts they are referred to as *miles*, which means warrior, although a Latinized form of a word from the spoken language, *caballarius*, means horseman or knight. The natural place for these men to perform their assigned mission was the fortress, where they gathered for limited periods to perform garrison duty. They also repaired to the fortress when, there being some threat to public peace, the "cry of the castle" resounded across the countryside. The master of the castle was commander of "his" knights. His authority over them, like the prince's authority over him, was familial. Each "castle warrior," upon reaching adulthood, pledged his body to the chief of the castle; the pledge was sealed by the giving and receiving of hands, signifying the gift of oneself, and by a kiss, a sign of peace and token of reciprocal loyalty. These rites sealed a kind of bargain, and between the parties to the contract there grew up bonds that could easily be confused with the bonds of kinship. Proof can be seen in the word *seigneur*, "the elder," which denoted the party receiving the pledge. Furthermore, the knights are included in the preambles to seigneurial decrees, indiscriminately mixed with the blood relatives of the seigneur. Finally, the patron felt obliged to feed his "loyal servants," to give them copious helpings of food from his own table, or else—but not always—to give them enough land to live on their own: a fief. The grant of a fief was accomplished by the rite of investiture, which involved the passing of a straw from one hand to the other. This custom appears to have originated in the mists of the very early Middle Ages, when the passing of the straw was a symbol of adoption.

In pledging himself the knight in effect joined the "family" of the master of the castle and became part of his private life. The acts of a council held at Limoges in 1031, in enumerating the men included in the upper echelons of lay society, mention first the "superior powers," then the "princes of the second zone," and finally the "knights," adding to the word *milites* the most appropriate qualifier, *privati*: private soldiers. Thus a fraction of the population was removed from the public sphere and divided into groups bound together by kinship-like bonds. Any disputes that might arise among members of these families were settled privately, in "battle" through judicial duels or conciliation by the patron. A knight served his patron as a nephew was supposed to serve his maternal uncle, offering aid and counsel; all participated in the administration of a common patrimony, the power of the "ban" associated with the fortress. One of the knight's duties, incurred in exchange for food received or the fief that took its place, was to keep the yoke on the rest of the populace by making regular tours around the castle for the purpose of intimidation. These were known as cavalcades, because their purpose was to demonstrate the superiority of the man on horseback, the agent of oppression.

The rest of the populace was subject to exploitation, which also became increasingly a private affair. Throughout the Middle Ages the people resisted, sometimes overtly but more often covertly and passively. In fortunate areas, especially mountainous regions, this resistance was successful, as it was too in the cities of southern Christendom, the only cities to maintain their vitality as trade dwindled in the eleventh century. In such places the knights were not alone in holding on to the prime perquisites of freedom, the ability to gather together with other free men for the purpose of rendering judgment or waging war. In addition to the knights, the texts speak of *boni homines*, men "of quality," or, in the cities, *cives*, "citizens." (In the camp of the Pisan army mentioned earlier, the citizens did not sleep in the tents of the inner circle yet stood armed and ready to attack Majorca. The prince-archbishop harangues them like an orator at the forum, to rouse them to action.) Still, civic attitudes and consciousness survived in at most a thin layer of the populace below the knights' *maisnies* and *masnades*. The masses were domesticated, but quite differently from the knights. The "public judge" (as the council of Anse as late as 994 was still calling the man who exercised the regalian power) treated his knights as he treated his sons, sons-in-law, and nephews; he treated the rest of the inhabitants of the territory subject to his ban as members of his *familia*, taking the word in its primary sense, meaning slaves of his household. Here the private model was one not of kinship but of servitude, and the image that shaped contemporary thinking was that of the great estate inherited from the rustic early Middle Ages. Here the castle was seen as a domanial court (*curtis dominicalis*), the enclosure at the center of any large Carolingian estate, surrounding the master's residence and its outbuildings. Similarly, the small enclosures or *curtiles* occupied by peasants were seen as analogous to the slave huts in which the Carolingian aristocracy had housed its inferior dependents.

What the Carolingians had done in fact was to settle slave couples on small plots, allowing them to bear and raise children. This proved to be the most efficient way of managing that portion of their capital, or livestock, consisting of *mancipia*; it provided for both the maintenance and the reproduction of the servile population. The only drawback was that by giving slaves huts, the masters allowed their animate possessions a modicum of private life. The gift was not generous: slaves fortunate enough to be given plots of their own were obliged to spend one out of every two or three days inside the domanial court doing whatever they were ordered to do; on those days they took their meals in the refectory and were thus reincorporated into the master's family. Their women were obliged to perform communal labor with the other women of the estate. The master took children from their huts as needed to replenish the ranks of his full-time servants. He could take whatever he wished from his slaves: their daughters to marry off as he pleased (and if a girl's father wished to reserve this right for himself, he had to pay for it), or a portion of their inheritance (livestock when a man died, clothing in the case of a woman). Slaves' courts, unlike those of free peasants, were not protected by law against confiscatory incursions; they were in effect nothing more than annexes of the master's house. The master was lord over men, women, children, animals, and belongings, just as he was lord over his oven, his stables, and his granaries.

As society began to be organized along feudal lines in the early eleventh century, those who wielded the remnants of what once had been public power sought to establish the principle that their territories were like the great old Carolingian estates. They attempted to extort from all the residents and all passing travelers other than knights what they extorted from their own slaves. As the instruments of public power were applied to the unarmed segment of the populace, they assumed an increasingly domanial character. The higher public tribunals were transformed into family gatherings, in which the prince or count was joined by his relatives, fief-holders, and private knights. Similarly, the assemblies that met in the countryside to judge free men of humble condition became domestic tribunals. The master of the castle assigned one of his servants to preside over these private courts, and the poor, regardless of status, were punished much as in the past slaves of an estate had been punished.

In the Mâcon region this transformation was complete by

1030. In other areas it came about later, but everywhere its effect was gradually to abolish the distinction between those of the poor who had once been considered free men and the rest. (I use the term *poor* as it was used at the time, to refer to all those who were without power and subject to the ban of the castle.) This was only natural, since the notion of freedom had been kept alive in village assemblies, where it was known that so-and-so was entitled to sit while someone else was excluded because he belonged from birth to another man, or that a woman (to cite a late-eleventh-century document transcribed in the cartularies of Cluny) could "legally prove" that she was not the private property of the man who claimed to be her master. When these once-public assemblies became indistinguishable from the domestic tribunals in which the master punished the misbehavior of his slaves, the notion of freedom evaporated. This took time: three generations passed before the charter writers in the rural Mâconnais ceased to draw a distinction between *servi* and *liberi homines*. Fifty years earlier, however, the expression *terra francorum*, land reserved for the use of free men (for communal purposes), had fallen into disuse, because by this time all peasants, free or not, had access to communal lands under the control of the lord of the ban. As early as 1062, one scribe, drawing up an act of donation, referred to the human beings who constituted the gift as slaves (*servi*). But he felt obliged to add, "these slaves, whether free or unfree," for the theoretical distinction had not entirely vanished from memory. Yet the fact was that they were donated indiscriminately by the man who owned them all, much as he might have donated a herd of livestock.

The second effect of the encroachment of the private sphere upon the right to dominate the "poor" was that those who wielded coercive power began to insist that not only knights but all human beings who resided in their territory but did not belong to them pledge themselves to their masters. A Cluniac charter tells of an episode that occurred around 1030 in a village on the banks of the Saône. A "free man" had come to settle there and had lived for a time "in freedom," but at some point he discovered that he must "commend" himself to the seigneurs of the place. The same word, *commendatio*, was used to designate the pledge made by a man of war, and the ritual gestures may not have been very different; but the consequences were. The *commendise* of the peasant made him not a kin of the lord but a member of the *familia*, the group of inferior dependents who were obliged to serve, not nobly or in a filial manner like knights, but servilely; such a peasant was no longer his own master but in part the property of another man. The wealthy men of the Mâconnais bought and sold *francs* (free men) in the eleventh century much as they bought and sold slaves. Though still called free, these men were hereditarily bound to the land. Their patron could enter their homes and confiscate parts of their patrimony; they could not marry without his consent. By the time the vocabulary of the charters caught up with this major change, a century after it occurred, two very revealing expressions had come into use to characterize dependents among whom no trace remained of the distinctions once sanctioned by law: the master said, this is my "own" man, that is, he belongs to me, he is my private property; or he said, this is my *homme de corps*, that is, his body is mine.

The lords of the ban rarely succeeded in subjugating all the "poor" in the lands dominated by their fortresses. Exempt were the humble folk who served in the households of knights settled in the district; they, too, were *hommes de corps*, but their bodies belonged to another master. The statutes of the city of Orange promulgated in 1282 declare such people to be *de mainada hospicii*, that is, part of the *manade* of a private house large enough and well-enough protected to remain to some degree independent of the castle. Also exempt were the men and women the statutes referred to as residents (*manentes*), on whom seigneurial power weighed less heavily and never entirely lost its public character. The charter of Tende, composed after 1042, mentions the services due the count, distinguishing between the unlimited obligation of slaves, *homines de sua masnada*, and the strictly limited services owed by the *homines habitatores*.

But even people of this sort, who had resisted the power of the lord with greater success, whose fathers had refused to perform the rites of submission and join one of the lord's ever-growing families, were subject to the demands of the man who called himself their *dominus* (because he claimed to dominate), and the payment required for the protection he claimed to offer took on a familial coloration. On specified days they were required to bring "gifts" to the lord; in lieu of military service, which they were no longer required to perform, they had to do *corvées*, or forced labor in the court of their sire, to visit his premises, live with him at close quarters, and submit to his orders. A similar effect was produced by rights known as *gîte, albergue,* or *recet*—the obligation to receive the lord as a guest in one's home. The public origin of these rights is beyond question: in late antiquity magistrates on their travels were given shelter by the citizens.

In the eleventh and twelfth centuries this obligatory hospitality periodically broke down the barriers that protected the private life of the village resident. The seigneur and his entourage came and fed their animals in the peasant's *courtil* and camped on his land; the man had to spend day and night in the company of the lord or one of his knights. Such offensive intrusion provoked resistance, but even when it was successful, winning a promise that in the future the right of *gîte* would be limited, the equivalent in kind still had to be paid. Supposedly free peasants had to provide wine from their cellars, bread from their kneading-troughs, and coins from their strongboxes; when the sire came to sleep in the village they had to furnish featherbeds. To win such a *franchise*, or exemption, was a victory for the people. At least the villager and his wife could hold on to what was theirs. Writers most confident of their vocabulary now referred to the subjugated people not as *populus* but as *plebs*; the protective shell around private life had been weakened and in places even broken. Feudalization at all levels of the social hierarchy had extended hitherto private relations throughout the power structure; the change was like a tidal wave that swept all dikes before it. Paradoxically, as society became increasingly feudal, there was less and less private life because power in all its forms had become more and more private.

Religion was not immune from the changes. Christians of the feudal era, at least those whose attitudes we know, adopted ritual postures of self-renunciation in the face of divine power. Like knights pledging themselves to the master of the castle, they threw themselves on their knees, hands joined, awaiting their reward, hoping to be nourished in the other world as in the home of a father, aspiring to enter into God's private realm, his *familia*, but with a rank appropriate to the order to which they belonged—at the bottom of a hierarchy of submission. They sought to assume a position in one of the interlocking networks of subordinate territories in God's private domain. God, they knew, was the supreme judge; Christ on the final day would render judgment, flanked by a council of intimate associates, whose advice he would seek as lords sought the advice of their associates in the feudal courts, listening in turn to each baron uphold the cause of loyal subordinates, of those who had pledged themselves to him. In heaven this assessor's role was filled by the saints, whose earthly power derived from the privilege they enjoyed, even before the Last Judgment, of sitting with the Master and stating their opinions. Sometimes the saints were terrifying and vengeful—think of the irascible Saint Foy—waging private vendettas against those who dared to touch their livestock or their wine, which is to say, the livestock and wine of their servants, of the monks who tended their sanctuaries or watched over their relics, their domestics as it were.

The Christian thus pledged himself to the saints, thereby becoming something like an arrière-vassal of God. The surest way of winning the saints' protection was to become one of their domestics, joining the monks who cared for their sanctuaries and making a profession of faith. How many eleventh-century knights decided on their deathbeds to don the habit of Saint Benedict and, by making a substantial donation to the nearest monastery, ensure that they would be counted, *in extremis*, as servants of a supernatural patron? How many sought to be admitted as lay brothers of some religious community (for which an entry fee was exacted)? How many participated in rites not of vassalage but of serfdom, making themselves the slaves, the property of a saint, his *hommes* or *femmes de corps*—like the so-called *sainteurs*, so numerous in Germany and Lorraine, many born into the highest nobility, who sought protection in this world and the other from their possessor and rallied beneath his banner, which as we have seen was a symbol of ownership?

The devout population came to resemble a vast household divided among numerous residences, each under the protection of a saint or the Virgin. Welcoming and expansive, these holy families spread tentacles like their feudal counterparts, and throughout the eleventh century the dream persisted that one day all mankind would inhabit one of the many mansions of the heavenly house. This dream sustained the promoters of the Peace of God. They hoped to slow the spread of power from the fortresses, to raise new barriers to its progress, to establish protected times and places—in short to trace the boundaries of yet another private domain, this one belonging to God. To violate the privacy of that estate by pillaging churches and the areas around them, "cemeteries" and other sanctuaries (*sauvetés*) marked by crosses, or to engage in plunder on holy days consecrated to God, was to attack his omnipotence and risk his private vengeance. Another affront to

God was to attack men and women deemed by reason of their condition to belong to his house: clerics, monks, unmarried women, and the poor. Another affront to God was any attempt to seize those whom he had received in his boundless hospitality in the many places of refuge available to the unarmed and to fugitives; these were the guests of God, placed in his *mundium*, under his hand.

The Peace and Truce of God, by attaching sacred significance to privacy, helped create a space in which communal gatherings could take place and thus encouraged the reconstitution of public space at the village level. The churches, where baptisms took place and the dead were absolved of their sins, became the seeds around which small closed societies of parishioners crystallized. In the eleventh and twelfth centuries many a village grew up in the shadow of the church, in the zone of immunity where violence was prohibited under peace regulations. There the "poor" lived in solidarity with one another, in communal "courts," so to speak, safe from intrusion. The villagers, who possessed in common the right to use that part of nearby land on which no crop was planted and from which no harvest was taken, were better able to withstand the pressures of the lord than if they had been isolated and alone. In some towns, particularly those revitalized by growing commerce, solidarity and "friendship" among citizens was institutionalized, fostered by age-old customs. Members of mutual defense societies, for example, met periodically to share meals and especially drink. Solidarity was also fostered by the ritual of swearing common oaths. These were a product of the peace movement; initially the idea was to control the aggressive impulses of the knights by obliging them to swear to uphold the peace. Later the practice spread to more humble folk, and it was not unusual for village heads of household to take a common oath to preserve "concord"— a matter of the heart—without outside interference. This was to be done through mediation by friends—through "the hands of neighbors," as the customs of the town of Cluny put it in 1166. Disputes were to be settled in private; the so-called public authorities were called upon only in cases of *fractus villae*, when the entire community was shocked by a very serious crime, like "public" adultery or larceny. The count reserved the right to prosecute such a crime if it occurred in his city, even within the limits of the cathedral's private territory and even if the guilty parties were personal retainers of the bishop and canons.

Enmity was not permitted in these associations. The institutions of peace promulgated at Laon in 1128, for example, not only prohibited violence within the protected zone but also forbade "anyone bearing mortal hatred toward another to pursue him if he left the city or to set an ambush for him upon his return." All aggressiveness was to be directed outside the group, against any threat to the common interest. It was therefore only natural that an internal power developed; groups of notables took responsibility for the chore of conciliation. The authority of the outside power was limited to so-called public expeditions and to the administration of what people in the twelfth century had begun to call "high" justice. Below this level we witness the re-creation, within the private space of the community, of a zone of public action and the delineation of zones of individual privacy.

Only adult males not in the domestic service of someone else were included in the associations. The text of a convention signed at Valenciennes in 1114 is very clear on this point: men (*viri*) undergo a ritual of initiation into the active community at the end of their fifteenth year. Excluded from membership, although included in the "peace of the city," are minor children, all women "regardless of status or rank," and monks, nuns, and priests, because they are serfs of God. Furthermore, "any master (*dominus*) can flagellate or beat any dependent (*cliens*) or slave (*servus*) in town without violating the peace." If slaves "living together *in the same house* and under the same domestic power (*dominium*) should fight among themselves, complaints and fines should be directed to their master, that is, the master of the house (*dominus hospicii*), and those who have sworn the oath of peace must refrain from taking any part, unless death occurs." Elsewhere we read: "The slave, who *eats his master's bread*, cannot bear witness with his master against someone for violation of the peace." In other words, within the pacified zone subject to common (that is, public) law, certain islets were excepted, namely, houses whose immunity was specially protected by the very same law. "Assault" upon one of these houses (breaking and entering) was subject to the highest fine, the same as that assessed for "public" crimes. Communal customs of Picardy, Athis, Oisy, and Walincourt, written down in the early thirteenth century, recognize the right of self-defense: a person is not subject to punishment for killing an assailant inside his house. A person who, inside a house, strikes a resident is subject to the very heavy fine of 40 solidi. If the aggressor attempts to gain entry

by force, he must pay 100 solidi, increased to 200 if he succeeds. Striking proof of the symbolic value attached to private
dwellings can be seen in the punishment inflicted by the community on one of its members who violates the contract of
friendship: his house is destroyed. This is vengeance, but vengeance of a public kind, as we see clearly in Valenciennes,
where it was left to the magistrates, to those who had "sworn
the peace oath," to decide whether or not a house should be
razed. Since those who took part were acting in the common
interest, they were to suffer no prejudice: "This act shall give
rise to no war [vengeance of one house against another, led
by a group of relatives or friends against another such group],
enmity, or ambush, since it is the work of justice and of the
prince."

At all levels of society we find an enduring distinction
between that which is public and that which is not. The exact
location of the dividing line is fluid, however, and because of
this there is nothing absolute about the notion of private life
in the feudal age. To illustrate, I shall examine an episode in
the history of Genoa, as reported by the commune's notary.
This "commune" was in reality a "company," an association
under private law for a limited period of time, not unlike a
commercial company; its members were the heads of the great
houses of the city whose towers loomed side by side, bluster-
ing back and forth at one another. The parties to the agreement
delegated power to magistrates known as "consuls," a title
borrowed from ancient Rome in an explicit allusion to the *res
publica*, since it was the function of the consuls to restrain
aggressive impulses. In 1169 an attempt was made to end a
"war" born of a fight on the beach between youths of rival
households, which had been raging for five years. All the
citizens of the city were required to swear a public peace oath,
pledging themselves to pursue anyone who caused trouble.
Although the consuls stopped short of razing the houses belonging to the heads of the two hostile clans, they did order
them occupied by public garrisons. A series of public combats
was planned: "six battles or duels on a closed field among the
leading citizens," to be held in the court of the palace—the
public palace—of the archbishop, the supreme patron, invested
with the *regalia*. The private powers opposed these measures,
however: "the blood relatives and allies of each party" urged
the magistrate to take a different approach and convoke an
assembly of reconciliation. A change of script: the story is no
longer one of civic peace. Now the entire city becomes a

sanctuary, a zone governed by the Peace of God. Crosses were set up in front of each doorway, and on the appointed day the archbishop arrived in ceremonial vestments, bearing reliquaries. The two "enemy captains" were called upon to swear peace oaths on the Gospels. One refused. He sat on the ground and would not move despite the supplications of his kin, "screaming" that he could not forget those members of his clan who had died "for the war." Ultimately he was dragged over to the Bible to put an end to the vendettas. This was unquestionably a case of private vengeance. But was the pledge to cease and desist also private, or was it public?

Let me turn to another episode in Italian history. (Italians were in the forefront in reflecting upon the logic of the law, and the early employment of notaries in Italy gives us a clearer picture of what happened there.) By the thirteenth century some families had grown so large that they occupied several households. To keep peace within them, so-called *consorteria* were adopted. These were agreements under which a kinship group was organized like a commune, and for the same purpose: "the general welfare and increase of the house." Under these agreements males sixteen and older were obliged to swear peace oaths. A code of conduct was promulgated. A "chamber" was set up to take charge of common funds, and a magistrate, called a consul, was elected to preserve "concord." He did so by having his brothers and nephews meet regularly to rehearse the terms of the agreement; on a specified date these same men met to elect a new consul. Thus we have a situation in which the commune was composed of an association of several *case* or *alberghi*, each subject to another authority, private and family-dominated to be sure but curiously like the ostensibly public authority that administered the still-larger household, the commune, of which each family household was a part. Each clan was like a molecule in which power emanated from the adult males of the race, penetrating and ensuring harmony among the more strictly private cells of which the clan was composed. But no attempt was made to impose the power of the clan by force over any individual household, for the resistance would have been fierce.

Merely to mention resistance suggests that we have finally struck the hard core, the elementary kinship group, the "family" consisting of a man, his wife, their unmarried children, and their servants. One household among many, which exchanged women among themselves, publicly, in noisy parades through public streets and squares. But this was a mere passage, a necessary, ostentatious interlude between two private ceremonies: the engagement, celebrated in the bride's house, and the wedding, celebrated in the groom's. Even here, was not the dining room in which the nuptial banquet was held less private than the bedroom, not to mention the bed, in which the marriage would be consummated that night? And the woman, before being given in marriage by her father, brother, or uncle, had been required to give a clear statement of her consent. Some stubbornly refused to do so; hence the power of the head of household faced obstacles, encountered still further barriers that protected areas of individual autonomy. Just as we thought we were about to grasp medieval life in its most private aspects, it eludes us. Our investigation must therefore go beyond the ostensible boundaries of the private to examine the individual man and woman, body and soul, in the depths of intimacy.

Land register of Saint-Paul-lès-Romans.

Beyond the castle gates dinner was shared, as was love. *Psalter* of Odbert, abbot of Saint-Bertin, ca. 1000. (Boulogne Library, ms 20.)

2

Portraits

Georges Duby
Dominique Barthélemy
Charles de La Roncière

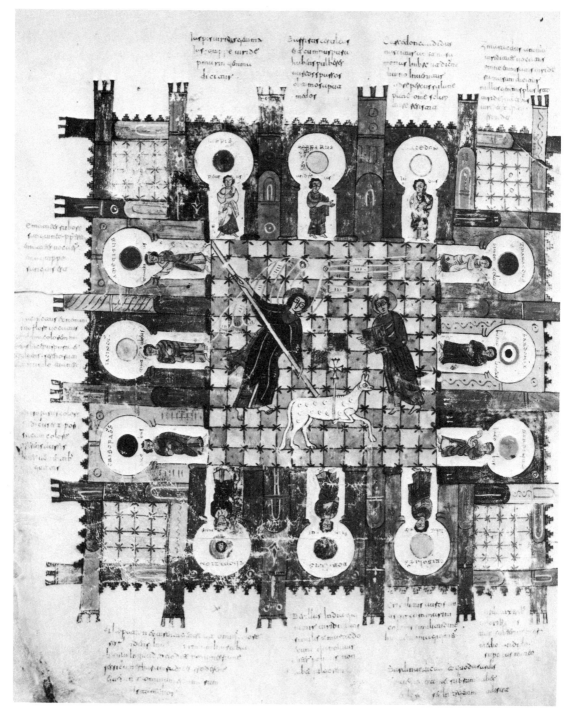

The heavenly Jerusalem, an image of the perfect abode. Beatus of Liebana, *Commentary on the Apocalypse*. (New York, Morgan Library, ms 644.)

❦ The Aristocratic Households of Feudal France

PRIVATE life in the feudal age—the eleventh and twelfth centuries—cannot easily be isolated from what surrounded, penetrated, and resisted it. To understand its nature, we must know a great deal about the society and culture in general. It would be imprudent to treat the entirety of western Europe, that mosaic of very different peoples and customs, as a single unit; nor would it be wise to attempt to treat all of society, when the sources are sufficiently informative only about the dominant strata. I shall deal, therefore, with only the northern half of the kingdom of France and only with aristocratic families. Subject to the private power of the head of household, members of these families were involved in relations of two kinds: those born of living together under a single roof, and those born of blood and marriage—kinship. Dominique Barthélemy will consider marriage and the family; I will discuss the household.

G.D.

COMMUNAL LIVING
Georges Duby

To understand the structure of power within the great feudal houses, as well as the customs and rituals of private sociability, we should begin with dreams—imaginary ideals of the perfect home—and Heaven—the lodging of the elect in the other world. According to the vision of Sunniulf, as reported by Gregory of Tours in the sixth century, souls that survive their trial in Purgatory eventually come to a "great white house." Two centuries later another visionary sees much the same sight: "On the other side of the river loomed huge, high, resplendent walls." But Saint Boniface, who recounts it, explains: "this was the heavenly Jerusalem." Not a house, then, but a city: the metaphor is political and urban; it refers to a city which, though in decay, continued to fascinate with its myriad monuments only recently fallen in ruin, a city to which memories of Rome also attached, a refuge—but a public one, ready to embrace all the children of God. The arches that frame the figures of the evangelists in Carolingian miniatures evoke not a court but the porticoes of a forum. Only later was the image of a house superimposed upon this ancient image: the Roman Catholic Church still wished to see heaven as a mighty city. Primarily, though, people thought of heaven as a kind of house. On the tympanum at Conques, for example, to the right (on the good side) of Christ the Judge, calm and orderly in contrast to the disorder evident on the left (where the reprobate are cast into the maw of hell), is an architectural symbol: niches open onto a space of concord, onto the peace that reigned in the center of the cloister; these niches are covered over as by a cloak, gathered into a single, communal habitation by a protective roof. In the same period Bernard of Clairvaux apostrophized heaven in these terms: "O marvelous house, preferable to our beloved tents." Heaven, then, is a solidly built house, a place to settle down and rest after the vagabond life of *homo viator*—undeniably a place of lodging.

So much for the fancies of churchmen; let us turn to those of knights. A text written in the late thirteenth century to divert people of good society is, though built around a sacred theme, to an almost sacrilegious degree imbued with the courtly spirit. Its title is *Court de paradis* (Court of Paradise). *Court* is here spelled with a "t" [the usual French spelling is *cour*], indicating that it derives from the Latin *curtis*. Yet this is also a *curia*: God the Father "wants to hold court," a plenary court, on All Saints' Day. He summons the lords and ladies of his house; his heralds scour "the dormitories, bedrooms, and refectories." The house is vast, divided as were the most up-to-date castles into several rooms, each assigned to a particular class of inhabitant: one room for angels, another for virgins, and so on. The assembly consists of all the residents of the household: the *maisnie* of Jesus Christ, "in joyful company," gazes upon its lord. "Joy" suggests a feast, in this case a kind of ball. The guest of honor is the Virgin Mary. There is music and dance; the whole society is invited to join in the

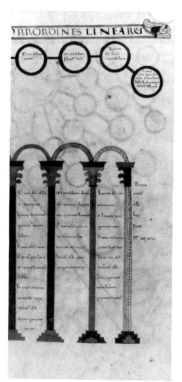

Arcades and genealogy. Beatus of Liebana, *Commentary on the Apocalypse*, mid-11th century. (Paris, Bibliothèque Nationale, Latin 8878.)

singing. In a naive way heaven is depicted as a household sharing in a joyous occasion, brought together to share in plainsong and round by its master, the *senior*, whose duty it was to "make the court merry." Clearly a sacred vision—ineffable joy, a choir of angels, universal love—is here contaminated by a profane one, in which courtly love, like divine charity, establishes order by assembling not the elect but the dining companions of the prince.

The poem suggests that the literature of diversion may prove to be a useful historical source; surviving fragments of this literature are much more common after the end of the twelfth century. In them the dream house eventually ceases to be regarded as a reflection of heaven. Three main impressions emerge from the most significant texts. First, the ideal house required an enclosure. Indeed, as the thirteenth century approaches, the population density inside the castle walls decreases; the court becomes a setting for individual exploits. Second, the ideal house was highly eroticized in these literary works composed for "youths," that is, unmarried males. It is depicted as a female preserve; women are watched, kept under lock and key, which makes them only more alluring. The towers are filled with maidens. Here we glimpse the recurring fantasy of free love—repressed and turned into a myth of origin in an early-eleventh-century tale by Dudo of Saint-Quentin, as it was three hundred years later by Father Clergues at Montaillou. Similarly, the defenders of orthodoxy imagined that heretical sects engaged in free love in their secret but

Paradise. Conques Abbey, 12th century.

fascinating nocturnal meetings; here, however, the fantasy has pejorative connotations. In courtly romance, whenever the game of love is given an explicit setting and the hero breaches the castle walls to seize a woman, the adulterous union tends to take place underground: making love is not something done in the open, and when that love is illicit, it must literally bury itself. Third, in the profane imagination the ideal house was light and airy: a thousand windows flooded every obscure recess with light. Further embellishing their image of the house, writers threw in souvenirs of the River Orontes, glimpsed on a Crusade, as well as Turkish art, fountains, and ornament of every sort. In imagination, heaven was a superb castle filled with people, and the ideal house was a dazzling paradise fitted out for the joys of life.

The Monastery: Model of Private Life

Imagination was not strictly necessary. Men could see with their own eyes, on earth, exact replicas of the heavenly abode. These were the Benedictine monasteries, which claimed to be antechambers and prefigurations of heaven in this world. Monasteries were therefore walled cities, "cloisters" to which access was strictly controlled, with but a single gate which, like city gates, was opened and closed at fixed hours. An important monastic office was the hostelry, which governed all relations with the outside world. Yet monasteries were essentially houses. Each was home to a "family"; in fact, the families of monks were the most perfect of all families, the most carefully organized. The organization of the monastery was governed by the Rule of Saint Benedict, a clear, well-thought-out, strictly conceived plan for perfection. Since the ninth century, copious resources had been flowing into the monasteries, enabling them to take the lead in developing new agricultural techniques. They are among the best-known medieval residences; quantities of explicit documents tell us a great deal about how they were organized and run. If we wish to discover how wealthy people behaved in the privacy of their homes, we should first look at the monasteries.

At the height of the Carolingian renaissance, between 816 and 820, while Emperor Louis the Pious was putting the finishing touches on a program of monastic reform patterned closely after the Benedictine model, a design was prepared of the ideal monastery. The celebrated plans for Saint-Gall, preserved on five pieces of sewn parchment, consist of a series of scale drawings with legends. They were sent, probably by the Bishop of Basel, to Abbot Gozbert, who was considering

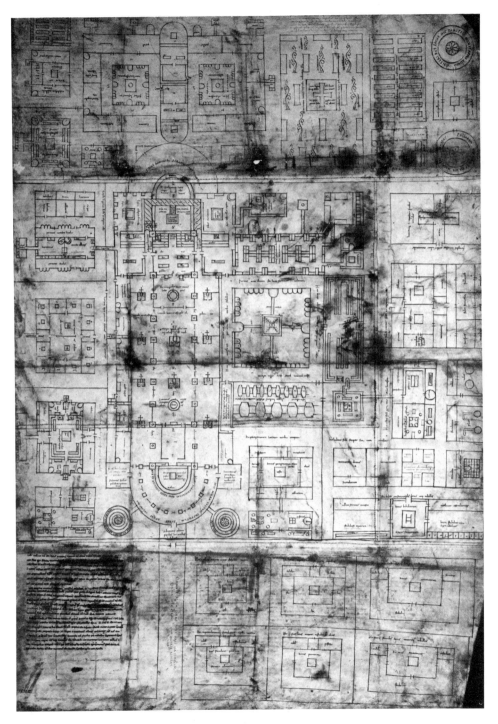

Plan of Saint-Gall, ca. 820.

rebuilding the abbey. The plans embody a theory of what a monastery should be: a place closely attuned to the harmonies of the spheres, cleaving to the axes of the universe, and perfectly balanced in a mathematical sense. The elementary architectural unit in the drawings measures forty feet on a side, with the nave of the church the centerpiece of the entire composition. The church was the heart of the whole organism, the point of contact between heaven and earth. Here the monks gathered to perform their main function: to sing God's praises in unison with the choir of angels.

The monks' residence was located south of the area reserved for the liturgy. Its arrangement resembles that of an ancient villa. There is an inner court abutting the church. To one side are the wine cellar, the food stores, the kitchen, and the bakery. On the other side is the refectory, above which is storage space for clothing. Along the third side is a hall, flanked by baths and latrines, and above it a dormitory, which communicates with the church. Adjoining the residence are

Plan of the Abbey of Cluny in the mid-10th century. (After K. J. Conant.)

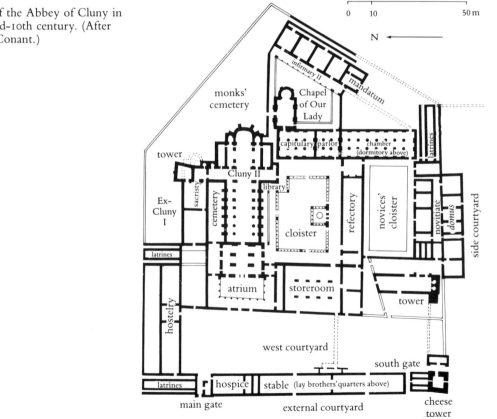

extensive annexes used for agricultural and artisanal purposes, gardens, granges, stables, barns, workshops, and servants' huts. To the north, beyond the church to which it is attached, stands the house of the abbot, equipped with its own kitchen, wine cellar, and baths. To the northeast, novices and monks suffering from disease, temporarily excluded from the community, were confined in a separate residence, divided into two parts; purges and bleedings were administered in the far corner of the building. Finally, near the gate, to the northwest, strangers admitted into the cloister were housed in two buildings as fully equipped as the rest. One, next to the abbot's residence, received the more important guests and pupils from outside the community; the other, closer to the monks, was reserved for pilgrims and the poor.

It is clear that the abbey's organization was intended to reflect the strict hierarchies of the heavenly court. The central place was God's: the sanctuary. On his right, beyond the north bay of the transept, was the place of the abbot, who stood alone; as head of the family he occupied a higher plane. To the left of the Almighty, occupying the third rank, were the members of the family: the monks were the sons, all brothers, all equal, like the angels forming a militia, a garrison sustained by servants who lived next to the refectory, since the ideal was autarchy, self-sufficiency. Farthest from the gate, that fissure open to the world's corruption, were confined the invalids and young recruits still undergoing training—the young, the old, and also the dead, since the cemetery was located here. The most vulnerable part of the community had to be kept separate on account of its weakness, sheltered, but also protected by the right hand of God. Here, too, were the areas reserved for spiritual functions, the school and the writing studio; the material functions, those which sustained the body, were relegated to the other side, to the left hand of God. Note that the graves were placed to the east, on the side of the rising sun, symbol of the resurrection, whereas visitors were lodged on the west, the side of the setting sun and worldly perversity.

These plans were employed in the construction of numerous monasteries in the ninth century, some of them immense, housing extraordinary numbers of people. In 852 one hundred fifty monks lived at Corbie; one hundred fifty widows were regularly fed at the gate, and three hundred guests were received daily in the hostelry. In some monasteries the staff was too large to be accommodated within the cloister,

Traces of a Cistercian abbey
abandoned shortly after its
foundation. (Vron, Somme.)

and large towns grew up outside the walls, as around Saint-
Riquier, where each street was occupied by a different type of
worker. In the feudal era most monasteries conformed in general outline to the plans for Saint-Gall, although a tendency
toward increasing concentration led to some variation. Consider, for example, the abbey of Cluny under Odilon in the
mid-eleventh century (prior to the sumptuous construction
program undertaken by his successor, Saint Hugh, who, faithful to another dream—the imperial—placed greater emphasis
on public spaces, in keeping with the ancient urban tradition).
The orientation is the same, as is the location of the gate. The
church is still the heart of the abbey, but here slightly off
center. The structure of the monk's residence is the same. The
infirmary and cemetery are to the east, and on the west is a
vast visitor's court and hostelry, again divided into two parts.
But here the abbot has no private residence and lives among
his sons. Nor are there workshops and barns inside the walls.
Under Cluny's interpretation of the Rule of Saint Benedict,
the manual labor that monks were obliged to perform was
merely symbolic. The ideal of self-sufficiency persisted, but
food was supplied by satellite farms called *doyennés*, scattered
throughout the countryside; these were replicas, on a more
modest scale, of the mother abbey, as is clear from the remains
of the doyenné of Berzé. At Cluny the only outbuildings that
remained were the stables. In this civilization of horsemen,

Dormitory of the Cistercian Abbey of Santa Cruz, Spain.

candū ficut pollicebaē cęnobiū tradere. capt. vuj.

Deprima hospuatione quam habuimus.

Monks on horseback, relics, and capitulary hall. *Life and Miracles of Saint Maurus*, late 11th century. (Troyes Library, ms 2273.)

the taste for riding extended even to the monasteries. The abbot of Cluny never ventured outside the abbey without a large mounted escort. Responsibility for making the *vestitus*, or items of clothing, and for supplying the *exteriora*, commodities purchased outside the monastery, was shifted to the merchants, artisans, and hired servants who inhabited the *bourg* (town) that grew up at the gates as monks began to be less stingy about disbursing money. Inside the cloister there was greater homogeneity: only a single residence existed. In private, life was governed by various customaries and statutes, which specified the monastic routine in great detail.

Communal life in Cluniac monasteries was conceived as a perpetual liturgy with strict ritual forms. At the center was the abbot, now integrated into the community he headed and neither taking meals nor sleeping apart. When ill, he joined other patients in the infirmary, and like other monks he took his turn at kitchen duty. Here we see one aspect of the new monastic life: the increased emphasis on togetherness and fear of isolation. So gregarious had private life become that the head of the family no longer had a place where he could be alone. In return he was shown greater deference by other monks. All rose whenever he entered or left a room and bowed when he passed by. Two candles were set before him in the refectory, and when he went to the church or capitulary hall for daily meetings, or if he needed to visit one of the outbuildings by night, a light was carried in front of him by one of his sons. When he returned from a journey the entire community dressed up and turned out to meet him. At the church door he kissed all the monks in a ritual of paternal embrace, and that day an additional dish was served, as for a festive occasion. At table the abbot was set apart from the other monks and served more sophisticated dishes and better wine. Thus the signs of the abbot's superiority included fire, the kiss, the wine, the ceremonial greeting, and the pomp of a "joyous entry" (as the kings would later call their entries).

The abbot was nothing less than the master. He reigned as sovereign over the monastery, but he did not govern alone. To assist him he had a group composed of monks referred to in the customaries as *seniores*, or elders. Here we see another important feature of monastic life: the subordination of the young to the old. The abbot was also assisted by department

Refectory of Poblet Abbey, Spain.

heads, the officers of the monastery. The prior (or premier) was a sort of second-in-command, ready to stand in for the abbot during his absence. Under him were the heads of the four major departments. In charge of the church was the sacristan, who opened and closed it at the prescribed hours and took care of the liturgical accessories and other items needed by the community for the purpose of prayer. The chamberlain had charge of everything kept in the "chamber," or inner sanctum of the monastery; in particular he was responsible for handling money and the things that money could buy. His role increased steadily throughout the eleventh and twelfth centuries. Everything that came into the monastery by way of gift, rent, or purchase—fabrics, wine, precious metals, common coins—passed through his hands, and it was up to him to oversee the wise redistribution of these items. He also replaced the monks' worn clothing every spring and distributed new mattresses and bedclothes every autumn, on the eve of All Saints'. He supplied shoes for the horses and razors for the monks and was in charge of all windows except those in the church. The *victus*, or food normally grown on monastery lands, was the responsibility of the cellarer, master of the cellar stores, where a light was kept burning all the time lest the monks be tempted to sleep there. Assisted by the wine steward and the corn chandler (responsible for water, hence also washing, as well as corn), the cellarer doled out each monk's daily portion of food; also assisting him was the constable, the man in charge of Cluny's ostentatious worldly pastime, riding.

Kitchens of the Abbey of Fontevraud, exterior and interior

Fountains Abbey, Yorkshire, England.

Saint Benedict spreading his rule. *Martyrology and Obituary of the Abbey of the Holy Sepulcher*, 12th century. (Cambrai Library, ms 829.)

The father abbot. *Collectaire* of Stavelot, 11th century. (Brussels, Royal Albert I Library, ms 1813.)

Relations with outsiders, less pure than the monks and of lower rank, constituted the fourth monastic office, shared between the hosteller and the almoner. The almoner distributed surplus food and clothing to the indigent. He also paid weekly visits to bedridden patients outside the cloister, in the town. (He did not call on women; lay servants under his orders took care of this.) Inside the cloister he maintained eighteen indigent prebendaries, or pensioners. The presence of such duly accredited representatives of the assisted poor was considered essential at the time in every wealthy household. The almoner was also responsible for visiting paupers; to give them lodging was a charitable duty.

A clear distinction was drawn between this and the duty to offer hospitality to more distinguished guests: visitors of quality, who shared the same background as the monks and who were received as friends. Such guests could be recognized by the fact that they arrived not on foot but on horseback; they were lodged in buildings administered not by the almoner but by the hosteller. In the course of Saint Hugh's ambitious program of construction in the late eleventh century, the guest house at Cluny took on imposing proportions; it measured 135 feet by 30 feet and was divided into two parts. Here, suddenly, a ray of light is cast on precisely what we are trying to discover: the domestic arrangements of the lay aristocracy. At Cluny there were two dormitories, one for men, with forty straw mattresses and forty individual latrines, the other

Monastic infirmary and oratory. *Life and Miracles of Saint Maurus,* late 11th century. (Troyes Library, ms 2273.)

for women—"countesses and other honorable women"—with thirty beds and thirty latrines. Between the two was the refectory, where both sexes ate at the same tables. The dining room was sumptuous, equipped with tablecloths and cups and a large staff including a maître d'hôtel, a cook, a porter, a boy to wash the feet of the guests and carry water, and a donkey-boy who kept the fireplace filled with wood. All these were paid servants who received their orders from the hosteller, the officer responsible for relations with the outside world and thus in contact with its corruption and filth. That is why his office was also responsible for cleaning the abbey latrines.

Strangers entered the monastery's private space and for a brief time shared the life of its permanent residents. The communal life was normally open, and the highest-ranking guests were received with much ceremony. Although at Cluny the monks lined up in ranks to greet visiting princes, everyone who crossed the threshold and passed from public territory into the private space of the monastery was required to adopt the penitent's way of life. Wives, for example, were not allowed to sleep with their husbands inside the cloister. Unmarried women and especially widows who chose to end their days in a religious community were admitted into the church for important services but lived outside the cloister in houses of their own. One such woman was Ide, countess of Boulogne, who lived with an entourage of protégées and servants. Another was the mother of Guibert of Nogent, who lived

Patron saint punishing a wicked lord. *Life and Miracles of Saint Maurus,* late 11th century. (Troyes Library, ms 2273.)

Healing abbot. *Life and Miracles of Saint Maurus*, late 11th century. (Troyes Library, ms 2273.)

Healing abbot. *Life and Miracles of Saint Maurus*, late 11th century. (Troyes Library, ms 2273.)

near the gate of the monastery of Saint-Germer-de-Fly. Although strangers had access at certain hours even to the area set aside for the liturgy—at Cluny, a sumptuous, semipublic festival not unlike the coronation festivals of the royal palace—they were always barred from the more private areas where the monks and their father-abbot lived and ate. (Also excluded were the household servants, who shared the black bread that was given to the poor.)

The fraternity of monks was divided, as prescribed by the customaries of Cluny, into four groups, each assigned to a distinct quarter of the monastery: the novitiate, the infirmary, the cemetery, and the cloister. Separated from the monks' residence by the church, the novices' residence was a place of transition and gestation. Here the slow process of spiritual reproduction took place. Children sent to the monastery by their families at a very tender age were fed and educated. When their apprenticeship was complete, when they had learned the complexities of monastic behavior and knew what to do when and how to sing and how to express themselves by signs during the periods of silence, they were solemnly initiated into the community of adult monks. The ritual was one of adoption, of integration. First came a personal pledge of commitment, the profession: this was a written formula that was signed and read and then placed on the altar in the presence of the assembled community. Next came gestures which, like the dubbing of knights, symbolized admission into a functional group: the former novice donned the one item of monastic clothing he still lacked, the cowled robe. Then there was a ritual of welcome: the kiss of peace was bestowed on the newcomer first by the abbot and then by each of his brothers. There followed three days of retreat, of time spent alone with one's most intimate, secret, private thoughts. All these signs, like the pre-dubbing rituals of vigil and bath performed by the prospective knight, suggested death followed by resurrection. But the three days of solitude are particularly noteworthy. The retreat was a trial. To become a monk the novice was required to spend three days in total silence, his head covered by the cowl and his body by the robe night and day. The new monk lived as it were in his own little house inside the big house that was the monastery. His robe was a cocoon in which the metamorphosis of man into monk took place; it was an inner cloister to which the young monk retreated, emulating Christ's withdrawal into the tomb from which he emerged, transformed and reborn, three days later.

The infirmary, too, was a place of waiting, to which some members of the community were sent for a time because tainted by disease. In effect, disease was seen as a mark of sin.

Child with endowment offered to monastery. *Gratiani Concordantia discordantium canonum*, 12th century. (Douai Library, ms 590.)

Odbert's *Psalter*, abbey of
Saint-Bertin, ca. 1000.
(Boulogne Library, ms 20.)

A novice becomes a monk.
Guillaume Durand, *Pontifical*,
14th century. (Paris,
Bibliothèque Sainte-Geneviève,
ms 143.)

Those who suffered from it had to be isolated during their
period of purgation. At Cluny two rooms in the infirmary
were set aside for purifying ablutions, one for washing feet,
the other for washing dishes. Four other rooms were furnished
with two beds apiece. The abbot, however, enjoyed the privilege of a private room. Adjoining the infirmary was a separate
kitchen, because ailing monks, made less pure by illness, ate
a different diet from the rest of the community. They were
not forbidden to eat meat, which supposedly replenished the
blood and helped warm ailing bodies. But because the ill
became meat-eaters for a time, they were even more excluded
from the community, and in particular from receiving communion. After extreme unction was administered, however,
meat was no longer served. From that point on the dying
received communion daily; as death drew near, the main concern was to bring them as close as possible to the angelic state,
to wean them gradually from the flesh. The less gravely ill
could be recognized by their canes, signs of weakness, and
their covered heads, signs of penitence. Sickness proved that
they were sinners, hence they were obliged to purify themselves through penance. Once cured, they had to pass through
a final stage of purification, receiving absolution before re-
joining their brothers.

Life of Saint Omer, late 11th century. (Library of Saint-Omer, ms 698.)

Most monks lay for a time in the infirmary before entering the other world. This transition was another occasion for collective ritual. No one died alone; death was perhaps the least private of a monk's acts. The death of a monk was rather like a wedding in profane society. Around the deathbed was staged a sort of festival, in which communal bonds were at their most visible. When his condition worsened, the dying man was carried by two of his brothers out of the infirmary and into the meeting hall known as the capitulary for his last confession, which had to be made in public. He was then taken back to the infirmary to receive communion and extreme unction and then to bid farewell to the community. After kissing the cross, he exchanged the kiss of peace with all his brothers, starting with the abbot, just as he had done at the end of his novitiate. Once the death agony began, an unremitting vigil was kept. Crosses and candles were placed at the foot of the deathbed, and all the monks, alerted by blows struck against the cloister gate, gathered to recite in their brother's stead the Credo and various litanies. When the dying man finally yielded up his soul, his body was washed by monks, his peers in the hierarchy of age and office. It then was carried into the church, where psalms were sung, and finally laid to rest in the cemetery, which was located in the most private part of the monastery, the third quarter of its familial space. The dead were by no means cut off from their living brothers. On the anniversary of a monk's death a tasty additional dish was served in the refectory. The dead, it was

The death of a monk. *Life and Miracles of Saint Maurus,* late 11th century. (Troyes Library, ms 2273.)

believed, gave nourishment to the community and ate with their brothers—and with their brothers only, since strangers were not allowed to partake of these meals, the crumbs of which were left for the poor. The dead thus shared once more in the life of the monastery, for the common meal was the essential ritual of communal life.

The fourth and final quarter of the monastery was the residence. In Cluny the monks' residence, which occupied the center of the *curtis,* was supposed to be the earthly embodiment of an ideal of private life, as far as possible a mirror of heaven. The inner court, what we call the cloister, combined the four elements of the visible universe: air, fire, water, and earth. With its covered walkway it was an introverted version of the public square, entirely given over to private concerns. Here the chaos of time was subdued; everything was strictly regulated according to the seasons, the hours of the day and night.

Different parts of the building were assigned different functions. The most ornate and carefully maintained was the section set aside for the *opus Dei*, the work of God, the special office of monks, that is, prayer, which was chanted at the top of the lungs in chorus: this was the church. Alongside it was the hall (*aula*), reserved for discussions and judicial proceedings. This was similar to the ancient basilica, but it, too, was turned inward: whatever was said here was private and secret. Every day, after Prime, all monks well enough to attend and not excluded as a result of some punishment gathered in the hall to renew the bonds of community by reading a chapter of the rule and a list of the names of the abbey's dead. The monks also dealt with temporal affairs in much the same manner as the council of a feudal prince. Finally, as a family they corrected one another's mistakes: the hall was a scene of continual self-criticism. Violations of discipline were denounced either by the guilty party himself or by others, for the purpose of restoring order within the community. The guilty were first flagellated. (This was the usual penalty in private, domestic justice, inflicted by a man upon his wife, children, servants, and slaves.) Then they were separated from the community for a period of purification. They took their meals apart and were made to stand at the church door. Their heads always covered, they lived in retreat, isolated from their brothers. Again it is important to note that solitude was envisioned as an exile, a trial, a punishment.

Their sins purged, the lost sheep rejoined the flock in the refectory. Meals, taken in common every day (and supplemented in some seasons by light snacks), were ceremonial occasions, celebrating the unity of brotherhood. The monks sat in prescribed order around tables whose linen was changed every two weeks. At these princely banquets each monk found a loaf of bread and a knife waiting at his assigned place. Bowls of food were brought in from the kitchen and wine from the cellar, served in what were called "just" measures, each one shared by two monks. The rule prescribed that wine was to be drunk in silence. The monks ate in perfect discipline, modulating their gestures as prescribed by the rule and waiting for the silent signals of the abbot, seated at the center of the table. Meals were a communion, and during them the spirit was occupied, distracted from the flesh, by the voice of one of the monks, who read out loud.

At dusk the time of danger commenced, for the devil was abroad. It was imperative that the community close its ranks

Sermons of Saint Bernard, ca. 1160. (Brussels, Royal Albert I Library, ms 9645.)

and keep a sharp watch. In the dormitory, the most private part of the residence, located on the second story, high above any creeping menace, no monk was allowed to be alone, and the abbot lived in the midst of his flock. Lights were kept burning throughout the night, as in a military camp. Each monk slept in his own bed, however; the rule strictly prohibited any sharing. The needs of community took second place in this regard, owing to an unarticulated but obsessive fear of homosexuality. Ultimately the communal life of the monastery was gregarious; every secret, every intimacy inevitably became common knowledge, and solitude was held to be a danger and used as a punishment.

Topography of the Noble Household

It was essential for us to look at life in the monastery before turning to the lay nobility, about whose homes there is far less information. Fortunately, noble households resembled the Cluniac monasteries in many ways, for both housed people of considerable wealth, certain that it was their role to govern the masses, spendthrift in their habits, and much given to luxury. There were, however, two important differences.

First, the leaders of the lay aristocracy contributed to the common good in a way that differed from that of the monks. Not having renounced the world, their vocation was to combat evil by force of arms, not by prayer. Accordingly, their private life was much more ostentatious and open than that of the monks. It unfolded, moreover, in a setting that for generations had been reserved for public functions, military and civil: the noble house incorporated aspects of the fortress and the palace.

Second, the monastic family, being pure, excluded the germs of weakness; women and children were not admitted. (Novices at Cluny were treated as small adults.) By contrast, the nobleman was duty-bound to marry and produce legitimate offspring. Fertile marriage was the bedrock of social order. There was no house without marriage, no marriage without a house. At the center of every household was a single married couple. When children married they had to leave. So did the elderly; widows were relegated to monastery towns and aged fathers sent into religious retreat or on trips to Jerusalem to prepare for death.

Let us begin by exploring the physical aspects of private space, or at least what we can still see of that space, since the remains are much less well preserved than those of the monasteries. In France archaeologists attentive to the artifacts of everyday life have been scrupulously exploring those remains for many years. Their research suggests that the number of aristocratic households increased considerably between the beginning of the eleventh and the end of the fourteenth century. The pace of construction seems to have accelerated at two points. The first expansion took place in the early eleventh century, when the major principalities disintegrated and the fragments of regalian power were dispersed. Fortresses and towers were erected in various places to justify the exploitation of the peasantry, the exactions made in the name of keeping the peace. The second phase began at the end of the twelfth century and continued for a century and a half. It witnessed the construction of large numbers of more modest dwellings, the so-called *maisons fortes*, or fortified houses. In Burgundy, in the Beaune and Nuits regions, at 240 inhabited sites, including hamlets, remains of 75 such buildings were found, several of them crowded together at times on a single *terroir*, or expanse of farmland. Many were seats of high justice, where public crimes were punished. This dispersion was encouraged by four factors: the growing wealth of the dominant class, which profited from increased agricultural production and the munificence of the reconstituted state; the breakup of large households, as the knights formerly housed in them were settled in residences of their own; the relaxation of the strict controls exercised by family heads over the marriages of sons (there was less reluctance to allow younger sons to marry, and each new couple required a house of its own); and finally, the disintegration of castellanies, which led to further fragmentation of the powers of command, henceforth held within the parish under the eminent authority of the state. It is clear that during the eleventh and twelfth centuries in northern France, there was a steady increase in the number of places in which aristocratic families lived. This led to gradual diffusion of models of behavior originally elaborated in princely households.

Aristocratic houses required both public and private spaces, areas for ostentation and retreat; this necessity dictated their structure. A description can be found in the biography of Bishop John of Thérouanne, which dates from the first third of the twelfth century: "The wealthiest and noblest men of the region customarily pile up earth to form a mound as high as they can possibly make it, around which they dig a moat as wide and as deep as possible. Then they fortify this

Saint-Martin-de-la-Brasque, Vaucluse.

LE CASTELAS
Overall plan, showing restitutions. (Contour lines at 1-meter intervals showing height before excavation.)

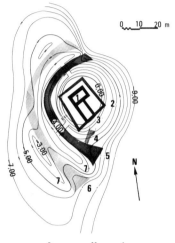

1: tower?   2: wall   3: house
4: entrance   5: interior moat
6: exterior moat   7: rampart.

Enclosure and two mottes.
(Vismes, Somme.)

mound with a fence of stout posts. Each enclosure is equipped
with towers, if possible, and a house is built at the center, a
fortress accessible only by a bridge, which dominates the
whole construction." Mounds of earth, a wall enclosing a
dwelling place, a single entrance: the features are similar to
those of a monastery. Here, however, the defensive character
stands out, even in periods of relative peace. Fortified houses
in thirteenth-century Burgundy are distinguished by their
moats and *terreaux*, or earthen embankments surrounding a
court, and especially by their towers, often the only fortified
element, and indispensable to their purpose. The tower was
the symbol of power, the *dominium* (from which derives not
only the word *danger* but also *donjon*)—the power to protect
and exploit. An emblem, sign of a function, like the banner
or the belltower of the abbey church, the tower was not
ordinarily inhabited; archaeologists have turned up very few
vestiges of daily life in their remains. Life was lived elsewhere,
in the house (*domus*), which was sometimes divided into two
parts.

These houses, less solidly built than their accompanying
towers, have left almost no traces. We can guess how they
were arranged internally, however, by looking at the remains
of some earlier houses, which, because they were occupied by
great princes, had been constructed of stone. At Caen Castle

there is a rectangular structure (100 by 36 feet, 26 feet high) dating from the second half of the twelfth century. It has two stories and no vault. There are no openings in the lower story save for three night-soil dumps in the ground; there is a central hearth and a well. No doubt there was once a cellar, part of which served the kitchen. The "noble" upper story consists of six large bays, several wall chimneys, and a door that was reached by an exterior stairway. A list of expenditures for repairs made to the castle in 1180 brings the ruins to life: the accounts mention first the tower, the walls, and the chapel, then the "chambers" and the "hall," which were probably located in the ruins just described. Michel de Boüard, the archaeologist who carried out the excavation, suggests that the terms imply a distinction between "the hall in which *public* power was manifested" and the *"private* apartment of the prince." Just as in the monastery, though more marked here, there was a distinction between space that was more or less open for the display of power and that which was more closed. The public portion was apparently suitable for banquets; here the master served meals to his friends for all to see. There were windows, halls, and lights. Dishes were ceremoniously served, brought up from below where servants prepared them

Caen Castle. Vestiges of the main tower and seigneurial dwelling, 12th century.

out of sight. The chamber, the space of privacy, of *privance*, may have been contiguous with the hall, separated by a partition that has disappeared or even by a simple tapestry, as at Vendôme or Troyes. Or it may have been a separate construction, of more fragile materials that have left no trace, situated perpendicular to the hall, as was the case at Angers. This princely model was copied in the fortified houses. A late-thirteenth-century house at Villy-le-Moutier in Burgundy, excavated by J.-M. Pesez and F. Piponnier, consisted of a large one-story wooden building approximately 66 by 33 feet, divided into two rooms, one equipped with a chimney for a formal fireplace, the other with a central hearth for cooking.

Archaeology can show us little more than carcasses. To restore life to them the historian must consult the written record. This gives some idea of how these buildings were decorated, mainly with perishable textiles, whose abundance and variety is evident from the inventories. In 1071, for instance, an inventory of the property of Arnal Mir, a great Catalonian lord, tells of a house filled with fabrics and furs and lists the gloves, hats, mirrors, and other indispensable accessories required by the master and his relatives. We learn of the candelabra and utensils of precious metal in the splendid dining hall. Finally we discover the bedchamber, filled with more intimate items of comfort, the most important of which was the "well-appointed" bed: the vocabulary takes on a special richness in describing the bedroom's many accessories—mattresses, feather cushions, covers, tapestries, rugs. On holy days, when the family paraded in splendor, persons, tables, and walls were handsomely decorated. In ordinary times, however, everything was kept in the most inaccessible part of the house, the lord's chamber. Here, according to the texts, was also kept the strongbox, the reserve of valuables, partly in coin, partly in objects that could be exhibited, for the lord needed to make a show of his wealth. When Charles the Good, count of Flanders, was murdered, the knights and bourgeois of Flanders apparently searched in vain for his strongbox, first in his house, then, during the great pillage of 1127, in the tower of Bruges. In the end they fought over the kitchen utensils, the lead pipes, the wine, and the flour; emptying the coffers, they left nothing but the skeleton of a building.

Only the written sources can tell us what parts of the house were used for various functions and activities. Perhaps the most explicit testimony is found in the history of the counts of Guînes, which describes, in minute detail because it

Men in the hall, woman in the chamber. Peter the Eater, *Scholastic History*, late 12th century. (Paris, Bibliothèque Nationale, Latin 16943.)

seemed so admirable, the house reconstructed in 1129 by the lord of Ardres; built of wood, nothing remains today except the mound on which it stood. On the ground floor, as at Caen, were "the cellars and granaries, the coffers, the barrels and jars." The second story included the *habitation* where "the household assembled," that is, the hall where meetings were held and meals eaten, equivalent to the monastic capitulary and refectory combined. This was flanked by small rooms reserved for use by the pantler and cupbearer. Then "came the great chamber where the sire and his lady slept, adjoining a room used as a dormitory by the servants and children. Part of the great chamber was a place where a fire could be built at dawn or in the evening, for the sick, or for bleedings, or to warm the servants and children . . . On the same level, but set apart from the house proper, was the kitchen." (The kitchen occupied a separate two-story building. Beneath the kitchen proper, which contained the hearth, were a pigsty and chicken coops. The kitchen was linked by a passageway to the dining hall.) Above the master's bedchamber "upper chambers had been built. In one the lord's sons slept, if they wished. In the other his daughters slept, of necessity," watched over by guards, whose guardroom stood nearby. A corridor led from the *habitation* to the *loge,* a place for relaxation and private conversation, and from there to the chapel. Just as in the monastery, there was a gradual transition from the entry gate to the most private inner recesses. The vertical arrangement is also worth noting: from the nutritive earth and the lower court where food stores were kept we move up to the lord's residence, which dominates the building. The residence proper is segregated from the common space, reflecting the two components of domestic society, masters and servants; similarly, there is a distinction between the fire that cooks and the fire that heats and lights the chamber and reveals the master in his glory.

Thus, the elevated, magisterial portion of the great aristocratic house was divided into three parts, three functional areas. In contrast to the monastery, prayer was an important but secondary function, hence the chapel was relegated to the periphery; at Ardres, we are told, it was richly painted. More primary were the military and judicial functions, whose place was in the great hall. An open space, the hall was located close to the court and the gate, because it exerted considerable influence on the outside world. Each person had his place in the ceremonial ritual, according to rank, just as in the cortèges in which the power of the family was exposed to public view; other nobles appeared dressed in their finest attire to hear the lord state the law and pronounce judgment. People came to pay him homage. A place for public acts, the hall was primarily a masculine preserve. Female relatives were admitted for round dances and banquets, however, because this was the place for festivities of all kinds. Their proper place, however, was the bedroom, where the third fundamental function was carried out: reproduction. This was so serious and disturbing a business that it had to be done in seclusion, in a protected place. By nature the bedroom was nuptial, conjugal. At its center stood the bed, the blessed bed to which newlyweds were led on their wedding night and the place where new heirs came into the world. The bed was the family womb, the most private part of the residence. Yet there was no more solitude in the bedroom than there was in the monks' dormitory. Not far from the lord's bed other people slept, surely women and perhaps also, for a time at any rate, men, family members; Tristan's nocturnal adventures suggest as much. The oppressive promiscuity stimulated the desire to escape. Everyone knows what a large part windows play in romantic fiction: unhappily married women stand beside them and dream of deliverance. Medieval women as well as men were used to the outdoors. Shut them up for too long and they suffocated. They escaped to the orchard. Open space—yet not open to the outside like the court—orchards, like monastery cloisters, were surrounded by walls. Often water flowed through these mock forests, as it did through the monasteries. Here a person could feel alone and lost. Here, too, clandestine loves were born and nurtured. But when the moment for the illicit embrace arrived, the lovers repaired underground.

Domestic Society

Social relations in these great houses were half private, half public, for, as a line from the *Roman de Renart* tells us, the house was frequented by "privés ou estranges ou amis"— by familiars or outsiders or friends, three different kinds of guests. The *estranges*, or outsiders, were those who had no special emotional bond with the master of the house. Possibly the "familiars" were distinguished from the "friends" by a blood relationship: "out of friendship," the *Roman* says, the wolf and the fox call each other uncle and nephew. More likely the difference was that familiars were official residents of the house, whereas friends, although they might have free access and enjoy close relations with the lord, did not reside there. They came and went, like the occupants of a monastery's hostelry.

The familiars formed what was referred to in medieval French as the *ménage* or *maisnie* (household), legally defined as follows in an article of the *Olim* dated 1282: "His own *maisnie* residing in his house (*ostel*), that is, composed of those who perform his private tasks at his expense." The defining characteristics of the maisnie are common lodging, common meals, and collaboration under the lord's orders on some common task. It is therefore a precise analog of a monastic frater-

nity. The household could be quite numerous: in thirteenth-century England Thomas of Berkeley's comprised more than two hundred people, and the bishop of Bristol needed a hundred horses to carry his whenever he traveled. What held together so large a group was the fact that all were subject to—or as people said at the time, "retained" by—one man's rule, kept alive by one patron. What twelfth- and thirteenth-century familiars expected from their patron was in essence no different from what, according to one formulary, a Merovingian pledging himself to his lord had expected some five hundred years earlier: "Food and clothing (*victum et vestitum*), both for my back and for my bed, and shoes, thou shalt procure me, and all that I possess shall remain in thy power." Thus a man pledged himself (much as a monk made profession) in exchange for all that his body and soul might require. The man who distributed food and shelter also obtained the right to punish, to flagellate his men. Lord and men formed a *corps*, or body, with a head, or *chef*, and members. A document dating from the eve of the twelfth century in the archives of Cluny refers to the *caput mansi*, the head of the *manse*, or residence and all it contained.

Like the monastic "family," the aristocratic maisnie was divided into two parts. One group, the *servientes* (those who serve), took its meals separately and ate bread less noble, that is, blacker, than the other. In very large households the servientes often lived in a town adjoining the main residence. (As

Preparations for seigneurial banquet. *Queen Mathilde Tapestry*, 11th century. (Bayeux Museum.)

the urban renaissance began early in the eleventh century, it is clear, I think, that the "bourgeois" population was composed largely of familiars of the lord—the bishop, count, or castellan—who practiced various "crafts.") The other group was composed of "masters." In profane society the masters included not only the lord but also those who assisted him, who shared responsibility for the two major functions, prayer and combat. In a house of any size the clergy formed a college of canons; the lord, though a layman, was a member of that college and sat at its center. The military function fell to the knights.

Among these servants of the first rank it is difficult to distinguish between public and private, friends and familiars. The prayers recited in the lord's chapel benefited the entire seigneurie, and his house was a fortress from which peace and justice emanated into the surrounding territory. Hence the warriors who actually lived in the house were periodically joined by other men whose vocation was combat but who resided in the vicinity in houses of their own. For a period of time they entered the private domain of the master of the castle, received their daily pittance and their harness and equipment from him, and became his familiars. After returning to their own homes they remained his friends, bound to him by homage, which established a kind of kinship. Most of the clerks and knights who assisted the lord were bound to him in any case by true kinship, by blood or marriage. They were

Reconstruction of one of the houses at Charavines (Isère), early 11th century.

his sons, nephews, and cousins, legitimate and bastard alike. To other servants the lord gave his daughters in marriage. Although they were then sent away from the castle to reside in homes of their own, they remained tied to it, bound from time to time to return, and to send their descendants to return, to the lord's maisnie.

Like the monastery, the aristocratic residence was a place where visitors were welcomed. Its gates were open to the poor, who were admitted to receive, as in Lazarus' house, the crumbs from the lord's table; it was a blessing for the master and his entire household to submit to this necessary and ritualized despoliation. The noble household also received youths for training. Young men of high birth—sons of the master's sisters and vassals—were taught the usages of the court and the arts of war. Travelers of noble rank were also received, "friends" and "foreigners" alike; these parasites, too, were essential. An important symbol of power was the gesture by which the master invited his guests to be seated in the dining hall to gorge themselves on food and drink and then to lie down for the night to sleep. On certain days the visitors included not only passing travelers but representatives of all the satellite households. On major Christian holidays—Christmas, Easter, and Pentecost—the hall of the princely house resumed its original function, that of a basilica in which the regalian powers were exercised; on those days the private was

Rural house and silos. (Buoux, Vaucluse.)

entirely dissolved in the public. In every house, great or small, the wedding feast was the apex of hospitality. The groom's "family" advanced beyond the walls to meet the bride, escorted by her own kin, who accompanied the young woman to the gate and eventually beyond, right into the nuptial chamber, pausing along the way in the intervening semipublic space to enjoy a lavish feast.

Order and Disorder

The power structure of this complex and rather fluid society was also strikingly similar to that of the monastery. At the head was a solitary male, a father, as in heaven. He was never supposed to act without seeking counsel, however; advising him were other males, who formed a hierarchy in which the young ranked below the old. The paterfamilias thus occupied the place of God: within his house all life seemed to emanate from him. Yet there was a considerable difference between the noble household and the monastery. The residents of the one did not live in such close proximity to the angels as those of the other. They were not so far removed from the flesh. The household was not asexual. As the leader of a dynasty, the head of the noble household was duty-bound to perpetuate its existence by engendering offspring. He was obliged to disseminate females among allied houses to secure their allegiance and ensure procreation. Because his primary function was genital, he required a woman for his bed. At the center of the network of power, then, was a couple. The females were entirely dominated by the males; nevertheless, the master's wife was mother to his heirs (and, in the eleventh century at any rate, if she failed in this function, her husband would have felt no compunctions about throwing her out). Hence the lady of the house (*domina*), legitimate sexual partner of the master and mother of his progeny, shared some of the powers of the man she called her lord; she, too, "dominated."

Reproduction meant expansion. Up to now we have looked at private life on the defensive, huddled behind walls, whereas in reality the household, like any living organism, tended to grow. Everything, especially the authority of the paterfamilias, was arranged so as to maximize this vital outward thrust. Every noble household was constantly in search of more relatives, more allies, more servants. The castle of Ardres contained at its heart a nursery, where governesses took care of the mistress' offspring so that the lady herself could get on as quickly as possible with the business of conceiving the next child. As soon as children attained the age of reason they were strictly segregated: girls were carefully watched to protect their virginity until the moment when they were conveyed in solemn cortège to the castle of their future spouse; boys were sent out into the world to seize whatever they could, particularly wives. They returned home only for brief visits, as guests.

The progeny of the paterfamilias' own loins were never enough, so his first duty, after marrying and fathering children, was to increase his maisnie still further by taking in "retainers," men with whom he dined. This aim ruled the domestic economy. Investment was alien to the medieval mind. The reserves accumulated in bedchamber, stores, and wine-cellar were merely provisions laid up for future feasts, in which the wealth of the house would be lavishly squandered. A Cluniac cartulary from the middle of the twelfth century contains a *constitutio expensae*, a "plan of expenditures" for adding to the resources of the house. The purpose was to assign the income of the estate to the imperious needs of indispensable largesse. Thrift was not the great domestic virtue of feudal times; expansive generosity was, its purpose being to attract additional allies to a house. True wealth consisted in allies, or "friends," a point made time and time again in profane literature.

The patron was obliged to meet the spiritual and physical needs of the members of his household. Spiritual needs took precedence over physical ones; accordingly the clergy were the highest-ranking domestic retainers. Their services were needed not only in the chapel but also in the dining hall and even the bedchamber, for the paterfamilias was chief among those responsible for ministering to the needs of the spirit. As in the monastery, the father was also a teacher. The eulogy of Count Baldwin II of Guînes describes him as an "illiterate," unable to read books himself yet a great collector of them, who ordered that Latin texts be translated into a language that he could understand and then commented on what was read to him, asked questions, discussed the answers—in short, a man who studied hard so that he could better fulfill his role as teacher. To aid in this he supported a staff of assistants recruited from among graduates of the schools, or "masters." Some lived in the count's house only temporarily, while working on translations or adding to the library. Canons or monks who belonged to a community of ecclesiastics might come to stay for short periods, aiding their brothers with their spe-

Hunter, 14th century. (Paris, Bibliothèque Sainte-Geneviève, ms 1283.)

cialized knowledge. Other ecclesiastics remained permanently in residence. Chaplains of the house, they preached to the count and his familiars. The count also employed them in other ways, setting them to write amusing plays or songs in the vulgar tongue, knowing full well that his friends appreciated these far more than the edifying sermons to which they also lent an ear.

The lord worked to dispel the boredom that overtook his men, by nature hunters and warriors, during periods when these more strenuous activities were unavailable. But he knew that the best way to please them and to win their loyalty and obedience was to satisfy their physical desires. As often as possible he led his retinue after wild game and against rivals in tourneys, as well as in battle. He made sure that his castle was well supplied with serving women and his wardrobe well stocked with "vests," which were handed out in ritual fashion on major holy days. Without such gifts and "boons," how could he maintain control over his maisnie? How could he honorably discharge his office as patron? In 1219 William, marshal of England, made ready on his deathbed to distribute his personal property. He left all his money to the Church, that it might pray for his soul. He was then reminded that in his bedchamber there were still quantities of scarlet robes with squirrel collars and at least eighty fresh skins, which could be sold for a good price to obtain money to buy more prayers. William became angry. Pentecost was coming, and on that day his knights were entitled to new clothing, which he was determined they should receive. Their lord could not fail them; even on the brink of death the duty of munificence outweighed William's concern for his salvation. Before clothing the bodies of his retainers the lord was obliged to satisfy their appetites, to serve them plentiful and savory dishes that not only pleased the tongue but also distinguished the lord's dinner companions from the vulgar; for them the *companagium* was not merely something eaten along with the staple bread but the main part of the meal. Hence a lord could never be stingy. Whether in bedchamber or dining hall, his power was proportionate to his willingness to give—in ever greater amounts.

Like the monastery abbot, the lord was aided in domestic management by household officers. In the feudal age administrative chores were divided much as they had been in the Carolingian palace. The lord's first assistant was his wife, who wielded power analogous to that of the queen in the ninth

Musician. Church of Saint-Donat (Drôme), late 12th century.

century. She had charge of everything that pertained to women (including young children, who were considered part of the female domain). She supervised the storage of supplies and everything that came into the house. The wife of the lord of Ardres, for example, oversaw the collection of taxes from the peasants. When one of them was unable to deliver the required sheep, the *dame* asked for a daughter instead. She then raised the girl and, at the proper time, found her a mate. Like a good shepherd, she husbanded her flock and exploited its reproductive capacities, assisting her husband in extending the "family." She also kept an eye on her domestic servants. When one maid became pregnant, the lady of the castle forced the putative father to marry the girl. Imperiously she punished and terrorized all the women in the house and forced them to obey her will. According to Jean de Marmoutier, the king of France wanted to marry off the orphaned daughter of a great vassal, but the girl refused. Unable to win her consent, he asked his wife to break the girl's will, and the queen obliged.

The master and mistress had other assistants, each in charge of a *ministerium*, or household department. A look at the organization of the court of Hainault tells us a great deal about how these departments worked. In 1210 two elderly men, the bastard brother and chaplain of the next-to-last count (among the most "private" of his familiars) came to recite publicly the most ancient custom of the realm, which the count wished to restore and record for posterity. At this time things were becoming more and more institutionalized and rigid. Profitable offices, already held as private property, could be sold with the patron's approval and bequeathed to heirs. Some were owned by women or by men through their wives, although normally, after his training as heir-apparent, a man's eldest son succeeded him when he died or became too old to discharge his duties. Despite such practices, the *ministeriales* continued to be considered full-fledged members of the family; they ate with the master, slept in the house, and were given horses as if they were knights. Every year they received clothing—a cloak and a tunic. In addition they received what was called a *livrée*, a sum of money to pay for whatever additional equipment they needed. In addition, those with military responsibilities received their soldier's pay. Among them were the count's *commilitones*, comrades-at-arms who rode at his side and formed what was called the *conroi*, the tightly knit group of warriors who fought at their prince's side. Although not mentioned in this particular document, these were men of the same age (*coetani*) as their leader. Most were his relatives and had been his comrades since childhood. All had been dubbed on the same day, and together they formed a particularly unified and "private" corps within the household, not unlike the college of canons and, like the canons, ranking above simple ministeriales. The latter lived, however, on intimate terms with the master and were obliged to accompany him on military expeditions to "defend his body."

Not all were of the same rank. This enormous and august household had a strict hierarchy of offices. The document speaks of three so-called major offices, direct descendants of the three lay ministries under the Carolingian prince, model for aristocratic households. These offices were held by the grand seneschal, the grand chamberlain, and the grand butler. They were seen as men who served the count throughout his principality, but quite obviously their offices, having become honorific, no longer required them to live in his house; they simply assured these high officials of access to the prince and a place at his side in formal processions. Each official ran an autonomous household department, serving the three comital residences (each of which served as capital of a political subdivision): there were two castles, at Mons and Valenciennes, each with a collegiate church. The church at Mons was the

Meal being served, 12th century. (Toulouse, Museum of the Augustinians.)

more important, because the ancestors of the dynasty were
buried there. (Bear in mind that the dead were counted as
members of the household and included, through periodic
ceremonies of commemoration, in its private life.) The third
house, less substantial than the other two, dominated a recently acquired seigneurie, Ostrevent. There was also an extra
chamberlain. In fact, when Mme Marguerite, "the wife of
Baldwin [V], who is buried in the choir of Mons"—she was
the sister of the count of Flanders—was given to her husband,
he was only the heir-apparent of Hainault; his father still lived
in the ancestral house. The new couple required a house of its
own, so they went to Lille and settled on lands belonging to
the bride. She had found a husband for one of her servingwomen and named him her own chamberlain. From that time
on, the countess maintained a "chamber" of her own "in all
places," according to the text. This chamber was not associated with any particular house but managed the woman's
portion of the movable property: the trousseau. A hierarchy
of many ranks: the count, the countess, three houses of different ranks, and in each principal house two major departments. One served the table, that is, the dining hall, under
the direction of the seneschal and butler; the other served the
more private chamber under the direction of the chamberlain,
who ranked below the seneschal but above the butler (who
supervised the cellar, the lowest portion of the house).

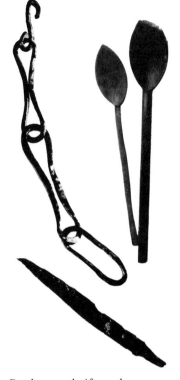

Pot-hanger, knife, and spoons,
early 11th century.
(Charavines, Isère.)

The table, or, rather, tables (*mensae*), were placed in the
hall or, weather permitting, outside. As in the monastery,
eating was a solemn, public act; it was not proper to eat with
the fingers while crouching or standing. Hence it was only
fitting that dining should be the responsibility of the highest-
ranking official in the household. The seneschal was responsible for the noblest part of the meal: the *companage* or *esques*
(*escae*), which was purchased from outside suppliers and prepared in the kitchen. This consisted primarily of meat, which
it was the task of the first servant to slice in the master's
presence. (The preeminence of meat is revealing.) Seven subalterns served under the seneschal: highest in rank was the
"buyer" and "guardian of the esques"; then came three cooks
(*queux*); below them, the concierge, responsible for stoking
the kitchen fires as well as the more impressive blazes in the
dining-room fireplace; next the porter, who welcomed and
seated the guests; and finally the cutler, who was in charge of
salt as well as cutlery. Wine was the responsibility of still
another important official, the butler (*bouteillier*). In the early

Knight in arms. Tympanum of
12th-century window. (Arles.)

thirteenth century at Mons, this post was held by a woman,
a knight's daughter who had inherited it from her father; but
she was also a canoness, hence not very available. "On her
orders," however, the wine was brought to the tables. She
could wait on the count and countess with her own hands if
she wished, but usually two surrogates served in her stead.
Of slightly lesser rank was the official who supervised the two
storekeepers and who "kept the wine and poured it into pitchers and cups." (This official, naturally enough, supervised the
potter, an artisan of very low rank.) Ranking slightly below
the wine steward, the pantler served the round loaves of bread
which, as a sign of the master's distinction, were served him
as a side dish. Under the pantler were four other servants: a
purveyor; a "hereditary" baker who lived in town, outside the
court, with other independent artisans; a guardian of the bread
or, more accurately, of slices of bread, canapés on which slices
of meat were placed; and finally, under the guardian, "the man
who placed these slices on the tables." Rounding out the list,
we have the official in charge of the larder; he ranks lowest
on the scale because lard, like bread, was what the common
people ate, and because the larder was located next to the
scullery, in the lower portion of the house.

At Mons the "minor chamberlain" (subordinate to a *camerarius*, himself subordinate to the grand chamberlain of Hainault) was in charge of the chamber and the precious items stored there. He was responsible not only for "robes" and other fabric goods but also for preparing the beds "for the entire court," most of which were unfolded every night in the hall. He provided the water that his superior presented to the count and countess; before the meal he himself brought water for washing to the clerks and knights. Finally, under the supervision of the serving chamberlain (who no doubt retained charge of the treasury), the minor chamberlain manufactured and distributed candles, in particular those that were stuck in a loaf of bread to illuminate the count, countess, and seneschal—and no one else—while they were seated at table.

On the one hand, table, light, open fire, pomp and circumstance; on the other, beds, nighttime, candles, retirement. The hall was fitted out primarily for celebrations, which were also representations, displays of the proper order of things. The count and countess, the ruling couple, occupied the center of the scene and were served, as a mark of special distinction, by the highest-ranking servants. But nearby, almost at the same level, sat the seneschal, who, as *major domus,* the highest official in the house, was entitled like the master to eat salted bread with his slice of meat and to have a light set in front of him. Since the meal was a public spectacle, a demonstration of power, the officers of the table had to be knights. They were given the same equipment, the same *livrée,* as the patron's comrades-in-arms. And whenever he mounted his horse they accompanied him, along with the cooks and the concierge. Their daily labors influenced the world outside the palace; their work was open and public. By contrast, the chamber, to judge by the customs, was hermetically sealed. Gone was the wine of the feast, offered freely to guests. In the chamber we are far from the sun, in the place where lustral water and prophylactic lights are used to wash away any bodily taint and push back the shadows.

Without crowds of witnesses and the use of ceremonial as an instrument of discipline the master could not have maintained order in the household. Trouble pressed in on all sides. Where the men were concerned, the peril stemmed from the overt, armed violence that erupted among these warriors and jousters. Constant effort was required to eliminate causes of envy and rancor and revivify friendship, a difficult task in

Land register of Saint-Paul-lès-Romans, compiled between 1339 and 1349. (Valence, Archives of the Drôme.)

view of the fact that the court was a place of unending rivalry, where the young were jealous of the old and all competed for the favors of the lord and his lady. Knights insulted and challenged one another and occasionally struck low blows. Emulating each other's behavior, they generated much sound and fury. Three methods were used to quell disorder. First, the most unruly knights were expelled from the court. (This was no doubt one of the more beneficial purposes of the Crusades.) For similar reasons the lord financed a two-year round of visits by his eldest son and other new knights immediately after their dubbing; excesses of youthful ardor could be vented harmlessly during these years of wandering. It also became customary to send adolescent boys away from home to receive their training in the knightly arts. One noble house simply exchanged its young men with another, but the change of scene probably helped to diminish conflicts. The rituals of courtly love were, I think, a second way of curbing the violence of youth. What we know about those rituals and their development from the middle of the twelfth century on suggests that the lord used his wife as bait, as a sort of decoy, offering her as the prize in a game whose rules, increasingly sophisticated as time went by, obliged participants—the unmarried knights and clerics of the household—to control their instincts ever more firmly. Finally, the head of the household wielded judicial power. He could arbitrate disputes and redress wrongs. Although he could say nothing without the counsel of his familiars, the latter were obliged to provide it, to speak in his presence and lay out their disagreements for him to settle. In the noble hall, as in the abbey's capitulary, the lord, having listened to all complaints and justifications, periodically distributed rewards and reprimands. He might, however, decide instead to appeal to the judgment of God. In that case the court became the scene of a battle or duel over which the *caput mansi* presided. Such battles were like organized riots, in which hostile rivals unleashed their violence on one another.

Was this system of regulation effective? Signs of failure are easy to detect in what little remains of family literature. In the history of the lords of Ardres—on the whole a panegyric, well documented over four generations—at least one domestic murder is mentioned: the *senior* was assassinated in the forest, allegedly by servants from his kitchen. In the history of the sires of Amboise (also a panegyric, and also well documented over four generations) we hear of a brother-in-law's murder, which was made to look like an accident of war. The two brothers of the last seigneur mentioned in the

Embrace. Church of Aulnay (Charente-Maritime), 12th century.

text were killed by their familiars, one in an ambush, the other by poisoning. There are constant references to the agitation of the castle knights, who formed opposing parties, one supporting the son, the other supporting the father; younger brother fought against older brother, son against uncle. These conflicts were not easily quelled. The master of the castle of La Haye (an intruder, who married a woman who had inherited the property) and his brother were ultimately killed by their own soldiers, who could no longer put up with them.

Despite this, women were held to be the principal, and insidious, source of domestic danger. They administered poison, cast spells, sowed discord, and caused weakness, disease, and death. If the lord was found dead in his bed, his body bloated, blame was laid at the door of the women of the house, the mistress first of all.

The threat to established order appeared to stem from the most intimate, private aspects of courtly society. The word *courtly* is quite appropriate here: there was little to worry about from the women who served under the oppressive power of the mistress. The problem of private peace concerned the well-born. Hence women of noble birth were kept under close surveillance and tightly disciplined. The cornerstone of the system of values that governed behavior in the noble household was a precept derived from Scripture: women, being the weaker sex and more prone to sin, had to be held in check. The first duty of the head of household was to watch over, punish, and if necessary kill his wife, sisters, and daughters, as well as the widows and orphans of his brothers, cousins, and vassals. Since females were dangerous, patriarchal power over them was reinforced. They were kept under lock and key in the most isolated part of the house: the *chambre des dames* was not a place for seduction or amusement but a kind of prison, in which women were incarcerated because men feared them. Some men were allowed to enter the ladies' chamber; the master in particular came and went quite freely. In romances he is shown going to the chamber to relax and eat fruit, his head cradled on the knees of maidens who tousle and comb his hair and pick out the lice. This was one of the pleasures reserved for *seniores*, the fortunate men who ruled the household. Other men were allowed into the chamber for various diversions such as reading or singing, but they were selected by the patron, summoned to enter, and received as temporary visitors. In fiction, virtually the only source of

Danger: Women and the Dead

Lord and ladies, 12th century.
(Toulouse, Museum of the
Augustinians.)

information on this subject, no male other than the head of
household and his very young sons is ever shown in residence
in the chamber—except occasionally the wounded and sick,
who were entrusted to the care of women until healed. Men
caught only brief glimpses of the gynaeceum, from which
they were naturally excluded. In their eyes it seemed a
"strange" place, a separate principality ruled by the lady of the
house, whose authority was delegated by the lord. Its inhabitants were a hostile, if seductive, tribe, the most vulnerable
of whom were confined even more securely in a religious
community, a sort of internal convent governed by a rule and
run by a mother superior—not the lord's wife but a widow

from his family or a daughter for whom he was unable to find a husband. The women of the family formed a state within a state, not subject to the power of any man except the lord himself. And even the lord's power was only one of supervision, that of a suzerain, and contested by ecclesiastics, who claimed the right to examine the consciences of the women of the house.

Specific tasks were assigned to this worrisome group, on the grounds that idleness was particularly dangerous for such feeble creatures. Ideally women divided their time between prayer and various kinds of handiwork. They sewed and embroidered, and when eleventh-century poets wanted to give voice to women they wrote *chansons de toile* (literally, linen songs). Women were responsible for the clothing that people wore and the ornate fabrics that decorated the chamber itself as well as the hall and chapel. They had a considerable share in what we would call artistic creation, both sacred and profane, but their work was embodied in such fragile materials that only shreds have survived. Yet all the prayer and all the work (group activities, much as males hunted and made war in groups) did nothing to appease the men, persuaded as they were that women were by their very nature perverse and obsessed with fantastic anxieties. What, men asked, do women do together when they are alone, locked up in the chamber? The answer was: Nothing good.

At this time the Church still practically monopolized writing; little besides the thought of ecclesiastics is accessible

In the heart of the house, why wouldn't the woman be captured? *Bible of Saint Lawrence of Liège*, 12th century. (Brussels, Royal Albert I Library, ms 9916.)

Nurse. Avicenna, *Canon of Medicine*, 13th century. (Besançon Library, ms 457.)

A good marriage is a prolific marriage. Latin Bible, 13th century. (Orléans Library, ms 41.)

to the historian. The moralists were obsessed with thoughts of the guilty pleasures which, they had no doubt, women enjoyed in the gynecaeum either alone or in conjunction with other women and young children. In the *Life* of Saint Godelive, composed early in the twelfth century, we read that women, particularly young women, are constantly vulnerable to the pricks of desire, against which there is no defense, and that they usually satisfy these desires through homosexuality (suspicion of which was encouraged by the common practice of having several members of the same sex share one bed).

Among themselves, women were believed to exchange secret knowledge of which men had no inkling. This knowledge was passed on to younger women by the "little old ladies" who appear in any number of stories. In the home of Guibert of Nogent's father, for example, they knotted and unknotted aiguillettes. In the thirteenth century Stephen of Bourbon attacked old women who taught magic to young village girls. Males were powerless in the face of spells and philters, which could sap a man's strength or heal his wounds, kindle his desire or snuff it out. Masculine power ended on the threshold of the room in which children were conceived and brought into the world and in which the sick were cared for and the dead washed. In this most private sanctum, woman ruled over the dark realm of sexual pleasure, reproduction, and death.

Domestic society was sharply divided between masculine and feminine, and this institutionalized division affected many kinds of behavior and attitudes. In each house there was only one official, visible, public marriage, that between lord and lady; the entire household was organized to ensure that the lord's marriage would be perfect, that is, fertile. But many other liaisons occurred, illegitimate and hidden. Innumerable signs attest to the irrepressibility of private sexuality, which flourished in secrecy and obscurity, in the shadows of the orchards, cellars, and palace nooks and during the hours of darkness, unrelieved even by the light of small candles. No door was secure, and it was easy for a man to slip into a woman's bed. To hear the moralists and writers of romances tell it, however, the opposite was more common. With nothing to impede fleeting unions, houses were said to be filled with willing and even provocative women. Of course there were servants, but they were small beer, and neither the domestic literature nor the romances have much to say about them. There were also the noblewomen: the mother-in-law, sisters-in-law, and aunts. It is not difficult to imagine what incestuous relationships might have been formed in such circumstances. The most active women, we are told, were the bastard daughters of the lord or his brother the canon; their children were future concubines. What about the "maids," the master's legitimate daughters? Were they offered as freely to knights-errant as fiction suggests in its depiction of the rites of hospitality? And were men roused from their sleep by insatiable females as often as the hagiographies allege?

In any case, with so many unmarried men and women living in close proximity to the lord and his lady, promiscuity

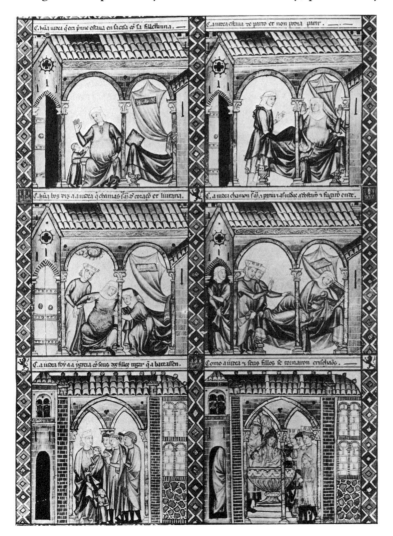

Scenes of childbirth. Illustration in Alphonse the Wise, *Cantigas*, 13th century. (Madrid, Escorial Library.)

was inevitable. Furthermore, it was considered proper to exhibit the women of the house to friends and visitors as though they constituted a treasure. Hence honor was a major preoccupation of the lord, who was responsible for maintaining order at home and protecting the glorious family name. Honor, although an affair of men, a public matter connected with shame, was essentially dependent on the conduct of women, that is, on private behavior. A man could be dishonored by women over whom he exercised power, especially his wife. The great game, as described in the literature of courtly love, was to exhort young men to demonstrate valor by seducing and abducting the lady of the house. This was a game, but its setting was real life. Undoubtedly the lord's wife was coveted, and the desire she inspired, sublimated into a sophisticated form of love, was used as a means of disciplining young knights. Stern taboos prevented the young knight from actually riding off with the lady. Yet occasionally she was taken by violence. The importance of rape in the romances obviously reflects reality. Sometimes of course the woman gave herself freely.

Adultery was an obsession in medieval society; envious eyes lay in wait whenever lovers chanced to meet. To avoid being shamed, men placed a screen between themselves and the public. For fear of dishonor women were kept shut away and closely watched, cloistered when possible, and allowed out only with an escort when required for public ceremonies or religious duties. When a woman traveled, a part of the household "conducted" her to her destination in order to make certain she could not be seduced. During a lengthy pilgrimage to Rome in the eleventh century, Adèle of Flanders remained shut up inside a sort of mobile home, a sedan chair whose curtains were kept constantly drawn. Prisoners of their castles, women sometimes escaped, like Corba of Amboise, who gladly allowed herself to be carried off by her cousin as she left mass in Tours. As long as women remained confined within the castle walls, their private mischief brought no dishonor on the house. Unless of course there were some profit in exposing the adultery, which might offer an opportunity to get rid of a sterile or tiresome wife or a sister in a position to lay claim to part of an inheritance. In such cases the paterfamilias unveiled the adulteress, shouted her name in public, so that he might legitimately punish her and turn her out, assuming he decided not to burn her alive.

Sophisticated love. Illustration in *Carmina Burana*, 13th century. (Munich Library, Clm 4660.)

In the chamber, a dying man's last words. *Code of Justinian*, 14th century. (Rheims Library, ms 807.)

Another danger faced by family members came from the dead, who expected a great deal of the living. Ghosts returned by night to haunt the chamber where their mortal remains had been prepared for burial, hoping to be cared for once more. As in the monasteries, the dead were part of the private life of the aristocratic household; everything possible was done to see that their souls did not suffer, so that they would not trouble the living. As soon as the money was available—and it took a great deal—a proper place for the remains of departed family members was constructed. Families founded monasteries or collegiate churches and buried their dead in them. Once such a necropolis was begun, everyone in the family had to be buried there, arranged in order of rank, as though the cemetery were an annex reserved for especially dangerous denizens of the household who needed to be confined like women. The anniversaries not only of the death but also of the birth of the deceased were celebrated here. On the birthday of a departed family member, the family shared its dinner, as in the monasteries, with the dead—or, more precisely, they ate for their loved one, in his stead, in order to secure his blessing. Immediately after the murder of the count of Flanders at Bruges in 1127, the killers repaired to the chapel, where they "sat down around the bier, upon which they set bread and cups as upon a table, eating and drinking over the body and believing, in consequence, that no one would exact vengeance," that the murdered count would pardon them.

Death itself was both a public and a private affair. The corpse was moved from one private place—the chamber, the bed—to another—the tomb—in what was a public, and therefore a festive, ceremony. In a procession similar to the marriage procession, the entire household marched in order of rank, demonstrating its unity for all to see. For the deceased this was the last public display, the last occasion for generosity; gifts were distributed to the poor, and a vast banquet was laid on. Also public during this phase were the signs of mourning, a spectacle in which the women played the leading roles, wailing, tearing their clothing, scratching their own faces.

This public demonstration was followed by very private rites—although the privacy was in fact gregarious, shared with many people. The ritual farewell began in the hall: in the presence of all his familiars and friends, the dying man expressed his last wishes, made final arrangements for transmitting his property, and established his heir in a loud voice and with visible gestures.

At Audenarde, for example, as Baldwin V of Hainault prepared to die, all the religious relics of the region were gathered together, as for a public peace assembly, and all his vassals were summoned to swear on those relics to maintain the peace. More intimate was the final agony, which took place in the chamber. A poem composed in honor of William, marshal of England, who died in 1219, gives one of the most detailed accounts we have from this period of the death of a prince. Wishing to die at home, William had himself transported to one of his manors when his illness took a turn for the worse. He convoked his relatives and friends, and in particular his eldest son, so that he might be seen arranging his inheritance and choosing his tomb; then changing his clothes, donning those of a templar, becoming a full-fledged member of another fraternity; and, in tears, kissing his wife for the last time. Once this farewell scene was over (and it was very similar to that which took place when the lord left home on a journey), the audience dwindled. Still, the dying man was never left alone. Night and day people watched over him, as he gradually rid himself of all his possessions. Once he had relinquished the patrimony (which was not his but had merely been given him to hold during his lifetime), he disposed of all his personal belongings: money, jewels, clothing. He paid his debts and begged pardon of those he had wronged in life. He turned his thoughts to his soul and confessed his sins. Finally, on the eve of death, the gates of heaven began to open. William saw two men dressed in white take up positions alongside him, one to his left, the other to his right. The next day, at noon, he bade farewell—this time in private—to his wife and knights: "I pledge you to God, I am no more. I can defend myself against death no longer." He thus departed the group whose leader he had been; divesting himself, he transferred his power to God. For the first time since birth, he was alone.

KINSHIP

Dominique Barthélemy

In the preceding section Georges Duby deliberately omitted discussion of blood relations, treating the medieval *familia* without reference to the "family" in the modern sense of the word. Kinship often interfered with the bonds that developed from living together under one roof, and vice versa. By failing to distinguish clearly between coresidence and consanguinity, and by using the ambiguous term "family" indiscriminately, many historians have become mired in time-worn ruts.

Kinship is as important to a study of private life as co-residence. Like metaphors of residence, metaphors of family played an important part in representing notions of religious and political solidarity. Like large households, the large clans studied by social and political historians tell a great deal about the privatization of power in the eleventh and twelfth centuries. Yet there is something paradoxical about the growth of kindred groups, for their very size tended to diminish the importance of private relationships. The autonomy of both individual and married couple was threatened as much by the irresistible ascendancy of the "lineage" as by the importunate presence of the domestic entourage. This was a time when private life was everywhere and yet nowhere.

Kinship, as a much more abstract relation than the fact of living together under one roof, raises problems of its own. To begin with, we must try to define precisely what a "lineage" was. The medieval sources show it in very different lights, and modern commentators have failed to give a sharp definition. Rather than review the historical literature, I shall comment on the two chapters that Marc Bloch devoted to the subject in his *Feudal Society* (1939), the seminal work of all medieval studies in France.

Bloch takes up the question of blood relations immedi-

The Contribution of Marc Bloch

Adam's lineage. Christians of the Middle Ages took a passionate interest in biblical genealogies. Kinship played an important role in both the ancient Hebraic and the feudal world. At the four corners of this sheet the progeny of the primal couple were fruitful and multiplied. *Apocalypse de Beatus*, 11th century. (Paris, Bibliothèque Nationale, Latin 8878.)

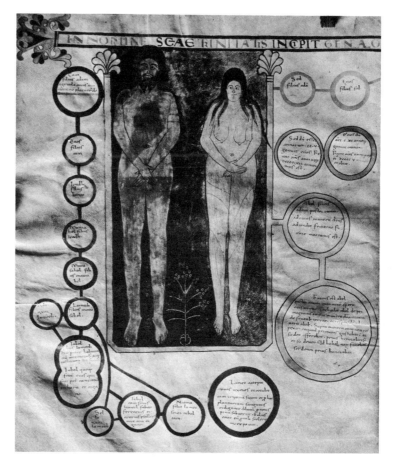

ately before he considers relations of vassalage; he plays down the importance of the latter by showing that they merely complemented bonds already formed by kinship, giving coherence to what might be called a society of vassals and clans rather than "feudal society." Vassalage and kinship were commonly linked by contemporaries, and the most durable groups were those that incorporated bonds of both kinds. According to Joinville, for example, it was the combination of *ligesse* and *lignage*, vassalage and kinship, that made Gui de Mauvoisin's troops so effective in the battle of Mansourah (1250). Bloch analyzes kinship in terms of legal relations (mobilization for private wars and common holding of patrimonial rights). Unfortunately, he is equivocal on the subject of coresidence, for he has not yet freed himself from the idea that relatives dwelt under one roof or at any rate in close proximity. But this does not prevent him from breaking new ground. He points out how different medieval society was from our own even in what might appear to be its elementary and natural fundamental unit. "Both in its emotional climate and in its size, the family of those days was quite a different thing from the small conjugal family of later times" [Manyon translation, p. 136]. The blood tie was less a matter of emotion than of constraint; for Bloch and his contemporaries, influenced by Lévy-Bruhl, this suggested a primitive state of development, with "primitive" intended pejoratively. Compounding this belief was a suspicion that the strength of the clan came at the expense of the couple: "But to place marriage at the center of the family group would certainly be to distort the realities of the feudal era" [Manyon translation, p. 136]. The wife was only a "half" member of her husband's clan, and widowhood automatically excluded (or liberated) her. Nevertheless, by grace of church and state, incontestable modernity emerges with the dawn of the thirteenth century, in the form of new attitudes toward individual rights and public peace. Seeking to further their own interests, church and state worked unremittingly to relax the coercive power of kinship.

Bloch's three main themes are to define the contours of the "lineage" and describe its functions; to investigate the relation of lineage to "conjugal family"; and to study changes that began around 1180. Research inspired by *Feudal Society* has refuted some of its author's conclusions, as is to be expected in a scientific work several decades old. The book's greatness is apparent from the insights that Bloch's successors have not sufficiently exploited as well as those that their work has confirmed. For example, Bloch anticipated the importance of the anthropological concept of "undifferentiated filiation" (which means that kinship is recognized through both maternal and paternal lines, with equal value and similar properties ascribed to both). Bloch does not merely remark in passing on the equivalence of maternal and paternal lines; undifferentiated, or cognatic, filiation made it impossible, he argues, for the "lineage" to serve as the fundamental social unit, as though it were a substantial reality. "This double link had important consequences. Since each generation had its circle of relatives which was not the same as that of the previous generation, the area of the kindred's responsibilities continually changed its contours" [Manyon translation, p. 138]. The nature of the clan is difficult to pin down for reasons having to do with the nature of the sources on the one hand and the structure of society on the other. What exactly were these extended families, which sheltered and absorbed feudal man in their bosom and which, in the case of a noble, were the source and symbol of his power?

Metamorphoses of the Lineage

Linguistics and the Feudal World. The French words *lignage* and *parenté*, translated, respectively, as lineage and kindred, derive from Old French and Latin forms that denoted relations rather than rigidly constituted groups. A person was said to be related to some powerful personage *par lignage* or *par parenté* (by lineage or by kinship—the terms being practically equivalent) and as a result enjoyed a privileged position in the social hierarchy. Enguerran IV, sire of Coucy, who was misused·by the royal courts in 1259, owed his rank to the fact that all the great barons of northern France were *de son lignage*, of his lineage, and therefore obliged to offer him their "counsel." Patri- and matrilateral cousinhoods and relations through marriage also helped to constitute an extensive network of kinship, which was given particular prominence by the dramatic circumstances; indeed it may have been specially reconstituted to cope with the situation.

The same words were applied secondarily to groups, as in the Arthurian romance *li parentez le roi Ban*, or when Gawaine deplores the enfeeblement of *nostre lignage*, our clan. This usage is less common than that evoking a definite (and/or contrived) relation. The group crystallized and particularized the kinship relation. *Genus*, a pure Latin word (not the direct ancestor of "race"), was used in the same way in the eleventh and twelfth centuries, primarily meaning that a man or woman was of "noble" or "illustrious" birth. It was applied only secondarily to a specific social group, for which a more exclusive term was *prosapia*. *Cognatio* was also applied to groups, but of slaves rather than aristocrats. To this list should be added such collective nouns as *proches* (close relations), *amis* [*charnels*] (friends [by blood]), and the more common *parents, cognats (cognati)*, and *consanguinei*. Clearly there were many roots and derivatives for expressing kinship. The only thing lacking is a word for "family"! Neither the couple nor the "conjugal" or "nuclear" family (couple plus children) is prominently indicated.

It would be wrong, however, to conclude from this that the nuclear family did not exist. Social description and interpretation cannot rely solely on what a society understood about itself, on the self-image that it was able to (or wished) to project. In fact, what the society failed to conceptualize or articulate deserves special attention. In his recent *Dialogues* with Guy Lardreau, Georges Duby brought up the idea of a history of silences, of those aspects of private life that went unmentioned, that words failed to capture. In particular, the question of kinship cannot be resolved simply by paying close attention to the vicissitudes of language, since, as Marc Bloch noted, the changing vocabulary may well indicate that kinship ties were less powerful than some scholars have suggested.

Feudal France was not linguistically homogeneous. The *langue d'oïl* [spoken in northern France] had regional variants. Hence Latin derivatives probably exhibited regional variations

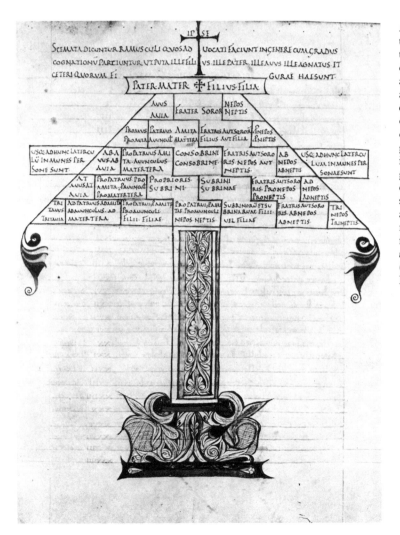

An exercise in abstraction. In this 12th-century kinship table, the reckoning of degrees is canonical, but the ascending and descending lines are arrayed along the left and right edges of the triangle, while the central axis is reserved for cousinages of the same generation. The terminology is interesting: *nepos* is used for grandson, whereas nephew is denoted "son of brother or sister." Paternal uncles and aunts were distinguished from maternal ones: *patruus* and *amita* for the paternal, *avunculus* and *matertera* for the maternal. (Paris, Bibliothèque Nationale, Latin 5239.)

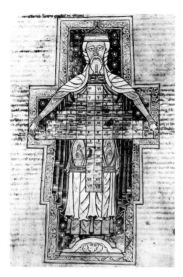

In the 11th and 12th centuries the human body often served as a metaphor for kinship, usually starting from the head (the common ancestor) and descending to the shoulder (first-degree kinship) and on down to the nails (sixth or seventh degree). In this 12th-century manuscript the figure simply serves as a support for the image: the table is read from the center out; the direct line runs up and down the vertical axis, whereas collateral relations are farther out to the right or left. Relatives are recorded to the sixth canonical degree. (Auxerre Library, ms 269.)

and failed to capture the richness of the vernacular. The absence of specific terms for various possible kinship groups is noteworthy. Kinship fulfilled a generic social function, linking different spheres of society.

Family names were not generally used. Modern historians have given names to major actors on the political stage, such as the Blois-Champagne and Erembaud, for the sake of expository clarity. The Giroie, a twelfth-century Norman clan actually known by that name, were a unique case, pioneers in the use of patronymics, which were slow to catch on. Their adoption was in some ways quite artificial, for it was enforced from outside by government authorities.

As for the nomenclature of kinship, Church Latin made distinctions that have since fallen into disuse. The two types of fathers-in-law were distinguished, for example; brothers-german were distinguished from half brothers. Such distinctions were necessary in a society where death claimed so many novice warriors and first-time mothers. Couples could not look forward to long lives together; this affected the way the notions of "couple" and "family" were seen. There were different words for the father's brother, *patruus*, and the mother's brother, *avunculus* (which is of course the root of the English *uncle*). But there is no evidence to show that attitudes toward the two kinds of uncles differed, and the nomenclature itself is rather confused. The medieval vocabulary made distinctions that we no longer make, but at the same time it conflated notions that we consider distinct. *Nepos* meant both nephew and grandson. The first sense was dominant and prevailed in the transition to the vernacular, probably because few children knew their grandfathers. Even among the Capetians, a sturdy lot, until 1214 no man survived long enough to witness the birth of his grandson.

Sources. The aristocracy encouraged and made use of genealogical literature, which developed first in Flanders and Anjou and flourished throughout northern France in the twelfth century. Georges Duby points out that it reveals at best an "ideology of filiation," a representation more concerned with lineal descent (*lignée*) than with lineage (*lignage*) in the strict sense of the word; in other words, more concerned with the vertical axis of kinship than with the space defined by combining that axis with a horizontal one. Nevertheless, this genealogical literature can be useful: kinship was as much a matter of the imagination as of "reality" in the narrow (and limited) sense of the word. To make use of the genealogical sources we must reconstruct the network of relationships and marriages by other means. We can then determine how the genealogists selectively distorted that network and thus deduce the social and political uses to which their work was put.

Historians commonly labor under the impression that charters and accounts preserved by churches reveal the raw stuff of social relations. The fact that these documents often mention relatives of the individuals with whom they are primarily concerned is considered irrefutable proof that kinship ties were quite strong. If someone wished to give or sell a piece of land or source of income to a church, that person required the approval of his or her close relatives, the so-called *laudatio parentum*. (Incidentally, most transactions were neither simple gifts nor outright sales but something more complex.) We therefore find the names of sons and daughters, brothers, sisters, and brothers-in-law, cousins, nephews, and so on inscribed on these official documents, usually at the bottom.

Foundation of a monastery: in this case a double investiture of laymen and monks, financial and sociopolitical, spiritual and libidinal. *Decretum of Gratian,* 14th century. (Laon Library, ms 372.)

This fact has led Bloch and others to the unwarranted conclusion that the medieval clan was a cohesive economic unit, often holding property in common. In the first place, large clans, though interesting, are rarely represented. Statistical analysis shows that the relatives participating in the *laudatio* were usually members of the "conjugal family." On occasion more remote connections, such as "friends by blood," were also included. This is particularly true since such participants may have been overlooked by those who prepared the briefs for each case; we find such omissions whenever we are able to compare the briefs with more extensive charters pertaining to the same transactions.

More important, the rights of *relatives* may have been overstated. They do not renounce actual enjoyment of a property but merely a potential right. Must we assume that the Church, exalting the individual, sought to diminish the importance of family ties? Is it not more reasonable to suspect that brothers and cousins were using kinship as a basis for claims that they knew were unlikely to be upheld but that might result in the payment of substantial compensation? Many were no doubt willing to wail the *calumnia* in the hope of receiving 10 solidi or a palfrey or vermilion slippers or jewels or furs or pigskins for their wives and daughters—thereby transforming a right to scrutinize or at most a share in indivisible property into personal wealth. In all likelihood in such cases the kinship group was artificially constituted to exert pressure on monks and clerics who were more compliant than has been thought. The group was not defined by coresidence and did not necessarily own property in common; these ambiguous documents should not be confused with the customs associated with inheritance, which were rarely recorded in writing in the period 1000–1200. Nevertheless, this sort of ruse was a common social practice: property and honors were often claimed in the name of the kindred. People were not confused about the law or blinded by some sort of mentality: they argued and vied with one another in subtle ways, using every means at their disposal.

The historian dissatisfied with the evidence of the practical record can turn to narrative sources. Though marred by errors, they contain a wealth of interpretation and comment invaluable for a retrospective sociology. A number of great historians and chroniclers flourished in northern France around 1100. The "Frenchman" Guibert of Nogent, the Flemish Galbert of Bruges, and the Norman Ordericus Vitalis paint, in a rather sinister light, a world not of "feudal anarchy" but of lineages engaged in brutal but rational competition. In dialectical fashion the power of the great is cited as both cause and consequence of the strength of their kindred and vassals, who often lived together under one roof. Yet the contours of the household are no more clearly delineated than those of the clan, no doubt because there was no reason to look closely at such matters; what counted were networks of relations, not homogeneous social formations.

Finally, there is no reason for us to reject the direct testimony of epic and courtly literature in the *langue d'oïl*. Carolingian and Breton subject matter is here couched in twelfth- and thirteenth-century settings and dialogues. Historians of material life have used these sources, so why not accept as plausible the social relations upon which these fictional plots are constructed? Here, at least, "feudalism" is not treated as though it were accursed, as it was by monastic authors blinded by contempt for the world. The colloquies and monologues of Guinevere and Lancelot come to us directly from the lay courts. If there is stylization, it serves as a magnifying glass; there is no better vehicle for the expression of emotion. Medieval romances, like contemporary ones, embody much more of reality (broadly understood) than supposedly more "objective" texts. Thus charters, narrative histories, epics, and courtly romance all deserve our attention. Each is attuned to a different level of authenticity; each constructs its own fiction.

The story of the rise, decline, and fall of great families or houses (though neither word was applied at the time to kinship groups) was a rich subject for the chroniclers of feudal times to explore. The theme has remained eminently suitable for romantic and historical fiction, ideal for illustrating subtle changes in social relations. The Erembaud clan furnished the material for a rich portrait of a decade of Flemish life; the Giroie did the same for more than a century of life in Normandy, enabling us to appreciate longer-range strategies.

The Erembaud. The kindred of Bertulf, provost of the collegiate church Saint Donatian of Bruges, achieved notoriety through a deed in 1127 that ultimately led to their downfall: the murder of Count Charles the Good. Several contemporaries, most notably the notary Galbert of Bruges, described in minute detail the plot, the crime, and the vengeance of God

Fortunes and Misfortunes of Great Families

(carried out by the hand of man). Galbert's account is part of the standard anthology of social history, for it has much to tell us about the rise of the *ministeriales*, those servants of princes and lords who, despite a rapid improvement in fortune in the twelfth century, were still struggling to cross the crucial threshold of aristocracy. Nobles or serfs? The ministeriales fell somewhere between the two extremes, these two hereditary social conditions preserved in the one case *by* the group itself and in the other case *in spite of* it.

The Erembaud no doubt would have succeeded in obscuring their servile origins had not a knight related to the clan by marriage been refused a judicial duel in the course of protracted legal proceedings. Though free initially, he had lost his free status, it was claimed, because he had been married for a year to a niece of the provost. Thus the knight, who had hoped to reaffirm his still precarious status through so illustrious a marriage, discovered that his wife bore a hidden taint: she was a serf. His in-laws found themselves embarrassed and therefore obliged to react politically against a rival faction which, conspiring to bring about the downfall of the Erembaud, had exhorted the count to enforce his claims upon those who had been born his serfs.

The intrigue had another cause. The *cognatio* accused of bearing the taint of servitude saw itself as a *genus*, a prestigious clan with fortresses of its own and the ability to wage private wars. Bertulf himself indirectly urged his nephews to do so for the sake of prowess and honor. Borsiard and the other *nepotes Bertulfi* were locked in unending conflict with the enemy party, the *nepotes Thancmari*, equally arrogant and just as roundly hated by the Brugeois. Relatives and vassals on both sides were mobilized. In punishment for the infraction of his public peace legislation, the count destroyed Borsiard's house, thereby incurring the wrath of the Erembaud.

The result was a conspiracy among several of the provost's nephews, joined by various other kin not so clearly defined, and even by one nonrelative. The conspirators murdered the count in the church and at once put into effect a well-thought-out plan to ensure that William of Ypres, a bastard of the comital family, would become count of Flanders, thus guaranteeing that the assassins would go unpunished. But neither the avengers of Charles the Good, men of his household who sallied forth immediately after his death, nor King Louis VI, who sought to achieve sovereignty over Flanders through his candidate William Cliton, was prepared to leave the field free to such lowborn conspirators. One by one, all the Erembaud were crushed by the weight of their crime, including those who had nothing to do with the murder. Galbert justifies this collective damnation by arguing, a posteriori, that a curse was inherent in the lineage. Indeed, it was Galbert (or the popular sources from which he drew his inspiration) who invented the Erembaud. The name comes from an ancestor, a rather lowly knight, who betrayed his lord, the castellan of Bruges (one Boldran, not mentioned in any charter). This knight committed adultery with his lord's wife, then cast her husband into a river and along with the unfaithful spouse seized the castellany. Thus the punishment of the count's murderers, some of whom were pitched from the top of a tower, mirrored and compensated for the initial crime, a fitting end to the history of an infamous—and fictitious—clan. Nevertheless, the counterfeit of the fabulous deed, which in the ordinary genealogical literature would have inaugurated the good fortunes of the *genus,* is worthy of note: as reward for some exploit, a young, unknown hero wins the hand of a young girl or widow, through whom honor (wealth and prestige of the blood) comes to the progeny in the male line.

This lineage, however, is actually a fabrication, as is evident from the fact that elsewhere the contours of the group are less rigid. Its central core is patrilineal: promoted to the rank of *caput generis* as a result of his holding high office in the principality, Bertulf manages the careers of his brothers' sons; having raised them in his house, he feels affection for them. Although the nephews have established their own homes, they still look to Bertulf to plan and coordinate their activities, and his residence remains the center of the group's prestige. Borsiard's father, Lambert, occupies a place on the system's periphery. Castellan of Reddenbourg, he sought (in vain) to keep his distance from a plot in which his son was a principal conspirator.

Lambert and other kin of the conspirators were victims of the notion of collective guilt. Several of them attempted to escape the count's avengers. Bertulf's brother, the castellan Didier Haket, tried to separate himself from the murderers before the leading men of Flanders: "We condemn their actions, and we would have sent them away unequivocally had we not been obliged, against our wishes, to consider the proximity of our blood" (and thus to give them refuge, aid, and advice). Was this simply a ruse or a genuine conflict of values? There are overtones of tragedy in the way in which Didier here struggles against the bonds of kinship. The struggle was not unfounded, however. As Galbert and his contemporaries were aware, some individuals did manage to detach themselves from the accursed clan. Beloved by the "people" and almost a noble, Robert the Child (Didier's son) was accorded two privileges not granted his "relatives": he was not held in the dungeon, and he was beheaded rather than hanged. The consequences of the blood tie were ineluctable.

Not all members of the lineage were equally responsible for the crime. Galbert identifies a core group of blood relatives, which can only be called a lineage; another chronicler, Gautier of Thérouanne, identifies a group linked more by coresidence than consanguinity. For Gautier, Bertulf is primarily a paterfamilias, the master of a household. He believes moreover that the conspiracy was a contractual arrangement. The two authors reveal another ambiguity seemingly concocted to confound sociologists: marriage apparently established a sort of solidarity between the two clans involved. So far as we know, the husbands of Bertulf's nieces did not escape his clan's downfall; yet throughout the chronicles they remain in the background, with but a single exception. This suggests that consanguinity and marriage interacted in complex and unpredictable ways.

Perhaps it was because this particular *genus* was of recent date that the details concerning it are so imprecise. In contrast to these parvenus, did not the aristocracy exhibit a more solid, less improvised lineal structure? The Giroie would seem to offer an excellent example. By the time Galbert's contemporary Ordericus Vitalis relates their story, or, rather, offers us glimpses of it in the course of his *History of the Church*, the family is already four generations old.

The Giroie. This family is typical of the upper strata of the Norman aristocracy, established by, or at any rate imitative of, the dukes of the early eleventh century. Lucien Musset has shown that this aristocracy was composed, as one would expect, not of legendary "companions of Rollo" but of well-born Frankish and Breton immigrants. Giroie, founder of the clan, was descended from "a great French and Breton nobility." Ordericus Vitalis knew the names of Giroie's father and grandfather, as well as that of his sister, Hildiarde, mother of numerous noble children. Giroie's descendants perpetuated his name by adding it to their own, either simply (Robert "Giroie") or in adjectival form (Guillaume *Geroianus*, William "the Giroie").

In the Middle Ages a man's first name was his real and basic identification. Family ties were indicated by the repetition of the same names generation after generation. Names were transmitted as hereditary attributes from father to son and uncle to nephew, but also (and perhaps primarily) from maternal grandfather or granduncle to grandson or grandnephew. Illustrious names were one of the essential contributions of women to their husbands' clans; such names could be used only by descendants of the first person to possess them, and they could be a major asset in a political career. The *virtus* of the ancestors flowed in the blood of the homonymous descendants; more than that, the progeny on occasion inherited the *honores* (offices and possessions) of their forebears.

In any study of an aristocratic kinship group we must attempt to understand what choices were being made when infants were named. For to choose a name was to choose a destiny. Here, the names William and Robert indicate a link (probably by marriage though possibly by spiritual kinship) to the dukes of Normandy. These names tended to replace Ernaud and Renaud, which apparently date from an earlier time and were patrilineal. Giroie was merely added as a sobriquet, to help the members of a patrilineage recognize one another, although the basic system was one of undifferentiated kinship, apparently well accepted and exploited, based on the traditional usage of first names transmitted by women. This ancient practice was what Karl Ferdinand Werner has called the "grammar of (cognatic) kinship relations." The male surname transmitted by agnation was an innovation—one is tempted to call it a pioneering discovery—connected with the new vigor and density, unknown before the year 1000, of the aristocracy established in the castles. To manage the new "castral system" and the power of command associated with it (the so-called lordship of the *ban*) was the difficult task that fell to the descendants of the first Giroie.

The Giroie settled near the border of Maine and Normandy some time between 1015 and 1027, with the duke's blessing and the support of the sire of Bellême, a companion-in-arms of Giroie. The only daughter of the powerful Helgon was promised to the soldier, but she died prematurely, before the wedding could take place. This did not prevent Giroie from assuming title to the *fiscus* (revenue) of Montreuil and Echauffour (an estate or fief on which a castle would soon be built). He then married another noblewoman, who bore him

THE GIROIE

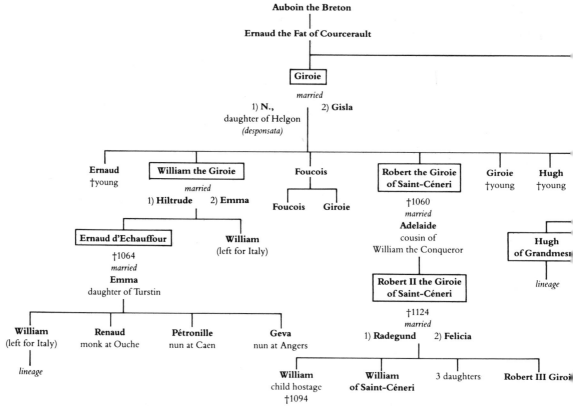

seven sons and four daughters. So fertile a marriage was not unusual at the time. In order to avoid destructive divisions of property, therefore, lineages were obliged either to follow an expansionist policy, competing with other lineages both "at home" and "abroad," or to subject younger sons to strict discipline. Ordericus Vitalis helps us reconstruct the strategy of the Giroie, but he does not show all of its aspects because he is committed to a particular representation, compatible both with what he knows and with what will serve the interests of his monastery, Saint-Evroul d'Ouche.

In the first generation of Giroie heirs only three of the seven sons produced male heirs. William the Giroie, eldest of the survivors (after the death of his brother Ernaud), assumed command over his brothers. Having obtained the château of Saint-Céneri, he left it to his younger brother Robert, who appears to have been an ally in his battle against Giroie's third son, Foucois. William's preeminence did not come about au-

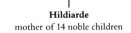

Hildiarde
mother of 14 noble children

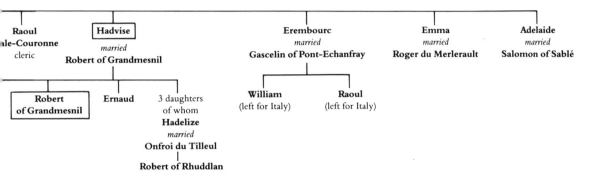

tomatically. Originally he and Foucois had divided the *honor* of Montreuil between them, and we can only imagine that a bitter rivalry developed shortly after 1035. Foucois was the companion and godson of Gislebert, count of Brionne, and enemy of William the Giroie and his retinue. But he lost the battle, and Ordericus Vitalis relegates him and his progeny to obscurity and illegitimacy: his mother is referred to as a "concubine."

Was this the only marriage of dubious validity in the entire history of the clan, powerful in an age when the canonical rules of marriage were so often abused? It is hard to believe. Perhaps the point was to discredit those sons who did not take part in the founding of the Ouche monastery (although they later contributed to it) and about whom the monks became concerned at a later date. Here we see one of those competitive stratagems to which Georges Duby alluded earlier. It is remarkable that in the internal struggles that divided Normandy, the great clans did not line up on one side or the other but split into factions reflecting their own internal divisions. The clans survived because they were represented in both camps. The question was which branch would eliminate its rivals or at least gain the upper hand over them. (By rewriting history, a younger branch could portray itself as the eldest.)

Of Giroie's four remaining sons, three had premature deaths; they died "young," unmarried. They included the eldest, Ernaud, and the fifth-born, "Giroie," whose "real" first name is not given. In his final moments this Giroie, who had been accidentally mortally wounded by a squire, urged his slayer to flee the vengeance of his brothers, who would have acted out of concern for honor as much as for brotherly affection. This was the kind of act of piety which, like gifts to churches, tended to isolate the individual from his kin. Another younger son, Raoul Male-Couronne, renounced the perils and sins of knighthood in favor of a clerical career, thereby acquiring leisure for the cultivation of letters and the study of medicine.

William thus won ascendancy over his brothers, vanquishing one, allowing another to pursue a vocation in the church. He held sway over a patrilineal group whose members approved one another's "gifts" and "sales" to Saint-Evroul, participating in the *laudatio* to the exclusion of all other relatives (but not of lords and vassals). Those who gave their

The burial of great personages in churches, *ad sanctos* (among the saints), was traditional, but the tombs of Henry Plantagenet and his wife, Eleanor of Aquitaine, attest to a new concern on the part of French princes about 1200 to take care with the burial places of their relatives and adorn tombs with sculpted images of individuals, although there was still no concern with accurate representation of features. (Abbey church, Fontevraud.)

approval were called *consentants* or *codonateurs*, as though the two terms were equivalent. The practice, however, did not always indicate that the property being transferred was held jointly.

By contrast, Giroie's four daughters did not transmit to their heirs either the patronymic or the equivalent rights over the patrimony. All married, because marriage posed no threat to preservation of the patrimony. On the contrary, matrimonial alliances served the interests of the lineage by putting others in its debt. Erembourc and Emma were married to lesser lords occupying lands that neighbored the Giroies' sphere of influence. The head of the clan exerted some influence over his sons-in-law. The group of "neighbors, men, and cousins" grew over the space of a generation. The marriages of Adelaide and Hadvise were, I think, of a different type (isogamic), to geographically remote partners of social rank roughly equal to that of their brides, one in Maine-Anjou, the other in Normandy. When it came to giving wives to other nobles or nuns to the Church, the lineage was always careful to divide its daughters equally between these two provinces.

Ordericus Vitalis gives particular weight to the alliance that was established through the good offices of Hadvise. In partnership with her sons, the Grandmesnil, William and Robert Giroie "founded" the abbey of Saint-Evroul around 1050. A special relationship with a monastery was an important milestone along the way to acquiring lordship of the *ban*. The holy relics in the abbey lent legitimacy and an aura of permanence to the power of the sword. In the abbeys, which have been called "family burial grounds," uninterrupted prayer was offered on behalf of the dead. Epitaphs in fine Latin verse exalted the family ancestors. The composition of the founders' group was the result of a deliberate strategy. William wished to emphasize the alliance with the Grandmesnil, whereas his nephews at first wanted to act alone, to build a monastery on the spot where their father had died. Ouche was therefore the sanctuary of two lineages rather than of the descendants of a common ancestor through a single line. Nevertheless, of the two lineages the Giroie was the more eminent. Robert of Rhuddlan, who wanted to be buried in the monastery, was added to the founders; his mother, sister of the Grandmesnil, was said to be "of illustrious Giroie stock" (*ex clara stirpe Geroianorum*).

Because of their association with the new monastery, an aura of sacredness surrounded both lineages. But they had

Alms to the churches, a gesture of salvation. The lay donor, William of Bezac, gives the cleric, who represents the saint to whom the monastery belongs, a symbolic object: the column itself. This decorative component of the building seems to play the role traditionally assigned to a knife, branch, piece of straw, or book. (Romanesque church of Saint Priest, Volvic.)

to pay dearly for it. Robert of Grandmesnil and Ernaud d'Echauffour became monks and literally "plundered" their "relatives" of a part of their wealth, in particular booty from southern Italy, on behalf of the saint. Their behavior mirrored that of the *calumniatores* who fill the pages of the cartularies. What is more, control of a monastery such as this one was never assured. The founders had to contend with both the Gregorian reform and, what proved an even greater threat, the power of the duke. The Giroie and the Grandmesnil would fade, but Saint-Evroul would not—not so quickly, at any rate.

The difficulties the families encountered were direct repercussions of a grave political crisis that developed around 1060. Robert I of Saint-Céneri and Ernaud d'Echauffour, who rebelled against the duke, did not survive the troubles. The latter lived just long enough to regain the good graces of William the Conqueror and recover his briefly confiscated property before succumbing to poison administered by Mabille of Bellême in 1064. The elder Giroies and Bellême had broken bread together, but their descendants now embarked on an endless round of warfare with a number of noteworthy episodes. The Grandmesnil reestablished themselves more quickly. Their destiny then diverged from that of their cousins. According to Ordericus Vitalis, the nobility of the *Geroiani* began to wane. Their descendants were forced to flee to southern Italy, an escape route that innumerable younger or disinherited branches availed themselves of.

But the Giroie returned. The name was kept alive in the Saint-Céneri branch. In 1088 the liberal Robert Curthose succeeded the implacable William as duke. Inheritors of great *honores*, more or less distant relations deprived of their property by Robert's father, hastened to beseech him to restore their possessions, which Robert did, thus consecrating the medieval legal concept of a hereditary right to land. When Geoffroi of Mayenne intervened on behalf of Robert II the Giroie of Saint-Céneri, he cited in support of his case not Robert's ancestry but his relation to the duke through his

Knights of the Grail. As prose fiction endowed these legendary warriors with a flesh-and-blood presence, they also acquired a patrimony, a heraldic identity, and kin. Robert of Boron, *Histoire du Graal*, ca. 1280. (Paris, Bibliothèque Nationale, French 95.)

mother, Adelaide, a cousin (*consobrina*) of William the Conqueror.

The descendants (*progenies*) of the Giroie survived numerous difficult situations because they were at once more and less than a pure patrilineage. An extensive, multilateral network of kinship helped them through hard times. In 1094, for example, Robert II found his first wife, his hostage son, and even his castle all fallen before the might of the Bellême, yet "with the support of relatives and friends" he regrouped his forces and rekindled his hope. On the other hand, because it was necessary to protect the integrity of the land, the lineage pruned itself back, admitting unmarried brothers and uncles but excluding cousins; those who made their fortunes elsewhere most likely lost contact with their relatives. In 1119 Montreuil and Echauffour were returned to Robert II. Thus he succeeded in recovering all of his ancestral patrimony before he was forced to divide it among his sons. The Giroie had a strong presence near Saint-Evroul when the old monk chose to include part of their predecessors' history in his vast fresco. With hindsight he is able to bring out the peculiar features of the family's strategy: its ability to multiply alliances while limiting the number of direct descendants. During one hundred years of solitude the family, with support from its kin, fought constantly to further its own interests.

This history—and its historian's viewpoint—is typical in more than one respect. Most of the castellans of northern France established their power, as the Giroie did, in the early eleventh century. For them the crystallization of a dynasty came later than for the prince and no doubt earlier than for the lesser knights. A peculiarity of Normandy was the power of the dukes, whose confiscations of property enabled them to alter the distribution of power at will. But in the even more troubled regions of the Loire Valley and the Ile de France, assassinations and ambushes could cause similar upheavals, though with no more effect in the long run on the power of the principal lineages.

This kinship structure was characteristic of the aristocracy, involved, by vocation as it were, in the great game of power politics and local domination. "Middling" knights occur frequently in Ordericus Vitalis' *History* but rarely as individualized figures; rather, they are satellites of the "powerful," caught up in the intrigues of the vast households to which they belong. As for the peasants, absorbed in productive labor, their fragile huts sheltered "small families." The peasant's strategy was to enlarge his plot of land, not to uphold honor through matrimonial alliance or private warfare. Incorporation of a peasant's land in a seigneurie or parish made him subject to the customs of the place and associated him with the anonymous *patres* buried in the church. Modern ethnology teaches the same lesson as the social history of the central Middle Ages: lineages and genealogies are a monopoly of chieftains.

They are also an ideological construct. Here, instead of referring frequently and directly to the oral tradition of the castellans' households, Ordericus has drawn upon the work of Lambert of Ardres and John of Marmoutier (and his adapters), invaluable gifts of the second half of the twelfth century. By comparing these works with some composite genealogies, Georges Duby has been able to identify their major concerns. Justifying possession of a patrimony, the genealogists followed the male line. They were also at pains to show how the clan added to its luster through splendid (hypergamic) marriages. Not that nobility originated with women rather than men. If any status in this society could be acquired through the mother, it was servitude. Yet even this legacy of the ancient slave gangs was made largely obsolete by the existence of genuine marriage and establishment of the couple in the husband's residence as an autonomous unit. Nobility was an innate quality, although it varied in intensity according to the degree of honor and proximity to kings. Only if the mother's or grandmother's line was markedly more illustrious than the father's was it thought justifiable to make a matrilateral detour from the royal road of ancestry. Had a twelfth-century domestic chaplain of the Giroie imitated the chaplain of the sires of Ardres, the Giroie ancestors might have been made, by careful selection, to shine more brightly in the firmament of the nobility. The merit of the more objective Ordericus Vitalis is that he offers us a middle stage between the raw data and the idealized image.

The *Chanson de Roland* is a precocious masterpiece, the earliest manuscript version of which stems from the same time and milieu as Ordericus Vitalis' *History of the Church*. Yet it paints a different picture of clan structure. Only two relatives of the hero are identified: Charlemagne, his maternal uncle, and Ganelon, his stepfather and enemy. Roland's hatred of his

Social Structure and Literature

stepfather may well have been a consequence of a struggle for power between two clans. Marrying the king's sister would have assured a man of a powerful position at court, and the woman's remarriage might signify that one of two rival groups had usurped the position of the other. None of this is explicitly stated in the text, however. Roland lives not among "friends by blood" but among companions-in-arms, members of the royal household. His kindred exist only in an abstract, virtual sense; he alludes to them in justifying his proud and fatal refusal to call for aid by blowing the trumpet:

> Ne place Damnedeu
> Que mi parent pur mei seient blasmet.
>
> May it please God that my relatives
> not be blamed on my account.

Ganelon's treachery is judged by the barons, before whom Charlemagne himself brings complaint, backed by the loyal young Thierry, his familiar but not a member of his clan. Opposing them is the felon, assisted by thirty "relatives," vague, nameless shadows. Only Pinabel stands out when called upon to fight a judicial duel, and his relation to the accused is not specified. Between blows he and Thierry exchange peace proposals and offers of mediation. Nevertheless, Pinabel cannot let Ganelon down. His cry, too, embodies the values of a "shame culture":

> Sustenir voeill trestut mun parentet
> N'en recrerrai pur nul hume mortel;
> Mielz voeill murir qu'il me seit reprovet.
>
> I want to support all my kindred; no
> mortal man shall force me to deny them;
> I would sooner die than incur that
> reproach.

His defeat leads not only to the torture of the traitor but also to the hanging of the thirty relatives who had backed his cause. An ill-defined, unsentimental, even inarticulate kinship: is this the primitive Germanic tribe?

The atmosphere of *Lancelot* and *Perceval* by Chrétien de Troyes (1170–1190) is more springlike. Chrétien's alert pen gives a more important role to female characters, who occasion more inward feelings in the males. The heroes' adventures frequently bring them into contact with named and identified relatives. This always occurs accidentally, however, and the

relative's identity is not usually revealed until after a spontaneous sympathy has developed. Does Perceval defend a damsel
against her friend's brutality? Does he bow his head sadly in
remorse upon hearing the words of a hermit? Only later does
he find out that the damsel is his cousin and the hermit his
uncle. Similarly, the good Gormemanz de Gorhaut admires
the natural talent of a boy undergoing accelerated training for
knighthood, whom he does not know to be his sister's son.
One almost waits for these episodes to end with an exclama-
tion worthy of Marivaux, such as "I sorely needed for that
boy to turn out to be my nephew!" or "At last I understand
the stirrings of my heart!" Such stories reveal the social prej-
udices of the audience as well as a subtle heritage of "class."

By 1200 both epic and romance had matured, perhaps not
without losing some of their savor. What is more, the distinction between the two had faded. There was need for a
synthesis of the French with the Breton subject matter, now
scattered through innumerable works. It was at this point that
the patrilineage made its appearance in both literatures. It
quickly took on a central dramatic role, providing a firm
structure for two fictitious societies. Arthur and Charlemagne
lost power to their barons, unlike Philip Augustus, from
whom they borrowed the traits of brutal ingratitude and unwillingness to take personal risks. What changed was more
than the appearance of an individual; it was the appearance of
the state. This developing literature tended to depict complete
worlds because of its own internal logic, apart from any kind
of determinism, dialectical or otherwise. It is surprising to find
such great similarity between the sources considered most
objective and the epics and romances of the so-called second
age of medieval literature.

Bertran of Bar-sur-Aube divided the heroes of the Frankish epic into three great *gests*, that is, "races" or "clans": the
clan of the kings; the clan of traitors descended from Doon of
Mainz; and the clan of loyal barons, for whom Bertran provides an ancestor in the fictional figure of Garin of Montglane.
The second- and third-named clans battle for preeminence in
the realm (*seignourie*). This status is of greater interest than any
particular castle or duchy; these are merely pieces in a chess
match. Genuine feeling was reserved exclusively for ancient
patrimonial lands.

Each work in the epic cycle could now be devoted to a
patrilineage representing a segment of one of the three great
gests. It becomes hard to distinguish between the principal

character and his brothers. (The chanson *Renaud de Montauban* is also known as the *Quatre Fils Aymon*.) In the first generation, the four direct heirs of Garin of Montglane follow the lead of the youngest, Girart of Vienne (who gives his name to Bertran's chanson). Insulted by the queen, he becomes enmeshed in a private war with King Charles. Unstinting, his brothers come to his aid with large troops of vassals. Here the youngest is in charge because he is the offended party. In the presence of their aging father the brothers hold a "family council," in which each states his opinion. Relations among adult members of the same clan were egalitarian; leadership alternates between Hernaut, the eldest son and master of the castle, and Girart, *chevetaigne* in battle. Girart, moreover, enjoys a special relationship with his nephew Aymeri, for whom he feels particular affection and over whom he wields greater authority than Hernaut, the boy's father. This establishes Girart as an educator and "nourisher" of youth, and the boy is admitted to

The gang of four. Riding a single horse and all roughly the same size, the Aymon brothers, like many other 12th-century knights, probably shared joint ownership of their steed, which in practice they would have ridden in turn. The ideology of the lineage depicted them as enjoying equal value; actually inequalities usually developed. *Renaud de Montauban*, 15th century. (Arsenal Library, ms 2990.)

his household after his sense of family honor has been tested: *Molt traoit à sa geste* [he was of his clan, or "conformed" to it in "many respects"].

When the clan is finally reconciled with Charles in a ceremony known as the *asseurement* (an agreement to ensure the peace jointly), young Aymeri at first refuses to offer the homage of peace. He avails himself of a right recognized in the customaries of Saint Louis's time to withdraw from a ritual traces of which are found in documents dating back as far as the eleventh century. Nevertheless, he allows himself to be persuaded that he cannot carry on the war by himself. He embodies the arrogance of youth within the clan. Ill-tamed by the authority of the *senez*, senior members of the lineage, at times he lampoons his grandfather in the presence of other family members; yet he is the first to defend the clan's honor at court when a disrespectful baron makes similar fun of the old man. In the Giroie lineage we saw vertical divisions emerge between branches. Here we see a horizontal division between generations, temporary to be sure and more the result of dynamic tensions than of fatal structural forces, but nonetheless real. This generational conflict was somewhat obscured by the Latin sources, where the contrast between the idle wisdom of the *seniores* and the thoughtless impetuosity of the *juvenes* tends to be couched in global social terms rather than set concretely within the lineage.

In the epic that bears his name, *Aymeri de Narbonne*, the young squire has become an aging lord on the brink of senility. Between him and the first six of his seven sons a conflict smolders, for Aymeri, dreaming of grandeur for his line, expels his older sons from the city, keeping only the youngest, still a child, by his side. His intention is to forestall controversy and keep the patrimony intact, but the effect is to frustrate the desires of the six sons and jeopardize lands that now lie defenseless before the Saracens. The author does not find in favor of the older generation but leaves his audience with contradictory arguments of equal force.

Can we not say that trouvères such as Bertran reproduced in their work the very process by which the clan came into existence in real life? In literature, taken out of its social context, we see a development in two stages, whereas in society the change was more subtle and gradual.

We witness the same evolution in the literature devoted to the Knights of the Round Table, from Chrétien de Troyes to the anonymous author who, wrapping himself in the authoritative mantle of Walter Map, completed the vast Lance-lot-Grail cycle around 1230 with a dramatic narrative of "The Death of King Artu." In the early romances individual rivalry in the noble courts proves fruitful, but in the later ones inter-lineal rivalry unleashes uncontrollable forces of vengeance and hatred that ultimately lead to the ruin of King Arthur's world. Though friends by predilection, Lancelot and Gawaine are tragically separated by the intrigue—and the blood—of three of Gawaine's brothers.

The two hostile patrilineages are not entirely comparable. *Li parentez le roi Ban* (the kindred of King Ban) include the king's sons (Lancelot and Hector) and nephews (Bohort and Lionel). Lancelot, as the eldest son in the eldest branch of the family, is the undisputed leader; he also enjoys control of the patrimony of Bénoic and Gaunes (while his two cousins enjoy rights of succession) and the rank of lord. His honor as lover in the affair with Queen Guinevere is also their concern, and they defend him. Although he attempts to seek his own des-tiny by withdrawing in disguise with his squire and wearing a borrowed coat of arms to detach himself temporarily from the group, his heart remains transparent to his kin, to brothers and cousins who feel the same affection and the same powerful obligations toward one another. Each of the four men heads a large household of his own, yet their unity is unshakable in war and tournament alike.

Such unity proves more difficult to achieve among the five nephews of King Arthur. (Whether these nephews were sons of a brother or sister of the king we do not know.) In mourning, he deplores the loss of his flesh and blood in these, his kindred. From their *ostels* in town they converged on the palace, where they could often be found gathered in dark recesses or corridors whispering and murmuring among them-selves as though in private. But their sentiments differed, and they formed no common plan of action. If Agravain was envious and conspiratorial and Mordret criminal, Gawaine was courteous and Gaheriet loyal. Had there been a prize for most *vaillans* (valiant), it would have gone first to Gawaine, then to Gaheriet. This lineage was less homogeneous than the other and lacked its hierarchical organization. Indeed, it is only the three deaths inflicted by the kin of King Ban that stir Gawaine's family feelings and impel him to vengeance. Like the heroes of the great Icelandic sagas (contemporaneous with these French romances), he is obstinate in quasi-judicial negotiations over compensation for Gaheriet's death, single-mindedly refusing anything but Lancelot's own life in return. He makes a public show of the "love" he feels for his lost brothers, but over the course of the romance the word is cast into disrepute. Make no mistake: what is at stake is the social rank of the lineage, and this royal dynasty has no intention of accepting anything less than the ultimate price for one of its members.

In the thirteenth century there was nothing anachronistic about this. Every man had a price or value, which relatives of a murder victim could legally collect in compensation from the murderer to restore peace between their respective families. Although these prices were no longer precisely fixed by statute as in the so-called barbarian laws of the early Middle Ages, the idea of compensation was still familiar in feudal times; it complicated the determination of a man's social rank. "Friends by blood" avenged one another not because of the emotional wounds that the death of one caused the other, nor even to compensate for the loss of a soldier in interclan rivalry, but because loss of honor was a matter of great consequence.

La Mort le roi Artu is sociologically interesting for another reason: the contrast it draws between the *parage* of Gawaine and the *frérage* of Lancelot. (These systems allowed the heirs of a fief to hold the property undivided under the authority of the eldest. In parage, the younger brothers aided the eldest by performing in his stead military services owed to the lord—or by paying the tax assessed in lieu thereof—but they were not obliged to do homage to their brother. In frérage, the younger brothers held their part of the undivided property in fief from their elder brother, to whom they rendered homage.) Frérage, a thirteenth-century innovation that introduced vassalage relations into the lineage, was accepted in some parts of northern France by the "feudal" aristocracy, the original audience of the romances.

Like the chanson of Girart of Vienne, romance was a mixture of social reality and fiction. Both chanson de geste and romance reveal or clarify matters that other sources neglect or obscure, such as the rivalry between young and old or the lack of an emotional distinction between brothers and cousins. The banishment of the maternal uncle (suggested, for example, by Bertran of Bar-sur-Aube's transformation of Girart into a paternal uncle of Olivier) may seem puzzling. Yet this is consistent with the exaltation of the patrilineage. The degree to which the abstract relation of kinship must be supported by the concrete fact of coresidence is striking; each manipulates the other. Moving away from the dreamy solitude and heroic isolation of earlier forms, this eclectic literature places the individual in his social setting.

What was fictional was the fact that all the kinship functions were ascribed indiscriminately to a single group. In practice, however, as we learn from the reportage of Galbert of Bruges and the monumental work of Ordericus Vitalis, kinship relations could not be shrunk to the confines of the patrilineage. The lineage may have controlled the patrimony, but war mobilized broader cognations. Thus, the literary sources are right about systems of relations but wrong (or at any rate stylized) when it comes to the constitution of groups.

Honor and Family Strategy

It will be useful in what follows to distinguish between (cognatic) kindred—*parenté*—and (agnatic) lineage—*lignage*—reserving kindred for relatives in general and lineage for the particular group defined by filiation through a single (male) line. With this distinction we can eliminate the apparent contradiction between Marc Bloch, who recommends caution on account of the vague nature of "family" obligations, and Georges Duby, who in his writings on the age of châteaus confidently fills the stage with battling and conquering lineages.

The writings of medieval jurists at times come close to sociology, though they were produced for other ends and according to different rules. Philippe de Beaumanoir, once the king's bailiff, began recording and commenting on the *Customs of the Beauvaisis* around 1283. In chapters entitled "On degrees of lineage" and "On war" he illustrates the properties of undifferentiated filiation. He counts degrees of kinship by the canonical method: the number of generations between each of two consanguineous (or more distant) relatives and their common ancestor. Significantly, his texts contain masculine *egos* and patrilateral liaisons, but the context makes it clear that for him kinship could pass through women as well as men. Definitions of kinship were relevant to four kinds of legal questions: war, marriage, inheritance, and *retrait lignager* (defined later).

Consider war. Beaumanoir raises the question of a judge who must hear a case involving nobles who excuse their misdeeds on the grounds that they were engaged in "warfare" on behalf of a relative. Under what circumstances can such a claim be accepted? In medieval usage such wars were not described as "private" (an epithet added by more recent commentators). Private violence had not yet been declared illegitimate by the state, which sought merely to limit its use to the noble class, to consanguineous kin of the fourth degree or less, and without regard to "relations of affinity" (kinship through marriage). Bourgeois and *hommes de la poesté* (common subjects of the seigneurie) could not serve as military captains, though they were automatically involved in the wars of their lord, if they had one. The offended or offending noble was flanked by his kindred, organized according to a principle of structural relativity: the contours of the group varied from individual to individual. This was a matter not of vacillation but of rigorous logic, which legists employed in reasoning about the rules of war. War could not be waged alone, after all; there was no reason to place in one camp rather than the other those men to whom both *chevetaignes* were related in the same degree. Thus two brothers-german could not fight on opposite sides; but two half brothers, sons of different mothers, belonged to different clans and therefore would have had means to fight (their common kin being obliged to remain neutral). And so it went throughout the zone of legitimate solidarity. Cousins of the same degree were not required to take up arms. If of unequal degree, they joined the side to which they were more closely related.

These observations point up some crucial differences between consanguinity and vassalage, so alike in so many ways, in particular in the kinds of obligations that each entailed, that Marc Bloch referred to the latter as a surrogate form of kinship. Besides lacking a natural hierarchy, kinship was a bond whose consequences were ineluctable. Once recognized and accepted, it was not negotiable. If a vassal found himself caught between conflicting obligations, however, he could declare that one *ligesse* took priority over the other and, with shrewd casuistry, apportion his military or financial contributions accordingly. Between relatives aid was unlimited, and the obligations of a cousin-german were no less than those of a brother.

Affection was not accepted as legal grounds in the courts of Beauvais. Nevertheless, Beaumanoir alludes to it in connection with bastards (who were, to be sure, semi-kin, for they had no right of inheritance but were obviously of concern in the rules regarding impediments to marriage). Bastards, he says, feel a natural love (and community of interest!) with their half brothers. The rigor of the bond of "friendship by

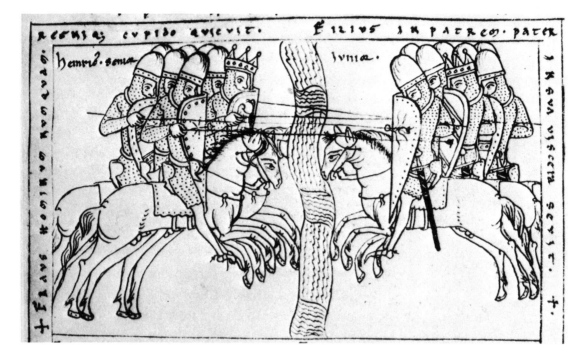

Was the only real combat, of which Beaumanoir says nothing, that between fathers and sons? Here, the emperor, Henry IV "the Elder" (*senior*), on the left, battles his heir, Henry V "the Younger" (*junior*). *Chronik Ottos von Freising*, 1177. (Jena University Library, Cod. Bose q. 6.)

blood" may shed light on the question, but the legist is still worried about the mobilization of other forces. He avoids the trap of arguing that relatives must come to one another's aid, which would have been detrimental to the public peace that he wished to uphold. Individuals are always free to refuse to make war, avoiding its perils; if avengers, they may refuse to haggle over the peace. On the other hand, they have the right to refuse *asseurement* against the wishes of the chevetaigne, the primary party involved: private interest could take precedence over clan honor. A combat troop was organized for a particular battle; it had no true hierarchy or firm structure of authority.

Undifferentiated filiation was useful in the abstract to the theory of private war. But in practice the theory was adjusted to give preference to patrilateral cousins. Was the Beauvaisis that far from the Cornwall of the imagination? The logic of the law was a long way from knightly ideology, but narrative and diplomatic sources provide the transition.

In conclusion, let us consider the interaction between the kinship function and clan structure. When I speak of kinship function, here limited to filiation (marriage will be discussed later), I use the word *function* in almost the sense it has in mathematics. Kinship induces egalitarian relations among men (all share the same "honor"), without distinction (the same aid and affection are due cousin and brother), and reciprocity is unstinting rather than fixed by schedule. Honor is a social capital that the kindred jointly maintain and exploit. With each new occasion for evaluation (whether murder or marriage), the group's rank and composition are called into question. So-called feudal society recognized the possibility of such close relations among "friends by blood" in all lines, a possibility that was in fact frequently realized. William of Grandmesnil's splendid marriage resulted in "great honor for his kindred" (*in magno honore consanguinitatis sue*). When William of Saint-Pan-thus, a knight-brigand, was hanged in the land of Nesle, his cousins had to bear the shame. Though they had no part in his crimes and little sympathy for his suffering, they complained to Saint Louis, but in vain. Such broad solidarities did not hamper the individual. On the contrary, they enabled him to exact a price in return for his favors, to extort a return gift from a religious institution or to live as a parasite on distant cousins or to go to war for the pleasure of the sport and the hope of booty. Aristocratic solidarity was the basis of the noble's freedom and social status, his springboard to fame and fortune in the public arena.

It was therefore important that accurate memories of all ancestors be preserved. When we examine the family consciousness of medieval man in its pure state, without interpretation, it seems as cognatic as our own; there are links to cousinages through all lines, via women as well as men. Consider Lambert of Wattrelos, canon of Saint-Aubert of Cambrai. Born in 1108, he composed his genealogy in 1152. The document is innocent of conscious manipulation, because it was the work of a cleric whose office left him relatively free with respect to his original lineage, a clan of the middling or minor aristocracy. Lambert is equally interested in ancestors on both his father's and his mother's side; the same number of relatives is cited on each. He is loath to neglect his mother's family because it seems to have been slightly more "honorable" than his father's; many of the churchmen who helped the young man on his way to the cloister were relatives of his mother. Similarly, Guibert of Nogent's autobiography (ca. 1115) contains scattered allusions to his *consanguinei*, suggesting a similar kind of family memory.

Lambert's order of exposition, however, gives priority to

men over women and to elder over younger. In the canon's mind, Georges Duby observes, "his paternal family is organized as a 'house,' a lineage of warriors, in which seniority is of great importance." It would be a relatively easy matter to distinguish, within this cognatic kindred, an agnatic lineage. If we did this, we would see a concrete structure defined by male/female, elder/cadet oppositions that remain latent in Lambert's text. The subtle selection effected by his memory already makes this clear. The center of this agnatic lineage is surely the family house at Wattrelos. Lambert fails to make this fully apparent because, unlike domestic genealogists, he was not a member of the household but a son who had left to make his life elsewhere.

The clan is what might be called "an elementary unit of political structure"—but not exactly. Using the properties of the kinship function, it unified its members against the outside world. More than that, it maintained disparities among its members and ensured that those disparities would be accepted by all. There were differences in the division of the inheritance and strict rules regarding social roles, most notably in the impediments to marriage of younger sons. By obscuring internal conflicts (which promoted change), genealogy legitimated the result; it also served the interests of the group in public competition.

The tower, symbol of the power of a lineage. *Bible d'Etienne Harding*, 1109. (Dijon Library, ms 14.)

It is here that we must look for the actual constraints on individual behavior. But those constraints were the reflection of a strategy rather than the emanation of a collective attitude. In northern France, the sacrifice of cadets was a curse peculiar to the aristocracy. The clan incurred the hostility of its clerical sons, who were suspicious of bonds of the flesh yet powerless to overcome them completely. It upset the equilibrium of couples made or broken by family policy. It invaded the private time and space of noble men and women.

The agnatic lineage is necessarily associated with a couple, master of a household and procreator of sons, from which it derives its substance. Although there was no word for this couple in everyday language, it was the heart of the family. In feudal times the most typical and active kinship group comprised a broad community of interest and affection (despite the absence of permanent coresidence); its members were adult brothers and cousins. All looked to a central residence on the family's ancestral property, the focus of the lineage's prestige, which passed from the couple to the eldest son and his wife. Reigning jointly over the castle (or at least over the residential part of the high court), the lord and lady were a prominent feature of this period.

The Misadventures of the Couple

In studying the condition of women and relations between spouses the couple is not the proper setting, nor is the triangle maliciously created by adding a lover. Mediocre but prolific writers lacking scientific intention or training have, in the guise of popular history, embroidered on two themes: the proud and adulated lady, and woman as victim of oppression. But "women" are not a good subject for history in the "age of cathedrals" or any other period. Social classes were too diverse, and women occupied too many different positions (wives, sisters, mothers, and so on), to permit a unitary treatment. We must examine relations between groups of men, groups of women, and groups of both sexes.

To what degree was the wife (and mother) integrated into the clan that received her, and what relations did she maintain with the one that gave her? These questions are of interest not just in the feudal era but in other periods as well. But they assume particular importance in the feudal context, where many aristocratic marriages were dictated by political imperatives. Was the woman a hostage of one clan or an instrument of the other? Although I do not believe that sociological factors

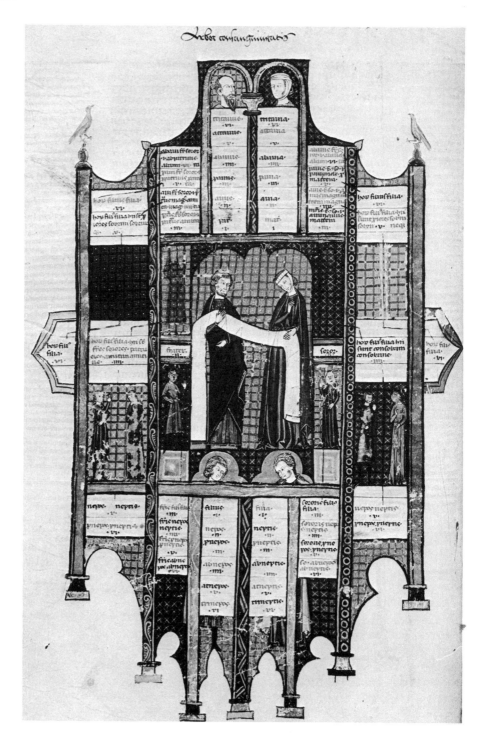

tell the whole story, I want to examine them before attempting to describe married life or raise the question of how free individuals were to maneuver within the constraints of the system.

Choice of Spouse. To analyze a kinship system we must understand how men exchange women among themselves. This stark Lévi-Straussian formulation should not be allowed to obscure the fact that women were not purely passive objects. It is true only at a certain level of interpretation and tells nothing about actual behavior or power relations. A father "gives" his daughter to a son-in-law, who "takes" her for his wife: these medieval expressions were still in common use not so very long ago.

In "primitive" and "archaic" societies marriage is carefully regulated. Incest, that is, marriage between close relatives or members of certain (parallel) lines, is prohibited, while more distant (cross) cousins are permitted to wed. The early medieval system of exchange is one of the most complex that has ever existed. Anthropologists call it *cognatic*, because there is no differentiation between the male and female lines: no man may marry a cousin in any line down to some specified degree, usually the fourth. Changing the number or method of computation of degrees of kinship does not necessarily alter the workings of the system, but it does force the groups involved in the exchange of women to extend and loosen their network of alliances. The sociopolitical game becomes more open. This system in effect marks a transition between that of archaic societies, in which each man's mate is more or less designated in advance, and that of modern society, in which the range of choice open to both man and woman is very wide.

Nevertheless, as Françoise Héritier has shown in her study of cognatic systems, there is a tendency to choose wives only from the first permissible degrees of consanguinity. Because of this, regular cycles of exchange are possible. Marriage retains its importance as a means of ensuring the cohesiveness of a relatively small group. Was this system practiced in the northern French aristocracy in the eleventh and twelfth centuries? Research on the question is lacking, for want of source material. We do not even know whether the extension of the degrees declared prohibited by the Church from the fourth to the seventh was ever seriously respected. Without family trees to use as evidence, Héritier points to an interesting paragraph

A kinship table intended for use in determining possible consanguinity between a man and a woman. It extends only to the sixth degree according to Roman (civil) law criteria rather than canon law and defines a more restricted zone of kinship. It indicates that even before 1215 common sense had led in practice to a wise moderation of overly rigorous standards. (Göttingen Library, Cod. inv. 27.)

in a text by the pre-Gregorian cardinal Peter Damian. I would add the preamble of a Laon charter (1177). Both indicate the advisability of a new marriage to revive *caritas* between two groups once the branches of the family tree have reached a certain length.

Héritier calls upon medievalists to refine the definition of the groups involved in the exchange of women. Undifferentiated filiation makes it impossible to define permanent groups; but if a patrilineage rooted in a principal residence and enduring patrimonial property was effectively in control of the cognatic kindred, then it, not the kindred as a whole, should be regarded as the real partner in matrimonial exchange with its counterpart in another kindred. Certain important aristocratic marriages were decided by the prince. (The Anglo-Norman monarch often exercised this right.) This does not mean, however, that the prince was a party to the exchange, simply that he was capable of regulating interlineal relations, or at any rate of appearing to act as regulator.

Groups of unilinear filiation (through one line only, in this case the paternal) may have practiced marriage according to the rules of undifferentiated filiation. This left room for maneuvering, hence for strategic calculation, which historians are just beginning to understand. Lineages in search of prestige sought to marry their older sons to women of equal or superior rank, choosing to wait rather than make bad marriages. The family trees of sires or castle knights reveal that this was a constant preoccupation. If a man married a woman of higher station, the blood of his lineage could be irrigated by that of kings, princes, and counts. This periodic infusion of good blood not only rejuvenated the family's nobility but ensured the cohesion of the dominant class. "Good" marriages were scrupulously recorded in house genealogies. By contrast, daughters given to lesser lineages were more readily forgotten. Yet wives were never given purely as a favor. Women numbered among the "gifts that create an obligation," to borrow a phrase used by Jean-Pierre Poly and Eric Bournazel in describing fiefs. The transfer of women from higher to lower levels of the social hierarchy entailed a compensatory gift of services in the other direction. Chains of obligation, often combined with the obligations of vassalage, linked the various strata of the aristocracy. It is not true in all societies, however, that women are given by the higher-ranking lineage. Comparative sociology suggests that cultural factors, possibly related to the feudal or parafeudal political system, exerted an influence on marital practices.

For a good illustration of those practices, let us return to the Giroie clan. It was in the interest of the group to marry off all its daughters, for a daughter's marriage brought with it new allies and even debtors. By contrast, it was important to limit legitimate marriages by male members of the lineage, for this could result in an unhealthy proliferation of heirs (agnation being the rule in matters of patrimony). The fact that Ernaud d'Echauffour's two daughters were relegated to a convent signals the decline of this branch of the family and its exclusion from the political contest in Normandy.

Women in this society were prizes to be won. They could bring to a lineage not only prestige but also valuable possessions such as châteaus. Hence competition was fierce. The social ascendancy of the knight lucky in love was really just promotion to a higher grade, however. Georges Duby has carefully analyzed the nobles and knights of the Mâconnais around the year 1100. Although all the members of this group have basically the same origin, the old aristocracy (composed, one is tempted to say, of those who had "always" been aristocrats but whose nobility dates, in any case, from before the year 1000) was divided into several strata, differentiated by the vicissitudes of the battle for castles and inequalities in the order of birth. The scarcity of *honores* meant that unfavored or excluded branches were constantly falling into disrepute. Men who married above themselves could bring about, or consecrate, a temporary revival of a family's fortunes.

Most marriages reported in the sources were concluded only after much deliberation by kindred on both sides. Each evaluated the other's degree of honor, and heads of both houses entered into negotiations. The young man and woman were asked simply to consent to their promotion to adult rank and to their settlement in a home of their own. What more did either dream of than this, the natural conclusion of their education and upbringing? Three by no means atypical examples from the second half of the eleventh century reveal the importance and difficulty of the negotiations.

Simon de Crépy-en-Valois, who in 1076 inherited three strategic counties along the northern border of the Capetian domain, had to marry to ensure the future of his house. "They chose for him [a wife from Auvergne], elegant in appearance, beautiful in visage, and noble in lineage." But Simon's monastic vocation prevented him from consummating the union, thus rescuing him from a political impasse. For he had received a rival offer from William the Conqueror, who, with anti-Capetian sentiments in the back of his mind, also wanted him for son-in-law.

In the Boulonnais in the mid–eleventh century, several suitors presented themselves to the parents of the future Saint Godelive, a young woman of the finest stock. A man from Bruges named Bertulf (the same name as the celebrated provost) was chosen, because he offered the handsomest marriage settlement. He had not solicited the advice of his own mother and father, however. His mother reproached him bitterly, regretting that he had chosen a woman from so far away and troubled by her daughter-in-law's black hair, a mark of evil. She said, according to Godelive's talented hagiographer, Dreu of Thérouanne: "Couldn't you, dear son, have found a rook from your own country?" The marriage began under the worst auspices.

A more adventurous tale comes from the ninth decade of the eleventh century via Hermann of Tournai. A cadet of Burgundy, Fulk of Jur, enamored of the nobility and fine qualities of Count Hilduin of Roucy, sought to marry Adele, one of the count's many daughters. The "French" father at first refused the offer of marriage on the grounds that the suitor was of foreign nationality. Some time later, however, while traveling in the service of King Philip I, Count Hilduin was caught in an ambush set by Fulk and redeemed his freedom and treasure only at the price of his daughter's hand. As soon as the promise was given, the count was treated with honor and showered with the customary gifts. This bold approach, more elegant and readily forgivable no doubt than a straightforward abduction, produced a fertile couple, most of whose children lived and made their careers in the orbit of their maternal family.

Unlike Simon of Crépy, a powerful heir to whom many clans sought in vain to marry their daughters, Fulk of Jur forced his way into that fortunate group of men who married above their station. In all three examples the kinship network was widened, even if the kindred sometimes hesitated about accepting a spouse from another region. Because of their ability to travel, young men seem to have enjoyed some freedom of choice, whereas any journey was perilous for women and girls. No evidence suggests that Godelive of Ghistelles or, more likely, Adele of Roucy made discreet advances to their suitors. Female initiative had no place in either hagiography or the warrior ethic. A century later the fictional Girart of Vienne spoke harshly to a duchess who, though a desirable catch, throws herself into his arms:

> Or puis bien dire et por voir afier
> que or comence le siecle a redoter
> puis que les dames vont mari demender.

> I can say, certain that I speak the truth,
> that the world has fallen into its second
> childhood, since women go begging for
> husbands.

Whereupon Girart shows the ardent duchess the door, reminding her that marriage is men's business—like war, which is suspended briefly for the occasion.

Women had few means of expressing their desires other than refusal. The *Lives* of saints are filled with stories of women who wish to consecrate their virginity to God and who flee in order to foil the marriages planned for them by their families. Even a few men shunned marriage, as the story of Simon of Crépy shows. Around 1150, Saint Ode of Hainault found escape too perilous, not so much on account of locked doors in the castle as of dangers outside; so to avoid an unwanted marriage, she disfigured herself. She had already refused, in the presence of a priest, to consent to the union, forcing her family to suspend the ceremony. But the family, determined that its strategy should succeed, continued to exert pressure on her. The power to give daughters in matrimony did not emanate from the father alone but depended on his ability to win the approval of the matrons of the clan.

Then, too, there were maids who died for love of a dismissed or slain suitor. In a story told by Ordericus Vitalis, a maiden in love with Harold, an Anglo-Saxon to whom she had been promised by her father, William the Conqueror, prior to the Battle of Hastings where Harold did battle with and was slain by her prospective father-in-law, wasted away aboard the ship that bore her toward another husband, Alphonso of Castile. Around 1080 the daughter of a castellan of Coucy threatened to kill herself. Her father and mother had chosen for her a husband of good family, but she preferred the prowess of the "famous knight" with whom she had fallen in love. On the advice of Saint Arnoul (in whose *Life* the tale is recounted) she is betrothed to the man of her dreams: "Canonical authority prescribes that a girl not be joined in wedlock with a man she does not want." But, as the text intimates, accidents will happen to those whose profession is knighthood. Soon widowed, the recalcitrant girl eventually comes to accept the man for whom she was originally intended.

There is an air of spontaneity about the seductive exploits of twelfth-century knights-errant (*milites gyrovagantes*) in the tourney season of northern France. Not all were cadets forced to leave their homes. Heirs, too, were sent on journeys as part of the family strategy. Their itineraries were carefully planned, more for purposes of initiation than for sport. The Church's opposition to marriages between close kin was undoubtedly one reason nobles roamed far afield in search of mates. Nevertheless, sons and daughters were unable to shake the subtle control of their families and the unperceived influence of sociological factors on their inclinations. Risks, occasional surprises, and a rebellion or two were not enough to put an end to a system of kinship.

Christian Marriages

The first liturgical rituals of marriage appeared in northern France around 1100. I am thinking, in particular, of those of the Anglo-Norman type (whether elaborated in Britain or on the continent we do not know), which have been commented on by Jean-Baptiste Molin and Protais Mutembé. These ceremonies indicate that the power of clerics had made increasing inroads into family life. Ecclesiastics verified that both bride and groom had given their consent to the marriage and conducted investigations to determine whether the degree of consanguinity was such as to prevent legitimate wedlock. Did the Church disturb the equilibrium of the aristocracy by thus allowing women to express their wishes publicly and perhaps by disrupting marriage cycles through insistence on a high degree of exogamy? The liberation of women, which for Michelet constituted, along with the liberation of the "spirit" and the "communes," one of the three great glories of the twelfth century, should be evident first of all in the marriage ceremony, which protected the religious dignity of the bride (and also established her economic prerogatives). Still, a comparison of the liturgical *ordines* with the brief remarks on noble marriages found in the hagiographies and chansons de geste shows that the ecclesiastical enterprise was not only incomplete but also inept.

Customary marriage involved two distinct procedures, as

Man puts asunder what other men's gods have joined together. The *Decretum of Gratian* considers the case of a married infidel who converts to Christianity. His wife refuses to follow his example, so he marries a Christian. (Autun Library, ms 80.)

described, for example, in the eleventh-century *Life of Saint Godelive*. His suit accepted, Bertulf received the young lady "under marital law." She became his *sponsa* at the moment that authority over her, the right and duty to protect her in the public domain, were transferred. Once assured of the constitution of a marriage settlement, the girl's father handed his daughter over to her husband. Thereafter the contract was unbreakable, and Bertulf's mother's reproaches came too late. With the wedding ceremony Godelive was installed in her husband's house (where she would henceforth live as *sponsa nova nupta*). Surprisingly, however, her husband, who already regretted his choice, was not present at this ceremony; he was represented by his mother, who was obliged to conceal her rancor with a smile. Bertulf, who did not arrive until three days later, departed immediately to live with his father, leaving his wife to reign alone—but under surveillance—over the conjugal home. The story ends badly. But the hagiographer's more or less fictionalized account must have had the ring of truth to its audience. In any case, it illustrates the clear dis-

The joining of hands. The
bride, her hair still worn long
in the manner of a virgin,
drops her father's hand and
takes that of her husband. The
transfer of a woman from one
man to another was replaced
by a more symmetric
ceremony, in which husband
and wife gave themselves to
each other. *Decretum of Gratian*,
14th century. (Dijon Library,
ms 341.)

A festive scene of musical
marriage. The priest is the
main witness, but he is not
responsible for joining the
hands of bride and groom. The
jut of the wife's hip draws the
eye of the onlooker. *Artus le
Restoré*, 14th century. (Paris,
Bibliothèque Nationale, French
761.)

tinction between the *espousal* (*épousailles*), which began the marriage, and the *wedding* (*noces*), which consummated it and made it indissoluble in the eyes of the Church.

The late-twelfth-century epic of Aymeri of Narbonne is a more humorous account of the two stages of traditional marriage. Aymeri, eager to marry the beautiful Hermanjart, sends his barons to ask her brother, the king of Lombardy, for her hand; he then goes to claim his wife in person. In the ensuing negotiations, carried on by men, Aymeri's side alternates between threats and generosity, although there is concern throughout that Hermanjart's wishes be respected. Was this because the trouvère wished to please his audience, or was he reflecting a real custom? In any case, the future bride and groom desire each other solely on the basis of reputation, since neither has ever seen the other. The words of the negotiators seem plausible enough. Aymeri, in extolling the value of the proposed marriage to his future brother-in-law, says:

> En totes corz en seroiz vos plus chier
> Et en voz marches plus redoté et fier.

> In all courts of justice you will be
> judged a man of greater value; and
> when you march you will be more
> feared.

Convinced, the lord gives Aymeri his sister's hand. Throughout the journey to Narbonne she is referred to as *espouse* or *moillier*, although the marriage has yet to be consummated. The wedding is delayed by a Saracen attack, but it finally takes place, and Hermanjart becomes the lady of Narbonne. Amusingly enough, the wedding night occurs before the official wedding ceremony, a mass celebrated by an archbishop, from which the guests depart in haste in order to take their places at tables set for a week-long banquet. This splendid celebration was intended to exalt both the count and France, at a time when wealth and power, the one inseparable from the other, were measured by liberality and sumptuousness.

Examination of eleventh- and twelfth-century sources reveals that the length of time between the *desponsatio* and the *nuptiae* varied considerably. The longest delays resulted from certain traditional characteristics of aristocratic life. The two families often lived far apart, necessitating a lengthy journey for which the husband bore responsibility. Sometimes delay was essential in order to allow betrothed children to reach the requisite age. (Ive of Chartres implicitly allowed marriages between children, provided both were seven or older.) Marriages between children were sometimes necessary to seal an alliance or to effect a reconciliation between warring clans. Threatened by an uncle, one only child needed a husband to defend her and her castle. A prince could not put off marrying a female relative to a recalcitrant lord who had been pillaging outlying parts of the principality. Accordingly, contemporary chronicles distinguish quite clearly and quite frequently between *desponsatio* and *nuptiae*, for which the terms "engagement" and "marriage" with their present connotations obviously are unsuitable translations.

Louis VI, heir to the Capetian throne, was joined by *desponsatio* in 1105 to little Lucienne, a "not yet nubile" daughter of Count Guy of Rochefort. This marked a temporary reconciliation between a prince who was having a hard time maintaining control over his domain and the dominant faction of a powerful patrilineage whose castles encircled Paris. But the king designate, advised to seek a marriage more in keeping with his dignity and long-term interests, bestowed Lucienne on a member of his entourage and yet showed himself in no hurry to marry anyone else. (He did not marry in fact until 1115.) The transfer was not easily arranged. The approval of the Council of Troyes (1107) was required to annul what Suger called a "contracted . . . marriage." The girl, however, had not left the donjon of Montlhéry, where she was chaperoned by her aunt. Considering, with some justice, that Louis was trying to make a fool of him, her father, Count Guy, unleashed a war in Ile-de-France.

Twelfth-century canonists and theologians, in Paris particularly, added a new dimension to the more realistic and pragmatic marital ethics of Carolingian times. Based on consent, marriage became a sacrament. Carolingian priests had been concerned mainly with the mutual oaths (*fides*) of bride and groom and with the crucial importance of consummation in establishing the marriage bond. The emphasis, after 1100, on more spiritual elements reflects the progress of clerical high culture. In practice, the "minor part" of the sacrament, the social and carnal elements, retained their importance. Until the Council of Trent, moreover, sexual relations between "fiancés" (which if complete established "carnal union" between man and woman) transformed betrothal into true marriage in

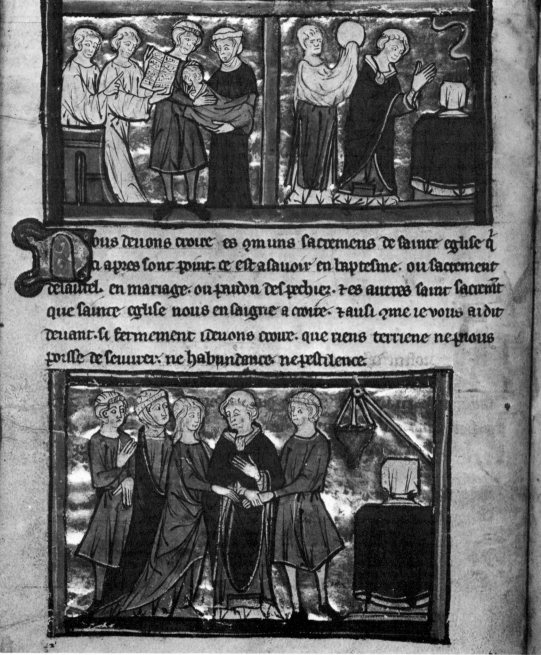

ous deuons croue es qui uns sacremens de sainte eglise q
a apres sont point. ce est asauoir en baptesme. ou sacrement
delautel. en mariage. ou pardon des pechiez. ¬ es autres saint sacremt
que sainte eglise nous enseigne a croire. ¬ausi qme le vous ai dit
deuant. Si fermement deuons croire. que riens terriene nepnous
poisse de seurrer. ne habundance. nepestilence.

Note the complex gestures of the hands, indicating three of the principal sacraments: baptism, eucharist, and marriage. *Credo du sire de Joinville*, 14th century. (Paris, Bibliothèque Nationale, French n.a. 4509.)

A new power of the priest, who is here the person joining the hands of husband and wife. *Commentary on the Decretum of Gratian,* 13th century. (Laon Library, ms 372.)

the eyes of canon law. Intercourse confirmed the consent given in the betrothal.

Was the ritual at the church door mentioned in the Anglo-Norman *ordines* anything other than a desponsatio, either the original one or possibly a public repetition of an espousal originally made in private? Molin and Mutembé note that there were "worldly and familial customs that naturally found their place in the liturgy." The Church revealed these rites by making them public and placing them under its control; at the same time it altered their meaning. Nevertheless, we can distinguish between the features inherited from the civil context and innovations introduced as part of the Church's spiritual designs. The priest first verified that consent had been given and that the rules of nonconsanguinity were satisfied. He was then satisfied merely to watch the ceremony unfold and to conclude it with a prayer. The bride (*sponsa*) was given to the groom by her father or another close relative acting as guardian. The joining of the right hands concluded the transfer of a gift—with all the artifice and ambiguity implicit in the act. (Later, in the thirteenth century, the Church would interpret it as pledge of faith by both parties, and the priest would join the hands of bride and groom.) The man then slipped onto three of his wife's fingers, one after another, the blessed ring that signified marriage—and was supposed to protect her from assault by demons. According to ecclesiastical theory, it was given for love and as a token of fidelity; the reciprocal gesture, the giving of a ring to the groom by the bride, did not appear before the sixteenth century. According to two of the twelfth-century ordines, the wife then prostrated herself before her husband. Later an attempt was made to transform this part of the ritual by having both bride and groom cast themselves at the feet of the priest. But this was too much to ask, and the Church, adept at the use of trial and error in its efforts to absorb the marriage ritual, preferred to eliminate the whole sequence, which was probably only one of many regional peculiarities.

However much theology extolled the gifts made on both sides, the ceremony clearly marked the precedence of the husband. He was the active party, bestowing not only the ring but also the "customary" gifts and presenting a charter of the marriage settlement along with 13 denarii as prescribed by Salic Law. The coins went eventually not to the bride but to the priest, the poor, or certain of the assistants, for the bride was not so much bought as invested with the mission of giving alms on behalf of the couple. Symbolisms would come and go over the centuries, but the coins remained. "With this ring I thee wed, with this gold I thee honor, and with this dowry I thee endow"—some such formula was spoken as the various acts of the ritual were performed.

Roland's "engagement" to the beautiful Aude, as she is called in the *Chanson of Girart of Vienne*, is similar to an espousal. Charlemagne, pressing his nephew's suit, applies first to the girl's uncle, a warrior captain, and then to the eldest uncle in the clan (but not to the girl's father, even though he is present). Hostilities are ended with a banquet, after which Lady Guibourc sends the richly dressed Aude out of her bedchamber. The charming young woman passes from the hand of her aunt to that of her uncle to that of the king and finally to her fiancé. He gives her the liturgical ring, and she pays him in turn with an *ensegne*, which is really part of the courtly ritual. An archbishop is present but only as a witness; he takes no direct part in the ceremony. Had the drama at Ronceveaux not interrupted this idyll, would the "marriage" have been

This depiction of the *velatio* (an ancient ritual in which bride and groom take their places under the nuptial veil) illustrates a 14th-century copy of the *Decretum of Gratian*. (Dijon Library, ms 341.)

anything other than a public repetition of this espousal, followed by "nuptials" that would have installed the couple as rulers of a household?

The sources offer numerous examples of ritual donations first made in private, in the donor's home, and then repeated in front of a church, or vice versa. The desponsatio, like other contracts, may have been subject to similar repetition. In that case the Church would have succeeded only in enforcing a public repetition of an act already accomplished in the privacy of the home, to which priests from the Carolingian era on were in any case frequently granted access.

It was impossible to transfer all of the nuptial ceremony to the public square. The key element was the blessing of the bedchamber or—not to put too fine a point on it—the bed. (It would be more accurate to refer to the home of a married couple as a bed rather than a hearth.) The *benedictio thalami*, well known to modernist historians bent on restoring life to "old France," figures in certain twelfth-century ordines from northern France. The blessing dispelled any curse that might have compromised the couple's fertility and wiped away any taint of female adultery. (Male escapades did not count.) Bride and groom then took their places in bed under the watchful eyes of a circle of close relations whose composition is hard

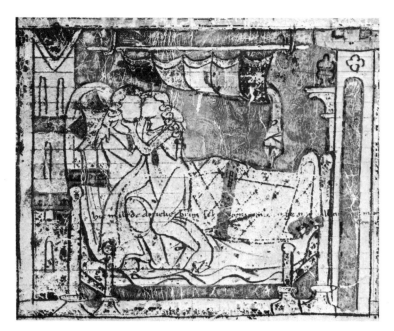

Alone at last. Rudolf von Ems, *Wilhelm von Orleans*. (Munich Library, Cod. germ. 63.)

to pin down precisely. Once witnessed together in bed, the couple may or may not have been left alone to consummate the marriage. A benediction by the priest became customary, though not without some hesitation on the part of the bishops. The priests had a rival in the groom's father, according to a passage in a text of Lambert of Ardres which discusses the last decade of the twelfth century. I am tempted to view this not as a survival of an immemorial spiritual patriarchy but as an attempt by the household powers to usurp religious authority.

The scene in the nuptial bed, which, as thirteenth-century clerical investigations show, either remained or became the crucial element in marriage, symbolized what was at stake: power in and over private life. Feudalism's tentacles touched even the minor aristocracy, barely free of the taint of servitude. The same Lambert of Ardres describes the misadventure of one unfortunate vavasoress, which occurred around 1100. Having gone to bed with her knight, she is unexpectedly interrupted by the ministeriale of a powerful neighbor, who has been sent to collect the *colvekerla,* a tax with all the unpleasant connotations of a *formariage,* or marriage out of rank and condition. The poor woman blushes for shame. It is not so much her modesty that is offended as her sense of social rank. Through the good offices of the Countess of Guînes she has the assessment annulled—a blow struck for the cause of women.

The value of the desponsatio in the eyes of the Church is evident in a judgment rendered by Ive of Chartres: in case of death or annulment prior to the nuptiae, the (surviving) party to the espousal is not free to (re)marry a brother, sister, or other relative of the other party. This judgment comes from a prelate who, like many of his contemporaries, was particularly concerned with the prohibition of incest, whose definition had been broadened considerably. Relations by affinity (that is, marriage) were taboo to the fourth canonical degree, and the more frequently invoked relations of consanguinity were taboo to the seventh degree. Since the canonical degree of kinship between two individuals was the smaller of the numbers of generations between each one and their nearest common ancestor, historians are faced with something of an enigma: the taboo zone was enormous, particularly in a society of such limited size. By extending the incest restriction so broadly, the Carolingian Church (and the even more rigorous Gregorian Church of the late eleventh century) considerably complicated the business of marriage. How did common folk, hobbled by their ties to a seigneurie, manage to leave their villages and find nonrelatives to marry? And how did the well-born avoid mésalliance without venturing beyond the borders of their provincial fatherland?

What exactly did the clergy want? The legal documents are silent as to motives, simply invoking the *auctoritates* (which could easily have been selected or interpreted differently). We are therefore reduced to speculation. If the purpose was solely to oblige Christians to seek dispensations from the Church, thus reinforcing the power of the clergy, the procedure was quite Machiavellian. But in advancing such an explanation, are we not mistaking effect for cause? As direct parishioners of the bishops, the aristocracy would have been the first target of such a move. But it would have been unreasonable for prelates and monks to place such an obstacle in the way of endogamic husbandry of their own "herds" of serfs. A more inspired, "European" outlook may have influenced the application of the incest taboo to kings. Eleventh-century monarchs who refused to marry beneath their station but shunned incest were forced to await the conversion of petty Slavic and Scandinavian kings and then hasten after their daughters. Or else they could wait, with all the patience required by diplomatic complexities, for the hand of a Byzantine princess. The cohesiveness of the ninth-century Franks would have been enhanced by maintaining the greater ethnic purity of the early medieval aristocracies. Are we to believe, moreover, that clerics of the noblest blood, known to be quite conscious of their families' strategic concerns, should have decided as a group, in a moment of elevation, to fragment the patrimonies of aristocratic lineages by preventing reconcentration through marriage?

The best hypothesis concerning the clergy's intentions is one of confusion. Bernard Guénée suggests that the Church chose to interpret a symbolic seven in a literal sense. The Bible and Fathers simply recommended banning marriage to any recognized relative, not systematically excluding all kin to the seventh degree as advocated by synods around the year 1000. I should like to propose a similar confusion, not incompatible with the former but more anthropological in nature. As Beaumanoir observed, the seven degrees once defined the circle of possible heirs and companions in private war; in 1283 they still defined those entitled to the *retrait lignager*. The origin of these customs was remote, lost in that "Germanity" to which the Carolingians wished to adapt all their norms of measurement. Hence they may well have regarded kin of the fifth to seventh degree, with whom marriage would have been prohibited, as non-kin, members of exogamous groups under the cognatic system.

We cannot say to what extent the rules of incest were respected. Kings themselves, models for the people, sometimes married cousins of the fifth or sixth degree. Ultimately the Church backed down: the Lateran Council in 1215 reduced the prohibited range from the seventh to the fourth degree. Did this decision mark a victory of the traditional cognatic system? Or had that system already been destroyed? However that may be, the Church became aware of the contradictory situation it had created. Intent on making marriage indissoluble, it had in fact provided an easy pretext for "divorce." Like so many misused fathers, Guy of Rochefort rightly attributed the annulment of his daughter's espousal to intrigue. The history of the period is full of husbands who discovered that they were related to their wives when it became expedient to do so. Fulk Rechin, count of Anjou in the late eleventh

Prerogative of the bishop: the dissolution of a marriage that has been declared invalid. *Digeste*, 13th century. (Paris, Bibliothèque Sainte-Geneviève, ms 394.)

century, was adept at drawing up genealogies for purposes of divorce. The same tactic could be used to thwart an opponent's strategy. Henry Beauclerc, duke of Normandy and king of England, prevented his disinherited nephew William Cliton from forging an alliance with the house of Anjou by spreading word that William was a cousin of the woman he sought to marry.

In short, prior to the thirteenth century the Church's attempts to influence the marriage practices of the aristocracy appear to have been superficial and ambiguous. The presence of the priest did little to change the meaning of the marriage ritual. Protections afforded the wife against changes in her husband's feelings or shifts in his allegiances, sometimes alleged to be a major achievement of Christian humanism, were all but nullified by blind attachment to the astonishing incest taboo (which facilitated "divorce").

Women, War, and Peace

The frequency of notorious divorces reveals that the system of aristocratic marriage suffered a crisis around 1100. Georges Duby has shown that a conflict existed between the dynastic strategies of the "warriors" and the demands of the "priests." As these strategies evolved, the disparity between the two groups sometimes increased, sometimes decreased, sometimes underwent qualitative change. The emphasis on legitimate marriage, with its espousal and nuptial phases, facilitated the exclusion of bastards. The extreme lengths to which the incest taboo was carried had more ambiguous consequences, augmenting an uneasiness of which it was probably not the initial cause. Was this malaise perhaps a sign of growing individualism? Young men and women did not oppose the will of the clan, but that will might be altered if the marriage proved difficult or barren. The failure of the system opened the way to individual protest. Nevertheless, we still must determine why this became increasingly apparent about 1100.

Among the nobility, instability did not affect marriages as much as it did the policies governing them. Religious history tells only part of the story. Changes in the condition of women are easily explained. It was one thing to be the wife of an eleventh-century warrior involved in the thrusts and counterthrusts of "feudal anarchy," and quite another to be the wife of a thirteenth-century lord, part of a fixed hierarchy under the pacifying influence of the "monarchic state." Yet this apparent progress produced a complex web of effects.

The tumult of war had spread from castle to castle; by the end of the eleventh century chaos reigned. Alliances based on marriage, necessary for securing truces between lineages and factions, were no more secure than peace itself. What became of a woman whose husband made war on her father or brother? Ordericus Vitalis and Suger tell of various ways such an untenable situation might be ended.

William the Conqueror used his nieces and cousins to spy on the men to whom he married them. Judith reported the conspiratorial plans of her Anglo-Saxon husband, Count Waltheof, yet mourned impressively after his execution in 1075. Robert the Giroie accidentally swallowed the poisoned apple that his wife, Adelaide, had prepared for another man (1060). By a troubling coincidence, however, this accident occurred at a time when Robert was leading a rebellion against his wife's cousin, the duke of Normandy. Wives were often used as ambassadors to urge their husbands to go to war on the side of the wife's kindred. In a sense, the wife ruled the donjon on behalf of her brothers.

More often, though, women took the part of their husbands. As mistress of the house, a wife had a great deal to lose by returning to the bosom of her own clan. Julienne, bastard daughter of Henry Beauclerc, was given to Eustache de Breteuil along with the château of Ivry. She was at his side in his battle with the duke-king in 1119, energetically leading the defense of the fortress. Henry, meanwhile, did not shrink from allowing his own hostage granddaughters to be blinded

Fortune and misfortune in the war of love. In this German version Tristan does battle with Nampotenis over Cassie. At the foot of the ramparts (in the scene on the right), Tristan puts down his adversary with a blow from his sword, but an enemy soldier wounds him with a poisoned lance. (Munich Library, Cod. germ. 51.)

and mutilated (their noses were cut off). A few months later, however, autumn brought peace, and the couple's surrender was accepted in the name of kinship: "Clemency softened the king's heart in favor of his son-in-law and daughter, and he regained his benevolence." Unfortunately nothing could be done to restore the martyred children.

The brutality of the feudal era often wreaked havoc on private life. Suger relates the heart-rending words spoken by the wife of Gui de La Roche-Guyon to her brother, who had killed her husband before her eyes: "Were you not joined by indissoluble friendship? What is this madness?" Attempting to defend her fallen husband with her own body, she is badly beaten, then wrested from the dying man's embrace. To cap the horror, her two infant sons are thrown from cliffs into the Seine—a somber scene from the "springtime of the Middle Ages."

Powerless to mediate or overcome by tragedy, women sometimes sought refuge in convents under the protection of the clergy. The order of Fontevraud served as refuge to the victims of the crisis of political marriage. But most of the women received by the order had been permanently abandoned or were simply too old to remarry.

Women were also instigators of revenge, throwing themselves wholeheartedly into the conflicts that disrupted and shattered their lives. Monastic writers describe with horror and disapproval *viragos* (the word is theirs) who, out of hatred for their husbands, unleashed wars against them. In 1090 "Countess Helvis [of Evreux] was irritated with Isabelle of Conches [a Montfort] on account of some contemptuous words, and out of wrath she put all her might to persuading Count William and his barons to take up arms. So it was that the jealousies and quarrels of women inflamed the hearts of courageus men." Shortly before 1111 a similar story led to conflict between Enguerran of Coucy and Gérard of Quierzy. Wives with forked tongues (and otherwise distinguished by notorious debauchery) had launched insults and accusations at one another "in private"—which is to say, with the assurance that their words would be widely repeated. Guibert of Nogent describes such women as lewd vipers. Serious study of these polemics would no doubt reveal that they merely provoked the eruption of latent conflict between seigneuries, objective political rivals. Still, they prove that certain wives exerted considerable influence over their husbands and played an active role in these feudal battles. Feudal warfare, in many respects a "private" affair, was a concern of women, who exercised undeniable, though not total, power over the private domain.

Women enjoyed the privilege, in practice as well as in principle, of being relatively less exposed to war's perils. This was true to such a degree that some of the proud women who instigated violent conflict seemed to exercise greater authority than the warriors who wasted themselves in futile and bloody cavalcades. Enguerran of Boves, first of the great sires of Coucy, gained control of the castle in 1079 when its mistress (and possibly inheritor of her father's rights) became his lover and, betraying her husband, turned it over to him. But with the knight's good fortune went the onerous duty of defending the premises. A more pacific though no less treacherous example of female power can be seen in Bertrade of Montfort, who, worried by steps taken by her terrible husband Fulk Rechin, made advances to King Philip I, who carried her off and made her his queen (1093). With the aging monarch under her thumb, she coordinated the strategies of his sons by two queens against the young Louis VI. (Conflict with stepmothers was another fixture of these troubled times.) In Bertrade's case, the failure of her maneuvers resulted in her being forced into a cloister after a remarkably long period of conflict.

Abduction remained common until the twelfth century. But was it merely an act of barbarism and oppression directed against women? Many women instigated their own abductions or at any rate aided their abductors. When lovers faced opposition from their clans, abduction was a means of asserting individual freedom; if the clans later recognized the *fait accompli*, it ended happily. A girl imprisoned in her own home or a wife abused by her husband might look upon her abductor as a liberator. Women gave themselves in order to attract a champion. Thus, the meaning of abduction is ambivalent. Proof of the oppression of women forced to resort to such measures to free themselves, it was one of their most effective weapons. Abductions were often rather theatrical affairs; in a more profound sense they were a kind of ritual. They symbolize the way in which high drama and fierce pleasure were combined in the lives of feudal women.

The fact is, however, that we know nothing about feudal woman except what men tell us. The texts that paint her in a fearsome light are suspect. In Ordericus Vitalis' *History* women are constantly shown administering poisons, latter-day Eves slipping their men venomous apples while hissing accusations against others. The influence of Old Testament

Abducted! *Roman de Tristan,* 15th century. (Chantilly, Condé Museum.)

models on the mind of a monk brought up on the Bible is evident. He suggests that his perverse heroines share "that obscure and powerful influence, one of the rare prerogatives of the half-savage woman." But like the accusation of witchcraft in other societies, was not the charge of poisoning intended to discredit any possible attempt to question the male-dominated social order? The constant suspicion of adultery may have served a similar function, whatever its factual basis. Incredulousness is the proper reaction to a report of letters allegedly written to the companions of William the Conqueror in 1068 by their libidinous wives, threatening that, unless their men hurry home to satisfy their desires, they will take lovers.

Women were not kept strictly under lock and key. The wives of the soldiers of the First Crusade were not locked in dungeons or forced to wear the legendary chastity belts (not mentioned in the sources until much later). If women were confined, it was in much more subtle—and no doubt more effective—ways. In the first place, they were kept under surveillance by older matrons. The division between youth and old age affected female as well as male society. Saint Godelive was murdered by an assassin in the pay of her husband after being subjected to various forms of persecution. Yet she was not utterly alone: she had run a household, albeit under supervision, and acquired many supporters. Her sad story proves that conflict with an oppressive matriarchal mother-in-law could have devastating consequences. In Ordericus Vitalis the model of the paterfamilias and just lord is Anseau of Maule, a man who takes it upon himself to educate and discipline his noble young wife. The trait that demonstrates Anseau's superior virtue, however, is his rare filial piety, exemplified by his willingness to maintain his aged mother, no less noble than his wife, in the house that had belonged to her late husband.

In the twelfth century war was repressed by legislation of councils and princes, turned outward by the Crusades, and transformed into a game by the vogue for tourneys. The clergy approved of the first two only, but all three produced similar effects, allowing the edifice of state power to be constructed while enabling couples to enjoy a more serene private life.

Raoul I, sire of Coucy, married Agnes, daughter of Count Baldwin IV of Hainault, in 1160. For a dowry she brought her husband the revenues derived from the annual tax that a city in her princely father's province was obliged to pay. In order to guarantee regular collection of the tax, Raoul had every reason to offer military aid and counsel to his father-in-law: just compensation (in the form of unreciprocated service) for the infusion of Carolingian blood into Raoul's clan. This unequal relationship was part of the logic of the hypergamic system. Either the sire himself or his predecessor had reserved for his sister (as dowry right) a share of the tolls collected on his lands; this was explicitly declared to be a fief-rent, held first by a brother-in-law of lesser rank and then by his son. In this second feudal age the aristocracy continued to stand out from the rest of society by the intensely sociopolitical significance that it attached to marriage. Pierre Toubert's observations about Latium can equally well be applied to northern France. The peasant, according to Toubert, was quick to sell off any land received in dowry if it was located far from his village. (The peasant woman who married a man from a village far from the one in which she was born was obliged by customary charters to accede to the sale.) By contrast, the lord who received a remote dowry was careful to hold on to it, because it extended his strategic influence and involved him in the preservation of his rights, obligations, and records of the alliance. The peasant wanted to enlarge the property that he farmed and acquired land in alodial (as opposed to feudal) tenure; the noble preferred to acquire feudal tenure, because his purpose was to maintain his rank and his interests ranged far more broadly.

Thus, noble marriages created common financial interests that promoted active alliances. More subtly, the ambivalent relations between brothers-in-law, because of structural tensions more profound than the vagaries of politics, were perpetuated in pantomime in the tourneys. Raoul I of Coucy and Baldwin V of Hainault fought by turns as allies and opponents in major jousting tournaments. And Gislebert of Mons is clear about the close ties that remain between Lady Agnes and her relatives: she is present at a "family reunion" in 1168, but the whereabouts of her husband at the time are not clear. Agnes is especially talented at winning the hearts of the "fierce" knights who hold power over the land along with the sire of Coucy, to whose court they belong. In this part of the world she is *the* lady of knightly romance, which, according to Georges Duby's interpretation, means that she is not an idol raised to the pinnacle of courtly society for her own qualities but an instrument skillfully manipulated by her husband to secure his own power. It is as though the role of instigating war, which women of the preceding generation had actually played in real life, had been transformed into mere sentimental sovereignty or transposed into fiction (and simultaneously attenuated). The woman exalted in this way could no longer be abducted in earnest, only in pantomime; she was the prize in a contest.

By 1200 women had gained security and stability, but at the cost of some freedom of maneuver. Nevertheless, women exercised regencies in many places: Blanche ruled in France; another Blanche ruled in Champagne; and there were women in command of innumerable seigneuries. This does not mean that a new career had suddenly opened up to women, or that the Crusade somehow permitted women to assume greater responsibilities than previously. The fact is simply that the conditions under which power was exercised had changed. What mattered now was not physical prowess in battle but the ability to keep accounts and preside over councils (with legists to advise).

This change in external conditions produced ambivalent effects. The royal and princely peace of the thirteenth century—far from uninterrupted—was not necessarily conducive to the exercise of greater power by women. Premodern aristocratic society was in many ways monolithic and rigid, as the sight of the fortified castles of the period suggests. Such a society was not made for the freedom of noble ladies and damsels.

Conjugal love often manifested itself as death drew near. There are some moving moments in Guibert of Nogent's account of the Laon commune. When the vidame Adon leaves home to aid his lord, the bishop, under siege by a rioting mob in 1112, his wife senses that death lies in wait. Before the assembled household she begs his pardon for any wrongs she may have done him; a long embrace precedes the couple's final kisses. Another scene of tender solemnity is when Anseau of Maule takes leave of his household three days before what he expects will be his death. In the presence of the knights of his castle he admonishes his eldest son to respect church and king and bestows his fatherly blessing. Turning to his wife, he preaches chastity in widowhood and asks her permission to become a monk. Here we see two practices common among eleventh-century nobles. Many donned the habit of Saint Benedict just before death, in extremis, or as the sources put it, *ad securendum*, in a moment when help was needed; a generous posthumous gift went to the monastery. It was also common to break the marital bond in favor of one more pure: this was the only form of "divorce" permitted by the Church, and it required the consent of one's spouse.

Marriage was thus exalted and put on display at the moment of death. Was this a revelation of life's most essential relationship at a time when falsehood was out of the question, or was it a final opportunity to shape an image of the ideal? All we can say with assurance is that the Church was determined to represent the couple in a certain way, emphasizing equality between men and women but at the same time portraying woman's subjugation. Such coexistence of contradictory principles or ideas is a feature of myth or, as here, of cultural stereotype and ritual. Marriage was supposed to be *both* egalitarian *and* hierarchical. In this respect it was exactly analogous to the relation between vassal and lord; indeed, the two shared common terminology, such as the use of *mon*

The Conjugal Family

seigneur (my lord) and *ma par* (my equal). As for Roman law, which was not without influence in northern France in the thirteenth century, its concern for individuals was coupled with an emphasis on the prerogatives of the husband and father. Its rationale was the same as that of canon law: in conjugal partnership (*societas*) the woman must consent to her subjugation.

It is not inaccurate to draw a parallel between the forms of family power and those of state power. The *franchise* (freedom) allowed the wife was in all likelihood little more than a new legal concept, with no more real content than the *franchise* granted to villages in the same period: a carefully specified set of rules and regulations, an affirmation of theoretical liberty followed by a precise delineation of constraints imposed upon that liberty. The liberation of women and the liberation of the communes, seen by Jules Michelet in the nineteenth century as important phenomena of the period, must be looked at skeptically. Communes were required to recognize their lord, and women were obliged to love their master.

Triumph of the couple. *Roman de la Rose*, 13th century. (Chantilly, Condé Museum.)

But did they? It is almost a commonplace to say that the couple as we know it was invented in twelfth-century France: at first, with the troubadours of disquieting Occitania, outside of—and opposed to—the bonds of matrimony; later, in the relative calm of northern France, within the confines of holy wedlock, which Chrétien de Troyes depicts as no less delightful or profound than adultery. Whether love and marriage were compatible was the great question that agitated the courts of Champagne and the Ile-de-France. There was no definitive answer. Was the debate based on actual marital experience? Did it influence that experience, or was it simply discussion of a world of fiction in which anything could happen or which compensated for what reality lacked?

Eleventh-century men were obsessed with the idea of wives' committing adultery. This obsession had some basis in fact, for it was relatively easy for outsiders to enter houses and the rooms within them. Queens and other noblewomen accused by hostile factions of suspect relations with men with whom they plotted in their bedchambers frequently proved their innocence by undergoing an ordeal: they were made to hold red-hot iron bars, or they were represented by knights in duels. In the one case the accused faced her accusers alone; in the other she needed to find a champion: a friend, relative— or lover. Isolde, Guinevere, and a whole gallery of heroines of epic and romance, not all of whom were truly innocent, managed in this way to escape judgment by the feudal court of their lord and master. In the late twelfth century, when the trouveres sent shivers down the spines of their audience with tales of these dangerous trials, ordeals were apparently already on the wane (and with them, perhaps, a kind of liberty as well). Yet they were in widespread use at the beginning of the century, as is shown by the letters of Yves of Chartres. To be sure, the great canonist wished to limit the use of this "illegitimate" (or, as we would say today, irrational) proof to cases where there was no other means of getting at the truth; female adultery was one such. (The ordeal was particularly shocking to the medieval mind in that it was a means of "tempting God." But in adultery there was no witness to virtue upon whom a woman could call other than the Lord.)

Male sexual excesses posed no threat to the household order or the purity of the lineage. Such innocuous escapades are mentioned in the sources only incidentally. The portrait of Baldwin II, count of Guines (died 1169), by the chaplain Lambert breathes authenticity: this nobleman's vitality—as

In a minor French tale of the 13th century, a jealous husband, seeing a form stretched out beside his sleeping wife, believes that he has caught her in adultery and slays her. Too late he discovers his error: she had taken a small dog to bed with her. In despair, the man stabs himself with his own sword. (Dijon Library, ms 526.)

Lambert puts it, "the intemperance of his loins"—manifested itself in an immoderate lust for virgins from the time he turned an adolescent until he was well on in years. He fathered bastards all around Calais and even tried to establish three of them (since illegitimate offspring had no recognized right to any part of a man's legacy). Nevertheless, he suffered greatly when his legitimate wife, the lady of Ardres, died in childbirth. In every way he seemed distressed and inconsolable. He began to do good works (*opera pietatis*) on behalf of the *domestici* (of his extended household) as well as minor nobles in difficulty, of whom there were many in the region. In short, he took the place of his late wife, who had been patroness to all these people. We can imagine what relations between her and Baldwin must have been like: theirs was a good friendship, in the Ciceronian sense, characterized by careful attention to the "offices" that each owed the other. Their marriage was a harmonious partnership, devoted to the management of the family business, the seigneurie, with its steady inward flow of revenues and outward flow of gifts.

In order to understand conjugal society we must first understand the domestic economy that supported it. Full community property was unknown, although acquests sometimes accrued to the community. Questions of inheritance of property belonging to couples of noble or knightly rank are complex and highly technical. The constitution of the widow's dower, traditionally provided for under Salic Law, was to some extent compensated by a dowry (share of an inheritance); both were considered in the desponsatio. The lengthy preamble to the charter concerning these matters, drawn up in 1177 on behalf of Arnoul of Monceau, affirms the dignity of marriage. It was directed explicitly against heretics, whose egalitarian, almost libertarian propaganda proved attractive to women refractory to the male order. Because he loves his wife, Arnoul designates the "best part" of his possessions, a toll at the city of Laon, as her dower. (This was the main purpose of the document.) But, as the proverb says, what is earned in bed is collected in widowhood.

In the Capetian realm it was customary in the early thirteenth century for a noblewoman to enjoy a dower right (*jus dotalitii*) to half of her husband's property. It was intended to provide for her after her husband's death in case she did not remarry. The practice took into account the fact that because the woman had been given a dowry at the time of her marriage, she no longer had any claim on the patrimony shared by her brothers. Her widow's dower was not always firmly established, however. Practicing jurists were careful to mention that the wife consented to any alienation of her husband's property. Both might appear, for example, before a church official, where the wife could agree to the gift or sale, relinquishing her share of the property or accepting in compensation an increase in her rights on some other component of the patrimony. The wife's agreement was said to be "spontaneous and uncoerced" (*spontanea, non coacta*). This ensured the validity of the agreement even if the husband's gifts proved extravagant or if children or, more likely, collateral heirs raised objections after his death.

After 1175 the documents indicate a decline in the *laudatio parentum* and an increased emphasis on the wife's participation

A woman before a male tribunal. In *Tristan und Isolde*, Isolde attempts to plead against the charges of adultery that have been leveled against her. (Munich Library, Cod. germ. 51.)

at her husband's side. Does this suggest a triumph of couple over lineage? The opposite interpretation is equally supported by the facts: that the lineage obtained the incontrovertible right known as *retrait lignager*, attested by Beaumanoir, which gave it the power to veto any sale, while the wife received in return nothing more than an incomplete and tenuous guarantee to a part of the inheritance. The image may be a negative of reality or a harbinger of things to come.

Widow and Orphan. Broadly speaking, the legists wished to defend the rights of the widow. Their concern is proof of the potential tension that existed between a man's wife and his blood relatives. Marc Bloch was sensitive to this problem, as is evident in his citation of a brother-in-law's cruel apostrophe to a widow from the gest *Garin le Loheren*: the brother-in-law claims that his mourning is greater than the wife's, because his loss is irreparable, whereas she will remarry. This speech reflects more than just the sudden, unthinking emotional re-action of the moment; it is a public plaint, a claim laid to a share of the inheritance—a *clamor* in the full sense of the word.

But was it not the knight's mission in life to "defend widows and orphans"? I believe that this formula (borrowed from the traditional definition of regalian rights) was a part of the Church's injunction to the knight because he was so likely to oppress them—beginning with his sister-in-law and nephew. The different branches of a patrilineage found themselves in conflict at each inheritance, battling for the means to maintain a way of life that required inherited wealth. Over the two centuries that concern us here, the form and intensity of the struggle may have varied, but the conflict was constant.

What became of the young widow? When Ernaud d'Echauffour died in 1064, poisoned by Mabille of Bellême, his wife returned to her own family, taking up residence with her brother, the seneschal of Normandy. The two young sons were sent to live in "strange houses," far from their mother, vulnerable to "penury and injustice." (This did not prevent them from eventually enjoying illustrious careers—one in the Church, the other as a knight.) The conjugal unit disintegrated in the wake of this misfortune.

A very different example is found in the story of Guibert of Nogent's mother. Guibert, a monk whose father was a knight, has left a gripping account of a childhood shaped by tension between patrilineage and conjugal family. His father

Quiet strength, 12th century.
(Andlau, Sainte-Richarde
Church.)

and mother had married quite young, in the mid-eleventh
century, and enjoyed a residence of their own, with their own
domestic staff, in an *oppidum* (a precursor of the urban castle
of later years) in the Beauvaisis. Other couples associated with
the father's clan lived in the immediate vicinity, and it is not
hard to imagine that there was both rivalry and mutual support
among them. (For instance, the families competed for the
services of a tutor for their children.) Yet between these young
households there must have been a veil of privacy, for seven
years passed before Guibert's future father admitted to his
relatives that he had been unable to consummate his marriage.
(He may have been intimidated by his wife's higher rank.)

Huntress. Equestrian seal of
Sibille of Beaujeu, regent of a
seigneurie as long as her son
remained a minor (until 1217).
(Archives of the Nord.)

The clan then attempted to end the marriage (despite its being
hypergamic) by driving the wife to commit some crime (perhaps by arranging her abduction). The couple resisted these
pressures, and, thanks to an extramarital adventure, Guibert's
father was able to overcome his inhibitions. He subsequently
fathered several children before dying while still a young man,
probably in the aftermath of a period of captivity. Then,
according to the orphaned Guibert, the fury of his father's
relatives was unleashed against his mother. Their aim was to
rid themselves as quickly as possible of this despised woman,
who, though besieged with suitors and lawsuits (possibly over
the dower), refused to remarry. Threat and intimidation were
coupled with blandishment. In a terrible scene the wretched
woman is about to collapse before a hostile castle court (composed of course exclusively of men), when she finds salvation
by invoking the name of Jesus Christ as *sponsus*, that is, by
declaring herself ready to embrace a religious vocation, which
gains her the support of the priests. Actually this strong,
almost biblical woman remains mistress of her house and of
the education of her children until Guibert, the last to be born,
reaches the age of twelve or so. Thereafter her only thought
is for the salvation of her soul and of the souls of her sons
and, above all, of her husband; this she proposes to obtain
through penitence, by going to live with other women at the
gate of a monastery. She even adopts a foundling to redeem
her husband's sin (for the experiment that had demonstrated
his virility had produced a bastard).

Conjugal love and maternal love clearly did exist in the
Middle Ages. They are present in Guibert's mother's struggles, visions, and dreams, all of which are closely related
(assuming that she transferred to her son her devotion to her
deceased husband). Other social and emotional aspects of kinship play a part in the story, each with a specific functional
role. The churchman reproaches himself for the detours (*dé-
cours*) that he followed on the advice of his "friends by blood"
and that took him away from God. The loving son, whose
worship of Mary is explicitly related to his feelings for his
mother, takes up her grievances against her in-laws. But his
father's clan, bent on obtaining social advancement for its
sons, took an active interest in his ecclesiastical career. Guibert
thoroughly detested the elder cousin who headed the clan, but
he nearly obtained a canonry thanks to the cousin's efforts on
his behalf. Although the mother's family was apparently of
more exalted rank, it is distinguished only by its failure to

intervene in the two major crises of the young woman's life. Apparently cognatic kin did not take an active part in social life but limited themselves to the passive function of representing social rank. Guibert encounters relatives in all lines throughout Beauvais and Laon. He cannot and will not disown his affection for Evrard of Breteuil or his worldly prejudice in favor of a female cousin who has married and settled in Laon. Despite his membership in that immense kindred known as the clergy, the monk is unwilling to renounce his true kin.

The impression remains that the widow is unwilling to return to her own family. Would they have welcomed her had she been willing to go? The attention learned thirteenth-century jurists paid to matters pertaining to the widow's dower may be related to a decrease in the frequency of remarriage, to an estrangement of the couple from their kindred. If correct, this would suggest that the importance of the couple had increased. Beautiful Hermanjart, who left her native Lombardy to live with Aymeri of Narbonne, was not destined to return home. And Lady Guibourc explained to her nephew, in her favors and her verses, the social reason for this practice (along with the prosaic but useful notion that accurate accounting makes for good marriages):

Seal of Gertrude, countess of Dabo, 13th century. (Archives of Meurthe-et-Moselle.)

> El n'a parant en iceste contrée,
> Seror ne frere, dont elle soit privée.
> De son doaire ne doit estre obliée:
> Car li nomez, sire, s'il vos agrée
> Plus en avra d'amor a vos tornée,
> Si vos en ert plus cortoise et privée.
>
> She has no relative in this region,
> no brother or sister with whom she
> is privately associated. Do not
> forget her dower: state it out loud,
> sire, if you choose. In return she
> will love you more, she will be
> more attentive and devoted to you.

The dowager widow played an important role in the great lineages of the twelfth century. In the Coucy clan, for example, we find a dowager aiding her adolescent son in the first years of his government, after which she was given a permanent residence and lived on the income from her dower, which, after her death, went either to a younger son or to the constitution of a new dower (which was kept within the patrilineage). She diminished this income somewhat during her lifetime, however, owing to an interest late in life in founding and maintaining churches. Between 1130 and 1138 the widow and son of the terrible Thomas of Marle, sire of Coucy, were subjected to attack by the count of Vermandois and to reproach by monasteries that claimed to have been plundered by Thomas. His vanquisher, King Louis VI, refused to be drawn into committing an injustice (or imprudence) by disinheriting Thomas' wife and children. He was content to appropriate the dead man's treasure, leaving his land to his family. Meanwhile, the bishops and abbots, who had no wish to see the heirs of the sinner expunged from society, were willing to settle for restitutions and alms.

In the history of any seigneurie, principality, or kingdom, the death of a young father and husband marked a period of weakness. At such times relations with vassals overshadowed kinship ties, for it was the vassals' obligation to defend—and opportunity to manipulate—the widow and children. The peers of a castellany supported and inspired their sire's heir; the king or suzerain prince defended and disciplined the sons and daughters of their vassals. It was sometimes hard to distinguish the child taken hostage from the youngster educated and encouraged by a patron. As for the great regents mentioned earlier, Blanche of Champagne was closely monitored by Philip Augustus, who held her son (1200–1216), and Blanche of France (née Blanche of Castile) saw her "lease" on the kingdom challenged by the great barons, who in 1229

Reign of a mother. Blanche of Castile supervises the education of Louis IX. William of Saint Panthus, *Life and Miracles of Saint Louis,* 14th century. (Bibliothèque Nationale, French 5716.)

sought to seize the young Saint Louis by force. Had not their dying lord, Louis VIII, suggested that they take the heir to the throne into safekeeping? As in the time of Guibert of Nogent, a widow's life was a bitter struggle. If she was a young woman, whether by tyrannical lord or insolent vassals, she was constantly urged to remarry; she had no choice.

To the end of the twelfth century the great seigneuries, to the extent that they were not subject to constraining feudal rule but remained alodial holdings, were largely controlled and protected by the patrilineage. Practical precepts and the traditional image of classical feudalism came to the fore later, and women and children did not thereby gain true freedom. Traditional histories of France argue that the Capetians took shrewd and peaceful advantage of the rules of suzerainty. This actually means that they cast marriageable daughters into prison, held inquisitorial investigations into questions of kinship, vetoed dangerous alliances, and unscrupulously wreaked havoc with the private life of the high aristocracy.

The private life of the high aristocracy? Perhaps I should invoke Duby's broadly defined "private domain" and say, rather, that the Capetians wreaked havoc with the kinds of strategies just described. The individual and the married couple enjoyed relatively limited freedom in a society that was more a society of lineages than it was truly "feudal," both in the period when violence was more or less unrestrained as well as after aggression had become more covert.

Conclusion

This essay has been guided by Marc Bloch's conception of the subject. Although my analysis is more detailed and in some respects different, it tries to answer the same questions that he posed. The distinction between lineage and kindred, the theory of cognatic systems, and the historicization of the ideology of the couple are ideas borrowed from anthropology. The number and importance of the ideas that I have taken from Georges Duby should be obvious.

Let me sketch what a history of aristocratic kinship structures might look like, given the current state of research. The broad, cognatic, essentially passive kinship group remains the backdrop, as the actors clash, redefine their relative status, and make and unmake alliances. The abstract legal concepts of Philippe de Beaumanoir waned in importance very gradually, as the functional necessities to which they corresponded slowly disappeared. At the other extreme, the system was composed of simple molecules: nuclear families. Because each couple established its own household, the composition of society was constantly changing. The transformation of this ancient unit into an emotional relationship of modern type was a lengthy process; yet, given the ambiguity of the evidence and the ever-present possibility of temporary regression, it seems almost imperceptible. The work of the militant (and not triumphant) Church was of considerable importance, but its impact was limited and society responded to the exigencies of Christian marriage in a variety of ways.

The aristocracy, the ruling minority, behaved in characteristic ways designed to quell internal rivalry and ensure continued domination over the rest of society. For a fairly long period the noble kinship group was more affected by history than was the peasant family, as can be seen in the way the aristocratic kinship system responded to two major changes in the forms of power and exchange. The first change occurred around 1000 and resulted in the unleashing of wars of unprecedented violence in the various regional societies that survived the breakup of the Carolingian Empire. The construction of a host of fortresses and fortified mounds was at once a cause and a symptom of this new kind of warfare. The "encastlement" of the aristocracy was accompanied by what can only be called its "enlineagement." Kinship became so important within the nobility that it resulted in the crystallization of highly structured groups known as patrilineages. These stood out against an undifferentiated background of cognatic kinship and for a time threatened to destroy the conjugal family. Politically, decentralized power proved more advantageous than centralized power, and lineal kinship acquired, or reacquired, major social functions. For a brief time the nobility rose to the surface, like an archaic society erected on top of a more modern one, before it disappeared forever.

A second change, which took place around 1180 in northern France, was among other things socioeconomic: increased use was made of money as trade revived and economic growth all but overwhelmed the century. A great consumer of wealth, the aristocracy was spendthrift in its behavior, and disastrous transactions by irresponsible "relatives" threatened whole segments of the nobility with ruin. The right to veto the sale of clan property (*retrait lignager*) was a fine thing, but it could not be exercised unless the relatives of the seller were in a position to equal the price offered by the prospective buyer. The rapid disappearance of the *laudatio parentum*, although it does not really demonstrate the triumph of the couple, does prefigure the decline of the clan, a decline hastened by the advent of the classical feudal order some time between 1150 and 1200. Establishing the right of daughters to transmit fiefs and of younger brothers to receive fiefs directly from the father's lord (as opposed to parage and frérage), and in particular from the king, eventually proved fatal to the patrilineage. Together the economy and the law conspired to ruin the barons of the first feudal age.

The broad historical overview can be seductive but superficial. An abstract, anthropological approach cannot hope to reconstruct the actual texture of medieval married life or clan relations. Nevertheless, if focusing on the kinship system makes this world seem peculiar and remote, the rare and indirect testimony of the men and women of the feudal age, their shouts and their equally significant silences, make us feel less distant.

Plan of the city of Florence, ca. 1470. A bird's-eye view, looking south, of the principal buildings (some eighty in all). Surrounded by cloisters or gardens and isolated from the city by walls, many of these monasteries, hospitals, and palaces formed islets of private social life, worlds unto themselves. (Paris, Bibliothèque Nationale, Latin 4802.)

❧ Tuscan Notables on the Eve of the Renaissance

Charles de La Roncière

THE CONTENTS OF THE PRIVATE WORLD

Man is not made to live alone, except for the few—hermits and brigands—whose vocation requires isolation. For the most part man is a social animal; as the Venetian Franciscan Fra Paolino expressed it in 1314: *Fagli mestiere a vivere con molti* (Make it your business to live with many others). With many others, yet without chaos. To live in society was to participate, according to Paolino, in three progressively more exclusive communities: the overarching political community (city, kingdom, or other entity); the neighborhood (*vicinato*); and the household. His view, widely shared, was that distinct groups coexisted within the public sphere, the city or kingdom; these groups enjoyed sufficient autonomy to be considered "private." Though centered in the house (*casa, ostau,* and so on), private life was not confined within its walls. It extended beyond the family and its dwelling place into what our Franciscan called the *vicinato*. This singling out of the neighborhood suggests that neighbors, people who rubbed shoulders daily, shared a special kind of solidarity. Through the network of neighbors the family thrust its antennae into the wider community—the city or canton.

The Family

To live in private was above all to live at home, in the midst of the family. The family was the heart of private life. The house or home, that warmest and most indispensable of private sanctums, was often defined in somewhat restrictive terms. According to Paolino, its inhabitants included a husband, a wife, their children, and no one else save a female domestic to wait on them, a luxury Paolino plainly considered essential. A hundred and twenty years later Leon Battista Alberti had a similar notion of the family. A husband, a wife, children, maids, manservants: "That is what people refer to as the family." If these moralists are right, the elementary unit of private existence was the married couple. But had couples in pre-Renaissance Italy really achieved autonomy?

Tax declarations prepared by every taxpayer allow us to glimpse the composition of the Italian household from the fourteenth century on. The average size of each household unit in many cities, especially after 1348, is slightly more than four persons: in Bologna in 1395 it was 4.3; in Tuscany in 1427, 4.42; in Siena in 1453, 4.28. In some places the average was less than four: in the city of Florence in 1427 it was 3.8, and in Lucca in 1411, 3.91. These small numbers seem to indicate strictly conjugal families: a father, a mother, and two children.

But these averages were below normal, mainly because of the plagues that ravaged the country after 1348. Households in the early Trecento were probably more robust, and in some cantons as late as the fifteenth century we find homes quite crowded with inhabitants. In San Gimignano an average of six peasants crowded around every hearth in 1290; by 1428 the number had increased to more than seven. These figures suggest that the typical home sheltered more than just a nuclear family; closer examination confirms this hypothesis. Not only the largest households (those with seven or more members) but also those of more modest size (four to five members) exhibit a notable variety. The remarkable work of David Herlihy and Christiane Klapisch-Zuber has shown that in Tuscany, where the average household size in 1427 was 3.8, households were of many different kinds: single individuals (widows, widowers, or unmarried persons); nuclear families (with or without children); extended families (including an ancestor, parent or otherwise, or a brother or cousin); and multiple nuclear families (several related families gathered around one hearth). The restrictive definition of the family given above was valid in the majority of cases (54.8 percent), but not in all. Many people lived alone (13.5 percent of all households), and not every family enjoyed its own private residence.

In the Tuscan cities of the Quattrocento few families shared quarters with other families; only 12 percent of all hearths served more than one nuclear family. Such sharing was far more common in the countryside, particularly among

Andrea Mantegna, *Wedding Chamber* (detail of north wall), ca. 1474. In this family portrait of the Gonzagas, lords of Mantua (eighteen in all), the hands of Marquis Louis III are recognizable on the left, his wife, Barbara of Hohenzollern, on the right, and around them, not all visible here, sons, daughters, a bastard(?), and familiars. A prince's strictly private world extended far beyond his household, and its limits were ill-defined. (Mantua, Ducal Palace.)

the better-off. One peasant dwelling in five sheltered more than one family, and among the wealthier peasants the proportion ran as high as one in two. It might even seem that such patriarchal households were in fact the original pattern, that the practice of allowing each nuclear family to establish a home of its own was a more recent development, but this is far from certain. In the twelfth and thirteenth centuries in rural Romagna, for instance, families were apparently quite small and very few homes sheltered more than seven individuals, at least in these villages that historians have been able to study. It was common in this period for rural Italian families to share houses. Around Bologna, for example, 22 percent of all hearths were shared in 1392; in the plain the figure rose as high as 36 percent in 1451. Around Lucca 18 percent of hearths were shared in 1411–1413, and in the Polesina of Ferrara the figure in 1481 was 30 percent. While the conditions of urban life impeded the establishment of multiple (or multinuclear) households in the cities, more affluent citizens were less affected by these handicaps. In 1427 some 15 percent of Florentine houses whose wealth exceeded 800 florins sheltered more than one family.

In the cities cohabitation was practiced to different degrees in different lineages and different generations. Among the

Domenico Ghirlandaio, *Scenes from the Life of Saint Francis,* "Miracle of the Resurrected Child" (detail), 1483–1486. Around the magnificent bed in which the child lies the artist has placed two groups of some twenty patricians in all, one of which is shown here, the other on the page opposite. The family, gathered near the patron, is in the minority. The patron, Francesco Sassetti, is here paying homage to such eminent citizens as the Albizzi and Strozzi, whom he has had painted mingled with members of his own family. (Florence, Santa Trinità, Sassetti Chapel.)

Rucellai, an important Florentine family, only two of twenty-six households (7.7 percent) included more than one couple in 1427, compared with seven of twenty-eight (25 percent) in 1480. Among the Capponi, an equally well-known Florentine family, multiple households accounted for 8 percent of all hearths in 1427, compared with 54 percent in 1469. There was no fixed rule. Circumstances were decisive. It was common for a household to undergo a complete transformation in the course of a few generations. In the earliest tax declarations we encounter a young couple and its children. Fifteen years later the parents are gone, but the children, now grown, continue to live together under one roof. Ten years later, still together, all have families of their own. Finally the "brotherhood" disintegrates and one brother, now an aging patriarch, remains in possession of the premises and prepares the final tax statement on behalf of his sons' families.

For many Tuscans, especially peasants and members of the bourgeoisie, living in a large family (whether extended—couple, children, and ancestors—or multinuclear) was a familiar experience. Anyone who lived, however briefly, with grandfather, cousins, brothers and their families, and so forth necessarily had a more complicated notion of family privacy than the moralists suggest. The memoirs (*ricordanze*) that many bourgeois Florentines composed in the fifteenth century frequently attest to their authors' attachment to large groups. Alberti, for one, frequently has old Giannozzo express his regret at seeing "families separate, come and go through many doors; and I have never allowed my brother Antonio to live apart from me, under another roof." Legislation often enshrined the notion of large family groups, and the moralists viewed them with approval. In Bologna in 1287 a statute defined the family as consisting of father, mother, brothers, sisters, and daughters-in-law. (The family envisioned by the law was of the patriarchal type, in which sons brought wives home to live under their father's roof.)

However animated and crowded such households may have been, they normally included only relatives in the male line. Relatives by marriage or in the female line were accepted only with the greatest reluctance, no matter how close or needy (orphans, say, or even bastards). Once received into the fold, however, even they were treated with hospitality and affection. As for servants, who Alberti insists were full members of the household, we naturally find a goodly number in the homes of the wealthy: in 1290 the Florentine merchant

Attributed to Pellegrino di Mariano, *Scenes of Hospital Life* (detail), second half of the 15th century. Distribution of food to the patients. This model hospital, Santa Maria della Scala in Siena, had modernized its treatment of patients, each of whom had his own bed, curtains for privacy, and a personal plate for food. (Siena, Pinacoteca.)

Bene Bencivenni employed a valet, five servingwomen, and a young maid; and Francesco di Marco Datini, the well-known merchant of Prato, in 1393 employed two valets, two servingwomen, and a slave. Wealthy households were not typical, however; artisans hired servants relatively infrequently. Domestic servants did not become a major presence until the sixteenth century.

The "family" extended beyond the bounds of the home. In city and countryside everyone had uncles, cousins, and other kin who shared the privileges of private intercourse. Here, again, the primary kinship group was the lineage, consisting of descendants of a single ancestor in the male line, and all aware of their common origin. Of the many lineages (*consortiere, casate,* or even *famiglie*) to be found in fourteenth- and fifteenth-century Italy, the oldest and best-known adopted names that manifested family pride. In Florence in 1427 the practice was sufficiently well established that one taxpayer in three indicated a family name. The proportion was smaller (20 percent) in other Tuscan cities and still smaller (9 percent) in the countryside, but occasionally signs of strong family pride are found even in peasants without a family name: they know their distant cousins and are aware of belonging to the same *consorteria.* Unostentatious solidarity of this sort is very common at all levels of society. Some lineages were organized by treaty into a *consorzio famigliare,* with its own institutions, leaders, and statutes; such groupings added a third dimension to private life (along with the household and the lineage).

Finally, marriage attached to each male a further network of kindreds (*parentadi*) through his mother, wife, and daughters-in-law. Marriage was an affair of state. The stakes were considerable. Alberti tells us that "many marriages have been, as everyone knows, causes of a family's ruin, because concluded with quarrelsome, litigious, proud, or malevolent individuals." On the other hand, wise, carefully planned marriages had won for families "the enthusiastic zeal of their allies" (F. Barbaro), "strengthened mutual affection among new kin and . . . reestablished concord" (San Bernardino of Siena), and induced families "brought together by kinship . . . to lend each other charitable assistance and offer mutual counsel, favor, and aid" (Matteo Palmieri). In short, marriage opened a whole new realm of possibilities, establishing new contacts and sources of information, winning new allies, and fostering sympathy that not only defined the private sphere but sometimes proved influential well beyond its limits.

Other forms of private solidarity sometimes complemented or competed with family ties. Moralists and other writers praised the values of friendship and neighborliness. Companionship in all its forms deserves comment here despite the staid silence of the sources; people were influenced by those with whom they associated for purposes of sport, amusement, education, and protest.

Private Life Outside the Family

In the standard formulas for describing a person's close ties, friends were always mentioned after relatives (*parenti, amici*); in Italy the two were never confounded, as they were in France. Every family relied on a stable group of friends who complemented and augmented relatives by blood and marriage. Often only a handful of these friends were on intimate terms with family members. The memoirs of the Florentine banker Lapo Niccolini (ca. 1410) mention perhaps a half-dozen. But when needed, those friends were always there, steadfast, loyal, affectionate, and ready to perform any service, financial or otherwise. Families took care to expand their circle of friends, and moralists and memoir-writers stressed the need for such effort and the advantages that it could bring. Friendship was in itself a great good. The humanists, won over by ancient exemplars of the virtue, were fervent in its praise. The question whether friendship was preferable to kinship or vice versa was widely and passionately debated, even in the entourage of Cosimo de' Medici (Platina). Alberti has no doubt that friendship is more durable than any *parentado*, and he does not hesitate to make even friendship with a person from outside one's home (*fuori casa*) a domestic and private (*privato*) virtue, just like honor. The Florentine Giovanni Morelli, a practical man with little liking for abstruse speculation, advises his children to emulate himself and his father by "winning the friendship of good men . . . , virtuous and powerful." The services that Giovanni says his father rendered to friends and expected of them in return show how intimate a role friends played in private life.

For the memoir-writers, relatives, friends, and neighbors comprised the standard trinity. Neighbors played a role in everyday life not very different from that of friends and relatives, a role for which proximity ideally suited them. Not much could be kept secret from neighbors, who were often useful and in some cases might even be accepted as friends. Boccaccio tells us that the Florentine patrician Geri Spini treated his neighbor the baker Cisti as a friend after the latter good-naturedly offered him a glass of wine. Proximity could efface social distance.

Certain friends and neighbors were selected to fill the enviable position of godfather, and it was customary for a child to have more than one godparent. Godparents were chosen from outside the family, and in families with many children this created another circle around the household, composed of godparents who were on terms of particular intimacy with the family. The Niccolini, for example, had thirty-two godfathers and godmothers for their thirteen children. Godparentage introduced a note of spiritual kinship (between, on the one hand, godparent and godchild, and between godparent and the godchild's parents, on the other), which people took quite seriously. If the Niccolini entourage is typical, godparents did not form a homogeneous group, any more than did the group of neighbors from which they were recruited. Half of the godparents of the Niccolini children came from the same social class as the family, but ten were drawn from much lower down the social scale. Yet all commentators agree that godparents enjoyed freer access to the family's home than did other outsiders. They could come and go and converse with servants or with the lady of the house without occasioning gossip among the neighbors. They were part of the family's private life.

Powerful men (nobles, bourgeois, businessmen) were also surrounded by what the sources call *amici* and *seguaci*; we would call them clients. Relations with clients were responsible for many political successes in fourteenth- and fifteenth-century Tuscan cities. In return, patrons recommended their clients for positions, favors, tax abatements, and many other rewards which could not be had in any other way. Although we know little about these client networks, evidence suggests that relations between patrons and clients were extremely close. Personalities like Cosimo de' Medici and the patricians who formed his entourage were besieged by requests for assistance. They were bombarded with letters, constantly asked for favors, heaped with gifts. Clients fawned for favors and treated these illustrious patrons like elder brothers, almost like fathers. They sought to establish between themselves and their patrons relations of protection and affection. Contemporaries called such relations *amicizia*, but they were in fact patterned

Pietro Lorenzetti, *Scenes from the Life of the Blessed Umiltà* (detail), 1341. Monasteries and convents offered their inhabitants a private life totally separate from that of the lay world yet sharing similar customs, such as meals in common or instruction of the young by their elders. (Florence, Uffizi.)

after kinship relations in the patriarchal clan. Clients constituted an artificial lineage, an ersatz family that grew up around powerful figures and was composed of men whose own families were too modest to help them win success or honors. It was impossible to rise in public life without powerful private backing.

Beyond the limits of the home and the family there existed a strange world that many people considered too dangerous to confront alone. Confraternities, corporations, and other structured institutions offered the necessary support, but people also ventured briefly into the dangerous outside world at times when they could not or would not rely on such institutional support. Under such circumstances groups formed spontaneously, extending or replacing the private circles of relations on which they were often based. For instance, children of all social classes played together in the streets, as they do in many societies. In cities neighborhood children formed *brigate*, or groups of friends, as did the youths who ran errands for artisans in the quarter. By playing together or amusing themselves repeatedly with the same companions, young people formed relations of their own. In the country (in Val d'Elsa, for example), the young companions of Saint Verdiana, shepherdesses aged six to fourteen who spent their days scattered about the meadows, occasionally met for a moment of recreation. In the shade of a tree or chapel the girls paused to chat about childish things but also about serious matters: religion and sanctity were among the topics discussed. Adolescents, too, formed *brigate*: youths might escort a companion lucky in love through the streets of the town or assemble for a raucous banquet, sometimes repeated year after year. There was no lack of inventiveness. At times these *brigate* were more formally organized; some had uniforms, customs, names, and more or less secret rituals and entered into rivalry with other, similar groups. Court documents reveal that in 1420 Florence two bands of youths, the Berta and the Magrone, often came to blows. Florentine men married very late; not until they were almost thirty were they permitted to assume family and political responsibilities. The resulting frustration encouraged marginal, extrafamilial forms of sociability, substitutes for private life in the form of pseudo-consorterie with "family" names and secret rituals.

Even after marriage many people, especially women, con-

Private Life on the Fringes of Society

Fra Carnevale da Urbino, *Visitation* (detail), 15th century. There were many occasions for women to gather and support one another, such as childbirth or illness. Their *brigate* were a valued substitute for other forms of privacy. (Rome, Barberini Palace.)

tinued to participate in various activities on the fringes of private life. Their involvement, though sporadic and informal, was nonetheless significant. Women had their *brigate*, which gathered to escort a member to confession or some other destination. There were few secrets among group members. For a woman to travel from village to town or city to city or to embark upon a more ambitious pilgrimage often meant joining other women following the same route. Young Agnes, later to become a saint of the region, traveled to Montepulciano with such a group. And when her emulator, the Blessed Verdiana, left Castelfiorentino for Santiago da Compostella, it was in the company of other pilgrims, most of them women of her village who set out together on purpose. Groups of pious women, sometimes members of a tertiary order, sometimes widows, used to meet privately in a member's home for ritual purification. And devout women frequently gathered around the cells of holy recluses (like the mother of the Blessed Verdiana).

Men as well as women felt a need for other forms of

privacy. Lonely men without families sought company for support, like Sacchetti's three blind men who went begging on the same highway and, when evening came, shared the proceeds in a rented room (Novella 140). Even married men were occasionally drawn to different types of privacy. On holidays and Sundays they sought refuge in the countryside, and the late-fifteenth-century description of holiday revelry at an inn in Pontassieve in Tuscany surely applies to many other villages as well: "Some thirty peasants had gathered, as was customary on holiday evenings, to drink and gamble and recount their follies." Finally, imagine the different forms of private experience shared by pilgrims, merchants, shepherds, and sailors—all occupations that took men far from home and family for long periods of time.

Everyone in the highly urbanized and sociable Italy of this period had the opportunity, the obligation, or the desire to join one or another informal group. Like the family in some ways, these groups were places where confidences could be exchanged in an atmosphere of warmth and affection. Friendly companionship was sometimes only a short way from complicity in crime. Groups of friends sometimes skirted the law or deliberately engaged in crime. Members of such clandestine groups felt a passionate attachment to them. In some way they were almost a caricature of the family.

Games of chance (*ad zardum*), especially dice, brought people together. Men everywhere gambled passionately by day and above all by night in private homes, in certain places where gambling was tolerated (fairs and markets), but most of all wherever there was space enough to hide a few players and a brief candle: deserted marketplaces, loggias, doorways, palace entries, alleys, streetcorners, riverbanks, and so on. Muffled voices could be heard as strangers from all parts of the city gathered. Such encounters were quite outside normal patterns of sociability, which brought together people who lived in the same neighborhood or parish. Yet those drawn to these nocturnal games were passionate about them, despite the discomfort, cold, and roving police patrols (from whose reports we know about them). Similar though more furtive, episodic, and scattered were the gatherings of homosexuals.

Of the same species but more picturesque and cruel (yet often quite disciplined) were the bands of outlaws, brigands, and soldiers of fortune recruited from among the victims of war and pillage. Camping together, gambling together, frequenting prostitutes together, these criminals created a private life of their own, a substitute for family life based on entirely different norms yet full of nostalgia for a more settled existence.

The Composition of the Population

Thus every individual belonged to many different milieus—household, lineage, kindred, friends, neighbors, companions, and more or less clandestine associations—and was therefore familiar with hundreds of other people. The demographics of the period tell us something about the nature of these acquaintances. Prior to the plagues households were apparently full of children, although our evidence is spotty

Ambrogio Lorenzetti, *The Effects of Good Government in the Countryside* (detail), 1338–1341. Patrician residence in the suburbs. Close to the city, spacious, with broad views of the countryside (the crenellations serving merely as inoffensive decoration), the country house stood ready to receive clients and friends. (Siena, Palazzo Pubblico.)

and impressionistic. We do have figures for the late fourteenth and fifteenth centuries, and they show that by 1371 the proportion of young people in the population of some rural areas had again reached an unusually high level. In the vicinity of Prato youths under fifteen accounted for 49 percent of the population, a far higher percentage than is found today in any developing country. Twenty years later, in the town of Budrio near Bologna, the percentage of youths was only slightly lower (43 percent). The epidemics that were such commonplace occurrences after 1348 cut down children in disproportionate numbers. In 1427 the under-fifteen age group had shrunk to just 37 percent of the population around Prato, and this figure remained fairly constant for some forty years throughout Tuscany, city and countryside alike. To be sure, the number of children per household was still high (slightly less than in Egypt today, slightly more than in China).

But the proportion of the population that was over sixty-five was also extraordinarily high (9 to 10 percent in rural Tuscany), much higher than in Egypt or China. The population was "elderly" in the demographer's sense, even though the relative size of this age group declined after 1430. Another unusual feature for which there is no good explanation is that men outnumbered women pretty much everywhere (in Tuscany, in the Bologna region, and around Ferrara). This was especially true in some rural areas and among the wealthier urban classes.

Thus, family life in the fifteenth century was lived among large numbers of children (although the numbers tended to diminish from generation to generation). It also meant frequent contact with the elderly, whose words were heeded by the young. And finally, given the shortage of women (especially noticeable among the bourgeoisie and in adult age groups), it meant much talk about women, but primarily from a male point of view.

Ambrogio Lorenzetti, *The Effects of Good Government in the Countryside* (detail), 1338–1341. Peasant dwelling: several sturdy buildings with tile roofs; outbuildings; three adjoining residences with multiple stories; an orchard surrounded by walls. Although this could be a hamlet of several hearths, it more likely was a well-equipped, isolated farm, on which the household of the farmer lived and worked in comfort. (Siena, Palazzo Pubblico.)

THE HOME

Fifteenth-century memoir-writers sought to foster a taste and respect for (not to say a mystique of) family life. In 1421 the Florentine Gino Capponi recorded in his diary advice to his children. He recommended that they "remain together for a time until you are ready to divide the estate harmoniously." Almost ninety years later, in 1510, another Capponi, Andrea, informed his uncle, bishop of Cortona, that he and his brother had decided to live together and pool their possessions, a decision that redounded to the honor of the house and satisfied the bishop's wishes. To live together was also the ideal of Leon Battista Alberti, who expresses his wish through old Giannozzo: "I would like all my family to reside under one roof, to warm themselves at one fire, and to eat at one table." By "all my family" he means his household, his family in the narrow sense already discussed. But this much of the patriarchal household everyone at this level of society (the upper urban bourgeoisie) wished to preserve. The desire was partially realized in the practice whereby several families shared a single dwelling, but the wish was broader and deeper than this. In their references to unity, honor, and the "house," the patriarchs expressed nostalgia for a time when family business was transacted on a daily basis in the home. Their ideal was a permanent alliance that included not only members of the household but also the entire lineage and other friends.

Types of Dwellings

For each type of household—small or large, rich or poor, rural or urban—there was a different type of dwelling. Diversity was apparent in the flatlands (around Bologna, in various parts of Tuscany, and above all in the area around Lodi and in Lombardy), where workers and small farmers lived in crude huts with cob walls and thatched roofs, often no more than 13 to 16 by 26 to 33 feet. Small, smoky, lacking interior walls, sometimes dilapidated, they offered little in the way of comfort or intimacy. Farmhouses (*poderi*) built in Tuscany for farmers and sharecroppers were better constructed: the walls and roofs were of sturdier materials (stone or brick for the walls, clay tiles for the roofs) and the dimensions were larger (33 to 39 feet by 16 to 20 feet by 16 feet), making these homes more habitable. Inside the space included a loft and was generally divided into several rooms, including a larder, a hall, and one or more bedrooms. Loggias provided space for working outdoors. This model had hundreds of variants throughout the Piedmont and in the Emilian Apennines; some had exterior staircases with a gallery and rooms on the second floor, a cowshed on the ground floor, and so on. In fortified towns and villages, where houses had to be crowded close together inside the town walls, dwellings were built to yet another pattern. In 1437 there were seven houses in the older portion of the town of San Colombano near Lodi of robust construction, with walls made of the same stone as the town walls,

which they abutted. They were quite small, however: four of them measured under 294 square feet of living space, divided into just two rooms. Here crowded conditions were not necessarily associated with poverty, for these homes were inhabited by the barber and other artisans.

Just as there was greater variety in wealth in the cities, so too was there greater variety in housing. Uniform building materials were used in larger cities. The wooden construction common in the twelfth century was vulnerable to fire. By the fourteenth century not all wooden buildings had disappeared from Bologna, Siena, Genoa, and Venice, but the use of safer materials such as brick and stone had become commonplace. In Florence brick was used for simpler structures, stone for the homes of the bourgeoisie. In Siena brick was used for both simple homes and palaces, at least as a dressing; stone came into use in the fifteenth century. In Genoa stone was used for the basic structure and brick for the second and higher stories.

Anonymous, *Surrender of Colle di Val d'Elsa in 1479*, 15th century. The Neapolitan and papal armies occupy Colle. The carefully drawn urban scene depicts a standard model house, large, with several stories, in which brick predominates over wood in the walls and the roofs are of clay tile. These sturdy urban dwellings were suitable for housing several hearths. (Siena, State Archives, Biccherna Register, 1479.)

But standardization of building materials in no way implies standardization of housing or living conditions.

For the poor, living in the city meant putting up with crude housing, often worse than that found in the countryside. In Florence in 1330 young bachelors newly arrived in the city shared a single room. Some families (we do not know how many) were reduced to similar conditions. In fourteenth-century Tuscany the poor typically lived in small, run-down wood or cob shanties or in one or two rooms in a multistory building. If they were lucky, their two rooms adjoined, but that usually meant living on the very top floor or on the *palco inferior* (a sort of mezzanine). Sometimes a family had several rooms on different floors: a living-dining room on one, a bedroom on another, perhaps a kitchen on a third, joined by the building's common staircase. These dark and impractical apartments, often lacking kitchens, were usually located off an inner courtyard, leaving the facade to the building's wealthier inhabitants. The building itself might be of good appearance, but, thanks to a strict horizontal and vertical zoning, apartments were strictly segregated according to the social station of their inhabitants. The majority of the poor probably congregated in neighborhoods, streets, and buildings of their own, and this segregation increased in the fifteenth century, at least in Florence. Apartments at this level were rented, usually for short periods (one-year leases in three out of four cases). Humble folk moved frequently. Poverty limited a fam-

Simone Martini, *The Blessed Agostino Novello*, "Miracles of the Saint" (detail), polyptych, 1328-1330. Around 1330 many buildings in overpopulated cities were expanded with light additions (like this one of wood), suspended over the streets. The towns opposed this anarchic, unaesthetic, and dangerous development, which contributed to fires and accidents. (Siena, Sant'Agostino.)

ily's private space and compressed the household (to the point of promiscuity). It forced people to break off relations with friends and neighbors before they could really become established. Of course they could still become clients of powerful patrons, since clientage relations were more flexible and less tied to living in a certain quarter; but clientage meant a sacrifice of independence, and it is not altogether clear that the poorest citizens were allowed to join wealthier circles of clients.

Artisans, shopkeepers, and other members of the group known as the *popolo medio* occupied more spacious quarters in most Italian and especially Tuscan towns. They lived in apartments or houses, usually rented though sometimes owned. At the heart of these residences we find the two groups of rooms present in all medieval dwellings: the hall (*sala*) and chamber (*camera*). There were additional conveniences: above all, a kitchen (rarely found in the homes of the poor), increasingly incorporated into the home itself rather than relegated to the courtyard, though often placed in a garret on the top floor; there were also a court, a garden, a larder, a stable, a private well, and other amenities. Real luxury meant having two or more bedrooms, located on different floors in a house or created by dividing a larger room in an apartment. Preferably the "halls," or living-dining areas, abutted the building's facade, the bedrooms (especially those of women) were off the courtyard. In fourteenth-century Florence a newly created grid of rectilinear streets opened up many new lots; houses were built to take advantage of the double exposure, to garden and to street. This established a new relation between house and neighborhood: whereas small squares had drawn people together, long, straight streets tended to alienate neighbor from neighbor. At the same time the intimacy of family life was enhanced: the garden assumed new importance, as did the private bedroom.

The wealthier bourgeois, the *popolo grasso* that comprised the *arti maggiori* and the nobility, dwelt more sumptuously. The fortified and crenellated dwellings, lacking in space and amenities, in which people of this class had lived in the thirteenth century were replaced by more open and spacious houses in Pisa, Siena, Lucca, Florence, and the Lombard cities. Constructed, like the homes of the *popolo medio*, of brick or stone, they stood out by virtue of their imposing facades, windows and doorways, and details of embellishment, including various kinds of ironwork (rings, lanterns, hooks), marble colonnettes flanking the windows (Siena), large windows with

This decorative ironwork, used for holding torches, is from the Palazzo Giandonati in Florence, 14th–15th century. Private luxury served as a stimulus to the minor arts.

full arches (Florence), crenellations along the edge of the roof, and so on. The earliest Florentine dwellings of this type (the palaces of the Mozzi, Frescobaldi, Spini, and Peruzzi) appeared before the end of the thirteenth century, and by the middle of the next century the leading merchants had adopted this pattern for their urban residences. Sturdy and livable, many have survived (including those just named), and we can still admire the long, austere facades, their severe aspects softened by series of shops along the ground floor and window bays above, which allowed light to enter and distinguished these homes from the fortresses of a bygone era.

This type of dwelling, somewhat misleadingly referred to as a "palace," continued to be built for some time. We do not know what changes were made over the course of the century. Not until after 1375 do we learn, from estate inventories, that interior arrangements were quite complex and varied. According to an inventory compiled in 1390, the Florentine home of Jacopo di Rosso included a grand entryway (*androne*), probably vaulted; a vaulted room used as wine cellar or larder (*volta*); two halls (the "first" and the "grand"); two bedrooms, one off each hall; a kitchen; and servants' quarters. In all there were five habitable rooms and enormous passageways. Two years earlier Serotino Brancacci had at his disposal three halls, an antechamber, four bedrooms, two *volte*, and a kitchen, all part of a two-story house built around a courtyard at whose center stood an orange tree. The vaults, one hall, and one bedroom occupied the ground floor; the second floor contained the other two halls and the remaining bedrooms.

There were a thousand variations on these themes. The bourgeoisie was quick to adopt new ideas, such as making private use of the ground floor. (In times past the ground floor had been used for commercial purposes or storage.) The number of halls and bedrooms was increased, yet the relation of hall to chamber was maintained. Reserves were augmented and new services provided in order to make the private home more independent as well as more comfortable. Family life spread out over two floors, encouraging greater differentiation between common and private areas. Parents, children, servants, and couples all enjoyed spaces of their own. The court (still absent or rudimentary in many buildings) became the aesthetic and festive center of the home.

The lots created outside the old city in the fourteenth century constitute a special case. Here, patricians built homes just as sumptuous as the more traditional palaces, but their

Iron flagholder, 15th century. (Siena, Piazza Postierla.)

situation, at the ends of long lots perpendicular to the street, made them look much like the simpler homes flanking them. Built to rectangular plans, these grand edifices shared the same double exposure to garden and street as their less imposing neighbors. The garden consisted of that portion of the plot on which nothing was built; there was no interior courtyard. These patrician dwellings took their place in long lines of other houses and were distinguished only by their size (for they often spanned two lots).

In the fifteenth century this pattern changed unmistakably. Construction of sumptuous housing continued in the late fourteenth and early fifteenth centuries, but more often existing buildings were renovated—by constructing additions, rearranging rooms, or joining neighboring buildings. Some buildings were conceived on an even grander scale than before. Inventories from Florence in the period 1380–1410 tell us of homes (like those of Palla Strozzi, the Bombeni, the Cappelli, and the Davanzi) equipped with interior courtyards (*cortili*) and twelve or more rooms distributed among three or four stories. The palace (in this case the word is appropriate) inhabited in the fifteenth century by the Da Uzzano brothers (via dei Bardi) contained some thirty rooms, nine on the ground floor, ten on the second floor, and eleven on the third. These immense houses respected the overall plan of the city, however. Often irregular in plan, they followed the outlines of lots that were frequently assembled out of haphazard purchases. Their facades were aligned with those of lesser houses, from which they were distinguished by nothing more than

Vittore Carpaccio, *Miracle of the Relic of the Cross* (detail), 1494. Patrician homes in 15th-century Venice were as elegant as their Florentine counterparts. They accommodated a large private circle, which on this festival day overflowed onto the Grand Canal. The public bridge, made of wood, is more fragile. (Venice, Accademia.)

Medici-Riccardi Palace (1444–1464), Rucellai Palace (1446–1450), Antinori Palace (1461–1466), Strozzi Palace (1489–early 16th century), Gondi Palace (1490–1501.) Five celebrated examples, designed by Michelozzo, Alberti, Benedetto da Maiano, and Giuliano da San Gallo, of palaces in the new style, distinguished either by their decor (Rucellai) or their overall design (the four others). Impressively monumental, set triumphantly in the midst of the city, with splendidly decorated facades, and as intimidating as fortified or holy places, these palaces combined the glorious might of a castle with the tranquil privacy of a convent. Ideal as a setting for private pursuits, on occasion they also served for public ostentation.

the care taken in cutting their stone and adding finishing touches. At ground level existing shops were maintained or new shops were introduced, as in the case of the Davanzati Palace, described by its owner to the tax authorities in 1498 as "a palace with three shops of the wool *arte*."

After 1440 palaces began to be built by people who deliberately set out to break with tradition. Among these were the great and renowned Medici (1446), Pitti (first version, 1446), Antinori (1465), Strozzi (1489), and Gondi (1490) palaces. These prestige projects were costly. Whole groups of existing houses were demolished to make way for the new structures. Isolated and surrounded by streets that in many cases touched them on two or three sides, the new buildings required several ornate facades. Without shops of any kind, these palaces were given over entirely to private space. They were immense and magnificent, with gardens and beautiful *cortili*, but completely closed in on themselves and protected from the outside world by high windows and walls and awe-inspiring gates. A vast courtyard, surrounded by porticoes, formed the heart of the building, on which all entries and staircases converged.

Contrary to the suggestion implicit in the majestic archi-

Davanzati Palace, 14th–15th century, Florence. Built about 1350, this palace respected the alignment of facades. Its plan remains irregular, but it stands out by its height (four stories); the number, size, and alignment of its windows; the care taken in ornamentation; and in livability. Occupied at different times in the 15th century by one or two households, it offered a choice of twenty rooms to live in.

tecture, and despite the enormous difference in scale between these palaces and the ordinary bourgeois and merchant dwellings just described, the former were not more livable than the latter and sometimes less. The four stories of the Davanzati Palace contained about fifteen usable rooms, whereas even the most spacious new-style palaces contained no more than a dozen, according to historian Richard Goldthwaite. A great deal of the available space in the new palaces was given over to courtyards and gardens, and the inhabited rooms were so grandiose that there was no way to increase the amount of living space.

The wealthiest Florentines thus lived in two kinds of dwelling. The more recently built palaces were by far the more prestigious, distinguished from other bourgeois homes in size and location. It is tempting to view them as the true model of aristocratic housing in Florence, revealing the real reason that such palaces existed: to provide a sumptuous and protective setting for the newly exalted conjugal family and the superior type of individual that it created.

We must take care, however, lest we be misled by the impressiveness of these palaces and the ambitions of their builders. Buildings of this magnitude account for only a small proportion of aristocratic dwellings. From 1430 to 1520, of the some two hundred households included in the various branches of the Capponi, Ginori, and Rucellai families, only two undertook to construct palaces. The rest lived in houses that they had inherited or purchased, houses of all sizes, generally old, in some cases dating back more than a century and, broadly speaking, medieval in design and appearance. Paradoxically, renovations, additions, and construction of new stories made these older houses more workable in some ways, more open and spacious than the new palaces. Such buildings contained from twelve to as many as thirty rooms, enough space to shelter large multinuclear families, who lived a kind of communal existence even when the dwelling space was divided into separate apartments. This type of extended, patriarchal family flourished in Florence among the aristocracy.

Furnishing the Home

The Use of Rooms. In the homes of the poor one room served all purposes. As soon as a family could afford more than one room, specific functions were assigned to each. Throughout Europe in fact, wherever homes became large enough to accommodate two rooms (which was the case in even modest rural and urban quarters), one was used as a *sala* (living room) and kitchen, the other as a *camera* (bedroom). The distinction between sala and camera seems to have been fundamental throughout Italy, from Genoa to Florence to Naples. As the number of rooms increased, their function was diversified still further.

In the countryside around Florence (probably typical of a more general tendency in Italy) peasants wealthy enough to enlarge their living space hesitated about what to do first: add space for doing useful work or increase the size of that part of the home reserved for private pursuits. Papino di Piero of Certaldo, who headed a family of six, added a second bedroom to his basic sala-camera as well as a *cella*, or storage room (1456). Another family of four, in addition to its sala-camera, had a storage room and a "bread room" (bakehouse?). Both families gave priority to working space. Sharecroppers were better housed. Maso of Montalbino received from his patron a house with kitchen, dining room, master bedroom, two smaller bedrooms, one for each of his two sons, and the indispensable storeroom (ca. 1450). He lived in comfort, as did a farmer who worked for the Carthusians near Lodi, who

Vittore Carpaccio, *Saint Trifone Exorcising the Daughter of Emperor Gordian* (detail), 1507. Carpaccio envisioned this scene as taking place in a loggia above a vaulted passage alongside a palace. The general appearance of the loggia—balustrade, columns, roof—is inspired by numerous Venetian examples. As often happened in loggias overlooking the lagoon, a dozen young people have come to watch the show, and tapestries create a festive atmosphere. (Venice, Scuola di San Giorgio degli Schiavoni.)

had five rooms at his disposal. But we do not know for sure whether this was common among people of this class.

In the city an increase from two rooms to three usually meant the addition of a kitchen or another bedroom. The latter was common, for it was easy to create a second bedroom by building a thin partition of wood, cob, or bricks placed on end; this, as storytellers will attest, offered little privacy.

The bigger the house, the more diversified the rooms. Even the simplest bourgeois home generally had a storage room. The wealthier the family, the greater its needs. To store provisions and their share of the crop, the well-to-do built storage vaults, woodsheds, stables, lumber rooms, and offices in space previously used for landings or corridors. They also added living rooms and bedrooms. The wealthiest constructed vestibules and anterooms, arms rooms, studios, and the like, especially in the fifteenth century. They added courtyards and arcades and, on the upper stories, loggias where they could relax and enjoy the air on hot summer days. Fourteenth-century aristocrats of Florence and Siena became enamored of these loggias, as did the Venetians, who liked to sit outside and gaze upon the lagoon from the *liago, termanza, coreselle,* or *altane,* as they called their innumerable variations on the theme.

Newly added rooms and other amenities were distributed among the various floors of the house according to a deliberate

Florence, central court of Strozzi Palace, late 15th century, work of Simone del Pollaiuolo, known as Il Cronaca.

plan. Naturally the storage and service rooms were located in the basement or on the ground floor, under the arches of the *cortile*, which was connected to the street by a vaulted entryway, the *androne*. If there was a garden, there was usually an access to it at ground level to the master's apartments. If the house did not have shops, rooms opening onto the street were sometimes turned into bedrooms. But most aspects of daily life unfolded in the upper stories. The second was the "noble" floor and contained the most prestigious rooms: the master bedroom, the anteroom, possibly an arms room, a studio, and above all the great hall, which sometimes occupied the entire facade (as in the Davanzati, Pazzi, Guadagni, and Medici palaces). There were exceptions to this general rule. The Davanzati Palace had halls on all its floors, with one or more adjoining bedrooms. Often the pattern of rooms was duplicated on each floor. Whether the house was divided up and rented to different families or occupied solely by one multinuclear family, separate private areas could easily be created on any floor.

Florence, central court of Gondi Palace, late 15th century. Thanks to the size, monumentality, and classical perfection of these courts, they are fine examples of late-15th-century Renaissance style. Their grandeur reflects their function, not only as centers of private life but as areas for receiving clients, celebrating holy days, and presenting the family to the public as prestigiously as possible.

Furniture. Comfortable furniture was an urban privilege. We are struck by the paucity of objects that even the well-to-do peasant home contained. An inventory of the estate of Zanobi, a peasant from Capannale (Mugello) who died in 1406, suggests that he was relatively well off. He owned his own farm and was well equipped with agricultural implements, barrels, beasts of burden, and farm animals (including three pigs). His stores of grain and wine were sufficient to tide him over to the next harvest. He had no debt. But in the single room in which he lived with his wife and three children, the only noteworthy item of furniture was a bed, quite large (measuring some 6 feet in width), along with bedding and several chests. We also find a kneading trough, a grain bin, two tables (one small and round), a cauldron, a skillet, and a few pots. There was no chair or lantern or basin, no dishes or utensils. Allowing for the usual omissions by the notaries (bowls and other pottery deemed of no value), it is obvious that Zanobi's prosperity and success were poured back into his farm, on which he lavished attention and expense. Many peasants no doubt shared Zanobi's view that furniture was of little importance, although a few prosperous farmers, influenced by urban tastes, chose to spend more on chests, benches, tables, lanterns, and other household amenities.

The furniture of the urban poor (wool carders and the

Vittore Carpaccio, *Birth of the
Virgin* (detail), 1504–1508.
From the bedroom a series of
service rooms leads to the
garden. From the kitchen, in
the foreground, the
monumental fireplace is visible,
as is a high shelf holding bowls
and pitchers. Note the maid
warming a towel at the fire.
(Bergamo, Accademia Carrara.)

Florence, central court of
Davanzati Palace, 14th century.
The architect had to adapt his
complex design to the
building's irregular plan. But
the care taken with the
arrangement and decoration
(keystones, columns, capitals,
benches) is an indication of the
cortile's social importance.

like) was equally rudimentary and often rented. In their case,
however, the choice was not deliberate. Furniture assumed
much greater importance in urban settings. Becoming wealthy
and moving up in society meant, among other things, acquiring better furniture. Consider the estate (1393) of Antonio, a
Florentine wool dresser (a relatively undistinguished trade).
His eight-room house (four bedrooms) contained 553 items.
Most of these were clothing, but there were also many pieces
of furniture, including nine beds, at least five of which were
fully equipped with mattresses and the like; seven benches
(measuring almost 50 feet in all); four other seats; two tables;
and a writing desk (*tavola da scrivere*); to say nothing of smaller

items such as lamps, dishes, and linen. This is still relatively sober wealth, but all the essentials are present: beds, chairs, and tables—enough for everyone in the household.

At a higher level of success, fabric merchants, fur dealers, and *mercatores* possessed more diversified furniture. They, too, owned a number of beds, each with its accessories, benches 6½ to 11½ feet long, stools (*deschetti*), and trestle tables 7 to 10 feet long. But this furniture was made of finer materials than that of the less well-to-do (oak for the benches, walnut for the tables), and there were many other items besides these basic essentials. To begin with, there were chests of many varieties. The widow of one furrier had ten in her bedroom, ranging from large *cassapanche* around the bed, whose covers served as benches; to *cassoni*, tooled metal chests that contained her trousseau; to *forzieri*, metal-reinforced caskets; to *cassoncelli* (a variant of the cassone) and simple painted boxes. Wealthy homes normally contained just as impressive a variety of trunks, chests, and jewel cases for storing the household linen and valuables. (Armoires are seldom mentioned in the fourteenth century.) There was a range of other comfort items, such as household utensils, lanterns, receptacles for meats, grains, and liquids, tools, and pots, pans, dishes, and the like made of iron, wood, copper, tin, and ceramic for use in the kitchen and dining room.

The quest for comfort assumed a more systematic form. The vogue for chests was associated with a keenly felt need for order. The poor hung their clothes from long bars attached to their walls midway between floor and ceiling. The well-to-do had chests. The need for organization also governed the way furniture and other objects were distributed among the rooms of the house. There was still no fixed arrangement, particularly in regard to provisions. The storeroom, or *volta*, and kitchen were the usual storage areas, but some patrons liked to keep a closer watch on their reserves. One bailiff of the commune of Florence stored grain and salted meat in his living room (*sala*) and transformed his bedroom into a pantry, heaping sacks of flour and bran, a keg of vinegar, and four jugs of oil around the three beds. Usually, however, rooms seemed to have been used for the purposes suggested by their names (sala, camera, cucina), especially the bedrooms, which were regarded as the heart of the household. Living rooms were generally furnished with a table or two and occasionally benches or stools, although some were left completely empty. Apart from these basic items, there were sometimes dishes,

Chest from the crypt of Sixtus V, 16th century. This strongbox has been specially reinforced for use in the apostolic chamber. Private citizens made do with less formidable storage. (Rome, Castel Sant'Angelo.)

food, and various objects such as a chessboard, an account book, or a clyster. Firewood and construction materials were temporarily stored here as well. Given the lack of decoration and scant furnishing, it is obvious that these uninviting rooms played only a sporadic role in private life. They came to life during the summer or on important occasions. Decked out for banquets, with flowers strewn about, these normally dreary rooms took on a festive charm. The situation may have changed somewhat after the turn of the fifteenth century. In 1434 Alberti described *sale* in much more flattering terms. It was in such rooms that men met to engage in the dialogues that he so skillfully recounts.

The Bedroom. Bedrooms present a different impression. They seem to have been in constant use for a variety of purposes, gay and animated. Their primary use of course was at night, for sleep and rest. No other place was consistently used for this purpose; servants, slaves, and children occasionally slept in the living room, anterooms, or storerooms, but this was the exception rather than the rule. The function of the bedroom was at times underscored in a monumental way.

In city and country alike the bed was the basic item of furniture. Not to own a cot or straw mattress was a sign of abject poverty. A couple's first investment in furniture (often financed by the father of the groom) was the purchase of the matrimonial bed. The bed was a prestige item, as literature, painting, and notarial records show. Its frame was generally made of wood, though sometimes of terra-cotta; its width (or length—the texts are not always clear) ranged from 5½ to 11½ feet, with about 10 feet the average. The size of these beds was impressive, but remember that several people often slept in them, and they were surrounded by trunks. The inventories distinguish several types, such as *lectica, lectiera, lettucio*, and styles, such as *lectica nuova alla lombarda*. This monumental piece of furniture was equipped with springs, mattress, covers, a pair of sheets, a bedspread, pillows, and sometimes *piumacci*, small cushions whose purpose is unclear. (They may have served as bolsters.) Additional sheets and bedspreads were kept nearby.

So huge a bed was an imposing presence in the room, its vast surface extended by a ring of chests and embellished by a colorful spread, sometimes a quilt of many colors in checkerboard or herringbone pattern, sometimes red or blue or even snow white, depending on the vagaries of fashion. The bed's

Sassetta, *Life of the Blessed Ranieri Rasini of Borgo San Sepolcro*, 1444. A prelate's sumptuous bedroom. Note the monumental bed with high headboard, spread that covers even the wooden bed frame, *cassapanca*, and vases. The sophisticated wall decoration (whether of leather, fabric, or fresco, we cannot tell) is elegantly repeated in the chest. (Berlin, Staatliche Museen Preussischer Kulturbesitz.)

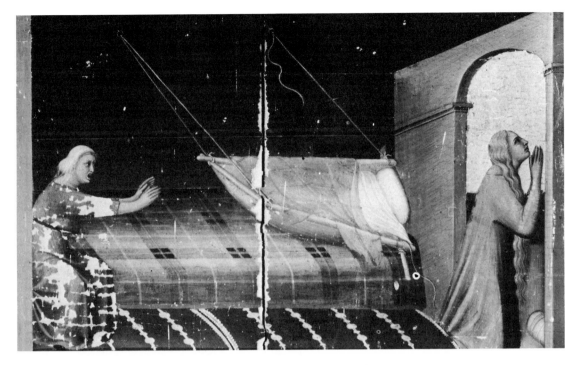

curtains further enhanced its monumental character. In the fourteenth century on the whole beds were still relatively modest. In the Scrovegni Chapel, Giotto (ca. 1306) depicts Saint Anne, a recent mother, resting on a simple, narrow couch without headboard or surrounding chests; its curtain is nothing more than a veil of inexpensive fabric hung from four wooden beams attached to the ceiling. Some twenty years later (ca. 1328) Simone Martini set one of the miracles depicted in his painting in the Church of Sant'Agostino Novello in a bourgeois bedroom. The main feature of the painting is an enormous bed, adjacent to which stands a gleaming red chest. Yet the bed has no visible frame and no curtains. A generation later a version of the birth of the Virgin, painted for Santa Croce by Giovanni da Milano (1365), shows a much fancier bed, more in keeping with the descriptions found in estate inventories from the end of the century. A long chest, now a commonplace feature of the bedroom, stands along one side, and the bed itself is raised to a higher level, almost as though it had been placed on a pedestal. A light but elegant curtain hangs from a rod concealed by the frame.

Still later, around 1430, the beds in which Fra Angelico paints his human figures in childbirth, sleep, agony, and death

Simone Martini, *The Blessed Agostino Novello*, "Miracles of the Saint" (detail), polyptych, 1328–1330. Here we see another era (14th century) and another milieu (petty bourgeois.) The room and furniture are simpler; there is no wooden bed frame and no wall decoration. The only luxury is the two red chests in the foreground, each with a lock. Note the ingenious but dangerous method of fitting a child's cradle into this crowded room. (Siena, Sant'Agostino.)

Giovanni da Milano, *Birth of the Virgin*, 1365. A bourgeois scene depicted with elegant realism (attitudes, clothing, bed) by a painter attentive to everyday life. (Florence, Santa Croce.)

retain many of the same features, some accentuated even further. A continuous chest surrounds the bed on three sides, enlarging it and emphasizing the height of the central portion. The headboard in some paintings is as tall as man. Because of the need for access to the chests, finally, these beds have been moved from the corner of the room to the center of one wall, making them seem even more ostentatiously monumental. Although such beds were found in wealthy homes, the beds of more modest folk often conformed to the same models on a simpler, more economical scale. Frames were made of fir or pine, for instance, but the wood was planed and surrounded by chests, the headboard was tall, and the bed was surrounded by curtains (as in the predella of the Pala da San Marco by Fra Angelico).

In Venice (1495), the bed on which Carpaccio's Saint Ursula lies dreaming is also placed in the middle, against one wall and surrounded by chests that serve as stairs. The headboard, which is part of the wall, is a masterpiece of sophisticated architecture. A light baldacchino, set very high and devoid of curtains, covers the whole structure; it is supported by elegant wooden columns. In other Venetian paintings we see beds with sumptuous curtains, figures, designs, hunting scenes—a whole panoply of luxurious embellishment.

The bedroom remained a bustling center of activity throughout the day, as the furniture and artifacts arranged around the bed indicate. Inventories from 1380–1420 list as many as two to three hundred such items, sometimes more. Benches, round stools, and even tables, to say nothing of the many chests, encouraged people to gather in the bedroom for conversation, work, and even prayer, which was facilitated by icons and pious artifacts on the walls and furniture. The bedroom, which the master kept under close surveillance, was also the strongroom where valuable treasures were kept. That

Vittore Carpaccio, *Legend of Saint Ursula*, "Dream of the Saint," 1495. Wainscotted bedroom, well lighted by large, partially glazed windows, embellished by a Renaissance woman of letters. Note the spaciousness, the refined decoration of common furnishings, and the books, objects, and sculpture, new indications of a worldly feminine culture. This late-15th-century bedroom reflects the tastes of its occupant more than did rooms of earlier periods. (Venice, Accademia.)

Vittore Carpaccio, *Legend of Saint Ursula*, "Arrival of the English ambassadors at the court of the king of Brittany," detail of bedroom, 1495. Icon of the Virgin, a common decoration in 14th- and 15th-century bedrooms This one, in a Renaissance frame, looks down on the bed. (Venice, Accademia.)

was one reason for the chests, which served not only as wardrobes for clothing (kept folded rather than hung) but also as a storage place for books and personal papers, jewels, table linen, and possibly china and silverware. Though full, the room was not overcrowded. Everything was carefully arranged, and few objects were left lying about. Fourteenth-century Italians apparently did not care to adorn their bedrooms with bibelots, which became fashionable only later on. The rich fabrics, protective icons, reassuring presence of the bed, and constant traffic and conversation made the bedroom the liveliest room in the house.

The great Florentine palaces in the new style are a case apart. How were their immense rooms to be furnished? At the beginning of the sixteenth century, fifty years after the Strozzi Palace was built, its largest rooms remained completely bare. The massiveness of Florentine furniture of the Cinquecento should be seen in light of the need to fill such impressive spaces in a manner that would not seem ridiculous.

Privacy and Comfort

To feel at home one needs more than just a pleasant room, and various innovations enhanced people's privacy and comfort. In inventories and descriptions we read constantly about locks and bars (*spranga*). Were houses generally kept locked? There are reasons to think so. Private space had to be defended. Great attention was paid to exterior door frames in both rural and urban homes, probably for reasons of security. Rural homes in the Lodi region were equipped with stout door frames. The best of them, which were built of stone, had wooden doors reinforced by stanchions and incorporating various devices to ensure a tight seal: embedded bars perpendicular to the two leaves of the door, bolts, and locks of many kinds, real masterpieces of the locksmith's craft. Windows were equipped with full shutters, bars, and frequently iron grates. Even cottages boasted wooden doors with bars and locks, though less care was taken than in the homes of the relatively well-to-do. Keys were lost, and some houses had entrances that could not be locked. But with few exceptions windows had shutters.

In the cities, tower houses (still attested in Bologna in 1286) were gradually abandoned; to enter one a person had to climb a ladder to a door situated halfway up the tower. Yet vigilance remained the order of the day. New urban homes were equipped with carefully designed locking systems. The best known are those used in bourgeois homes, which had double doors reinforced by thin boards attached by large-headed nails. Of forbidding aspect, these doors were very sturdy. They were sealed with a horizontal bar on the inside together with a lock and possibly a bolt. The mechanisms were maintained in good working order. Decent women were supposed to lock the main entrance the moment their husbands left home. At night the man of the house made sure that everything was locked up tight and that the key to the main entrance was itself locked up in his bedroom (Paolo da Certaldo). If ground-floor rooms had windows, they were equipped with grates, especially if the windows were small and intended mainly to admit air, hence not provided with shutters.

The house was supposed to provide protection against the weather. This need became greater as homes became more sumptuous, especially after urban houses ceased to resemble fortresses and added many new openings and windows throughout. The first concern was to block the breeze, and the oldest solution to this problem was inside shutters. These were common in Siena before 1340 but may not have been in use elsewhere. The twin windows in the Gothic palaces painted by Lorenzetti seem to lack them; in these houses curtains, hung from long rods stretched horizontally across the windows at mid-height, provided a lighter, more tenuous barrier against wind and sun. In any case, closing the shutters kept out the light as well as the rain and did nothing to stop the cold. Shutters were but a first step toward comfortable living.

In order not to dwell in darkness during periods of bad

Florentine tower, 13th century, via delle Terme. In the 13th century tower houses like this one were the linchpin of a lineage's defenses. (Note the side openings and brackets for supporting movable defensive platforms.) They were also used, at least temporarily, as residences. In the 14th century these same buildings served as symbols of the lineage's strength, unity, and political influence.

Window and interior shutters in the Davanzati Palace, Florence, 14th century. The reconstruction of the glazed windows is based on guesswork. The full shutters are hinged vertically but not horizontally.

weather (without using lanterns), complex shutter designs were invented, with extra hinges on each leaf and, at the base, a system of panels that could be pivoted on both horizontal and vertical axes. But this was a relatively late innovation and does not seem to have been widely used in Siena in the 1340s or even in Florence in the 1420s, when the frescoes and paintings of Lorenzetti, Martini, and Masaccio show massive shutters kept partially ajar. Sliding window covers and venetian blinds are not mentioned until the last decade of the 1390s, when they appear in the accounts of the Florentine hospitals. This was a time when great solicitude was shown to the sick, and these devices may have been designed expressly for use in hospitals before being widely adopted in the second half of the fifteenth century. Window covers did not, however, eliminate all the drawbacks of shutters, which kept rooms dark, allowed drafts, and so on. A more elaborate device made its appearance early—possibly as early as the beginning of the fourteenth century—but seems to have been slow to catch on: *finestre impannate*, "draped" windows. Their use is most readily observed in the Florentine hospitals in the 1370s and 1380s, probably related once again to concern for the patients' welfare. Linen was stretched over a frame and impregnated with oil to make it translucent; then this frame was fitted into the window opening to block the breeze without shutting out the light. Use of this device gradually spread throughout central Italy in the fifteenth century; it is attested in Pisa, San Gimignano, Montefalco, and Genoa. It was widely used in the Florentine palaces of the late Cinquecento, especially in the noble rooms: halls, bedrooms, and offices. It was also adapted for use in the studios of painters and mosaicists. Glass windows did not appear until much later. We know of one in Bologna in 1331, which was equipped with a latticework of copper wires to protect the glass. And in 1368 one was installed in Genoa. In 1391 glass windows were used in at least two rooms in the Carmelite convent at Florence: the infirmary (with two windows) and the studio. In the fifteenth century modest use was made of glass windows in bourgeois houses. Bear in mind that glass at this time meant small round pieces of glass joined together by a framework of lead.

The problem of nighttime darkness due to crowded conditions remained. The Florentine patrician Alessandra Mazzinghi-Strozzi complains in a letter that a neighbor's house robs her light. We can only imagine what the poorer streets were like. The cheapest form of lighting was the tallow candle, widely used in the countryside, where special mortars were used for beating tallow. Peasant inventories mention oil lanterns (*lucerna*), but forty-eight of the sixty poor to moderately well-off peasant homes studied by M. A. Mazzi lacked them. The candle was the peasant's faithful companion through his daily rounds and nocturnal labors, but its feeble rays were quickly swallowed up by darkness. Only the light from the hearth illuminated the faces and gestures of the family members gathered round it. The hearthside was the peasant's nighttime gathering place.

Urban houses (or at any rate the bourgeois houses that we know about) were better equipped. There were lights of

French lock, 15th century. This superb ironwork reflects the importance of the lock in the defense of private property—and private lives. (Florence, Bargello.)

Key, 15th century. It has a very beautiful handle, but note especially the minute working of the bit and teeth; the complexity of the design made the lock inviolable. (Florence, Bargello.)

Masolino and Masaccio, *Resurrection of Tabitha* (detail), ca. 1425. (Florence, Church of the Carmine, Brancacci Chapel.)

Iron lantern, Davanzati Palace, Florence, 14th–15th century. Light was a luxury indoors and out.

many kinds, ranging from simple oil lamps (made of earthenware, tin, or iron) to lanterns, "portable lamps," and chandeliers of every description, long and short, made of copper, iron, or in the "English" style. All these objects were found in well-to-do Florentine homes in the 1400s. They were located throughout the house but principally in the bedroom (six cases) rather than the living room (two cases) or kitchen (one case). These lightweight lamps were portable, but light seems to have been a luxury reserved primarily for the bedroom. Every room contained from two to six brackets in well-chosen locations from which lamps could be hung. Unlike the candles used by peasants, these large lamps produced enough light to illuminate a whole room, so that families and *brigate* could gather at night to converse or transact business. In addition, lamps were kept burning through the night at the corners of major palaces, around which they created a mysterious and dramatic aura.

Mere candles could do nothing to alleviate the cold, which was a problem in these poorly caulked, poorly insulated rooms from November to April. In rural Tuscany in the fourteenth and fifteenth centuries the fire used for cooking (in the hall or kitchen) was the only source of heat. Rustic fireplaces were simple, bare hearths erected on the packed earth with a few bricks for support. The same was true in the Lodi region in 1440, except for the really well-off households, especially those of the *castelli*, whose houses, however modest, included one and sometimes two fireplaces (for just five rooms). Fire was more fully domesticated in the cities, where the wall fireplace with mantelpiece, conduit, and external chimney was no longer a novelty in the fourteenth century. There were fireplaces in Venice as early as the thirteenth century; the first ones in Florence began to appear around 1300. The fireplace was slow to catch on, however. There were none in Piacenza in 1320 according to the chronicler G. Musso, nor were there any in Rome in 1368. At Siena in 1340 Lorenzetti's fresco reveals only a half-dozen chimneys on the roofs (and these were not necessarily connected to wall fireplaces). Musso adds that in Piacenza in 1388 every house contained several fireplaces (but were they true wall fireplaces?). Fireplaces gradually became popular in Florence; the pace seems to have picked up in the period 1370–1420, as the central hearth finally gave way to the "French-style" fireplace.

Not every house derived the benefit, however. Some were too small or insubstantial to allow the installation of

fireplaces. Paradoxically, this was true of many of the new houses built on outlying plots in Florence between 1280 and 1340, where builders were reluctant to erect tall chimneys against their relatively thin walls. Kitchens were located on the top floor and equipped only with a central hearth. Was it easier to install fireplaces in bourgeois homes in the older, more spacious, less rigidly aligned areas of the city? By the end of the fourteenth century most of them contained at least one heated room apart from the kitchen. Of eight interiors known to me, six kitchens, six bedrooms, and two living rooms contained equipment associated with a fireplace: andirons, tongs, grates, or shovels. Hearths are described in only two cases, however: a wall fireplace in one master bedroom and a brazier in a guest room. In this period (late fourteenth to early fifteenth century) it is certain that wealthy Florentine homes contained heated rooms adjoining the bedroom (but not in more than one out of three cases) rather than the living room. The fireplace had not yet won out, however, and poorly ventilated hearths were still common, with implements moved from room to room.

Ambrogio Lorenzetti, *The Effects of Good Government in the City* (detail), 1338–1340. (Siena, Palazzo Pubblico.)

Vittore Carpaccio, *Miracle of the Relic of the Cross* (detail), 1494. Chimneys proliferated in Venice (up to eight per building) as the Venetians learned how to vanquish the cold of the banks of the lagoon. (Venice, Accademia.)

Wherever we are able to observe the use of fireplaces, we find that they became increasingly common as the fifteenth century wore on, capturing the fancy of city after city. As soon as a few residents adopted the new invention, others were quick to follow. Masons were familiar enough with the construction of fireplaces to be able to install them in several different places within a single house, and by the end of the fifteenth century there were fireplaces in all the principal rooms of the great palaces. Their hoods took on monumental proportions, and andirons, tongs, and other related objects, tastefully sculpted, turned hearths into veritable art galleries. Venice too was won over, and in Carpaccio's *Miracle of the Relic of the Cross* (1494) the presence of numerous chimney pipes of impressive size makes the roofs of the city resemble a field of mushrooms.

The Domestic Scene

Sumptuous clothing was out of place in the privacy of the home. Peasants simply wore their work clothes, which changed somewhat over the fourteenth and fifteenth centuries owing to the remote influence of urban fashions. But the fabric used was still primarily *romagnolo*, a coarse brown or gray material. People dressed in their holiday best (which everyone owned) only when they left the private setting. In the cities too people dressed simply at home. Alberti insists on it: new clothes are for holidays; slightly used clothing is for everyday business; and really worn clothing is for the home. Palmieri's view differs slightly: for everyday home use, wear only the same clothing that everyone else wears. Two types of clothing were thus declared fit (and probably actually worn) for private use: simple clothes and fancy but worn or outdated costumes inherited from an ancestor or purchased from the ragpicker. But as a rule people wore simple clothing around the house. A woman at home, no matter what her station, was likely to wear a *gonnella* (fourteenth century) or *gamurra* (fifteenth century, also known in Lombardy as a *zupa*); it was a simple wool tunic with sleeves (which, after 1450, were removable), worn over the *camicia*, a long chemise of linen or cotton. So dressed, she could go about her household chores and even run errands or make informal visits in the neighborhood. In cold weather a cloak was added. But the moment one left the private realm to be seen in the outside world, the gamurra ceased to be appropriate. At such times the chests were opened and the richest fabrics brought out, for the clothing worn in public was a matter of individual and social distinction.

Other liberties could be taken at home. The moralists recommended that household attire, especially in the living room where the family gathered, should be perfectly correct, but in reality it was not considered shocking to appear at certain moments partially or entirely nude. For sleeping, people sometimes wore chemises but might just as easily go naked, simply because it was hot. Ladies did not worry about the little daughters who lay beside them or the neighbors who watched, through windows kept wide open to let in the cool evening air, as they prepared for bed or rose in the morning. Women warmed or dried themselves in front of the fire (there was no lingerie), and men removed their breeches and settled down to warm themselves by the hearth. Sacchetti advised men in such circumstances to beware of the cat, which, creeping beneath their stool, might easily mistake certain pendulous objects for amusing playthings.

Life at home may have been simple and informal, but this does not mean that it was not often gay, animated, and colorful. Flowers were plentiful; fourteenth- and fifteenth-century painting from Florence and Siena often shows vases filled with them decorating tables and credenzas or standing on window sills. In frescoes by Lorenzetti and Masaccio birds can be seen in cages of cane hanging in windows; caged birds were sent as a gift to a sick child, Michele Verini, so that their songs might cheer him up. (The youthful humanist replied in perfect Latin.) And there were pets: playful, friendly cats; dogs; even a goose (which Alberti thought did such a good job watching over his house); and, last but not least, a bear,

Fireplace in the "Parrot's Room" on the first floor of the Davanzati Palace, Florence, late 14th–15th century. This monumental fireplace is decorated but well equipped and functional. The large flat hood became more fashionable than the conical as fireplaces moved into patrician halls and bedrooms in the 15th century.

Carlo Crivelli, *Annunciation* (detail), second half of the 15th century. (Frankfurt-am-Main, Staatkunstinstitut.)

which despite its leash, performs acrobatic stunts on the ledge of a house in a painting by Masaccio (Carmine in Florence).

With wealth one could do much to embellish the home, adding more durable improvements such as tapestries or frescoes in the major rooms. Genoese inventories from the 1390s frequently mention tapestries (but without description), and the fashion continued into the fifteenth century. In Genoa there were also "rooms of painted canvas" (mentioned in the late fifteenth century), genre paintings done on canvas and designed to fill entire rooms, in this case bedrooms. Fabrics and tapestries were all the rage in Florence as early as the fourteenth century. Small pieces were used on tables, chairs, and benches, even in strictly private rooms. Larger pieces, including true tapestries (*arazzi*) intended to be hung on walls, headboards, and even doors, were normally kept in chests and displayed only on holidays to impress. Fabric items were also used to embellish fancier clothing, along with makeup, jewelry, and other showpieces.

As Dante's *Vita nuova* attests, paintings in fresco and tempera had been used since the thirteenth century as a less costly alternative to tapestries; they too are closely related to private existence, of which they were unflinching witnesses. Standard and relatively inexpensive motifs such as simple geometric designs (multicolored checkerboards, lozenges, and so on) are found in combination or alternation with more complex arabesques and, already, the more sophisticated imitations of fur (vair or ermine). Such motifs, sometimes used to cover an entire wall, also embellished trompe-l'oeil wall hangings, which featured painted imitations of brackets, folds, and fringes. Fashionable and cheap, fresco paintings became a common feature of inner courtyards, mezzanines (as in the late-thirteenth-century Tuscan castle at Poppi), reception halls, loggias, and even toilets.

The infinite possibilities of painting could be more fully realized in the houses of the truly affluent, where painted scenes were common as early as the fourteenth century. Fashionable subjects included trees, elegantly painted on separate panels, and gardens filled with flowers, birds, and even human figures, depicting scenes of sport, hunting, or other noble diversions. One room might well contain paintings on several different themes. The Davanzati Palace, which has been magnificently preserved and restored, offers a superb sampling covering three generations, from the late fourteenth well into the fifteenth century. The hall and two bedrooms, the only rooms in the palace that are fully decorated, all contain careful, sophisticated, but easy to paint geometric motifs, which cover the walls up to more than eight feet in height. Above this is a strip from eight inches to more than a yard wide. In the hall this contains a frieze of palms with birds against an alternating background of blue and red. In one bedroom the frieze also depicts trees, each decorated with an escutcheon and framed in a Gothic arch. In the other it tells the story of the castellan of Vergy, the episodes of which take place in a sylvan setting filled with birds beneath a trompe-l'oeil arcade of semicircular arches bearing the arms of France. The more affluent the home, the more sophisticated the embellishment, which diverted the inhabitants from their cares and worries.

Painted room (detail), Davanzati Palace, Florence, ca. 1400. The frescoes were painted in honor of the marriage of the young owner, Davizzi. From bottom to top: imitation tapestry with key and lion motif; series of panels partially masked by a painted net; trompe-l'oeil ledge on modillions; imitation arcade decorated with the arms of France under which are depicted episodes from the *Castellan of Vergy*, a 13th-century French romance; and, finally, coats of arms and a painted cornice. This sophisticated decor was intended to exalt the owner's family line as well as to create a private world into which he could escape amid visions of knightly exploits.

A Nurturing Privacy. The wise family head was careful to store up reserves in case there should be any interruption to the supply of vital necessities. If nature or the public authorities failed to do their part, private families had the means to cushion the blow. That paragon of bourgeois common sense, Paolo of Certaldo, had this to say in the fourteenth century: "Always keep a two years' supply of wheat on hand . . . and the same for oil." The poor of course were unable to abide by this cautionary rule, and many peasants, especially in periods of famine, had to sell their wheat before it was ripe. Still, any extra cash was put to use replenishing supplies at the best possible price. In Prato in November 1298 the authorities, seeing that the price of grain was on the rise, conducted a survey of supplies. In the San Giovanni quarter 30 percent of the families had no supplies at all; 20 percent held a six months' supply; and the rest, fully half the population, had enough to tide them over to the next harvest. In other words, it was not only the upper strata of the bourgeoisie, the judges and merchants, who kept reserves on hand. Shopkeepers and artisans did the same, and, given the modesty of their resources and the size of their reserves, they must have placed a higher priority (in terms of time and budget) on maintaining adequate reserves than did their more affluent fellow citizens.

The bourgeois of Cinquecento Florence did not abandon this custom, but their reserves formed a less conspicuous part of their inventories. Almost all the households about which we have information kept reserves of wine (a few barrels) and oil (several jugs). Two out of three kept vinegar, and at least one in two stored supplies of wheat, other grains, dried vegetables, and dried or salted meat. This sample is not as rigorous as that from Prato. Wheat reserves were certainly more common among the Tuscan bourgeois, most of whom owned one or more farms. It is certain that the habit of maintaining ample reserves was not abandoned, although we cannot be sure just how much was kept on hand. Special rooms were set aside for holding stores. Chests of grain (*arca*) were kept in the hall or more often in the bedrooms; barrels were always stored in the *cella* or *volta* (storeroom) found on the ground floor of every bourgeois house.

Between pantry and table food naturally had to be prepared. There were kitchens in most dwellings and in all bourgeois houses. In the thirteenth century these had been located in the court or garden, but later they were moved into the main house. For various reasons (including fear of fire and the

problem of smoke and cooking odors) they were usually confined to garrets, though for convenience at times they may
have been installed on the "noble floors." This urban luxury
soon spread to rural areas, and in the fifteenth century we
know of several affluent rural houses in the Apennines and
parts of Lombardy that were equipped with kitchens, and they
must have existed elsewhere as well.

Kitchens were not the least well equipped of rooms. They
often contained more objects, of greater variety and in some
cases more costly, than living rooms; Florentine inventories
list anywhere from twenty-five to eighty items per kitchen.
In the way of furniture we find kneading troughs, bread bins,
armoires (in the fouteenth century only, and quite rare), and
shelves. Most important of all were the innumerable utensils
of iron, copper, tin, terra-cotta, and wood used for preparing
good meals and excellent banquets. Good food put the master
in good spirits, but even more it was a means of ostentatious
display. Technically advanced kitchens existed in Venice at the
end of the thirteenth century; by the fourteenth century they
could be found in all good houses throughout Italy.

Progress in visual and culinary amenities was facilitated
by improvements in the water supply to private homes. Public
wells, located at streetcorners and public squares and maintained by the residents of the neighborhood, were in common
use in Bologna, Piacenza, Florence, and many other cities in
the thirteenth century. The water from these wells was not
always good, however, and not available in sufficient quantities, and river water, when available, was not necessarily any
better. Various communes therefore set out to improve matters. Fifty public cisterns were constructed in Venice, while
Siena undertook to build an ambitious network of underground pipes and public fountains. Residents of other communities took it upon themselves to make the necessary
improvements. In Florence, for example, in new lots laid out
north of San Lorenzo in the period 1320–1380, each building
was equipped with its own private well; there were at least
149 of them.

Wells were not available everywhere, however. Out-of-
the-way streets and poor houses did without; in the via Guelfa,
for instance, there was only one well for every thirty-three
houses. The finer the street and the more costly the construction, the greater the number of wells; in the better neighborhoods, such as Campo Corbolino, as many as 39 percent of
the houses had wells of their own. Water was thus conven-

Domestic well with upper-story access, Florence, 14th century. The well is directly under the building, with a shaft running up to the roof. A pulley enabled residents to haul water up to the floors. Double doors offer access from two different rooms.

iently available to anyone who needed it, with well shafts running as high as the third story in some buildings and an arrangement of pullies, pails, and access doors permitting water to be hoisted directly from the well—a great boon to hygiene, cleanliness, cooking, and thirsty people.

LIVING TOGETHER

Shopkeepers and craftsmen usually worked outside the home. In Florence most artisans rented workshops in a different part of the city from where they lived. Instances are known in which workshop and residence were combined, but these were rare. During the day working people left their homes—men, women, and even children (who began work, in some cases, as early as age eight or ten). Some trades were traditionally practiced at home, however: weaving (practiced by both men and women) and above all spinning (practiced by women). Inventories of woolworkers' furniture (1378) often include a loom and a *filatoio*, or spinning wheel; these work-related items were listed along with the furniture and installed in private residences. The same was true in Siena in the mid-fifteenth century and in many other places. When husband and wife were both weavers or the husband was a weaver and the wife a spinner, they could work together at home throughout the day and sometimes late into the night. In the countryside work was even more inseparable from private life. In the cities it was quite rare for families to work together at home and more of a threat than a boon to family intimacy, for work could easily swallow up both day and night, especially in poor households.

Collective Activities in the Home

Fortunately there was no lack of opportunity for family members who dispersed for work in the morning to spend time together in the evening when work was done (at vespers in the case of Florentine masons) or all day long on Sundays and holidays.

Washing was one good opportunity for seeing other family members. The mother supervised the washing of the children (according to Giovanni Dominici). When adults washed, they were not always alone, and the early morning hours were not the only ones reserved for doing one's toilette. It was normal for a wife to assist in her husband's ablutions. Matrons had servants help them wash (at least their feet), dress, and put on makeup. Mutual delousing was so common among the ladies of Ravenna that a thirteenth-century regulation forbade anyone from engaging in the activity under public arcades.

Family members were together at and sometimes before meals. At Fiesole, in July 1338, an observer sketched a housewife preparing the evening soup while her fifteen-year-old daughter sat on a low chest, her elder daughter sat in the doorway with her chin on her knees waiting for her beau, and a young rascal of a son paced up and down. Eventually all sat down for dinner. Eating together was both an ideal, as Alberti reminds us, and a reality. Rich or poor, Florentine households owned at least one table, either rectangular and mounted on trestles or round, and obviously used at mealtimes. (Some inventories are explicit: "round dining table," for example.) Storytellers take it for granted that husbands and wives eat together, probably along with children above a certain age. Servants did not eat with the family, except possibly in rural and relatively modest urban homes.

After supper the family's evening began. There was much work for everyone, including daily chores such as shelling beans, scouring, mending, cleaning, and repairs. There was also a great deal to say; evenings were for conversation, as they are everywhere. People discussed their daily labor: they talked "sheep, wheat, buildings, and other usual topics of married couples," according to a witness reporting the conversation of a peasant couple. They discussed their plans for the future, such as whom their daughter should marry, and their worries: oppressive taxes, children who were born one after another and "did nothing but eat," and all the other complaints that one can read about in the tax declarations, which record so many tales of woe and echoes of marital squabbles. Some conversations were absorbed by such matters as a daughter's dowry, possible investments, and (in the case of sharecroppers) relations with the landlord or patron. Moralists complained about the licentiousness of private conversation, but there was also talk of religion. Even the most pious and well-bred families were at times shaken by moments of

A family meal, from an illustrated manuscript of the *Decameron*, 1427. An ill-fitting rectangular table cloth with fringes has been placed over a round, three-legged table. Father, grown son, mother, and children have taken their places on stools around the table. There are several goblets and one knife to be shared by all. The son is being asked to divide up the food, presumably because he is so well educated. (Paris, Bibliothèque Nationale, Italian 63.)

Painted room (detail), Davanzati Palace, Florence, ca. 1400.

anger in which each member "exhaled his bitterness in violent words," as Saint Catherine's biographer said of her family. Grandparents sometimes recalled their childhood and discussed the family genealogy (not always with great confidence). There was outraged comment on local scandals: bigamy, murder, clerical misconduct, and so on. All these examples are taken from fourteenth-century Tuscan sources. The range of conversation among the humanists and the urban bourgeoisie was naturally broader, but on occasion even they chatted about the simple matters of daily life. Alberti praised the charm of relaxed conversation about "cattle, wool, vines, and seeds," in which vacation permitted him to indulge. But he could rise to whatever heights the occasion demanded. At the home of one of his uncles, "the custom was never to speak of futile things, always of magnificent ones." In real or imaginary dialogues the humanists liked to display their erudition.

In addition to conversation there were games: dice (frowned upon), chess (often mentioned in bourgeois homes), and, later, cards. Or the children might be called in (Palmieri tells us) for alphabet games. When they were a little older, there was evening reading, as in the home of the dignified and pious notary Lapo Mazzei of Prato, who spent winter evenings reading Saint Francis' *Fioretti* to his children (1390). A hundred years later (1485), an uncle of the young humanist prodigy Michele Verini read to him from the Bible after dinner (and from Euclid for an apéritif).

The structure of the house, not all parts of which were equally well heated (or cooled), lent itself to evening gatherings. During the summer the family often sat together on the steps or in the garden or in various kinds of loggias. In winter everyone gathered around the fire in the *sala*, as the wife read and the master talked and kept the fire going, while the children sat on stools in a variety of attitudes, listening—the scene formed the subject of innumerable illuminations. On certain occasions, such as the birth of a child or a case of illness, the family gathered in the bedroom. To purists, however, this was an encroachment upon space that properly belonged to the lady of the house or the couple; in their eyes the place for family socializing was the living room. This certainly had its role, but a nuclear family—married couple and children—was probably more comfortable in the warmer, more intimate surroundings of the bedroom. The great halls of bourgeois houses were used mainly to receive large numbers of relatives and guests, while only a select few were allowed access to the bedrooms.

The Paterfamilias

A household had to be run. Decisions needed to be made every day. The patrimony and the children were areas of major responsibility. Much had to be done for children from early childhood until marriage. In each child two lines and two traditions converged: the father's and the mother's. Which would prevail? The same question applied to the patrimony. Except for households declared in tax documents to be *nihil habentes* (propertyless), all had possessions, if only a few pieces of furniture and items of clothing. These possessions were a composite of the "patrimony" in the narrow sense of the word (property brought into the marriage by the husband), acquests, the wife's dowry (and possibly the dowries of daughters-in-law), and the sons' *peculia* (obtained by gift or acquisition). The dowry itself was not treated uniformly. Jurists distinguished between the "estimated" part, which was carefully inventoried, and the "nonestimated" part, which consisted of furniture and other items of daily use. Questions pertaining to the patrimony involved husband, wife, and children alike. The responsibilities had to be shared or delegated.

In Italian tradition power belonged incontestably to the husband. During the twelfth and thirteenth centuries his authority, identified with that of the king, continued to grow in the eyes of the jurists, especially those at Bologna. The general view was summed up in the popular thirteenth-century adage, "Every man is king in his own castle" (*Quilibet, in domo sua, dicitur rex*). The father exercised this authority, called the *patria potestas*, over his children. It was his alone; as the jurist Azzo explained, "neither mothers nor maternal grandparents have power (*potestas*) over the children." The father's power extended to all his descendants, in particular his grandchildren, no matter how old he was, even over sixty (*etiam sexagenarius*), and no matter how old his children were. This doctrine was not confined to jurists' manuals. Worked out in response to vital questions, it had an impact on everyday life, in part through statutes and customs adopted by cities in the thirteenth and fourteenth centuries to regulate private life, among other things. Through those statutes the jurists' thinking impressed itself on people's minds.

The paterfamilias was in the first place the sole trustee of all family property. He managed his wife's dowry (all of it, *estimata* or not, in the thirteenth century) and in some cases the dowries of his daughters-in-law as well. He could even sell it, and there was little his wife could do to stop him. In practice the courts tended to grant the husband full power to govern the property brought into the marriage by the wife, who was rendered powerless to thwart decisions potentially harmful to her property and to her children's future inheritance. The jurists also held that the income from the dowry should become part of the common family treasury which the husband managed (rather than reinvested in the wife's property). This was to enable the husband to cope with the "unbearable burdens" of marriage (that is, current expenses); naturally it left him free to reinvest his own income in land

Tacuinum sanitatis. Pavia or Milan, 1390–1400. Seated on his throne, the paterfamilias has just tasted from a spoon held out to him by his anxious wife. He is pleased. The two women are comforted to know that the master is satisfied. (Paris, Bibliothèque Nationale, n.a. Latin 1673, fol. 50v.)

Gentile da Fabriano, *Polyptych Quaratesi*, "Story of Saint Nicholas" (detail), early 15th century. Honor thy father and mother. A woman shows deference toward her elderly father by helping to remove his shoes. He is so poor, however, that he is about to put her and her sisters to work as prostitutes in order to survive. (Rome, Vatican Museums.)

or commodities. Similarly, the father had full control of his sons' cash reserves and property, again in virtue of the patria potestas.

The father was master not only of the family property but also of all family members. His wife and children were subject to his potestas and obliged to show him obedience and respect. The teachings of the leading Dominican confessors upheld the doctrines of their colleagues, the jurists. In 1398 Giovanni Dominici, repeating a precept known to all preachers, reminded a female penitent that a wife was subject to her husband's command (as long as he ordered her to commit no sin). The same note is sounded by the moralists Fra Paolino,

L. B. Alberti, and E. Barbaro: "Sole master in his own home, the husband does not disclose all the family secrets to his wife. He trains her to perform her wifely duties and, with due consideration for the fragility of her body and character, assigns her none but minor responsibilities in the household." In practice this subordination of wife to husband could have tangible and painful consequences. Communal statutes like that of Gello in Tuscany (1373) authorized men "to punish their children, their younger brothers, and also their wives." Legal texts, laws, and moralistic writings accorded a father even greater authority over his children, who were obliged to treat him with respect and total reverence, as though he were sacrosanct. Whatever public responsibilities a son might have, they vanished in private. The father's authority and priority were total (Palmieri). Any failure to respect one's father, any rebellious behavior, insult, or neglect (of an elderly father) could lawfully be punished by either the father himself or the public authorities. As late as 1415 a Florentine statute authorized fathers or grandfathers to have wayward offspring thrown into prison. Preachers embroidered upon a related theme: he who honors his father shall be rewarded in his sons, receive God's blessing, and so on. Moralists and clergy agreed that all education stemmed from fathers willing to "adorn the lives of their sons with the most virtuous morals" (Palmieri). Giovanni Dominici, author of a treatise on education that obliged him to be concrete, insisted that children should preface any remarks addressed to their fathers with the words "Messer si," remain standing in the presence of their parents, humbly bow their heads when given an order, and in short always show respect for the man to whom they owed their existence.

Law and policy reflect custom, and the known facts about Tuscan family life confirm various aspects of the precepts and doctrines reviewed above. The statute allowing fathers to imprison sons was applied in Florence as late as 1463. In the great bourgeois families of the fifteenth century patriarchs were living testimony to the preeminence of the father. Some retained total control over family finances. In 1480 the aged Gino Ginori prepared his own tax declaration, in which he stated of the grown sons who lived under his roof that "they work with me in my fabric business and do not yet know enough to strike out on their own." Other patriarchs established dowries for their granddaughters. The father's power in economic matters was also firmly established in the more modest world of sharecroppers. Around Siena (ca. 1400) share-cropper families appear to have been organized as small corporations, with labor, debts, harvests, and stores all managed, controlled, and divided up by the father.

Fathers frequently took charge of education, starting with their wives. At marriage most women were young and inexperienced, hence necessarily dependent on their husbands' knowledge. Many husbands must have inflicted on their attentive and frightened young wives pompous harangues such as the one that old Giannozzo, according to his nephew Alberti, addressed to the young woman he had married, whom he intended to teach to be a good housekeeper: "Her natural gifts and upbringing, but above all my instruction, made my wife an excellent mother." The father's best efforts, however, went to the moral and intellectual upbringing of his children (conducted in part during family evenings, as we saw earlier). What joy when his pains were rewarded! Affectionate pride is evident in the letters from Ser Ugolino Verini, a fifteenth-century notary, to his son Michele, the young humanist prodigy. A demanding father, Ugolino encouraged his son, offered advice, reprimanded him from time to time, but usually, aware of the ten-year-old's exceptional gifts and affection for his father, allowed his tender sentiments to speak: "What joy your visit [from Florence to Pisa] would have brought me! No one is dearer to me than you; there is no one I want to see more than you, my son, who have made my every wish come true."

Obedience and respect please the master; rebelliousness and arrogance provoke his anger. Legislation gave him the right to punish members of his family. His use of this right, particularly with regard to his wife, met with general approval. Sacchetti tells of a family of innkeepers in Romagna in which the wife grumbled one night when asked to help her husband, offending a client who happened to witness the scene. Later, the client's wife died, as did the innkeeper husband, and the former guest married his hostess of one night with the express intention of punishing her for her past insolence. Which he did, starting on their wedding night, beating, brutalizing, and otherwise insulting the unfortunate woman. Whipped, thrashed, and pummeled into obedience, the new bride swore in a broken voice that she would be an irreproachable spouse. From this Sacchetti pompously drew the conclusion that the quality of a wife depends entirely on her husband.

Sacchetti may not have subscribed to the popular proverb that "good wife or slattern, all women want a beating," but he was willing to concede that the club was useful for dealing with the latter. The subject must have rankled, because he devotes an entire novella to the strained dialogue between another young bride and one Martin Club. As for children, the motto was spare the rod and spoil the child, and Giovanni Dominici pointed out that "punishment, frequent but not furious, is of great benefit to them."

Though beaten and subjugated, women did wield some power in the home, and with strength of character they could fare rather well. Humanist moralists even approved of this to a certain degree. Women should confine themselves to the home, they said, but there they should occupy first place, "ahead of all the rest of the family." In other words, women were allowed real authority, albeit in a narrow domain. That authority was delegated by the husband, who closely supervised his wife's activities. But when it came to everyday decisions, the wife had her say and was sometimes free to act without her husband's approval: on journeys, for instance, which were common among the merchant class. "She is in charge of household items, servants, and education of the children. As princess of the family, it is up to her to govern and to distribute with care and prudence whatever her husband gives her . . . to develop and improve it." With these bombastic and ambiguous words Ermolao Barbaro paid homage to the wife's role. San Bernardino of Siena was more direct and illuminating. His description is picturesque but long; it shows the wife busy from cellar to attic, keeping an eye on the supply of oil, salting meat, sweeping, spinning, weaving, cutting, washing, cleaning clothes, keeping the house in order. A servant's work? Yes, San Bernardino admits, but a wife performs such tasks so much better than a servant. And the work was essential, the foundation of a whole edifice which the wife controlled: the children's education (upon which Barbaro places great emphasis); support of husband and family; assistance to the poor; and, last but not least, peace and concord. Concord was a primary goal of all government: to assign responsibility for domestic concord to the wife marks the beginning of a new way of thinking about the meaning and purpose of female domestic labor.

Wife and Mother

A wife's daily lot, her moods and humors, are well illustrated by the letters of Monna Margherita, wife of Francesco di Marco Datini, a Prato merchant. At first husband and wife were nearly always together, but eventually Francesco's work took him away more and more frequently; hence they exchanged letters. By the time their correspondence reveals her most fully, Margherita is a more mature woman, rather hardened and less willing to put up with her subjugation to a sometimes difficult spouse. Relations between husband and wife are therefore more complex but also more vivid. Francesco, whose occupation made him a particularly vigilant *massaio* (administrator), harries his companion with daily orders and warnings so distrustful as to become offensive: "Do not forget to keep the kitchen windows closed and to water the orange trees. Do not forget . . . and do not forget . . ." In the beginning Margherita complies docilely, but eventually relations between husband and wife become tense. Her sterility, about which nothing can be done, and her husband's extramarital adventures depress and embitter her. Her replies to her husband's tiresome reproaches become sharper, and she knows how to wound. We see her draw attention to the difference in their backgrounds; she is of noble birth, he is not. She silences his whining by reminding him that it was his decision to leave home. And she scolds him, vehemently at times, for his misconduct: change your way of living, she says, and look to your soul. Her letters exhibit not only remarkable bluntness but also independence, and Francesco, in moments of lucidity and contrition, acknowledges that she is right and encourages her to "do as you think best . . . if only God had willed that I should listen to you." Thus, a woman of character who, because her husband was away from home for long periods, was forced to make hundreds of decisions by herself, could to some degree stand on her own. Left a widow, such a woman was better equipped to deal with the new responsibilities that were suddenly hers.

Nevertheless, a woman's fulfillment came primarily through the education of her children. Because she was sterile, Margherita felt particularly frustrated. But her case was far from the norm. Women assumed the role of educator for a number of reasons, age first among them. They were generally younger than their husbands by seven to ten years, having married at age sixteen to eighteen. Thus they stood midway between the father's generation and that of the children and felt particularly close to their older offspring. Mothers stood for stability and permanence in a world where the men (especially in the cities) put in long hours as merchants or artisans and were often forced to travel for long periods. Hence women exerted great influence over their children—too great according to some moralists, who feared that the children were being made soft by being brought up in an overly effeminate environment. Despite laws backing the authority of the paterfamilias and the moralists' cult of the father, in some segments of the bourgeoisie the father's role in his children's existence may have been relatively limited.

In theory, then, a hierarchy existed in the household, a hierarchy approved and idealized by the moralists, in which the father enjoyed precedence above the mother. This hierarchy was reflected in modes of address, formalities, and other concrete signs. A husband never used the formal *voi* (you) in addressing his wife, but the wife did in addressing her husband. If the husband had a title (*messer, maestro*), the wife never forgot to use it: she addressed him as *Maestro, voi* (Boccaccio). Among the urban bourgeoisie children too apparently addressed their fathers as *voi*.

A Couple Nonetheless. This hierarchy of rank and deference was often ignored, particularly by common folk, among whom wives used the informal *tu* in addressing their husbands, to whom they could speak quite forthrightly when the occasion required. Monna Margherita herself uses *tu* with her persnickety spouse. Indeed, the use of *voi* seems to have been limited to certain noble and patrician families faithful to tradition or, like Alberti, deliberately reactionary. The use of *voi* by children seems to have been more common, but where it persisted one has the impression that both parents are being addressed. Much the same thing can be said about other marks of politeness. Dominici holds that certain marks of respect, such as bowing and maintaining a respectful silence, are essential for children to learn, but these are to be observed with both *genitori*. In stressing the distinction between parents and children, Dominici is proposing an ideal, but he is surely reflecting widespread attitudes. Parents in Tuscany and indeed throughout Italy probably appeared to their children as a couple, a tutelary pair enveloped in an aura of joint authority that obscured differences and tended to equalize the partners in a marriage.

PERSONAL PRIVACY

People gathered at home for meals and conversation and dispersed for work. Everyone had a task. Alberti's Giannozzo, who omits nothing, warns his wife that she had better have a suitable job for every person in the household. Since he is talking about a wealthy household, he means the servants. In humbler settings, particularly in the countryside, family members divided the household chores.

The division of labor could become rather complicated, as is clear from what we know about the sharecroppers who worked for the monastery of Monte Oliveto near Siena (1400–1430). The women spun flax, wove wool, and washed woolen cloth for the monks. In addition to working their farms, the men performed various kinds of seasonal work. Boys worked in the monastery as servants, though with the approval of the monastery's bursar, families could call them home in busy times. Because the monastery was so near, sharecropping entailed duties that extended beyond the strict boundaries of the farm. Each person tried to find a niche between two powers, that of the paterfamilias and that of the bursar, hence independent of both. Individuals looked for work that would be both interesting to themselves and beneficial to their families. Diversity was not uncommon in rural areas. In the Val d'Elsa, for example, a cobbler lived with a family of sharecroppers and plied his trade. Children could leave home to work in the city or in a profession without disrupting the harmony of the family, a situation even more common in towns than in the countryside.

Isolation

This diversification of employment became manifest at the time when the documents note increasing signs of a more intense desire for individual privacy. People began to feel a need to be alone; a privacy *within* the home developed beyond the privacy of the home. The need for privacy was reflected in the arrangement and use of space. The number of rooms increased, particularly bedrooms. Moreover, the new bedrooms could be locked with a key or even more securely bolted. The house began to be organized as a series of private spaces of varying degrees of intimacy. Boccaccio shows us a jealous husband taking leave of his unfaithful wife: "I am going out for dinner," says the husband, lying, "so you must take care to bolt the door to the street, the door to the stairway, and the door to the bedroom." Obviously this family occupied the entire house. To enter, one had to penetrate a first barrier, the street door. But this gave access only to the ground floor, used for storing food and other supplies and on occasion for guests. There was a bedroom on this level, but it was unoccupied. (The jealous husband hides in it.) The residence itself, the rooms that were normally occupied, were located on the second floor, which was separated from the guestroom and storage area by a stairway door, equipped with a lock. Finally, the residence was compartmentalized: the couple's bedroom could also be locked, establishing yet another barrier. Three doors, three protected spaces, three levels of intimacy: guests, family, couple.

Sienese master, Italian manuscript of the *Meditationes Vitae Jesu Chrisi* (detail), 1330–1340. A door with a heavy bolt for security and intimacy. (Paris, Bibliothèque Nationale, Italian 115, fol. 40v.)

The Intimacy of the Couple. We are familiar with the master bedroom, with its chests, tapestries, icons, benches and stools, bed, and lock and key. Or rather keys. In this ultimate sanctum the chests themselves were often equipped with locks, which are always carefully mentioned in inventories. We know, for example, that in 1380 the bedroom of Bartolo of Castelfiorentino and his wife, Catherine, contained a long chest-bench (*cassapanca*) with three locks, as well as a regular chest with two; their anteroom contained two even longer chest-benches, each equipped with six locks, plus an ordinary chest with two locks. Households of equivalent wealth were just as well equipped, while more modest families made do with less impressive storage. Still, practically every artisan's house had its locked chest.

Bedrooms were warm, inviting places, and married couples liked to spend time in them, after supper for example. The husband instructed his young wife, who listened with deference and (according to Sacchetti) washed his feet. She also deloused him (although the storytellers describe this practice as limited to peasants). By and by the wife might feel emboldened to bring up her concerns, minor marital frictions: "I have nothing to wear. You neglect me . . . So-and-so has better clothes than I do, and so-and-so is more respected. Everyone thinks I'm ridiculous . . . What did you say to the neighbor? And the maid?" (Fra Paolino). Eventually calm would return. Then there might be talk of family business, etiquette, the children (Alberti). Topics discussed earlier by the family as a whole were now discussed privately by husband and wife. There was no shortage of subjects.

Finally the time came for sleep or making love. Prepa-

Couple. From an illustrated manuscript of the *Decameron*, ca. 1370. The preliminaries are not without importance. (Paris, Bibliothèque Nationale, Italian 2212, fol. 151.)

rations for the night began, perhaps with a prayer. After bolting the door for the first time some young couples inaugurated their life together by falling to their knees and praying for prosperity, concord, fertility (many sons), wealth, honor, and virtue (Alberti). We do not know if such nocturnal prayers were common in more normal circumstances; confraternities and confessors made evening prayer obligatory, but whether or not it was widely practiced cannot be ascertained with certainty.

In the privacy of the bedroom husband and wife made themselves at home. The man, in shirtsleeves, and the woman, in chemise with little or nothing under it, did the last bits of tidying up (Sacchetti). With nothing more to hide the wife's flesh, her husband became aroused: "You know what somebody told me tonight? When you go to the bathroom, you can't even wipe what I'm thinking of!" (Sacchetti). Then, a final kiss.

Exhausted by the day's work, some husbands fell asleep at once—so much for marital intimacy. Fortunately, this was not the case with all. Moralists and preachers were much concerned about these moments of intimacy, about which they issued innumerable warnings and minute regulations. Storytellers were quick to seize the opportunity for ribald humor. Both shed light on sexual practices.

The preliminaries were not without importance. One lingered over the *ragionamenti amorosi* (amorous persuasion) before disrobing. Nudity had its fascination, yet one example was cited of a Florentine gentleman who was incapable of recognizing his wife in the nude without seeing her face. As a matter of modesty, some wives came to bed in nightgowns. Physicians held that in order to have a good pregnancy and a handsome child, the woman's desire had to be fully aroused: *farsi ardentemente desiderare.* Their view lent authoritative support to the liking of some couples for *toccamenti . . . de la bocca . . . e con mano,* which San Bernardino deplored.

Storytellers and gossips were highly skeptical of the virginity of women at marriage. When a valet took a wife, no one in the kitchen had the least doubt that "Lord Rod entered Black Mound without spilling blood and to the great delight of the inhabitants" (Boccaccio). But where bourgeois brides were concerned, the scullery maids were probably wrong. Since the daughters of the bourgeoisie were kept under close surveillance until marriage, which came early (age sixteen to eighteen), the fortress of their virtue probably never opened its gates until they said "I do." The first night may have been traumatic for these young maidens, deliberately raised in ignorance. Afterward they were free to acquire every possible *astuzia* and *malizia*, artifice and ruse. Despite the reticence of the moralists, we divine from their writings that couples knew and used positions that grew naturally out of long years of lovemaking. That is why the fool Calendrino, whose companions have convinced him that he is pregnant, attacks his wife: "*Non vuoi stare altro che disopra*" (You only want to be on top) (Boccaccio).

From the repeated denunciations of the moralists we also gather that conjugal sodomy was common in Tuscan cities in the fifteenth century (but had probably become so only recently). The preachers blamed the naivety of young brides, who did as they were asked without realizing the gravity of their acts. Women, it was said, had too much to do with the education of boys, who were kept celibate for too long. Sodomy also may have been connected with contraceptive practices (coitus interruptus?), which demographic statistics suggest were almost certainly used, at least by women over thirty belonging to the petty bourgeois and artisanal class (who ceased to have children long before menopause).

The storytellers liked to dilate upon the sexual perform-

Memmo di Filippuccio, *Couple Preparing for Bed*, ca. 1320. On the night of the *ductio ad maritum* the young newlyweds discover their wedding chamber, with its large bed, chests, and intimate atmosphere. They are naked except for their headpieces. In a moment the maid will let the curtains fall around the new couple. (San Gimignano, town hall, chamber of the podestà.)

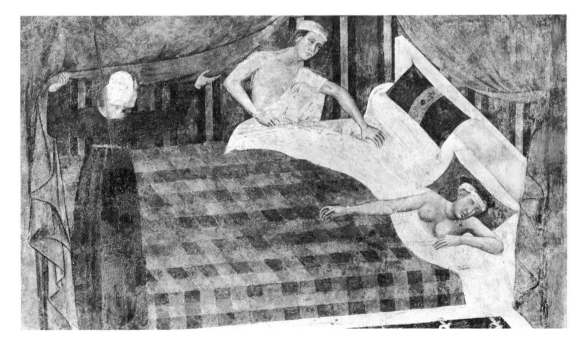

Masaccio, *Charity of Saint Nicholas* (detail), fragment from predella of polyptych of Pisa (no longer together), 1426. Because the bed is so narrow, only the father can sleep in it. His daughters sleep sitting up, leaning against a chest. (Berlin, Staatliche Museen Preussischer Kulturbesitz.)

ance of males. In homage to those greatest of sexual athletes, the priests and monks, the sexual act was referred to as a "psalm" or "*Pater.*" One monk was said to have recited six psalms during the night and two more in the morning—surely a zealous excess of devotion.

Medical beliefs, propagated by oral tradition, held that a woman who wanted children should pass the moments after sex in quiet relaxation. Even a mere sneeze could propel the semen out of its receptacle. Of course if she did not want to become pregnant, she could sneeze to her heart's content and move around as much as possible. In the poorest peasant cottages, with only one room and in some cases one bed for the entire family, sexual mores must have been quite different.

A Private Room for Everyone. In bourgeois homes the proliferation of rooms often made it possible for unmarried adults and even children to have their own bedrooms. Among the elite individuals soon acquired a private space that they could call their own. These bedrooms were equipped in much the same fashion as the master bedroom: they had doors with locks and bolts, locked chests (found even in guest rooms and maids' rooms), lamps, benches, stools, perhaps an icon or a hearth, and of course a bed with all its accoutrements. These rooms offered true comfort and permitted independence, the need for which seems to have considerably predated the fifteenth century; the availability of additional rooms simply ac-

celerated a preexisting tendency. By the fourteenth or fifteenth
century it was no longer utterly utopian to dream of living as
one wished in one's own home.

Alberti recommended that husband and wife each have a
room so that neither would burden the other unduly—in case
of illness, oppressive heat, or pregnancy, for example. The
two rooms should communicate so that husband and wife
could meet without attracting the attention of gossips. A quiet,
heated, private room was even more indispensable to an elderly person, Alberti added. Most of all, however, a private
room was needed by the head of household, particularly if he
belonged to a great lineage. The bedroom was the secret
chamber, where the master of the house contemplated his most
precious possessions and consulted his most valued family
documents as he decided on a proper course of action. Family
documents were "sacred and religious objects"; poring over
them, the father resembled a priest performing a ritual of
commemoration and propitiation in his private temple. In
some houses there was an office or a studio off the master
bedroom, a sort of inner sanctum in which the patron drafted
the *Memoirs* that he would pass on to his offspring. Preservation of family tradition thus depended on the father's privacy. Alberti, as was his wont, couched his recommendations
in rather theatrical bombast, but his advice—that the father
should have a private space all his own—had in fact been
followed since the fourteenth century, perhaps widely. Some
men had bedrooms apart from their wives, a practice attested
among the upper strata of the bourgeoisie by Boccaccio as
well as by inventories (1381). In the fifteenth century there is
mention of such *studii* in several palaces.

Vittore Carpaccio, *Vision of Saint Augustine* (detail), 1502. Adjoining Augustine's large study, this tiny, well-stocked room is reminiscent of those in which patricians gathered books and personal belongings and shut themselves away, sometimes under lock and key. (Venice, Scuola di San Giorgio degli Schiavoni.)

The family books were not always confined to these masculine inner sanctums. Sometimes they were kept (not necessarily under lock and key) in the husband's bedroom (two
instances), sometimes in vast rooms containing two or three
beds and accessible to the entire family (three instances), sometimes in anterooms (one instance), sometimes in all the bedrooms of the house (one instance), without any apparent
secrecy or reverence. Nevertheless, men usually had their own
retreats, where they kept family papers and other books, including works by Livy and Sallust and Villani's *Chronicle*, all
of which are cited in the inventories. On Saturday afternoons,
Sacchetti tells us, or in the evening these books were taken
out of the chests, opened on writing tables, and read attentively. As early as the fourteenth century men attached im-

portance to having a room in the house in which they could pursue private interests without losing touch with their families (and it was often for the sake of their families that they withdrew into their private rooms).

Women, too, had moments of solitude, sometimes by choice, sometimes not. Some had their own bedrooms on a temporary or permanent basis. Great ladies, such as Lucrezia, the mother of Lorenzo de' Medici, had rooms of their own, as did aristocrats and wealthy bourgeois women in Naples, Florence, and Venice. Circumstances sometimes required temporary isolation. In case of illness, for example, it was normal for a woman to have a bed in a separate part of the house, maybe in the ground-floor guest room, which was often unoccupied (Pecorone). Pregnancy was another reason for a woman to take to her own bed. Affluent women had enough room to withdraw during the day as often as they wished, particularly since they had no work other than their household responsibilities. Some patrician women (or their confessors)

Anonymous, *Annunciation*, 15th century. The reading stand, the Bible opened to the prophecy of the virgin birth (Isaiah 7:14), the sumptuous decor, and the meditative attitude of the Virgin evoke and inaugurate the iconography of the cultivated, scholarly Virgin who meditates upon pious works. (Florence, Santa Maria Novella.)

set their sights on personal sanctification and turned their bedrooms into chapels, cloistered refuges from the outside world, complete with prie-dieu, crucifix, and icon. Here the lady of the house came to kneel and pray several times each day; here she came in the evening to escape idle after-dinner conversation in reading and prayer. Touched by grace after a youth spent in fornication, Saint Margaret of Cortona retired to her bedroom to cry.

But she and others like her were exceptional. Other women, less pious and less hostile to the world, found more human uses for their private space. The bedroom was first of all the sanctum of sentiment and secrecy, an aspect of its function emphasized by storytellers. In the master's private space the atmosphere was one of cultivation and almost sacred devotion to the family; the woman's private space was more sentimental. Alone with her caskets, a woman reread or answered correspondence and dreamed of her husband or lover; she became emotional. Separated from the man she loved, Madonna Fiammetta often retired to her bedroom "more readily alone than with someone else . . . Opening a casket I removed an object that had belonged to him and looked at it as filled with desire as if he were there in person; I contemplated those objects again and again and kissed them, holding back my tears . . . Afterwards, I reopened one of his many letters and, in rereading them, felt comforted almost as if I had spoken to him."

The matrons who inhabited the cities were sturdier and more realistic than those who inhabited romances. They went to their rooms alone or with a servant (if they had one) to discharge various household responsibilities. They did write to their husbands and children, but not necessarily in tears and on subjects in which the emotions played but a small part, matters of health and above all administration. Women also drafted correspondence connected with business deals that they organized themselves, often quite astonishingly complex and numerous, including speculation on flax, fabric, foodstuffs, and the like. They dealt with problems of administration and management in their husbands' absence or after his death. And of course, in a more feminine vein, they also attended to their toilette and tried on new clothes.

The wife's private space was in some ways not unlike that of her husband. Her bedroom was in a sense her office, from which she presided over activities for which she bore joint responsibility with the master (such as household management and education) or which belonged to her private province. Later, as women acquired humanist tastes, their rooms filled with books and the little writing desks seen in late-fifteenth-century *Annunciations*. Yet women made their private spaces more domestic and frivolous or else more mystical than their husbands' offices. The woman's room was a more emotional place, where it was easier to cry but also to laugh. Women were less often alone in their rooms than men in theirs. Children, servants, and governesses formed an indiscreet, sometimes annoying court around the lady of the house, whom they kept busy, helped, and if necessary comforted. This description applies only to well-to-do urban families. Women elsewhere worked all day long, and these remarks on private space would have left them aghast.

The Place of Children

Very young children often shared their mother's lot. Among the bourgeoisie, however, infants were rarely nursed by their mothers. Most were turned over to wet-nurses, only 23 percent of whom lived in their employer's home. Three out of four young children spent their first months away from home; indeed, 53 percent were not reclaimed by their families until they were at least eighteen months old. One memoir-writer says that his father stayed with his nurse until he was twelve years old!

Some contemporary experts warned parents against the child's attachment to its nurse, that affectionate, caring surrogate mother. If it persisted after weaning, they said, such an attachment could weaken, even permanently damage, the child's natural love for its mother. Sooner or later children were reclaimed by their parents (assuming that they survived the first months of life) and reintegrated into the bosom of the family.

Children slept in cradles of simple construction, equipped with a light mattress and placed next to the bed or sometimes even above it, suspended from the ceiling and free to swing like a hammock (Simone Martini, fifteenth century). According to inventories, such cradles were found in guest rooms, maid's rooms, and storerooms, suggesting places of storage rather than use (unless the maid's room off the kitchen, the *camera di cucina*, was used by the nurse). None of the cradles mentioned in our inventories were found in the mother's bedroom. The child's cradle was in the mother's bedroom for only a short period, between the time of its return from the

Filippo Lippi, *Miracle of Saint Ambrose*. Women bustle and confer around an infant. Notice that the child is sleeping in a scaled-down model of an adult bed. (Berlin, Staatliche Museen Preussischer Kulturbesitz.)

Veronese master of the 15th century, *The Birth of Mary*. Matrons attend to the newborn, to whom they show natural affection, mingled in this case with respect. Inspired by the example of Elizabeth, Anne, and Mary and orchestrated by the female entourage, maternal love developed immediately, although sometimes it had to be held in abeyance until the child returned from the nurse. (Siena, Museum of the Opera del Duomo.)

Italian school of the 15th century, funerary statue of an infant. This fine piece of sculpture is moving in its evocation of the precariousness of the newborn's existence. (Paris, Louvre.)

wet-nurse and the momentous moment when it was sent to sleep with the older children. Diapers, swaddling clothes, and other infant items were usually kept close to the mother (in the bedroom or an anteroom) and under her surveillance, as though, nursing or not, she personally supervised the condition of the often extensive and well-maintained layette. One chest was known to have contained as many as fifty items of infant clothing.

The fourteenth-century moralist Francesco di Barberino has many sensible things to say about the care of young children. But he addresses himself to the nurse, presumably a good peasant woman. Did she follow his advice—or even know about it?

Pietro Lorenzetti, *Charity of Saint Nicholas of Bari* (detail), ca. 1330–1340. The poor often had no private space. Here three sisters share one bed. Their father is sleeping on the chest beside them. (Paris, Louvre.)

Giovanni di Pietro, *The Birth of Mary* (detail), fragment of predella, 15th century. An elderly man shows tenderness to a young companion. (Paris, Louvre.)

The infant mortality rate among the working class and peasantry was high during the period of plagues (1348–1430). Infanticide (by smothering) ceased to be rare after 1348; in the fifteenth century it became even more common. So many children were abandoned that hospices were established to care for them—San Gallo and Innocenti in Florence in 1445, for example. The existence of such facilities encouraged even more parents to abandon their children. Infants, particularly girls, were so vulnerable that impoverished parents thought it better to part with them, assuming they cared about the child at all.

As soon as a child was old enough to walk and talk, attitudes changed. The fact that cradles of various sizes have survived shows that these were not reserved exclusively for infants. But young children were soon given beds, often shared with brothers or sisters or a relative or the entire family (up to six in a bed). Giovanni Dominici describes the children of affluent families as adulated. He himself was kissed and licked and sung to sleep. He delighted in hearing frightening ghost stories. In his playroom were rocking horses, tambourines, drums, painted birds made of wood and ceramic, and a hundred other gifts. At first sight, to judge by certain inventories, it would seem that some children were spoiled. Chests in the mother's bedroom held enough clothes to outfit a little king: clothes of all kinds, solidly made, superbly dyed, and gleaming with silver buttons. (One item of child's clothing contained 170 of them.)

Dominici's account, addressed to a lady of very exalted rank, apparently applied to only a limited number of families, even within the bourgeoisie. An inventory of a furrier's possessions showed that his two children had only one coat and four black tunics, only one of them lined; the daughter of a communal bailiff possessed only four nightgowns, a house dress, two simple tunics, and a skirt, all made of ordinary fabrics. Costly toys are extremely rare. However their parents may have felt about them, the children of the affluent were not necessarily spoiled, even if their education became less strict over the course of the fifteenth century. The wardrobes of children of the common people were even more meager; toys are never mentioned.

Children had games and playthings of course, and parents did not withhold affection. But the child soon shared a room and bed with elder siblings and therefore also shared their activities and concerns. The poorer the family, the sooner the carefree days of childhood came to an end. Many children began working at an early age, with little girls hired out as maids as young as age six.

Growing Up. Not all young bachelors slept in their own beds. In one, rather special case, three young eremites shared a sofa, on which they were joined one night by their confessor. Shared beds were common in poor and rural households, but it seems to have been usual for young men to have beds of their own, even among the artisan class. Sleeping in one's own bed did not always mean sleeping alone, since several beds could be fitted into one bedroom. In 1390 a communal bailiff who had two bedrooms in his apartment installed all three of his beds in one of them; only one of the three had curtains. Catherine of Siena, daughter of a dyer and twenty-fourth child in a family of twenty-five, had her own bed at least by the age of fourteen (fortunately for her sisters, who were thus spared from lying on the boards that Catherine preferred to a mattress). After sharing a room for several months with one of her brothers, Catherine finally obtained her own room, which had been denied as punishment for her stubborn refusal to marry.

Young people wanted to be by themselves, and their wishes were often granted. Many in the cities and lesser numbers in the countryside enjoyed rooms of their own. This advance favored the development of an inner spiritual life as well as an emotional life. Some children, like Agnes of Montepulciano and Catherine of Siena, were quick to acquire the habit of private prayer, while others, somewhat older, privately boasted to their friends of those other "psalms" so dear to the storytellers. Young humanists used their private rooms in the city as well as in their country homes to store and read their books and compose their works.

Parents called upon the services of their older children. Saint Catherine was sent on errands at age seven. At thirteen she was put to work in the kitchen (as punishment). As soon as she was big enough, she was made to trudge up and down the two flights of stairs in her house, carrying bundles delivered to the doorstep. To Francesco di Barberino it seemed perfectly natural that the daughter of a merchant (even a wealthy one) should participate in all household activities in which the mistress of the house was involved. As Paolo of Certaldo points out, these included baking bread, cooking, washing, sewing, spinning, and embroidering purses, activities also held to be appropriate for the daughters of judges and knights. As for common girls, daughters of peasants and the like, their work was nothing more or less than that of a servant. Boys also made themselves useful. When young they ran errands, and by the time they had grown a little they were ready to exercise authority. Morelli praises his cousin, a boy of twelve or fourteen who handled all business matters for his family of twenty when plague forced them to flee Florence and take refuge in Bologna.

The chores, daily life, and even working life of children were controlled by their parents. Even such matters as the location of a bed or whether to sleep on the porch were controlled by parental decision, especially in the case of young girls, whose rooms, beds, locks, hairdos, and household occupations were subject to the scrutiny of their parents. Parents influenced the choice of a profession. Apprenticeship contracts were signed by the father. More generally, fathers administered their sons' fortunes, regardless of where the fortunes originated, whether by gift, wages, inheritance, or purchase. The *paterna potestas* gave the father the right to decide what the son should do with his wealth, though often emancipation upon attaining the age of majority limited that power.

Family pressures were particularly intense where marriage was concerned. The stakes were too high to leave the decision to the child. The first question was whether or not to marry. Many boys, particularly in less affluent families, were reluctant to marry: marriage was too costly, tedious, and burdensome. Alberti, who deplored this state of affairs, preached firmness: "Youths must be induced to take wives by persuasion, reasoning, and reward, by means of every argument, stratagem, and artifice." He proceeds to outline a shrewd argument in favor of marriage. We can well imagine the innumerable discussions and scenes that must have taken place, the tears that must have flowed, in connection with the subject. Unlike boys, girls were not handled with kid gloves. When Catherine informed her mother of her irrevocable vow of chastity and showed her shaved head, Monna Lapa nearly choked with rage. The whole family was furious; reproach and mockery were showered upon the poor girl's head. A warning was issued: "Even if it breaks your heart, you will marry." Catherine's room and keys were taken away; she lost her freedom and was sent to the kitchen as a scullery maid. At stake was not only the daughter's fate but also the family's. Catherine was a perfect little girl, and there was every reason to hope for a good marriage, an "illustrious son-in-law."

Children sometimes were able to influence the exercise of parental authority. Popular opinion, in some cases backed by urban statutes (which contradicted Roman law), held that the son had a right to participate in the father's *dominium* (exercise of paternal authority) over the family patrimony, and this opinion was widely put into practice. In rural areas sons joined their fathers in drawing up contracts for sharecropping and helped in the management of the farm. When a girl married, her brothers sometimes had a major say in the matter; the brothers of young Catherine of Siena did. At age fourteen a boy was considered ready to share his father's responsibilities in the village assembly. Brothers and sisters supported each other. As children grew older, they sought to create a private space for themselves that was more than just a separate bedroom; they wanted some measure of authority to act independently.

Despite the impediments of custom and the hesitation of

Benozzo Gozzoli, *Procession of the Three Magi* (detail), 1460. Like these young squires attending the three magi, many youths joined the groups of pages at court or, more commonly, the armies of the condottieri. Although their enlistment might be brief, no more than a few months, they would receive a soldier's pay and come to know the special camaraderie that exists only in camps. (Florence, Medici-Riccardi Palace.)

parents, boys did achieve a degree of autonomy. They sought freedom in many areas: religion, sex, work, and marriage. Not all their efforts met with success. When youths were able to join together in societies that were in a sense substitutes for the private life of the family—confraternities, youth groups, associations of apprentices—they were more likely to get what they wanted. Little is known about these numerous groups, whose rites and revels helped integrate young men first into private communities and then, little by little, into the fabric of urban life. For girls there was little if any hope of emancipation. Their only option was to take refuge in prayer, mysticism, or the ultimate assertion of freedom: refusal of marriage. Their difficulties were compounded by the misogyny that remained strong in many traditional households, reflected in the works of such memoirists as Paolo of Certaldo. Girls had to be kept alive of course, and they had to be clothed in such a way as not to bring shame upon the household. But it was pointless to overfeed them, and there was no question of their ever going out, except to carefully selected events. Such was the principle, at any rate, and it was not limited exclusively to the bourgeoisie, but widely shared.

Growing Old

Contemporaries differed as to the threshold of old age. For Dante it began at age forty-five, for Palmieri at fifty-six, when *virilità* ended. This was where decline set in. Real old age, as we think of it, or decrepitude, as it was called at the time, began for Dante at age seventy; Palmieri agreed. To define old age as beginning at age forty-five or even fifty-six was to classify many fathers of young children as old men: the Tuscan cadastre for 1427 lists many men between thirty and forty with children under one year of age. By age fifty-six a man had hardly begun to know his sons' children, the grandchildren who would carry on his name and lineage. Attitudes toward the elderly really concern those over sixty-five or seventy.

The number of elderly was relatively small: 3.8 percent of the population of Prato in 1371; 4.8 percent of that of Florence in 1480. Circumstances favored the elderly at certain times, however; in 1427, 10 percent of the Tuscan peasantry fell into the category, as did 11 percent of the working class and petite bourgeoisie, but only 3–4 percent of the more opulent classes. Their role in the family was out of all proportion to their numbers, however, particularly in affluent families and in rural areas, where the old man was always the head of the family, often presiding over several families. His children and even grandchildren lived with him under one roof. Memoirists like Alberti exhibit great respect for these patriarchs and encourage others to ask them questions, heed their answers, and obey on account of the experience that lies behind them. Special care was to be taken to ensure that their bedrooms were comfortable.

In reality, however, these precepts were at times honored more in the breach than in the observance. The wives of old men who had entered into second marriages with younger women sometimes tired of their not very dashing, occasionally repulsive, and naturally jealous mates, to judge by the fondness of Boccaccio, Sacchetti, and other storytellers for this stock character of fiction. In his memoirs the money changer Lippo del Sega, aged sixty-four, recorded with annoyance the insults heaped upon him by his young wife, who called him *vecchio rimbambito* (doddering old fool) and declared that "*il cesso dove ella cacava era più bello . . . que la mia bocca*" (the pot she shit in was handsomer . . . than my mouth). His children often found the old fossil's interminable rule unbearable; the sources are full of reports about the tension such a situation could create within the family. But the daily life of the elderly was more tranquil. Age made them talkative, and they may have done more to enliven evenings by the fireside than Alberti's Giannozzo, who, spurred on by the flattery of all present, was a crashing bore.

Old women had a harder lot than old men. Young widows enjoyed power and authority, even if they had to share it with their children's tutors, often brothers of the late husbands. But households headed by widows less than thirty-eight years of age accounted for only 1.6 percent of all households in Florence in 1427 and for less than 1 percent in the countryside. Elderly widows were far more common, and their position was far weaker. In Florence 8.4 percent of urban and 5 percent of rural households were headed by widows over fifty-eight. But these were relatively small households, numbering scarcely two persons on the average, and their average wealth was extremely low (200 florins in the city of Florence, compared with 800 florins for households headed by men). For a woman, growing old meant confronting widowhood: 46 percent of Florentine women were widows by the age of sixty, 53 percent by sixty-five, and 75 percent by seventy. It also meant loneliness and poverty unless the woman had a son willing to take her in. One elderly woman confided to a young companion: "What the devil are we good for once we grow old, other than to stir the ashes in the fireplace? When we women grow old, no one wants to look at us, neither our husbands nor anyone else. They send us off to the kitchen to inspect the pots and pans and talk rot. And that's not all. Songs make fun of us, and worse!" For a woman, growing old meant watching her children grow up and disperse. It meant feeling burdensome and abandoned, a useless relic, the warmth and tenderness of the past gone and forgotten.

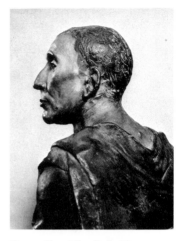

Donatello, *Niccolò da Uzzano*, polychrome terra-cotta bust, early 15th century. A masterpiece of observation, lively detail, and interpretation (reminiscent of ancient sculpture), this bust was for a long time a prized possession of the Uzzano clan, whose ancestral residence it decorated.

The family included domestics and other servants. The staff of the typical bourgeois household in fifteenth-century Florence was relatively small; the great influx of servants did not come until the sixteenth century. (By 1552, 16.7 percent of Florence's population consisted of servants.) Even the great Renaissance palaces employed few servants. Giovanni Rucellai's vast extended family required a half-dozen servants and

The Private Life of Servants

Paolo Uccello, *Birth of the Virgin* (detail), ca. 1440. A graceful servingwoman hastens from the kitchen, on an upper floor, with bouillon and a chicken wing for the mother in labor. (Prato, Duomo.)

Francesco Datini employed five, but an ordinary household, even in the upper bourgeoisie, could make do with two or three. Staffs of this size were common in the homes of physicians, notaries, judges, and merchants. Lower down on the social scale, artisans, shopkeepers, and brokers belonging to the *popolo medio* generally employed only one servant, usually a woman. In Pisa (1428–29), large domestic staffs were even more unusual.

Youth was an advantage. It has been calculated that in Florence in 1427, 40 percent (456) of the known male servants and 39 percent (280) of the known female servants were between eight and seventeen years of age. Being so close in age to the children of the household, domestics were treated the same way: with severity, but as much as possible with justice and even generosity. They were not beaten for trifles, and their mistakes were forgiven. At least this was the advice of writers like Paolo of Certaldo, Alberti, and Giovanni Rucellai. Youthful servants were assigned a variety of chores, reflected in the range of words used to describe them: *famulus, domicellus, fante, ragazzo,* nurse, chambermaid. It is unlikely that all servants were admitted into the family's private life to the same degree. In houses with several maids, the chambermaid was by definition more involved than the others in the private affairs of her mistress. But this distinction was meaningless in families where there was but a single maid to perform all chores, and there were many more of these. The mistress of the house, who generally married at about age eighteen, found in her maid a companion of approximately her own age; it was tempting to turn to her as a confidante, especially since women were confined to a home which they often shared with an elderly, strict, and frequently absent husband. Maids could be pressed into service as accomplices in their mistresses' romantic affairs. But such stories, while common fare in fiction, have no statistical basis. Be that as it may, maids assisted their mistress in the most intimate of times—while dressing, in the bath, trying on clothing—and were their officially designated companions.

In late-fourteenth-century Florence well-to-do masters provided proper quarters for their domestics. A room was often set aside for them near the kitchen or elsewhere in the house. The servants' quarters sometimes doubled as a storeroom for provisions, old furniture, wood, raw material, and other items. The presence of kneading troughs and other equipment made some look like workrooms. But there was always a bed with its accoutrements and often chairs. The bed and sheets were cruder than the masters' and often acquired secondhand. The mistress kept the servants' bed linen in her own chest and supervised its use, but this was not intended as punishment; children were treated in the same way.

Although watched closely and punished when necessary, servants were also shown consideration and respect. Bonds of affection often developed between masters and servants, particularly in the case of nurses. Servants who became attached to the household were rewarded in the master's will with fine clothing, gold coins, or a plot of land. Sometimes they were offered permanent room and board in the household of the heirs, a provision similar to that made for widows. The moralists lavishly dispensed advice for maintaining household harmony to masters and servants alike. Francesco di Barberino placed particular stress on the duties of the chambermaid, who had access to the very heart of the private home. He advised her to be deferential, clean, chaste, frank (without flattery for the mistress), devoted to the children, and above all discreet—very, very discreet.

Pietro Lorenzetti, *Birth of the Virgin* (detail), 1342. The young woman on the right, a servant (as is evident from her hair), has dressed up for the master's celebration of a birth. She has donned her gilt-trimmed *gamurra* and gold belt. (Siena, Museum of the Opera del Duomo.)

However much good will there was on both sides, and however well the moralists' warnings were heeded, difficulties remained. The servants' mere presence in the home was bound to cause problems. Gifts willed to servants by their late masters were sometimes in lieu of wages that had gone unpaid for years, exhortations from the confessor notwithstanding. Many other frictions, if they did not altogether extinguish affection between master and servant, at least dampened it. Masters complained that servants were incompetent, lazy, underhanded, and light-fingered. Pretty servingwomen were overly flirtatious, in the judgment of their mistresses, while the "old monkeys" who replaced them were too ugly, in the judgment of the masters. If servants had been able to write letters, they would have accused their masters of brutality, stinginess, lasciviousness, and many other vices. Rancor was obvious: "I would like to see him hanged. I wouldn't lift a finger to save that arrant liar . . . drenched in vice and cunning," an exasperated Margherita Datini wrote about one of her servants. Distrust seems to have been rampant on both sides, judging by the frequency with which masters changed servants (and servants, masters). In theory, domestics signed a notarized contract that specified how long they would serve (up to six years was the most common duration for service

Memmo di Filippuccio, *Couple Bathing*, ca. 1320. A maid assists the couple in their private bath; she will also be present when they go to bed. (San Gimignano, town hall.)

contracts in Genoa). In reality, however, such contracts were not always used or respected. Of thirty engagements mentioned in the fifteenth-century memoirs of three Florentine families, only four were for more than one year. Most servants were women, and maids normally served from three to six months, with a median of four months.

Under these circumstances servants were potentially hostile witnesses to what went on in that most intimate of rooms, the master bedroom; an indiscreet domestic was in a good position to relay family secrets. Feelings and bodies were exposed to the view of dozens of pairs of eyes as new servants came and went. In a fresco at San Gimignano a servant is present as a newly wed couple take their bath. Masters took precautions to hide their feelings and their escapades, but they seem to have been indifferent to gossip about their naked bodies. The real secrets were secrets of family and fortune, which is why the mistress always wore the keys to doors and chests on her belt.

Domestic Slaves. Coexisting with the free servants in great houses were the slaves (*servi*). Mostly from the Near East, slaves were used in rural Sicily and Spain as well as in the cities, but they played a particularly important role in the larger urban households. A 1458 census in Genoa counted more than two thousand slaves, 97.5 percent of them women and almost all employed as household maids. Many people preferred slaves to free servants because they cost less. Even the most expensive slave cost less than six years' worth of a servant's wages. Venice, Florence, and other cities all had large slave populations.

Slaves were purchased when still young. Of 340 slaves recorded bought in Florence between 1366 and 1397, 40 percent were under twenty-three. They were also penniless. Everyone in the house reprimanded and beat them, including the master, mistress, and older children. Witnesses in court often depicted them as living in fear of being thrashed. As months passed, however, slaves, especially those admitted into their mistress' private sanctum, became more sure of themselves. Female slaves were supervised primarily by the mistress of the house. In certain cities such as Friuli and Ragusa, many wealthy women traditionally kept a devoted slave; in other cities such as Genoa and Venice, the custom was less a matter of obligation than of prestige: noble and wealthy matrons took slaves as their servants. These humble companions often lived on fairly intimate terms with their mistresses.

The least desirable and most tiring jobs were assigned to the slave rather than the free servant. But some were put to work as seamstresses, which left time for conversation. Others were used as nurses. In 1460 Maria, a slave owned by a family of Florentine shopkeepers, was left alone in the house all day long. She entered her mistress' bedroom several times daily, knew where the jewelry box was kept and where to find the key. We have the impression that she was totally familiar with the bedroom, that domestic sanctuary, yet that her masters harbored no suspicion of her. Sometimes a master became so enamored of a slave that household affairs were placed largely in her hands. Alessandra Strozzi joked with her son Philip about this on several occasions (1463).

Slaves carved out a private niche for themselves. Unlike free servants, many served the same family for many years. Some were housed in their own quarters, often attic garrets, filled with provisions and unused furniture (Florence, 1393). Or they might have to sleep in a storeroom alongside firewood and building materials (Florence, 1390). We do not know if they had beds, but in any case they slept alone. The lucky ones were given better accommodations, perhaps a bedroom of their own. One slave kept her clothes in what she referred to as "my room" (Florence, 1450). Slave clothing was simple, like the clothing worn at home by the masters but made of cheaper, older fabric. The young slave just mentioned had complete charge of her wardrobe; she put away her own clothes and was free to cut up old clothes and use them as she liked. She was also allowed to wander about the city, visiting friends who included both freeborn men and women and emancipated slaves.

The presence of slaves was often an inconvenience. Families found their behavior strange and sometimes hostile; it reflected alien tastes, choices, and secrets and posed a constant threat of rebellion. If other members of the household tended to conform, slaves could at any moment raise the specter of disobedience. Many slaves were disturbed, even deranged, by the trauma of capture and exile. Slaves were condemned for their exotic behavior. They were criticized for gaps in an education they never received and blamed for pilferage, lying, argumentativeness, and even unpleasant odors. Last but not least, wives were frightened by the way the slaves' young bodies, enticingly exotic, ravished their husbands' senses. Be-

Florence, Davanzati Palace, "Peacock Room," ca. 1400. Beneath superimposed trompe-l'oeil designs (trefoil arcs and a blind arcade on corbels), 56 escutcheons (6 visible here) are set in a decorative motif of vegetation and birds. Above, from left to right: the arms of Robert of Anjou, the Commune of Florence, and the Florentine Church; below: the arms of the Cafferelli, Bardi (related to the Davizzi through four marriages prior to 1400), and Guidotti families.

tween a quarter and a third of the inmates of Florentine hospices for foundlings in the period 1430–1445 were children of slave women, hence also of their masters. It was impossible to maintain, in a situation of childlike dependence, adults eager to lead autonomous lives. The slave's desire for privacy eventually expressed itself in the form of seduction, sedition, violence, or flight. In the end, many were manumitted.

PRIVATE SOLIDARITY

Among the affluent—and not just the aristocracy—particularly in the cities, the notion of privacy extended beyond the household to include kin. Reinforced by affection, kinship ties were strongest among brothers, cousins-german, uncles, and nephews, many of whom spent part of their childhood together in an extended household. Mourning was limited to brothers and other intimates; widows, brothers, and sisters-in-law all dressed in black. But the feeling of kinship went further, as can be seen in the work of Alberti and other Tuscan memoirists, whose recollections are celebrations of their *gens*, or clan.

Escutcheon of Mariotto Sengini, 1442. Note the lion, the crest, the two escutcheons of the Commune (silver with gules lily) and People of Florence (silver with gules cross). Mariotto, like all his predecessors, wanted to leave a memento of his service as governor of Pescia (for Florence) and a symbol of his family's prominence. (Pescia, wall of the vicar's palace.)

In Florence, Genoa, Bologna, and many other places this unity of the kindred was sustained and symbolized by many things. Lineages were distinguished by family names (which became increasingly common in the fourteenth and fifteenth centuries)—a sort of label attesting to a community of blood. A small number of first names tended to be used repeatedly, generation after generation, in every lineage or branch. Each name was supposed to bestow upon the newborn not only the memory but also the vital force of the ancestors who had borne it previously. A family coat of arms embellished weapons, clothing, houses, chapels, altar decorations, tombs, and banners reminded everyone of the (supposed) antiquity of the house, its strength and valor. Land, buildings, and other highly symbolic possessions such as towers, squares, streets, chapels, and church patronages were held in common. These had little importance economically (the rest of the patrimony was divided among the sons at each succession) but a great deal of importance symbolically, and kinship is first of all a matter of consciousness. In the church decorated with the family coat of arms the family maintained altars, chapels, and tombs, so that its spiritual energies were directed toward the same saints, the same ceremonies, and the same ancestors. The dead were not forgotten, and much was done in the fourteenth and fifteenth centuries to embellish their memory. Memoir-writers in Florence vied with one another to claim the oldest ancestor. Giovanni Morelli begins his *Memoirs* (ca. 1400) by mentioning not only an ancestor who was alive in 1170 but also that ancient relative's great-grandfather. Paintings and busts of ancestors began to fill palaces after 1450. After 1480 they were joined by what Vasari calls an "infinite" number of death masks, which were hung everywhere—on fireplaces, doors, windows, cornices, and what have you. These were "so natural they they seemed to be alive," innumerable faces that hung in the privacy of the home and reminded everyone that the conjugal family was but a single cell in that larger organism, the lineage.

Fifteenth-century Florentine memoirists advocate extending kindness and familiarity as far as possible. Obsessed by financial problems and the vicissitudes of politics in a city governed by a small number of families, they feel that an extensive network of close and fervent allies is the best defense against caprices of fate. Giovanni Rucellai eloquently supports this widely shared view in a memoir composed for his sons: "In our city of Florence, I must advise you, it is impossible to hold on to your wealth without braving enormous difficulties. [He means taxes.] . . . I see no other way to defend oneself than to avoid making enemies; one enemy can do more harm than four friends can do good. In the second place, stay on good, indeed excellent, terms with your *consortes* [members of the same lineage], allies, neighbors, and other residents of the gonfalon [district]. I have never been anything but proud of mine. They have always helped me to obtain tax abatements in the gonfalon, they have assisted me and shown compassion for me. On such occasions good friends and devoted relatives are quite useful. They keep your head above water when you are about to go under and rescue you from danger . . . In order to be on the best terms with citizens, relatives, and friends, I exhort you, my sons, to be good, just, honest, and virtuous and to devote yourselves to good works . . . so as to make yourselves loved. I urge you equally to be most generous to your truly just, honest, and good friends. I would not hesitate to make them loans or gifts or to confide in them completely, sharing with them all my plans, thoughts, success, and failures (without neglecting to make new friends) . . . I still have to speak to you about the requests for assistance that family members may address to you; it happens every day. My opinion is that your duty is to help them, not so much with your money as with your sweat, blood, and everything else, even your life, as long as the honor of your house and your family is at stake."

The homily goes on to elaborate on what has already been said, but the meaning of the passage is clear. It is in the family's interest to defend its property against the fiscal authorities; for this something more than mere courteous relations with relatives and neighbors is required. Relations are particularly close with the extended family (*casa*), for which everything must be sacrificed, and with close friends, who are worthy of complete trust. But to be on "good terms" with other citizens requires treating them, too, as intimates, inviting them for meals, sharing confidences, exchanging letters and visits. This of course is the view of a wealthy merchant. But the fiscal and political problems with which he is trying to cope were the same (or similar) for everyone. In reading Rucellai's advice, we become aware of the increasing importance for every family of extending its circle of intimates as a bulwark against the obtrusive solicitude of the state.

Yet this advice, however sound, is hard to put into practice; full of self-denial, it is too utopian. Nevertheless, there were numerous opportunities to invite others into one's private domain, though at a simpler, more modest level than Rucellai's grand strategy.

Privacy in the Larger Sense

The way space in cities and villages was organized encouraged the formation of bonds between households. The first to benefit from this phenomenon was the nobility. Families of the Italian aristocracy had long built towers and houses in compact sections of a city, which they then in a sense colonized and in some cases fortified. Each family was rooted in its own district. These patterns, with their resulting neighborhood solidarities, were not disturbed in the fourteenth or fifteenth century in Florence, Pisa, Siena, or Genoa. In Florence the several houses of great families were often grouped together around a tower, church, loggia, or small square. In Pisa and Siena, *castellari*, groups of buildings that formed a fortification around a central palace, continued to house the leading clans. And in Genoa the *alberghi*, or leading families and their clienteles, occupied houses concentrated in rather small areas. In the suburbs of Genoa the same families built rural residences, which they were careful to surround with similar dense neighborhoods. In 1447, for example, the Spinola family owned eighteen houses in Quarto. Peasant families imitated the nobles. In certain Tuscan villages one can identify veritable hamlets or sections of town which in the fourteenth century gradually expanded so that growing families could continue to live together.

Italian cities were therefore agglomerations of separate cells, sometimes isolated by walls or mazes of tiny streets. In the fourteenth century cities such as Genoa, Siena, and the old quarters of Florence retained their original character. Residents were united by familiarity, complicity, alliances, and common interests, whether they were members of the same family, clients, friends, or merely tenants (excluding tenants who rented for only short periods, as was common among the poor). In such circumstances it was only natural that people living in the same neighborhood should meet, converse, and gossip with one another; sometimes these meetings were formal, organized by the parish, gonfalon, or whatever, but more often they were private and informal.

Various simple devices were used to facilitate such meetings. In the homes of the affluent, a room on the ground floor was often set aside for them. The inventory of Piero Mostardi (Florence, ca. 1390) mentions benches and stools (enough to seat fifteen to twenty people), tables, as well as pitchers, carafes, and goblets obviously intended to provide the *brigate* with refreshments, which were in plentiful supply in the nearby storeroom, where six hundred liters of red and white wine were kept. When the weather was good, people liked to be outside, so benches were placed along the walls of buildings. There people could sit, perhaps sheltered by a corbelled window. The squares of Sienese *castellari* (fortified houses) and Florentine family seats were often surrounded by such benches, like miniature agoras suitable for discussions of all kinds. Cloisters, public wells, bakeries, church parvises, and cabarets (for men) all provided opportunities to exchange a few words with a neighbor. The two edifices that best typified the solidarity of noble family, clients, and neighbors were the parish church (a sacred place during services and a profane meeting hall at other times) and the loggia, an open space surrounded by arcades where family members (and on occasion others) met to gossip, argue, settle disputes, administer their properties (by receiving vassals and farmers), and show off. In Genoa some loggias were open to everyone, and people loitered there throughout the night.

The rural houses of the aristocracy were always adequate

Giovanni Bellini, *Architectural Study*, drawing, second half of the 15th century. Plan for a Renaissance palace with columns and capitals, full arch, niches, and *oculi*. Outside provision is made for two customary centers of sociability: a covered upper porch (*altana*) where the family and servants could go for fresh air, and a large lower loggia, where larger groups of relatives, friends, and neighbors could meet and public ceremonies could be held. (London, British Museum.)

and sometimes ideal for large private gatherings. Alberti, in his book *De re aedificatoria* (On Architecture), describes the model country house under the imposing title: "On the villa of masters and noble persons with all its parts and its best location." He recommends that the house be situated so as to enjoy an extensive view and surrounded by parks suitable for hunting and fishing. "It should consist of several parts: some accessible to everyone, others open to a more select company, still others reserved for intimate uses." The open areas, patterned after princely houses, should consist of immense fields suitable for use as racecourses. More select areas should include promenades, bathing pools, meadows, streams, and loggias for the use of the *brigate*. Here the old could stroll and the *famiglia* frolic (famiglia being taken here in the broad sense to include the family proper, plus its relatives, servants, and guests). Indoors, this extended private zone would include various rooms ringing the cortile, different ones for use in winter, summer, and the in-between season. The winter rooms were to be heated, and all were to be spacious and gay. Rooms near the main entrance were to be set aside for guests.

Except for the palaces of princes, Alberti's dream may never have come true in quite such handsome style, yet it reflects the sensibility and taste of wealthy Italians from the fourteenth century on. Alberti's vision was an amplification and embellishment of what was already common practice. Between 1310 and 1320 the Peruzzi, a noted family of Florentine bankers, renovated a recently purchased country house not far from the gates of Florence, adding a garden dotted with pools and fountains and a walled enclosure. At the end of the century the Alberti property was so famous for its splendors that it was dubbed *il Paradiso*. Stands of fragrant pine and cypress were planted near fountains, and "strange and marvelous" animals grazed in the meadows. Here, close to the city, Florentines gathered to enjoy the charm of the countryside, as did other brigate in equally fragrant gardens outside Naples, Genoa, and Venice.

The Private Life of Youth

The friendly familiarity characteristic of the wider sphere of private relations began in Italy, as it does everywhere, in childhood. Neighborhood children played together in groups, boys and girls alike, without regard to social distinctions. In fourteenth-century Florence the son of a wealthy merchant could play with the daughter of an ordinary tailor without causing any concern. Florentine girls and boys attended the

Master of the *cassone* Adimari (?),
Game of "civettino," 15th
century. Adolescents play in a
square, while others look on.
The setting was conducive to
forming friendships and
hatching plans. Children had a
hierarchy of their own, a
juvenile private world.
(Florence, Davanzati Palace.)

same schools (attested in 1338), so there were opportunities
for acquaintance beyond play. We do not know whether boys
and girls attended the same classes, but in any case young
children make friends more readily with members of their
own sex, whether by predilection, modesty, or obedience.
Young Catherine Benincasa (admittedly more frightened of
the presence of males than most girls are) surrounded herself
with a group of loyal female friends, whose principal delight
in the pursuit of perfection was to flagellate themselves in
secret. Through games and secrets children discovered a private world of their own, and at the same time they sowed the
seeds of the future. Allegiances sealed in childhood could be
called upon later: "Even as kids we were pals, we were friends,
as you well know" (Florence, 1415)—a weighty argument
when, as in this case, a man needed support. Such allegiances
were important, providing a firm basis for adult relations.

Among adolescents (children aged twelve to fourteen and
older), friendships were even stronger and more independent.
Francesco di Barberino considered it permissible for young
girls (except daughters of a prince or king) to meet friends of

Ambrogio Lorenzetti, *The Effects of Good Government in the City* (detail), 1338–1341. Proper young ladies could dance at home or in the family territory around the home. Public dancing was allowed only on holidays, and the commune collected a tax. Maidens loved dancing, which permitted them to display their grace and be close to other members of the *brigata*. (Siena, Palazzo Pubblico.)

their own age in the neighborhood. In frescoes such as the *Buongoverno* (Siena, 1338) we see them dancing and singing to the music of tambourines. Boys, who were allowed to range more freely outside the family, also sang and danced with each other (and with girls). Magnificent suburban parks offered abundant opportunities to the spoiled children of the nobility and bourgeoisie, typified by the young dandies in the *Decameron*. They played chess and checkers, wandered about, frolicked in the fountains, and so on. At the age of eighteen they were old enough to go hunting, embark on military expeditions, and so forth. In the more peaceful and plebeian climate of the cities and towns, boys were boys: they told coarse and bawdy stories, which only the most exigent and well-organized families could prevent. The young husband of Bonaventura Benincasa (sister of Saint Catherine), "deprived of his parents, regularly saw youths of his own age; these youths, totally unrestrained in their speech, indulged in more than their share of coarse talk, and he was not left out!" Poor Bonaventura, so well bred yet so sad! (Siena, 1360.)

These young gallants organized themselves in gangs, each with its own name and rituals. They created disturbances and occasionally fought with rival gangs (Florence, 1420). Some of these endured for long periods, while others formed spontaneously. They amplified youthful emotions and encouraged seditious behavior. Once, when a Ghibelline was executed, a gang of *fanciulli* (children and young adolescents) seized the body, dragged it to the man's home, cut off his hands and used them as footballs, and for four days prevented his burial vault from being sealed (Florence, 1381).

On a more sober and routine note, youths also worked for a living. At work they entered a different circle of private acquaintances: their employer, his wife, and other apprentices. Some apprentices lived where they worked. (Saint Catherine's father lodged his apprentices under his roof.) Their wages, which after 1348 were quite substantial, stimulated their tastes and goaded their desires: to go out on the town, to dress well, to be in fashion. Young men were interested, as they are everywhere, mainly in young women; they talked about strat-

Anonymous, *Decameron*, "Prologue," 14th century. The young protagonists of the *Decameron* (three boys, seven girls) surround their queen for a day. Near the castle are meadows, groves, and a fountain, all features of the "park" customarily available to members of the upper classes for their private amusements. (Paris, Bibliothèque Nationale, Italian 482, fol. 4v.)

egies of seduction, paraded in front of the houses of pretty girls, ventured out in *brigate* on amorous expeditions, serenaded their beloved, and savored each victory among themselves. Festivals were also in fashion. Rich or not so rich, young men were like tinder, ready to be kindled by the first report of a festival or joust. These were staged frequently in Tuscany, Genoa, and perhaps even more in Venezia, where particularly impressive festivals were held at Treviso (involving an attack upon the Castello d'Amore), Padua, and above all Venice, where there was year-round activity. Through work, festivals, and the like, young people established their right to a personal privacy of their own. Young men, frustrated by exclusion from the established model of private life—the couple—until they were twenty-seven or twenty-eight years of age, compensated with coarse language and conquests, male and female. Young citizens for whom there was no real place in established institutions erected a counterpower in their gangs, whose rules remained their own affair. As they grew up, adolescents did not abandon their world but, in search of identities, sampled new kinds of experience.

Relations within the Family

Families came into informal daily contact with outsiders: neighbors, friends, allies, and strangers. Loggias, neighborhoods, and city squares (surrounded by convenient benches) were places where men went in the morning or evening when the weather was good. People came from all parts of Florence to the most famous squares, like the New Market or Saint Apollinaris. Many other people preferred the intimacy of benches near their homes, where neighbors customarily gathered in the evening. The elderly discussed the past, travels abroad, foreign countries, and so on (Boccaccio). Men laughed, telling each other stories (Sacchetti). Above all they talked about women. One night all present might tease a neighbor's wife; the next evening the conversation might be a little naughtier, discussing why women always seem to get their way in bed (Sacchetti). The conversation was just as lively in the loggias of the aristocracy, where from early morning on men gathered *a cerchio*—in circles—where communal affairs were often discussed and private family business sometimes spilled over into the public domain.

People often invited guests into their homes, and there were frequent comings and goings between one house and another. Children went to visit their grandparents; mothers, "as was customary, visited their married daughters to make sure that everything was going well" (Siena, 1360). Cousins exchanged visits. "Constanza [a cousin of Alessandra Strozzi, whose 1459 letter I am quoting] comes to the house often to gossip." Clan members could not avoid meeting constantly in the streets of their fortified neighborhoods, and even a minor incident could quickly assemble an army of avengers. One night a young woman of the Acciaiuoli clan cried for help in jest; that was all it took for her room to fill in an instant with worried relatives, male and female (Florence, fourteenth century). Friends exchanged visits, and visits to neighbors were a part of the daily routine. During the day people exchanged words from door to door or window to window—moments frequently recorded by painters. At night, if the weather prevented outdoor conversation, several couples or perhaps a small group of women would gather in a house. This custom is attested in fourteenth-century Florence as well as in Genoa, where in the fifteenth century the matrons were apparently in charge, "exchanging visits with one another and inviting guests to pass an evening at home."

People were attentive to the needs of the sick. Alberti once again lays it down as a duty that one must "not abandon a sick relative . . . but visit him and offer him assistance." And that was indeed the custom. Monna Alessandra Strozzi visited the bedsides of her ailing cousins. Friends came to show their affection for the young humanist Michele Verini before and after his operation (1485). They talked and played with him and cheered him with a little music. Similar solicitude was shown to the ill at all levels of society, whether a dying innkeeper, an old man paralyzed with gout, or a housekeeper stricken with colic (she was being poisoned). Old friends came to share food and jokes with the man suffering from gout. An old woman comforted the dying man, "as she did with all of them" (Sacchetti). Such attention to the sick was so expected of friends and neighbors that the ailing person was often installed in the ground-floor bedroom, ideally placed to receive visitors from outside the family (and perhaps also to prevent the contagion, although there is no evidence for this). Only the terror caused by plagues could stem this concern.

Perhaps the most important of all occasions for cementing private relations outside the family involved food and drink. To offer a neighbor a glass of wine was a small favor. People frequently gathered to toast the arrival of a neighbor's new wine, and some brought strangers with them (Sacchetti). To

Anonymous, *Birth of Saint John the Baptist*, 14th century. Female cousins and friends hastened to the bedsides of the ill and women in childbirth. Here we see two visitors—a cousin (the Virgin) and an older friend or relative— keeping old Elizabeth company and playing with the child. (Avignon, Petit Palais.)

be invited upstairs for a meal was a mark of greater familiarity, limited to relatives, friends, and neighbors with whom one had fairly close relations. A wider circle was invited to major banquets. Priests liked to receive their parishioners, whom they plied with drink, all priests, according to the storytellers, being jolly topers. In return, people liked to invite priests with whom they were friendly or perhaps the local curate. When a priest came to dinner, he presided over the meal; on his right sat the master of the house, flanked by his wife and daughters. Painters employed in the house were sometimes invited to dinner, and close friends were constantly present. But dinner invitations were reserved primarily for relatives; for example, cousins in the Strozzi entourage continually invited each other to breakfast as well as dinner (Florence, ca. 1450).

For reasons associated with the aristocratic way of life (with its vacations and obligatory travel) and with the times (marked by warfare and plague), the aristocracy developed more comprehensive forms of hospitality. Rooms were set aside for guests who stayed overnight and sometimes lingered for weeks. Alessandra Strozzi often availed herself of the privilege, staying with her daughter in the Mugello or with a brother or cousin in a nearby suburb. She also knew how to receive others, such as a cousin-german of her husband for whom her two sons worked in Naples and who happened to be passing through Florence in 1449. She put him up for eight days, opened her living and dining rooms to the host of relatives, allies, and friends who came to greet him, and served him sumptuous meals day after day. Hospitality was not limited to the bourgeoisie. Less well-to-do families opened their homes to friends and relatives as their means allowed. If there was no guest room, they made available a bed in a room occupied by a family member, or a place in a bed, or at the very least a bale of straw in the stable.

Major occasions. The broad circle of private relations came into its own on major occasions, when the close ties between a family and its relatives, friends, and neighbors were reaffirmed. When a woman became pregnant friends and relatives were attentive in a thousand ways, and gifts of fine fabric, silver, and the like poured in. Some births were occasions for joyful toasts, as when Bernardo Velluti came into the world, the first son after five daughters (Florence, ca. 1330). Relatives surely took part in the "great feast" that marked the event. Clan members were less involved in baptisms, which were deliberately used to foster artificial kinship with neighbors, clients, and business associates, from whose ranks the vast majority of godparents were drawn (Florence, 1380–1520).

The true kin reaffirmed their rights and reclaimed their rightful place whenever a wedding was held. When Giovanni del Bene decided that his daughter Caterina would marry, he wanted the negotiations kept quiet. People told him that this was impossible. The fiancé had so many relatives, and they were so happy about the news, that they would never be able to hold their tongues (Florence, 1380). The custom of consulting both families was no mere formality, especially if one or the other boasted an illustrious member. Donato Velluti reports that, when consulted in connection with the marriage of a second cousin, he gave his assent (Florence, 1350). On the wedding day all clan members were present. In Florence the exchange of vows and bestowal of the ring often took place in the presence of a small group; the regulations required only that the groom be accompanied by four close relatives.

Masaccio, *A Birth*, 1427. A
woman who has just given
birth amid a host of friends and
acquaintances. This is a *desco da
parto*, a decorated plate, a
traditional gift for young
mothers. (Berlin, Stattliche
Museen Preussischer
Kulturbesitz.)

But other kin soon resurfaced. On the day of the wedding or
the day after, fifteen to twenty relatives of the groom presented
the bride with rings that they had received on similar occasions. Presented by women but supervised by men, these ritual
rings established the bride as a member of her new family and
gave physical embodiment to the welcome afforded the new
couple by the current as well as past generations, whose possessions the rings once had been.

For the actual marriage feast, which celebrated the beginning of the couple's new life together, invitations went out to
family members as distant as the third canonical degree (great-
uncles, cousins-german of the parents, and second cousins of
the bride and groom). Friends too were present, in undeter-
mined numbers. Relatives and friends helped make a sumptuous feast: those on the groom's side sent provisions for the
banquet, and all sent gifts for the bride. They also served as
witnesses, as Bianchi, a fifteenth-century chronicler from
Modena, points out; the witnesses testified to the fact that the
consent of the spouses was genuine. These feasts became so
ostentatious that worried communes sought to restrain them.

In Bologna in 1401 it was forbidden to invite more than twenty-four ladies to the banquet, not including those of the host family, and the cortege from one house to another was regulated accordingly. Florence, Siena, and Modena adopted similar ordinances.

Clan members turned out in equally large numbers for funerals. According to Sacchetti, "all the relatives, men and women," gathered at the home of the deceased, where they were joined by neighbors. The women wailed and moaned. The burial of a great personage was often accompanied by heart-rending screams. When the mother of Giovanni di Marco saw her son's body returned home (he died in Orvieto), "she bemoaned her fate with such cries, accompanied by all the women present, that it sounded like a riot" (Siena, 1394). Then the body was raised and the funeral cortege formed; naturally all the clan members participated. Thirteenth-century statutes governed these processions in order to discourage

Veronese Master, *A Marriage: The Exchange of Rings*, 1490–1500. The groom takes his fiancée's right hand and places the ring, of gold or gold-plated silver, on her ring finger. As was often the case in Italy, there are few witnesses and no priest. (Berlin, Staatliche Museen Preussischer Kulturbesitz.)

Sano di Pietro, *Marriage of Nobles: The Exchange of Rings*, 15th century. Here there is more pomp and a larger crowd of relatives and probably friends. Behind the groom a man prepares with an exaggerated flourish to give the customary slap on the back, which is often indicated in paintings. (Siena, State Archives.)

possible mischief by the alarmingly large crowds of relatives. In Ravenna only close relatives were allowed to take part and wailing in church was prohibited.

Thus there was no lack of major family events. In addition to weddings and funerals, there were the first masses of newly ordained priests and the dubbing of knights, to name just two. On all these occasions relatives and friends were drawn into the family's private sphere, or, rather, the private sphere became common to all, since a dubbing, a marriage, or a funeral involved an entire lineage. The family honor, posterity, or survival was at stake. A key role was played in these ceremonies by women—mothers, wives, sisters-in-law, that is, women who did not belong to the lineage (or who would leave it when they married). They represented their own families, allied by marriage with the celebrating family. But they also took part as individuals, and their participation, even when ritualized (such as wailing at funerals), gave these occasions a special stamp, compounded of spontaneity, warmth, and feeling.

In the intervals between major occasions, family and clients were bound together by the exchange of advice and services. Family members intervened on behalf of relatives with the authorities and the courts and helped each other in innumerable ways. Hence relatives had access to one another's homes; they felt solidarity with other family members and often affection as well (though at times difficulties did arise). The humanist Platina emphasized the importance of these services at even the highest levels of society by having Cosimo de' Medici present to his son Lorenzo the following precepts for family harmony: "Love your brother, and love all your kin. Do not merely show them esteem, but invite them to take part in your deliberations, whether they concern private or public affairs. The counsel of relatives will in all probability be worth more than that of individuals with whom you have no blood ties."

Anonymous, *Decameron*, 14th century. Women mourn beside the bed of the deceased. Their wailing, followed by the pomp of the funeral ceremony, made the death of a wealthy bourgeois more than a private affair. (Paris, Bibliothèque Nationale, Italian 482, fol. 79v.)

SOLIDARITY PUT TO THE TEST

The solidarity of the family was often put to the test, and that of cousinages and lineages even more so. One threat to family solidarity was the fact that individuals were obliged to travel in connection with their work (and many liked to do so); others were forced into exile by the vicissitudes of politics. Death could strain family ties, particularly if common ancestors were forgotten—a very grave matter in a society where ancestors were supposed to live on in memory as well as in heaven and continued to play a role in the lineage even after death. Italians, especially those belonging to the merchant bourgeoisie (along with the humanists), sought to protect themselves against these dangers in the fourteenth and fifteenth centuries.

Far-flung families were an ancient part of the Italian tradition. Merchants had plied the seas and traveled the world for centuries. Dealers in wheat, livestock, oil, and other commodities combed the countryside for many miles around their homes. Even peasants frequently went into town, where they usually stopped for a moment to visit a relative or a former neighbor who had moved to the big city. In the fourteenth and fifteenth centuries the situation was aggravated by the need for citizens to shoulder the burdens of the increasingly extensive state apparatus; ambassadors, provincial administrators, and court officials were often forced to reside away from

Private Correspondence

Anonymous, *Italian Bankers Abroad*, 14th century. Three bankers with their books and a host of clients. Thousands of Italians—merchants, bankers, lenders, artists—lived abroad for long periods. They kept in touch with their families by means of oral and written messages. (London, British Library.)

home. Political purges swelled the ranks of exiles. Many families had to adjust to having a father or son living in exile several days' journey from home, if not farther.

Fairly regular contact could be maintained with persons living abroad. Among the steady flow of travelers some were always willing to carry news and information. "Impatiently I await the arrival at any moment of Gherardo [who was coming from Bruges] so that I can finally hear from a living soul news of you and all about your health and welfare," Alessandra Strozzi wrote her son Lorenzo in 1459. The family might take to the road to rejoin an absent member. Alessandra and her children considered it on several occasions. Because they lived at opposite ends of Europe—Naples, Bruges, and Florence—why not all meet in Avignon? Complications put an end to this plan as to many others; people talked of visiting Pisa or Bologna, but they stayed home. Waiting for people to visit could mean losing contact with them altogether.

But there were always letters. Private correspondence was the pride and joy of fourteenth-century Italians. Exchanging letters with commercial information had been a tried and true technique of Italian business for a century or more. As the generations passed, these business letters increasingly became joined by purely private correspondence. People gradually accustomed themselves to the writing desk: men to impart information and convey orders; women to respond and give advice; children to send a word of affection; stewards and notaries to render accounts. Not all women knew how to write. The lower down the social ladder, the less likely they were to possess that precious skill, and the problem of illiteracy seems to have grown worse in Tuscany in the fifteenth century. Some men, laborers and peasants in particular, were also illiterate, but they were less numerous than illiterate women. By 1380 there is abundant evidence of a clear need and desire to write; innumerable letters have been preserved. It may be that, in Florence at least, the period 1360–1380 marks an upturn in the volume of private correspondence.

Antonello da Messina, *Saint Jerome in His Study*, 1475. A model for intellectuals: bookshelves, a quiet, spacious study, a place to think and experiment—everything that humanist merchants wanted for their studies and reading rooms, where they wrote their memoirs and prepared their correspondence. (London, National Gallery.)

Anyone could send or receive letters. Sharecroppers sometimes received instructions from their landlords by letter (Siena, 1400). Other letters were strictly private, concerned exclusively with family matters, with private emotions and concerns, particularly those of women, who wrote some truly admirable examples of the genre. Alessandra Strozzi, whose sons were sent into exile by the Medici, kept them informed of domestic affairs for twenty-three years (1447–1470). Her son-in-law, her daughters, and her little Matteo (from the time he was twelve and a half) added missives of their own. The two exiles responded. Family life remained intense.

Certain *carteggi*, or bodies of correspondence, covered a much wider range. Letters sent to relatives, friends, and clients reveal not only the scope of private relations but also their connections with public affairs and institutions and the role that letter-writing played in overall administration. To take one example, the Florentine Forese Sacchetti, who was prior of the commune in 1405, returned to power in 1411, and many times served as captain (*podestà*) of towns in the *contado*, or countryside, was bombarded with notes written on pieces of paper folded several times and bearing an address on the back. To judge by those that have survived, sometimes several arrived each day, especially when responsibilities took him away from Florence. The range of correspondents was wide. Members of Sacchetti's entourage are of course prominently represented. His steward, Piero di Giovanni, kept him informed with perfect regularity of the state of his various properties (with information about harvests, farmers, sales of provisions, and so forth). When necessary he sent letters one after another: four were dispatched between 15 and 30 November 1417. Sacchetti's close relatives do not appear to have been great writers, but those of his friends who thought about him told him so in affectionate letters or charming little notes. Little yet substantial: "Forese, I went hunting and had a good day. I am sending you this hare. Eat it if you like with my loyal and excellent brother Giovanni." Present or absent, Forese remained in the hearts of his friends, who found both words and things to prove it. Other letter-writers inquired about their wives' and children's health and occupations; concern turned to worry if something was amiss. Ser Bartolomeo Dei, away in Milan, wished to be kept informed about a daughter or daughter-in-law who was about to give birth. His brother-in-law wrote him as often as three times in ten days (1, 5, and 10 May 1489) with a detailed report on the health

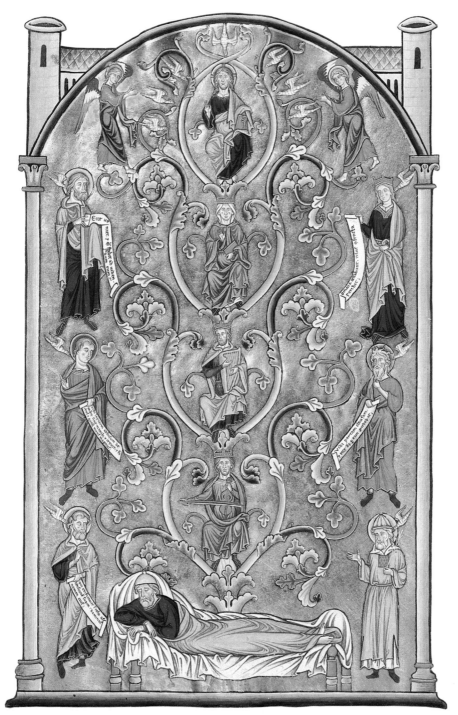

Psalter of Ingeburge of Denmark. Christ, his coming heralded to his ancestors by prophecy and dreams, takes his place at the summit of a genealogical tree. At the root of the tree is Jesse, father of King David. Then come Solomon and, twenty-six generations later, the Virgin Mary. (Chantilly, Condé Museum, ms 9.)

Gaming table. Alphonse the Wise, *Book of Games*, 1282. (Madrid, Escorial Library.)

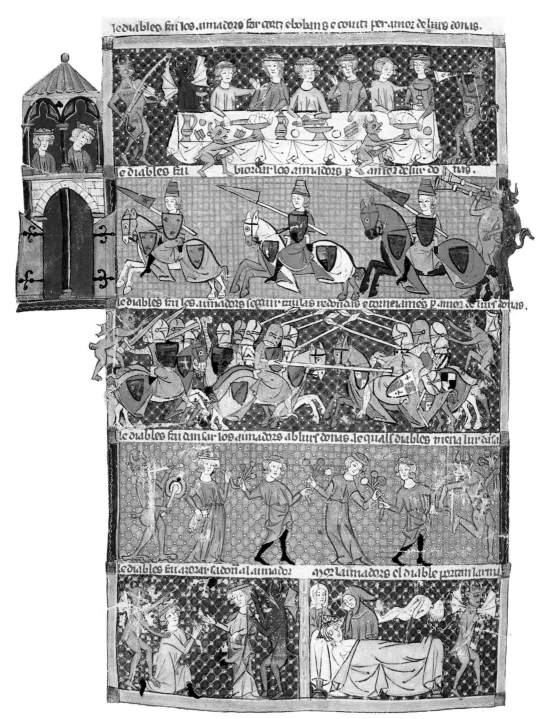

The perilous pleasures of worldly life. Master Ermengol, *Love's Breviary*,
13th century. (Madrid, Escorial Library.)

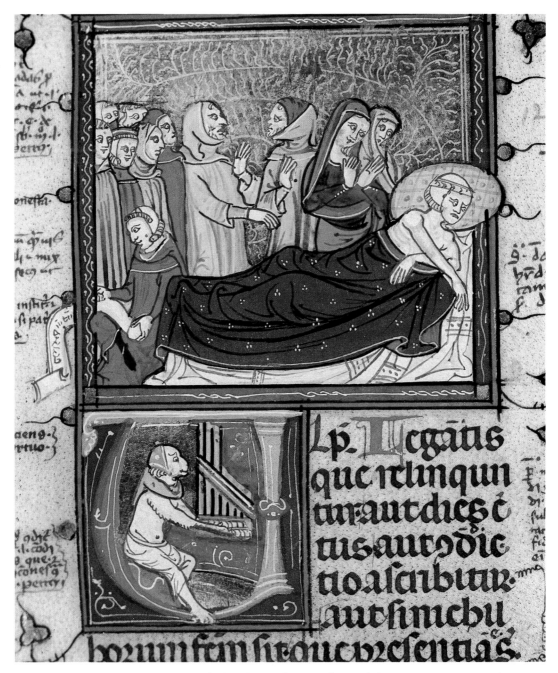

Justiniani in fortiatum, 14th century. With the rebirth of Roman law and the growing authority of written documents (12th–13th century), wills again came into use. They enabled an individual to make known to his relatives his wishes for the disposition of his property after death. (Madrid, Escorial Library.)

Attributed to Paolo Uccello,
Birth of the Virgin, 1436. An
episode from the Bible
transposed to Tuscany, as
indicated by the setting (a
patrician bedroom), the decor
(trompe-l'oeil fur tapestry), and
the elegant audience. A birth
was a marvelous occasion for
women to give free rein to
their sympathy and joy and to
employ their skills: a high
point of a woman's life. (Prato,
Duomo, Chapel of the
Annunciation.)

Andrea Mantegna, *Wedding Chamber* (detail of west wall), 1474. Two small boys caught between the public and the private. Francesco da Gonzaga, the future marquis, and his brother Sigismond, the future cardinal, are dressed for the occasion in the family colors. How long the ceremony is, and how intimidating! Hands seek each other out. (Mantua, Ducal Palace.)

Jacopo et Lorenzo Salimbeni, *History of Saint John the Baptist* (detail), 1416. Two young men dressed in the latest French style share the emotions of their elders as they listen to the saint. (Urbino, Baptistry of Saint John.)

Meo di Guido of Siena (active 1319–1334), *Retable* (detail), "The city of Perugia presented by its patron, Saint Ercolano." With two gloved hands, consecrated and maternal, the prelate presents and protects his city and his spiritual clientele. (Perugia, National Gallery of Umbria.)

The happy (female) citizens of the City of Ladies in the kingdom of Femenia. Christine de Pisan, *Le Livre de la Cité des Dames*, 15th century. (Chantilly, Condé Museum.)

"A small book which would have for name *Les Evangiles des quenouilles* [The Gospels of the Distaff] in lasting memory and souvenir of those women, for all women to come." 15th century. (Chantilly, Condé Museum.)

French translation of Cicero's
De senectute. In this elegant late-
15th-century manuscript, two
elderly men engage in
philosophical debate: Cato, on
the right, in his professorial
chair with reference books
close by, argues with Atticus
on the left. A fire warms the
room. Another room with a
bed can be seen through the
door in the left rear. (Chantilly,
Condé Museum.)

Christine de Pisan presents a
manuscript of her poems to
Isabeau of Bavaria. The queen
of France, flanked by her
ladies-in-waiting, receives
Christine in her bedroom.
Sumptuous draperies bear the
queen's arms (French fleurs de
lis in dexter, Bavarian
diamonds in sinister). Note the
comfortable chairs and
cushions, the carpeted floor.
The windows are shuttered,
glazed, and barred; the ceiling
is paneled. (London, British
Library, Harley ms 4431.)

Master of Tolentino, *The Faithful Listen to the Word of God* (detail), 16th century. God's word penetrates hearts and illuminates faces. The artist captures the expression of the innermost feelings. (Tolentino, San Nicola Chapel.)

Lucas van Leyden, *The Fiancés*,
ca. 1519. Note the hands, the
intensity of the looks, the
gravity of love. (Strasbourg,
Fine Arts Museum.)

German master, *The Resurrection of Lazarus* (detail), 15th century. From the ornamental pool to the imaginary river, from the decorative peacock to the conventional sheep, nature bursts in through a breach in the urban decor, establishing a steady current between interior and exterior, private and universal. (Mexico City, San Carlos Museum.)

Benedetto Bonfigli, *The Body of Saint Ercolano Is Buried Outside the Walls of Perugia* (detail), 1461–1496. Note the forbidding facades of the fortified city, inhospitable to the toil of man. (Perugia, National Gallery of Umbria.)

of the young woman, then in her ninth month, whose condition caused concern: her legs were quite swollen.

These familiar missives are swamped by a mass of other letters from distant relatives, clients, and even unknown correspondents, people of every stripe, class, and walk of life. This flood of correspondence was addressed to the public man, the one in a position to use his authority or influence in his correspondents' behalf; most had some favor to ask. To explore these letters would take us beyond the private domain. But the dividing line between public and private was not always clearcut. In asking for help, many letter-writers adopted the warm and familiar tone, sometimes even the vocabulary of private life, hoping by means of affectionate deference to create a relation of adoptive kinship which would oblige the recipient to intervene. Everyone called Forese Sacchetti *maggiore*, in homage to his superior status. More moderate correspondents added *onorevole*. Deference (not to say sycophancy) reached a crescendo with words such as *magnifico, carissimo*, or, rather more presumptuous, *onorevole maggiore come fratello* (most honorable, like a brother, used by peers, other members of the bourgeoisie) and *come padre* (used by others). The word *padre* recurs three or four times in one letter, in expressions such as "placing my hope in you as in a father" or "begging you as a father." Forese was not unmoved by these pleas, which were sometimes repeated in more threatening tones. He made inquiries, consulted jurists, and in general showed himself to be an understanding patron to his clients. Unstable as a man's clientele might be, it offered definite political advantages, and the Florentine memoirists are categorical: be obliging, don't make enemies. But the mask of familiarity worn by his correspondents (who were not entirely hypocritical) worked on his feelings and induced him to act on behalf of his clients as he would have acted on behalf of his own family.

Among educated Italians (not all of whom were members of the urban bourgeoisie), letters were seized upon as a marvelous way of maintaining cherished family ties and friendships during periods of separation. Letters not only maintained relationships, they enriched them. Of course the farther letters had to travel, the longer one had to wait, so distance slowed the epistolary dialogue. The answer to a message sent from Naples to Alessandra Strozzi in Florence on 18 December 1464 did not arrive until 18 January 1465, even though Alessandra answered within four days of receiving the letter. But everyone was aware of the difficulties. The delays only made letters more precious to those who received them, and correspondence was composed with the slowness of transit in mind. The correspondent was kept abreast of intimate household affairs, but they were presented in a particular way. Letters were sometimes warmer than conversation would have been. In writing one was forced to find words to express affection, anxiety (redoubled by distance), relief, and joy, words that came less easily to women's lips in daily intercourse owing to convention and modesty. Sometimes the gravity of the situation was concealed from the absent party: Bartolomeo Dei's brother-in-law confided after his daughter had given birth that "the swelling of her legs was much worse than I led you to believe." People went out of their way to keep an absent family member informed of events at home. They showed greater interest than usual in those around them. An uncle might ask for news of his niece. A young son might listen attentively to the conversation of adults so as to be able to write knowledgeably to his father about dowries, mortgages, and taxes. A mother might be especially solicitous of anyone who had seen or might see her son.

Letter-writing expanded the circle of private relations even further, at least at this level of requests for favors. Many such requests were composed by third parties, and it was often easier to write a letter than to arrange a visit. The letter-writers expressed themselves in terms that created, however artificially, a relation of dependence, which sometimes outlived the granting of the favor.

Memoirs and Diaries

The dead, though beyond receiving letters, were not necessarily out of touch. To begin with, there was prayer, a plea without explicit response yet widely viewed as a way of requesting a favor from God or a saint. Through prayer one also addressed the souls in Purgatory, where many ancestors were presumed to reside. There were endless opportunities to pray for deceased members of one's family at masses and memorial services instituted by the deceased themselves through their wills and regularly celebrated (in some cases in perpetuity) at churches they had attended while alive or in chapels they had founded. It would be hard to prove, however, that family members actually participated regularly in these services or that they used them to revive the memory of the deceased. Unless a special effort was made, the dead were soon reduced to little more than an annual proclamation of a name inscribed in an obituary.

Special efforts were made, however. In some lineages oral traditions concerning ancestors dating back as far as the twelfth century were still current two or three centuries later. Giovanni Morelli claims on several occasions (ca. 1400) that he obtained information from elderly relatives, male and female, which they in turn had obtained from their elders, concerning an ancestor born in 1150. Giovanni Rucellai reports that he benefited greatly from conversations with elderly kinfolk, who shed light on his family's history. Some great families, especially those in which groups of relatives lived close together, seem to have been at pains to preserve a rich oral heritage from which they derived much knowledge of their ancestors and a fierce sense of family pride.

In the fourteenth and fifteenth centuries some sought to learn even more about the past by consulting family papers—notarized contracts, account books, affidavits, and the like—and by painting more detailed, lifelike, and convincing portraits of their ancestors. People were also careful to leave accurate information about themselves and their children: age, name of godfather, hour and day of birth, and so on. Alberti was the first to recommend this precaution "for many reasons" (which he does not cite).

People thus ceased to rely on memory alone for such precious information. In the fourteenth century many families set aside a few pages in an account book or a notebook purchased specifically for the purpose in which they recorded whatever information they could glean about their ancestors. Some listed only direct ancestors and very close relatives (Morelli); others included more distant cousins (Velluti). The purpose of this portrait gallery was not necessarily to flatter but rather to illustrate how a family lived, to commemorate the high points of the past, and to emphasize the length and continuity of the family's participation in a particular line of business. It was intended, in short, to foster family solidarity in regard to property, religion, politics, and so on, without obscuring the uniqueness of each individual member (sometimes marvelously sketched, as in the case of the Velluti, as far back as the cousins of two generations past) and without hiding the inevitable frictions and quarrels. Memoirs of a lineage, these albums (*ricordanze, ricordi*) helped to create an informed and personal appreciation of the family past, thus extending the private realm backward in time.

Filippino Lippi, *Portrait of an Old Man*, second half of the 15th century. A taste for observant and penetrating family portraits, encouraged by family feeling as well as by humanism, was even more striking in painting than in the *ricordanze*. (Florence, Uffizi.)

The known memoirs are the work of individuals, family heads interested mainly in their own generation. Ancestors are worth a tip of the hat, but when the narrative reaches the author's own time, when it describes his parents, uncles, cousins, and children, the emphasis changes. Giovanni Morelli's finest and most sensitive pages are devoted to his uncles, brothers, and sisters. These personal memoirs were jealously guarded by their authors and their authors' offspring. They might be shown to intimate friends or lent to brothers and even cousins (Corsini, Florence, 1476), but generally the authors inisted on the private character of their work. Memoirs were addressed primarily to the author's children and direct descendants, who frequently continued the narrative. They were for the family, more specifically for the males of the family. Even the wife was suspect: she belonged to a different lineage, so the *ricordanze* were kept secret from her as well.

Two different points of view coexisted in the memoirs. The portraits of ancestors and elders encouraged family feeling and perpetuation of family traditions, habits, and traits. Readers were meant to be inspired by past triumphs and chastened by past mistakes. This aspect, however, sometimes was all but overwhelmed by what the memoirist had to say about the present generation. Observations of close relatives and friends were more detailed and accurate, warmer in tone, and more strictly private in point of view than were passages based on historical hearsay. Consider what Giovanni Morelli says about his brother Morello: he was born on 27 November 1370, "the evening of Saint Peter of Alexandria; it was a Wednesday night, when the bell for 8:30 struck at Santa Croce. He was baptized the following Saturday, 30 November. His four godparents were [names and addresses of two men and two women]. He was given the names Morello and Andrea, Morello on account of his grandfather, and Andrea, patron of the day . . . He took for his wife Caterina . . . Castellani." This was followed by details of the marriage.

Apart from the mention of the grandfather's name, every detail relates to a strictly private world, centered on the basic family unit. City, church, and everyday details merely form a backdrop. In this and similar reports the emphasis is on the importance of private relations, of solidarity with family, godparents, and allied clans. The nuclear family is the hub; more extensive family solidarities take second place. Family memoirs not only recorded this state of affairs, they helped to create it. They gave concrete embodiment to the nexus of solidarities and relations that defined the new and more extensive private world of the basic nuclear family, its connections with in-laws, godparents, and so forth. These were the relations that distinguished each family from others belonging to the same lineage.

Each individual had commitments to his or her spouse and children, his or her extended family, and him- or herself. Where there was conflict between these various commitments, there was also tension. Consider conflict between husband and wife. Some wives found their husband's absences hard to bear; the private life of the family requires two people. Other couples found living together more difficult than living apart. Husband and wife often had been brought up in very different settings, for the mores of different occupational groups varied widely. Such situations were quite common, and the inevitable family crises revealed and aggravated these underlying differences. Some time between 1350 and 1380 a Sienese painter of crucifixes caught his proud wife in the act of adultery. The insults and invective that poured out on both sides reveal the tensions that may have precipitated the break:

Individual Privacy Versus Collective Privacy

> He: Filthy whore! You call me a drunk, but you're the one who hid your lover behind my crucifixes.
> She: Are you talking to me?
> He: No, I'm talking to a pile of donkey shit.
> She: That's just what you deserve.
> He: Shameless hussy! I don't know what's stopping me from sticking this poker you know where.
> She: Don't try it . . . by the cross of God. If you touch me, you'll never finish paying for it.
> He: You filthy sow, you and your pal over there . . .
> She: Curse anybody who forces his daughter to marry a painter. You're all touched in the head, crazy, the whole lot of you. Always boozing it up, you gang of debauchees.

This lively episode of Sacchetti reveals the kinds of tensions already alluded to. Living with Mino (the painter) meant being forced to put up with a coarseness of manner that was a legacy of his previous bachelor life. Painters were rootless and intemperate, and a girl raised in a different milieu would have found these traits difficult to endure. For this marriage to have worked, the customs of three different private worlds

Tacuinum sanitatis, 1390–1400. Wife-beating was a husband's sacred right, but if he availed himself of it while under the influence of drink or in a bad humor, the consequences for the couple could be serious. An adequate diet offered protection against this evil, according to the *Tacuinum.* (Paris, Bibliothèque Nationale, n.a. Latin 1673, fol. 50v.)

would have had to be reconciled: that of a well-bred young lady, that of a gang of youths, and that of the milieu of painters. It is easy to see why the woman was upset, and why she might have succumbed to temptation.

Troubles and difficulties in the nuclear family also resulted from a clash of different forms of privacy. Problems sometimes began with the birth of a child; in a poor home another mouth to feed could spell disaster. Bastards were another source of trouble. And young widows could not keep their children by their late husband if they followed their in-laws' advice and remarried. All three situations could lead to infanticide or abandonment (especially of daughters), for reasons of necessity in the first case and social convention or self-interest in the latter two. Bastards and daughters of poor families were turned over to hospices; children of widows were left for long periods with their nurses and finally turned over to their father's family (Tuscany, late fourteenth to fifteenth century). In the case of bastards and widows, the interest of the lineage won out. Its honor and unity prevailed over the feelings of the mother, whatever they may have been.

There were also problems as the children grew up. Some suffered from a brutal nurse, a cruel mother, or a father's frequent absence. Paolo Morelli was left with his nurse until he was twelve, and his son, Giovanni di Paolo was abandoned by his mother when he was four; neither man overcame his bitterness in later life (Florence, 1380). In other families dissatisfaction sometimes reached the point of open insubordination. In 1380 in Florence a member of the Peruzzi family devoted an entire page of his book to explaining why he was reduced to cursing his son. The boy, he said, was disobedient; the word occurs five times: "Deceitful, treacherous, and false, he has always disobeyed, betrayed, and ridiculed not only me but also my neighbors, my commune, my kin, and my allies." In Cortona the father of the future Saint Margaret evinced similar hostility to his daughter. After several years of concubinage God's servant returned home in tears, dressed entirely in black. Margaret's father, egged on by her stepmother, refused to receive her (Cortona, thirteenth century).

Sometimes too a father's actions irritated or exasperated his son. In the Lanfredini family the father arranged an inopportune reconciliation with a hostile lineage against the express wishes of his children. His wife heaped opprobrium upon his head: "Lanfredino, you are a traitor to yourself and your children! [She used the formal "you."] How dare you inflict on your sons the shame of this reconciliation without saying a word to them or to me! You have deprived them of all their worldly goods—property, honor, everything." Appalled, one of the sons wrote to his brother thus: "I tell you, when I left the house I made an irrevocable decision never again to call myself his son and to change my name" (Florence, 1405). Extreme as they are, the examples just cited indicate the two directions in which children sought to assert themselves. Sometimes they asked to take a full part in major family decisions, while other times they wanted to act in full independence, to make lives for themselves outside the confines of the family.

I shall have little to say about the innumerable quarrels over inheritance, which involved first the dowry and second the patrimony. These disputes, which concerned not just the nuclear family but the entire lineage, were a constant stumbling block to family solidarity. Not all the families within a lineage were intimate with one another, and there were plenty of factors to aggravate natural divisions. Housing, for one: some families were forced to settle outside the quarter colonized by their kin, ceasing to take part in the daily contacts that tended to create a private world. No one would accept such exile unless forced to do so by poverty or isolation. For those who did, the one wish was to return to the fold. In the great Florentine clans about which we know a great deal (the Ginori, Capponi, and Rucellai), they form a small minority. Fortune played its part: the poor presumably lived differently from the rich relatives who were their neighbors. But to judge by the families just mentioned, in the cities differences of wealth were not always as decisive as some have maintained. Disparities of wealth between households belonging to the same lineage were not as great as once thought; more important, family fortunes were unstable. Between one fifteenth-century cadastre and another (in other words, every decade) the identity of the wealthiest Ginori changed. Members of the three families cited were much more uniformly wealthy than the urban population as a whole. No Ginori household was counted among the poorest of the poor in the fifteenth century, and even those whose tax payments were relatively low had access to the same education, the same responsibilities, and the same style of life as their wealthier relatives. (Often their poverty was of recent date.) Solidarity played a part; family members supported one another.

Lineages were solid enough and had sufficient esprit de corps to cope with the tensions inherent in their structure. They were less well equipped to deal with other challenges, in particular the temptation on the part of some individuals to strike out on their own in business or investment. Consider the Velluti family. In the thirteenth century all the males in the family were partners in a single trading company. Families sought to keep the patrimony intact or at least to administer a part of it in common. But in the period 1310–1330 independence was the rule. Estates were commonly divided, and portions were even sold to outsiders. Divisions, inheritances, and sales sowed discord that often lasted for years or even increased with time. Donato, author of the Memoirs on which this account is based, reports ten conflicts among his cousins, several of which degenerated into open breaches. Donato himself was involved in six of them. The result was that the natural family hierarchies fell apart. The authority of Donato, the leader of the family (reflected in consultations and arbitrations in which he took part) was reduced to just one of the five branches of cousins-german descended from a common paternal grandfather. Indeed, the real scope of his power was limited to his brothers and children. Perhaps the most eloquent sign of the waning of family solidarity was that the vendetta fell into disuse, at least among the Velluti. No one was willing to avenge offenses against the clan, and when, after much shilly-shallying, one cousin finally drew blood in vengeance for a murder committed in 1310, the rest of the family took the view that he was a dangerous eccentric (Florence, 1310–1360).

As time passed the solidarity of the lineage gradually waned in rural areas as well. One village in the Val d'Elsa between Siena and Florence was dominated by the Belforti, a family of petty nobles. Three brothers ruled the family at the beginning of the fourteenth century. Years went by, and the three founders eventually gave way to their children, three groups of cousins-german (1330–1340). The once proud family spirit had meanwhile lost some of its luster. Members of its main branch were all engaged in thriving professions as moneychangers or landlords and did not hesitate to overdower their daughters so as to attract illustrious husbands. (Each daughter received, on the average, more than 1,000 lire in dowry.) They all settled in the city. As for the brothers of the family's third branch, all were engaged in modest occupations (farmers), could afford to give only small dowries to their daughters (less than 100 lire on average), and continued to live in their native village. Solidarity of some sort survived, since people still referred to the family as a *consorteria*, but there was no longer any private intimacy among the cousins (Tuscany, 1300–1340).

The conclusion to be drawn is the same as that suggested by our study of the memoirs. The old duties imposed by the lineage were no longer consistent with the new needs of individuals for greater freedom to choose a profession and to invest their wealth; for greater autonomy in matters of justice (and freedom from implication in the crimes of a kinsman); and for a more effective defense against the gargantuan appetite of the fiscal authorities. Though still useful, the support of one's lineage needed to be supplemented by other forms of solidarity, better tailored to the needs of the individual and less constraining than the family solidarities of old: neighbors, friends, and freely chosen allies filled the gap. This new network of allegiances defined a new private sphere, larger than before and in some ways warmer (with its exchanges of letters, visits, and invitations to dinner), and different for each individual household.

THE PRIVATE CELL

Individual personalities were not submerged in the private milieus of which they were a part. Within a given lineage, branch, or even nuclear family personal choices were possible; the well-to-do even enjoyed private space of their own (perhaps a bedroom) within the home. But families helped individuals develop their potential in ways other than just leaving them alone. They took an interest—not always welcome—in what their members were doing and set an example for the younger generation to emulate. The stimulus of the family was particularly important in a society in which the role of educational institutions and other surrogates for the family was quite limited.

Mutual Knowledge

Living together day after day was an ideal way to gain intimate knowledge of others—and for women, the only way. From letters and family record books we learn how attentive families were to the activities of their members, regardless of sex, importance, or public position.

Until the first cadastres were compiled in the fifteenth century, only parents knew the exact ages of their children. Vital statistics were conveyed by mothers as oral tradition. When one merchant sat down in 1299 to write his memoirs, he began by saying that he had been born in 1254, "according to my mother's memory." A peasant estimated his daughter's age as ten years, "having heard it from her mother." Alessandra Strozzi knew all the major events in her children's lives and could date them almost to the day. In 1452 she imparted some of this information in a letter to her son Lorenzo. "Filippo's age? On 29 July he will have completed his twenty-fourth year. Next March the seventh he will have been gone from Florence for twelve years. You were twenty years old this past August twenty-first. You left Florence in that month seven years ago." This was followed by similar information about her three other children. Biographical reports (as well as obituaries) were a common feature of the increasingly popular memoirs, composed by men; but it may be that such information had previously been the province of women, transmitted orally and therefore particularly private. Knowledge of precise birth dates was important for planning feasts, casting horoscopes, and establishing a hierarchy within the extended family.

Children grew and developed physically under the watchful eye of the private entourage. Memoirs frequently attest to the fact that the physical graces of clan members, young and old alike, did not go unnoticed by members of the private inner circle. Giovanni Morelli's descriptions of his brothers, sisters, and cousins are quite accomplished. Bernardo, a cousin, was "robust, very big, muscular, very dark-skinned, and covered with freckles." Bartolo was "fat and fresh, with white, or rather olive-colored, skin." His elder sister Mea was "of normal size with a lovely complexion, fresh and blonde, well turned out, pure charm. Among her many perfections were her ivory hands, so well made that they might have been painted by Giotto, long, soft hands with long, thin fingers that tapered like candles down to beautifully shaped, shiny red nails." Family members naturally made fun of one another, but to live at home was above all to be known, recognized, distinguished, and admired.

The memoirists have left us not only portraits of what their kinfolk looked like but even more astute sketches of their character. Donato Velluti has a few words to say about the moral qualities of all of his cousins, not only first and second but even third, male and female alike. Yet he never stoops to banality or cliché but always seeks to demonstrate his perceptiveness and insight. In describing his relatives' character and behavior he uses no fewer than seventy-nine different adjectives. As a man of the world, Donato is not always admiring, and he has no compunctions about recording deviant behavior. His judgments, moreover, are inspired by the values of his time, milieu, and generation. He is especially appreciative (as the nuances of his seventy-nine adjectives suggest) of wise

Vittore Carpaccio, *Legend of Saint Ursula*, "The Saint's Dream" (detail), 1495. Attentive to the profile, features, character, and personal charm of the subject, portraits of women, which sometimes indulged in rather suggestive poses behind an ostentatious facade, reflected the higher status enjoyed by 15th-century patrician women in their private world. (Venice, Accademia.)

Filippo Lippi, *Scenes from the Life of Saint John the Baptist* (detail of Herodiad), 1464. In the guise of a biblical figure, this is supposedly a portrait of Lucrezia Buti, the painter's companion. Elegant and shrewdly observed, the painting emphasizes the young woman's features (especially her forehead and ears) and her dazzling throat as well as her rather gauche modesty. (Prato, Duomo.)

judgment, prudent management, and polished high spirits and comes down hard on wickedness and waste. Given these limitations (his judgments are neither very social nor very Christian), he is generally benevolent, admiring, and optimistic. (Seventy-five percent of his adjectives are positive.) His private circle is very wide indeed, though perhaps not quite ample enough for his cast of characters to display all their qualities fully. Yet it remains the center of mutual knowledge and esteem and the focus of individual development from early childhood on.

The private world was also the cradle of the emotions. Situations viewed with indifference when they involved outsiders were here experienced more personally and directly, with emotion and even passion. Individual sensibilities were shaped by such experiences.

A subject frequently touched upon in letters was the absence of loved ones—an absence from which people suffered. Michele Verini, barely eleven years old, said as much repeatedly to his father, then in Pisa. The slightest delay in the mail was worrisome, especially if illness was believed to be the cause. Whether a letter arrived or not, "your absence," Michele told his father, "causes me real suffering," and the confession, coming as it does from a sensitive and precocious young man, has the ring of truth.

Physical suffering, harbinger of death to come, was the hard anvil on which sensibilities were forged. Since hospitals were intended primarily for the poor, well-to-do patients were nursed at home. They took to their beds, suffered, agonized, and died. Suffering and death, and the sight of suffering and death, were private experiences, common owing to the size

The Sophistication of Sensibility

Domenico Ghirlandaio, *Scenes from the Life of Saint Fina* (detail), 1475. Saint Fina, who has taken to her bed voluntarily (as a form of penitence), is watched over by two other women as a saint announces her impending death. (San Gimignano, Collegiate Church.)

of the family, the precarious health of the population, and treatment that was often nothing less than brutal.

Correspondence, private diaries, account books, stories and tales, all illustrate the persistent presence of illness. In Michele Verini's family, an uncle of thirty-five, stricken with dropsy, had been bedridden, his stomach swollen like a wineskin, for six months (1480). Michele's thirteen-year-old contemporary Orsino Lanfredini saw his two sisters stricken with measles (May 1485); they were treated in their parents' home. It was common to have a relative bedridden for weeks at a time. Marsh fever was common. Still more serious, cases of plague were treated at home, and many a will was dictated by an invalid *in domo sua*, in his own house. Moralists recommended that domestics be treated in their patrons' homes, advice that was certainly followed. If the servant's condition worsened, however, there were no compunctions about sending him or her to the hospital; patrons like Alessandra Strozzi comforted themselves with thoughts of the good care that the hospitals dispensed.

Thus, people were treated at home for relatively minor illnesses (of the sort still treated at home today) as well as for

Andrea del Sarto, *The Patients of San Matteo Hospital*, first quarter of the 16th century. The great hospitals of the 15th century were remarkably well equipped, with individual beds, benches for visitors, airy rooms, and solicitous personnel. For the patients, all poor, the private world provided was warmer and more comfortable than their own homes. (Florence, San Matteo Hospital.)

Ambrogio Lorenzetti, *Scenes from the Life of Saint Nicholas,* "healing of a child" (detail), 1330–1332. This child's serious condition is blamed on diabolic magic (worked by a devil disguised as a pilgrim). The saint's intervention rescues the onlookers from their helpless plight. (Florence, Uffizi.)

major diseases (which nowadays require hospitalization). Familiarity with sickness often meant familiarity with suffering, sometimes for brief periods but often chronic, painful, or even unbearable; no one could escape the ubiquitous presence of pain. Michele Verini's dropsical uncle was constantly thirsty and woke the entire household with his screams for wine. Five years later, Michele himself suffered greatly from an injury for some time (1485–1487), and surgery to remove a testicle caused still further torture. Afterward unremitting pain kept him awake through many a night. His friends' attentions diverted him but hardly put an end to his suffering. The longer he lived, the more he suffered "from excruciating pain."

Simone Martini, *Saint Louis of Toulouse Crowning King Robert* (detail of a *pala*), 1317. In the absence of effective therapy, the saints were often called upon to heal the sick. Saint Louis is here healing an injured child (note the child-sized bed). (Naples, Capodimonte Museum.)

Monna Ginevra, wife of the memoirist Gregorio Dati, remained bedridden at home after giving birth to a child. She never recovered and died a martyr's death (Florence, 1404). The sight of excruciating pain was particularly upsetting to family members. Giovanni Morelli never got over the experience of watching his son Alberto die. One Sunday morning the poor child, aged ten, was stricken at school with bleeding from the nose, nausea, and colic. He then developed a fever, which never abated. After two days of vomiting, a sharp pain developed in his groin. His condition worsened with each passing day. So intense was his suffering, from which he had not an hour's respite for sixteen days, that he never stopped moaning and crying. Even the most hardened members of the family were overwhelmed.

Many died at home: children like Alberto (aged ten) and Orsino Lanfredini (six or seven); adolescents like Michele Verini (nineteen) and Lucrezia Lanfredini, Orsino's sister (twelve); young women like beautiful Mea with the ivory hands (aged twenty-three, eight days after giving birth to her fourth child, who lived no longer than the other three, all of whom died before they reached the age of two); and of course adults and elderly people. People at home repeatedly witnessed scenes of death: the fear, the preparations (confession, viaticum, extreme unction, preparation of the will, prayers), the funeral (with its wailing women, pomp, and solemn ceremony), and finally the cortege. When Valorino di Barna Ciuriani completed, in 1430, the memoirs begun by his grandfather in 1324, he may have cast a melancholy eye over the vital statistics of his family, recorded in the final pages. Between his twenty-fifth and thirtieth year he had witnessed the death of a month-old daughter and a father of fifty-eight. When he was thirty-seven he lost a daughter of fourteen and an eleven-month-old baby. When he was forty-seven he lost two daughters, aged thirteen and fifteen. And after reaching the age of sixty he lost three sons, all around thirty-five, his wife, a son aged fifty-four, and a granddaughter of seventeen. (I have omitted from this list any mention of the deaths of

Simone Martini, *Blessed Agostino Novello*, "A Child's Accident" (detail), polyptych, 1328-1330. While playing by the gates of the city, a boy is attacked by a wolf but saved by Saint Augustine's miraculous intervention. (Siena, Sant'Agostino.)

newborns.) Yet he did not begin his diary until he was twenty-five. The experience of death came very early: Valorino's son Luigi, who died at thirty-six, had already mourned these same deaths (of sisters aged fourteen, fifteen, and thirteen, a younger brother aged eleven months, and a brother aged thirty-one) when he himself was, respectively, nine, ten, nineteen, twenty, and thirty-one years of age.

There was nothing new about dying young and in pain, but the epidemics that ravaged Europe after 1348 made the experience of early and painful death quite common. The plague was particularly hard to bear because it took its greatest toll among the youngest and most innocent and struck them at home, in private, where they were supposed to be most secluded and protected, most tranquil and isolated.

The Development of Feelings

The foregoing suggests that the private world was the place where feelings were most likely to flourish. People obviously had frequent and powerful cause to vent their emotions. Such basic emotions as fear, joy, and sadness first revealed themselves in the intimacy of home, family, and neighborhood. After all, the private world was inhabited by the people to whom one felt closest and whose fate was particularly likely to elicit an emotional response. Women, whose lives rarely extended into the public arena, expressed their feelings most fully in private. Emotions were reinforced by other family members, who experienced them simultaneously. Fortunately, the period offers an abundance of family records and private correspondence, sources which enable us to see those emotions unfold.

Painting is an invaluable source of information. For the first time in Italian history, we have religious paintings, frescoes, composed of episodes in which various figures, who constitute a sort of Holy Family, give vent to their deepest feelings. Not all painters were equally successful in capturing these emotions, so let us concentrate on Giotto, the undisputed master of the fourteenth century, considered such and universally admired even at the time. Take, for example, the figures in the Scrovegni Chapel at Padua (ca. 1305). Anne and Joachim meet at the Golden Gate. In their embrace and features we read the indestructible love of a husband and wife long abused by fate but profoundly glad to be reunited at last. With the same look of grave tenderness, Saint Anne reaches out to her newborn daughter and later accompanies her to the high

Giotto, *Saint Joachim and Saint Anne at the Golden Gate* (detail), 1304-1306. According to a pious legend in the Apocrypha, Saint Joachim was forced into exile by the priests of the Temple. Upon his return to Jerusalem, he was met at the Golden Gate by his wife and her servants. (Padua, Scrovegni Chapel.)

priest. Later, in another scene, the Virgin, still lying on the rough boards where she has just given birth, receives for the first time from the midwives (mentioned in the Apocrypha) her swaddled child. Her gesture reveals all the respect, and her face all the tender, watchful veneration (mixed with fore-knowledge), that she feels for her son and creator. Years pass. Bending low over her dead son, she looks at him with the tearless desperation of one who can cry no more, determined in her grief to engrave in memory the features of the son who is soon to vanish forever. In the presence of Jesus' body she seems no more courageous or hopeful than any mother would be. Around her saints wail and moan.

The next century brought new talents, new styles, and new names to the fore, but Madonna and Child continued to inspire countless variations on familiar themes: tender feelings toward children, suffering, and death. With ever-greater technical and psychological mastery, the artists with their sacred iconography surely contributed to the sophistication of private sentiments. Free vent was given to innumerable feelings in-

Giotto, *Lamentations over the Body of Christ* (detail), 1304–1306. The curved, veiled silhouettes and pitiful gestures heighten the effect of the moment: a mother's final embrace of her tortured son. (Padua, Scrovegni Chapel.)

spired or heightened by the example of the painters, the popularity of an urbane and humanist literature, and the very structure of private life.

Harmonious family life, which was happily quite common, depended on creating and maintaining a climate of affection in the home warmer than could be found anywhere else. Of this the moralists, starting with Alberti, were convinced: whatever value was ascribed to friendship (for him the paramount virtue), he was obliged to admit that usually it was ranked second to conjugal love. Family conversation, open-hearted frankness, sex, children, household concerns—all contributed to the closeness of the married couple. As for paternal love, everyone knew how deep, tenacious, and even violent it could be. Nothing in the world was greater, more constant, or more all-embracing.

From literature and letters we learn how strong the mutual devotion of family members could be. Husbands and wives in this period were reticent about expressing their feelings for each other, but other emotions were poured out freely. Separated from her exiled sons, Alessandra Strozzi cannot refrain from filling her letters with sighs of frustrated love, which the passing years only rekindled: "I think I shall die of the need to see you again . . . With all my heart and soul I want to live where you are living. My only fear is that I shall die without seeing you again" (1450–1451). As one Florentine woman confided to another, "If you had had children, you would understand the strength of one's love for them."

Fathers were no less tender-hearted. Boccaccio, in his offhand way, uses and abuses the noble sentiments of fathers;

many a cuckold is deceived by feelings of tenderness toward his children. What is a monk in nightshirt doing in a woman's bedroom? Reading verse to a poor, sick child. The father effusively embraces his son's healer. But in memoirs and letters there is no shortage of more clear-sighted if equally powerful instances of paternal solicitude. In the writings of Giovanni Rucellai, Piero Guicciardini, Piero Vettori, Guido del Palagio, Cappone Capponi, Giovanni Morelli, and Ugolino Verini we find an attitude summed up by an aphorism that I borrow from one of them: "People say that the greatest love there is is that of a father for his son" (Florence, fourteenth–fifteenth century). The smile, indeed the mere presence of an infant very quickly elicits the love of both father and mother. According to Alberti, "the care given an infant by its mother is far more attentive and diligent than that of a nurse, and so is the mother's love." Reality was not always so benign, however. As we saw earlier, affluent Italians were the first to send their children off to a wet-nurse. Young widows in their haste to remarry abandoned infants still at the breast. Lower down the social ladder, we note a suspiciously small number of little girls relative to the number of little boys. For there were cases—perhaps a good many—in which poverty, disease, and the harshness of life eclipsed the feelings of parents for scarcely formed yet already burdensome children; infanticide was sometimes the result.

Affection between husband and wife was communicated to the children. It reinforced and rejuvenated the bonds that held the extended family together; even friends were included in its warmth. The child who was raised at home, particularly among the urban bourgeoisie with its many contacts and relations, became part of a dense and for the most part stable network of affections. Michele Verini, who so admired and cherished his father, was also very close to his Uncle Paolo ("you love me in a special way"), his tutor Lorenzo ("you love no one more than me"), and his friends; and the word he used to describe all these relations was *amore*, love (Florence, 1480). For him, to have a friend was to love someone (especially during his illness). Alessandra Strozzi, who commanded the affectionate respect of her daughters and sons-in-law (redoubled by the sight of the suffering she was forced to endure), lavished on her nephews and cousins all the affection that her exiled sons were not there to receive. But everyone acted this way, even men, whose feelings were held in check by respect for the proprieties. Between uncle and nephew,

Giotto, *The Massacre of the Innocent* (detail), 1304–1306. The mothers' gestures, movements, and faces reveal their impotent agony. (Padua, Scrovegni Chapel.)

cousin and cousin, friend and friend, esteem, with all its nuances—*fidanza, fede, stima*—was often coupled with affection. Men said as much and allowed their wives to repeat and write down their words: "You always showed him so much affection; help him." And people acted on their feelings, helping relatives with advice, jobs, and business assistance. Despite quarrels and disagreements, the family remained the prime breeding ground of an affection that extended to friends and relatives alike and was active and productive, the cornerstone of private solidarity.

Along with affection went the usual host of other feelings, which flourished in the private setting. Fortunately there was no lack of occasions for pleasure. The election of a cousin as prior could gladden the hearts of the entire family. News from an absent family member or of the birth of a child could make everyone happy. The height of joy, described several times by Boccaccio, was a private event with symbolic value: the surprise reunion of a scattered, perhaps desperate family. A mother is reunited with her long-lost son: torrents of tears, a thousand kisses, an "overflowing of the purest happiness." A father recognizes his daughter: his "joy [is] immense." Then he spies his son: a thousand stories are told, "punctuated by mutual tears of joy." Everyone agreed this was the ultimate happiness.

Yet affection was more often a matter of concern in an age when separation, exile, disease, and death were constant threats. Families worried about their absent members, as their letters attest. If an expected answer failed to arrive, waiting was tinged with *malinconia* (anxiety): "How can I describe those two months of anxiety, with no news of them! I was certain that something had happened to them!" (Alessandra Strozzi, 1451). If, in the end, the news was not good, anxiety turned to anguish: "Not knowing the nature of his illness, I was gripped by anguish" (the same, 1459). If someone at home fell ill, took to his bed, and was racked by pain, the worry and anguish were just as intense.

Death cut a swath of devastation. Families knew every shade of grief, from melancholy to despair. Yet they survived, because grief was simply the obverse of the feelings of affection that held the family together. The worse the pain, the more it was shared among family members, who were drawn together by their suffering. When twenty-three-year-old Matteo Strozzi died in Naples in 1459, everyone around Alessandra was greatly concerned. Their letters of condolence, each more

Giotto, *Death of the Knight of Celano* (detail), very late 13th century. A sudden death dumbfounds and frightens onlookers. The facial expressions are rather clumsily rendered in this very early Giotto, but at the time they were seen as remarkably truthful. (Assisi, Convent of Saint Francis, Upper Church.)

tactful than the next, are filled with sorrow. The news was broken by a cousin, who had heard it directly from Naples. He invited a number of relatives to his home; Alessandra was sent for, the news was broken to her gently, and all who had gathered at the cousin's house offered their compassion. There was much mutual consolation in letters and conversations, and friends and relatives exhorted one another to stand by Alessandra and support her in this time of trial. The bereaved mother did more than her share to aid in this general process of healing. As the living heart of her household, she made sure that the tokens of affection she had received were shared by the entire family. The rude shock of Matteo's death actually drew the family together and even renewed ties with its more distant allies.

Tears, it seems, were usually shed in private. We do not know whether people cried in public, but at home they did cry, at funerals and reunions, when they suffered and when they were happy. Were they especially sensitive? Yes, but it was more that tears were a kind of language whose place was in the private sphere. Letters and storytellers tell of lonely tears shed by those suddenly made aware of a solitude enforced by death, absence, or abandonment, that is, by the abrupt end of a comfortably domestic private existence. But more often tears were shared with relatives and friends when a family suffered a loss beyond words; in such circumstances no other language would do. When people met after years of separation, they embraced in tearful silence (Boccaccio, II, 6 and 8; V, 6 and 7). They cried tears of compassion (Boccaccio, II, 6; III, 7; VIII, 7) and tears of repentance. And they cried when they shared a common pain. Still shaken by the news of the death of his young brother-in-law Matteo, Marco Parenti received two letters in quick succession. One, which described his wife's suffering, caused him to break down and cry. The other, which focused on his mother-in-law's distress, completely overwhelmed him: "My tears were doubled." Marco's tears signify that he has made his in-law's suffering wholly his own. Although his subsequent letters are filled with expressions of compassion, he presents his silent tears as the most eloquent witness to his deep feeling for his wife's family. Shared tears, even at a distance, speak louder than words. Men as well as women used the language of tears; crying transcended all conventions.

Only women cried at funerals, but these ritual tears were intended to communicate the family's pain to the public at large. Not to shed them was an insult to the honor of the deceased. But such tears were of necessity extravagant, a travesty of true feelings which did nothing to enhance family intimacy.

Training the Body and Mind

The mind, like the sensibility, was shaped at home. Training of body and mind was initially a private concern. School, however important it may have been, came later, in every sense.

Education began at the nipple, and the child's nurse was its first teacher. Families were advised to exercise care in choosing a wet-nurse, and to beware, as Palmieri put it, of the epidemic of "Tartars, Saracens, barbarians, and other energumens." The same author offered a myriad of other recommendations concerning the prospective nurse's breasts, breath, age, demeanor, and so on. There was good reason for caution. Important tasks awaited the successful candidate: besides giving of her milk, the nurse was expected to sing the baby to sleep, correct its speech, and even manipulate its face to correct a misplaced mouth or nose or a case of nearsightedness (Francesco di Barberino).

The child's "natural" teachers began their ministrations even before the nurse had completed hers. Alberti, Francesco Barbaro, and other moralists recommended that the mother take charge of the child's early education: "The care of very young children is women's work, for nurses or the mother," as Alberti put it. But she was soon joined by the father, who, in the eyes of the moralists, bore primary responsibility for the child's moral and intellectual upbringing. It was recommended that training begin quite early. Palmieri reports that some people delayed their children's instruction until they reached the age of seven. This, he says, is pure laziness. Teaching should start while the child is still with the nurse, beginning with the rudiments of the alphabet. Parents who followed this advice enjoyed a two-year head start. Boys required a teacher from the time they were seven. Maffeo Veggio insists that boys should be sent to school, where they can make friends with other boys. Other moralists favored a private tutor, advice that was adopted by Giovanni Morelli in the fourteenth century. Later, Lorenzo de' Medici and many others were taught by private tutors.

Domenico Ghirlandaio, *Scenes from the Life of Saint Francis*, "The Confirmation of the Rule" (detail), 1483–1486. Patrician families often entrusted their sons to tutors. Angelo Politiano, who here leads the way, filled this post for the children of Lorenzo de' Medici, who are shown following behind him. (Florence, Santa Trinità, Sassetti Chapel.)

Thus, in affluent families most if not all of the children's education could take place in the home. In this respect the wealthy were closer to the peasants and the working class than to the middle classes. Homes were increasingly well equipped with educational facilities. As the Renaissance proceeded, bourgeois houses became more and more suitable places for intellectual pursuits, equipped with quiet rooms, writing desks, lecterns, bookcases, and sometimes even libraries (found in palaces in Florence, Milan, Venice, Naples, and Rome). The adults who provided these facilities were the first to take advantage of them, but the children also profited.

Teaching the young was an absorbing task that involved many household members. The young humanist Michele Verini was first taught by his father, who began his lessons quite early, surely before Michele reached the age of seven. But the further he progressed, the larger his household teaching staff grew; between his tenth and fifteenth years his father employed a half-dozen teachers for the boy. His uncle Paolo, a

Benozzo Gozzoli, *Scenes from the Life of Saint Augustine*, "The saint is taken to the grammar teacher," 1463–1465. The artist was inspired both by the *Confessions* and by his own school experience. In Italy children of different ages were taught by a single teacher. The school was another private world, in which the schoolmaster took the place of parental authority. (San Gimignano, Sant'Agostino.)

physician in his mid-thirties, taught him the rudiments of mathematics and the Bible; his instruction in the former subject was eventually completed by another uncle, the mathematician Lorenzo Lorenzi. A priest and a grammarian taught him Latin until Cristoforo Landino and Angelo Poliziano learned of the boy's gifts and agreed to offer him their invaluable assistance; he was not yet fifteen. Michele took some lessons outside the house, others at home. He found touching phrases to tell each of his teachers how much he cherished them and how, by teaching him, they were discharging a paternal duty, a *paternum officium*. As the boy's tutors, all these eminent persons, most of them professors at the *studio* (university) of Florence, entered into his private domain. The domestic faculty, composed of father, uncles, relatives, and illustrious *amici*, devoted much time and attention to the education of their young pupil. They exchanged visits, wrote letters, solicited advice, and consulted one another about their plans. It was impossible to do too much for a brilliant young man.

The objectives of this domestic education were not exclusively private, however; far from it. The purpose of a boy's education was to put him rapidly in possession of the tools of his trade, so that he could properly and efficiently discharge his public functions. Bourgeois families prided themselves on equipping their sons for political careers. As Palmieri points out, a boy's education consisted not of separate lessons on "how to organize a business, how to converse with one's fellow citizens, and . . . how to run a household . . . but of a unified, practical course of instruction" that covered all these things. Given the decisive role that family and lineage played in political life, public success depended on fidelity to private family values.

Families were less ambitious when it came to educating their daughters. Although children of both sexes attended the schools of Florence in 1338, the wisdom of education for girls was passionately debated, and many moralists were opposed. Women of leading families were a case apart. Their social responsibilities required a certain level of culture. They were therefore taught to write, and some of them did it very well. Many liked to read. In the fifteenth century the most gifted knew Latin and sometimes Greek well enough to earn the *satisfecit* of a humanist like Leonardo Bruni. Those who aspired to be nuns learned to read and write, and some studied Latin. Apart from these privileged few, however, women were educated with an eye to marriage, childrearing, and other private responsibilities and values. This was the recommendation of both Francesco Barbaro (*De re uxoria*, 1416) and Maffeo Veggio (*De educatione liberorum*, 1440). As a future mother, teacher of morality and religion, and model for her own daughters, the adolescent girl, Veggio said, should "be raised on sacred teachings to lead a regular, chaste, and religious life and to devote all her time to female labors," punctuated by prayer. Barbaro placed greater stress on practical training. But the two authors were in agreement as to general principles, principles to which many others also subscribed. Since mothers were in their eyes the repository of private values, it was desirable for them to devote themselves entirely to the defense and inculcation of those values. The education of young girls was predicated on this belief.

Relations with the Outside World

Protected though they were by doors, locks, distrust of outsiders, and solidarity with relatives and neighbors, individuals and households did interact with the outside world as a matter of everyday necessity. Even the best guarded of houses was not impervious to visits by the indiscreet or importunate. Domestic arguments became known outside the house. Changes in mood, behavior, and appearance did not go unnoticed by local gossips (Boccaccio IX, 5). Neighbor spied on neighbor whenever a glance across the way seemed worth the trouble. Narrow streets made voyeurs of everyone. A judge asks: "Did Monna Selvazza live as a prostitute?" Her honest neighbor replies: "From a window with a view of Monna S.'s house, she [the neighbor] saw her countless times naked in bed with naked men engaging in all the turpitudes commonly associated with prostitutes" (Florence, 1400). Nothing went unnoticed for long by nosy neighbors, and gossips reported on everything, starting with affairs of the heart.

Visitors

It was as easy to enter someone's home as to spy on him. Beggars, street musicians, and would-be suitors congregated in front of the gates of great houses, and many actually crossed the threshold. Apart from professional beggars and neighborhood children, many people who performed indispensable services came and went daily. Sharecroppers paid their landlords with crops stored in the attic or cellar; some needed as

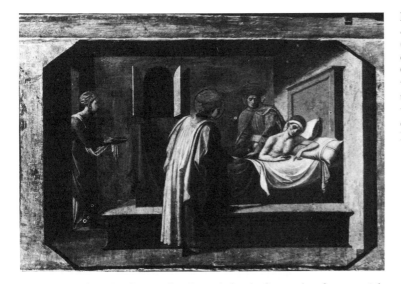

Pesellino, *Scenes from the Life of Saint Como and Saint Damian* (detail), fragment of predella, ca. 1450. Like their patrons, Como and Damian, physicians were regularly admitted into the intimacy of the bedroom, which occasionally served as an operating room. (Paris, Louvre.)

many as a hundred trips back and forth from the farm, with sacks loaded on the back of a donkey. A street vendor might hawk his wares in the entryway. A neighbor's servant might come to visit a comrade employed within. The barber arrived to do his duty. (In Ravenna barbers were required to go to the homes of knightly clients.) The physician might come to visit his patient, or the midwife to attend a pregnant member of the family. Notaries and witnesses came for the signing of contracts. Marriage negotiations were conducted by intermediaries. Priests came to discharge their functions—visiting the sick, administering extreme unction, and so on. One could easily multiply examples. In addition there were the occasional drinking companions, banquet guests, paupers invited in for a meal, and guests who were received for a night or two or even longer. Wealthy families considered it a duty to receive guests, in keeping with the ethic of opulence defined, for example, by the Neapolitan Giovanni Pontano at the end of the fifteenth century. Liberality and hospitality were among the inescapable duties of the rich.

Not all guests were admitted very far into the privacy of the home. Many barely made it across the threshold. Drinking companions were apparently received in a ground-floor room off the storeroom; the upstairs living room was used for business discussions, suppers, and conversations with acquaintances and associates. The bedroom was more private, though not totally inaccessible. Jesters were allowed in, as were farmers sometimes, and of course those who attended the ill: barbers, physicians, midwives, and priests with all their retinue. In the *rocche*, rural castles of the feudal nobility, the bedroom often enjoyed the same prestige as in a royal palace; here nobles stored the documents on which their power was founded and in the presence of notaries and witnesses registered important contracts.

Hospitality required that guests be offered a place to sit in front of the fire or at the dinner table. Priests and physicians seated themselves familiarly on a patient's sickbed to hear confession or take a pulse. Guests received for the night were sometimes offered a place in a bed that was already occupied. This standard practice in the inns and hospitals was also accepted in the home.

Receiving guests did not violate the intimacy of the household. True, stories might be told outside; there was a risk, or at any rate a fear, of robbery (as Saint Bernardine recounts); and improvised sleeping arrangements could provoke quarrels or arouse caresses. But none of this was particularly serious.

School of Ghirlandaio, *Succor in the Home Offered by Members of the Confraternity of San Martino dei Buonuomini*, late 15th century. The private life of the poor—often women living alone—was alleviated by charitable visits, generally by men, since organized charity was controlled by the confraternities—male institutions—of which San Martino was the most important. This woman who has just given birth must have suffered some temporary reverse in her fortunes, for she lies in a grand bed surrounded by impressive chests. (Florence, San Martino dei Buonuomini.)

It was not easy for a woman, especially a young, unmarried woman, to go beyond sporadic contact with outsiders and confront the world on her own. Women were watched closely; most people thought this was as it should be, and certain moralists agreed. For Paolo da Certaldo, "woman is a vain and frivolous thing . . . If you have women in your house, keep an eye on them. Survey the premises often, and while going about your business keep them in a state of apprehension and fear." Later he adds: "Women should emulate the Virgin Mary, who did not leave her house to go drinking all over town, ogle handsome men, or listen to a lot of idle talk. No, she stayed home, behind closed doors, in the privacy of her own home, as was only proper."

Little girls could be indulged. Of course by the time they were three they were made to sleep in separate rooms and beds and obliged to sleep in nightgowns (as were boys); modesty was essential (G. Dominici). But no one thought of preventing them from roaming the neighborhood doing favors for the neighbors or from going home with uncles who came to visit or from meeting at a friend's home (as did the companions of little Catherine Benincasa, whose mother was very strict).

By the age of twelve, however, a girl's freedom was finished. Catherine was locked up at home, as was customary in Siena. Her father and brothers (brothers played a major role in protecting their sisters) kept her under close guard, and the moralists, in their insistence on this theme, reveal how seriously it was taken by the public at large. Fra Paolino considered twelve the age when fathers were well advised to heighten their vigilance by forbidding their daughters to idle about town or even engage in private conversation. Diligent and silent work at home was the only way to deal with the foolish dreams that filled the heads of these brainless creatures. Francesco da Barberino paid greater attention to rank. Young ladies of high station were to be brought up strictly, though not as strictly as young princesses. Attention was to be paid to the men they saw, to the flattery they received, even to the looks directed at them. Young ladies should be kept at home and away from the windows. Fewer precautions were necessary in the lower classes. Maffeo Veggio warns against bad company: boys, girls from outside the family, servants of dubious moral character. For this the woman of the house bore responsibility. People were so circumspect that they even refrained from bringing their daughters to church, despite angry

Women and the Outside World

Filippo Lippi, *Scenes from the Life of Saint John the Baptist,* "Dance of Salome" (detail), ca. 1450–1465. Ostensibly a portrait of Salome, the painting in fact depicts a girl dancing at a sumptuous Tuscan banquet in the painter's own time. It was permissible for a girl to dance alone in front of her parents' guests, but only in a strictly private setting. (Prato, Duomo.)

words from the preachers. Piety, chastity, and honor were the watchwords of maidenly behavior.

Marriage brought only a partial relaxation of this imprisonment. Despite their newfound household responsibilities, wives were subject to the will of their husbands as far as relations with the outside world were concerned. Some husbands were odious and ill-tempered: "Say nothing of going to weddings, celebrations, or church or even leaving the house; this wife [of a Rimini merchant] did not dare stand next to a window or so much as glance outside for any reason" (Boccaccio, VII, 5). Such extremes were rarely encountered, and all women were indignant about them. But if that was the way the master was, what could be done about it?

The moralists' long-winded severity toward these fifteen-year-old "scatterbrains" shows that there is more going on here than meets the eye. For all the bluster, the women's quarters were not impenetrable. The moralists' tone awakens our curiosity. Just how porous were the walls?

Even the most severely cloistered homes had doors and windows, at which we have already seen censorious critics level a finger of suspicion. Windows were a diversion and a temptation: open to the street, they were nevertheless protected against prying eyes by shutters. From windows one could watch and stare, converse, or show oneself. Indolent beauties "sat there all day long, leaning on their elbows, holding in their hands an excuse in the form of a book that seemed

Antonello da Messina, *Saint Sebastian* (detail), 1475. An evening chat between two women on a Renaissance balcony that surrrounds their palace, while the handsome young Sebastian sighs in the courtyard below. (Dresden, Gemäldegalerie.)

Vittore Carpaccio, *Saint Trifone Exorcises the Emperor's Daughter* (detail), 1507. From decorated windows in which they show themselves in their finest attire, the ladies contemplate the great urban spectacle, in this case a battle between the saint and the beast. (Venice, Scuola di San Giorgio degli Schiavoni.)

Cosme Tura and Francesco Cossa, *Triumph of Minerva* (detail), ca. 1470. Moralists recommended finding tasks to occupy the women of the house. A sampling of their work (weaving, embroidery) is shown in this celebrated composition. (Ferrara, Schifanoia Palace.)

never to end" (Alberti). Near the main entrance of the house ladies sat in the evening to chat and watch the passersby (Saint Antonino). Because the door was so close to the street, this area was reserved for matrons; young girls were not allowed to sit here unless chaperoned. Yet this was a place of some prestige: on traditional holidays the women of the household assembled here to show themselves off to the town. In Milan we find "matrons and maidens sitting in the doorway on holidays. With so much gold, silver, enamel, and the occasional pearl sparkling on their finest attire it would be easy to mistake them for queens or princesses of the blood" (G. Fiamma).

Contact with the outside world for young girls as well as mature women seldom was limited to such occasions. Domestic and religious duties provided daily opportunities to venture outside the home. Some women, especially among the poor, held jobs outside. Others gathered in the market, around the well, or at the mill. The church was a favorite destination, especially of well-to-do women whose servants deprived them of the excuse of having to run errands and who had plenty of time on their hands. The devout had ample opportunity to spend hours in church, especially on holidays and during Lent, and it was fashionable for upper-class women to gather in church for certain ceremonies: "Sunday morning all the women go to the Franciscan church" (Pecorone). Even young women (of relatively modest background, at any rate) took part in local pilgrimages, visiting two or three churches in succession without any kind of chaperonage (Boccaccio, IV, 7).

To cast a glance or take a step outside the home was to risk meeting people, and in particular men, from outside one's private world. For adolescent girls such encounters often led to infatuation. Certain attachments grew out of childhood friendships or long familiarity, others out of a chance meeting at an inn. In urban bourgeois families, however, where girls were strictly supervised and not permitted to discover the world except through the window, romance often began with a glance. Innocent young girls fell for young gentlemen merely because they happened to pass by. (In Palermo in 1280, the daughter of a pharmacist, while "stationed at the window with other ladies," made the blunder of falling for the king himself.) Far more disturbing were the exchanges of glances. Young dandies strutted up and down beneath the windows, and woe unto the unfortunate girl who happened to meet one of their fatal stares! Such an encounter could mark the beginning of a long seduction, conducted sometimes without the parents' knowledge, sometimes with their tacit approval. Let us eavesdrop for a moment on a dialogue between a Venetian mother and her daughter:

"Where is your scarf, dear?"
"I don't know, mother. Somehow it came loose last night while I was on the balcony, and I have no idea how it could have fallen. A young man picked it up."
"How long has this ruse been going on?"
"Nearly a year, mother."

—Lionardo Giustinian, early fifteenth century

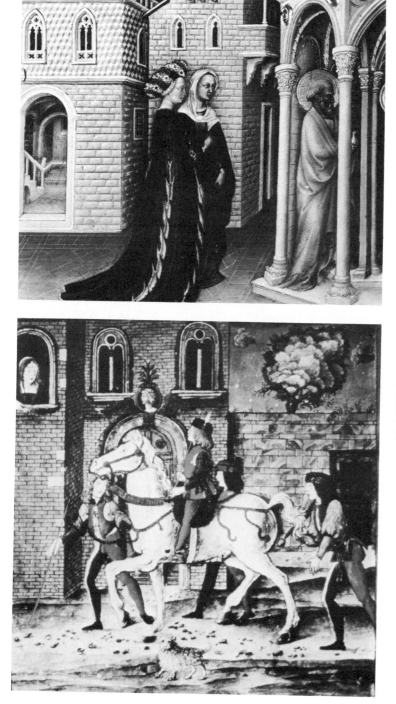

Gentile da Fabriano, *Presentation at the Temple* (detail), predella, first quarter of the 15th century. Two well-dressed patrician women alone in the street? Yes, but with the appropriate dignity and modesty and the excuse of a religious ceremony. (Paris, Louvre.)

Disciple of Cristoforo da Predis, *Massimiliano Sforza in Milan*, 15th century. Galloping into Milan in search of romantic adventures, the young prince draws glances and sighs from the women in the windows. (Milan, Trivulziana Library.)

Giovanni Mansueti, *Miracle of the True Cross* (detail), ca. 1506. For a procession, mansards, windows, transoms, grills, shutters, and every other opening onto the square are filled with female figures. Windows here play the role of pulpits in churches. Among the spectators, dressed to the nines, devotion is rivaled by curiosity and vanity. (Venice, Accademia.)

Girls in Genoa were no different. A local poet describes them as "young nymphs of marriageable age. Anyone can spot them, stationed in their windows so as to see and be seen. Every damsel smiles at her beau. Or perhaps she will toss him flowers, fruits, nuts, anything that can serve as a token of love. Confessions of love and light banter pass back and forth . . . If a father catches his daughter in the act, he does not punish her, even if the beau is a good friend. Imprisoned as she is, she can do no harm by speaking tender words to her chosen one. Nothing of consequence will come of it." Everywhere one heard the strains of dawn and evening serenades. (Boys and girls also met, more prosaically, at innumerable holiday celebrations.)

Marriage

Marriage was the crucial moment in a woman's private life. In the Trecento the period of infatuations ended early: girls were married off quite young. In 1370 the average age at marriage was sixteen in Prato (Tuscany). In 1427, again in Prato and in Florence, the average was seventeen and a half. Around 1350 in Siena parents began planning a daughter's marriage as early as age twelve. A hundred years later they delayed a little longer, until age fourteen, and girls actually wed at sixteen or eighteen. There was further evolution after

this date. In 1470, in Prato, Florence, and the surrounding countryside, most brides were twenty or twenty-one. The long delay may account for the new exuberance of romantic scenes such as those just described, which rarely led to marriage.

Marriage was what counted. Whatever the girl's age, her parents did not casually make a decision with such important consequences for their private lives. The choice was subjected to lengthy scrutiny, sometimes for years. Negotiations were conducted by the parents and in some cases by third parties, sometimes professional marriage brokers. At the same time the girl began her seduction, for unless the boy was won over, the negotiations would not succeed. Nothing was done that might compromise the girl, but she could be presented in a window or doorway, flanked by chaperones, with all the pomp and circumstance of a tableau vivant. She must be well scrubbed—Monna Pica scolds her daughter Catherine (of Siena) for her carelessness in this regard: "Wash your face"— carefully coiffed, perfectly trim, and careful not to smile too much: a little icon, who everyone hoped would succeed in capturing the devotion of the eligible young men. If all went well, there was no lack of suitors. Then the problem was to choose. All sorts of considerations were taken into account: the dowry, the prospective groom's social background, his occupation. Was there a possibility of partnership? Would the marriage better the girl's social position? (At Fiesole in 1338 an artisan was considered a worthy son-in-law for a peasant.) Did the groom's family wield political influence? Where did they live? (The closer the better.) Did the lineage give at least tacit consent? How did the girl herself feel? Once again the moralists are not short on advice. Dominici: "Marry your daughter to someone of your own class, with the desired dowry." Alberti: "To take a wife is to search for beauty, kindred, and riches. Seek advice from all your elders. They know all there is to know about the families of the candidates, including generations past." No marriage could be successful unless both sides knew each other well.

Master of the *Cassone* Adimari, *The Marriage of Boccaccio Adimari and Lisa Ricasoli* (detail), painted on a *cassone* (wedding chest), 15th century. Procession in front of the Florence Baptistry of young men and women participating in the sumptuous rite of the *ductio ad maritum*, the installation of the bride in her husband's home. (Florence, Accademia.)

To marry first her daughters, then her sons, was Alessandra Strozzi's chief concern. After succeeding with the former, she turned her attention to her sons, in which she was aided by her two sons-in-law. Innumerable negotiations, consultations, and hesitations ensued. Some of the prospects were ravishing, in particular the Tanagli girl, glimpsed at Santa Maria del Fiore just as sunlight, filtered through the windows of the church, limned her charming silhouette in angelic radiance. Alas, all of them left something to be desired. One was brainless, another penniless (and of undistinguished stock). Alessandra finally came to a decision, but only after much anguish. No effort was too great when the family's happiness, honor, security, and survival were all at stake.

At last the wedding day arrived, with all its pomp. Worked out over centuries, the complexity of the ritual suggests the importance of the occasion for both families, joined together for one brief moment. In his diary for 1393 the merchant Gregorio Dati notes: "On 31 March 1393 I consented and pledged myself under oath to take Isabetta for my wife. On 7 April, Easter Monday, I gave her the ring in the presence of Ser Luca, notary. On 22 June, a Sunday, after nones, she moved into my house, the home of her husband, in the name of God and good fortune." Without undue romanticism, quite in the impersonal style of the merchant, this young newlywed faithfully recorded the three customary stages of Tuscan marriage in the early modern period. Negotiations between the two families having reached a successful conclusion, a first contract was signed to record their mutual pledge. In the days, weeks, months, or years that followed, the espousal was celebrated. In a formality omitted from Gregorio's account, the fiancé delivered a receipt for the dowry in the presence of a notary, who then heard the consent of both parties and presided over the exchange of rings—with nary a priest in sight. To the question "Do you, so-and-so, take you, so-and-so . . . ?" bride and groom responded "Yes" or "Yes, sir" (*Messer si*, according to Poppi and Casentino, 1388). Then the groom placed a gold (or gold-plated silver) ring on the right ring finger of his bride and a similar ring on his own ring finger. (In some cases there was a mutual exchange of rings.) In Bologna knights and doctors were entitled to two rings, and three gold rings were needed when Leopold of Austria married Verde Visconti in Milan in 1350. Then the venerable paterfamilias (or his eldest son, if the father was deceased) officially transferred authority over his daughter to his new son-in-law.

In burlesque counterpoint to this solemn ceremony, an on-looker would occasionally give the groom a vigorous clap on the back at the moment he spoke his "Yes," presumably to indicate the vexation of the local male population. (This blow is often reproduced in frescoes depicting the marriage of the Virgin.) The wedding ceremony proper was followed by stage three of the marriage, the installation of the bride in her husband's home. This blessed moment was often delayed, sometimes for months or even years (often for financial reasons), and families had to bear the continuing burden of young maidens who were *maritate* but not *ite* (that is, not yet physically settled in the husband's house), because her kin had not been able to assemble the required dowry. These difficulties were usually ironed out in the end, and a new household was constituted, like a tiny cell splitting off from its parent cell and beginning life on its own.

Clandestine Escapes

Brief flirtations rarely led to marriage: lovers were contemporaries, husbands seniors. But flirtation could lead to other things. Not all marriages were happy or faithful. Escapades were conducted discreetly. The subject of clandestine loves is a vast one, thoroughly explored by storytellers and thoroughly obscured by participants; there is no way of counting secrets, no matter how calamitous. Such love affairs were common, however: everyone said so, and everyone laughed or complained about them. Many considered them a fundamental right.

Servants and slaves, many of them radiant young girls, offered the men of the house a distraction that discouraged outside escapades. Bourgeois memoirs are filled with the names of bastard offspring. Margherita Datini complained about her young maids (1390), and the moneychanger Lippo del Sega celebrated his seventieth birthday by raping his servant (Florence, 1363). So much for the backdrop. The presence of cousins and nieces could also be disturbing, particularly when they shared the same bedroom. Cases of incest were occasionally heard in the courts, as at Pisa in 1413, where a cousin and niece were involved; this form of deviant behavior was perhaps more widespread than it appears.

Outside the home there was ample opportunity for fleeting adventure or regular rendezvous, and perhaps even for enduring attachment. Every city, even every town (in Liguria) had its prostitutes. As centuries came and went, the prostitutes

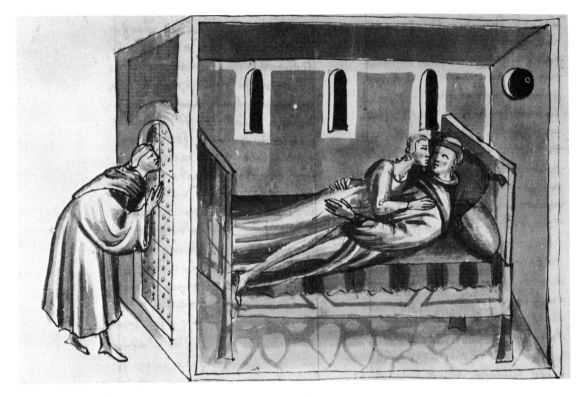

remained, despite attempts by the communes to hamper their trade (by regulating their attire, residence, comings and goings, and taxes). Yet even these regulations could be relaxed. Bordellos were set up in Florence in 1325 and 1415 and in Genoa before 1336. In fact cities sometimes encouraged prostitution as the lesser of two evils, a means of preventing graver problems such as homosexuality (Florence, 1403). The omnipresence of prostitution; the surprisingly large numbers of prostitutes, especially in Venice (where there were more than 11,000 in the sixteenth century), Rome, and Naples; the wealth and social success of certain prostitutes in Roman and Venetian high society in the fifteenth century—all illustrate the success of the profession and the role played by prostitutes in breaching, however furtively, the barriers that protected the family's strict privacy.

Homosexual encounters were similar in their effect, although they sometimes led to more lasting relationships. Homosexuals were everywhere—in Naples, Bologna, Venice, and Genoa, for instance. But the sermons of the most brilliant Tuscan preachers (Giordano of Pisa, ca. 1310, and Bernardine

Anonymous, *Decameron,* illustrated manuscript, 1427. Two monks, champions, according to the storytellers, of the sport of love. At the door of his abbot's bedroom, a monk spies on the amorous activities of the woman he held in his arms a few moments earlier. (Paris, Bibliothèque Nationale, Italian 63, fol. 20v.)

of Siena, ca. 1420), Dante's barbs (*Inferno*, XV and XVI); and alarmed discussions by the authorities, coupled with quite stringent repressive measures in the early fourteenth and early fifteenth century suggest that Siena, and especially Florence, were the principal centers. (*Florenzer* meant homosexual in German.) The preachers dotted their *i*'s and crossed their *t*'s, leaving no doubt that the primary offense was pederasty involving males between the ages of eight and thirty, all or almost all unmarried. These practices may have been not so much an alternative to married life as a range of substitutes, invented by young men compelled to wait many years before they were allowed to marry and therefore forced to seek other means of forging their identities and creating a private life for themselves. Nevertheless, homosexual activity was at variance with traditional moral norms, and the vogue for it posed a problem. Without delving into causes, let us note Saint Antonino's observation that permissive parents were to blame for their unhealthy indulgence of "childish games," which suggests that there was a link between pederasty and changes in the private life of the family. It is possible that in a world where such traditional masculine outlets as politics and warfare had lost some of their luster, boys were increasingly susceptible to values such as gentleness, politeness, and affection, which were perceived as feminine. Furthermore, many fathers were frequently absent from the home or much older than their sons, hence by the time the latter reached working age the father's authority over them had diminished or evaporated.

As for true clandestine love, think of it as a vast theater whose actors were drawn from every family and where men shared the stage with the coquettes and maidens we met earlier, now grown older and perhaps a trifle gone to seed. Those who remained unmarried were testing their independence; those who had married were asserting theirs, creating for themselves a second private realm outside the home, just as their men did. The storytellers regale us with an endless variety of amorous adventures, recounted from the first sigh to the final moment of ecstasy. Gifts were exchanged, servants (often the lady's maid) shuttled back and forth, rendezvous were set at home, in the garden, at the baths. The jealous husband's stratagems were circumvented and the goal achieved: Long live love! Twists in the plot occasionally resulted in wife-swapping (Boccaccio VIII, 8) and bigamy. Laws against the latter (Venice, 1288; Genoa, thirteenth century; Bologna, 1498) also publicized it, but without concrete details.

Sometimes events took a darker turn; the lovers rid themselves
of the encumbering husband; farce turned to tragedy. In the
archives of justice we can read minutely detailed interrogations
of the murderers and their accomplices and watch the poignant
drama unfold.

On numerous occasions, usually dictated by tradition, the   *Ostentatious Display*
family, extended or narrow, shared its intimacy and its private
affairs with the public. Private events sometimes required public witness or participation: weddings, funerals, baptisms, reunions, a son's accession to knighthood, and so on. At all
levels of society these ceremonies were staged with particular
publicity, and the throngs that attended far exceeded the limits
of the family and its private associates. In the lengthy marriage
process, the betrothal and transfer of the ring were private,
but the final rites—the initiation of cohabitation and the visit
to the paternal home (which, at Chioggia in the late thirteenth
century, occurred eight days later)—were the object of a splendid public celebration, especially among the *popolo grasso*.
Guests, acquaintances, clients, onlookers—hundreds of persons participated in the festivities staged in June 1466 by Giovanni Rucellai in honor of the marriage of his son Bernardo to
Nannina de' Medici, Cosimo's granddaughter. Sideboards,
stables, and storerooms were heaped with gifts (mostly wine),
sent by entire villages, monasteries, and even nameless peasants as well as by friends and relatives.

The *ductio ad maritum*, or escort of the bride to her husband, was traditionally public, so much so that in many places
(Piedmont, Lombardy, Tuscany) fourteenth-century custom
permitted local communities to take part. Remarriages were a
special target, particularly in the fifteenth century, and bands
of youths or even the entire village demonstrated loudly and
memorably as the cortege passed, taunting the bride and making weird noises and obscene speeches, ending with a distribution of money or wine

When someone died, especially if he was a great personage, the public for miles around was apprised of the fact by
the piercing screams of women. The women of the family
gathered around the body, left to lie in state in the church.
Men stationed themselves outside (Florence, fourteenth
century).

Other public celebrations included homecomings, reunions, and banquets staged to honor a reconciliation between

Pisanello, *Wedding Banquet*, panel of a wedding chest, first half of the 15th century. A banquet was held to celebrate the final rites of marriage. A podium and dais for the newlyweds are seen, as are squires and valets. Engraved silver plates are displayed on a sideboard. (Venice, Correr Museum.)

feuding clans (an event of considerable importance in Italy). In all these ceremonies the family honor was at stake. To lose face in front of strangers was unthinkable. Eventually there came to be a set decorum for such events, the purpose of which was to avoid embarrassing blunders and to show the family off to advantage, while private secrets remained hidden beneath a splendid facade.

A proper reception required abundant food and drink. Banquets were showpieces. For Bernardo's wedding Giovanni Rucellai had a platform of nearly 2,000 square feet erected in the street and filled with tables, at which as many as five hundred people a day feasted, served by fifty chefs and kitchen-boys working in a nearby kitchen, which had been built expressly for the occasion. Not every affair could boast of such magnificence, but all ended with a banquet. The decor rivaled the cuisine. An eminent personality like Rucellai carefully decorated the festival platform with tapestries, rich fabrics, and fine furniture. To protect the diners in case of inclement weather, an immense cloth canopy, light blue in color, brocaded and festooned with garlands of greenery mingled with roses, was stretched over the platform. A credenza of chased silver stood on the platform. People of more modest means spread greenery over the floors and decorated walls and windows with tapestries, woven fabric, or just plain cloth.

Most feverish of all was the attention paid to personal appearance, to makeup and above all to clothing. People dressed up whenever they appeared in public. For major occasions such as weddings the bourgeoisie spent impressive amounts on clothing. Along with many other gifts, Marco Parenti gave his fiancée two ultrasumptuous items for their wedding, a *giornea* and a *cotta*, plus a hat of peacock feathers, for which he spent a total of 1,000 lire, or four to five years' wages for a good mason. The case is typical. When ladies of good society paid even an informal call on a pregnant friend, they took care about their dress. When Lucrezia Tornabuoni posed as Saint Elizabeth for the frescoes in Santa Maria Novella, she wore a magnificent *guarnacca* of old pink silk studded with gold stars and worn on top of a white silk *gamurra*, embroidered with pomegranates and flowers, whose slashed shoulders permitted bloused sleeves to protrude. In this attire she stood for Ghirlandaio.

Over the generations fancy clothes, particularly those of women, grew steadily more varied and sumptuous. The quality of the fabric improved as silk, and silk of a richer sort,

Domenico Ghirlandaio, *Scenes from the Life of the Virgin*, "Birth of Saint John the Baptist" (detail), 1486–1490. Dressed for visiting and flanked by two matrons, Lucrezia Tornabuoni enters the magnificent home of a patrician friend who has recently become a mother. (Florence, Santa Maria Novella.)

came into common use. Wardrobes became more varied, and a taste for precious accessories developed. In a Bolognese document that dates from 1401 and describes nearly two hundred female costumes, we note 24 decorated with silver, 68 with gold (fringes, embroidered ornaments, brocades), and 48 lined with fur. Our impression, one reinforced by surviving household inventories, is that fifteenth-century noblewomen were increasingly able to indicate their rank by their dress. What is more, they did so without explicit reference to clan or family; their paramount concern was to distinguish themselves personally by means of dress, makeup, and even a hairstyle that showed off their individual features. Dress publicly demonstrated the illustriousness of a woman's family but without identifying which family was involved. By thus emphasizing the individual, clothing affirmed the value of women and avenged their private subjugation.

THE AUTHORITIES AND PRIVACY

The crucial place of private, primarily family, values and concerns in people's lives and the lives of their communities called for attention from the authorities, and occasionally for action.

Communal Legislation

The communes took notice of the existence of private groups at an early date. The words consortes, family, offspring, and brothers recur frequently in official documents, indicating a human, social, and above all political reality with which the authorities were obliged to reckon. Families were suspect; private groups usurped the functions of still fragile thirteenth-century governments. Rival families clashed, each seeking to further its own interests and ambitions. Against these powers—*magnati*, contemporaries called them—the communes raised ramparts of law. This was the first legislation concerning private groups, and it was defensive, aimed at imposing peace.

Suspicious or not (those who ruled the cities favored the families that supported them), this legislation would have had little effect on what went on in private had it not sought to regulate the content of private life as well as external relations between private groups. Roman law codified private as well as public matters, and we saw earlier that in the twelfth and thirteenth centuries Bolognese jurists commented extensively on such questions as the role of the paterfamilias. Following

their lead, the communes constantly leveled their sights on the
content of private life, a subject evoked in many different
contexts in statutes adopted in the thirteenth and fourteenth
centuries. Even at this early date municipalities were passing
laws concering private housing, specifying the maximum
height of buildings, the materials of which they were to be
constructed, and their alignment (Siena, fourteenth century);
or they were levying taxes on corbelled construction, limiting
the height of towers, and so on. Many insisted that private
wealth be declared to the authorities, so that it could be
properly taxed. The earliest known cadastres were compiled
in the thirteenth, fourteenth, and fifteenth centuries in Verona,
Venice, Perugia, and Florence. Communes also regulated the
way in which private wealth was to be managed, touching on
such matters as who bore responsibility, inheritance, and dowries. They penetrated even further into the intimacy of the
home to delineate and regulate the authority of the husband,
the rights of women and children, emancipations, majorities,
and marriages. (In 1266, for example, in Parma, Guelphs were
forbidden to marry Ghibellines.) There were also laws forbidding the most serious sexual offenses: incest, bigamy, and
above all homosexuality.

The communes were especially interested in areas where
private decisions had or might have public consequences.
Weddings and burials, particularly suspect, were covered by
prolix regulations that omitted nothing: the number and sort
of guests (particularly women); the timing of banquets (Venice, 1339, 1356; Bologna, 1276, etc.; Genoa, 1484); the value
of the trousseau and wedding gifts (Venice, 1299, 1360; Bologna, 1401); the procedure of funerals, and so on. Surprisingly, the most dreaded of all legislation was that concerning
fashions. The expense and luxury of women's clothing worried city fathers, who responded with ordinances that read like
fashion catalogs: the sumptuary laws instituted in Bologna in
1401 list sixteen possible categories of infraction of the dress
code, including jewels, belts, rings, embroidery, fur, fringes,
dresses, shoes, and buttons; these categories were themselves
subdivided. Money from fines poured in; but the job of enforcing the laws was a thankless one. The Signorie shut their
eyes when it came to their own feasts. Venice was notorious
in this regard. And women proved devilishly clever: when
one representative of the authorities, a notary, spotted a lady
of fashion wearing a dress that sported a long row of buttons,
he pointed out that buttons were forbidden by law. "Buttons?"

she replied. "What buttons? These are cupels! Look closely if you don't believe me. Where are the stems, where are the buttonholes?" (Sacchetti). Humbled perhaps, the authorities persisted nonetheless, maintaining their vigilance as the years passed. At stake were morality and public order, and as power was gradually concentrated in a smaller and smaller number of hands, it became more inquisitorial. The Medici went so far as to scrutinize private correspondence. Thus the private sphere was constantly infiltrated by values and precepts formulated outside it.

The Authority of the Church

Private homes were used spontaneously as places of worship. The poor hung medallions and sacred boughs on their walls, and in many inventories of more affluent homes we find valuable religious items, such as amber rosaries, crucifixes (very rare in late-fourteenth-century Florence), an occasional pious book, but above all portraits of the Virgin.

These icons and other objects were found only in bedrooms (including guest rooms and maids' quarters), where they were apparently used for personal worship; they were not found in living rooms (Florence, 1380–1420). But private worship was not necessarily associated with icons. At times the entire family would gather in the living room to hear the father read some sacred text or to listen to his dinnertime prayers. In any case, it was in the home that children learned their first religious acts and recited their first prayers.

As the focus of the hazards, anxieties, and worries that affected the lives of individuals and those close to them, the private realm was in a very tangible sense governed by Providence. Every man, woman, or child was aware of this, and said so. To watch a loved one grow weak, suffer, and die was to feel the hand of God, to recognize His power, and to call upon His mercy. When people spoke in private letters of trusting to God, they were not merely repeating a habitual formula but were perfectly sincere. Deceased ancestors provided another mediation between the private world and heaven. Honored by masses and prayers that helped speed them on their way to paradise, the dead—especially the innocents among them, the children—kept family members in close touch with the other world.

Customary and daily awareness of heaven and its powers could lead to true piety. But was it really of a nature to train the conscience? This was the question anxiously raised by moralists and preachers, who saw innumerable dangers lurking on the fringes of private life or even within its bosom—dangers that only a sound private education could combat. Aware that jealousy might lead outsiders to try to vex a family by magical means, such as tied laces or the *mal occhio*, evil eye, cast on children, the moralists recommended attaching a piece of coral to a child's neck as protection. Some painters show such charms attached even to the baby Jesus. The Church, for its part, was not unduly worried about such dangers. Its moral reflections followed a different line.

To open one's doors to others was in itself a disturbance that clerics, on this point in agreement with lay moralists, denounced with melancholy indignation. Weddings, funerals, baptisms, banquets, indeed all public occasions, were all too often the cause of misbehavior, *disonesta,* ranging from culpable indulgence and vanity to brushes with emotion and desire; even a furtive squeeze of the hand could be a mortal sin (Saint Antonino). Every outside excursion offered a hundred opportunities for suspect conversations and encounters, especially for boys who kept dubious company. (Saint Catherine, Palmieri, Saint Bernardine, and Maffeo Veggio all agree.) Even the most innocuous of encounters might awaken the most corrupting of tempters, the senses. Dominici emphasizes the dangers inherent in the sense of smell. Glances, those "darts of love" (Francesco di Barberino), were also arrows that pierced the soul and killed it (Saint Antonino). With the ears one heard words of flattery, ribaldry (whispered or in song), and foolishness of every kind. (Again I am paraphrasing Saint Antonino, who here is addressing a great lady and accordingly limits his list to misdemeanors with which she is likely to be familiar.) To speak is simply to become involved in the same conversations. And taste leads to gluttony.

Staying at home is no protection against these temptations, however. Even in private it is possible to eat too much, lose one's temper, or engage in idle chatter. Our words and deeds tell our children about "our vices, our mistresses, our feasts" (Palmieri), entailing the risk that "those who show no sign but understand everything . . . will be corrupted by our depravities" (Saint Antonino). Even at home children could see people in shocking states of undress, and such dubious gestures as raising the middle finger, learned in the streets, were tolerated by everyone, with the result that children learned to look upon such misbehavior as natural. Last but not least were the depravities of the marriage bed.

Detail of bedroom, Davanzati Palace, Florence, 14th–15th century. In a Gothic niche covered by two doors, a 14th-century artist painted a crucifixion with the Virgin and Saint John, an unusual theme for a home. The statue is a 15th-century procession statue.

The Church was much concerned about the moral and spiritual failings of private households. Every family was supposed to be a mirror of the Holy Family and thus a cornerstone of Christian society, an exemplar of progress toward spiritual perfection. The most powerful moral lessons would be unavailing if the family did not provide fertile soil for them to take root. The family was also the wellspring of religious vocations and the holy life. Its failure would spell disaster for spiritual life in general.

Intervention was therefore felt to be urgent, and by the fourteenth century Dominicans and Franciscans were beginning to assemble the elements of a pastoral of private life. Brothers soon began family visits; as their efforts expanded, many became close confidants and friends of numerous households. Saint Catherine's parents counted a Dominican among their intimates (Siena, 1360), and two Franciscans of the Observance volunteered their advice concerning family decisions to Monna Alessandra Strozzi in the name of their old friendship for her late husband (Florence, 1449).

Sano di Pietro, *Saint Bernardine Preaching Before the Church of Saint Francis in Siena* (detail), 1430. Preaching often took place on the squares in front of churches. Men and women are separated by a fence. Saint Bernardine of Siena was fond of moral themes that touched on aspects of private life. (Siena, Duomo.)

Master of Tolentino, *Scenes from the Life of Saint Nicholas of Tolentino*, "Saint Nicholas as a Child Listening to a Sermon," 14th century. Young boys and girls were allowed to hear the great preachers, but for the most part their religious education was obtained at home. (Tolentino, Chapel San Nicola.)

The close relations that the mendicant friars established with families laid the groundwork for more specific and "technical" interventions such as confession (more commonly practiced, it seems, by women than by men); spiritual guidance, achieved by means of religious pamphlets (such as those authored by Dominici and Saint Antonino); letters and conversations (again, primarily involving women); and of course preaching, especially when, after 1350, it came to bear most heavily on morals. Saint Bernardine invited all members of the household, even young girls, to come to church and hear the words of the preachers.

By these various means the friars were able to spread teachings of which a major, if implicit, objective was to reassert ecclesiastical control over private life. They insisted, as did the humanists, on the importance of private space, of the home as a structure for educating the Christian individual (for the humanists, simply the individual). The home environment, they stressed, should be calm and conducive to meditation, a retreat and a refuge, a defense against aggression of all kinds, and physical aggression above all. The home offered protection against the night, that "forest in which, away from home, all evils lie in wait" (Ser Ugolino Verini, 1480). The most private rooms of the palace were also supposed to be proof against domestic noises and odors (Alberti, *De re aedi-*

Giovanni Mansueti, *A Confraternal Procession* (detail), first half of 16th century. A Gothic church with an old jube and retables and a Renaissance altar and mural monuments. A pope welcomes penitents, each of whom carries a cross. The many confraternities offered companionship (on a private model), piety (liturgical as well as personal), and moral teaching (concerning chastity in marriage, the family spirit, charity, and dignity) whose implications for private life were of the utmost importance. (Venice, Accademia.)

ficatoria). At home the agitation and temptation of the world were attenuated in an atmosphere of peace and quiet.

Once this preliminary goal was achieved, it was possible to move on to the second stage of the program: to free the soul from all vanities and desires by means of a discipline acquired in early childhood. Educators took this task upon themselves, as did confessors, the former subjecting their pupils and the latter their penitents to a strict discipline, a conditioning, understood and accepted by all. Of primary concern were the most dangerous agents of lust, the five senses. Sight: "Turn your eyes to God . . . Open them to heaven, the forests, the flowers, all the marvels of creation. In the cities and wherever occasions for sin are met, lower your eyes" (Dominici). "Train the child to turn his eyes away from disturbing sights, starting with paintings" (Fra Paolino). "Look to your eyes . . . to your eyes . . . to your eyes" (Saint Antonino), and to the eyes of others, whose curiosity may prove corrupting for your good works and yourself. Hearing: be careful of what you say and listen to. Language was sufficiently suspect for Saint Antonino to devote three long chapters of his *Opera a ben vivere* to it: "Take care with your tongue, so as not to offend God," "On the sin of talking too much, and how deserving of blame are idle words," and "Use even decent words only with discretion." To be master of one's tongue was also to control one's laughter (an excess of which was a sin), one's gestures, and one's play. Nor did taste and touch go unnoticed. Of course the ascetic program also extended to sexuality—true sexuality, that of the married couple (all other forms were proscribed). Marriage was prohibited during certain periods

specified by the Church (and it was a mortal sin if consummation occurred). Marriage rights were to be exercised only in appropriate places, only during canonical periods (not during Lent or days of penitence), and only in natural ways, meaning no sodomy (a mortal sin of the most serious kind) and no unusual positions (a mortal sin).

These difficult precepts could be put into practice with the help and support of the family. Its members were exhorted to help one another along the path of virtue. Fra Paolino urged older children to help younger ones obey their parents. And Giovanni Dominici told parents that if they chose their children's friends carefully, offered them good advice, and set them a good example, God's blessings would reward them.

The pastoral perfected by the Church was diffused widely not only by its leading spokesmen but by hundreds of friars scattered throughout Italy's cities and towns in the late fourteenth and the fifteenth century. The Church's efforts probably did bolster the faith and improve religious observance by families. But were these convinced Christians also persuaded of the need to take a more active role in public, that is, social and political, life in the world?

Certainly not in the case of women. They were offered spiritual guidance (and many tertiaries and great ladies accepted), but its chief purpose was to deepen their inward sense of piety, their solitary devotion. No sooner were the senses muzzled, than one found inward solitude everywhere, in churches, salons, banquets, even on the streets. But the most propitious setting for this private devotion was the bedroom. The devout woman's bedroom became her refuge, her cell,

Giotto, *Saint Anne Receives a Visit from an Angel*, 1304-1306. Praying in her room, Giotto's Saint Anne illustrates the view of some religious authorities, that a woman's bedroom should be the focal point of her religious devotion. From the 13th century on, this precept was put into practice by generations of penitents, tertiaries, and pious laywomen seeking to find sanctity in the only place available to them, their private rooms (Padua, Scrovegni Chapel.)

the center of her spiritual exercise. She filled it with the necessary objects, in particular a crucifix, more suitable for penitential meditation than the usual icon of the Virgin. Among women true private devotion led to estrangement from the world.

The objectives of private religious education for men were more controversial. Saint Bernardine pointed out that men have a duty to act in the world, but neither he nor his brethren showed much interest in pursuing the subject. In cultivated circles the voices of the humanists could now be heard above those of the mendicant friars—not without some discord. Opinions were divided. Circumstances led Coluccio Salutati (d. 1406) to write a brief apology for the life of retirement (*De saeculo et religione*). This current of opinion never completely died out in the fifteenth century; we encounter it again, for example, in Cristoforo Landino's reflections on the contemplative life (*Questiones camaldulenses*, 1475). But the majority of humanists held the opposite view. Salutati considered the life of the city too important to accept the view that "to shun company, avert one's eyes from pleasant things, and shut oneself up in a cloister or hermitage is the way to perfection." The wise man has the duty to use all his gifts for the common good. In their different ways, Poggio, Bruni, and Valla, to mention only the greatest names, all emphasize this obligation; they do so, Bruni especially, in the name of a Christian ideal. On the other hand, they are quite hostile toward preachers who, among other sins, "preach hypocritically to foolish little women and simpleminded and no less foolish men," in whom they inspire a daydreaming faith that diverts attention from serious matters. The humanists, who believed in civic participation, thus rejected a pastoral program according to which the objective of Christian education for men was the same as for women: to encourage retreat into a world of private devotion. (They did not formulate their objection in these terms, however.) Contrary to this, they held that a man's training ought to prepare him for public commitments. But they looked toward a world whose authorities increasingly were not those of Christian religion, to a modern world whose presence was already strongly felt in the fifteenth century.

Domenico Ghirlandaio, *Scenes from the Life of the Virgin*, "The Visitation" (detail), 1485–1490. Dressed grandly for a religious festival, a patrician woman is divided between curiosity and reticence, vanity and modesty, public ostentation and private devotion. (Florence, Santa Maria Novella.)

René d'Anjou, *Le Coeur d'amour épris* (Vienna, National Library.)

3

Imagining the Self

Danielle Régnier-Bohler

René d'Anjou, *Le Coeur d'amour épris* (Vienna, National Library.)

❧ Exploring Literature

IN studying the emergence of the private sphere, the growing importance of the individual, and the new contours of domains henceforth regarded as secret or reserved, literary sources, whether in the *langue d'oïl* (spoken in northern France) or the *langue d'oc* (spoken in the south), offer a rich vein of information. At times we may labor under the illusion that literature presents a "slice of (private) life." But in fact the representation of places and communities is governed by literary codes, and the intimate secrets that appear to yield themselves up are actually subservient to metaphor.

Fiction can, however, claim *narrative* verisimilitude, which is subject to laws of its own. Literature brings to life what would otherwise be mere description. It fills in the very gaps that it seems to create (between scenes, or between conflict and resolution). Even the most fantastic tales suggest finely wrought judgments of the relations between the individual and the collectivity; in literature the fluctuating boundary between the one and the many is imagined or, in utopian writing, transformed. In some stories the individual is excluded or banished from the community. In others he excludes himself, voluntarily, in order to strike roots in a private territory all his own. In still others he remains within the community and subject to its values but seeks to discover "private" truths. Sometimes the family cell seems to be coming apart in the face of malevolent forces, yet in the end the initial unity is restored, improved, and enriched.

I shall concentrate on a few aspects of issues that have proved especially congenial to the literary imagination. In particular, I am interested in individuals excluded from society, whose gradual reintegration tells us something about the na-

Arthur said to Mélion: "I have a castle that looks out upon the sea, unequalled in all the world! It is magnificent, surrounded by woods, rivers, and those forests that you loved so much!" *Lai de Mélion.* (Paris, Bibliothèque Nationale, French 8266.)

ture of the underlying culture. I am also interested in the obsession with doubles and their reconciliation (a fictional transfiguration, I think, of family rivalries); in clothing, adornment, and nakedness, which tell us about what the community kept secret or forgot and what the individual had to rediscover for himself; and finally, in the symbolism of the gynaeceum, the often prisonlike women's quarters. Here, we lack the abundance of detail found in genre painting, so useful for reconstructing the history of everyday life. Instead, the focus is on the status of the individual, the knight-errant of courtly literature, who abandons his community of origin and is wafted like a seed to distant soil; there he again takes root, recreating a communal structure that, legendary though it may have been, was at least safe from decay. In Arthurian romance, the royal figure, Mark or Arthur, is never tainted by the tragic transgression that has become one of the myths of the West, or by the suspicion that, grown endemic, shook the Arthurian world to its roots. Nevertheless, in the thirteenth-century *Châtelaine de Vergi* the sovereign is compromised in a private drama, and the resolution of the plot lies in a private anecdote (even if other tales focus primarily on the exaltation of courtly life and collective joy). Later still, the world of fiction reveals a notable shift in the individual's relation to the community. Instead of the Arthurian ordeal, which combined love and adventure and joined the hero to the community, we now have secrecy. Jean de Paris wins his fair lady because of his looks; self-fulfillment is no longer part of courtly romance.

As literature evolves over a long period, new representations of the individual slowly emerge. Instead of poetry we have the expression of a lonely conscience, a more individualized lyricism that owes nothing to the rhetorical subjects marshaled by the troubadours and trouveres. As for nonfiction, memoirs and chronicles no longer pretend to be neutral; authors wish to be part of the scene.

The literary sources are still capable of evoking the relations between individual and community by means of "biological" symbolism. Sleep, for example, symbolizes the transition from prenatal "amnesia" to full communal life; in sleep the mind is filled with the cultural baggage required by social life. But the men of the Middle Ages, we know, were suspicious of solitude, which they regarded as an invitation to the devil; hence any positive evaluation of intimacy, retirement, or introspection is worth noting. I especially want to call attention to the striking use of dreams as a frame for fiction, for exploring the mind's certitudes and obscurities. Clearly, we are far from regarding the literary sources as mirrors of reality, reflections of everyday life. The imagination runs according to its own timetable, governed by authors' revisions and reworkings of their predecessors; hence I want to avoid any over-rigid chronology. Works of fiction should be seen as responses to obsessions, instincts, and tensions— responses whose purpose is simply to satisfy the mind. The nature of those obsessions, instincts, and tensions to which literature responds may be gathered from other, more nor- mative texts, which pretend to prescribe the proper relation of the individual (especially the female individual) to the com- munity. Fiction can be used as evidence in a literary archae- ology of the private. I am interested in how people conceived of what eventually came to be known as the "individual," that is, one who had the right to speak or remain silent, to assume an identity or wear a mask.

SPACE AND IMAGINATION

Was enclosure a threat or a form of protection? Walls sometimes imprison, as in Rutebeuf's description of the resi- dence of Avarice, the very antithesis of conviviality, a trap in which the unwary visitor is caught and subjected to the whims of the mistress of the place, a woman "more dead than alive." Robert of Blois contrasts the open house with the one that is shut up all too tightly. Raoul of Houdenc's *Songe d'enfer* (Dream of Hell) tells us that in France, alas, everyone keeps his house shut tight, whereas in Hell people eat with "open doors." And in *Blancandin et l'orgueilleuse d'amour* (Blancandin and the Proud Lover) we encounter nostalgia for an earlier time when doorkeepers were unnecessary. Thus, walls were seen as an impediment to the ideal of free intercourse, free circulation of people and things, and in particular to the free- dom to eat together. For as Robert of Ho's *Enseignements* (Lessons) pointed out, "the meal, you must know, is the cornerstone of friendship."

From Oppressive Confinement to Desired Inclusion

In contrast to this negative representation of enclosure, we find, interestingly enough in a thirteenth-century text that champions the cause of women, an argument of a different order: women enjoy the good fortune of "being born in- cluded." After creating Adam, the Lord caused him to fall asleep and from his side extracted the rib from which Eve would emerge; thus she was doubly protected, enclosed by both Eden's walls and Adam's flank. For the author, who contrasts the space without and the space within, this enclosure is a positive thing: "Judge you, then, if He did not show greater love to woman than to man, since He created man on the outside."

Space Possessed by a Glance. The all-embracing glance construes space, generally in a reassuring way, as a series of enclosures. What emerges from the panoramic view, from the "total" space, is a complex of protected subspaces, readily viewed in an aesthetic light: "This place fears assault from no quarter; to starve it is impossible. It was fortified by King Evrain, who has held it freely all the days of his life and will so hold it as long as he lives. If he caused the walls to be sealed up, it was not because he feared anyone but because the city is the more beautiful for it" (*Erec et Enide*).

Protection continues to be functional: the traitor who betrays Arthur in *Cligès* fortifies the castle with a double wall, "stockades, moats, drawbridges, trenches, barriers, lists, sliding iron gates, and a great dungeon of square stones," a job so thoroughly done that there is no need to close the gate. In private settings vegetation supplemented this protective and defensive shield. In *Le Vair Palefroi*, for example, a fortified house built on a cliff is surrounded by a moat, a thorny hedge, and, for good measure, a "thick and deserted forest."

The rule of the imagination is this: enclosing walls must be surrounded by ample open space, and they must connote not only strength and protection but also interdiction. In the lays of Marie de France, based on mythical material, the institutional taboo is surprisingly precise, even though the narrative laws at work here are remarkably economical. In *Guigemar*, for example, the wounded knight comes to a place where a man has imprisoned his wife: the woman's prison is surrounded by a wall of green marble breached by but a single door, guarded day and night. In *Yonec* a young woman in search of her mysterious bird-lover undergoes initiation in a city's beautiful environs; the city is surrounded by ramparts and filled with superb buildings, while beyond it lie swamps and forests and, in the distance, a river. Imaginary architecture was often based on the realites of the feudal age, as the fairy castle in the *Lai de Guingamor* illustrates. In *Floire et Blancheflor* the fortified city of the emir who possesses the "art of enchantment" is quite large and surrounded by high walls built with strong mortar and punctuated by 140 gates and 700 towers; in the center stands a tower 1,200 feet high—the hyperbole is typical of utopian literature.

In other texts we find economic symbolism as well as signs of power. The castle in *Le Bel inconnu* (The Handsome Stranger) is set amid mills, rivers, meadows, and vineyards, and in *La Gaste Cité* the hero's comprehensive gaze takes in the city's impregnable, high-walled dungeons and many houses, surrounded by woods, vineyards, and meadows. Taking Chrétien de Troyes as our standard of reference, we find, as the thirteenth century progresses, an increase in the frequency of spatial representations. The choice of viewpoint is not fortuitous: the individual hero is often denied (or only grudgingly allowed) access to the enclosed spaces his eye can see. Walls deliberately divide those who are outside from those who live within, those who are admitted from those who are banned. In many tales of Celtic origin the hero is required to cross a transitional space: an open area, perhaps a moor or a huge forest through which a river runs, like the forest in which Graelent encounters a doe that flees in the direction of the moor. In *La Quête du Saint-Graal* (The Quest for the Holy Grail) the enclosure may be of divine origin: arriving at the imposing castle of the Grail, Lancelot manages to pass through a gate guarded by two lions. Following the main road inside, he comes to the dungeon, where he finds not a living soul. He then goes to the castle's great hall and encounters a firmly locked door, a symbolic barrier that denies him access to the Grail. The doors of the room close "without anyone's touching them," which is considered an "extraordinary occurrence."

Closed spaces can be opened, however. If cities sometimes resemble castles and castles sometimes resemble cities, fictional space also connotes an active questioning of authority. Indeed, the space that opens up before the hero as he leaves the feudal world leads only to a new enclosure, that of love and its taboos, a space defined by social taboos; the fairy is often a "lady" from "another earth." If the theme of individual versus collectivity forms the heart of the romantic adventure tale, it is often coupled with another theme: that of crossing boundaries, particularly boundaries that only a chosen few can step across. In twelfth- and thirteenth-century literature collective space is not a mere backdrop; it is sometimes an enclosure from which the hero can escape or be banished, sometimes a

"Nearby stood a city entirely surrounded by walls. Not a house, a hall, or a tower did not seem to be made entirely of silver." Marie de France, *Yonec.* (Paris, Bibliothèque Nationale, French 20127.)

fortress for him to conquer. Space is defined by a dense network of enclosures, and even a place as intimate as the orchard, usually reserved for love, can symbolize a power over the Other World, as in the final ordeal of *Erec et Enide*.

The Anguish of an Empty World. The strangeness of the wilderness is underscored by innumerable imaginary dwellings, monuments to the laborer's toil and the architect's imagination; what is missing or left out is oddly redundant. During their perilous quest Erec and Enide neither drink nor eat, "for within a day's march in any direction there is neither castle nor village nor tower nor fortified house nor abbey nor hospital nor inn." In *Le Chevalier à la charrette* (The Knight on the Cart) the maid who goes looking for Lancelot wanders aimlessly: "Before coming close and learning anything of him, I do believe that she may have explored in every direction many and many a country. But what would be the point of recounting every one of her stops for the night and each and every lengthy day? Though she followed thousands upon thousands of trails and let more than a month go by, she knew just as much, not one bit more or less, than she knew before: all of it amounted to nothing. One day, while crossing a field in a glum and pensive mood, she suddenly saw in the distance, on a shore bordering an arm of the sea, a lonely tower, with not another house, hut, or manor for a league in any direction."

"There was, it seemed, no castle, no fortress, no tower, and no house fit for human habitation." *La Quête du Saint-Graal*. (Paris, Bibliothèque Nationale, French 1438.)

The Solitary Man. In the Middle Ages the solitary man was considered dangerous. In Béroul's *Tristan*, Mark, having learned that the adulterous couple is in the forest of Morrois, summons his entourage to announce that he wishes to go out alone: "Go out alone?" they say. "Was ever a king so imprudent?" To which Mark responds: "I shall therefore go without escort and leave my horse. I shall take with me neither companion nor squire. For once I reject your company." Similarly, Erec's father responds to an unusual and dangerous situation by begging him to take along at least some of his knights: "A king's son must not go alone!" Thirteenth-century narratives occasionally give quite a realistic account of the dangers to be expected in such circumstances. In *La Fille du comte de Pontieu* (The Count of Pontieu's Daughter) a husband makes up his mind to reinforce his wife's escort but takes the wrong trail through the forest and is rewarded with the sight of his wife being raped by five men. In *Le Vair Palefroi* a young woman is able to join her lover and marry him only because the escort conducting her to her intended spouse does its job "badly." A woman who traveled alone so upset the hero of one lay that he married her, to his great misfortune.

Sometimes, though, solitude was deliberately sought and prolonged for extended periods. Hermits lived in cells, some with crude openings providing minimal contact with the outside world. These men performed a definite function for the community they had abandoned, invariably located some distance away. Ogrin's hermitage, located in the forest of Morrois where *forbannis* (banished exiles) built wretched huts, is not described. Instead the narrative stresses its remoteness from civilization and the long journey through the *bocage* (hedged fields) required to reach it. After a similarly long journey Yvain finds a small, low house with a narrow window, where the hermit stored food for the wild. In *La Quête du Saint-Graal* the many encounters with hermits and recluses are set in specific locales (a hidden trail, a chapel, a hermitage on a hill) and at a specific time—in the evening, the time of conversation. Perceval, for example, loses his way: "Nevertheless, choosing the direction he judged best, he eventually came to a chapel and knocked on the recluse's tiny window. She opened at once, for she was not asleep, and, sticking her head out as far as possible, asked him who he was." She then explained that after her husband's death she had chosen to retire to this wilderness because she feared for her life, and that she had had a house built for her chaplain and his men and a cell for herself.

Upon reaching the foot of a mountain, Gawain and Hector follow a narrow trail that leads to the summit, a trail so rugged that they are soon exhausted. Only then do they notice a poor house and a tiny chapel, next to which stands a small garden in which a hermit is gathering nettles for his dinner. Thus solitude is evoked by the distance that must be traveled in order to reach it, making its protective value clear.

Solitude and Meaning. All the landmarks encountered in the territories traversed by the Knights of the Round Table on their various quests are basically symbols of the subordination of the "earthly" to the "celestial." These zones of voluntary seclusion are pregnant with meaning, but it is no accident that the meaning is secret and almost inaccessible and must be ferreted out. Late-fourteenth-century literature heightened the obscurity still further. Raimondin, husband of Melusina, obtains from the pope a pardon for his perjury regarding his wife and then goes to visit the hermitages of the Montserrat abbey. Seven of them line a path that ascends a steep cliff. Raimondin is to occupy the fourth. These are so remote from all other dwellings that the church and abbey, seen from above, look quite minuscule.

In literature encounters with religious solitaries are never fortuitous. One who has chosen to live in solitude has established a very special relation to the values of the community that he or she has abandoned. In *Yvain* the hermit serves as a link between the wild and civilization. In *Tristan*, Ogrin, who speaks the language of Good and Evil, is able to help Isolde rejoin society. He becomes the instrument of reconciliation, traveling from Cornwall to Mont-Saint-Michel, where, on credit or by bargaining, he purchases furs and silk garments so that Isolde can dress as befits a queen. In *La Quête du Saint-Graal* the meaning of the various adventures is a secret known only to a hermit or recluse. The hero is aware that there is a meaning, but he cannot decipher it; the hermits are the interpreters, which explains the narration's lengthy discourses and repeated confessions. Dreams, vehicles of the intimate, must be interpreted. To Lancelot the hermit says: "Know that this vision is far richer in meaning than many might think. And now, listen to me if you wish, and I will tell you the origin of your race." Indispensable intermediaries between God and those in search of the Grail, the hermits and recluses have captured the meaning of each adventure in their lonely words.

Symbolic Places

In the fictional imagination certain frequently mentioned spaces, such as the tower and the orchard, serve special symbolic functions. Furthermore, although the division of the interior into hall and chamber was apparently functional, objects such as beds possessed such a multiplicity of meanings that they too may be considered symbols.

The Tower. A symbol of power, the tower signaled conquest. Unlike the *Chanson de Roland*, which takes place almost entirely in the open (with the exception of the orchards in which Charles and Marsile assemble their respective vassals), the *Prise d'Orange* offers an interesting view of the tower, which William, disguised, enters with his companions. They go first to the reception hall and from there to the Gloriette tower, whose "pillars and sections of wall are made of marble." No ray of sunshine or breath of fresh air can enter. In the heart of the alien power, William heads for the private domain of the "Other." Along one side of the chamber a terraced orchard has been constructed, and there William discovers the object of his desires: the woman. Symbolizing the power coveted by the conqueror, the tower is simultaneously a defensive edifice, a habitable space, and a place of pleasure.

A prison for captives, the tower also stands for the exercise of undue authority, as many a heroine of the *chansons de toile* (songs sung by women while weaving) was aware. Sometimes, though, the tower serves to protect lovers from prying eyes. Thus, the enclosed spaces of feudal architecture had many meanings. Prizes in battle, walled enclosures also figured in private affairs, in the violation of taboos established by authority. In the *Lai du laostic* a wall becomes an emblem of institutional and social taboos in a barely plausible way. The young woman's love for her neighbor thrives on the obstacle that stands in its way: "Their houses stood next to each other, as did the great halls of their dungeons. Between them there was no obstacle, no separation, other than a great wall of gray stone."

Dancing in the orchard. "Then you would have seen the round dance and the people dancing their pretty ballet and performing many a beautiful dance and many a fine turn on the new lawn." Guillaume de Lorris, *Roman de la Rose*. (Paris, Bibliothèque Nationale, French 19153.)

The Orchard. A private place as well as a place of sociability, the orchard similarly reflects an obsession with boundaries and their ambivalence. The wall around the orchard made it the ideal spot for lovers to meet, for seductions to take place, for secrets to be exchanged. Circumscribed, the orchard was a theater in which woman's charms were exposed, as in the *Lai d'Aristote*; a place in which women could vent their woes; a scene of espionage; and a place of magical silence, as in the *Lai de Tydorel*, in which a fairy discovers that the queen is sterile. For Erec it is the site of a final ordeal of initiation, yet it is also a place of delights. For lovers, however, the orchard was mainly a refuge; the castellan of Vergi conducts her love affairs in secret, in her orchard. But it was also a place of social gathering, usually reserved for small groups, particularly of women, as in the *Lai d'Ignauré*, where the women, playing at confession, discover that they are all mistresses of the same seducer; or, again, in the *Lai de Tydorel*, where the queen and her damsels are in the habit of eating their after-dinner fruits in the orchard and then taking a nap.

When lovers were alone, the orchard was ideal for intimacy, but indiscreet and hostile eyes were naturally drawn to it. In the thirteenth-century *Lai de l'ombre* the lovers' solitude is shattered when the elusive woman encounters her Double reflected in the water of a well; the Double does not refuse the ring the lover offers.

The orchard sometimes symbolizes not the secret rendezvous and perilous seductions of courtly love but an enchanted landscape in which nature's beauty is enhanced by man's artifice. Derived from the tradition of the *locus amoenus* (in such twelfth- and thirteenth-century fiction as *Floire et Blancheflor, le Lai de l'oiselet, le Bel Inconnu,* or even *Huon de Bordeaux,* in which the orchard contains a fountain of life and youth), the artificial garden was an enclosed space ideally suited for the exploration of sensuality. These man-made paradises symbolized the pure joy of repose; every object appealed in some way to the senses. The arrangement of the garden, the flora, the various fragrances and sounds all contributed to the effect. Precursor of the mannerist garden, that apotheosis of sensuality, the medieval orchard promised endless pleasure. Nature, refined to the height of exquisiteness, became a benevolent place filled with saving grace, rich not only in fragrances but also in "good herbs," remedies for disease and old age. Here the ground has been leveled, whether by the hand of man or by some magician one cannot say. The orchard in the *Oiselet*

"More than ever I liked his sweet, measured gestures, which silenced me." Christine de Pisan, *Le Dit des vrais amants*. (Paris, Bibliothèque Nationale, French 836.)

seems to be a product of black magic. The light is gentle, and a bird sings songs of oblivion, desire, youth, or eternal life. In this hyperaesthetic world the ephemeral reigns supreme. Yet it is a fragile paradise: when the bird disappears, the trees wither and the spring runs dry.

Abolition of time or eternal recurrence? The social fable is explicit in the *Oiselet*, which condemns the chaos of its time, the inversion of social hierarchy: a villein becomes owner of the orchard, supplanting knights and their ladies. The suspension and retention of time are evoked by the sensuous qualities of the cenotaph in *Floire et Blancheflor*: death is transcended by rapture of the senses and reiteration of the gestures of desire, aided by the rhythm of the winds. How better to deny the lapse of time than by exalting every imaginable sensual pleasure? Far from being a mere ornamental motif or a theater of the senses, the orchard suppresses even the perception of time's passing by its celebration of pleasure.

Color is all but absent from this utopia of the senses. Paradoxically, it is the volatile, the fragrance of trees and grass, the passing sounds that make happiness last. As fragile as the body itself, the violated orchard withers away.

L'Offrande du coeur (The Heart's Offering), tapestry. (Paris, Cluny Museum.)

Inner Space: Hall and Chamber. Literature, which depicts different strata of society, reveals various ways of dividing up domestic space. The commoners' homes described in the fabliaux are quite rudimentary; houses are small, frequently with but a single room. In one fabliau, a room contains barrels and chests as well as a bed. When the miller's·daughter had to be protected, she was locked in a hut to which her father possessed the only key.

By contrast, the literature depicting aristocratic society reveals more sophisticated arrangements. It is tempting to describe the hall as being reserved for collective purposes, for the more gregarious aspects of private life, while the chamber was for more secret and intimate uses. But there are problems with such oversimplification. To be sure, the hall was the center of collective life: isolated from the street, it was the usual gathering place, the ideal room for social functions. The mythical King Arthur used his great hall almost entirely for social purposes. Grand entries were made there. In the *Chanson de Roland*, Charles, returning to Aix, goes to the palace and enters the hall to inform Aude of the hero's death and the grief that overwhelms him. The vassals gather in the hall to discuss

Celebration at the court of King Arthur. "It would have been difficult to say which one was the most beautiful and the most elegant." *Lai du mantel.* (Dijon Library, ms 527.)

important affairs: in the *Charroi de Nîmes*, William, returning from the hunt, learns from his nephew of Louis's ingratitude. Hastening to the palace, he "crossed the hall with such impetuosity that he broke the thongs of his leather sandals. All the barons were frightened. When the king saw him, he got up and went to meet him."

Yet on ritual occasions, when the group gathered to reaffirm its solidarity, the hall was a place for recreation. At the Feast of the Ascension, King Arthur presided over a magnificent court, his hall replete with barons; the queen and her ladies were present too. The knight who kidnaps Guinevere in the *Chevalier à la charrette* throws down a challenge to the entire assembly. The hall was also the place where, at the end of a tale, the group gathered to honor the hero. The banquet honoring Erec's coronation took place in six rooms "so full that there was hardly space to move between the tables. At each table there was, truly, a king, a duke, or a count." As the primary location for the beginning of an adventure, the hall was not surprisingly subjected to hyperbole in the parodic lays: in the *Lai du cor* thirty thousand knights attend the banquet, accompanied by thirty thousand maids!

Even when guests were received on more modest occasions, meals were served in the hall. The "knight in the cart" and Gawain follow a midget toward a dungeon where they are to be put up for the night; Lancelot follows a damsel who gives him shelter in her manor, a "fortress surrounded by high walls." For her "living place she had had built a vast hall flanked by many lavishly decorated chambers." A sumptuous meal is served in the hall: "From the hall shadows were banished, yet stars already shone in the heavens. A huge number of twisting, heavy, ardent torches spread a festival of light." The hall was for receiving guests. When Enide arrives, the king escorts her first to the great stone hall; next the queen takes her into the "mistress' chamber," where she dresses her

"Furthermore, as you know, wherever knights are found, whether in pagan or Christian lands, they come to the Round Table, and if God accords them the grace of being seated, they consider themselves more fortunate than if they held the entire world in their possession." *La Quête du Saint-Graal*, 14th century. (Paris, Bibliothèque Nationale, French 120.)

"All who came into the king's company were shown a seat, provided they were knights." *La Mort le roi Artu*, 14th century. (Turin National Library.)

in royal style. The two women then rejoin the king in the hall, and the many knights who have gathered there rise to greet them. On this day of jubilation, part of the wedding feast, all barriers are lifted. Doors and windows are left open, entrances and exits are left free all day long, so that nothing separates the rich from the poor. For a brief moment the solidarity of the group obviates the need for defenses.

The chamber, on the other hand, was more a place of solitude. But what was the meaning of solitude? In *Erec et Enide*, Arthur submits to being bled—a procedure, one would think, best carried out in the strictest privacy. Nevertheless, the king "had with him, in his chambers, in private, only five hundred barons of his house: never in any season had the king been so alone, and he was bored not to have more people in his court." Did the royal image exist in solitude? Or was it perhaps an artifact of the perception of the king by others? Be that as it may, Arthur is always seen in the midst of a bustling crowd.

Nevertheless, the chamber was the ideal place for escaping from other people and therefore the place where a person could give vent to his pain. The afflicted retired to their rooms. In general the chamber was a place for isolating and protecting women. In *Guillaume de Dole* the heroine stays in her room: "No man can see her, since her brother is not here." In a lay by Marie de France the young woman who loves Milon laments that "I am not free . . . Innumerable guards dog my every step, young and old, and even my domestics." The wounded or exhausted man was carried to the chamber; in such cases the detail emphasizes health, calm, and isolation. The chamber to which Erec is taken is "pleasant, far from noise of any kind, and quite airy"; in the *Chevalier à la charrette* Lancelot, after enduring the harsh ordeal of captivity, finds "healthful air and secure retreat" in the home of the damsel who gives him shelter.

The chamber was also available for more sophisticated forms of social intercourse and amusement, for music, stories, and games. In *Eliduc*, Guilliadon's father enters his daughter's apartments, sits down to play chess with a knight from across the sea, and teaches his daughter, seated on the other side of the board, how to play. Clearly the division between collective space and space reserved for individuals was fluid, and men were allowed access to areas set aside for women. In the fourteenth-century *Dit du prunier* (Sayings of the Plum Tree) we see diners washing their hands after a meal as the lady of

the house distributes wine and spices. The guests then gather in the chamber: "The lady, who knew many a trick for making a young man fall in love, gathered the company around her to play 'the king who does not lie.' . . . In this game she was queen, and she wanted to know what each person thought. One after another the guests were obliged to tell their secrets of love." The count in *Escoufle* "had a custom that was a great source of pleasure to him: nearly every evening when he was alone with his men, he had a huge, beautiful fire built in the maidens' chamber, and there he went to eat his dessert and relax among the damsels. The beautiful young Aélis well knew the art of making herself agreeable to him. Couches and beds were placed around the fire to sit on. The count had given the order for this on the night when the event occurred. After supper the count went to the chamber for his pleasure, and while his fruit was being prepared, he undressed so that he might be scratched, keeping nothing on except his breeches."

The Bed. Did people sleep in the hall or the chamber? Did they sleep alone or together? Were beds shared with a spouse or with a member of the same sex? Nocturnal promiscuity seems to have been commonplace. When Guinevere plans a rendezvous with Lancelot, she makes it clear that she does not sleep alone: "Do not think of joining us; opposite me, in my

A game of chess. *Guiron le Courtois*, about 1370–1380. (Paris, Bibliothèque Nationale, French n.a. 5243.)

"Here begins the testament of Master Jean de Meun . . ." (Stockholm, Royal Library.)

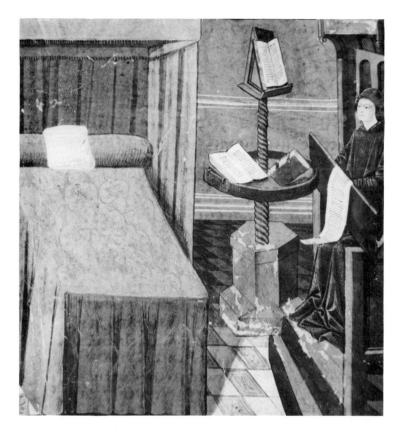

chamber, lies Keu, the seneschal, who though covered with wounds still lingers on." (Deep in sleep, the wounded man would hardly have bothered the lovers.) The queen tells Joufroi of Poitiers that he cannot come into her chamber; instead, she has two beds installed in the great stone hall: one for the count, in which she will join him, the other for his companion.

When a person slept alone, it was because someone felt that he needed his sleep. King Arthur offers Erec a bed of his own: "The king felt a great affection for Erec; he had him sleep alone in a bed, not wanting anyone to sleep alongside him, touching his wounds." Enide and the queen slept side by side in the chamber next door. Healed, Erec found his wife "in the same bed." Yet in the lay *Equitan* the couple seem to sleep in two beds, for they take their pleasure on "the husband's." A bed of one's own could be a mark of honor. In the *Quête du Saint-Graal*, Arthur gives Galahad his own bed, "in order to pay homage to his high birth." Arthur himself goes off to join Lancelot and the other barons. Later we are told that in the morning Arthur entered the chamber in which Lancelot and Gawain had slept, a tacit indication that the king had been afforded some measure of solitude during the night.

A peninsula of privacy, the bed heightened private pleasure. Nowhere else could a person give free reign to his or her feelings. Thus, in the *Quête*, Guinevere, "in order to show the extent of her pain" at the departure of the knights, goes to her apartments and casts herself down on her bed in a state of affliction. But the bed could also be a symbol of guilt, a shadowy place, a scene of crime; the truth of what went on here could never be revealed. The bed lent itself to all sorts of maneuvers and substitutions, particularly in the case of women accused of giving birth to monsters or bastards. It was a place of subterfuge, of manipulation of reality. Taking the place of Isolde, Branwen served Mark as a virgin bride. In stories involving doubles, the bed was that dark place where the deceived bride could no longer tell the two brothers apart. Mistakes were always possible in the dark, as were crimes.

Troilus was plunged into melancholy: "Within a short time, his room was full of ladies and damsels and all sorts of musical instruments." *Roman de Troilus*. (Paris, Bibliothèque Nationale, French 25528.)

Christine de Pisan, *Le Dit des vrais amants*, 15th century. (Paris, Bibliothèque Nationale, French 836.)

The bed was also a symbol of adultery: Tristan's was "but the length of a lance" away from the king's. Tristan plans to speak to the queen as soon as his uncle has fallen asleep, but his wound opens and blood flows onto the sheets. Similarly, Lancelot's blood stains Guinevere's bed, so that she is accused of having slept with the wounded seneschal. Seeing is not always believing, and what seems to be proof is not. The bed could easily become a dangerous place.

Finally, the bed symbolizes the alternation of day and night; the nocturnal life it evokes can be troubling. Tydorel, hero of the lay that bears his name, a half fairy whose eyes never close, cannot sleep and therefore cannot dream. This makes him unsuitable for social life and thus for the exercise of power. He rejoins his fairy father in a world from which time is banished, in a parable of the necessary alternation of diurnal and nocturnal rhythms, of sociability and respite from sociability. In many stories people stay up late with their guests, but they seldom say that they cannot sleep. Wakefulness can cause trouble, as when the wife of the *Chevalier au cygne* (Knight with Swan) succeeds in wresting confidences from her insomniac husband. Spurred by the devil, she asks the fatal question. In bed too the duchess extracts from her husband the secret that will precipitate the death of the chatelaine of Vergi and her lover. Thus the bed is a place of vulnerability, where identity can easily be concealed and grave crimes committed, including crimes perpetrated solely by means of words.

SOCIABILITY

In literature space is almost always represented as being occupied by a domestic group: couples, children, different generations coexisting under one roof, servants, fluctuating family groups, Arthurian *maisnies*, or households—in short, a hierarchical, domestic society, a power structure in which various intrigues are played out. Mothers die in childbirth, fathers disappear, children are lost, reconciliations take place, sometimes murders. The very redundancy of the plots reveals that the fantasies being expressed create a coherent universe all their own. In the chanson de geste the lineage is the center of interest; in romance it is the family, whose members' relations are corroded by a kind of corruption, and in which certain roles are consistently represented as evil—the mother-in-law, for example, and sometimes the concubine or seneschal. Others are consistently victims, generally children and young wives. Here we see certain powers at work. In particular the women of the house are subject to the authority of husband and father. Stories of twins, real or fictitious, were often debates about the respective rights of the older and younger sons: twinhood is the sign of a type of affective association, a form of partnership between brothers. Fiction offers not a portrait of private life as it was actually lived but a compendium of private difficulties and tensions, pertaining to both communal life and the status of the individual. The sites and rituals of sociability, and especially of conviviality, shed light on the difficult but necessary process of integrating the individual into the group.

Private Life: Self and Others

Boundaries. Walls were gradually erected within the house so that people could be alone and enjoy personal freedom. Chrétien de Troyes's stories are structured as journeys of initiation: individuals leave the community and embark upon a period of solitary wandering; eventually they return, covered with glory and prepared to receive the adulation of the group. In the thirteenth century, moreover, the body increasingly came to be seen as a private possession. Normative discourse concentrated on it, because it was felt to be open to abuse and hence a potential disturbance to the life of the group.

Consequently, a notion of "other people's privacy" emerged. Within the community discretion was essential, according to Robert of Blois's *Chastoiement des dames*; too much curiosity about the privacy of others was inadvisable. The admonitions to respect the privacy of others primarily concerned women, as if the female body were the focal point of all virtue and vice: "Any time you pass by another person's house, be careful never to look in and never to stop. To stand agape or idle in front of a person's house is not wise or courteous behavior. There are things that one does often in private, in one's own home, that one would not want others to see, should someone come to the door. And if you want to enter the house, cough a little upon entering to alert those within to your arrival, either by this cough or by a word. To speak plainly, no one should enter without warning."

To Be Alone. How could one be alone in the gregarious privacy of the home? The organization of domestic space shows that some areas were more public, others more private.

Fiction reveals how difficult it was to find the right time

and place for private conversation. The texts generally portray these difficulties realistically. Cligès summons his serf Jean to a private meeting and asks for a safe place where he can meet his lover. Private conversations are especially common in thirteenth-century fiction. Compared with the well-ordered Arthurian world in Chrétien de Troyes, the early-thirteenth-century *Mort le roi Artu* (in which there is precious little adventure and the Round Table tragically succumbs to faction) is a theater of intrigue and denunciation. And in *Le Vair Palefroi* a man who wishes to convince his uncle to speak to a girl's father on his behalf searches for a good meeting place, such as a *loge* (a small room over an entranceway, or perhaps an upper-story bedroom): in other words, a place apart.

In *Guillaume de Dole*, a tale exalting the social virtues of the good sovereign, private conversation serves a real function. The partner in these conversations is Jouglet, the minstrel and friend of the emperor. When the sovereign wants to hear a good story, he grabs the bit of Jouglet's horse and leads him off the trail. "Tell me, dear friend, a story to wake me up!" Even out in the open, private conversation requires a place to retire to. In a conversation on a balcony the emperor announces his marriage plans to the seneschal. Later the emperor (who is said to be "in small company") invites the hero, William, to come amuse himself in the orchard, scene of yet another conversation. After learning of the calumny of which young Lienor has been the victim, the emperor sets out alone across the fields, his heart filled with sadness. As for the seneschal, a final conversation results in his being duped. In the midst of a full assembly, Lienor's messenger entices him "outside the palace, near the high wall," a place of safety, sheltered from all prying eyes, but in fact a trap where the felon is finally captured. Thus, the lovely transparency of the Arthurian world is gone, supplanted by intrigues carried on in secret palace niches. In the fourteenth-century *Lai du blanc chevalier* (Lay of the White Knight) and the later *Jehan de Saintré* window embrasures lend themselves to secret encounters and less than honorable negotiations.

The growing role of writing. *Roman de Troilus*. (Paris, Bibliothèque Nationale, French 25528.)

The Secret Language of Signs. The late twelfth century saw the development of secret means of communication. Lovers exchange symbolic gifts and letters. As the number of written messages increases, many are lost, diverted, or tampered with. Containers such as jewel boxes, clothes chests, and weapons cabinets are exalted to such a degree that they become precious reliquaries, metaphors for the secrets of courtly love, and, on occasion, key elements of plot and pretexts for a rhetoric of opening and unveiling.

Some signs of love are visible, others secret. Thirteenth-century courts were invaded by secret signs. A little dog, apparently nothing more than a household pet, informs the lover of the chatelaine of Vergi of the times of their rendezvous. In the *Lai du chèvrefeuille* Tristan wraps honeysuckle around a hazel branch on which, having removed the bark, he has engraved his name, a secret sign that says: "My beautiful beloved, this is the way it is: neither you without me nor I without you!" Yet another sign is the knot that Guigemar's beloved makes in his tunic in such a way that no one else can undo it; Guigemar, for his part, wraps a belt around his naked lover's waist which no one else can break or cut. This secret sign language establishes an affective space upon which others are forbidden to trespass. Later, in the masked world of *Jehan de Saintré*, the young man's initiation into courtly life includes an initiation in the use of a secret language, a hidden code.

Conversations, Communal or Private. (Paris, Arsenal Library, ms 5117.)

By contrast, the token of love is a gift—a ring, say, or a piece of clothing—whose meaning may not be incomprehensible to others. An element in the representation of self, the ring is also the most obvious sign of sexuality, a major prize in stories that incorporate taboos. The liaison with the fairy dissolves the moment the hero reveals to the hermit the secret of the seduction. The ring has disappeared! Better integrated among the signs of sociability are the necklaces women give their lovers, a gift that we find as late as the work of Guillaume de Machaut. The damsel "was very nimbly going to make a very pretty necklace, which seemed most sweet to me for it was made of nutmeg, roses, and violets. When she finished, she came and placed it over my head"—a living bond that is in effect an extension of the woman's embrace.

Forbidden Speech. The law of secrecy is a well-known component of courtly love; its violation inaugurates the tragedy of the chatelaine of Vergi: "So it came to pass that he who had delivered up the secret lost the happiness of it, for the more intense love is, the worse it is for ideal lovers when one suspects the other of revealing what should have been kept secret. And often the result is such woe that love must end in pain and shame."

"As long as you want me by your side, do not ask who I am and never ask where I come from." *La Chanson du chevalier au cygne.* (Munich, Bayerische Staatsbibliothek.)

Roman de Flamenca, second half of 13th century. (Library of Carcassonne.)

Encounters between mortals and fairies frequently involve secret taboos. The mortal is not allowed to reveal the existence of the fairy or to ask where it came from, as in the *Lai de Tydorel* or the *Chanson du chevalier au cygne*. In fairy tales we find an extreme form of the taboo against revealing the existence of some private secret (possibly having to do with the other world). Melusina hides her serpent nature by invoking such taboos: no one may look at her or inquire about her past. She attempts to maintain a wall of opacity around her person, but Raimondin breaches it when he presses his guilty eye to the door behind which she is bathing.

The importance of writing as an element of fiction increased over the course of the thirteenth century. In *Flamenca* the lovers for a long time rely on brief messages, written as well as spoken, in their search for one another. A letter plays an important part in Béroul's *Tristan*, in which Mark has Isolde's missive read to him by the chaplain: its contents become known publicly. The chaplain breaks the seal, reads the text, then reads it out loud line by line. Mark then orders that the barons be summoned and the text read aloud to them.

In *La Mort le roi Artu*, Arthur himself reads the message from the damsel whose body has come floating down the river in a mysterious bark. Here as well as in *Tristan* the purpose of the written communication is to reveal information intended to be public and which had been either genuinely private or made to seem so; as Ogrin says, "To reduce shame and avoid scandal, it is useful to lie a little." When it came to sad revelations, visual images may have been preferred to written messages. At dawn Arthur, a guest in the mysterious castle of his sister Morgan, sees the paintings made by Lancelot while held in captivity and deciphers in them his own misfortune. In *Philomèle*, attributed to Chrétien de Troyes, a poor mute girl comes upon skeins and spindles in a chest and spins in colored threads the story of her rape, mutilation, and imprisonment—a message that her sister will know how to read. The image will say what no one has yet dared to voice: the unspeakable transgression.

In the case of a wild man deprived of reason and memory, writing informs passersby of the cause of his affliction. The hero of *Dit du lévrier* flees into the forest, taking with him parchment and ink; there he writes about his affliction, his long years of waiting, and the lady's scorn. The document becomes the only memory of the man; it is affixed to a tree so that all may learn of its contents.

Containers. It is an occasion for rejoicing when hidden things are revealed. When a werewolf regains human form in *Guillaume de Palerme*, the trunks are opened and clothing is gladly offered to the former scourge. A traveler's chest hides a coat of arms made of green silk in which the fairy cloaks the savage in the *Dit du lévrier* (Sayings of the Greyhound). In *Escoufle* a stolen purse is the source of the drama as well as the pretext for a reconciliation. In *La Mort le roi Artu* not only does writing reveal the secret of the beautiful corpse, but the message itself consists of many layers: bark, tapestries, purse. Containers were frequently given as presents, thus encouraging the proliferation of ritual acts of opening (*la gestuelle de l'ouverture*).

Symbolically, objects might become reliquaries, like the small chest in one of Marie de France's lays in which the body of a nightingale is encased, a metaphor for the eternity of secrecy—guardian of a quintessence and a memory. A woman's husband has killed the nightingale, so, in order to let her lover know what has happened, the lady wraps the little bird in a brocade in which their story is embroidered in golden threads. A courtly man, the lover has artisans make a "chest of pure gold" covered with precious gems and has the reliquary sealed. Other reliquaries convey the symbolic value of their contents, like the "straw basket" that miraculously preserves beautiful Helaine's arm; and, most of all, that strange object which for many years preserved the severed hand of the Manekine, a sturgeon's stomach from which emanated sweet fragrances that delighted the hearts of all who smelled them.

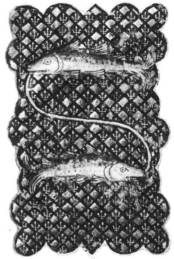

"You will find in your stomach something like the imprint of a glove: that is the place where the hand was preserved, winter and summer alike." *La Manekine*. (Cambrai Library.)

Domestic Society: Fluctuations and Restorations

The structure of the medieval tale reflected both the structure and internal problems of the family, especially the obsession (no doubt widespread in the feudal era) with rivalries between heirs. Narrative often ventured outside the closed circuit of the family; after exogamic episodes of one sort or another, unity was finally restored. Although the ways in which the family figured in literature are extremely complex, certain basic types can be identified. Sexual themes are common: incest between father and daughter, mother-in-law and son-in-law, brother-in-law and sister-in-law; rivalries over women; sexual slanders that lead to the exile of young mothers.

The Family Domain. In the fabliaux couples were often beset by tensions and dissidence. Chrétien de Troyes, on the other hand, stresses the fulfillment of the couple in marriage, the culmination (as he patiently demonstrates) of courtly love. In his anti-Tristan romance adultery is replaced by free choice in legitimate marriage. Nevertheless, tension and misunderstanding are far more common features of fictional marriage in this period. Unless adultery is involved, however, couples often survive their marital difficulties. In the short tale entitled *La Fille du comte de Pontieu*, a man traumatized by having been forced to look on as his wife is raped protects himself by breaking off all sexual relations with her. Or in stories of incest like *La Manekine*, the reunited husband and wife temporarily master their desire (for the duration of Holy Week) and embark upon a new life together.

Affectionate feelings toward children are manifest in numerous texts from *La Manekine* to *Tristan de Nanteuil*, where a miracle finally increases the flow of milk from the breasts of a mother who would rather commit suicide than see her baby suffer. In a more hierarchical context Ide, countess of Boulogne, will not entrust the task of suckling her infants to anyone else. She discovers, however, that during her absence a nurse has given suck to her hungry son. Seized by holy wrath, she shakes the child, causing it to vomit up the substitute nourishment, then feeds it with her own milk. This episode from the *Chevalier au cygne* establishes a connection between the private world of women and the grandeur of the lineage. The gynaeceum becomes the symbolic locus of the mother's capital role within the domestic cell; the transmission of mother's milk becomes a sacred act, such that the child's biological mother is the only nurse worthy of her glorious progeny.

The Frantic Search for the Father. Another obsession of medieval literature is ancestry and the question of relations between parents and children. Relations with the father are quite obviously a major preoccupation of those tales in which a woman is accused of giving birth to a monster that cannot be a legitimate child of her husband. The question of paternity is even more at issue in stories of combat between father and son, tragic adversaries who do not know or do not recognize each other. In *Gormont et Isembart* the renegade son strikes his own father in the melee; other examples are found in *Doon de la Roche, Baudoin de Sebourc, Florent et Octavien*. The late romance

Valentin et Orson is an instance of parricide. Valentin, who is carrying a Saracen shield, is attacked by his father. They clash with such violence that the son's lance passes right through his father's body: "Today you have killed the father who engendered us!" cries Orson, the murderer's twin brother.

Uncles and Nephews. The questioning of blood ties suggests the degree to which medieval notions of kinship remained ambiguous. The father's fascination for the son and vice versa is especially explicit in fairy tales, where the one belongs to the feudal world and the other to a supernatural world. Father and son are at once close relatives and total strangers, as in the *Lai de Désiré* or, in an even more fantastic way, in *Tydorel*. King Tydorel, after learning of his descent from fairies, abandons his crown, spurs his mount, and gallops fully armed into the depths of the lake from which his father had emerged to engender him.

The great heroes of the chansons de geste frequently have no sons, or else their sons are ridiculous figures, like the feeble Louis in *Charroi de Nîmes*. Nephews serve as surrogate sons and enjoy a special relationship with their uncle. R. Bezzola has pointed out that there is no precedent for this kind of relationship in Greek, Roman, German, or Celtic mythology. The symbolic value of the father-son relationship is not hard

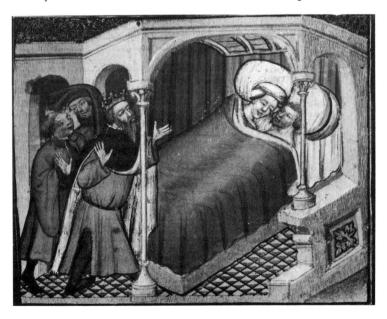

"When Gawain had fallen asleep, the damsel, who was young and plump, also fell asleep, soothed by her friend's tender presence." The king of Norgales then surprised his daughter in the arms of the knight. (Paris, Arsenal Library, ms 3479.)

King Arthur and Queen Guinevere leave the banquet; 14th century. (Turin National Library.)

to imagine; but this was joined by the nephew–uncle relationship, one of close kinship but without direct succession. Nephews are extremely close to their uncles, who feel a special affection for them (consider William of Orange and his nephews); they are therefore "distinguished" personages. Yet there is ambiguity, as in the case of Roland and Charles. The emperor's only nephew, Roland is assigned an individual mission, but "might he not have been more than a nephew? Might he not have been the emperor's own son?" (Bezzola). According to a Nordic saga, Roland, to whom the *Chanson de Roland* assigns only a stepfather, is in fact the son of Charles and his sister Gisèle, but this incestuous parentage is not attested in any French text prior to the fourteenth century. The theme of the nephew as love child is paramount in the story of Tristan as related by Gottfried of Strasbourg. Raised by adoptive parents and kidnapped by Norse merchants, Tristan is taken in by Mark and learns that he is Mark's nephew. The uncle so loves his sister's child that he does not want to engender a successor. Ambiguity also prevails in the antinomic couple of Gawain and Mordred, Arthur's nephews. Faithful companion and close adviser to the king, the courtly Gawain becomes the enemy of Mordred the traitor, who conspires to deprive Arthur of both wife and kingdom. According to one version of the legend, Mordred is the product of Arthur's incestuous love for his sister, the wife of King Loth of Orcania and mother of Gawain. But his incest was innocent, because at the time of the act Arthur did not know whose son he was, hence had no idea that Anna was his sister!

Exiles. Closely related to the problem of relations between the individual and the collectivity (which, even as it imposes limits, defines the individual's status) is the question of exile. Women are particularly interesting in this regard. Consider the daughter of the count of Pontieu, who marries the son of her father's sister. She proves sterile, however, and having lost all honor and social value, is cast adrift in a barrel; but she washes ashore in a Muslim country, where she regains both her social position and her fertility. Sterility turns to fertility via an initiation that begins with the attack on her body, with a murder attempt for which she will never repent, and finally with her coming under the jurisdiction of pagan law. Are we to assume that this exogamic journey, this temporary rupture of relations with family and society, was for her a necessary

and fruitful experience? In any case, exile is frequently a consequence of incestuous relations. The father's desire, barely
suggested in *Le Vair Palefroi*, is more explicit in Marie de
France's *Les Deux amants* (The Two Lovers): "Powerful vassals
asked for her hand and would gladly have taken her for their
wife, but the king would not agree, for he could not do
without her. She was his only refuge, and he stayed at her
side night and day." It is quite clearly perverse in *La Manekine*
and *Le Roman du comte d'Anjou*.

Courtly Love and Jealousy. Not the least of the causes of domestic tension was jealousy. Indeed, in one sense the institution of courtly love was a fantastic elaboration of the theme
of jealousy, since the husband, who made love possible, also
made it dangerous. In Arthurian literature the king is little
affected, however. (Arthur does not appear to be either jealous
or suspicious in the *Chevalier à la charrette*, a story of adultery.)
The effects of adulterous love on private life do not begin to
appear until the thirteenth century. In the *Roman du châtelain
de Coucy* the jealous husband makes his wife eat the embalmed
heart of her lover, who has died on a Crusade. In exaggerated,
parodic form, jealousy figures in the *Lai d'Ignauré*, in which
twelve husbands take their revenge. In the *Châtelaine de Vergi*
the jealousy of the duchess leads to a profanation of love. In
Flamenca, jealousy reaches pathological proportions: the jealous lover appears out of control, repulsive, the antithesis of
the courtly ideal.

Accused Women. Some domestic plots are so common in medieval fiction that they must have been more than mere en-
tertainment, providing at the very least imaginary release in
the form of a happy ending (after a household has endured
some threat to its well-being). One such plot involved an
accusation of wrongdoing against a woman, particularly a
pregnant woman. As a result of the alleged crime, the woman's child is tainted; her offspring will be illegitimate or even
monstrous. Or a chaste woman is accused of being the object
of her brother-in-law's lust. Sometimes the heroine's perse-
cutor is afflicted with a disease and cured by the victim herself
after confessing his misdeed. The importance of public confession cannot be overstated, especially confession of guilty desire. In *Florence de Rome* the confession is repeated obsessively.

Accusations of monstrous loves are frequent. In the *Chevalier au cygne* Queen Beatrix, having maligned a mother of twins, herself gives birth to a litter of six. In the later *Theseus de Cologne* the queen, having laughed at a deformed cripple, gives birth to a monster, and a spurned lover accuses her of having had relations with a midget. Her outraged husband condemns her to the stake, but the baby is graced by God with beauty, and the midget defeats the slanderer in single combat. In some stories the children of accused mothers are banished from their legitimate families, disinherited, and cast out into the world.

Brothers. Between the twelfth and fifteenth centuries literature offers innumerable examples of a model nuclear family, usually with twin brothers for children. This apparently was seen as an ideal solution to the underlying problem of conflict over power between two occupants of the same private space. Drawing upon the ancient enigma of dual birth, the brother stories seem to be a response to the tendency of feudal society to fill the lives of younger brothers with endless frustration. By making the brothers twins, the stories restore equality to the less favored brother (or even superiority, since the younger brother sometimes supplants his double, with the latter's full accord). Occasionally the twin metaphor made it possible to touch on issues that could not be broached in stories about real brothers. It thus served as what Georges Duby has called "social therapy": the rights of the last-born were asserted, and the need for coexistence was stressed.

Some pairs of brothers were involved in bloody episodes. The descendants of Oedipus figure in the *Roman de Thèbes*; the story of Romulus and Remus is briefly sketched in the prologue to the *Roman d'Athis et Prophilias* and, in a more feudal context, in the thirteenth-century *Florence de Rome*, in which there is a battle over walls and a deadly struggle for power. In stories where the brotherly theme is used as a vehicle for the expression of hatred, one brother is always older, and the dispute hinges on the rights of the first-born. Fratricide always involved an older and a younger brother, never twins.

Twins in fact were always exemplary in some way. Frequently victims, they were banished from society in order to tell the story of their progressive resocialization. Sometimes the twins' mother is herself an exile—such as the queen of England in *Guillaume d'Angleterre* or the beautiful Helaine, sister of Pepin in *Valentin and Orson*. Often the children are born in the wild, where they lose their mother and are raised by an animal or brought up by peasants or merchants in a social setting very different from that into which, by right, they should have been born. Clearly their close relation to the mother suggests a survival of archaic materials: the twins remain tied to the mother's womb. An example is Helaine's severed arm, which her son Bras (*bras* means arm), to whose body the arm has been attached, will preserve until adolescence, carrying it as a relic until his brother, the future Saint Martin, miraculously reattaches the sacred umbilical cord to the mother's body.

Deliverance and reconciliation are quite common in these

A knight visits his lady; 15th century. (Chantilly, Condé Museum.)

tales, especially those involving the mother's rehabilitation. Twins are thus the nucleus of the parent-child cell, and there is a centripetal structure to their stories: the disintegrated family is reunited, drawn back toward its center. Yet the children retain a name that is at variance with their recovered identity: in one version of *Valentin et Orson*, Orson, who has been raised by a bear, is called Nameless, and he keeps this name, as if the mystery of his birth and of his ejection from the community had made him in some way unnameable. The twin tales are stories of acculturation: before they can be reunited with father and mother, the twins must first recognize each other as brothers. In *Valentin et Orson* a savage child is vanquished by his already acculturated brother. He then acknowledges an allegiance that casts Valentin in the role of lord: Orson "reached out his hands toward his brother Valentin, begging his pardon in sign language and indicating that henceforth he wishes to obey and satisfy his brother's wishes. And he shows him by signs that he shall never fail to respect his brother's person or property."

Here there is an apparent paradox: one of the twins is cast in the role of the elder brother. Yet no situation was more egalitarian than that of twins. Nevertheless, *Guillaume d'Angleterre* clearly indicates that there is a first-born. Remember that an article in the customs of Beauvaisis held that testimony by women was inadmissible except in cases where a mother was obliged to indicate which of her two male children was born first: "There is no way to tell which is the elder except by the testimony of women, and for this reason *in this case* they must be believed."

Fictive Twinship. Metaphorical twins were in a sense a hyperbolic version of real twins. The origin of their twinship was different; it was accompanied by new compacts and tested by new trials. Yet the role of twins as benefactors of the community was the same, and the idealized, exemplary vision of flawless solidarity was comparable. These twins are artifacts, for their twinship is the result of peculiar circumstances: they are bound forever by a contract of partnership, not unlike actual documents of *affrèrement* (adoptive brotherhood). But the bond between them is purely emotional; the partners share neither blood nor homeland. Ami and Amile come from Berri and Auvergne, Athis and Prophilias from Rome and Athens, and Artus and Olivier, the heroes of a fifteenth-century tale,

"The bear showed great affection for the child and suckled it for an entire year. Because of this feeding, the child became as hairy as a wild beast and ate raw meat." *Valentin et Orson*; manuscript illustrated by J. Bourdichon, 15th century. (Paris, Ecole des Beaux-Arts.)

from Algarve and Castile. From their first meeting relations between them are sealed by an explicit contract, whose language is quite vigorous: "And when they began to know each other, they were bound by such perfect love that they formed an alliance together as stalwart companions, promising each other that nothing would ever make either abandon the other except death. For apart from the will of Our Lord God, it was their opinion that hatred and malevolence could never come to be where there existed such great love and good company" (*Histoire d'Olivier de Castille et Artus d'Algarbe*).

From that day forward the partners agreed to offer the world "*un semblant et une feiture,*" an appearance of identity. We are asked to believe that their appearance, similar to the point of possible confusion, is a result of the contract they have signed. Even relatives cannot be sure which is which. In other cases the contract has to be tested before it is valid; frequently one party is required to search for his double, from whom separation is unbearable, using some token of recognition. The crucial test involves the prized woman, however. Athis, aware that Prophilias is dying of love for his, Athis's, intended wife, imagines a subterfuge in which he marries the girl but then hands her over to his double on the wedding night (and for long months thereafter). Another test involves the gift of children, or, rather, of the blood of children. A twin who contracts leprosy is cured by blood from his brother's children. In this we may be detecting an echo of traditional rites involving the exchange of blood.

Twins, both real and contractual, always engaged in a contest for power. Indeed, there is reason to view twinship not as a matter of kinship in the narrow sense but as the kernel of a special type of relation to the community. The sons of Oedipus and the founders of Rome were consumed by covetousness; by contrast, medieval twins were always associated with prosperous and expanding kingdoms. Fed by that charismatic pair Claris and Laris, the Knights of the Round Table extended their conquests into new territories. In medieval literature an individual and his double often act jointly, the one reinforcing the power of the other. In some cases, however, both twins renounce power. Ami and Amile end their days piously in Lombardy. Valentin and Orson end theirs in a manner worthy of hagiography. The serene renunciation of property is, it seems, the best way to extinguish a dangerous rivalry. Even in the *Histoire d'Olivier de Castille*, a territorial romance rooted in the designs of the fifteenth-century court of Burgundy, the twin who assumes the role of elder brother has the good grace to vanish rapidly from the narrative, bequeathing all his kingdoms to his brother.

Brotherhood, real or fictive, could also be experienced as the inversion of hatred, an acceptable solution to latent conflicts which were presented in literature in sublimated form. Twinhood symbolized a primitive undivided state, a sharing of the womb. Twins filled the world with a spirit of conciliation, of solid ties, of restored community (and their metaphoric homologues depended on the same utopian notions).

Women and Marriage

The Gynaeceum. By "gynaeceum" I mean a group of women living together in an area set aside for the purpose. Literary representations may be found in the chansons de toile, chansons de geste, romances, and, at a later date, in *veillées*—stories told by groups of women who gathered together after sundown. From the thirteenth to the fifteenth century a space was explicitly or tacitly reserved for women. How constant was its structure? The question is important for understanding the relation between women as individuals and groups and the larger community.

Information about women's space is hard to come by. Clearly it was sharply delineated from the rest of domestic space; a distinctly feminine sense of time prevailed within it. In the chansons de toile women are seen to be dependent and in a state of virtual rebellion against the institution of marriage. Woman's time is a time of waiting; time is experienced inwardly, and in despair. Occasionally, as in the *Roman du comte d'Anjou*, women flee their threatened private space only to recreate a new female space elsewhere, in which the temporal dimension is both the same and different. The boundary of woman's space sometimes is breached by an accursed female, such as the *maistresse* of beautiful Euriaut in the *Roman de la Violette.*

By contrast, in the *Chanson du chevalier au cygne* woman's space is closely guarded, for within it reside the women in whom the quality of the lineage is vested. In the gynaeceum woman is exalted in her role as mother; men may enter, but only for a limited time. In parts of the household where multiple female functions are on display (lady, retinue, nurses) spatial references are absent. In the gynaeceum the child receives its earliest education; the segregation is functional. The internal time of the gynaeceum is consonant with external (or male) time.

Later, in the *Evangiles des quenouilles* (Gospels of the Distaff), a work that is the heir of the *Decameron* and precursor of a flourishing sixteenth-century genre, the narrator reports: "It is a true story that one night after supper during the long nights between Christmas and Candlemas of this past year, I went to visit the house of a rather elderly damsel not far from my neighbor's, where I was in the habit of going to talk, for several of the neighbors from thereabouts came to spin and talk of idle and happy things, from which I took great solace and pleasure." In this women's talk, which must be recorded by a narrator, the women's group has a very distinctive character. It defines itself in terms of boundaries. Deliberately setting themselves apart from the male world, women discuss an almost magical form of knowledge and convey a kind of mastery over the community. Here women's time is all-embracing, womblike in the strict sense.

Memory of gesture. Boccaccio, *Des clercs et nobles femmes*, ca. 1403. (Paris, Bibliothèque Nationale, French 598.)

The modalities of various scenes in which females figure as protagonists depend on the milieu, whether the aristocratic world of the romances or the peasant world of evening vigils. These women are made to act and above all to speak in ways that signal their retirement, their spatial, emotional, or ritual separation from the community at large. The economy of means reveals the way in which the literary code functions; a variety of signs supplement the rare spatial notations. In the chansons de toile women's private space is a place of reverie, openness, expectation, and confidence. The visual framing may be slight, but the verbal notations clearly suggest two separate spaces: one private and female, and another upon which the first depends for everything. The heroines of the chansons de toile seem to live on the brink of rupture with the authoritarian world of laws. Frames (a window or a tower crenellation) suggest boundaries crossed by the gaze. By contrast, the orchard, an open space, frequently indicates that private space is about to dissolve, that the gynaeceum has already broken into fragments. Belle Beatris' lover meets her in the orchard, from which they plan to make their escape.

Withdrawal is another constant. The heroine frequently lies in wait or delves inward by means of reading, but usually she is absorbed in women's work, which we find in lyric as well as in romances like *Guillaume de Dole, Escoufle,* and the *Roman du comte d'Anjou.* Seated women sew, sing, and speak, at times with a spatial and temporal organization that is not without consequence for the functioning of collective memory within the gynaeceum. For example, William's mother and sister sit by themselves embroidering in the chanson that Lienor sings to welcome the emperor's messenger. In the six veillées of the *Evangiles* there is a striking redundancy of objects; each is introduced and ended by this reminder of what the women are doing with their hands: "All brought their distaffs, flax, spindles, standards, happles, and all the agoubilles useful in their art."

In narrative fiction the fate of the gynaeceum often depends on a governess. Governesses exhibit either the most exemplary or the most malicious behavior. In the *Roman du comte d'Anjou* a young girl, accompanied by her governess, flees her father's house. The fugitives hide in the home of a poor woman, where they pass their time in prayer and work. (They are skilled at embroidery.) Forced to flee once again, they are engaged to teach embroidery to a castellan's two daughters. The governess, who is referred to as the "good lady" and who calls her young charge "girl," is the younger woman's confidante; it is she who persuades the girl to flee, who knows how the house is run, and who gathers together the gold and silver needed for the escape. Their *chambre et maingnage* (chamber and household) open onto an orchard from which it is possible to reach the forest. Later, the heroine is persecuted by a malevolent stepmother who starts a rumor that the girl has given birth to a monster; she is condemned to be thrown into a well along with her child. The governess dies of sorrow, a figure of the exemplary mother. The story suggests that the slander of incest could be used to malign all womankind. The individual woman stands for the group as a whole, because in this and other stories the group functions through doublets. (In two different stories the beautiful Helaine of Constantinople is "doubled" by another woman, who goes to the stake in her place.) The value attached to handiwork in this romance is redundant. The women obtain *manentise* and *herbergage* (food and lodging) because they know how to work with their hands; they gain security and reintegration into the community because their function is to pass this knowledge on to two young apprentices, the daughters of the castellan. Thus the gynaeceum is reconstituted. Indeed, this gynaeceum is mobile, its cohesion mantained through the remembered craft of embroidery. Under threat, the enclosed women's space dissolves but only in order to seek out a new

"The old woman led him to the peephole she had made. The count peered through it and saw the violet on the right breast." *Roman de la Violette*, 15th century. (Paris, Bibliothèque Nationale.)

space in which it can exist in freedom, a space that will be both private and protected. It spreads like a vine.

In contrast, the *Roman de la Violette* illustrates the disintegration of the gynaeceum. The nurse, by aiding in the violation of the enclosed woman's world, stands for dissension among women. She senses the man's nascent desire, offers to aid in its fulfillment, wrests from the girl the secret of the intimate sign (the violet), and finally penetrates the symbolic barrier whose fragility reveals a flaw in the utopian values of the gynaeceum, the plural harmony of women.

In the *Evangiles des quenouilles* we move outside the aristocratic maisnie. One day, a group of wise and prudent matrons decide upon an amusement for the group: "One of us will begin her reading and recite her chapters in the presence of all assembled, in order to hold them and fix them perpetually in memory." By reading maxims and commentaries, then, together with their experience of everyday life, these women attempt to exercise a magical power over domestic society. Since some of them have had contact with the occult sciences, they offer age-old nostrums for making the land productive and animals fertile along with more superstitious advice for, among other things, preventing nightmares. Their seclusion is linked to active leisure and a collective ritual, hence the repetitive is here sovereign: a moment of cyclical time that

Very skillfully, Marcia paints her own portrait with the help of a mirror. Boccaccio, *Des femmes nobles et renommées*, 15th century. (Paris, Bibliothèque Nationale, French 598.)

links past, present, and future. The women form an organized society, electing one of their number to a term as president, assigning another to act as secretary and take minutes, while their audience grows with each passing day. These peasant women possess a secret knowledge, as is indicated by the abundance of marks of interpretation, the relations that they establish among various deciphered "signs," and their ability to interpret the hidden meaning of things. The group is held together by the exchange of knowledge. These secrets can only be passed from woman to woman: "They thanked lady Abonde for her true Gospels, promising that none would whisper them in a calf's ear but would divulge and publish them through all their sex, so that from generation to generation they might be continued and augmented."

Thus, today's gynaeceum gives rise to tomorrow's. Society's future is governed by the authoritative and regulative utterances of women, who attempt to exert control over all areas of individual and collective life, from animal husbandry to the sexual act, from marital disputes to the control of emotions by means of witchcraft: "If a woman wants her husband to prefer one of his children to another, she should make him eat half the tips of his dog's ears and make the child eat the other half, and by the truth of the Gospel they will love one another so much that they will scarcely be able to bear being apart." The gynaeceum embraced wholeheartedly the magical and oracular function, as the secretary who recorded their sayings clearly understood: "It seemed to them that, through these constitutions and chapters, the world should henceforth be governed and ruled by them."

Surrounded by boundaries (in some cases imposed by others), the gynaeceum could create boundaries of its own, giving rise to a powerful dialectic of inside and outside which could prove fruitful for the community as a whole. Here it takes on the status of a sovereign motherland (*matrie*). Always hemmed in by language, misfortune, or power, the gynaeceum possessed, despite or even because of its segregation, a strength that preserved and maintained it as an inexpugnable component of domestic society.

The Couple Alone. Before 1200 depictions of marriage were often stereotyped, but in the thirteenth and fourteenth centuries increasingly sophisticated accounts of the state of matrimony began to appear, especially in didactic literature. The

Chevalier de La Tour Landry chastises women who are tempted to disobey their husbands, "especially in front of other people," but he adds that "when you are alone with him privately (*priveement seul a seul*), you can express your wishes more freely, according to your knowledge of his demeanor." He thus defines a private space and time in which relations are freer and more intimate, as though it were necessary to maintain a facade in the presence of other household residents, while in private one could speak more freely. The *Ménagier de Paris* contains some fine examples of marital intimacy. For instance, the young wife's husband reminds her of how she had asked him—in private—to correct her behavior in an affectionate way: "You humbly asked me in our bed, as I recall, that for the love of God I never scold you in a disagreeable way in front of strangers or servants, but instead that I speak to you every night in our bedroom and remind you of the mistakes and naive remarks that you made during the day or over the past several days, and that I point out to you how you ought to behave and give you advice on the subject. You would then not fail to change your ways by following my advice and you would do your best to do what I asked of you."

In the *Ménagier*'s "Quint article" (fifth article) we discover a hierarchy of intimacy, a series of concentric circles centered

From the beginning of the book that the Chevalier de La Tour Landry addressed to his daughters, "still very young and devoid of wisdom," 15th century. (Paris, Bibliothèque Nationale, French 1190.)

on the husband: "You should be *very loving and very private* (tres amoureuse et tres privee) with your husband above all other living creatures, *moderately loving and private* (moiennement amoureuse et privee) with your good and close blood relatives and your husband's relatives, *very distantly private* (tres estrangement privee—aloof) from all other men, and *completely distant* (du tout en tout estrange—have absolutely nothing to do with) from presumptuous and idle young men." Affection in marriage is depicted in even greater detail in the seventh article. A good wife soothes her husband's body and lets him rest his head "between her breasts." Treated well, the husband will feel for his wife the same attachment as a child for those who love it, who show it "love, care (*curialités*), privacy (*privetés*), joys, and pleasures." Some call this "bewitchment." The *Ménagier* heartily recommends such bewitching intimacy, reminding women of the country proverb according to which "there are three things that drive a good man from his house: a bad roof, a smoky fireplace, and an unruly wife."

Women in the Community. Didactic works in the vernacular give us a good idea of the individual's place in the community. Books of advice to women, aimed at preparing them to perform a suitable function in the community, are particularly interesting. Women are urged to fashion an image of themselves in private and not to show others too much of themselves. Misuse of privacy (abuse of the body, of language, or of sleep, for example) can have adverse repercussions on the workings of the community. Women are tools; their use must be carefully controlled.

In the *Chastoiement des dames* advice to women concerns the social proprieties as well as proper behavior in what some would call private, namely, an area of freedom which nevertheless remains under the scrutiny of the larger community. The status of women is fragile. Robert of Blois stresses how hard it is for women to regulate their behavior in society. If they are warm and courteous, there is a danger that men will misinterpret their intentions. If, on the other hand, their courtesy falls short of what is expected, people will accuse them of pride. A woman must be above reproach at every step. She must always maintain control over her body, for she is constantly exposed to view (the eye of course being a source of evil). She must be careful whenever she does expose herself and worry about hiding any ugliness. Even in church she must

"Here begins *Le Livre de la Cité des Dames* [The Book of the City of Ladies] whose first chapter states why and for what motive it was written." About 1405. (Paris, Bibliothèque Nationale, French 607.)

know how to look while assuming an attitude of piety: she should not laugh or speak and, as always, she should be careful about where she allows her eyes to wander.

In the *Book for the Instruction of His Daughters* La Tour Landry holds up a "mirror of old stories" for the benefit of his daughters, still "petites et de sens desgarnies," small and lacking common sense. This is a book of exemplary virtue composed of brisk chapters designed to appeal to a young girl's mind. Echoing Robert of Blois but written with greater subtlety, it is a program for shaping feminine nature by teaching proper attitudes toward the body in such a way as not to hinder the performance of daily chores and communal rites. A veritable rule of secular life, the book takes the view that a well-balanced life depends on performing each activity at the appropriate time, especially sleeping and eating. The one constant throughout the day is piety, which assures a good sleep. "Eat at the right hours, between prime and tierce, and take supper at the appropriate hour, depending on the season." To chasten the flesh still further, the young woman must also know the proper way to fast, three days a week according to chapter 6, which depicts a girl whose life is "dissolute and disorderly from morning till night," who says her prayers as quickly as possible, who gulps down "soup or some *lescherie* (jam?)," and after her parents have gone to bed gives in to the impulse to eat again. This excessive, gluttonous behavior, which fails to respect the hours set aside for the day's activities, will infallibly persist after the girl marries. Another example of an improper use of time can be found in an anecdote about a knight and a lady who, from early youth, liked to sleep late in the morning (*dormir a haulte heure*), thereby missing mass and, worse still, causing others in their parish to miss mass as well.

Such practical advice is based on a surprising mixture of moral counsel and anecdotes about posture, attitude, and so forth. A woman's bearing is of the utmost importance: "When saying your hours at mass or elsewhere, try not to look like a turtle or a crane; women look like turtles or cranes when they turn their faces this way and that and stretch out their necks and dart their heads back and forth like weasels. Keep your eyes steady and your back straight like a female bloodhound, which looks straight ahead without turning its head to one side or the other. Stand still and look straight ahead, and if you want to look to one side, turn your body and your face together."

Order depends upon striking the proper balance between regard for one's own body and regard for the community. Infractions of the social code result in punishment of the body. For having known a false joy the body is chastised. A good example of misuse of the body can be found in chapter 26: a woman refuses to dress in her finest clothes for a feast in honor of the Virgin, on the grounds that no important people will be present. As punishment her body is afflicted with swelling and paralysis, and she is quick to repent in a sort of public confession: "I had a handsome and pleasing body, or so everyone said in order to please me, and because their words filled me with pleasure and pride I wore beautiful dresses and handsome furs, which I made sure were cut carefully and tight. And it came to pass that the fruit of my womb suffered many dangers as a result, all that I might enjoy worldly glory and praise. For when I heard men who wished to please me say, 'Look at that fine woman's body, worthy of being loved by a good knight!' my heart filled with joy!" No sooner are these words of repentance uttered than the woman regains her original form. Thereafter she adopts a more measured attitude toward fine clothes and men's regard.

Women were also capable of unseemly haste, for example, haste in taking up new fashions. In chapter 47 we see a group of women in church, many dressed in the latest fashion. A bishop tells them that they look like slugs and unicorns. They are much aggrieved when they grasp that their *cointises* (coquetries), *contrefaictures* (artifices), and *mignotises* (affectations) are like the spider's stratagems for catching flies. Nevertheless, La Tour Landry can adapt his preaching when necessary. Sometimes it is best to do as everyone else is doing, "since state and novelty are current everywhere, and everyone takes part." Excessive concern with elegance leads first a young lady and then a young man to ignore common sense in dressing for the cold. One must learn, La Tour Landry advises, to avoid "uncivilized dress unsuited to the nature of the season."

Concern with the legitimate and illicit is evident in his counsels of modesty. Bathsheba washed and combed her hair in a window where King David could see her, an unfortunate act of exhibitionism whose consequences were only too well known: "This sin stemmed from her fondness for grooming herself and her pride in her beautiful hair, the source of numerous evils. Every woman should therefore groom and dress in secret; she should not take pride in her hairdo; and to please the world she should not show her beautiful hair or her throat or her bosom or anything else that ought to remain concealed."

In advice about physical contact with other people. La Tour Landry and his lady disagree. Relatively tolerant, he is willing to countenance some touching; his wife is more prudent: "As for my daughters, who are here, I forbid them to kiss, caress the chest, or be familiar in other ways" (*le baisier, le poetriner et tel manieres d'esbatement*, terms that reveal just how ambiguous the interpretation of promiscuity could be). Even earlier, in the thirteenth-century text *Flamenca*, familiar gestures are interpreted in two different ways. "Out of familiarity" the king places his hand on a young woman's breast: "He thought he was honoring Lord Archambaut when, in his presence, he embraced his wife and kissed her; he did so without thought of evil." Although such a gesture could be interpreted as normal, it clearly suggested the violation of a boundary.

Heat and Light in the House. Visitors were seated as close as possible to the fire, which stood for togetherness and sociability. When Erec is received by Enide's father, the vavassor, a fire burns brightly. "Brightly and without smoke," the fabliaux always insisted. Fires provided both physical and moral warmth and gave relief from the fatigue and hardship of travel. The hearth is the center of the family, and we often see scenes in which husband and wife sit on cushions near the fire to eat

Conversation around a fire. *Guiron le Courtois*, ca. 1370–1380. (Paris, Bibliothèque Nationale, French n.a. 5243.)

their meals (food and heat both being ingredients of domestic bliss).

In the fabliaux light is scarce, in contrast to the luminous debauch of aristocratic tales. In some conjugal scenes light is used to suggest that love is either legitimate or illegitimate. In La Tour Landry's *Livre*, for example, a gentleman and a damsel become involved in a rather heated argument during a game. The man says that if his partner were really a decent woman, she would not enter the apartments of men at night to "hug and squeeze them in their beds, without a candle." A woman whose lascivious husband always keeps one or two extra women around the house behaves in an exemplary manner; when the man returns from his debauches or, as he claims, from his "comfortable chambers," he finds a candle lit and a towel and water ready so that he can wash his hands.

The fact that in the fabliaux women tend the fire supports the notion that the wife was all-powerful in the home. If, in the misogynist world of *Quinze joyes de mariage*, a man takes over this chore, the reason is that things in his house are going badly. This work, which belongs to a tradition of writing hostile to women and marriage, is an anthology of the late fourteenth (or early fifteenth) century. It depicts a wife, mother-in-law, and female servants who, according to the introduction, conspire to turn their house into a "constricted and painful prison, filled with tears." Space is divided between chamber and hall, or, better still, between a sphere of heat and a sphere of cold, with a tactile realism that penetrates to the very quick. The work is confined entirely to this inhospitable household; people gather in the garden only before the marriage "trap" is sprung. The wife, a wily woman, takes refuge in her chamber. Pregnant, she is surrounded by other women, who plan ways to allay the husband's suspicions. Consensus and conviviality reign; the women eat and drink. The man, the husband, is condemned to solitude. Remote from the fire, he often goes to bed without supper, freezing, wet, and dejected. And when he wakes up he has neither fire nor candle at his side. In this topsy-turvy world the husband stirs the fire for his wife; while she dresses, he prepares the meal. When his relatives and friends come to visit, hospitality is denied. The wife sends all the servants away and permits no welcome to be prepared. The man is reduced to entertaining his guests in an unheated hall, his one wretched refuge.

By contrast, the women of the house (wife, chambermaid, mother, sister, and cousin) gather in winter around a warm fire and in summer in the garden, bound together by shared knowledge and song. Domestic space is compartmentalized, and the place of each individual within it signifies his or her status. Whether isolated in his room and subjected to hunger, thirst, and cold, or forced to receive guests in an icy hall, the husband's life is a nightmare. There is permanent conflict in the household. The children and the wife conspire against the husband, especially the eldest son, who wants to assume command and who cannot wait for his father to die. In vain the father dictates a domestic charter, but it does not help him escape from the trap.

Members of the household entourage, far from being minor characters, play roles that suggest great concern with the cohesion of the household unit. In *La Belle Helaine de Constantinople*, for example, when the mother-in-law wants to send a forged letter, she calls upon *gens estranges*, people with no connection to the family. In *Escoufle*, the emperor, influenced by wicked advisers, forgets the promise of marriage that linked William to Aélis. When William's father died, the sovereign surrounded himself with *noviax conseilliers*, new advisers, traitors, *losengiers*, and the text tells us that the emperor would have done better to have plucked out his own eye, for these men are always plotting "to stir up evil and do harm."

In a more strictly domestic setting we have the advice to the young wife in *Ménagier* concerning the judicious choice of servants. The twelfth-century *Lai du blanc chevalier* shows a young wife who suffers from a poor choice of companion. Her first companion is good: she exhorts the woman to do good, does not hesitate to correct her, warns her of false statements and misleading appearances, and above all is careful not to flatter. But she is replaced by another, who passes for a *preude femme* (honest woman) but exerts a thoroughly harmful influence, advising the young woman to take a lover in order to profit from her youth.

The Active Life and the Contemplative Life. With the aid of a recently discovered text containing a dozen or so rules for a Christian life, which was composed some time between the thirteenth and the early sixteenth century and which complements a handful of other sources in Italian and Spanish, we can see how a woman who wished to secure her salvation was advised to spend her days. (Here I am indebted to Geneviève Hasenohr's work on family and married life.) The texts reveal a tension between individual life and the life of the group, between sociability and self-fulfillment. These clerical writings help us to understand better the work of lay moralists like La Tour Landry and Christine de Pisan. The clergy classified women as married, widowed, or virgin; marriage ranked below chastity. Because of the value attached to the contemplative life, books of spiritual guidance were composed in the fourteenth and fifteenth centuries for the use of "simple folk." They echo the thoughts contained in thirteenth-century sermons in the vernacular.

"The life of contemplatives is better than the life of [those who are] active," the *Sept conditions d'une bonne femme* (Seven Conditions of a Good Woman) reminds us. Compared with the widow or the virgin, the married woman, burdened by a heavy handicap, finds it much more difficult to control her time. Although pastoral texts occasionally propose an active life for the married woman, there is a clear bias in favor of a contemplative life lived within the framework of an active one. According to the *Stimulus amoris*, attributed to Saint Bonaventure and widely available in translation from the early fifteenth century on, a person wishing to combine a contemplative with an active life had no alternative but to turn inward, to explore "the entrails of his heart," to lose himself entirely in God. But the attempt to graft a contemplative life onto an active one created tensions, as has often been pointed out, for temporal duties were disparaged by the spirituality of *contemptus mundi et carnis*. Certain "programs for life" like the *Decor puellarum* suggest that women's lives were tightly organized from morning till night; it was not easy to find time or space for private piety. Daily life was filled with "impediments." Yet a woman could always turn to the "ark of contemplative prayer, for the higher the waters of tribulation mount, the higher the ark of prayer must rise." The most suitable hour for prayer was the dead of night: "I believe, my dear daughter, that the most profitable hour for you and us might be in the middle of the night after going to sleep, after digesting the meat, when the labors of the world are cast off and set aside, and when, too, the neighbors will not see you and no one will look at you except for God, and there will be no one to see our moans and tears and sighs coming from the depths of the heart, nor all our bitter clamors, plaints, and laments, punctuated by heavy sighs, nor our prostration and kneeling in humility, nor our moist eyes and sweaty, changing faces, now red, now pale" (anonymous manuscript, Arsenal Library, 2176).

If the ideal time for meditation was the evening, after supper, the entire day was filled with moments of contemplation and self-regard. Instead of reading at dinnertime, as monks did, a program of silent prayer and meditation was proposed for wives. Husbands, it should be noted, were rarely present, particularly at bedtime, for wives, like widows, slept alone and in silence.

The ideal, then, was to maintain within the active life a state of devotion and meditation capable of sanctifying every minute of the day. This otherworldly ideal led to forms of seclusion within the home and even within the bedroom, the last refuge against the "worldly" life. In the fifteenth century San Antonino's *Opera a ben vivere* (Works for Good Living) is careful to allow time for silent reading and prayer. After dinner the wife is advised to withdraw as soon as possible into her bedroom: "In retreat in your room, occupy yourself usefully by reading, praying, or meditating until vespers is rung." For those who wish to live a spiritual life, manual labor must be more than just a palliative for boredom and lack of fervor. Limits are set on the amount of time that should be devoted to the household or group, for spiritual improvement depends on preserving a measure of personal freedom. In Jean le Chartreux's *Decor puellarum* (Maidenly Decorum) much of the advice is concerned with the wisdom of refraining from idle chatter. By praying until everyone in the house had gone to bed and then making sure that all doors, windows, and chests were tightly closed (symbolically sealing the soul off from all temptation), an autarchic inner world was eventually created. The individual, wholly devoted to God, stood in the dead of night face to face with herself.

Reading was always prescribed—at least "one or two pages of some pious book for the recreation of your soul." In this respect, women's daily schedules resembled those prescribed by monastic rules. A letter of spiritual guidance, composed in the late thirteenth or early fourteenth century and concerned with "the right form of life" for the soul, stresses solitude in the home. Remain "as secluded as possible in your room," it counsels, "for it was in her room that the glorious Virgin was hailed and there that she conceived the son of God."

THE BODY

In literary representations the body's status and gestures are coded in accordance with established conventions. A structure of self-consciousness gradually emerges in which the body is not only the sign of an exaltation of the individual (viewed as giving pleasure to self or others) but also the focus of proper and improper attitudes toward oneself. On the one hand, the body is said to be ripe for hyperbolic description; on the other, it is seen as needing correction (or condemnation). Far from being a random component of a plausible narrative, the body "states" the problem of the individual vis-à-vis the community; it is a mode of apprehending the world, whether through the positive evaluation of beauty or the rejection of ugliness and mortification of the flesh. The flesh looms large against the backdrop of salvation. As early as the late twelfth century, Hélinant of Froidmont, whose verses show signs of a nascent subjectivity, addresses death in these terms: "You who claim free land and use white throats as whetstones" (*Vers de la mort*).

Representations of the Body

Models and Seductions. Exaltation of the body is found in the literature of amusement. Like Gothic sculpture, much given to depicting the body in twisted and awkward postures, this literature encodes the body in a quite specific way. A recurrent topos describes feminine beauty in canonical terms: a creamy complexion enlivened by a touch of pink; blond hair; harmonious features; a long face; a high, regular nose; bright, happy eyes; and thin, red lips. There is a corresponding male stereotype, so that a Cligès or an Aucassin is in fact a double of the woman he loves. The topos of the female body lends itself to metaphor. Thus the trajectory of love's arrow enables Chrétien de Troyes to ascribe to each part of the arrow an element of the female anatomy. Thirteenth-century descriptions of the body were more explicit and concrete: firm breasts are compared to nuts, for instance, and although the literary code had no precise counterpart for the tilted hips of sculpture, a woman's hips were emphasized as a kind of caesura, the waist being indicated by the laced garment in such a way that the body's curves could be imagined from the glimpses offered by the gaps.

As for male beauty, while the chansons de geste relied on conventional formulas emphasizing muscular development, courtly narrative did not stint in its description of male perfections. Flamenca's lover is described thus: "May's rose when it blossoms is not so beautiful or vivid as was his complexion, which combined creaminess with color wherever it was needed. A more beautiful complexion never existed. He had shapely ears, large, firm, and red; and a lovely, intelligent mouth, loving in all that it said. His teeth were quite regular and whiter than ivory. His chin was strongly etched and, what made it even more gracious, slightly cleft. His neck was straight, long, and powerful, and no nerve or bone protruded. He was broad in the shoulder, as strong as Atlas in that regard. His muscles were well rounded, his biceps developed, his arms reasonably thick. His hands were large, strong, and hard. The joints of his fingers were flat, his chest broad and his waist narrow. As for his hips, he did not limp! They were strong and square; his thighs were shapely, thicker on the inside. His knees were quite smooth; his legs healthy, long, straight, and close together; his feet were arched on top and his instep high. No one had ever been able to catch him in a race."

From these stereotypes, which proliferated throughout romanesque literature, we see how important complexion was as an element of physical beauty. The ideal was cream slightly tinged with pink. Color was taken as a sign of physical complexion, that is, of the body's constitution. As for temperament, the "sanguine" was preferred, for it yielded a clear complexion and a happy face, whereas the "melancholic" or "saturnine" temperament was associated with darker skin.

Chaucer, introducing the Canterbury pilgrims, tells us that the franklin is of sanguine complexion: a true son of Epicurus, he likes a wine-based soup in the morning. In La Tour Landry the good lover, the one whose suit is likely to be accepted and who is careful not to risk appearing with an "insipid color" because he failed to dress warmly enough in cold weather, is "red as a cock," a fact appreciated by the lady being courted, for whom complexion is a sign of virility and health.

Given this exaltation of the male body, it is not surprising to discover that male beauty figures prominently in any number of skillfully wrought scenes of seduction. In certain scenes (in *Flamenca*, for example) the male character is aware of the advantages to be derived from his body, grooming, and a certain strategic nonchalance about his appearance. People were conscious of the liberties they could take with their bodies in certain situations. In *Guillaume de Dole* young men and women of fashionable society are invited to frolic about "barefoot and sleeves afloat" in the water of a spring; the ladies' chemises are used as towels, enabling the young gallants to "graze many a white thigh." Here the association between clothing and body is weakened, offering glimpses of the flesh, of nature's own attractions, in a festival of gesture which is at the same time a festival of the court.

Nature Improved. Fiction and medical treatises agree as to the place of cosmetics and grooming. Henri de Mondeville describes parts of the body as items of clothing, as if there were no way to disclose the body's secrets other than in terms of social signs. The skin is a cloak, internal membranes are undergarments, and other internal parts are like a fabric wrapping. The body's architecture becomes a social metaphor.

Fictional characters well endowed by nature can afford to dispense with makeup. In the *Roman de la rose* Cupid is seated beside a lady named Beauty, who shines as brightly as the moon, compared with which the stars are but tiny candles; she is neither "painted nor made up." For her, embellishment and artifice are unnecessary. Those less blessed may seek to improve on nature's handiwork in a variety of ways. In Mondeville women exchange advice about seduction. Depilatory techniques include the use of quicklime, removal of hair with pincers or fingers dipped in pitch, and—a technique requiring much patience—sticking hot needles into the follicle. Such techniques, though useful, were best not talked about, even to one's husband. If burns resulted from their use, Mondeville recommended telling the spouse that the servant had overheated the bathwater. A pale complexion could also be remedied. In *Les Trois méchines* one of three girls getting ready for a dance sets out on a long journey to obtain a magic powder that is supposed to cause the blood to rise from the heels to the face. Robert of Blois in the *Chastoiement des dames* says that eating a good breakfast can do wonders for a woman's complexion.

Smell, or the lack of it, was an important part of seduction. Henri de Mondeville provides several techniques for eliminating body odors and adding fragrance to the hair with the help of musk, cloves, nutmeg, and cardamom. In one allegorical lay, women living in a lover's paradise wear crowns of rose and eglantine and give off a pleasant fragrance. The Idle Lady in the *Roman de la rose* has the seductive advantage of a "sweet and perfumed breath," and in the *Chastoiement des dames* women are advised to eat anise, fennel, and cumin for breakfast. It is wise not to get too close: "In the course of amorous combat do not allow yourself to be embraced, for unpleasant odors are more of a problem when you are overheated."

In Chaucer's "Miller's Tale" the handsome lover Absolon rises at the first crow of the cock, combs his hair, and chews cardamom and licorice to sweeten his breath. In attempting to seduce the young girl, he uses an olfactory metaphor connoting sweetness and physical pleasure (l. 3698): "My faire bryd (bird), my sweete cynamome (cinnamon)!" Advice about clothing was aimed at satisfying the sense of smell: Mondeville recommends washing clothes occasionally with soap, scenting them with large numbers of violets, and then sprinkling with fresh water in which finely ground iris roots have been allowed to soak.

Caring for the Hair. Hair was an important element of a person's self-image. Blond hair was considered a canonical ingredient of beauty, as is indicated by the numerous words for blondness and the many heroines whose names connote blondness, such as Clarissant, Soredamor, and Lienor. Although narrative literature preferred blondes, some very elegant women were nevertheless described as "a little brunette" (*Roman de la violette*). Laudine is blonde, but her servant Lunete is an "excellent brunette." In the *Geste des Narbonnais* Aymeri's third son,

"The history of Griselidis and of her astonishing patience: its title is 'The Mirror of Married Ladies.'" *L'Histoire de la marquise de Saluce miz par personnages*, 1395. (Paris, Bibliothèque Nationale, French 2203.)

"She looked at herself in a handsome and particularly luminous mirror and saw her pleasing, colored features and the shape of her white bosom." *Beuve de Hantone.* (Chantilly, Condé Museum.)

the one who represents the third or nutritive function, has red hair; the color seems to have had pejorative connotations:

'Tis true, I have heard it said,
that one cannot find a quiet redhead.
That all are violent cannot be gainsaid!

In *Lancelot en prose* Méléagant has red hair and is covered with freckles.

Formulas for turning white hair blond again recommended applying to it overnight a paste made of the ashes of vine stems and ash trees boiled for half a day in vinegar. Abundant information on hair care can be found in a thirteenth-century Anglo-Norman text entitled *Ornatus mulierum*. This work is almost contemporaneous with the celebrated painting commissioned by Adam de La Halle, which depicts the ravages that time has wrought on his wife since their marriage; once her hair was "brilliant as gold, full of body, wavy, and shimmering," but now it is "sparse, dark, and limp." The text is concerned about the color and health of the hair, which must be preserved and in some cases encouraged to grow. Bleaching and dyeing of red, black, and brown hair are discussed, as is the use of olive oil to keep hair supple. There is advice about how to cope with dandruff and lice. Hairwasher is an occupation occasionally mentioned in the texts: in *Escoufle*, beautiful Aelis manages to survive in Montpellier by washing the heads of important people; her skill is the object of much praise.

There were still other ways to amend nature and make full use of a woman's capital. Tresses, often praised for their length, could be turned into architectural edifices: in the *Roman de la rose* the Idle Lady holds a mirror in her hand and elaborately braids her hair with a precious ribbon. Jean de Meung offers the following advice: "If she has not a beautiful face, let her use common sense and offer to the eye the beautiful tresses that fall upon her neck, because she knows that her hair is beautiful and nicely braided! The beauty of the hair is indeed a pleasant sight to see!" On the other hand, undone hair has high erotic value; the fairy Melusina is perhaps the emblem of this form of seduction. Wild hair is a sign of sadness. The allegorical figure Sadness in the *Roman de la rose* pulls at and tears out her hair in an access of sorrow. Unruly hair is another sign of mourning. Laudine, afflicted by sorrow, tears out her most seductive blond hair before Yvain's eyes. In the *Roman de la violette* Euriaut, desperate over the death of her lover, thrusts her fingers violently into her braids and undoes her hair.

Care of the Body. *La clé d'amour*, an anthology of thirteenth-century works in the tradition of Ovid, combines advice about songs, games, and table manners with information concerning the health and exhibition of the body, useful material for a history of fetishism. We learn that it is important to make a proper show of the feet, to use décolletage, and so on. Breasts that are too large should be bound, and ample clothing can conceal excessive thinness. The *Chastoiement des dames* is insistent on the care of the hands; fingernails, Robert of Blois says, should not extend beyond the fingertips. More concerned with propriety than with seduction, he also indicates the proper way to hold the body: "A lady acquires a bad reputation if she does not carry herself properly. A careful and agreeable bearing is better than neglected beauty."

The same text discourages any attempt to exhibit the body in an unseemly manner. The games of the flesh are perilous, and it is all too easy to become the cynosure of all eyes. A sober, controlled display of those parts of the body that can legitimately be shown, however, is enough to suggest that the body is beautiful in its entirety. "It is not good for a lady to bare her white body to anyone other than her intimates. One woman allows a glimpse of breast in order to show how white her skin is. Another deliberately allows her side to show. Another exposes too much leg. A wise man does not praise this way of behaving, for lust takes possession of the heart by ruse when the gaze is brought into it. For that reason, the wise man usually says: 'What the eye does not see afflicts not the heart!' A white throat, neck, face, or hands indicate, in my opinion, that the body is beautiful underneath its garments. The woman who bares those parts does not behave badly, but every lady should know the maxim that she who exposes her body to the gaze of others does so behave."

Bathing and Bleeding. Medieval texts refer constantly to the washing of hands before and after meals. Failure to observe this custom could be greeted with consternation. In the course of a journey that takes him from Scotland to Norway, Sone

Water of the right temperature. *Tacuinum sanitatis*, ca. 1390–1400. (Liège, General Library, ms 1041.)

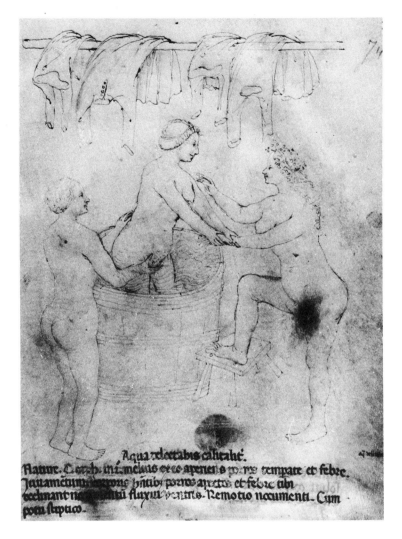

Aqua rclec̃abis cãlı̃cahc̃.

flauurc. C. crab. ıñ.meliu̇s eı̇ts aperıeı̇ a pı̃rc tempate et febre.
Jauanıc̃tum .... bıñtıbı pı̃rto apetto ef̃ febre ubı
declınãt n................bu fluxuı .... Remoı̃ıo nocumentı. Cũm
poı̃u ſtıptıco.

of Nansay, hero of a thirteenth-century romance, discovers that customs differ from one country to the next: among other peculiarities, the Norwegians do not wash their hands after eating! Bathing played an even more important role in literature, for it fulfilled a symbolic function. The bath represents intimacy, both spatially and temporally. Although a group of ladies who belong to the court of the *Châtelaine de Vergi* dress together, women usually groomed themselves in private. There was opportunity for transgression in modest solitude, however, so, as in the *Roman de la violette*, young girls were watched when they bathed. Baths encouraged eroticism, and it is not surprising to discover that public baths and steam rooms were regulated and closely watched. Going to the public baths seems to have been a risky business, and steam closets were often installed in private homes by jealous husbands.

In fiction there seems to have been a close connection between eroticism and the "feminine" moistness of steam. The significance of this is clear from the Old Lady's words in the *Roman de la rose*, when she sees Good Welcome "look at himself to see if his *chapel* suits him": "You are still a child and you do not know what you will do, but I am sure that sooner or latter you will pass through the flame that burns everyone, and you will bathe in the tub where Venus steams the ladies. I am quite sure that you will feel the fire! I therefore advise you to prepare yourself before you go to bathe, and that you take me for your teacher, for the young man who has no one to instruct him takes a perilous bath."

The baths of Bourbon-l'Archambault are the focal point of *Flamenca*, the place where lovers meet. These are therapeutic baths, whose virtues are spelled out by a sign placed in each. The sick, lame, and halt flock to the baths from all over. In each one there is a source of boiling water as well as cold water to mix with the hot. Each bath is closed and isolated; there are rooms to rest in after the treatment. Bathing is governed by the phases of the moon. Flamenca, who claims to be ill, informs her husband that she would like to bathe on the following Wednesday, for "the moon is in its last quarter, but in three days it will be totally dark and my condition will be improved." Her future lover is offered a bath by his host: "Today," he says, "I will not use it, because we are too close to the first of the month. It is better to wait. Tomorrow is the ninth day of the moon, and the moment will be ripe for me to bathe." Thus the lovers gained their moments of solitude, but they were not quite alone: Flamenca's female entourage went with her to the baths, carrying basins and unguents. But the heroine hits upon a subterfuge so that she can meet her lover: she invites the ladies of the court to bathe with her, but since these are volcanic springs with an unpleasant odor, the ladies will refuse. This narrative is unusually rich in its documentation of explicit eroticism and of the sociability of the baths. In reality sexual promiscuity may have been avoided by admitting men and women on alternate days or by having segregated baths. Such regulations prove how delicate a matter bathing was, and the degree to which public morality was at stake. In Occitanian fiction, moreover, Flamenca's husband

Bleeding. *Recueil de traité de médecine et Image du monde*, 15th century. (Paris, Bibliothèque Nationale, French 12323.)

"In a large marble basin with stairs going down to the bottom, Melusina was bathing." *Le Roman de Mélusine ou l'Histoire des Lusignan.* (Paris, Bibliothèque Nationale, res. Ye 400.)

locked her in the baths; when she wished to exit, she was required to ring a bell.

The bath was part of the ritual of welcome, an important item of comfort. The daughter of the count of Anjou is received along with her child by the wife of the "mayor," who immediately has a bath made ready for her. In the *Chevalier à la charrette* Lancelot is offered baths and massages by the damsel who rescues him. Were these baths signs of hospitality, were they therapeutic, or were they erotic in intent? Generally it is men who benefit from such attentions, as can be seen in numerous texts, including *Erec et Enide, l'Escoufle,* and *Sone de Nansay.* In *Guillaume de Dole*, after the tournament the weary knights return home, where they are glad to be given hot water to bathe their wounded necks. In the *Lai du blanc chevalier*, in the fourteenth century, the unknown victor in the tourney "bathed and cupped himself" upon returning home. In the fabliaux, baths are closely associated with meals. "Bath on the fire, capon on the spit"—such are the pleasures savored by the three canonesses of Cologne, as they bathe, eat, and drink, all while watching the jongleur perform.

Bleeding marked the beginning of a withdrawal into a private realm, not always without elements of parody. In *Erec et Enide*, when Arthur has himself bled: "Never at any time had the king been so alone, and he was bored not to have more of his court with him." But the text explains that he was accompanied, in his "private" apartments, by some five hundred of his barons. Marie de France has Equitan use bleeding as a device to be alone with the seneschal's wife. When the king says that he will undergo "bleeding without witnesses," the doors of his chamber are closed. The seneschal presides over the court as long as the king is indisposed. Here, privacy is culpable. In the realm of punishment, the Bel Ignauré, who twelve times defiles the institution of marriage, will also undergo a bath and bleeding.

Discovering the Body

In the *Lai d'Aristote* a young girl determines to prove to the elderly philosopher that he is just as fallible as young Alexander; the weather being mild, she strolls around the orchard as though she were alone, naked beneath her chemise, which floats in the breeze as she sings. This theatrical seduction contains signs of a fetishism that is quite up-to-date. The hidden parts of the body are as alluring as the visible. When Lanval is seduced by a fairy lying on a magnificent bed, the harmonious proportions of the fairy's body are suggested by her "bare flank," face, neck, and chest. In contrast to both patristic tradition and books of etiquette, which counseled prudence in physical display, literature liberated man's gaze.

Nudity. Medieval literature has much to say about exposure of the naked body to oneself and others, as well as about the ambiguous function of clothing (were clothes worn for protection, modesty, or embellishment?) and the perception of nudity. The fact that clothing was worn reveals exhibitionistic impulses and latent feelings of shame. Literature shows us the embarrassment that people felt when stripped naked, as well as their implicit or explicit rejection by others; yet nakedness could also be an occasion for jubilation, at least for men, in whose self-image the nude body played an important part. Nakedness could be a sign of exile and rejection. Medieval nudes are always covered with shame; nudity violates a social taboo. Initially, however, female as well as male nudes are seen as segregated from the community. Sometimes this segregation simply marks the observance of some private rite, such as bathing. But for men it also indicates a transition in their lives, as they shed their clothing and for a time revert to the savage state.

Lettuce was supposed to cure insomnia and gonorrhea but interfere with sexual intercourse and eyesight, effects which could be alleviated by mixing it with celery. *Tacuinum sanitatis*, ca. 1390–1400. (Paris, Bibliothèque Nationale, Latin n.a. 1673.)

The child born outside society or expelled from it at an early age (such as Tristan of Nanteuil, who was raised by a doe, or Orson, raised by a bear) recovers his clothing at the same time that he is reintegrated into the human community. In addition to stories of acculturation, there are many tales in which a person perfectly well integrated into the community (like Yvain of the Round Table) suffers an injury of some kind and flees society in a deranged condition; in other stories men are transformed into werewolves. These fictional characters are separated from society for long periods of time, often for years; escape from their predicament involves them in a ritual comprising a number of stages. Naked women are also segregated, but for shorter periods of time and generally within the confines of private space. In the *Roman de la violette*, for example, Euriaut is degraded when prying male eyes catch a glimpse of her as she bathes.

What does this tell us about the nature of modesty? That nakedness was supposed to be kept hidden and private, revealed only to a select few, hence that it was a source of embarrassment, shame, and weakness. It is hardly surprising,

In the course of their quest, Heart and Desire encounter the midget Jealousy, who has hairy arms and head and wears two lion skins. René d'Anjou, *Le Coeur d'amour épris*. (Vienna, National Library.)

therefore, that those who encounter a naked man along their route take the attitude of healers confronting the afflicted and seek to restore the clothing that has been stripped away. The male nude was always seen as an exile from a world of authority and order, or as a destroyer or opponent of order; nudity signifies anarchy. The nude is often hirsute in appearance, lawless in behavior, deranged in gesture, and incoherent in thought. In other words, the male nude signifies a break with society. By contrast, the female nude almost always responds to the logic of absolute sovereignty, to the will of the king or emperor. "We shall accede to your lawful will," say the young girls in the *Roman du comte de Poitiers* when the emperor insists that they disrobe so that he may choose the one he wishes to marry. In the tales that constitute the *Cycle de la gageure* (Cycle of the Wager), the female nude, whose privacy has been illicitly violated, is associated with a prize, a material reward of some sort, such as land. Female nudity functions in an autarchic and felicitous manner only in stories of a matriarchal stripe in which the woman uses her nudity as a decoy.

Nudity is a transitional state. Savage children emerge from the animal kingdom and progress toward the world of culture. Or males regress toward savagery, abandoning the group's cultural signs. The Bisclavret and Mélion, temporarily excluded from human society, retain human wisdom and memory; eventually they regain their human form. Some

men, deranged by love, are likened to werewolves. Social
reintegration begins with the donning of clothes. But the
transition to savagery is like amnesia: the individual loses all
marks of social identity and forgets the laws of behavior.
Spurned by a scornful damsel after completing a pointless
series of trials, the hero of the *Lévrier* breaks his sword, shreds
his clothes, and wanders deranged into the forest. Yvain flees
all human companionship, hunts game, and eats raw meat.
Amadas sleeps on the rocks. The return of memory, or anamnesis, is thus also a matter of taming or domestication: the
twin of the savage Orson, who brings the strange hairy creature to court, indicates that he "is behaving badly, which fills
Orson with shame." The deranged are notable for their aggressiveness and incommunicativeness. Significantly, the values
of the knightly ethic are also gone: bravery, frankness, and
loyalty. Hairiness, signifying the transition from the human
to the animal realm, is common: the savage man is both naked
and covered, as though the texts scarcely dared to portray the
"naked man." The new skin serves the same functions as
clothing; it mimics the habitable spaces and structures of society. Later, when the civilized appearance returns, it is domesticated, pared down, polished, in contrast to exuberant,
unruly nature. The rites of reintegration are specifically intended to contain abnormal excrescence. The hero is asked to
submit to techniques of exhalation, exudation, and purgation
designed to eliminate harmful elements as a necessary prelude
to the reintegration (or reception) of the savage. The treatment
that draws the "rage and melancholy" out of Yvain is not
unlike the therapy the fairy dispenses to the hero of the *Lévrier*:
having folded back his hood, she attaches to the young man's
forehead herbs that cause him to sweat profusely, thereby
quenching his madness. The sleeping hero wakes and says,
"Lady, I have regained my reason. Blessed is he who has
restored it to me!"

The ritual of the bath, an essential feature of any reintegration into society, occurs in almost all these stories. A damsel in love with Orson finds him nicely built and thinks, "if
he were bathed and steamed, his skin would be white and
soft."

After the hero returns to social consciousness, he divines
how insane his behavior must have been during his period of
amnesia and feels shame for having violated the social code.
He must suddenly confront the stares of other people, stares
in which communal values are crystallized. Amadas learns

Wild men and women. Jean
Wauquelin, *Histoire d'Alexandre*,
ca. 1448. (Paris, Bibliothèque
Nationale, French 9342.)

what a "repulsive and vile" life he led *in the city*; it is no accident that the city—communal space—is mentioned. From his incongruous appearance the hero reconstructs his nightmare, recalling the disorderly behavior that others have witnessed. In order to evaluate the significance of these stories as symbols of relations between the individual and the community, we must examine the role that the group plays in reintegrating the individual. The group must offer comfort and protection. In the werewolf stories a room is set aside for the creature so that, when it regains human form, it need not expose itself to public view. In the *Lai de Mélion* Gawain counsels Arthur: "Take him into a chamber for a private, secret interview, so that he feels no shame in front of onlookers." In the *Dit du prunier* there is even a series of communities into which the hero is welcomed one after another, proceeding from secret space to secret space.

Layers of Clothing. After the body has been cared for, it must be shrouded once more in its material wrappings, layers of clothing that are described in detail and constitute a metaphor of the social body. This metaphor is explicitly developed in Baldwin of Condé's *Li Contes dou wardecors*, in which the lord's vassals, his loyal protectors, are compared to body-armor. The werewolf that returns to human form, the amnesiac who regains his memory, are given sumptuous wardrobes. In the *Dit du prunier* the hero receives "robes, horses, coins, and companions." The association of signs of rank, social instruments, money, and human fellowship is worth noting. If clothing is a complex sign of the social surroundings and, conversely, the social matrix is seen as a protective shield against desocialization, is it correct to view male nudity as the carnal form of desocialization fantasies or of that exile which so struck Freud when he encountered it in his patients' dreams? Certain passages in *Amadas et Ydoine* suggest that the community plays an important part in the derangement of the individual cut off from the group. Amadas is a ritual victim who submits to daily beating by his fellow citizens. Has he taken upon himself the collective guilt for some fantasized crime? Seen in this light, the werewolf tales of folklore may have been parables of the individual unsuited to social life and therefore rejected by society, only to be reintegrated later on. Repetitive in structure, these provide a key to resocialization ceremonials in general. Nudity in the male seems to serve as an initiation trial. Anamnesis accompanies the preparation for amorous ritual, the epitome of true social integration. The instruction that Tristan of Nanteuil, no longer a fleeing animal, receives from a beautiful woman concerns not only clothing but also matters of love and manners.

"Shame Is To See a Naked Woman." Thus shouts one of the girls ordered to be stripped naked before the avid gaze of an emperor in search of a wife. Just as fragile privacy is always in danger of being exposed to the view of the group, so, too, is woman stripped naked before society; deprived of her clothing, she becomes prey to every man's illicit gaze. Unlike the naked man, the naked woman is always associated with a nascent or confirmed desire. The process of denuding is sometimes described in violent terms. In the *Roman du comte de Poitiers* the emperor summons thirty young women. "Each one shall be stripped," he commands, "as naked as when she came from her mother's womb. That is an order, not a prayer!"

Her perfection and beauty are the author's reward. *Les Douze Dames de rhétorique*, by the Lord of Montferrand. (Paris, Bibliothèque Nationale, French 1174.)

Female seduction. *Les Quatre Fils Aymon.* (Paris, Arsenal Library, ms 5073.)

If, however, a woman enters willingly at her husband's behest into a game of exhibitionism, she then becomes one of the signs on which male power rests; in the *Lai de Graelent*, for instance, the vassals are required to acknowledge the queen's beauty once a year. Just as clothing, a form of self-representation, was apparently the only legitimate form of exhibition for a man, the naked woman in this case seems to have been a means to an end. In *L'Atre périlleux* (The Perilous Lair), moreover, female nudity was explicitly linked to the affirmation of manly power.

By contrast, the function of male nudity apparently was closely connected with rites of sociability and signs of social cohesion. Exhibitionist tendencies in men are enveloped in clothing. Woman, on the other hand, is generally depicted in a situation of shame ("being seen"); her mode of exhibitionism is not a happy one. A woman is just one sign among others; her body mediates her relation to society, whereas, for a man, clothing is a sign of social integration. A metaphor for desirable social inclusion, the transition from naked to clothed is rich in communal symbolism: ritual expulsion and reintegration are the principal stages in medieval man's relation to his body. Woman is excluded from this way of looking at things: stripped, admired, punished, she serves to incite desire and remains an asset for man in his pursuit of self-enjoyment.

Modesty and Immodesty. Before the fall, nudity served the pretty function of cloaking innocence: "And because he committed the sin, Adam lost the robe of innocence and knew shame. And then the angel drove them out of Eden, in shame; and they found themselves naked of all grace" (*Ci nous dit*, chap. 7).

In an era now given over to shame, modesty is evident when a creature regains its former human appearance. It is even more explicit in women who are ordered stripped, with the exception of the haughty queen in the *Lai de Graelent* whose only interest is to hear her beauty confirmed. But the women who are ordered to undress in the emperor's tower (in order to submit to a test of virginity) challenge the iniquitous order by undressing slowly, under coercion. They remove their belts, tear their silk laces, and tremble so as they open their bodices that the clasps break. By contrast, bathing exemplifies a man's virility and confirms his manliness. Modesty is out of the question. In *Tristan de Nanteuil* Blanchandin is granted a delay of four days before consummating the marriage. The wife has a basin prepared for a public bath, but the "husband" flees. An angel appears and offers him/her a choice: to remain a woman or become a man. The latter alternative is chosen, and the transsexual prepares for his public bath: "When he was completely naked, he headed toward the basin. In the presence of numerous maidens he entered totally nude, and his member was visibly firm and thick."

Clothing, which seductively emphasized the sex of the wearer, could also serve, rather paradoxically, as a sexual talisman, protecting the wearer's modesty. Desire was no sooner aroused than it was defeated. Aye of Avignon and the wife of Dieudonné of Hungary were protected by a jewel: a ring or brooch. In *Florence de Rome* the brooch explicitly causes impotence. A jewel has a different power in *Le Moniage Guillaume*, in which the loudmouthed soldier-monk is sent to the sea for fish. Because his route is infested with bandits, the monk asks how he should respond, since monks are not allowed to fight. His companions answer that he should not defend himself unless it is a question of defending his breeches. Whereupon the man fastens his breeches with a clasp of precious stones which will catch the bandits' eye. This gives him the opportunity he has been waiting for: to cut them to pieces! This is a sort of integration rite, for following this episode the monks are obliged to accept their stalwart companion, even though he remains close to a savage condition.

THE INDIVIDUAL

Fictions of Inwardness

Men and women increasingly turned inward in search of their identity. Reading took on new importance, for it involved such absorption that it altered the very object of the reader's perception. The sense of reality fell away, replaced by an inexpressible feeling of happiness. In the fourteenth and fifteenth centuries stories often were framed as dreams. A divided self first imagined itself in pursuit of the beloved, then witnessed discussions that ostensibly had to do with the dream but in fact were closely concerned with political matters. Literary texts struggled to define reality and illusion. Dreamers, unable to grasp the meaning of their dreams, felt anguish; heroes, caught in a state between wakefulness and sleep, could not be sure whether or not they existed. The mirror, symbol of vice or self-idealization, stood for illusion, for the danger of believing an ostensibly true vision. By the late Middle Ages the misleading subjectivity of a first-person literature had staked out new limits to individual territory. Memoirs and chronicles incorporated elements of personal time in the representation of the individual. And even as individuals were attempting to define themselves, later medieval poetry developed an obsession with time and a perception of a lost era.

Self-Absorption. Vulnerable to the caprices of fate, absent from the world around him, the individual of fiction was often called "pensive," that is, absorbed in and by his own thoughts. Thus, the knight in the Pastourelles dreams on the moors amid heather and ferns until he spies the shepherd girl. Watched by Perceval, Arthur, lost in thought, sits at the end of a table, "pensive and silent," while his knights happily go on talking. "The king thinks and says not a word." they say, "the king thinks deeply and utters not a sound." Later, pensiveness becomes a sign of moroseness frequently associated with melancholy, as in the case of Charles d'Orléans; in the fifteenth century the hero of *Coeur d'amour épris* (The Heart Smitten with Love) calls himself "pensive and melancholy." Of particular significance in this allegorical tale, he has just encountered Lady Melancholy, a disheveled old woman, "glum and pensive," who with hands folded sits next to the fire. Pensiveness thus signifies not only a state of readiness or a refusal to communicate but also a search for an object worthy of the mind's attention.

"All the songs that I composed I did in praise of her." Guillaume de Machaut, *Le Remède de Fortune*. (Paris, Bibliothèque Nationale, French 1586.)

"One night this past month . . ."
René d'Anjou, *Le Coeur d'amour
épris.* (Vienna, National Library.)

Other situations of withdrawal are associated with read-ing, a solitary act that encourages projection into another place or another time. In one chanson de toile Belle Doette "is reading a book, but her mind is elsewhere." Reading puts real-life experience in perspective; the self-absorption it implies can easily stir fantasies and spur the imagination. There is a clear cause-and-effect relation in thirteenth-century tales: a person first reads, then falls in love. In *Claris et Laris* one of the heroes reads about the death of Pyramus and Thisbe and becomes susceptible to a confession of love. Flamenca, imprisoned in the tower, learns about love through books, so that reading for her is a suspension of time. The present is distanced—made unreal or surreal—by the way in which reading creates an aura around the written word, a space of silence and med-itation. For a brief moment the individual becomes self-sufficient.

First-Person Literature. The troubadours and trouvères sang of the most intimate pains and pleasures, those of love and the flesh. The "I" that occurs in their lyrics, however, is not a unique and fully realized individual but a universal "I." Based on repeated motifs, the lyric did not embody a voice that revealed the individual, not even when the name Vidas or Razos has been applied retrospectively to the poet's work. The lyrical "I" is an ego of eternal recurrence, an artifice that persisted throughout the Middle Ages. Even in a writer like Villon, what seems to be poignant self-avowal remains rigidly governed by a set of conventions. Nevertheless, in the last decade of the twelfth century a more individual voice seems to have made itself heard. In a fierce apostrophe to death (in *Vers de la mort*), Hélinant of Froidmont employs bodily imagery, which, while it may not refer to the poet himself, does indicate that the entire individual, body and soul, is concerned by life's end:

> Mort, toi qui m'as emprisonné pour muer
> dans cette étuve où le corps extirpe en suant
> les excès qu'il a commis dans le monde,
> tu lèves sur tous ta massue,
> mais, pour autant, personne ne fait peau neuve
> ni ne change ses vieilles habitudes.

> Death, to rehabilitate me you have imprisoned
> me in this steam bath, in which the body
> sweats away the excesses it has committed in
> this world; you raise your bludgeon over
> everyone, yet no one sheds his skin for a new
> one or changes his old habits.

The well-known ancient therapeutic techniques of sweating and purging are here applied to the rehabilitation of the soul.

A more personalized, individualized view of reality is found in the *Congés d'Arras*. Before the gates of the leprosariums closed behind them, Jean Bodel in 1202, and later Baude Fastoul and Adam de La Halle (whose fate is less tragic) tried their hands at a genre that is a combination of personal poetry and occasional poetry, in which some have found what they consider realistic details of decaying flesh and realistic accounts of such emotions as worry, depression, and loneliness. As for love poetry, many scholars have seen a transition from stereotyped love songs to a more subjective lyric. But the poetry of Villon, the "stereotype of poetic anarchism," is in fact comparable to that of his thirteenth-century predecessor Rutebeuf. Both men write poetry that pretends to recount the poet's life, a poetry of false confidence. This deceptive quality is shaped by a cultural model. In what some scholars call the evolution of lyric poetry, the poetry of generalizing abstraction, associated with singing, was supplanted by a poetry based on confidence, which was associated more with reading. In the

former, the poetry sung by the great troubadours and trouvères, the interpreter appears to identify with the subjectivity
expressed in the poem, with an "I" that is not the poet but
could be. With the disappearance of the singing that enabled
the public to enter into the poetic world, the poet sought to
make this process of appropriation impossible, thus permitting
what has been called "a concrete dramatization of the Ego."
Vidas and Razos seem to have increased the distance between
the reader and the subjectivity expressed in the poem, creating
a "novel of the Ego" (M. Zink).

Even with the inception of such personal writing as memoirs and chronicles, we find in lyric poetry a new effort to
define the individual: the impersonal periphrases of old gave
way to phrases like "I am he who . . . ," indicating an attempt
to animate the individual, to set him in action. Examples
abound in Charles of Orléans: "I am he whose heart is clad in
black," for instance. Allegory fragments the self. The poet
multiplies the number of possible selves with whom the audience might identify, hindering the process of identification.
René of Anjou assigns a mission to a part of the self, the heart,
a synecdoche which assumes responsibility for locating the
beloved. At the close of the Middle Ages, moreover, subjectivity took on spatial attributes. As early as the thirteenth
century Thibaut of Champagne described his loving captivity
as a prison built of desire, whose gates were longing looks
and whose chains were hope; still more visual is Charles of
Orléans's "citadel of the self," a "hermitage of thought."
Christine de Pisan and Alain Chartier also stressed the gates
that barred the way to the inner self, while the high value
placed on solitude and self-absorption is clear in Charles of
Orléans:

> Tristesse
> m'a si longuement tenu en son pouvoir
> que j'ai totalement relégué ma Joie.
> Il vaut mieux que je m'écarte de mes semblables:
> celui qui est pris d'affliction ne peut qu'embarrasser.
> Pour cette raison, je me cloîterai dans mes pensées.

> Sadness has held me in its power so long that I
> have cast off Joy completely. It is better that I
> separate myself from my fellow man. He who is
> afflicted can only embarrass. For that reason, I shall
> cloister myself in my thoughts.

A sign of the times: in *Voir dit*, letters and poems that the aging poet Guillaume de Machaut exchanged with a very young woman, the messages received by Guillaume are read in secret.

> Les lettres pris et les ouvry
> mais à tous pas ne descouvry
> le secret qui estoit dedens,
> ains les lisoie entre mes dens.

> I seized and opened the
> letters, but the secret that
> lay within was not revealed
> to all, because I read
> them between my teeth.

Memoirs and Chronicles. After Joinville, the writer's emotional investment in his life and times becomes a powerful motive for writing. Memoirs and chronicles incorporate two different time scales: one implicit in the narration and another that the narrator wishes to relate. As the author of the first vernacular autobiography, Joinville has been credited with "the sensational introduction of the subject into French literature." As guarantor of the truth of his narration, the writer who wished to write "a book of the holy words and good deeds of our holy King Louis" occupies the stage alone and presents himself as the subject of his book. Along with the individualization of the writing subject we find a new emphasis on authentication of his testimony by means of proofs and guarantees that strike us as very strange indeed but do not seem to have caused Joinville's contemporaries any problems. Although Joinville assumes partial responsibility for what he reports, he relates facts that he could not have witnessed personally, yet remains, as M. Perret puts it, "extremely aware of the gravity and seriousness of his testimonial function." And, as J. Monfrin has shown, he quietly reworked his notes concerning the capture of Damiette with the aid of documents and calendars.

The chronicles that flourished in the fourteenth and fifteenth centuries are a veritable *mise en scène* of the individual. In the prologue the author of the chronicle establishes his authorial status and defines himself as an individual, often using a formula which, after 1300, became a fixture of such introductions, on the pattern of "I, Jehans Froissars, treasurer

David Aubert writes under the watchful eye of Philip the Good the *History of Olivier de Castille and Artus d'Algarbe*. Manuscript illustrated by Loyset Liédet, 15th century. (Paris, Bibliothèque Nationale, French 12574.)

and canon of Chimay," or "I, Christine de Pisan, a woman submerged in the darkness of ignorance compared with the bright intelligences."

Similar formulas can be found in the work of Enguerran de Monstrelet, Georges Chastellain, Olivier de La Marche, and Jean Molinet: the first-person pronoun followed by the author's name and surname, title and rank (which situate the writer socially), followed by a verb indicating the act of writing. The individual thus designates him- or herself as a unique person in a "precise social context" and stakes his or her claim to truthfulness. Indeed, to write seems to mean the same thing as "to write the truth." The declaration is almost like swearing an oath, as the authors invoke the mission they have been assigned, namely, to serve as historiographers (C. Marchello-Nizia).

Time is a presence not only in memoirs and chronicles but also in late medieval poetry, where the legacy of the thirteenth and fourteenth centuries is considerably modified. Rutebeuf had made use of images of destruction and of his

"For [Fortune] is neither assured, nor stable, nor just, nor lawful and true. When it is thought to be charitable, it is greedy, harsh, changing, and frightful." Guillaume de Machaut, *Le Remède de Fortune*. (Paris, Bibliothèque Nationale, French 1586.)

friends' deaths in what seemed to be personal confidences. Later, Eustache Deschamps was particularly obsessed with instability and fragility, by old age and the vanity of all things human, and by his awareness of the "cycle of life, modeled on the clock that had just been invented." In the work of Charles of Orléans, personal time is tamed, though not without bitterness. It seems to accord with the seasons and the rhythms of the cosmos, yet it can also be a source of pain: the poet describes himself as searching through "the chests of his memory," aware of how amusing it must seem to others to see an old man follow "the amorous path" more commonly associated with the young. Michault Taillevent writes that "past time never returns," and Pierre Chastellain wrote a *Contre passe-temps* (Against Pastime), which he later entitled *Mon temps perdu* (My Lost Time), a history of his life interrupted by digressions that he would later amplify in a little book called *Mon temps recouvré* (My Time Recaptured). Poets now became sensitive to the inner sense of time. Villon calls the self the "minister of wasted time," and Chastellain, who in some ways anticipates the temporal sense of the Renaissance, calls it the "magistrate of time regained" (D. Poirion).

The Inner Voice. In romance we find love stories in which solitude and its associated inner voice play an integral part. Roland in his solitary agony offers three prayers to God. More significantly, in so-called antique romance, and especially in Chrétien de Troyes, the inner monologue is developed as a narrative technique that offers occasions for self-explanation, self-analysis, and self-judgment. The long parallel monologues of Soredamor and Alexander in Cligès are secret investigations, attempts to ferret out the emotional mechanisms that the subject wishes to describe. Joy, delirium, and pain, all occur in courtly lyric.

The thirteenth century saw the development of a more elaborate form of inner monologue, in which the narrator's account of intimate feelings is paralleled by another, lyrical voice. There were many forms of inner monologue. Guillaume's soliloquy about his love for Flamenca is both a lament of the power of love and a statement of his plan to enter her bath via an underground tunnel. Death is the ultimate moment of solitude. The *Châtelaine de Vergi* gradually gives up hope of any possible communication with her beloved, whom she rightly or wrongly believes guilty of abandonment and be-

"By her aspect she seemed unstable or at least readily changeable; her eyes were blindfolded like the god Cupid. In her right hand she held a royal scepter and in her left hand a wheel that never ceased to turn." Pierre Michault, *La Danse des aveugles*. (Chantilly, Condé Museum.)

trayal; she also feels cut off from the community. Her words are overheard by a young girl crouching in the alcove and conveyed to the lover, who takes his own life on the body of his beloved. If death in the *Chanson de Roland* was the occasion of a final speech in which the "I" is echoed by a "we," the chatelaine's final speech is one of tragic isolation. It is not unlike that of the Lady of Fayel, who faints upon hearing the final words of her lover, killed by a poisoned arrrow. After learning that by a cruel ruse of her husband's she has eaten her lover's heart, she begs to be killed, and, in a typical dying gesture, presses her arms to her chest, pushing the last breath from her body.

Identity

The literary imagination was obsessed by problems of identity—a lost or unknown identity that must be found or discovered, or an identity that must be concealed and that is known only through signs whose meaning will later become clear.

Clandestineness. Gesture, clothing, observance of the proprieties—all are discourses by which the body speaks. But the body can also remain silent, taking advantage of its absence. In fiction this absence makes sense. The body can be stripped of the marks that make identification possible. Its appearance can be modified; the face, for example, can be disguised by means of a magical herb. Threatened with marriage to a pagan king, Nicolette, in the thirteenth-century chante fable *Aucassin et Nicolette*, rubs an herb over her head and face to darken her skin. Disguised as a hurdy-gurdy player, she goes to her lover, Aucassin, whereupon she applies another herb called *éclaire* (chelidonium?) to her body, restoring its former beauty. Sometimes a skin covers the body: in *Guillaume de Palerme* the fleeing lovers obtain two white bearskins and a snakeskin from a kitchen and from these patch together two quilts with which they disguise themselves.

Another disguise was to dress in one color, as did the Red Knight and the White Knight. Of course colors had legible meaning: red indicated evil intentions; green indicated rage; black at first had many meanings but gradually became increasingly pejorative; and blue revealed the true nature of those who appeared incognito, as Froissart showed in *Le Dit du bleu chevalier* (M. Pastoureau).

Danse macabre. (Paris, Bibliothèque Nationale, Latin 1402.)

In certain circumstances men and women could refuse temporarily to reveal their identity. For a long period of time this was true of girls who, faced with the incestuous behavior of their fathers, saw no solution other than to flee; their silence may have been influenced by a desire to conceal what might be construed as a stain on the family. For the courtly hero, such as Lancelot in the *Chevalier à la charrette*, the temporary absence of a name signifies that a search is under way for a name worthy of the community's expectations of the hero. In the *Histoire d'Olivier de Castille* the hero refuses to reveal his identity, and the heralds are forced to proclaim as vanquisher the "red, black, and white knight." Ghosts, too, traveled incognito through this world, as in *Richard le Beau* or *Olivier de Castille*. Clandestinity is an excellent means of adding suspense to a story.

Monochrome knight. *Tristan en prose*, 1463. (Paris, Bibliothèque Nationale, French 99.)

Interpreting Signs. "Such was Cligès, who possessed wisdom and beauty, generosity and strength: he had the wood as well as the bark." The perceived dissonance between appearance and reality caused uneasiness. In women particularly a contrast was often drawn between the ideal appearance and the inner being, as in *Galeran de Bretagne* or the fourteenth-century *Dit du lévrier*, in which a sweet-faced girl is seen to have a heart filled with pride and "melancholy."

To discover the identity of a fictional character often requires detective work. The hero's weapons may be a clue, as may be the color of a knight's costume. The theme of the masked knight was an important one in thirteenth-century fiction. The knight chose anonymity and loss of social rank in order to be recognized by others for his physical valor alone; only later would he cap his renown with a name. In order to be recognized and valued for himself, the individual first had to appear masked. The point may have been that any identity has to be earned, and once earned must be proven repeatedly. In the romances of Chrétien de Troyes initiation is associated with concealment of identity. Perceval himself will not learn his name until he reaches the court of the Fisher King, after having failed to ask the question that would have healed the king and saved the Wasteland from desolation: "And he, who knew not his name, experienced something like a revelation, and said that he was called Perceval of Wales. He did not know whether he was telling the truth or not, and yet he spoke the truth, but without knowing it."

The armorial bearings of Bohort, Knight of the Round Table. *Lancelot en prose*, mid-15th century. (Paris, Bibliothèque Nationale, French 115.)

Further messages about identity lay in secrets that awaited decoding: mysterious inscriptions, embroidered patterns, and nameless portraits. In *La Belle Helaine de Constantinople* the reproduction of the heroine's face signifies that a search for her is under way, conducted by her guilty father and the husband who lost her. The father has an effigy of his daughter painted on a column of the papal palace in Rome; the husband carries his wife's picture on his shield. The redundancy of the motif tends to merge father and husband into a single, if disjoint, figure, whereas the reproduction of the wife's image separates her from her identity. A heroine without an identity, Helaine is yielded up to public regard by both father and husband.

The Portrait. Oddly, people are not recognized by their features (except in portraits). In many stories, when father and son meet after a long absence, they know each other not by their appearance but by a surge of emotion. This is true in the *Lai de Doon*, or again in the *Lai de Désiré*, in which a fairy sends a beautiful child to meet its father, from whom the child's birth has been concealed. In a rather different context, the king feels a strange affection for the Manekine, who has been found by a Roman senator and who, unbeknownst to the king, is actually his own son. The only explanation for his fascination is a "voice of the blood." Yet a portrait is a good substitute for an absent lover, whose beloved traits it recalls. Tristan worships the statue of Isolde: "He speaks his mind to the statue and wants to remain with it forever. His gaze falls on Isolde's hand, which reaches out to him with its gold rim, and he again sees his beloved's haggard face as she says her farewell."

Images may take unusual forms. Guillaume audaciously uses Flamenca's husband to send her a message. He writes a poem supposedly addressed to a mysterious beauty. The message contains two images, drawn "with such perfection that they seemed truly alive. The figure in the foreground knelt in an attitude of supplication toward the other, who faced her. A flower in her mouth touched the first word of each verse." The paintings do not mirror the lovers' features, but Flamenca has only to fold and unfold the pages of the poem "to kiss Guillaume's image a thousand times, and a thousand times more when she folded his lines, for one image seemed to kiss the other." Copies of the two lovers embrace in fantasy; the portrait both deceives and satisfies. Similarly, Guillaume de Machaut enjoys the "lovely image," the "sweet likeness" that his servant brings him. No sooner does he receive the portrait of his lady than "I went quickly and alone to my room, where I closeted myself away." Above his bed he places "the pure, pleasant image, represented in painting," not only to contemplate but also to touch and embellish.

Daughter and pupil of the painter Cratin, Irene surpassed her father in talent. Boccaccio, *Des femmes nobles et renommées,* 15th century. (Paris, Bibliothèque Nationale, French 598.)

Dreams. The dynamics of an individual's inner life can prove all-absorbing. In the thirteenth century the state of inner absorption is described in *Flamenca* in almost clinical terms. The senses rally to their "lord and father," the heart, leaving man unconscious, stupefied, deprived of sight, hearing, and speech: "The heart is the lord and father. If something good or ill happens, each of the senses immediately seeks to know his will, and while they are thus gathered within, man sees nothing outside and remains as though dumbstruck. And since good and ill force the senses to turn in this way to the heart, I am not surprised that when the joy of love, which is a compound of good and ill, is in the heart, it makes them gallop to their lord, should he require them. And all the senses are such that, if one of them delivers its message, the others are concerned only with offering their help and service, so that all share but one concern. That is why a person who is preoccupied sees less, smells less, speaks less, and hears less. And though you hit him very lightly, he will not even feel the shock. Everyone knows this from his own experience."

Dreaming invests the very substance of the dreamer, who imagines himself with a mission to perform in a concrete physical setting. Twelfth- and thirteenth-century penitentials and "dream keys" were greatly concerned with the relation between dreams and visions, the nature of sleep, the dreamer's responsibility for his dreams, and the connection between physical sensation and dreaming. Literary texts refer frequently to Macrobius, and dreams are frequently exploited in romance and allegory. Although dreams may not be under the control of the conscious mind, the dreamer is responsible for them. Merlin's virgin mother forgets to make the sign of the cross, thus giving Satan the opportunity to father a son. The priest who commands her to renounce the sins of the flesh till the end of her days adds the proviso, "except in dreams, for man can do nothing about dreams."

Dreams, apparently impervious to rational investigation

"King Nebuchadnezzar while dreaming saw things that later turned out to be true, and often things that we have thought during the day appear again at night when we are dreaming." Philippe de Mézières, *Le Songe du verger*, 15th century. (Paris, Bibliothèque Nationale, French 12442.)

and lodged in the most intimate depths of the individual, occur frequently in medieval fiction. For nearly three centuries (1200–1500) they served constantly as "frames for literary fiction" (C. Marchello-Nizia). In the *Chanson de Roland* Charles, on his way back to France, experiences several dreams in which he imagines himself being attacked by Ganelon and again by a leopard or a boar. As he sleeps, an angel predicts that a battle will take place and shows him the signs: tempests, thunder, wind, ice, fire, and flames. The emperor's army is assailed by monsters, dragons, demons, and griffins, but none of these terrifying visions disturbs Charles' sleep.

In the *Quête du Saint-Graal* dreams establish the dynamic of the narrative, forcing the hero to seek out hermits and recluses who possess the secret of their meaning. The tale has much to say about the anxiety of dreamers to grasp the significance of their dreams. We see Perceval, "greatly troubled" after an "extraordinary vision" of two ladies, allegories for the two laws. He sleeps until the sun is high and then encounters

a priest: "Lord," he says after much talk, "I beg you to explain
to me a dream that I had last night, a dream so strange, as it
seems to me, that I shall have no peace until I know its
meaning." Later, exhausted by fasting and vigils, Lancelot falls
asleep and sees coming toward him a man surrounded by stars
and accompanied by seven kings and two knights. From a
hermit Lancelot learns that "this vision is far richer in meaning
than many might think." Gawain and Hector, who take shelter
in an old chapel, have dreams "so extraordinary, so charged
with meaning, that they cannot be omitted." Hector awakens
"filled with anguish, tossing and turning, unable to sleep."
Gawain then says: "I had a very strange dream, which woke
me up, and I shall not rest until I know what it means." Every
dreamer insists upon more comprehensive knowledge of the
values upon which the allegory is constructed; meanings that
stem from the deepest recesses of the self await their revelation. Thus every dream calls for interpretation. The dream is
conceived as a world unto itself, and its elusive meaning becomes an object of conflict. Not until an appropriate maieutic
brings it to consciousness do its elements acquire their true
significance.

"I went to bed one night as
usual, and while in a deep sleep
I had a very beautiful and very
powerful dream." Guillaume de
Lorris, *Roman de la Rose.*
(Chantilly, Condé Museum.)

Misleading Dreams. The allegorical tradition, and in particular
the *Roman de la rose*, lavishly invests the ego. The hero, who
still says "I," embarks upon the most dangerous of quests.
The inner territory is related to the traversal of actual space,
and two time scales are superimposed, one of sleep (true time)
and one of waking (but fictive) consciousness. Here we are on
the threshold of dream: "I went to bed one night as usual, and
while in a deep sleep had a very beautiful and very powerful
dream . . . I dreamed one night that I was in that wonderful
time when every creature was impelled by the desire to love.
As I slept, it seemed to me that it was very early in the
morning. I got up from my bed at once, put on my breeches,
and washed my hands."

Sleep is dangerous, however, because illusion can take
hold of the dreamer: thinking he is awake, he may grasp at
shadows. Cligès' uncle, who wants to marry Fenice, possesses
her in nocturnal delusion, when in reality she sleeps unmo-
lested at his side. In *Claris et Laris* a lover becomes obsessed
with the illusion that he has embraced his beloved; oneiric
confusion leaves him in a hellish hall of mirrors. In the fif-

teenth century an incestuous mother-in-law dreams that her son-in-law is a diabolical dancer who constantly persecutes her.

Erotic dreams are our best evidence for states apparently not under the control of the conscious self. A monk dreamt of a series of female sex organs parading before his eyes, but when he reached out to touch one encountered instead a bundle of thorns: a case of cruel dissonance between desire and its object. In courtly literature dreams are occasionally gifts from Cupid. In *Flamenca,* William of Nevers, unable to possess his lady, feels sleep coming on and implores Cupid to "make me fall asleep, make me dream as only you can. Show me, at least in my dreams, the one I cannot see when I am awake. My Lady, it is of you that I want to speak, and if I can sleep in you, good will come of it, and profit. Then I shall repeat constantly: 'You, you, you, Lady, I shall call you My Lady always, as long as I am awake. If my eyes close outside, inside I want my heart to remain awake with you. Yes, with you, My Lady, with you.' But before he finished speaking he had fallen asleep, and with nothing to stand in his way he contemplated his lady in peace. It is common in dreams, moreover, that we see the object of our desires when we fall asleep with thoughts of it in mind."

If not all dreams were managed quite so rationally, dreaming was nevertheless a tried and true method of escape. William of England, in the romance that bears his name, is at the mercy of the uncertain boundaries between consciousness and unconsciousness. While sitting with company, he dreams of a hunt and falls into a state of such deep insensibility that the narrator feels called upon to say: "Do not take me for a liar, and do not be astonished, for it does happen that people dream while awake. As in dreams, their thoughts may be either true or false." William's dream precedes and indeed brings about his reunion with two sons lost since childhood. The dream is a kind of revelation, and when the dreamer later reenacts his dream he takes possession in reality of what the dream had given him in imagination.

The truth value of the oneiric message is discussed in the *Roman de la rose:* "A dream is a way of announcing to human beings propitious or unfortunate events. Most people dream at night, in the secret of their minds, many things that subsequently come to pass." In the tradition of amorous dreams, the fifteenth-century *Coeur d'amour épris* depicts the heart as a personage in its own right, separable from the self. The author,

René of Anjou, insists that evaluating the truth of a dream is a delicate matter. He describes himself in his bed, over-whelmed, tormented, deeply absorbed in thought and entirely possessed by love:

> tant confus
> Me vy que pres de mourir fus,
> car moictié lors par fantasie,
> Moictié dormant en resverie,
> Ou que fust vision ou songe,
> Advis m'estoit et sans mensonge
> Qu'Amours hors du corps mon cuer mist.

> So confused was I that I lay near death,
> whether imagining or dreaming or having
> a vision or daydream, it seemed to me
> that, truly, Cupid had removed my heart
> from my body.

Objectivity is imparted to this entry into the matrix of dream when, at the end, the author describes himself emerging from the dream state, filled with sorrow and anguish. (In the prose sections interspersed with the verse, the author himself becomes the narrator; this structure is a departure from the model, the *Roman de la rose*.) He opens an eye, calls his chamberlain, who is sleeping nearby, and confesses his fear that his heart has been removed from his side: "I am afraid that Cupid has stolen my heart and carried it away, because when I place my hand on my side I feel that it is gone. Verily, I cannot feel it beating." The chamberlain calls for a candle—an instrument of truth—to be brought in and makes a quick diagnosis: René's side is intact. He advises the dreamer to go back to sleep in peace, which he does, but not without difficulty. The next day, René takes up his paper and records his dream "to the best of my knowledge," a humorous allusion to the imaginary investigation which, solely through writing, is given reality. The dream is obliterated by the faint ridicule implicit in the gesture that relegates its illusory truthfulness to the murky realm in which it belongs. The evaluation of the dream, the attempt to verify it by objective means, the smile at the illusion, the redundancy of the attestation (whether awake or asleep, one cannot tell)—all confer upon the dream the rather ridiculous status of a theater that represents its own rhetoric: metaphor. Between metaphor and reality the link is sometimes tenuous. In the *Coeur d'amour épris* the courtly quest has be-

come a bad dream about a kind of impotence, which may be
what it always was.

The state between sleep and wakefulness—called *dor-
veille*—accurately reflected medieval concern with the uncertainty of consciousness, the ambiguity of "to be or not to be."
Consider Raimondin, Melusina's future husband, who wanders into the forest in shock over his uncle's accidental death:
"At midnight he came to a spring known to some as the
Fountain of Thirst and to others as the Enchanted Fountain
because many a miraculous adventure had occurred there in
the past and from time to time still did occur. The spring
bubbled up in a striking setting: between a steep and wild
slope with overhanging rocks and a beautiful meadow that
ran the length of the valley from where the tall forest left off.
The moon shone brightly, and Raimondin's horse went its
own way, for its master, overwhelmed by grief, was stripped
of his will as though he were asleep. Near the fountain three
ladies were frolicking. We shall now recount what the story
tells about one of them, the noblest of the three and mistress
of the other two. According to the story, then, the horse bore
on with Raimondin, pensive, unhappy, desperate over what
had happened, on its back; he no longer guided his horse, the
animal took him where it wished. He did not pull the reins
either to the right or to the left. He had lost his sight, his
hearing, and his understanding. Thus he passed in front of the
spring and the three ladies without seeing them."

Later, a poet of the court of Burgundy, Pierre Michault,
described (in *Danse aux aveugles*) his inner theater as the place
where his "sensuality" (his sensory perceptions) reposed
in the midst of a bright, clear night. Extreme concentration
("l'assiduité et fréquentation de mon poignant penser") then
developed the faculty of understanding. Note that this differentiation of thought from sensuality (the essence of rational-
ism) required the death of the senses.

Rationalization of another sort occurred in political
dreams, really debates in which the secrets of the unconscious
served as backdrop. The dream was part of a ruse, for political
dreams were really fables about power. In less than a half-
century nearly a dozen works used dream material to reflect
on power, including the *Songe de pestilence,* the *Songe du vieil
pèlerin,* the *Quadrilogue invectif* by Alain Chartier, and the *Songe
du vergier.* Rhetoric challenged the social order, and "in such
cases it is better to pretend that one is dreaming." The canonical formula for dreams (*il me fut advis,* followed by the
imperfect of the indicative, suggesting that the dreamer him-

self was caught up in the dream process) was dropped in favor of a process in which the dreamer became "the focus (*siège*) or scribe of a vision that always involved the royal power." The dream form must have guaranteed impunity for the writer or dreamer, who claimed not to be the originator of his tale (C. Marchello-Nizia).

The Mirror. The author of a book of religious instruction based on moral examples (ca. 1320) recounts the story of a lady who sends her chambermaid to buy a mirror. When the maid returns with a mirror that is not to her lady's liking, she is sent to buy another. This time she returns with a skull and says: "Here, look at yourself in this. In all the world there is no mirror of glass in which you can see yourself better."

Although the Idle Lady in the *Roman de la rose* uses a mirror simply as a beauty aid, mirrors were frequently associated with moral education. In La Tour Landry's book of advice to his daughters, a misused mirror ultimately focuses the beam of diabolical horrors. Bewitched by her own image into spending a quarter of the day ministering to her appearance, a lady exasperates those who are waiting for her in church: "What! Will this lady never be done combing herself and staring at herself in the mirror?" But it proves to be a mirror of evil omen: "And as it pleased God to make an example of her, even as she stared into the mirror she perceived the enemy, who bared his behind, so ugly and horrible that the woman lost her reason, as if possessed by the devil." If the mirror could be used to reveal imperfections of dress and hairdo, it also served, even more effectively, to bare moral imperfections and narcissistic excesses. In many texts the mir-

Cleopatra in front of her mirror. Boccaccio, *Les Cas des nobles hommes et femmes.* (Bergues Library, ms 63.)

"A lady must look in a mirror for two reasons: to see her face and to see her conscience." *Le Parement des dames en vers,* by Olivier de La Marche, 16th century. (Paris, Bibliothèque Nationale, French 25431.)

La Roue de fortune (The Wheel of Fortune), anthology of drawings, 15th century. (Paris, Bibliothèque Nationale, French 24461.)

ror appears as an instrument of edification. Sometimes it was doubled to guard against illusion or deception. In John of Condé's *Dit du miroir*, for example, a man insists on having a double mirror so that he can look at himself "inside and out"; indeed, there exists a mirror "à belle gent" which must be present night and day, a mirror whose obverse is "obscure and diverse." Yet it is advantageous to look into this mirror, because by doing so one can profit by the wicked deeds of others:

> Dou miroir par double maniere
> Pues tu veoir oevre pleiniere.

> Gentle mirror, in two ways you can
> fully expose everything.

The mirror can also be an instrument of seduction, as in one fabliau in which a woman, upon receiving the squire who comes to herald her master's arrival, asks the messenger to hold her mirror so that she can adjust her hood, a narcissistic gesture that makes her so irresistible that the master is inevitably preceded by his man.

The reflection (or shadow) of being that appears in the mirror deprives reality of a part of its existence and thereby promises reality to what is in fact ephemeral. Now, the essence of reality (in courtly love at any rate) being its elusiveness, a reflection (in the *Lai de l'ombre*) can elegantly absorb it. After repeated rejections by his lady, a knight has his ring returned to him. Rather than replace it on his finger, however, he completes by reflection the gesture that guarantees him happiness. Leaning on the edge of a well, he sees, clearly reflected in the water, the beautiful and pure image of the woman he loves most in all the world. He says: "Take this, my dear friend. Since my lady does not want it, you shall have it without further ado." As the ring falls, the water is disturbed; when the turbulence dissipates, the lady, touched by such a fine courtly gesture, at last grants her love. Elusive reality is caught by duplication and finally possessed.

If Cupid is to be believed, the *Roman de la rose* should have been called "The Mirror of Lovers," after the fable of the two fountains. In the depths of one lies the lethal mirror that kills Narcissus. By contrast, the circular fountain in the park is a source of knowledge, for by leaning over it at any angle a person can take in all the contents of the garden. If the first fountain connotes loss of touch with reality through infinite regress, the second mirrors the unity of the entire work.

Yet in the "Book of Regards," said to have been included in the *Roman de la rose* "as a mirror within a mirror," Nature denounces "distorting mirrors and other illusions engendered by the eyes' infirmity, the mirage of distance, and visions of wakefulness and sleep, to say nothing of contemplation . . . warning against any gaze that would attempt to present its vision as the truth" (R. Dragonetti).

The fountain of Narcissus. *Roman de la Rose.* (Paris, Bibliothèque Nationale, French 12595.)

La mort de Narcisse

Sur la fontaine alors se penchant,
il vit dans l'eau claire et nette
son visage, son nez et sa petite bouche;
aussitôt alors il s'étonna,
car son ombre l'avait trahi:
il crut voir dans l'eau
la figure d'un jouvenceau extrêmement beau.
Alors Amour sut bien se venger
du grand orgueil et de la fierté
que Narcisse lui avait opposés.
Son salaire alors lui fut bien donné:
il s'attarda tant sur la fontaine
qu'il aima sa propre image
et à la fin il en mourut.

The Death of Narcissus

Leaning over the fountain, he saw his face, his nose, and his small mouth in the crystal clear water. He was immediately surprised, for his shadow had betrayed him. He thought he saw in the water the figure of an extremely handsome youth. Then Cupid saw how he could avenge himself on Narcissus for his proud and haughty opposition. He reaped what he sowed: he lingered so long over the fountain that he fell in love with his own image and ultimately died of it.

Like a mirror, the fountain duplicates reality; it is a simulacrum of creation. In reflection the Other flees and the One lives, but in danger of death. The poet, too, is in danger, because it is in the mirror that he has seen the rosebushes laden with roses and the one rose whose fragrance stands out above all the others.

The master with his pupils. *Chronicles of Hainault*, 15th century. The landscape and environment have been transformed by human action. (Paris, Bibliothèque Nationale, French 20127.)

4

The Use of Private Space

Dominique Barthélemy
Philippe Contamine

Restormel, Cornwall. Built atop a motte whose circular form it duplicates (thereby reducing construction costs), this late-12th-century donjon typifies the concern for improved housing. The roof is missing, allowing the hall (perhaps a guardroom) and smaller rooms to be seen.

Civilizing the Fortress: Eleventh to Thirteenth Century

Dominique Barthélemy

WAR raged in the eleventh and twelfth centuries, separating couples and decimating families. It also wreaked havoc with the physical environment in which the aristocracy lived. Families were forced to crowd into towers with few windows owing to fear of missiles fired from below or assaults by ladder. To impede access, ground-level doors were blocked up, leaving only narrow entrances 18 to 26 feet above ground, which had to be reached by climbing a removable ladder or dangerous staircase. In these centuries of iron the shadow of the *donjon*, the castle's principal tower, weighed heavily on private as well as public life. No doubt it impressed the subjects and enemies of the seigneurie, but above all it seems to have confined knights along with their wives and children in discomfort and promiscuity. Such, at any rate, is the common view of life in the feudal era as recounted in countless histories of France and England.

The best-preserved vestiges of secular architecture from this period are the donjons, owing partly to their stone construction and prestige status, partly to chance. Some of them were abandoned and left to fall into ruin; others were converted, hence maintained though not without alteration. Renovations made in the late Middle Ages or afterward frequently impede archaeological reconstruction, making it difficult to determine if surviving ruins are typical of the period's architecture or whether stone buildings are similar in structure and appearance to those built largely of wood, which have long since rotted or burned.

How can we revive everyday life in its entirety, following men and women as they made their daily rounds and identifying the changing uses to which rooms were put? It will not do to stand before the donjons and dream, as nineteenth-century historians did. The archaeologists started out with a fairly good analysis of construction techniques, but they soon degenerated into pure impressionism, evoking the sadness of what they saw as cramped and crude dwellings but without asking whether the inhabitants experienced their surroundings in this way. More energetic as well as more passionate, today's researchers are also more cautious. Their learned articles usually stop short of any discussion of the intimate life of the household, so hard to grasp by any conventional methodology. Because they believe that exact knowledge of a way of life is fundamental, they refrain from prejudicing the case by ascribing definite functions to any room or building, and they resist the temptation to "aesthetically reconstruct" dilapidated buildings or dead sentiments.

But we are not dealing here with a fascinating but virtually unknowable civilization, a Minoan culture or a Toltecan tribe, for which the absence of written sources invites bold hypotheses and forces scholars to content themselves with the delights and delusions of the imagination. We can turn to

Excavation at Doué-la-Fontaine (Maine-et-Loire.) Vestiges of several eras have been found at this site in the floor of the great hall.
0: underlying clay
1: foundation of west wall
2: west wall (ca. 900)
3: floor of previous building
4: floor of building (ca. 900–950)
5 and 6: holes for posts that belonged to a previous wooden edifice.

documents as well as ruins; the section in this book entitled "Communal Living" is based on a fairly rich lode. In chronicles and biographies we find praise for master builders and details of their more official designs. In fiction we find ourselves looking at feudal dwellings from the inside. We are usually more interested in the characters than the decor, in the social relations and distinctions that existed among them. In short, documentary evidence can complement the study of ruins. Nevertheless, a gap remains, a penumbral zone about which the scrupulous historian had best admit his ignorance.

Doué-la-Fontaine, main entrance (ca. 900).

Most vexing is our inability to say precisely what words applied to what physical structures: pairs of terms like *turris* (tower or donjon) and *domus* (house or abode), or, again, *camera* (chamber) and *sala* (hall), appear to have been used sometimes as opposites, sometimes as equivalents. There must have been significant ambiguity in such terms. The history of noble habitation seems encapsulated here. Did the aristocracy condemn itself to live in the donjon, to the point where it came to be seen as the principal residence, and, if so, what did the residents do to make it more habitable?

From the middle of the tenth century towers or donjons were erected either in the midst of what had been groups of residences or on new sites where the tower was the sole or principal edifice. In neither case, however, were these towers necessarily inhabited permanently.

The Tower and the Dwelling

With every palace, whether inherited from the early Middle Ages or of more recent construction, a city or town was associated. The palace ruled the town, from which it was set apart by an "internal" wall; the main rampart encircled both palace and town. A similar arrangement was found in what eleventh- and twelfth-century texts call the *castrum*, or major castle; it was the kernel of what would develop into a true city as the pace of economic growth accelerated with the approach of the thirteenth century. The seigneurial residence—the castle in the proper sense of the word—was its focal point, frequently located at the center of a series of concentric enclosures.

These architectural complexes fulfilled a number of functions. Within a rather extensive oval or polygonal area, measuring from 2.5 to 12.5 acres, surrounded by earthen walls and moats, stood a number of not very high buildings, arranged in a fairly loose order and separated by open space. A

Montcuq (Lot): donjon dating from perhaps the 13th century, whose crude appearance shows that not all buildings of this period benefited from the most advanced technology.

court (*aula*) in the strict sense, that is, a reception area, built atop a half-buried storage room, flanked by what commentators have called, rightly or wrongly, "apartments," and communicating with a chapel: such was Charlemagne's establishment at Aix, one duplicated in many other places, whether because it was widely imitated or because form followed function we do not know. Outbuildings were set aside for work of various kinds: storage of food and arms, stables, possible additional noble residences, and a collegiate church. The presence and extent of such buildings is a measure of the importance of the place and the variety of its uses. All these features are found in the comital *burg* of Bruges, quite a large complex, which furnishes the backdrop for the drama narrated by Galbert. The first Capetian palace in Paris was already more constricted, but it did include a distinct royal hall that abutted the city's ramparts, a residence adjoining it at right angles, and a chapel.

Towers were slow to appear in both places. At Bruges, where as was so often the case the lay and clerical powers were materially and symbolically balanced, the murderers of Charles the Good were forced to take their last refuge in the bell tower of Saint Donatian, the collegiate church—and this as late as 1127. In Paris it was not until the dawn of the twelfth century that the king erected a donjon alongside his hall, doubtless for reasons of prestige more than defense. Yet as early as the tenth century (during the reign of Louis IV d'Outremer) the Carolingians had a tower in their palace at Laon—or else a highly fortified *aula*. In all these places there was plenty of space but neither luxury nor calm. Princes wanted not cosy rooms but exaltation of their power, evident in the ostentation of hall and balcony. *Aula* and donjon were important symbols of princely might.

Indeed, they may spring from a common source. Michel de Boüard's excavations at Doué-la-Fontaine (Anjou) have perhaps unearthed an ideal type. A spacious *aula*, dating from the early tenth century, measures 76 by 53 feet; the walls, of modest height (16 to 20 feet), were built level with the ground. This place served as secondary residence for the prince of the region, Robert. Following a fire, a second story was added in 940, with external access: this was a donjon of the most elementary type. Finally, shortly after the year 1000, the whole structure was buried in a bank of earth, converting the first two levels into an underground storage area and prison; a donjon was built on a classic motte. (It burned in the middle

Doué-la-Fontaine (Maine-et-Loire): excavation of the 10th-century *aula*, which had lain buried in an 11th-century motte; here, the west wall and entrance. On the left the cross-section of the motte can be seen.

of the eleventh century.) Clearly architectural continuity between court and tower, and between the Carolingian era and the time of so-called banal seigneurie (that is, lordship of the *ban*, in the eleventh century), did exist. It is also possible that contemporary towers at palaces in Compiègne, Rouen, and elsewhere were donjons that had gradually been constructed on top of *aulae*.

Not all existing castles acquired towers, however, and the process proceeded quite slowly. There were regional variations; in the cities of southern France the larger castles were without towers. The building of donjons seems to have been concentrated primarily in northwestern France, chiefly in Normandy and the Loire Valley, areas rich in good stone and home to powerful princes and lords. The oldest surviving example, at Langeais, dates from 994 and was built at the behest of Fulk Nerra, count of Anjou. When the castle is studied closely it becomes clear that the count's intentions wavered. At first he wanted a military bastion, but later he modified the structure for use as a residence. His successors restored its military value in the late eleventh century by

Langeais (Indre-et-Loire): quadrangular building, known as the "donjon of Fulk Nerra" (after the famous and terrifying count of Anjou), constructed in 994 and later equipped with buttresses.

reinforcing the walls. In this region the most common arrangement consisted of a donjon with an abutting residence, whose inhabitants could take refuge in the donjon when necessary. The donjon did not play a central or active role in the defense of the fortress; it was a redoubt, protected by its isolation or eccentric location relative to other defenses. Only in Norman England after 1066, at that time an appendage to northwestern France whose conquerors lived for a long time in a constant state of alert, did immense and imposing donjons serve as permanent residences—and even here this was not always or exclusively the case. The Tower of London was an often-copied model.

Let us take a brief look at some of the lesser seigneurial residences, which proliferated in the eleventh century as the population grew and local wars erupted in many places, especially on the fringes of the *pagi* (ancient counties) and castellanies. Over the past three decades archaeologists have uncovered traces and inventoried ruins of a large number of mottes and towers (either erected on the mottes or standing alongside them). These isolated fortifications were brigands' hideouts basically; scattered about the region over which the lord wished to exercise control, they were more regularly exposed to danger than were the castle complexes.

These secondary fortifications, totally artificial, sometimes carved out of terraces or barred counterforts, were not necessarily used as residences in either southern or northern France. Those that did house a knight's "family," however, tended to have a private dwelling separate from the tower. So it was at Grimbosq in Cinglais; the highest point of the motte of Olivet was not the site of the residence, which was situated in a small courtyard between the tower and the most vulnerable part of the wall. Another courtyard, larger and more easily defended, was used for keeping animals and for equestrian exercises. The residence, whose aristocratic character is amply attested by jewels and gaming rooms, is in the form of an *aula*: a trapezoid 56 feet long by 23–33 feet wide, whose frame rested on a stone foundation. The kitchen is separate (another distinctive sign of a noble abode), and a chapel and second building adjoin the main residence. What we have here is a reduced-scale model of a prince's or castellan's residence: the functional distinctions and arrangement of house and for-

Houdan (Yvelines): cylindrical donjon (50 feet in diameter, 100 feet high), built at the beginning of the 12th century by Amaury III, sire of Montfort. It is bounded by four towers, one of which (on the right in the photo) contains a spiral staircase to the second floor. The door is 20 feet above the ground. The interior centers on the great hall (following what has been called the Ardres plan).

tress are the same. As for Occitanian residences in this same period (eleventh century), interesting clues are found in accounts of the miracles of Saint Foy (Faith) of Conques. The tower in this case is usually described simply as a garrison for warriors; the wives reigned over an adjoining or separate house, the *mansio*.

Based on this evidence, I believe that tower and residence were usually separate, that one complemented the other. There are various possible explanations why the texts so frequently confuse *domus* and *turris*. One is that the tower was a metonymy for the house, the most prestigious part being taken for the whole. Second, if it is true that over time aula tended to evolve into donjon, then the tower in a sense symbolized the future. Some rural houses were built like donjons but had habitable first floors (as, for example, an early-twelfth-century residence at Longueil in Caux). The existence of such mixed types may have justified the writers' uncertainty. Or again, the tower may have been a part of the house, not just the place where people took refuge in case of danger, as in Loches Castle, but one where a part of the family—the men—lived permanently. In such a case the tower would have been the aula, and the "house" a mere supplementary "apartment." This was not the most common situation, however, for in many palaces and castles the tower was simply a military and, more important, a symbolic annex to a dwelling that can only be called an *aula*.

War or the pressure of political and military aims left its mark on noble dwellings, inside the tower and out. Even where the aula was separate, it took on some of the charac-

The donjon of Hedingham (Essex), ca. 1140. The second floor (built above the ground floor) is entered through a vestibule. The third floor contains the great hall, which actually occupies two levels, with a gallery opening onto it. The top floor contains a series of bedrooms.

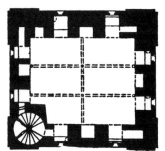

upper story with bedrooms

3rd floor

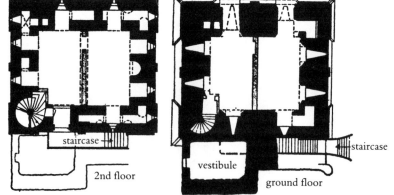

great hall

staircase

2nd floor

vestibule

staircase

ground floor

Rochester (Kent): royal donjon built ca. 1130, in the first century after the Norman conquest. It is typical of the series of donjon-palaces inaugurated by the Tower of London: massive cubes with 75-foot vaults, three stories, and access through a small donjon (here on the left.)

teristics of a donjon. There are many buildings in France and England about whose proper appellation the specialists in castle archaeology remain in disagreement.

Degrees of Discomfort

There is sometimes little to distinguish between aula and donjon. Add buttresses to the aula and wall up the door at ground level and you have a donjon. Cut windows in the upper stories of the tower and build staircases into the thick walls and you have something resembling an aula. Yet specific differentiae can be noted: thick walls, few and small windows,

Chevreuse (Yvelines): external outlet of latrines.

and access to the upper stories placed high above the ground typify the true donjon. Abandonment of the quadrangular plan in favor of a square or cylindrical structure and increased height also distinguished the tower from the aula. But characteristics of the latter are evident in the classical trapezoidal donjon. People did not hesitate to apply the term "aula" to a large hall, generally placed high above the ground (for less vulnerability) and equipped with large and beautiful "twinned Romanesque" windows.

Anglo-Norman donjon-palaces (as Pierre Héliot has dubbed them) deserve the dual appellation because their dimensions (approximately 66 by 42 feet internally) are the same as those of princely aulae and because their upper floors served many of the functions that had previously been discharged at ground level. The chapel was on the second floor, for example, and additional living space was accessible from the higher floors. The military function is not obtrusive in these mighty fortresses of the eleventh and twelfth centuries. The approaches were guarded, particularly the external stairway, a veritable bastion sometimes referred to as the "little donjon," and positions were staked out on the roof, usually crenellated and accessible via independent staircases built into the wall. Still, in this, as in any residence based on the donjon, however large or small, crude living conditions caused problems.

Archaeologists once tended to take a pessimistic view, doubting that such amenities as fireplaces, recessed walls, and latrines were part of the original plan. Recent excavations cast doubt on such skepticism. The beautiful fireplaces found at Doué-la-Fontaine and in various eleventh-century halls and the presence of three hearths and two latrines on the second floor of a primitive (eleventh-century) donjon in the castle of Ghent suggest early attempts to increase comfort, at least in the primary and secondary residences of princes. As we approach the year 1200 we find pipes supplying water to the upper stories and more elegant wall decorations, as at Ghent, where a sophisticated masonry structure was imitated. These findings both support and contradict the conclusions of Raymond Ritter, who allows a few rays of light from the luminous central Middle Ages to penetrate the darkness of the towers: "By the late twelfth century the greatest feudal lords had just begun to discover how terribly sad, how poorly lighted and ventilated, were the dwellings in which family and servants lived crowded together in the most peculiar promiscuity."

There were enough windows in the wall of the Vendôme

residence of Geffroi Martel, count of Anjou, so that, when he awoke one morning in 1032 next to his wife, he was able to take in at a glance all the surrounding countryside as well as a sky filled with shooting stars. There was no lack of openings in an aula or in any floors of a donjon that served as an aula. Interiors were undoubtedly rather drab: there was little decoration, not much more than a series of capitals with elegant colonettes and a few ornaments, perhaps, to accentuate the relief of a wall, and this in the finest palaces. It takes imagination to visualize the many tapestries that covered these bare walls and helped divide interior space into compartments, alleviating the "promiscuity" deplored by Ritter. There was also a good deal of furniture, which unlike that of today was frequently transported from house to house, as princes and lords together with their entourages made their normal rounds. Admittedly the construction was crude, but drabness and crowding were not as serious as was once thought.

There were degrees of discomfort, depending on how fully the residence was differentiated from the fortress and whether or not ladies and damsels lived in the place. The upper stories of the great donjons were better lighted and probably better heated than the lower ones. There is reason to believe that progress was made in the construction of don-

Doué-la-Fontaine (Maine-et-Loire): kitchen adjoining the great hall and wall fireplace, ca. 900–930.

jons over the course of the eleventh and twelfth centuries, although the increasing habitability of some late-twelfth-century examples of the genre probably resulted from the fact that people now lived in them, that there was an abrupt (albeit not irreversible) change of function.

The Late Twelfth Century

At the end of the twelfth century the aspect of castles changed: structures were massed more compactly than before around a fortified center. Military concerns in this period are said to have been more pressing than ever before, and thus likely to take precedence over the private life of the nobility. Henceforth the plan of the fortified residence would be dictated by the cold geometry of angles of fire. Yet there was progress in domestic amenities. Comfort and gaiety did not actually flourish; the breakthrough would not come until the next century, perhaps not before the Renaissance. Nevertheless, the austerity of the castle was undeniably diminished.

One detailed and quite illuminating document tells of work on the ancestral castle at Noyers (Burgundy) commissioned and financed by Bishop Hugh of Auxerre, tutor to his nephew, the castle's young sire. A keen student of military architecture, Hugh turned the fortress into an organic unit. Instead of reducing the donjon to a passive redoubt, as in the previous period, he made it an active defensive headquarters. Attention was concentrated on the *praesidium principale*, the main fortress, situated on the peak of a promontory dominating the valley of the Serein. Ditches and catapults were arrayed in front of it for protection. The *castrum*, already distinct from the bourg below, was divided in two by an interior wall. "Outside the wall of this main portion," Hugh's biographer explains, "he constructed a palace of great beauty, which completed its defense: a pleasant seigneurial residence, which he decorated with numerous ornaments and much taste. He built underground galleries leading from the wine cellar—located beneath the donjon—to the palace, which was situated lower down, so that it was not necessary to enter or leave the main part of the fortress to procure wine and other supplies . . . In addition, he equipped the principal part of the fortress with a remarkable array of arms, war machines, and other devices necessary for its defense. He bought, for a large sum, the houses of the knights and other houses located within the walls of the upper fortress and transferred the property to his nephew. Thus, both in this part of the fortress and in the

Château-Gaillard, in the Andelys (Eure): an application of the science of fortification.

palace residence, as a measure of prudence, the comings and goings of those who wished to see the lord in his palace but outside the walls of the main fortress aroused no suspicions, and since all foreign residents were excluded in times of danger, the lord of the castle was no longer obliged to allow anyone into the upper enclosure of whose loyalty he was not fully certain." [This English rendering is based on the French translation in G. Fournier, *Le Château dans la France médiévale* (Paris, 1978), pp. 335-336.]

This operation typifies nearly all aspects of the change that occurred in the second half of the twelfth century. First, progress was made in integrating donjon, turrets, and trenches into a coordinated defensive system, ranging from the rather early attempt in the south of France, at Carcassonne (ca. 1130, without donjon), to the extraordinary edifices built at Château-Gaillard (1190) and Coucy (1230) in the north. Strategy was the dominant concern. Although the "palace," where the lord normally resided, was not entirely devoid of military value, its contours were less constrained by the precepts of ballistic science than those of other parts of the fortress. At

Ghent (Flanders): the castle, modernized after 1178 by Count Philip of Alsace, dominates the waters of the Lieve.

Plan of the castle, which covers more than an acre of ground, showing entrance (8 and 1); walls (4, 5, 13, and 15); donjon of 1180 (3, 24); 13th-century additions to the donjon (11, 12); the "Romanesque gallery" (10); the "count's residence" and its annexes (16, 17, 18, 19); the gallery linking the count's residence to the donjon (14); and the cellar entrance (9.)

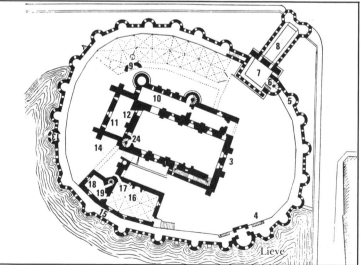

Château-Gaillard, Richard the Lion-Hearted's "manor" was situated outside and below the citadel. As in the previous period, residence and bastion complemented and communicated with one another, yet remained distinct. Advances in construction techniques benefited both.

Second, Bishop Hugh decorated the palace sumptuously, proving that not all available funds were sunk into military equipment. It was important that both strength and wealth be displayed and exalted.

Third, the knights of Noyers Castle sold their houses in the main portion of the fortress. The job of persuading them to do so was probably eased by the fact that in most castellanies at this time the knights' group was breaking up. Knights no longer garrisoned the principal castle; instead, they went to live on their own lands (in some cases paying a tax to underwrite replacement guards), thus inaugurating a second age of lordship of the *ban*. In the late twelfth century we find some trouvères rather nostalgic for the conviviality of the previous age, which existed partly in their imaginations and had not been without conflict. Such sentiments helped draw together the members of the sire's household.

Finally, along with the new household solidarity went a certain suspiciousness of outsiders. No doubt many old donjons had been delivered into enemy hands by cunning and treacherous visitors. Ordericus Vitalis tells how Ranulf of Chester and William of Roumare seized the strategic royal tower at Lincoln in 1141: they sent their wives to visit the wife of Lincoln's castellan and then, on the pretext of fetching their women, insinuated themselves into the most private sanctum, the very heart of the tower. More than one miraculous delivery of captured prisoners can be explained, in more mundane sociological terms, by the size of medieval *familiae*: with such a crush of people in the castles, it was impossible to monitor all comings and goings. By the thirteenth century the lord's desire for security had grown keener.

Still, if no château or fortress was entirely safe from treachery or surprise attack, why did thirteenth-century nobles find it necessary to seal their walls ever more tightly? Two plausible explanations are that, as peace spread and the power of the monarchy increased, the nobility suffered from fantasies of insecurity and from fits of pride.

Nevertheless, around the turn of the thirteenth century it became possible both to withstand far more serious sieges and to live in greater comfort than ever before, whether in the

Soussey (Côte-d'Or): square three-story tower with vaulted ground floor, the oldest portion of an early medieval castle.

fortress itself or in nearby buildings. Progress in defensive technology and in domestic comfort were in fact identical. To make the discussion more concrete, let us consider two examples. Count Philip of Flanders undertook to rebuild his castle at Ghent in 1178. He reduced its fortified area in order to strengthen the walls, and he diverted the Lève to create a moat. In an oblong donjon (86 × 33 feet) he installed two rooms, one above the other; adjoining the donjon were two residences. Thus the same logic that governed the work of the engineers in improving the castle's defenses also governed the integration of the various elements of the complex. In this case there was no other choice, owing to lack of space; but the limitation of space might have been a consequence or at least a concomitant of stricter household administration. With residence and donjon linked, it surely was easier to monitor the activities of castle inhabitants.

What is true overall is also true in detail. In the twelfth century donjons began to be built with twisting, angled, zigzagging corridors, vulnerable to loopholes above, so that if by chance the donjon's narrow door was breached, the enemy did not suddenly become master of the tower, able to occupy or burn it at will. But are these new arrangements not the same as those that Lambert of Ardres revealed in the structure of the château of Guines, in whose twisting passageways and mazes knights and maidens, creatures of the great outdoors, discovered "courtesy," and where, if the evidence of literature is to be believed, subtlety in the art of private living made rapid progress?

I would like to propose the somewhat optimistic conclusion that the thirteenth century saw progress in resolving both the military problem and the residential problem. Its donjons are both more livable and more easily defended than those of earlier times. And when one feels more secure, it is only natural that more time and money be spent on amenities.

Fortified Houses

In the late twelfth century the knights of Noyers, Coucy, and many other French castellanies ceased to live in the major castles. Previously they had spent only a part of their time in the castles, the rest in their rural homes. But now smaller seigneuries, seigneuries of the second rank, perhaps not really seigneuries at all, began to prosper. Vulgarized, the word *dominus* was now applied to simple village sires, and every castellany had a dozen *hobereaux*, or minor lords, rather than

one master residing in the principal castle. But anyone who wished to be considered a dominus was obliged to enhance the prestige of his *domus*, to raise its height, surround it by a moat marking his noble freedom, and perhaps add a tower to bolster his title of sire; defenses also needed to be shored up. The proliferation of *maisons fortes*, fortified houses, in the thirteenth century has impressed the archaeologists engaged in cataloging them, dating them precisely, and, through excavation, reconstructing what they looked like. The situation had changed dramatically since the eleventh century, when private wars had suddenly erupted all over northern France. Now the kingdom was pacified, and instead of warfare, or perhaps in compensation for its absence, aristocratic pretensions were rampant.

The history of rural seigneurial residences in the eleventh, twelfth, and thirteenth centuries is less well known than that of the great châteaux. The work of numerous archaeologists has begun to fill in missing details; I shall use only a few of their results. Although it is premature to draw any firm conclusions, there are signs that the proliferation of new lords

Villy-le-Moutier (Côte-d'Or). Aerial photograph showing ditches around a fortified house (right) and a barn (left.) Excavation proved that the earth removed from the broad but not very deep ditches was used to enlarge the platforms.

At Villy-le-Moutier (Côte-d'Or) numerous bronze and copper ornaments, pieces of copper, and the presence of glass indicate an aristocratic dwelling. These two oil lamps symbolize the gap between two levels of material civilization: "One is a simple iron cupel with no mouth, typical of the lamps used in rural villages; the other is made of bronze and has four mouths and a reservoir enclosed by decorative arcs. It hung suspended from four projections that end in animal heads and would have been used in a fortified house" (J.-M Pesez and F. Piponnier).

between 1180 and 1200 marks either another sudden transformation or the beginning of a new evolution.

At this level of society the problem was not so much to erect defenses as to distinguish the house of the minor noble from that of the peasant. From the eleventh to the fifteenth century a house was distinguished as "aristocratic" by its furniture, arms, and game rooms; rooms remained quite rustic in construction and feel.

At Colletière in Dauphiné, mounted warriors were stationed before 1030 to guard a section of the border; they lived by hunting, fishing, and raising livestock. An area of some 15,000 square feet was delineated by a stockade, which in the early Middle Ages served more as a means of staking out a private space than as a defensive perimeter. Within this fence stood several large houses, whose traces, preserved by immersion in Lake Paladru, have been unearthed by Michel Colardelle and his coworkers. In each house a northern section was used for domestic animals, while a better-lit southern section served as a residence. People did more than just pass the evening hours and sleep here. Game rooms and musical instruments suggest a more complex cultural life and active participation in the exchange economy.

Somewhat later, noble residences began to be built on mottes. Fewer vestiges of daily life have survived in these places. A house at Andone (Charente) is distinguished from nearby peasant houses by the presence of iron objects, backgammon and chess pieces, and dice. This was an ancient site on which a small castle, or *castrum*, was built around 975. At the seigneurial house in Rubercy (Bessin), which dates from the mid-twelfth to the early thirteenth century, horseshoes, nails, arrowheads, crossbow bolts, children's rattles, and scabbard chapes, all of iron, and pendants, dice, and backgammon pieces of gilded bronze have been found. Claude Lorren notes that these items suggest "possibilities for leisure that can be found only among the aristocracy." During its early years, from about 1150 to 1190, the house itself, rectangular in shape and with packed earth floors and a hearth at ground level, could scarcely be distinguished from that of commoners in the neighborhood. Even the improvements made after 1190, dividing the interior into a hall, a chamber, and a kitchen (not separate from the building), remained relatively modest in scope.

At Rubercy as in Burgundy, the fortified house was characterized by its setting, somewhat apart from the village, on a flat, rectangular, and slightly elevated platform (quite unlike the old-fashioned motte); the platform was built of dirt removed from the moat or series of ditches that surrounded it. Whether or not the tower was used as a residence, it was a status symbol attached to a rustic dwelling. In this pairing of tower and residence, the fortified house was not unlike the great castles.

Thus, the home of the minor aristocrat resembled both that of the common peasant, distinguished from it only by its location and size and by the richness and variety of its furnishings, and that of the high nobility, whose prestige the country lords attempted to appropriate for themselves. In the thirteenth century the minor nobility led the way in the improvement of rural housing and finally succeeded in crossing the threshold of honor and prestige. Consider the fate of a typical family of allodial landholders of knightly rank. Its house was at first the center of a farm, a small domain (*curtis*). The family wanted to turn it into a small castrum, but the prince or castellan (sire of the region's principal castle) remained steadfastly opposed. Throughout the eleventh and twelfth centuries tension persisted, with the scales tipping in favor of the minor nobility in periods of "anarchy" and in

Chess pawn, 12th century. (Paris, Cluny Museum.)

favor of the great nobles during periods of "order," that is, repressive reaction. Around 1200 an unprecedented compromise resulted in feudalization of the land in exchange for the right to bear titles and build towers. This inaugurated the age of the fortified house.

The same tensions are evident in the cities of the north and south. Urban patricians aspired to build *steens* even larger than before—and they were already impressive in Galbert's time for their structure (upper story over storage cellar on an aula plan) and their capacity to withstand assault and protect treasures. Ghent Castle, as reconstructed by Count Philip in 1178, may have been a riposte to the turrets erected by wealthy bourgeois. In the south the *solier* (multistory dwelling), conceived along similar lines, was the ancestor, or perhaps the neighbor, of the *tour gentilice* (noble's tower). In the cities as in the countryside, the history of noble housing is fundamentally just a chapter in the history of power.

Residence or fortress? Was it really an issue? If the military aspects of both the principal castle and the fortified house were intended partly or even primarily to impress the populace, and if improvements in the residential quarters were aimed mainly at heightening that impression, then the question is not of defense or comfort but of something which can only be called prestige or status and which played a powerful role in forging the medieval social imagination.

Hall and Chamber

The results of archaeological research are less directly useful for studying interiors. Texts—words used as antonyms and synonyms—tell us more about how people moved and gathered and sat by themselves than do empty rooms whose arrangement we cannot visualize. The best we can do is to verify that the arrangements revealed by the written sources could in fact have existed in the structures that have survived or been restored. In the past art historians and archaeologists concentrated exclusively on the remains, speculating on the basis of their reactions to what they saw.

Rigorous scholars whose work on their own special subjects remains irreproachable could not resist the temptations of rhetoric or ideology when it came to the private lives of barons and their ladies. The great Emile Mâle, like many of his contemporaries moved by "the hero of our epics, the soldier of our crusades," in 1917 attempted to capture what he took to be an organic unity linking the compact severity of the donjon to the character of its inhabitants: "This crude construction shaped feudalism, upon which it bestowed its flaws: the disdain, the pride of the man who has no equals in his entourage. But it also gave him more than one virtue: love of tradition and ancient ways and a profound sense of family. Here, as opposed to the Gallo-Roman villa, there is no gynaeceum, no summer triclinium, no winter triclinium, no baths, no galleries, no host of rooms in which a person could be alone; there is but a single hall. Father, mother, and children lived together all day long, crowded one upon the other, often under threat of danger. In this somber room a warmth of affection had to exist. The wife especially benefited from so austere a life; she became the queen of the house."

Artful as this passage is, it presents the critic with an easy target. It is full of arbitrary assumptions: that the husband always lived with his wife and that they raised their children themselves, for example, or that familiarity always breeds affection rather than contempt, or that the castle was a refuge rather than a base of attack. In effect, the bourgeois Catholic family as idealized by Léon Gautier has simply been transplanted into a feudal setting. Mâle relies on the artificial device of explaining the nature of social life by the character of the setting as it appears to him. The relation between human behavior and its physical surroundings is more dialectical and perhaps less determinate than this analysis suggests. It is simplistic to contrast the sophistication and self-indulgence of Antiquity with the alleged austerity and purity of the Middle Ages. And to say that the lady of the house reigned as a queen is neither adequate nor acceptable.

Nevertheless, even though Mâle fails to place his ideal family in the midst of an entourage of obliging and importunate servants and forgets to mention that rooms were divided by lightweight partitions, he is right on two important points: first, the household was organized around a single, dominant couple—a pair of masters; and second, they sat by day and slept by night in the same space. But did not lord and lady have private areas to which they could retire? And did not other members of the household—children, guests, and servants—have rooms of their own?

In describing the multistory donjon, scholars have tended to place the hall below and the chamber above; thus, the higher one climbed in the tower, the more private, secluded, and "feminine" the space became. According to this view there must have been a gradual transition from the horizontal order

Royal luxury. Curtains and columns compartmentalize a space dominated by the sovereign without disrupting its solemnity. The king is dictating sacred love songs, accompanied by musicians on the left and a choir on the right. *Cantigas* by Alphonso the Wise, 13th century. (Madrid, Escorial Library.)

of the older palace (aula with adjoining apartments) to the vertical order of the new donjons. I do not deny the validity of this interpretation, but more needs to be said. Some donjons had well-lit, spacious rooms on the upper floors, rooms certainly better suited than the rest for formal receptions. Hall and chamber were not strictly opposed spaces in a feudal residence, as bedroom and living room are in a modern home. They were whatever men and women wished to make of them. And we know from certain ambiguities of language that they used these rooms in sophisticated ways.

Hall and Chamber. In reading eleventh- and twelfth-century texts, we are sometimes surprised to discover the term *camera* used to describe what is in fact an authentic aula (one large room set atop a cellar). In Bruges (1127) both the count's hall and Bertulf's are called *camera*. Similarly, the *Miracles of Saint Foy* tells how a prisoner managed to climb from his cell to the upper story, the *herilis camera*; he then crossed the room discreetly to a window open to the outside and jumped to make his escape. Or consider the house, or "wooden tower," at La Cour-Marigny (Orléanais, mid-eleventh century), where Lord Aubry "spoke, ate, and spent the night" with his *familia.*

Finally, the "famous" description of the house at Ardres, built of wooden timbers in 1120, shows that the whole structure centered on a *herilis camera*, a "large chamber in which the lord and his wife slept." Archaeologists have found no trace of a distinct aula in the vicinity; hence the chamber must also have been the reception room. Furthermore, some of the titles ascribed to household servants are highly ambivalent. The chamberlain of the duke of Normandy, for instance, is the "first [servant] of my aula and of my camera" (twelfth century).

How could hall and chamber have been so confused? For

Loches (Indre-et-Loire): large donjon, built at the end of the 11th century, altered in the middle of the 12th century. There were three stories, with wooden floors. Access from the first to the second was via a staircase in the wall, from the second to the third, via a spiral staircase. The fireplaces with conical hoods are contemporary; the windows open into covered niches (secret passageways?), whereas from the outside they look like simple loopholes.

one thing, the study of great palace halls reveals that a wooden partition may have divided a larger reception area from a smaller sleeping area. At Troyes, in the palace of the counts of Champagne, we know that in 1177 there was a partition on one side of which stood a dais where the prince sat during banquets, dominating the guests who sat at two large tables arranged along the longitudinal axis of the room. On the other side of the partition was the *thalamus comitis*, the count's "bed" or "bedroom."

On each floor of a donjon, the large room could serve as both hall and chamber and could be divided into at least two parts. Thirteenth-century literature gives an exact picture of the arrangement: at Camelot, in *La Mort le roi Artu*, two distinct banquets are held simultaneously. The king presides over one in the great hall, while Guinevere presides over the other in her chamber, where Gawain and his entourage are seated along with a host of other guests, all served and subjugated by the lady. The text does not make clear whether this chamber is a floor of the building or a residence abutting the "hall." It makes no difference: regardless of whether the order is horizontal or vertical, entering Guinevere's chamber marks a step toward greater familiarity. (She forbids a disgraced lover from entering.) Yet the functions of her "chamber" are scarcely different from those of her royal husband's "hall," where the full court assembles.

The precise information gathered by Queen Marguerite's confessor, William of Saint-Pathus, concerning the private habits of Louis IX during the last twenty years of his life clearly show that the private sphere was really a series of concentric shells. Closest to the king were the *mout privé*, his more or less familiar companions such as the chamberlains. The next shell, the *assez privé*, included such people as Joinville, a high-born knight who could not serve his lord in privacy. The most secret place of all was the wardrobe (*garderobe*), an isolated section of the royal chamber. There Louis IX slept, watched over by a single servant; there he prayed in private and washed the feet of three paupers, careful to hide this act of personal piety from prying eyes. He also hid his body, if it is true that a chamberlain who served him for twenty years never glimpsed his leg above the bulge of the thigh. The "chamber" was far larger than the wardrobe, large enough to permit the performance of quasi-public acts, such as the reception of the sixteen paupers and the touching of scrofula victims. Seated at a table in front of a great fire, the king could receive knights here, but his more intimate entourage ate separately in the wardrobe. There was little to distinguish "chamber" from "hall," other than the fact that the former could accommodate fewer guests. The difference was in the degree of privacy, not in its nature. For us it is difficult to appreciate the distinction between valets of the chamber and valets of the hall. Taken together, they constituted the *hôtel du roi*, which played a fairly important role in politics and followed the king as he moved from castle to castle. In Paris, Vincennes, Compiègne, and Noyon, as well as in Normandy and other provinces, the king's *hôtel* accommodated itself to different locations without altering its structure. Like the house of the Lord, that of the king had many mansions; but his *hôtel* was a stable unit.

Additional residential space became available in the late twelfth century. At Ghent Castle, for example, the hall was located in the central donjon; it was elevated and reinforced. The two other residences abutted the tower's avant-corps and probably housed separately the men and women of the court. In courtly literature, much in demand at Ghent, we sometimes see a hall from which one or two *hôtels* can be entered; in the thirteenth century a structure of this sort formed the heart of the typical great house.

Was this segregation of the women's quarters without precedent? From careful study of the *Miracles of Saint Foy*, Pierre Bonassie has concluded that the *herilis camera* at Castelpers, where the lord lived with his "familiars," actually housed only warriors and their concubines, prostitutes whom monks in the early twelfth century blasted tyrants for frequenting; wives and children lived apart. Thus, domestic society was indeed divided in two, but we must take care in reading expressions such as *cum familia* and *cum familiaribus* to interpret the word "family" in its medieval sense. The great edifices that benefited from the advances made in the twelfth century are distinguished from earlier abodes simply by the fact that the women's chambers were prettier, not unlike earlier halls.

Thus, the really pertinent distinction in the language of the time is not that between hall and chamber but that between a central room, a hall-chamber, and the smaller rooms arranged around or alongside it, between a singular and a plural. This plan—a nucleus surrounded by its satellites—was unquestionably the atom of private life in the feudal era.

Rooms: Major and Minor

At Angers in 1140 a distinction was drawn between the "count's aula and all the chambers." Before 1125, in his palace at Yvré the bishop of Le Mans disposed of an "aula of stone with chambers and a cellar." Last but not least, we have the description given by Lambert of Ardres, who distinguished between the residential chamber and the *diversoria* in which women, children, and invalids lay curled around the fire. Lambert described the model household. Pierre Héliot has noted how frequently the "Ardres formula" was applied in twelfth-century English donjons, such as those at Rising and Bamburgh; each floor could be divided by light partitions into from two to six rooms.

Once again it is romance that best reveals the daily activities of men and women, though in the guise of dream. Perceval approaches Beaurepaire, a slate-roofed palace; a maiden spies him through a window of the hall. He climbs a majestic staircase and discovers this same hall, long and broad and with a sculpted ceiling. He sits down on a bed covered with a silk bedspread and there converses with Blanchefleur, the young mistress of the premises, who is attended in her public appearances by two white-haired knights. A meal is brought in. (Note that the bed both embellishes the room and serves as a couch for conversation, which explains how hall and chamber could have been confused.) Later everyone apparently retires to a bedroom of his or her own. Blanchefleur, no doubt using one of those hidden corridors that architects became so adept at constructing, rejoins (secretly?) the man who will henceforth be her "friend," and together they shed a few tears and pass a chaste and tender night dreaming of future knightly exploits.

A few pages later, at the Fisher King's castle, Perceval admires a hall situated in front of a square tower. At the center of the hall he finds the king lying fully dressed beneath a canopy supported by four huge brass columns and in front of a roaring fire. In this room the visiting knight is given food and a bed. During the meal he sees the cortege of the Grail pass by: valets and damsels parade past with the lance, candlesticks, and precious plates; dazzling arms and gleaming gold objects are removed from one chamber and placed in another after being carried in procession through the hall. The treasures stored in chests in the heart of the castle are exhibited, without undue mystery, to important guests.

The prose of thirteenth-century romances became more

Etampes (Essonne). Guinette Tower, built in the 12th century, was decorated in the 13th with rare elegance. Here a corner of the great hall (upper story) is shown, well lighted and equipped with a series of arches that made it possible to dispense with the central pillar.

dense. We are shown private conversations and allowed to eavesdrop on individual soliloquies. In *La Mort le roi Artu*, characters speak asides and whisper confidences either at the windows of the hall of Camelot (where they risk being overheard) or in private chambers. The king takes his nephews into his chamber to hear their denunciation of the queen's adulterous love for Lancelot, carefully closing the doors. "Secret niches" played an important role in fiction. Such niches were in fact located in the vaulted halls of the great castles, which today seem cold and austere.

Preludes. *Le Chansonnier de Paris*, late 13th century. (Montpellier, Atger Museum, ms 196.)

Even amid the bustle of a great household, there was a place for everyone. In the palaces, châteaux, and noble abodes of the central Middle Ages there flourished a characteristic form of private life. It is pointless to compare it at every turn to our own, either to point up differences or paint it as a distant precursor. From Castelpers to Ghent we see the male and female sections of the household staring at one another in fascination and fright, occasionally joining together or furtively communicating and interpenetrating. The precise layout is unimportant, since the structure of the "household" was largely independent of variations in internal topography.

It is time to abandon the image of the medieval castle as a place of "terrible sadness." The lay aristocracy preferred fine clothing to tapestries and easily transportable metal objects to artworks sculpted in stone. Its fondness for objets d'art was combined with a taste for the monumental. King Arthur, visiting the castle of his sister Morgan, first enters a beautiful hall filled with richly dressed people and illuminated by the reddish glow of many candles glinting from shields hung on the walls and filtered through silk hangings. He then passes into a chamber where a sumptuous table setting of gold and silver awaits him, and from there into another chamber where he is greeted with sonorous harmonies, and from there into still another room. But, someone will object: this was all a dream. Not at all. It was an amplification of what we can detect in the fragments of "positive" evidence, which permits us to conjure up an image of a strange yet familiar feast.

La Couvertoirade (Aveyron). The main street of the village, fortified in the middle of the 15th century on order of its lord, the Order of the Hospital. The stone houses have external staircases that lead to the kitchen and hall; storage rooms are at ground level.

Peasant Hearth to Papal Palace: The Fourteenth and Fifteenth Centuries

Philippe Contamine

Hearth, Family, Household

When the authorities, primarily for tax purposes, under-took to make a census of the population of late medieval France, they generally counted not heads or houses or even heads of household but hearths. The practice was traditional, not an invention of the Christian Middle Ages. Horace in one of his Epistles mentions a "small estate" or "hamlet" of five hearths (*agellus habitatus quinque focis*). In the ninth century the polyptych of Irminon repeatedly mentions *villae* consisting of so many hearths (*foci*), some *ingénuiles*, others servile. Never-theless, the term does not seem to have become current until after 1100 (when, for example, the hearth tax, or *focagium*, was introduced in Normandy; it would have important con-sequences later on). It remained in common use, at least among those concerned with matters of demography, until the end of the eighteenth century. In the *Livre des métiers* (mid-thirteenth century), Etienne Boileau prescribes that "no one may take an apprentice if he is not *chef d'ostel*, that is, of hearth and home (*feu et leu*)." These expressions and others like them are quite common in the late Middle Ages.

The word "household" (*ménage*), though less commonly used, had the same meaning, as is shown by the following passage from a Burgundian document (1375): "Faire cerche et inventoire des feux et mesnaiges de tous les habitans" (Locate and inventory the hearths and households of all inhabitants). Also found in the sources, particularly in eastern France, is the word *conduit*, which probably refers to the chimney pipe of a fireplace. In fourteenth-century documents concerning Bar-le-Duc and the surrounding region we find: "Dix conduis ou maisnages, chascun conduit ou mesnaige garni de trois per-sonnes" (Ten chimneys or households, each chimney or household being associated with three persons); or "Trente et six conduis tenant feu en la dite ville" (Thirty-six working chimneys in said city).

Historians of population and the family have long wondered what the precise meaning of the word *hearth* could have been. All agree that some hearths were rich and others poor; beggars had hearths, the *menus* (little people) had hearths, as did the *gros* (the "fat cats," so to speak). But on the average, how many individuals should be counted per hearth, household, or chimney?

Voltaire raised the question. "Population" in his *Dictionnaire philosophique* criticizes a writer who settled on the uniform figure of three persons per hearth: "I have computed the figure for all the regions that I have visited as well as the one in which I live, and I count four and a half persons per hearth." Though plausible, Voltaire's figure cannot be accepted uncritically for the fourteenth and fifteenth centuries. It seems clear, however, that the word "hearth" had long referred essentially to the nuclear family: father, mother, and unmarried children.

A good example is provided by the Florentine *catasto* of 1427. This extraordinary document lists 59,770 households containing 246,210 persons, an average of 4.42 per hearth. There is a noticeable difference between the cities, where the average is only 3.91 persons per household, and the countryside, where it is 4.74. Clearly, these are average figures that conceal fairly wide disparities.

Mid-14th-century documents. The hearth constituted a tax unit for the prince or lord. Whoever kept the books for Saint-Paul-les-Romans, a seigneurie belonging to the Hospitallers of Saint John of Jerusalem, has listed each tenant's name and, next to it, a list of amounts owed. The list includes a woman, no doubt a widow, with her three children. (Archives of Drôme, 40 H 2.)

The composition of Tuscan households in 1427

Group	Percent
Living alone:	
Widows	6.66
Widowers	0.10
Unmarried	0.84
Unknown	6.01
Without family:	
Frérèches	1.60
Unrelated individuals	0.69
Households with single conjugal family:	
Couples without children	10.26
Couples with children	36.35
Widowers with children	1.83
Widows with children	6.36
Households with extended conjugal family:	
With parent, grandparent, aunt or uncle, grandchild, nephew or niece	9.44
With brother, sister, or cousin, or combination of this and the preceding category	1.20
Multiple households:	
Vertically related	
with two nuclei	11.28
with three or more nuclei	2.11
Horizontal (frérèches)	
with two nuclei	3.55
with three or more nuclei	1.69

Source: based on David Herlihy and Christiane Klapisch-Zuber, *The Tuscans and Their Families* (New Haven: Yale University Press, 1984).

Some households included ancestors or collateral relations, and in 1422, in the parish of Saint-Pierre at Rheims, 23 percent of the hearths fell into this category. In 1409, according to a document duly registered with the *tabellionage* of Rouen, Jean le Monnier and his wife, Jeanne, *delivered* themselves (*se rendent*) to Tassin le Monnier, their son, and Perrette la Monnière, their daughter-in-law, along with all their worldly goods, retaining nothing for themselves, on condition that they be provided "with all necessities for drinking, eating, sleeping, getting up, lying down, clothing, hearth, bed, and board, well and sufficiently." In particular, they were to receive each week, as long as they lived, 20 denarii tournois "to buy bread or whatever they pleased," as well as a gallon of

Hours of Charles of Angoulême,
late 15th century. The carefully
tiled hall adjoining the kitchen.
(Paris, Bibliothèque Nationale,
Latin 1173.)

barley beer daily, plenty of meat on days when eating meat
was permitted and, when it was not, "such food as would be
served to other guests, such as herring, eggs, or other dishes."
On Sundays they were to receive a more copious meal, including among other things a pâté costing 5 denarii tournois.
Along with their young son Jehannin, they were to occupy
either "the upstairs bedroom or the ground-floor room in the
back," which was equipped with a fireplace, as well as the
adjoining room. In other words, they were promised a small
apartment, which was either heated or heatable and more or
less independent of the rest of the house, but they would take
their meals in common with Tassin and his family. Tassin was
supposed to invite his father to dinner personally, each time
repeating the words, "Monsieur, come and be seated." The
first to sit down, the father should also be the last to rise, "if
it so pleased him."

Similarly, documents pertaining to the seigneurie of
Choiseul in the late fifteenth century show that grown children
"did not keep hearths of their own but stayed with their father
or other relatives."

Throughout much of France a hearth could be associated
with an extended family of patriarchal type, with two brothers-in-law, or with two married brothers who pooled all their
resources—labor, wealth, and reserves—and lived from one
stew in a single "*hôtel.*" *Bibendo unum vinum, comedendo unum
panem* (drinking one wine, eating one bread), read the contracts drafted in Latin and signed before notaries to establish
the *afferamentum, frérèche,* or *comparsonnerie.* In some cases two
friends not related by blood joined together in lasting partnership, to share "a bread, wine, food, victuals, and alimen-

tation." Evidence for such associations and partnerships exists from the twelfth to the nineteenth century, but they seem to have enjoyed renewed popularity in the late Middle Ages, perhaps owing to an increase in the hardship of daily life. Enlarging the size of the household was one response of people in southern and mountainous regions of France to the major demographic depression resulting from a high mortality rate, insecurity due to the Hundred Years' War, and the laborious effort to rebuild the base of agricultural production in preparation for the return of peace.

Even in northern France the average household size increased, though to a lesser degree. Jean Merrey, a plowman, died at Choiseul (Haute-Marne) shortly after Easter 1494; he left a widow, who still maintained her own hearth in 1500, and at least two sons. One of them, also named Jean, settled in a nearby village in 1494 and was still living there in 1502. The other, Nicolas, headed a household in Choiseul by Easter 1496. "Here, in less than two years' time, three hearths replaced the one that the father had kept during his lifetime" (Hélène Olland). Western France was no different. According to J. Gallet, Carnac counted 173 hearths in 1475; of this total, 131 could be characterized as nuclear families (a couple and its children) and 42 as extended families (including one household of 19 persons).

Care should be taken not to exaggerate the extent of the phenomenon. Various documents, particularly wills, suggest that the majority of households were relatively small in the period 1350–1450 (when the life expectancy and the birth rate were at their lowest). By contrast, at the beginning of the fourteenth century and again at the end of the fifteenth, a higher infant survival rate may have increased the average household size slightly. I am speaking of course of averages.

Missal from the abbey of Montierneuf in Poitiers, late 15th century. After returning home, a man warms his feet by the fireplace, a familiar gesture reproduced in innumerable miniatures. (Paris, Bibliothèque Nationale, Latin 873.)

When the sources allow, we find that the range of household sizes was quite broad, from 1 to 12 or even more: the record for Tuscany in 1427 was held by Lorenzo di Jacopo, whose household in a Florence suburb sheltered ten families, 47 persons in all, distributed among four generations.

At Axat (Aude) in 1306 the average household size was 4.9; in the same year in the village of Caramanly (Pyrénées-Orientales) it was 5.6. At Rheims in 1422 the figure was 3.6 in Saint-Pierre parish and 3.8 in Saint-Hilaire. In Ypres in 1412 we find districts with an average of 3.2 and 3.4 persons per household; by 1437 the numbers had risen to 3.6 and 3.7. At Carpentras in 1473 (a time of demographic recovery) the average was as high as 5.1; at Ypres in 1491 it was 4.3.

It is not enough to show that small- to moderate-sized households predominated in the late Middle Ages. We would also like to know whether each hearth corresponded to a distinct dwelling, such as a house. Examples abound, particularly among the middling to high nobility, of families that owned numerous residences—manors, castles, even urban hôtels—not all of which were rented out; some were left vacant for a portion of the year. These residences were not always totally unoccupied; a caretaker, porter, concierge, or, better still, a castellan or captain kept watch over the premises during the owner's absence. The demographic crisis also led to the abandonment of numerous houses inside walled cities as well as in the open country. Buildings left to the ravages of pillagers and the weather quickly fell into ruin, leading to a noticeable and sometimes irremediable decline in the available housing stock.

By contrast, we find some evidence of overpopulation, particularly in more active urban centers. In Paris, for instance, a housing crisis reduced many families to lodgings of a room or two in an upper story or to rudimentary huts or cabins crowded into building courtyards; the situation did not improve until the fifteenth century. Cities such as Lyons and even Cambrai experienced similar overcrowding, reflected in the subdivision of rental property. In the cities of Brittany, "crowding appears to have increased as the end of the fifteenth century drew near. In any case, the records generally show two or three families sharing a single roof, necessitating the construction of garrets, additional floors, and the like" (Jean-Pierre Leguay). At Chambéry in the late fourteenth century each house sheltered two or three hearths (a population of perhaps 3,000 people occupied 306 houses).

It is difficult to estimate how many houses contained more than one hearth and how many were allowed to fall into ruin and to be swallowed up by vegetation, with nothing but a heap of stones and tiles to mark the spot where a building once stood. It is not impossible, moreover, that some houses stood empty while others nearby were overcrowded. Nevertheless, in many cities, a hearth and a house meant the same thing, regardless of the number of people included in the household. In Rennes, for example, in the middle of the fourteenth century, one parish counted 453 houses and 460 tax-payers, 189 of whom were owners and 271 tenants.

At Porrentruy in 1518–1520, 251 heads of family occupied 280 houses and barns. In the mid-sixteenth century the city of Montbéliard contained 375 buildings (including 82 outbuildings, such as barns and stables), whereas 267 bourgeois and other residents turned out for inspections of arms. "This shows," says Pierre Pégeot, "that the typical Montbéliard house sheltered just one family."

In this regard, housing in Rheims was fairly representative of the late Middle Ages: the typical house was of one story with a storage loft above; it was not large enough to accommodate more than four or five people (that is, one hearth). To be sure, some houses in the archepiscopal city had more than one hearth, but these "contained one or two rooms for rental apart from the principal residence" (Pierre Desportes). When war threatened, relatives and friends came seeking shelter inside the city walls. Some houses were shared equally between two heirs, but these were exceptional cases. Not until much later, in the late eighteenth and early nineteenth century, did overpopulation and impoverishment lead to profound changes in interior arrangements (construction of additional stories, and so on); at that time the population density increased to as much as 7 to 10 persons per house. Similarly, inside the old fourteenth-century walls at Tours 1,750 houses sheltered 4,511 families or 13,939 persons in 1836–1840; these figures work out to 3 persons per hearth and two and a half hearths or families per house.

Some rural houses contained more than a single hearth. A house at Dracy in Burgundy was apparently divided in two in the middle of the fourteenth century. In the villages of Lorraine in the late fifteenth century, tenants renting a portion of a house were called *chambriers*. As a result, complex legal problems arose involving easements, because the tenants needed access to wells, barn, stable, and threshing ground.

Parks, Plessis, Enclosures

Around 1460, in the celebrated *Debate Between the Heralds of France and England*, the herald of England undertakes to praise his kingdom's *belles chasses*: "There are so many parks that it is a beautiful thing, marvelously full of venisons like stags, goats, and deer." To which the herald of France replies: "Ahem, Sir Herald, you cause wonderment with this vaunting of your parks, which are in England; I beg you, tell me if you have parks as magnificent as those of France, such as the park of the Vincennes Wood, the park of Lesignan, the park of Hesdin and several others [added in margin of the manuscript: 'named are all the parks enclosed by walls that are found in France'] which are enclosed by high walls like closed cities. Those are parks fit for kings and princes. It is true that you have in England quite a number of parks, but they are enclosed only by a small moat, hedge, or picket, as are the vineyards and pastures of France, except for the park of Wyndesore; and in fact they are only village greens. So it is not a wise occupation to praise them so."

A polemical passage, surely, yet it is full of details useful for envisioning the French countryside as it looked in the late Middle Ages. In most regions the land, particularly arable land, was delimited by simple markers that could easily be removed or relocated, or else by a brook, path, tree, rock, or natural feature of some sort. In the *bailliage* of Senlis in the early sixteenth century, the jurisdiction of the high court of Cugny was delineated by a series of markers: a place known as the "thicket of Fourches," a large linden tree, a small road, a grave, a fountain, a roadside marker, and another marker. Wherever common grazing was the custom, there came a time, generally after the harvest, when the fields ceased to be private for a specified period of time. In addition, many peasant villages had commons—collective pasture, wood, or fallow land. Public areas existed both inside and outside the village: not only roads (*carreria publica, caminus publicus*), fountains, and major waterways but also areas set aside for markets and for herds of livestock. The tragic depopulation of the fourteenth and fifteenth centuries increased the amount of uncultivated land, adding what appeared to be no man's-land; however, when agricultural reconstruction was courageously begun after 1450 it became apparent that the old boundaries of *finages*, seigneuries, parishes, and tenures had not been forgotten. In one way or another, "agrarian memory" had survived.

Despite the use of common lands, private property and private farming were by far the dominant modes; in fact, farms and plots were increasingly separated by enclosures of one kind or another, as is evident from miniatures, plans, perspective drawings (after 1500), travelers' accounts, and daily records. Walls, fences, and hedges served as tangible guides for surveyors, census-takers, and land-recorders. This passion for *seisin*, possession, reflected the landowner's desire to define the boundaries of that valued and productive region within which his and his family's private life could unfold safe from prying eyes, and where in normal circumstances his stores, movable property, agricultural implements, and livestock would be safe. People needed protection not only from neighbors and strangers but also from wild animals, whose numbers started to climb at the end of the Middle Ages, as well as from domestic animals allowed to roam freely. Before harvests, fields were surrounded by temporary enclosures; in some cases *messiers* kept watch day and night. In Flanders the term *bock de vylls* referred to the crime of making an opening in the village enclosure at the time of plowing or harvest. Medieval farmlands were punctuated by *defens*, physical barriers that established zones where trespassing was prohibited by law. In 1460 an important Czech lord, Leo of Rozmital, traveled through Brittany and was struck by the large number of low stone walls, called *murgiers*, surrounding the fields: "Because of these, the peasants do not need to remain with their grazing livestock, and the livestock can do no damage to neighbors' lands."

In regions such as Anjou, farms were grouped closer together and were easier to isolate. Michel Le Mené writes: "All descriptions agree. Enclosure was not the result of the desire for protection alone; it was the physical expression of possession and in a sense the legal definition. It is no accident that the customs of Anjou consider the question of enclosures in the chapter on property. Forming great patches outlined by trails, estates and plots composed a huge jigsaw puzzle encompassing farmland, meadows, marshes, and woods." To cite one example among many, the sharecropper's lodge at Grand Thorigné comprised "two abutting houses with fireplaces, covered with tile, *estres*, an orchard, lines of huge ornamental trees, farmland, meadows, pastures, woods, brush, and warrens, along with ditches, hedges, and enclosures all around."

In Brittany the word *park* referred to vast domains that served for hunting and recreation as well as farmland, forest,

Hours of Louis de Laval, 15th century. A man and woman working in a vineyard, which is surrounded by a stockade fence; a gate in it can be seen in the distance. (Paris, Bibliothèque Nationale, Latin 920.)

and pasture: for example, the "duke's park" near Morlaix and the parks of Vannes, Lesneven, and Rhuys. In the park of Châteaulin a distinction was made between the great and the small domain, possibly corresponding to an ancient reserve and its tenures (Jean-Pierre Leguay).

In "open-field" regions, by contrast, plots belonging to a single peasant were normally scattered over different quarters or "breaks" of the region. But as we move closer to a rural village, we see increasing numbers of enclosures made of stone or trees or cut wood indicating the boundaries of a vineyard or a meadow, a hemp field or willow plantation, a cottage garden or toft, a poupris or a boille, a casal or a maine, a

Le Livre des eschés d'amour, 15th century. A clearing planted with fruit trees. The dogs and hunters are a reminder of the real forest nearby. (Paris, Bibliothèque Nationale, French 9197.)

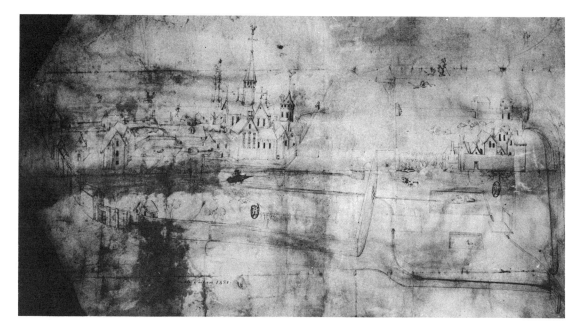

garden or an orchard. The French, Brunetto Latino writes, "are better at making meadows and orchards and apple orchards around their houses than other people."

At a more elevated social level, lay and ecclesiastical lords sought to enhance their prestige, their profit, or their pleasure by dividing their estates into smaller segments emphasizing their control over the land and their rights of ownership. Forest wardens were employed to keep intruders out of the forests and to oversee the exploitation of an invaluable capital resource. Temporary and permanent warrens kept the lands well stocked with small game. Castles had both a great court and a lesser court, the latter reserved for more utilitarian purposes and even mundane agricultural tasks. No noble abode was without its "pleasure garden" (the expression occurs as early as the end of the fifteenth century), which does not mean that herbs, vegetables, and fruits did not occupy most of the space. The enclosed orchard (*hortus conclusus*), sometimes surrounded by a crenellated wall, included fountains, trellises, loges, and wooden fences; nature was domesticated, tamed, divided into squares with benches and galleries. Literature and iconography tell us that this was where people came to rest and enjoy themselves, to sing, to make love openly or secretly, to debate and disport themselves. The orchard was also the symbol of the Virgin and virginity, a symbol of paradise lost,

A design for the convent of Saint-Antoine-des-Champs in Paris from the late 15th century; it is drawn on parchment. The cloister on the left includes the church, the convent buildings, and a dovecote, as well as a common and even a small park. On the right is the abbey farm with a barnyard for animals. (Paris, National Archives, N III Seine 730.)

A manuscript from the 15th century. The convent garden is enclosed by solid walls with a high tower and loopholes. Paths are clearly indicated. (Paris, Arsenal Library, ms 5216.)

a place sheltered from the omnipresent dangers and disorders of the outside world (Elisabeth Zadoura-Rio).

Clumsy in composition but precise in detail, a "panoramic view" done in 1481 of the convent Saint-Antoine-des-Champs near Paris shows clearly the location, within the cloister, of a copse, several ponds, fish hatcheries, streams, orchards, a garden, and, in the distance, a barnyard surrounded by farm buildings.

Christine de Pisan has left us a verse narrative about her visit in 1400 to the notable priory of Saint-Louis de Poissy, where her daughter was a Dominican nun. She lists all the buildings of the convent, which enjoyed a particularly illustrious reputation at the time because a daughter of Charles VI was also in residence. The beauty of the courts is described:

> Ainsi partout traçasmes maint pas
> Et par grans cours
> Larges, longues plus d'un chenal le cours
> ou grans chantiers de busche furent sours,
> Bien pavees et belles a tous tours.

> We walked everywhere, many steps,
> through great, broad courts, longer than
> a river's course, where great wooden
> structures were going up, handsomely
> paved and beautiful from every angle.

Later, we come to the garden, a "very lovely paradise, enclosed by high walls on all sides," with more than 140 fruit trees growing inside. There is also a *beau cloz*, a handsome walled park, in which deer, hare, rabbits, and wild goats frolic; the ponds are well stocked with fish.

Court, garden, hatchery, pond, park: no late medieval castle could do without these essential items. So much is clear (despite overtones of envy and mockery) from the *Songe veritable*, which contains a description of the *bel chastel* of Marcoussis, rebuilt at great expense by that most energetic of parvenus, Jean de Montagu, *grand maître d'hôtel* to Charles VI: "It is a pleasant and delectable place, as old as it is new, surrounded by walls and water."

A century later we have the no less magnificent Gaillon Castle, prideful project of Cardinal Georges d'Amboise, archbishop of Rouen and at the time principal adviser to King Louis XII. A description by Don Antonio of Beatis, chaplain and secretary to Cardinal Louis of Aragon, begins with the

Le Nouvelin de la vénerie, early 16th century. A hunter and his dog between two impenetrable forests. In the distance are three castles separated by hedges or copses. (Paris, Petit Palais, collection Dutuit 217.)

exterior, namely the park, two leagues in circumference and surrounded by high, thick walls which also protected the castle garden. This park was all the more remarkable in that it included both wooded and open areas, small houses to serve as rest stops during hunts, and of course game of every species. The square garden enclosed a series of still smaller squares, all surrounded by a wooden fence, painted green. There was even an aviary and a huge meadow. Only after admiring all these marvels did the visitor come to the galleries that led to the castle itself.

The royal parks were by no means put in the shade by these splendid places. The park at Vincennes, mentioned in the *Debate Between the Heralds*, also figures in the journal of the Florentine ambassador to Louis XI (1461–1462), from which we learn that the perimeter of the park was four miles, as well as in a roughly contemporary poem by Antoine Astesan: "Nearby stands a magnificent forest, from which the castle, I think, took its name, and which is interspersed with meadows and copses and surrounded by an unbroken wall. It is commonly called a park, and I once saw one like it near the castle of Pavia. This park is subdivided internally into several parts, one for boars with their dangerous tusks, another for timid deer and stags with huge antlers, and still another for nimble hares and wild goats. There are such quantities of rabbits that at times one sees thousands of them all gathered together. Thus, all the pleasures of the hunt are to be found in this wood."

Urban Space

Building walls was a reflex of the medieval mind, born perhaps of profound feelings of insecurity (for which events in France during the Hundred Years' War provided ample justification). This was just as true in the cities as it was in the countryside. The typical city was surrounded by a wall and accessible only through imposing gates, although in France some cities did not acquire walls until relatively late, and unprotected, vulnerable suburbs remained or were created, usually near city gates and along access routes. Then, as the danger waned and peace returned, many cities tended to neglect their ramparts for reasons of economy, and stout walls quickly degenerated into porous sieves.

Perhaps the most striking feature of the medieval city was the scarcity of public places and buildings. Streets and squares were under the jurisdiction of the municipal, seigneurial, or royal authorities, and the right of eminent domain was not unknown. Nevertheless, one has the impression that the public sphere was limited and residual; worse still, it was constantly threatened by private encroachment. Such encroachment was discreet because generally illicit, even if sometimes legalized by official recognition. In 1437 Master Jacques Jouvenel complained to Charles VII about illicit activities carried on near his residence in Paris's Ile de la Cité by *fillettes de joye*, prostitutes, who occupied "several small houses" on "a small public street named Glatigny." It must have been quite narrow, because it was "not a place where horses or carriages can pass" and by no means indispensable to the "public good," since other, parallel streets offered more convenient passage through the quarter. Yielding to Jouvenel's pleading, Charles VII, eager to show his gratitude to a member of a great family that had remained steadfastly loyal throughout the period of "divisions," authorized the incorporation of the street into the private property of Jacques Jouvenel. The royal charter reads: "Said street, which was a public way, we have revised and do hereby revise to be private property in favor of aforesaid Master Jacques Jouvenel and his posterity."

Between 1439 and 1447 the consuls and citizens of Saint-Flour found themselves embroiled in a lawsuit against the

The *Livre du gouvernement des princes*, a French translation of *De regimine principum* by Gilles de Rome, early 16th century, showing half-timbered urban dwellings, signs, workrooms, and shops along a paved street. Real cities were often less attractive. (Paris, Arsenal Library, ms 5062.)

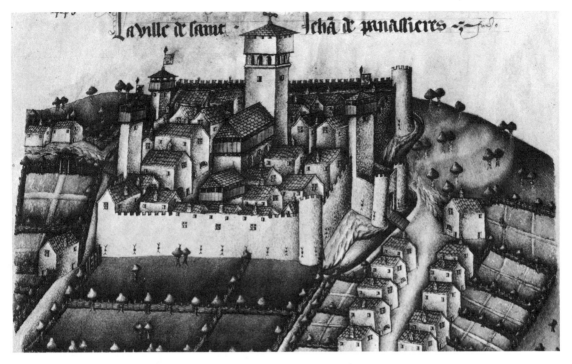

canons of the collegiate church of Notre-Dame. The subject of the litigation was a small street, 4 to 5 feet wide, which passed through the chapter's cemetery on its way to a communal oven. The chapter attempted to prohibit passage by erecting a wall around the cemetery. The municipality of Saint-Flour argued not only that the road was communal property but also that cemeteries in Auvergne were "public places" and that it was therefore improper to wall them in.

The cramped, fragmented nature of the public sphere reflected, in the very topography of the city, the weakness, lack of resources, and limited ambitions of the state. Streets were generally so narrow that an avenue 20 or 22 feet across was considered impressive. Cities were mazes of twisting, tiny streets, impasses, and courts; squares were small, and there were few broad vistas or buildings set back from the street; traffic was always clogged. In fifteenth-century Brittany many streets were nothing more than corridors, darkened by overhanging corbels (Jean-Pierre Leguay).

People did not necessarily look upon the medieval city, with its picturesque and labyrinthine hodgepodge of streets, vaulted passageways, and massive walls, as an unalterable and on the whole unlivable environment. They adjusted to their

View of Panissières (Loire) from the *Armorial* by Guillaume Revel, 15th century. This important town of the Forez is hemmed in by its walls and dominated by the square tower of the Church of Saint John the Baptist. Nearby orchards and walled gardens can be seen, and small houses with chimneys and tile roofs are lined up along a road. In the distance is the countryside. (Paris, Bibliothèque Nationale, French 22297.)

Carcassonne in 1462. In the foreground is the town; in the background, the cathedral city. In between are the bridge over the Aude, which dates from the 14th century, and a fortification or outwork that extends the walls northward.

cities, which they may have seen as offering protection against not just the weather but intruders of all kinds. But various indications suggest that many people, and particularly leaders of the community, wanted to improve living conditions and deplored the many inconveniences resulting from uncontrolled growth and uncivic actions by private individuals. New cities, planned in the thirteenth century by the appropriate authorities, were built with significantly wider streets; the *magna carreyra* in Libourne was more than 36 feet wide. We also find spacious squares and a grid of streets laid out at right angles. Similarly, the few medieval attempts at urban renewal reflect a genuine feeling for space and harmony of proportions, as do miniatures depicting the ideal city. A city fortunate enough to possess a nicely proportioned square did its best to preserve it from the greed of real-estate promoters and if necessary made improvements at municipal expense.

In 1484 the city of Troyes sought to obtain from the king the right to replace the just-abolished Lyons markets. Without excessive modesty the city fathers described their town as "a beautiful, large city with fine houses and beautiful, broad and spacious streets, fine squares, and public areas for fairs and markets."

Travelers occasionally remark on a city's sites. Antonio of Beatis has this to say about Mechelen (Belgium): "Superb city, very large and highly fortified. Nowhere have we seen streets more spacious or more elegant. They are paved with small stones, and the sides slope down slightly, so that water and mud never remain standing. In front of the church, which is quite beautiful, is a square longer and much wider than the Campo dei fiori in Rome and paved in the same manner as the streets. The city is traversed by canals, whose waters rise and fall with the tides."

Municipal ordinances and regulations were promulgated in various places, more in the fifteenth century than in the fourteenth, to protect the public health and safety and to regulate the circulation of men and merchandise. In this respect France lagged behind other countries, slowly and unenthusiastically following examples set in other places. But attitudes were beginning to change, perhaps because things had deteriorated to the point where something had to be done, perhaps because new diseases like bubonic plague were decimating the population, or perhaps because a genuine civic spirit had begun to develop. Most towns had aldermen, aediles, or town councillors of some sort; these municipal authorities were probably less strapped for resources than in the past and had the necessary manpower to enforce their decisions. To be sure, they used their powers to further their own interests and the interests of their class, but that does not mean that they did not also feel responsible for the welfare of the citizenry as a whole, and even more for the city which they so proudly claimed the right to govern.

I would be presenting only a very partial view of things if I were to look solely at the public aspect of the medieval city. Most cities contained numerous churches and religious communities. These in turn owned many buildings (among the better built) and often considerable amounts of vacant land; property in mortmain was urban as well as rural. Cathedral and collegial chapters, old monasteries, and convents founded in the thirteenth century or later often reserved the right, sometimes the exclusive right, to use courts, cloisters, and gardens. There were also cemeteries, sometimes isolated like the Cemetery of the Innocents in Paris but more often adjoining a parish church (sojourn of the dead and the living, as the phrase went). Furthermore, most of the houses in many cities had courtyards in the rear, used for both professional and domestic purposes, as well as gardens of some sort. Even

Pierre de Crescens, *Le Livre des prouffitz champestres*, 15th century. An urban garden in which gardeners toil under the master's eye. (Paris, Arsenal Library, ms 5064.)

southern cities, generally more cramped, boasted such amenities. The earliest cadaster of Arles mentions a garden in the Arenas. The archbishop of Arles had a garden inside the archepiscopal city, as did the Pope at Avignon (more precisely, Benedict XII had a garden and Urban V an orchard). Gardens were even more common in northern and western France, and not all were located outside the city walls in a sort of suburban "green belt." Most were located close to the walls, but on the inside. Even the most densely built areas contained gardens hidden behind high walls and unbroken facades. At Besançon, however, in the area bounded by a bend in the Doubs River, enclosed vineyards belonging to religious establishments formed islets of green that stood apart from residential sections. At Rheims in 1328 a property census (which omits some or all church property) lists eighteen houses with adjoining gardens and twenty-eight independent gardens in the episcopal city; for the adjacent bourgs the figures are thirty-nine and seventy, respectively.

Yet the street, narrow, noisy, and foul-smelling as it was, retained its power of attraction, for it represented communication, in every sense of the word: distraction, action, life. Houses turned their best, most ornate side toward the street, as well as their biggest windows, their signs, and the doors to their workrooms. The finest rooms faced the street rather than the court, in particular (to judge by the evidence of several inventories) the bedroom of the *chef d'hôtel* and his wife. Bernard Chevalier observes: "Unlike the cities of the Orient, whose beehive structure encourages clans and ethnic or religious groups to live turned inward on themselves," late medieval cities "forced the members of an extroverted urban society into the street."

Histoire de Renaud de Montauban, 15th century. Game room of an urban hôtel. Note the large windows and doors and the rudimentary furniture. (Paris, Arsenal Library, ms 5073.)

The Peasant House

How was space used in the peasant house? Various approaches to this rather difficult question are possible. We can begin by looking at regional house types in the recent past and asking whether such features as method of construction, social and professional uses, available materials, climate, and so on can be traced back to the Middle Ages. In other words, did, say, the Norman-style farm, the Alpine chalet, and the blockhouse characteristic of certain southern provinces have medieval precursors? Listen to Jean Dolfuss: "Leaving the question of construction material aside, urban buildings, endlessly diverse in purpose and design, are far more influenced by the period in which they were built than by the place. By contrast, rural houses, directly influenced by the geographical setting and local conditions, exhibit local characteristics that resist historical change and foreign influences; from province to province these are the buildings that give the best idea of the original diversity of French habitations . . . There is every reason to believe that today's rural house, built on the same soil and using the same materials as in the past, must in many cases be quite similar to the dwellings of the remote past." In other words, we are asked to believe that the rustic house, child more of its region than of its time, has for centuries remained an immutable reflection of the eternal rural order. More prudent than Dolfuss, Jean-Marie Pesez nevertheless holds that "the important differences appear to be not those which divide the social classes but those which define distinct economic and cultural regions, such as northern France and southern France."

There is nothing wrong with assuming that there is a rough correlation between types of peasant housing and prevailing regional agricultural techniques and economic conditions. Whether livestock-raising is flourishing or declining in a region cannot fail to have an impact on the way in which farm buildings are built and situated. It matters whether the region is one where grapes are grown or chestnuts gathered or silkworms raised, whether irrigation techniques have been perfected, and whether one type of production dominates all others. Speaking of nineteenth-century farmhouses in Picardy, Albert Demangeon notes: "There are no superfluous amenities; everything contributes to the agricultural product." The same remark holds true for houses in the medieval period considered as tools, as agricultural implements. Such routine necessities as ovens, mills, and presses required that buildings

Village of Hermes (Oise), early 16th century. Note the scattered homes, the two mills on the Thérain (one for corn, the other for textiles), and the church with its cemetery. (Oise Archives, H 4530.)

be built and made available, on certain conditions, to the community; each farm could not have its own oven, mill, or press. One consequence of the disintegration and subsequent abolition of "feudalism" (in the eighteenth-century sense of the word) was the proliferation of private mills and even presses. Furthermore, such things as the layout and maintenance of the house were affected by the status of its inhabitant: freeholder, perpetual tenant of a lord, farmer, sharecropper, or subject to mortmain.

The peasant house must be seen in relation to its environment. Was it an isolated farmhouse or a house in a village, flanked by other, similar houses? Were farms in the region scattered across valleys or grouped together on a hill to form a fortresslike castrum? Each of the many communal possibilities affected the plan and structure of individual houses.

In addition, some houses were designed for single women, others for nuclear families, still others for "patriarchs" with large numbers of offspring. There must have been at

French translation of Boccaccio's *Decameron*, 15th century. People and animals share the same roof. (Paris, Arsenal Library, ms 5070.)

least a rough correlation between the size of the house and the number of human beings (and animals) it was intended to shelter.

Finally, there were houses for cotters, living on the verge of poverty; other houses for day laborers who owned few tools and fewer animals; and still others for well-to-do plowmen who owned several plows and harnesses and who would have needed to store quantities of grain and straw and to house a number of domestics. Obviously the shape of the peasant house must have depended on the wealth of the peasant who occupied it.

Among the wide variety of medieval rural houses one type stands out: the so-called long house (*longa domus*), sometimes called a mixed house because, in the words of Robert Fossier, it "sheltered under one roof, at opposite ends of the building, both human beings and livestock. Occupants of both kinds shared one or two entries. If there were two entries, they were often arranged opposite each other in the center of the long side of the building." A document from Forez, dated 1314, describes a *hospitium* (inn) under whose roof stood a main room (in the center) with hearth and oven, a storage room (at one end), a cowshed (at the other end), and above all three, a hayloft.

It is now generally accepted that the long house was quite common throughout western Europe. It gradually disappeared, mostly because of people's growing unwillingness to live in permanent proximity to animals. Yet this type of habitation survives even today in certain regions: the Alps, France's Massif central, Brittany, Wales.

"Civilized" observers were quick to express surprise and pity at the sight of such archaic and rustic customs. When Dubuisson-Aubenay visited Brittany in the seventeenth century, he had this to say: "In most houses you must pass through the dining room or kitchen to go to the stable or cowshed. As in the rest of Brittany, the livestock use the same

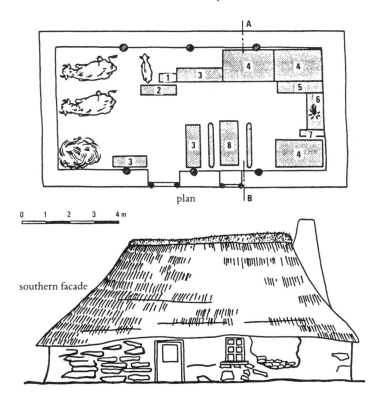

plan

0 1 2 3 4 m

southern facade

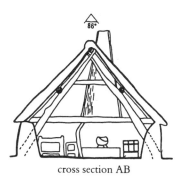

cross section AB

Long house at Plumelin (Morbihan), a modern survival of the medieval mixed dwelling, in which people and animals shared a single roof.
1: clock
2: bench-chest
3: closet
4: covered bed
5: chest
6: foyer
7: bench
8: table-chest

entrances as the people, and they are not far from sleeping together. And since the houses are made partly of a slatelike stone and mostly of wood, rats and mice are present in greater numbers than I have ever seen in any other place. The furniture is like everything else: the beds are very short and very high off the ground, the tables are high, and the chairs are very low. There is no shortage of fleas and lice." In 1618 a traveler staying at Erbrée (Ille-et-Vilaine) complains of being unable to sleep "because of the cows, there being where we were only yourself and the four walls."

Nevertheless, even under a single roof there were more and less elaborate ways of compartmentalizing space. The long house is not incompatible with separate entries for men and animals, and substantial internal partitions could be built to divide the human part of the habitation into several rooms. The mingling of men and animals was part of a way of life that must be looked at as a whole; it was not simply the result of extreme economic hardship.

Long houses had courts, a point often overlooked. Here there were sometimes pigsties, threshing grounds, a sheep pen, a *scure* (for storing grain), and perhaps an oven for drying grain. The long house seems unsuited to farms with more than a few head of livestock. A peasant with a dozen cows and fifty sheep would have required a different type of construction.

In the English village of Wharram Percy in Yorkshire there is a site containing several long houses which archaeologists have been exploring for the past thirty years. The earliest settlement on the site was apparently abandoned, but in the twelfth century a rather small village (albeit large enough to have a parish church) seems to have sprung up around a seigneurial manor; it was deserted around 1510 in the wake of an extension of livestock-raising and enclosures. All the houses, regardless of construction technique or building material, are rectangular in shape, ranging from 40 to 90 feet long and from 15 to 20 feet wide. The entrances are in the center of the long wall. The section reserved for human habitation possibly included a separate bedroom followed by a room with central hearth with a hole in the roof to allow smoke to escape. The roof consisted of a handsome, high wooden frame covered with thatch. The walls are of soft limestone, in some cases held in place by wooden members resting on a stone foundation.

These houses stood within an enclosure—hardly surpris-

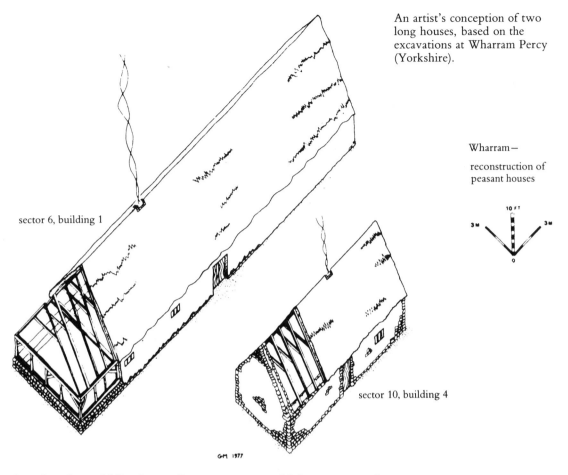

An artist's conception of two long houses, based on the excavations at Wharram Percy (Yorkshire).

Wharram—

reconstruction of peasant houses

sector 6, building 1

sector 10, building 4

GM 1977

ing for the Middle Ages. But, as one would have guessed simply from reading the texts, there was nothing intangible about the boundaries. Houses did not last very long. On one site, near the manor, no fewer than nine houses were built in the space of three centuries, each slightly different from its predecessor. It is as though houses were not expected to last more than a generation.

A small number of the houses at Wharram Percy are not of the long-house type. One of these, dating from the late thirteenth or early fourteenth century, is divided into two rooms, one with hearth; it probably sheltered no animals.

At Wawne, also in Yorkshire, traces have been found of a dozen houses built in the twelfth, thirteenth, and fourteenth centuries of wattles or wood frames, typically measuring 50 feet by 15 feet. Eventually these houses were abandoned and

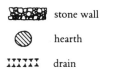

stone wall

hearth

drain

0   5   25 *feet*

0   1   5 m

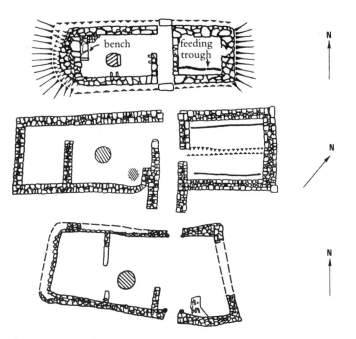

Plans of long houses in
medieval Devon and Cornwall,
some with two, others with
three rooms. There is as yet no
true fireplace, only a central
hearth.

destroyed, and wheat was grown on the site. Still later, in the
second half of the fourteenth or the fifteenth century, sixteen
new houses were built, possibly at the behest of the lord; they
were oriented in the same way as the old houses and of approximately the same width (about 16 feet) but only 33 to 43
feet long. Their two rooms, constructed of wood frames on
a base of small stones, were separated by a hearth on a platform
of brick; the roofs were of tile rather than thatch.

There is evidence of long houses of a relatively late date
with adjacent outbuildings or adjoining other long houses or
single-room dwellings. Finally, examples exist of long houses
with habitable upper floors, but these are fairly recent. Were
houses of this type completely unknown in the Middle Ages?
I shall assume that for northern France and England, at any
rate, the answer to this question was no. The typical long
house, then, measured 15 by 50 feet. Assuming that half of
its space was reserved for humans, and subtracting the space
taken up by the common entry, we can calculate that barely
350 square feet remained for a household of five or six persons.
These calculations are confirmed by the plans of long houses
in Devon and Cornwall, where a careful distinction was made
between the space reserved for people and that assigned to
animals.

Other types of rural housing were built. In the so-called

blockhouse, dwellings and farm buildings were contiguous and may have shared a single roof, though each retained its independence. In the court plan buildings were arranged around a courtyard. Whether these existed in the early Middle Ages we cannot say with certainty, though written documentation of such types of construction becomes plentiful in the thirteenth century.

The sources frequently concern farms occupied by a wealthy or well-to-do freeholder, a sharecropper, or a farmer. In the late fifteenth century Philippe de Commynes repaired the sharecroppers' farms on his estate at Argenton; they comprised "houses, lodges, silos, sheep pens, animal sheds, and other things." At about the same time in Lorraine we find a type of construction in which buildings were aligned along roadways. Between the facade of the house and the road was

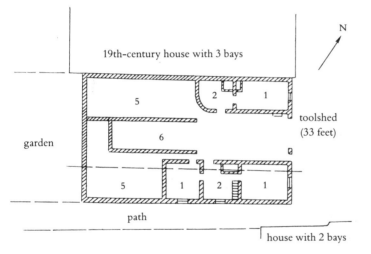

House built in 1619 at Rugney (Vosges). A similar interior arrangement probably existed in Lorraine in the 15th century.

1: bedroom   2: kitchen   3: cellar   4: attic   5: stable   6: barn

scale: 1/200

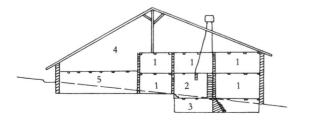

a space called the *usoir, usuaire,* or *parge*; then came the house proper, containing, from front to rear, a front room with door and window, a windowless kitchen, and finally a back room, in some cases heated by a *fournot* (stove). Normally there was no hallway; one room opened into the next. Parallel to the long axis of the house, a second building contained the *arault*, threshing ground, and the cowshed, topped by a loft for storing hay, straw, or grain. Sometimes there was a third building, again built parallel to the house and used for additional storage. Beyond lay the garden and hemp field. In some cases the cowshed was removed to the back of the house, as in a house built in 1619 at Rugney (Vosges); in its present state it contains two hearths, but renovations were made at dates that cannot be ascertained.

Blockhouses and houses with courtyards were also found on seigneurial as opposed to peasant farms; they may have served as models for the peasant houses described in the preceding paragraph. A typical seigneurial residence of this type is that of Tristan de Maignelay at Fontains near Nangis in La Brie, as described in a document dated 1377: "The *ostel* called Les Clos contains a great hall with three chambers above and two below, with four fireplaces above and below. Also, a large loft, and cowsheds below. A chapel, kitchen and pantry above, adjoining said chambers and halls, roofed with tile, well and sufficiently. Also, a barn with ten stalls, roofed with tile. Also, a rotating dovecote, well stocked with doves. Also, another house [possibly for farm laborers] containing two chambers with a cellar ten stairs below and a tile roof. A henhouse and beneath it a pigsty, with tile roof, surrounded by walls around the entire abode, including the three gardens." In other words, not all farmhouses were simple one- or two-room thatched-roof dwellings with hearth but no fireplace; some were veritable manor houses.

In 1450 the Grand Prior of France undertook to repair the commanderies of the Hospitallers, many of which had suffered grave damage during the war. Seven years later he inspected the work that had been done on the commandery at Lagny-le-Sec. Its commander, Brother Jean Le Roy, had begun, as was only proper, by repairing the chapel. He had then turned to the main building, the *grant maison*, where the knights of the order lived. Other prominent features of the premises included a "lower hall and chamber, kitchen, wardrobe, and loft," all covered by a tile roof; two great halls, also with tile roof and used for the time being as barns; a stable with five stalls and thatched roof; two animal barns with thatched roofs; a sheepfold with ten stalls and a tile roof; a square tower, also with tile roof, containing a pigsty at ground level and a dovecote above; another sheepfold, brand new, with seven stalls, covered with thatch; a *hostel* where the farmers were housed; a well, covered by a tile roof; a bedroom above the gate to the courtyard; a square tower with tile roof used as a prison and containing an upper-level bedroom with fireplace. "All these buildings, including those that have been repaired as well as those that remain in ruins, are situated in an enclosure of approximately three to four acres, surrounded by walls in fairly good and adequate condition."

A farm like this can survive only in a prospering rural economy where agriculture is both diversified and balanced. The master of the premises, at least, must have lived quite comfortably. However ancient farms of this type may have been, their numbers appear to have been growing slowly but steadily in fourteenth- and fifteenth-century France and England. There is general agreement among English historians that a variety of improvements were made to farm dwellings during this period: second floors were added; rooms were divided; and distinct areas began to be assigned to different functions, such as work, food preparation, food consumption, rest, and sleep. Animals were banished to separate buildings, distributed around the courtyard. The central hearth gave way to a wall fireplace, which drew better and reduced risk of fire. In 1577 William Harrison wrote: "Houses in our villages and towns are generally constructed so that neither the milk barn nor the stable nor the brewery is attached under one roof (as is the case in many places abroad as well as in the north); rather, they are separate from the house and independent of one another."

Finally, there were simple one- or two-room dwellings, just big enough for a widow or a farm laborer and his family; these went by a variety of names: *cahutes, loges, cabanes, bordes, burons, maisoncelles, masurettes, masureaux*. We read, for example, in a document dated 1391, that a man "called hut (*quahute*) an old house in which he lived."

In 1417 Jean Petitpas, a plowman at Jaux (Oise), lived with his wife and three small children in a house that consisted of a *foyer* and *chambre*. In 1416 the movable chattels of Marie the woodcutter, *femme de corps* of the Duke of Orleans, were distributed among the three rooms of her abode at Rocourt-Saint-Martin (Aisne): a kitchen, a bedroom, and a *solier* (upper

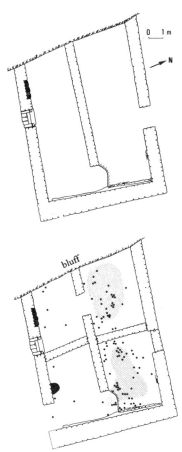

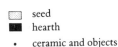

seed

hearth

• ceramic and objects

Plan of house at Dracy (Côte-d'Or); first phase, late 13th century. Open to the north and south, the house at this point had only two rooms. The lower drawing shows the same house in the second phase of its existence (14th century). It is now divided into two dwelling units, both open to the south. In the final phase, which ended around 1360, the building was again inhabited by only one family, which occupied both parts.

story). In the same year another *femme de corps* of the Duke of Orleans lived in a house with just two rooms, a kitchen and a bedroom. A cowherd at Rosoy (Oise) lived in a single room, which contained his few kitchen implements and a broken-down bed.

Like Wharram Percy in England, Dracy (a hamlet of the parish of Baubigny in Burgundy) has been the focus of intensive research; a team of French and Polish archaeologists has been excavating the site since 1965. Established at an unknown date at the foot of a high limestone bluff, this agricultural and winemaking hamlet boasted some fifteen hearths in 1285, but its population dwindled in the late fourteenth century as a result of pestilence and war and finally died out entirely shortly after 1400. The last survivors probably moved to a nearby village where economic prospects were brighter and life was somewhat easier to bear.

Perhaps the most useful information obtained thus far comes from a house that burned some time around 1360. It was a ponderous structure which abutted the limestone bluff and therefore needed only three walls, constructed of uncut or rough-hewn stone held in place by a yellowish clay. The building is roughly square, measuring 27 to 30 feet from north to south and 35 to 36 feet east to west. Of the 900-odd square feet thus covered, only about 600 square feet of living space remained, owing to the thickness of interior and exterior walls.

This building originally was divided into just two rather long rooms, one on the north side, the other on the south. Intended at that time for use by a single family, the house contained just one hearth, located in the southernmost room. It was quite remarkable for that time and place, in that the hearth was a true fireplace, with a chimney of clay-lined wood supported by the southern wall. In addition, there is a very carefully wrought stone threshold, which provided a solid base for the door frame and prevented barnyard filth from being tracked into the house. The northernmost room also has a door, on the other facade of the house. The room might have been used initially as a barn; there is no sign of a fireplace. Above this room was another floor, or, rather, a loft, probably accessible by ladder and used for storing grain. A single sloping roof of limestone slabs covered the whole structure: it started from the north wall, 16 to 20 feet high and descended rather abruptly toward the south, where it rested on a wall not more than 8 feet high.

At some point, perhaps as a result of inheritance or over-population, the house was divided. A partition separated the western part (abutting the cliff) from the eastern. The western section retained the fireplace and the original entrance and had access to half of the old north room and probably to half of the upper story as well. But the back room was now window-less; perhaps it was used for storage rather than as a bedroom. To make the eastern portion independent, a hearth and a door were cut into the south side; the northeastern room lost its entrance because the north door was blocked up. The remains of furnishings and kitchen utensils turned up by the archae-ologists do not indicate a doubling of all necessary items, which suggests that at some later date the two portions of the house were reunited and the building again occupied by a single household.

Jean-Marie Pesez sums up the findings: "a ponderous building, made entirely of stone, with few openings and fairly low despite the second story, yet a sturdy dwelling that was used for at least several decades and probably for several gen-erations, since it was transformed to accommodate a larger number of inhabitants." Bear in mind that people spent a great deal of time outside on the exposed platform, a few yards wide, that extended almost to the next house. Assuming that a fire was kept going throughout the day (which is by no

Vestiges of houses at Dracy. The walls, even the interior ones, were thick, and the rooms small.

An artist's conception of the village of Dracy (Côte-d'Or) as it might have been in the 14th century.

means certain), several generations of people may well have found even the dark, crude interior a reasonably warm and pleasant abode.

Few documents from the late Middle Ages give a more concrete picture of the peasant home than the fascinating records of an inquisition carried out at the behest of the future Pope Benedict XII when he was still Jacques Fournier, bishop of Pamiers (1318–1325). Among other things, this remarkable source clearly reveals the essential role of the *hospicium*, *domus*, or *ostal*. In the upper Ariège Valley, where Fournier displayed inexhaustible ingenuity in the persecution of heretics, the house represented stability; it was the center of life for every man, woman, and child. Though by no means isolated and cut off, the house was the nest of heresy, the place where heretics took refuge and waited in hiding until the moment was ripe. Here, secrets could be exchanged, parleys held, thoughts spoken freely. Of the various houses mentioned by the inquisitors, nearly all contained nuclear families: father, mother, and children. Some two hundred people lived in Montaillou's forty houses—five per hearth. The only exceptions were one "Catholic" household with five brothers and a "Cathar" household in which a widow lived with her four grown sons, all still bachelors.

The central portion of the house (sometimes called the "house within a house") was the *foganha*, elsewhere called the foyer, kitchen, *chas*, or *foconea*. A document dated 1377 reads: "Colin Basin entered said *hostel* and opened two chests that were there, one in the *chas*, the other in the chamber." A century later (1478), another document was even more explicit: "The supplicant, who was made uncomfortable by the cold, lit a big fire in his *chas* or kitchen . . . and afterward went to lie down in his bed in a small bedroom off said *chas* or kitchen." And further: "Jean Mariat holds the following inheritances: . . . the house in which he lives, a *chaps* and two bedrooms on either side, and a court, orchard, yard, and outbuildings."

The *chas–chambre* distinction current in northern France corresponds to the distinction between *foganha* and *chambre* in Montaillou. One of the tasks of the housekeeper, or *focaria*, was to keep a fire going in the foganha at all times during the day and to cover it carefully at night for fear of fire.

Normally no one slept in the foganha, which was used for both cooking and eating. Here, in the central room of the home, with direct access to the street, the women of the household spent most of their time; the door generally remained open from morning until evening. In winter the bed of an invalid might be placed close to the fire, much as in Noë du Fail's sixteenth-century description of a villein's home: "the good man's bed was placed next to the hearth, enclosed and raised fairly high."

In Montaillou there were usually several rooms around the foganha. One of the best descriptions is of the house of Pierre Michel in the nearby village of Prades d'Aillon. According to his daughter Raimonde, there was first of all a lower room, which "was arranged in such a way that it adjoined the room known as the foganha, and on this side it had a door which closed, so that no one could see into the lower room from the foganha when the door was closed. On the other side there was another door to this lower room, which led to the threshing ground. Through this door anyone who wished might enter without being seen by those in the foganha, if the first door was closed. And no one slept above this lower room or in the room except for my father and mother, and the heretic when he was in the house. My brothers and I slept in another room which was next to the foganha, which was in the middle, between the lower room and the room where we slept, my brothers and I."

It was not impossible, therefore, to be alone (and in this case the isolation was probably deliberate); the sources frequently speak of doors with bolts and even locks. Keys (as well as locks) are found in all excavations of medieval sites, even rural villages. Admittedly, partitions were not solid, and it may have been possible to listen to or spy on people in the next room through the cracks.

Besides the foganha and the bedrooms, located on the ground floor, some houses owned by wealthier villagers included a second story (solier) of wood and cob; after climbing a rudimentary staircase or simple ladder, one could light a fire for heat or cooking, but the solier served primarily as a bedroom. The solier (also called sinault or sinal) existed throughout France, from Metz to Toulouse, from Tournai to Narbonne, as well as in England; it may have been more common in southern France, however.

The typical Montaillou house also contained a cellar, a storeroom, and perhaps a pantry, balconies, or gallery (elsewhere called a valet). Housing here was fairly sophisticated. Roofs were of shingle and flat enough so that wicker could be set out to dry. Windows were covered with heavy wooden shutters. Outside, people placed benches along the street where they could sit and chat with neighbors or have the lice removed from their hair in bright sunlight. Animals seldom cohabited with humans. Most houses had a courtyard (cortile) that extended into a threshing yard and garden, equipped with the usual outbuildings: a bread oven, a boal (cowshed), a cortal (sheep pen), dovecote, pigsty, straw yard, and storage barn; shepherds, farm laborers, and female servants slept in the barn but had neither heat nor light.

Thanks to the combined efforts of archaeologists and historians, it has been possible to learn something about the evolution of rural architecture in the Middle Ages. In broad outline we witness the transition from rudimentary huts built with whatever materials happened to be at hand (earth, wood, branches, leaves) to more solid structures, designed to last, requiring sophisticated construction techniques and a considerable investment of time and money. More substantial homes became increasingly common from the twelfth century on: here the family could feel more at home, both materially and psychologically. The new housing provided better protection against cold, rain, and wind and permitted better care and storage of work and household implements and stores, what the Middle Ages called *estorements d'hôtel*. The family in a sense identified with its house, much as a noble lineage might identify with its castle.

The fourteenth-century Anglo-Norman poet John Gower penned this verse version of the proverb we encountered earlier about the three things that could drive a man from his home—a leaky roof, a smoky fireplace, and a scolding wife:

Hours of the Virgin, ca. 1500. Beating flax in the courtyard of a farm in northern France. Note the series of half-timbered buildings with thatched roofs. Each building was designed for a specific purpose: on the right, for instance, is a pigsty with a dovecote on top. (New York, Morgan Library, ms 399.)

> Trois choses sont, ce dist ly sage,
> Que l'omme boutent du cotage
> Par fine force et par destresce:
> Ce sont fumee et goute eauage
> Mais plus encore fait le rage
> Du male femme tenceresse.

> Three things, the wise man says,
> Can drive a man from his cottage
> By force and distress:
> They are smoke and dripping water,
> But even more maddening
> To the male is a scolding wife.

If the historian is not in a very good position to appreciate the last of these three nuisances, he can at least hazard a judgment that the severity of the first two diminished over the course of the Middle Ages. Limited as these improvements were, they had an enormous impact on private life. Before they could come about, changes had to take place in attitudes as well as in social and economic realities. Building techniques and social uses of the home may have been affected by what was happening in the cities as well as by the example of manor houses constructed in the country. For it was in the cities that people began to build durable structures, to invest in quality real estate, to replace open hearths with fireplaces, and roofs of thatch or shingle with tile and slate.

"Bourgeois" houses built in rural villages were not without influence on their neighbors. Take rural presbyteries. In 1344 the bishop of Bath and Wells ordered that the pastor serving the parish of West Harptree should have a house including a hall, two upper rooms, two storerooms, a kitchen, a barn, a stable for three horses, five acres of arable land, two acres of meadow, a garden, and a fence. This was not far below the level of a squire's house. A fourteenth-century presbytery still stands in Alfriston (Sussex). It is of half-timbered construction with a thatched roof; the great hall, equipped with a fireplace, is flanked at both ends by two-story soliers, one of which has its own fireplace.

In the late fourteenth century in Normandy, Guillaume Blesot of Touville (in the *doyenné* of Pont-Audemer) was paid 70 gold francs to build a half-timbered house for the curate of the parish, Master Jean de Paigny. The house was to have a "foundation of good stone," 54 feet long by 16 feet wide. Several stories were planned, to be linked by a staircase "of stone or plaster," and there were to be no fewer than four bedrooms and four fireplaces. The doorframes were to be of oak. At one end of the house a penthouse was to be provided, "a room for taking one's ease" (in other words, a privy). The job no doubt called for meticulous craftsmanship and an ability to copy urban models, but evidently it posed no particular problems for the contractor, whose agreement specified that the work was to be completed in just under six months.

The Urban House	Urban houses, like rural ones, were of many types. Stone predominated in some, wood, dried clay, or brick in others. Some had roofs of slate or flat stone, others tile; thatch and other natural coverings were still to be found. Factors that must be taken into account in assessing urban housing include the climate, the size of the city, the density of its population, the nature and intensity of urban activity, and the historical period. Some cities, ruined or bled white by war, beset by epidemics and economic change, were unable to maintain existing buildings, while others grew in size even during the Hundred Years' War and managed to create or appropriate new wealth, thus permitting a steady stream of new construction. In many cities the second half of the fifteenth century was a happy time: the hardships of the Bourges kingdom were in the past and the unhealthy overcrowding of the next century had yet to come. Significantly, many houses from this time are still standing today.

Medieval cities were home to a substantial number of monks, nuns, and clerics, some residing in religious communities, others not. Nobles—great lords, princes, kings—permanently or temporarily occupied urban hôtels. Such notable personages as men of affairs, jurists, financiers, and renowned physicians—*bourgeois*, the texts referred to them—also owned hôtels. Far greater numbers were lower on the social scale, with quarters often wretched or uncertain. Tramps and beggars went "searching for bread, lurking and idling everywhere, lying under the stalls" and sleeping "in the streets" (François Villon). For them the city of Tournai built a roofed barracks in 1439. Vagabonds were joined by students refused admittance to colleges; elderly men and women; and valets, maids, and companions who were not lodged in their master's homes.

Artisans and shopkeepers, though prevented from assuming any major role in government or administration, were typical of urban society; in some cities they were organized into guilds and confraternities. Around them gravitated a host

Renaissance house in Chartres, with a half-timbered spiral staircase. No doubt the building survived because of its fine sculptures.

Work and family: the workshop of an urban artisan. In this late-15th-century miniature Jean Bourdichon gives a good idea of the decorative wood carving that flourished at the time.

House in Rheims, no longer standing. A specimen of the quality housing of northern France, with two stories above a workroom, topped by a huge attic.

of other people who shared the same lot; all together they accounted for perhaps half of the urban population. Among the *commun*, or common people, as they were called, some were no doubt richer than others; some were engaged in more prestigious trades or exhibited greater savoir-faire or served a more important clientele. The less fortunate suffered from any number of handicaps: large families, old age, sickness, business reverses. Differences aside, most tradespeople lived in private residences, of which they occupied, if not the whole house, then at least the greater part. They used their homes not only as residences but also as studios and shops. A majority of the 3,700 houses in Rheims, 2,400 houses in Arras (not including the episcopal city), and 6,000 houses in Lille fit this description.

The value of an artisan's house depended on its location, size, type of construction, and general condition; some were appraised at 20 livres, others at four times that amount. In describing the typical artisan's house, I shall oversimplify; this is necessary but in some ways misleading. In most French cities in the fourteenth and fifteenth centuries the houses of the common people were built directly on the street, without forecourt of any kind, whether the house was gabled or built with roof ridge parallel to the facade. Facades were generally narrow, ranging from 16 to 23 feet in width, sometimes a little more, sometimes a little less. In the Bourget district of Nancy some fourteenth-century houses were squeezed into just 11 feet of space, while others spread as wide as 33 feet (Jean-Luc Fray).

Many houses had two floors, one of which was already referred to (in Paris at any rate) as the *rez-de-chaussée* (ground floor). There was usually a basement whose vault (or ceiling) protruded slightly above ground level, so that one had to climb two or three steps to reach the slightly elevated ground floor. Houses varied in depth from about 23 to 33 feet. The first-floor ceiling was generally 10 to 11 feet high; the second-floor ceiling was slightly lower, 8½ to 10 feet high. The upper story was often corbelled, which increased the amount of space available, though at the cost of light, ventilation, and perhaps decreased structural stability. Above it an attic was accessible via ladder through a trap door. Wood was the predominant building material, although stone was used in some areas, especially for first-floor walls. For better protection against fire and rain, thatched roofs were often replaced by slate or tile; this tendency was encouraged or even enforced by some town governments. Assuming, then, overall dimensions of 20 by 25 feet, we have, counting both floors, a living space of approximately 1,000 square feet per hearth (say five persons), plus the cellar, attic, and whatever outbuildings were constructed in the rear court, such as a separate kitchen.

In theory, there was no overcrowding. One Parisian source indicates that the ground-floor entrance, called a *huis* or *huisserie*, was often propped open all day long by means of a chair: "Une selle apuyee servant a mectre a huis," a chair used to prop the door, is mentioned in a fifteenth-century inventory. We also hear of chairs "for sitting by the door" or "placing outside the door." In 1535 the Venetian ambassador Marino Giustiniano observed that in Paris it was "customary for men and women, old and young, masters and servants to sit in their shops, on their doorsteps, or in the street."

The front door opened onto a narrow corridor, 3½ to 5 feet wide, which led to two rooms: the front room was called the *ouvroir, échoppe, boutique,* or *atelier,* and the back room the *salle* or *basse chambre,* which opened onto the court. An inside staircase led up to the second floor, also divided into two or three rooms. At Montbéliard early in the sixteenth century external spiral staircases (*viorbes*) became increasingly common.

For greater comfort and convenience, some houses had private wells, which obviated the need for the women of the house to fetch water from a spring, river, or fountain; the chore, though no doubt diverting, remained a chore. In Paris, houses without wells often used the services of hired water-carriers. Other amenities included shutters (visible in innumerable miniatures) for protection against wind, rain, and cold; oiled paper, parchment, or fabric in the windows; and, in the most fortunate cases, especially after 1400, fixed or movable glass panels. Most of the rooms of an artisan's house were equipped with fireplaces, but this does not mean that all were used simultaneously or continually. Packed earth or wooden floors were eventually replaced by beautiful polished tiles on both stories. Finally, even ordinary houses were equipped with latrines, more commonly than one might think. By the late fifteenth or early sixteenth century these were considered normal and indispensable by many municipal authorities. In 1519 the parlement of Rouen voiced public sentiment when it ordered all property owners to "construct and equip their houses with *retraitz en terre* [cesspits], and seats placed and affixed above said conveniences . . . and identical

A 15th-century miniature illustrating an episode in a French translation of the *Decameron*. Note the latrine between two upper stories. (Paris, Arsenal Library, ms 5070.)

for each apartment." Neighbors sometimes agreed among themselves about how to deal with the problem. In 1433 Martin Hubert and Pierre Fossecte lived in adjoining houses on the rue du Fossé-aux-Gantiers in Rouen. Having just built "brand new cesspits (*aisements*)" on his property, Hubert agreed that Fossecte and his wife, in exchange for a payment of 12 livres, should enjoy the use of a "seat for relief of the body" as long as they lived: "Which seat shall be located in said Hubert's gallery at the height of the second floor of the house of said married couple, at the place where they presently keep their chamber, in which chamber shall be provided a new door through which to enter and be seated in this gallery on the toilet seat, which seat shall be appropriately placed and shall have a glass window placed at a reasonable height." If the Fossectes moved, the access door was to be blocked up. Finally, when the cesspit was cleaned, the cost was to be divided, one-third for the Fossectes and two-thirds for Hubert. Nevertheless, there were still too few of these private latrines, so enlightened municipalities such as Loches, Tournai, and Rouen built common latrines in the fifteenth century, some-

Heures de Paris, 15th century. Estate inventory. The notary writes while his assistants open the chests and lay out their contents on a table. (Paris, Bibliothèque Nationale, Latin 1176.)

times on the city walls, sometimes next to rivers and streams; there were separate latrines for men, women, and sometimes children.

Evidence of more modest houses of just two or three rooms has also survived. These may have been the same houses classed in tax documents in Rouen, Romorantin, and Tours as *appentis* or *maisons appentisées* (houses covered by a single sloping roof) as opposed to gabled houses or houses with ridged roofs.

The estate inventory of Berthon de Santalène (died 1427), a barber in the village of Crest (Drôme) who was neither poor nor insignificant, lists the following in the home (known as *Dretche charriere*) where he lived with his father: a back room (*camera posterior*) with two beds, one small and one large; a front room (*camera anterior*) with a bed and kitchen utensils; a workroom (*operatorium*) with three barber's chairs, five basins, ten razors, four sharpening stones, two mirrors, and three silver lancets for bleeding; a storage loft behind the workroom, used mainly for storing grain; and a cellar. Thus this house had only three rooms, and "hall" and kitchen were combined: "Aula sive focanea," as the Provençal sources put it. The inventory of Guillaume Burellin, blacksmith at Calvisson in Gard (died 1442), describes an even simpler dwelling, with a workshop (*la botiga de la forja*) and a second-floor room (*lo solié de l'ostal*) serving as kitchen, bedroom, and hall.

One step closer to poverty, widows, valets, and students lived in single rooms. No doubt the "poor girl who spun wool" and whose house, described in the *Ménagier de Paris*, "had no kitchen or larder, no oil or charcoal, nothing but a bed and cover, a spinning wheel, and little other furniture," lived in one room. So did Perrin le Bossu, a poor Parisian wool carder, who in 1426 was excused from paying the fine incurred for having picked the lock of one Thomassin Hébert, goldsmith, whose room "is above that in which said Perrin resides." Many families in early-fourteenth-century Paris lived, according to Raymond Cazelles, in a single room, a *mansion, domuncula,* or *estage.*

At the other extreme we find the classic canon's house, about which we possess particularly abundant information. Canons generally lived near a cathedral or cloister; their houses consisted of approximately ten rooms, with garden and courtyard. There were several bedrooms, the canon's being the best furnished and no doubt the most pleasant, if not always the largest; one or two rooms called *sala* or *aula* in the Latin documents; a kitchen and pantry; a study (sometimes called a *scriptorium*); a chapel; and numerous annexes, such as stables, storeroom, cellar, gallery, lumber room, *charbonnier* or charcoal room, and so on.

At a still higher social level, the hôtels of bishops sometimes followed the model of the canonical house, sometimes that of the seigneurial or even princely residence. An inventory of the *domus episcopalis laudunensis*, the bishop's house at Laon, compiled after the death of Bishop Geoffroi le Meingre in 1370, oddly enough makes no mention of either a chapel or a study. But it does note a kitchen and pantry, a lower hall, and seven bedrooms: one for the bishop, complete with wardrobe, and others for the official, chaplains, keeper of the seals, collector, cook, and porter. In 1496 the *oustel episcopal* at Senlis was somewhat better equipped: still no study, but we do find a chapel, a small hall, a kitchen and pantry, six bedrooms, porter's *logis et hôtel*, and a number of outbuildings, including a *foulerie* for treading grapes, a bakehouse, large and small lofts, stables, cellar, and storeroom.

The inventory of the episcopal house at Alet, which dates from the death in 1354 of Guillaume d'Alzonne (or de Marcillac), bishop of Alet and abbot of La Grasse, gives some idea of the magnificence of the place, which contained not only a chapel and great hall (*aula major*), also called the *tinel*, but also two studies and no fewer than twenty bedrooms, including a so-called dressing room, distinct from the bishop's bedroom, which was called the *retrocamera*, chamber of retirement. The same distinction between dressing room and bedroom is found in 1389 at Porte-Mars Castle, the urban residence of the archbishop-duke of Rheims. Here, rooms were assigned by name to the majordomo, the chaplains, the squires, the kitchen boys, the butler, and the secretary. In other episcopal residences rooms were assigned to both lay and ecclesiastical subalterns, such as the collector, treasurer, vicar, lackey, camerlingo, and provisioner.

We learn a great deal about how the occupant or occupants of a house lived from the distribution and identification of its rooms. For example, it was "bourgeois" to have a *comptoir*, a counting room, rather than an *ouvroir*, a workroom, and even more bourgeois to have a study instead of (or in addition to) a counting room. A stable of horses or mules indicated that one had reached a station where travel on foot was unthinkable.

The grande bourgeoisie, the most illustrious notables,

obviously emulated aristocratic habits. Nevertheless, their hôtels generally continued to bear the marks of their professions.
In Rouen, for example, the house of Pierre Surreau, chief tax
collector for Normandy during the reign of the House of
Lancaster, contained two counting rooms, one on the ground
floor near the main entrance where official clerks discharged
their duties, the other on the second floor being "the private
counting room of the deceased," according to his estate inventory (1435). Pierre Legendre, treasurer for war and later
treasurer of France, was an eminent financial official under
Louis XI, Charles VIII, and Louis XII and connected with the
most prosperous families in the kingdom, such as the Briçonnet; he was ennobled and even dubbed by the king, owned
several seigneuries in Vexin and surely hoped to gain access
to the highest nobility. An inventory of Legendre's property
compiled in 1525 suggests that he had plenty to back up his
ambition, beginning with an extraordinary collection of tapestries. His hôtel in the rue des Bourdonnais in Paris was so
splendid that until the recent investigation by André Chastel
it was thought to have been the hôtel of an authentic and pure
aristocratic family, La Trémoille. Nevertheless, despite the
presence of a chapel and parlor, the hôtel also contained three
counting rooms in which work was done.

L'Histoire du Grand Alexandre,
15th century. The comforts of
a bourgeois home. Note the
interior shutters, lozenge-
shaped window panes, and
decorative floor tiles. (Paris,
Petit Palais.)

Renaud de Montauban, 15th century. The writing room of an aristocratic residence. Note the clerks on one side, the messengers on the other. Between the two sits the master, who dictates, supervises, and gives orders. (Paris, Arsenal Library, ms 5072.)

The journal kept by Dauvet, prosecutor in the trial of Charles VII's chief financial official, Jacques Coeur, contains inventories of several houses owned by Coeur and his business associates. In Lyons and Rouen the presence of counting rooms and shops reminds us of the nature of the accused's occupation. As for the *grant maison* in Bourges, its owner's pride and joy, "although incomplete at the time of the trial, [it] shows that good taste was not incompatible with a par-venu's penchant for comfort" (Michel Mollat). The towers, the chapel, the coats of arms sculpted in stone, the galleries and rostrums all called attention to the princely dimensions of this noble abode. There were four halls (a record for this type of residence), and prestigious names were ascribed to many of the rooms: *chambre des galées, chambre des galeries, chambre des évêques, chambre des angelotetz, salle des mois de l'an.* Never-theless, this aristocratic hôtel was the scene of lucrative busi-ness activities. In a sense it "derogated from nobility," as is suggested by the presence of numerous counting rooms, in which wooden desks covered with the traditional green cloth provided convenient services for scrutinizing financial and commercial documents.

Only in literary accounts did bourgeois hôtels cease—in the imagination, at any rate—to be distinguished from genuinely patrician residences. In a description of early-fifteenth-century Paris, Guillebert de Mez associates, though not without second thoughts, the "hôtels of bishops and prelates" with those of "lords of parlement, lords of the Chambre des comptes, knights, bourgeois, and various officeholders." In the hôtel (rue de la Verrerie) of Sire Mile Baillet, member of an old Parisian bourgeois family who was first a money-changer then an official who held various financial offices under Charles V and Charles VI, Guillebert notes the presence of a chapel "where services were celebrated daily," as well as two residential levels, one for winter, the other for summer: "There were halls, chambers, and studies [the author is careful not to mention counting room, *tablier*, or even writing room] downstairs for summer use at ground level, and the same upstairs, for use in winter."

Even more revealing is the hôtel of Jacques Duchié (or de Dussy), who died a *maître de comptes* in 1412. The house was again located on the right bank in the business section of the city, more specifically in the rue des Prouvaires. Guillebert de Mez deliberately emphasizes the military aspect of the place, which was equipped with an arms room, as well as its convenience and comfort. He shows how anything that might be regarded as overly utilitarian has been eliminated: in the courtyard there are peacocks, *oyseaux a plaisance*, rather than chickens or ducks. He calls attention to the owner's sophisticated tastes, his disinterested feeling for culture, and his aristocratic passion for gambling and music, the latter appreciated not as a connoisseur but as a participant. "In the court were peacocks and various other birds of pleasure. The first hall was embellished by various paintings and instructive documents attached to and hung from the walls. Another room was filled with all manner of instruments, harps, organs, hurdy-gurdies, guitars, psalteries, and so forth, all of which Maistre Jacques knew how to play. Another hall was graced by chessboards, gaming tables, and all manner of games. [These two rooms prefigure the gaming and music rooms of the eighteenth century.] Also there was a beautiful chapel with exquisitely made lecterns, which were brought to long benches on the left and right. Also a study, whose walls were covered with precious gems and fragrant spices. Also a chamber with furs of various kinds. Also several other chambers richly furnished with beds and ingeniously carved tables covered with rich fabrics and gilt cloth. Also, in another chamber on an upper floor, there were many crossbows, some of which were painted with beautiful figures. There were standards, banners, pennants, bows, picks, *faussars, planchons,* axes, guisarmes, mail of iron and lead, shields, bucklers, breastplates, canon and other devices, with plenty of arms, and in short there was military gear of every sort. Also there was a window most wonderfully crafted, through which a hollow iron head could be projected out of doors; through this head one could look about and talk to those outside if need be, without revealing oneself. Also, atop the entire *ostel*, was a square room with windows on all sides to look out at the city. And when one ate, wines and meats were sent up by pulley, because it was too high to carry them up. And above the pinnacles of the *ostel* were beautiful gilt images."

The Palace of the Popes at Avignon

The study of urban housing leads naturally to that of palaces, which in this period were almost obliged to be located in town. The term *palace* does not really designate a type of building in the architectural sense; rather, it refers to the status and rank of the building's owner. Thus, certain texts suggest that the château de Vincennes ought to be called a palace, since it was a royal residence. As for the arrangement of space, there was no hard and fast distinction between palaces (like the king's palace on the Ile de la Cité in Paris), hôtels (like the Hôtel Saint-Pol, also in Paris, and the primary residence of Charles V and Charles VI), and châteaux in the strict sense, like the Louvre. Appearances, such as the presence or absence of fortifications, matter little when the inner arrangement and order of the rooms are determined by a common set of rules. The same types of rooms are found in the Hôtel Saint-Pol and in the donjon in the Bois de Vincennes. One of the most remarkable of all palaces was that of the popes at Avignon. My remarks about it apply not only to other palaces, both lay and ecclesiastical, but also to castles of comparable size and purpose.

In 1305, when Bertrand de Got, archbishop of Bordeaux, was elected pope, he chose to remain on the French side of the Alps rather than go to Rome or even set foot on Italian soil. After much wandering he settled in Avignon in 1309; for the next half-century his successors would follow his example.

John XXII, who was bishop of Avignon at the time he was elected pope, continued to live in his former episcopal palace, located well inside the twelfth- and thirteenth-century walls in the northern part of the city, near the cathedral Notre-Dame des Doms. Improvements made to the palace during his pontificate (1316–1334) proved insufficient. Benedict XII (1334–1342), therefore, had the existing structure demolished and built on its site a residence befitting the prestige of his office. During the years between 1335 and 1345, extending into the pontificate of Clement VI (1342–1352), master builder Pierre Poisson and his successor, Jean de Louvres, constructed a "grandiose palace," to borrow the words of a contemporary chronicler, "of marvelous beauty and extraordinary power, with its walls and its towers." I am concerned primarily with this edifice, known as the Palais-Vieux (Old Palace) after Clement VI undertook to build the Palais-Nouveau (*novum opus, palatium novum*); in particular I shall describe the state of the Old Palace in 1345, so far as can be determined from the fairly detailed sources and with the help of specialists.

Benedict XII's palace was built around the court of a cloister in the form of a quadrilateral. It also included, on its east side, a garden surrounded by a thick wall.

> Bien est sa geoille gardee
> En son palais se tient fermez.

> His jail is well guarded; He
> remains shut up in his palace.

These were among the reproaches addressed to the pope by Jean Dupin in his *Melancolies*. Questions of defense, or at any rate security, were much on the minds of the builders, as is shown by the massive, high towers adjoining the long buildings that border the four sides of the cloister; several of these towers stand very close together, forming veritable mountains of masonry. Such precautionary measures were by no means unwarranted, for in 1398 the papal palace was subjected to a full siege, with mines, cannonades, and an attempt at arson. The indomitable Benedict XIII emerged victorious, at least for a short while. The life of the palace was not directed exclusively inward. Most of the buildings, as well as the papal bedroom, offered views of the city and garden through numerous substantial openings, located of course primarily in the upper stories.

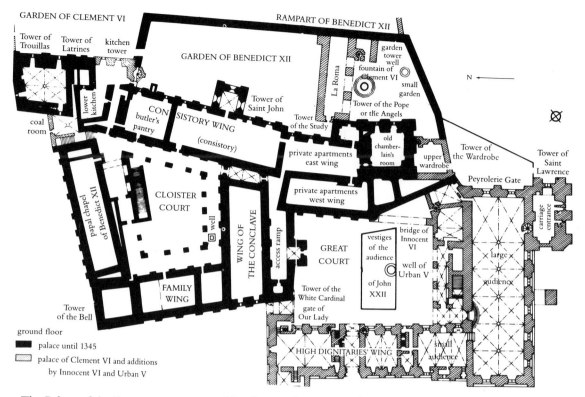

The Palace of the Popes, Avignon: plan of ground floor at the end of the pontificate of Urban V, 1370. The heavy black lines indicate the outline of the structure as it existed in 1345.

North, south, east, and west: four wings surrounded the cloister, each with two or three stories. Each tower had four or five levels, linked by stairs cut into the thick walls. Thus the towers were independent, at least in their upper levels; the middle and lower levels were linked to the main buildings, by stairs where necessary. This mingling of horizontal and vertical organization, common in medieval castles, made circulation relatively easy.

Let us begin our tour with the southern wing, the pontiff's own. Here the Great Tower, some 150 feet high, was built in 1335–1337; known originally as the Tower of the Pope, the Tower of Lead, or the Tower of the Treasury, today it is called the Tower of the Angels. Ordinarily, this was where the pope lived. His chamber (*camera turris, camera papae*), a room 33 feet square, with polished floor and wood ceiling, contained an enormous fireplace and was well lighted by two large windows, on the southern and eastern sides. Descending the tower by degrees, we come first to the room of the papal chamberlain, the pope's minister of finance, the lower treasury, and, finally, to a cellar where it is said that precious

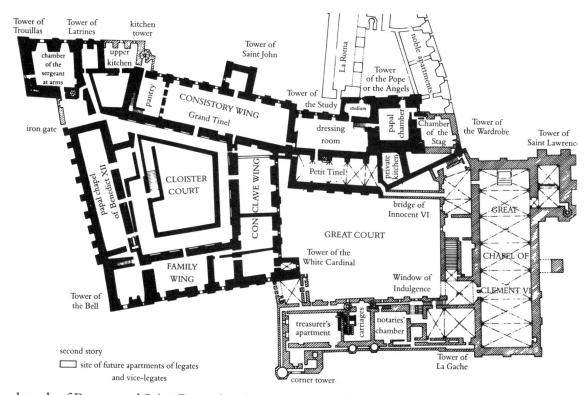

Tower of Trouillas

Tower of Latrines

kitchen tower

Tower of Saint John

La Roma

noble apartments

chamber of the sergeant at arms

upper kitchen

Tower of the Study

Tower of the Pope or the Angels

studium

pantry

CONSISTORY WING
Grand Tinel

dressing room

papal chamber

Chamber of the Stag

Tower of the Wardrobe

Tower of Saint Lawrence

iron gate

papal chapel of Benedict XII

CLOISTER COURT

CONCLAVE WING

Petit Tinel!

private kitchen

bridge of Innocent VI

GREAT

GREAT COURT

CHAPEL OF

FAMILY WING

Tower of the White Cardinal

Window of Indulgence

CLEMENT VI

Tower of the Bell

treasurer's apartment

carriages

notaries' chamber

Tower of La Gache

second story

☐ site of future apartments of legates and vice-legates

corner tower

barrels of Beaune and Saint-Pourçain wine were stored. Above the papal chamber was a large room, which in the time of Innocent VI was divided to form, on one side, the upper treasury and, on the other, the library; still higher was a guardroom used by soldiers of the garrison.

This tower was not self-sufficient; other, indispensable buildings complemented and supported it. To the north, for instance, was the Tower of the Study, only three stories high. At the very bottom was a secret room, headquarters of the pope's financial operations. Above it was a robing room, and above that, at roughly the same level as the papal chamber, the pope's *studium*, a tiled room measuring 16 by 23 feet. To the west a quadrangular building adjoining the papal chamber housed the pope's private kitchen, beyond which stood the papal dining room, called the Petit Tinel. To the south rose the so-called Tower of the Wardrobe, 130 feet high, built by Jean de Louvres in 1342 and 1343, at the beginning of Clement VI's pontificate. At the bottom of this tower was the pope's steam room with boiler and lead bathtub; the next two levels were occupied by private chambers, one above the

The Palace of the Popes, Avignon: plan of second floor at the end of the pontificate of Urban V, 1370.

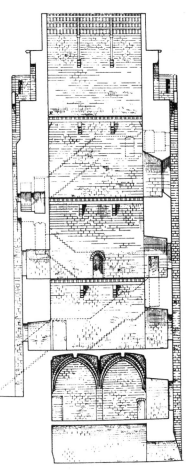

The Palace of the Popes, Avignon: Tower of Angels. From top to bottom: the *châtelet* for the sergeants at arms; the upper treasury and library; the pope's bedroom; the chamberlain's room; the lower treasury; the cellar.

other. Above them was the so-called Chamber of the Stag, which was used as a study by Clement VI and which stood on the same level as the papal chamber; and, at the top of the tower, the pope's private chapel, dedicated to Saint Michael.

North of the Great Tower stretched a wing of the palace flanked by the cloister on one side and the garden on the other. On the ground floor of this building we find the Great Treasury and the Hall of Jesus (so called because of the monogram of Christ that decorated its walls); on the second floor was the Petit Tinel, already mentioned, and perhaps also a private chapel; finally, following a classic model, a dressing room preceded the papal chamber.

As far from the papal quarters as possible, the northeastern corner of the palace contained the various household departments and storage areas: the butler's pantry, pantry, and butchering room; the kitchen of Benedict XII and the even more impressive kitchen of Clement VI; rooms for storing wood and charcoal; cellars and storerooms; as well as a prison, an arsenal, and quarters for part of the garrison (the so-called Tower of Trouillas). And let us not forget the Tower of Latrines, whose sheer size—it was two stories high—is evidence of the large number of people (several hundred at least) who resided permanently in the palace.

The east wing of the cloister linked the pope's personal wing to the service area of the palace; it abutted the Petit Tinel and the dressing room. On the ground floor we find the consistory and above it the Grand Tinel. Used primarily for official banquets, the Grand Tinel may have served ordinarily as a common dining room. This wing included a tower, the Tower of Saint John, with two small chapels, one on the ground floor and another directly above it.

The largest chapel in the Old Palace occupied the entire north wing. It was built on two levels; the lower one, referred to in 1340 as the "big, dark chapel," was soon transformed into a warehouse and lumber room, and only the upper retained its liturgical function.

The Tower of the Bell defended the northwest corner of the palace. It was 150 feet high and had four stories, containing rooms for the pope's relatives, members of the papal court, guards, and the offices of the grand majordomo. Broadly speaking its functions were the same as those of the adjoining building, situated on the western side of the cloister and called the family wing, which housed the pope's servants and other members of his *familia* who lived and worked here. Benedict XII had one of his studies here.

Finally, to the south, just beyond the fortified entrance gate, the Wing of the Conclave housed important guests. King John the Good of France stayed here, as did Emperor Charles IV of Luxemburg some years later. Completing the quadrilateral, the Tower of the White Cardinal housed pantlers and butlers and may have had other uses as well.

Having completed our tour, we can see that the papal palace was well designed to perform a diversity of functions. It was first of all a fortress, equipped with a garrison whose size varied according to circumstances. It was a palace, providing all the facilities necessary for the display of wealth and power expected of the pontifical court. And it was the headquarters of a bureaucracy, widely known for its competence and zeal.

Undoubtedly too little space had been provided for the bureaucrats in the Old Palace, for Clement VI's New Palace was designed primarily to house departments of the papal administration, in particular the courts (with large and small courtrooms).

It would be a mistake to think that Benedict XII and his architect were innovators because they adopted a relatively rational or at any rate "legible" plan for the palace. What little we know from the few written documents concerning John XXII's palace suggests that it was planned in a similar spirit: on one side the pope's private quarters and reception rooms, on the other the kitchen and other household departments, with the offices relegated to a third area.

Was this type of plan new in the fourteenth century? It is by no means impossible that both lay and ecclesiastical castles and palaces built in the twelfth and thirteenth centuries had been designed in similar ways, inspired by the monastic model, which in turn may have been an adaptation of late imperial palaces and villas. All we can say is that before the fourteenth or, stretching a bit, perhaps the thirteenth century, historical and archaeological documentation is either lacking or, if it does exist, too imprecise to permit anything more than a largely imaginary reconstruction.

The Palace of the Popes, Avignon: Tower of Latrines, built by Benedict XII.

In fourteenth-century Avignon the Palace of the Popes was far from being the only building structured around an interior courtyard or cloister. On a smaller scale, the resi-

Courts and Gardens

dences—"liveries," as they were called—of the cardinals and their suite of pages, chaplains, and servants were designed according to the same principles. A fiscal document dated 1374 gives us an approximate idea of the now-vanished livery of Cardinal Guillaume de la Jugie, a nephew of Pope Clement VI, who ordered that the house be built some time after 1350. The house had two parts. The "small livery," built around a court, was a rather confused arrangement of upper and lower chambers, towers, halls, and galleries, apparently used to house the cardinal's servants, horses, and mules. The "grand livery," where the master resided, consisted of three buildings erected around an orchard. It contained a basement for storage; a ground floor with covered walkways, a Grand Tinel with fireplace, a painted portico, a "great dressing room," and a spiral staircase; a second floor, again with covered walkways linking the five rooms, which included a chapel, a bedroom, an anteroom, and old and new dressing rooms; and a top floor with a wardrobe, a covered veranda (for taking the air or drying the wash?), and, circling the chapel roof, a tiled walkway protected by a crenellated wall and topped by a campanile and four corner turrets. Small and grand livery communicated by means of a bridge over the street consisting of a gallery at the second-story level and a bedroom at the third. The exterior must have had a severe, even repellent, aspect, but that was because every effort was made to give the rooms a view of the orchard, which had a griffin at its center. The whole is reminiscent of fifteenth-century Florentine palaces or of Jacques Coeur's hôtel in Bourges or, on a somewhat smaller scale, of the *Fondaco dei Tedeschi* in Venice. Yet traditional monasteries were rather similar in design, as were the quadrilateral castles so common in France since the time of Philip Augustus. Perhaps the most original feature of the Cardinal de la Jugie's grand livery was the use of ambulatories to link the various rooms on a given level.

Plan of the *livrée* of Cardinal de la Jugie at Avignon, 1374. To the left of rue Bouquerie stood the "small livery," which housed the working departments; to the right, the "grand livery," the cardinal's residence.

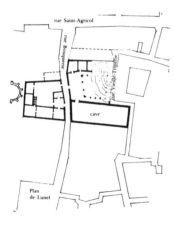

Pierre Legendre's hôtel in Paris (ca. 1500) presents a somewhat different aspect. The entrance courtyard off the rue Bourdonnais was surrounded by galleries and offices, while the main residence opened onto both the court and a garden (or rear court) adjacent to rue Tirechappe. Similarly, the hôtel of the abbots of Cluny, built for Jacques d'Amboise between 1485 and 1498, included an entrance courtyard, a main building, an adjacent wing, and a rear garden. Both buildings were early examples of hôtels built between courtyard and garden, a plan that became commonplace in the seventeenth and eighteenth centuries. By now won over to urban life, the aristocracy—whether of Church or court, office or trade—sought to set itself apart from the rest of the urban environment, to create for itself the most private possible space.

Between court and garden: the hôtel de Cluny in Paris, built between 1485 and 1498 at the behest of Jacques d'Amboise, abbot of Cluny; restored by Viollet-le-Duc.

Castles

Outside the cities, seigneurial residences in the late Middle Ages were based on a division of space among great court, lower court, and garden, indicating a desire to separate "noble" functions from matters pertaining, on the one hand, to domestic and physical needs and, on the other hand, to private

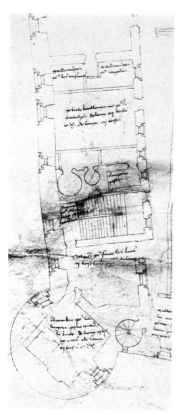

Plan for the reconstruction of the château de Gaillon submitted to Cardinal Georges d'Amboise, archbishop of Rouen, early in the 16th century. On the facing page is an overall plan of the project. Dimensions are in cubits, feet, and inches. In some rooms the location of the bed is shown. The detail above shows (top to bottom) the pantry; the bakery, with ovens and kneading troughs; a ladder to the second story; a washroom; and the bedroom of the chief washerwoman. (Vienna Archives, carton 37, document 8.)

life and its distractions. At Angers, Tarascon, and Saumur castles built or renovated by the princes of the House of Valois and Sicily (Louis II, King René) reflect these concerns. Perhaps the best example of all is the château de Gaillon: not the castle actually built in the early sixteenth century by Cardinal d'Amboise, whose imposing remains can still be seen today, nor the plan drawn up by Androuet du Cerceau, but the original and rather Italianate plan for the project, which fortunately has survived intact.

The unknown draftsman included a legend on his plans, from which we can deduce that the castle was to be built around a vast quadrilateral measuring 34 by 18 *toises*, 220 by 120 feet, more than 24,000 square feet or three-fifths of an acre.

This vast space was to have been divided into three parts: in the rear a garden with fountain bordered by a gallery; in the middle a great courtyard of more than 10,000 square feet; and just beyond the entry portal, to be built into what was to be left standing of the old medieval castle, a lower court, including a "place for an herb garden to serve the kitchen" and a washhouse.

The layout is only of the ground level, which contained three main centers. At one corner the large chapel and its oratory were to have stood. The chapel was an obligatory and regular gathering place for all castle residents, regardless of status, function, or position in the hierarchy. Around the lower court and herb garden, but extending a long way to both right and left, were rooms assigned to the various departments of the household: the bakeries, kitchens, harness-maker's shop, quarters for maids, cooks, and other servants, and so on. In the far corner and with the best view, close to the fountain, garden, and gallery, were the master's apartments. They consisted of a very large hall (52 by 26 feet), followed by a dressing room smaller by perhaps a third, and culminating, as was customary in seigneurial houses in this period, in a private retreat, a wardrobe, and—sign of the owner's high position in the Church—a study and an oratory.

In addition to this tripartite division, there was a vertical division between the first and second floors, the nature of which we can only guess. There was also a left-right division: to the left of the court stood the kitchen, butler's pantry, and pantry serving the common dining room; and on the right side the same rooms but serving the master's dining room.

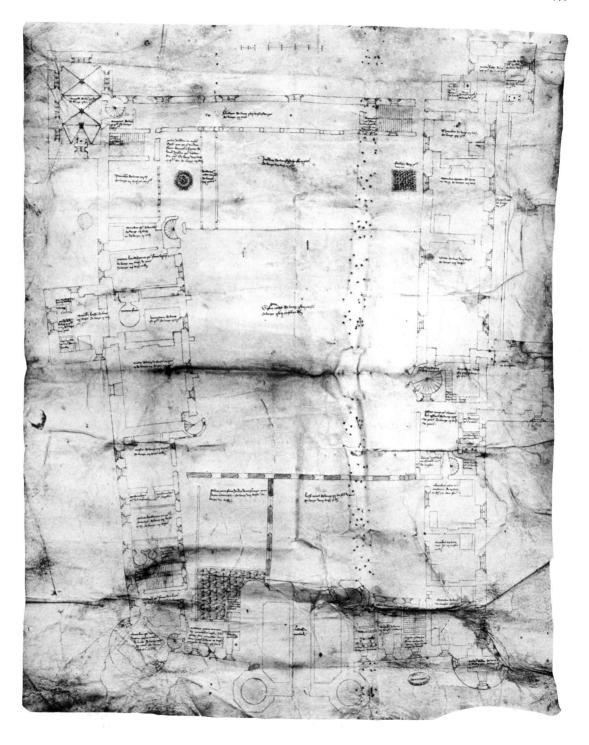

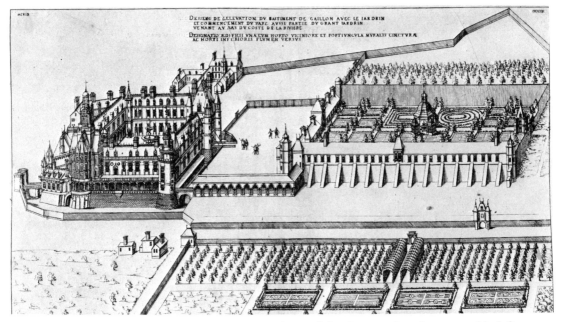

Engraving by Androuet du Cerceau, 16th century, showing the château de Gaillon as it was actually built for Cardinal Georges d'Amboise. (Paris, Bibliothèque Nationale.)

Just as in the Palace of the Popes, the plans provided for two separate kitchens.

Starting in the fifteenth century, construction estimates, often provided along with building plans, attest to the fact that French aristocrats sought sound, solid construction with such amenities as spiral staircases, garrets, and galleries. They wanted houses that were easy to live in and to heat, rooms with wainscoted walls, windows with good shutters, and carefully tiled floors. It is sometimes specified that occupied rooms are to be caulked. Steamrooms and bathrooms are not unusual, and libraries, tennis courts, billiard rooms, and other game rooms are often mentioned; for the ladies there were dressing rooms. A curiosity, undoubtedly unique, was the hunting gallery at Blois Castle. Beatis professed his admiration in 1518: "Below the palace stretch three gardens, full of fruits and foliage; to reach them one follows a covered gallery decorated on both sides with real deer antlers mounted on very good painted wooden sculptures of deer; they are mounted in the wall at approximately ten palms' height, and one sees only their neck, throat, and forelegs. On stones that protrude from the walls numbers of wooden dogs have been placed, as well as hares being chased by dogs, absolutely perfect likenesses as to size, features, and coat. Similarly, a few falcons are mounted on artificial hands, also attached to the wall."

Some seigneurial houses were of such fine quality that the construction costs were enormous. During the English occupation of Normandy, Edmond Beaufort, count of Dorset, Mortain, and Harcourt, wanted to build a three-story "fortified house and edifice" at Elbeuf on the banks of the Seine. Each of the first two floors was to have been 12 feet high, and the third floor was to have been 8 feet high and topped by garrets, which, given the installation of skylights, would have been usable living space. Rectangular in shape and equipped with a number of fireplaces, the building would have measured 80 by 33 feet. Turrets and meticulously designed latrines at the four corners would have extended the quadrilateral even further. A great spiral staircase was planned, along with one or two smaller staircases. Stone walls three feet thick were envisioned, plus a slate roof, "gilt and painted copper banners" with the count's coat of arms mounted on it; a court and garden; and a tiled kitchen. Naturally such ambitious plans inflated the projected cost of construction: for a building whose useful surface area, not counting the garrets, was less than 8,000 square feet, the cost of masonry, carpentry, plastering, roofing, plumbing, and landscaping would have come to 6,700 francs. Additional costs incurred for purchase of the land, as well as for "chests, locks, glass, and other equipment," would have resulted in a total of perhaps 8,000 francs—one hundred times the cost of the presbytery of Touville, with its 2,000 square feet of usable space.

The area reserved for the household departments was organized as in the urban hôtels, with a place for each of the traditional métiers. At Angers in 1471, besides the kitchen and pantry, there was a *saucerie* for preparing sauces, an *eschançonnerie* for drinks, a *paneterie* for bread, and a *fruiterie* for fruits.

Although manor houses and castles were primarily residences of a man (or woman) and his (or her) family, they also housed fairly large numbers of servants to perform highly and less highly esteemed functions; married as well as single, these servants enjoyed temporary or permanent room and board. The typical household staff of a very high noble seems to have comprised several dozen people; a middling member of the nobility, a dozen or so; and a minor noble, perhaps half a dozen. Hence many castle rooms resembled dormitories or barracks, with four or five beds and an equal number of locked trunks for each servant's personal effects. Other rooms were set aside for the exclusive use of an important household officer, such as a majordomo, treasurer, collector, or chaplain.

Such an official might enjoy the services of a personal valet, who would have slept in the same room or an adjoining one. Most servants took their meals in the common dining room, although a few privileged individuals might be permitted to receive their *livrée* of food, candles, and drink in their own rooms.

Communal Residences

Castles, like palaces and large urban hôtels, furnished one of many models of communal living. Barracks did not appear until much later, but already we find university dormitories, hospitals, lazar houses and leprosariums, and, most important of all, a whole spectrum of monasteries. For centuries many of the largest, most beautiful, most complex, and most carefully thought-out buildings had been occupied by the regular clergy, which still flourished as the Middle Ages waned.

One type of monastery combined communal life with solitary life. The Carthusians, in particular, had success with this model: in the fourteenth century they added 110 new foundations throughout Christendom, and 45 more in the fifteenth century. The official 1510 catalogue lists 191 active Carthusian establishments, 7 of which were reserved for nuns.

The charterhouse of London, built outside the city walls, to the north, in the 14th century. The large cloister dominates, with the cells arranged around it, each with its own garden. By comparison, the communal buildings, upper right, seem cramped.

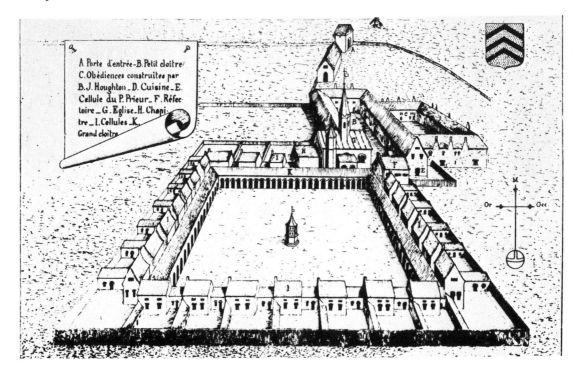

Carthusian cells at Villeneuve-lès-Avignon, 14th century.

In accordance with the wishes of Saint Bruno, founder of the order, the Carthusian was fundamentally hermitic but with cenobitic elements in the choir, chapter, refectory, and recreation. Daily attendance at common services was required, but the refectory was used only on Sundays, with chapter on holy days, during the weeks of Christmas, Easter, and Pentecost, on days of burial, or for a new prior's installation. The rest of the time the Carthusian ate alone an austere meal handed into his cell through a trap door by an anonymous servant. Monks' cells were located in individual houses. According to the statutes of the order, the Carthusian "must take diligent and due care not to create reasons to leave his cell apart from the regular and common observances; rather, he should regard his cell as being as necessary to his salvation and his life as water is to fish or the sheepfold to sheep. The more he stays in his cell, the more he will like it, provided he occupies himself in a disciplined, useful manner with reading, writing, chanting psalms, prayer, meditation, contemplation, and work, whereas if he leaves frequently and for frivolous rea-

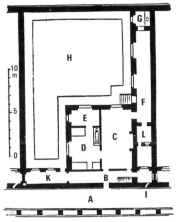

Typical plan of a Carthusian house according to Viollet-le-Duc.
A: cloister gallery
B: main corridor
C: main hall (heated)
D: cell, with bed and three pieces of furniture
E: oratory
F: covered walkway, with latrines (G) at end
H: garden
I: tower for storing food
K: small portico to allow prior to see into the garden and supply the monks with wood and other necessary items
L: storage area.

sons, he will quickly find that his cell is unbearable." In 1398 Philip the Bold donated ten small Bibles to the Carthusian monastery at Champmol, to be divided among the "cells, so that any monks suffering from infirmities requiring them to leave the church may say their service without preventing the sickroom attendant from attending church and for study if they lack the opportunity to leave their cell to study the church Bible or to talk among themselves."

The plan of a typical Carthusian monastery suggests the extent to which solitary life predominated. Relative to the vast cloister around which the monks' houses are situated, the other buildings seem quite insignificant. The houses themselves, built on one or two levels, offered decent and even comfortable lodging. The ascetic aspect of the life lay not in the quality of the housing, which was far superior to the medieval norm, but in the voluntary confinement and strict isolation.

The *béguinages* that flourished in the region of the Rhine and northern France in the thirteenth and especially the fourteenth and fifteenth centuries were a quite different type of establishment. An element of communal life existed in them, but the hermitic aspects of the Carthusian life were here totally replaced by individual life in the ordinary sense of the word. Consider the beguinage of Paris, founded by Louis IX in 1266. This "enclosure of houses" occupied quite a large space on the right bank of the Seine near the Porte Barbel but outside the wall of Philip Augustus; in principle it was cut off from the outside world after sundown. According to the perhaps optimistic testimony of Geoffroi de Beaulieu, the king's confessor, four hundred *honestae mulieres* or *povres beguines* resided there, some of noble birth. They were supported by numerous public and private charities and also earned their keep by doing various kinds of work inside and outside the beguinage. The mistress of beguines, appointed by the king's chaplain and assisted by a vice-mistress, a porter, and a council of seniors, was responsible to the prior of the Paris Dominicans for her charges' behavior, dress, and activities; no one was allowed to enter the enclosure for any reason without her permission. Beguines took no religious vows; they pledged themselves to remain chaste but were free at any time to break that pledge and return to a worldly life. Normally they were required to eat and sleep inside the beguinage and to attend certain services in a chapel, which, incidentally, was also open to residents of the neighborhood. A few "convent beguines" slept in a common dormitory and ate in the refectory, while other beguines

had rooms in houses distinct from the convent's main building; they were supervised by a *maîtresse de chambre*. Discipline
in this largely female institution was on the whole rather
flexible. Residents were young and old; some were authenti-
cally devout, others, as was often charged, out-and-out hyp-
ocrites. All retained a considerable degree of personal freedom
while enjoying the comforting benefits of a protective
institution.

Monks of all orders must have been keen to remain loyal
to a way of life meticulously elaborated by their predecessors,
often in the eleventh or twelfth century. In principle there was
no reason for the layout of Cistercian and Benedictine abbeys
and priories to change, and in many cases it did not, as is
evident from study of the ruins of such English monasteries
as Rievaulx, Fountains, and Tintern, where monastic life came
to a sudden end with the Dissolution. Yet defense needs,
coupled in some cases with dramatic decreases in revenue as
well as numbers of monks, did bring about profound changes.
In many monasteries, Francis Rapp writes, "once the prior,
hosteller, infirmary attendant, and cellarer had been appointed,
no ordinary monks remained. Without troops, the general
staff found it impossible to respect the rule of isolation, silence,
and meditation which was supposed to be the essence of the
monastic life. Because abbey finances were insufficient to meet
their residents' most basic needs, superiors were obliged to
close their eyes to infractions of the rule of personal poverty.
Monks paid for authorization to live outside the cloister, to
officiate at services, and even to obtain benefices." These remarks, based on a study of monasteries in Alsace, hold true
for many other regions. One very important change involved
the monks' dormitory, which was supposed to be locked every
night by order of the superior and furnished simply with rows
of straw mattresses; now, however, it was sometimes divided
into cells by means of partitions or curtains, sometimes abandoned in favor of *camerae* or *camerulae* in which monks slept
alone or in groups of two, three, or four.

Inspection reports from Cluniac monasteries are filled
with complaints and injunctions on this subject. After visiting
the Saint-Victor monastery in Marseilles in the early sixteenth
century, Beatis notes: "In this abbey reside approximately fifty
monks of the order of Saint Benedict; they eat here and live
separately." The dormitory of the Benedictine priory at Lit-
tlemore (Oxfordshire) shows signs of having been subdivided
into separate rooms, all of which remained, however, under

the surveillance of the prior, who had his own room but on the same floor. Other English cloisters contained pleasantly wainscoted "studies" with stained-glass windows. Infirmaries now had private rooms for sick and elderly monks. Not only abbots and priors but other principal officials had private rooms or even apartments, and rooms were assigned to monks who held university degrees or were working toward them. The following injunction, issued after an inspection tour of one English monastery in the fifteenth century, contains only pertinent recommendations: "Eat and drink in a single room, sleep in a single room, pray and serve God in a single oratory . . . completely renounce all private retreats and individual rooms and apartments."

It is tempting, given such widespread flouting of the most venerable rules of the cenobitic life, to speak of moral and spiritual decadence, of a growing lack of discipline on the part of monks without vocations who placed too high a value on their own comfort and too little value on the monastic rule. Three points, however, should be made. First, circumvention of the constraints of communal life occurred long before the "crisis" of the late Middle Ages. "Decline" almost always set in early in the history of religious orders, and in some cases the waning of the initial fervor began even before the first pioneers had vanished from the scene.

Second, all generalizations are misleading. Some monasteries surely remained faithful to the official customs. This was apparently true of the Dominican priory at Poissy, according to Christine de Pisan; the *parloir* remained the only place where

Life in the School of Ave Maria (or Hubant), Paris, 14th century. This miniature, which belongs to a series illustrating the worship, good deeds, games, and labors of the pupils, shows six of them sharing three beds and joining their hands for evening prayer, the first words of which are inscribed on the symbolic scrolls held in their hands. (Paris, National Archives, AE II 408.)

outsiders and nuns were allowed to meet, and the dormitory appears to have conformed to the rule. During the visit by the celebrated woman of letters, the men in her train were prohibited from entering the dormitory:

> Mais encor volrent
> Plus nous monstrer les dames, qui moult sorent,
> Car leur dortouer ordonné comme ilz l'orent
> et leurs beaulx liz que sur cordes fait orent
> Ils monstrerent
> Mais en ce lieu de nos hommes n'entrerent
> Nul, quel qu'il fust, car hommes ne monterent
> Oncques més la, par droit s'en deporterent
> A celle fois.

> But they still wanted to show us the ladies, of
> whom there were many, for their dormitory
> was arranged as was fit, and their beautiful beds
> with webbing [see below for more on this
> bedding]; They showed us; but in this place
> none of our men entered, for by rule men never
> came up here.

Third, and most important, the evolution of spirituality in itself may have encouraged and to some extent justified the decision to allow some monks to have rooms of their own in which to engage in intellectual work and solitary prayer and perhaps even to sleep. Practices permitted by the mendicant orders may also have had an influence. Saint Dominic had had cells built on the upper story of the cloister in Toulouse where his companions could study and sleep. To be sure, these were very small rooms: barely large enough for a small bed, just 5 feet wide. But at least each brother could be alone. Subsequently cells grew less cramped, if only to make room for a desk and chair. In the convent of Saint Eustorge in Milan, wooden partitions were replaced in the late thirteenth century by walls of light masonry, but in such a way that the proctor, as he made his rounds along the central way of the dormitory, could see at a glance that the brothers were either studiously seated at their desks or else lying properly in bed. Only senior professors (*lectores actu agentes*) were entitled to a room in the strict sense, one that could be entirely closed off, and most of these were located in another part of the convent.

In pious and charitable foundations in the late Middle Ages it was not unusual to dispense with the common dormitory. William de La Pole, founder of the hospital of Ewelme, stipulated that the residents should dispose "of some space of their own . . . a small house, a cell, or a room, with a fireplace and other necessities of the sort, in which each person can eat, drink, and rest by himself."

In 1380, at the college of Dainville in Paris, a room was provided for each pupil, yet all remained under the master's watchful eye. "Day and night, until they go to bed, the door is not to be closed, so that the master can visit whenever he wishes and so that the pupils will increase their zeal for study and fear to fall into idleness or bad habits. If he deems it necessary, the master shall be allowed to hold the key to each room."

In 1443 the statutes of King's College (Cambridge) prescribed a room for every two or three fellows (*socii*), with a bed for each and a corner set aside for work (*loca studiorum*). There were no individual rooms, to be sure—these may have been considered too costly or too liberal; but we are a long way from the common dormitory and overcrowded study hall. What is more, the fellow most advanced "in maturity, discretion, and knowledge" was assigned a measure of authority over his companions. Significantly, the poor student Nicholas, principal character in Chaucer's *Miller's Tale*, lives in a carpenter's house at Oxford, where he enjoys a room of his own, "allone, withouten any compaignye" (l. 3204).

In the middle of the sixteenth century the jurist Hermann von Weinsberg of Cologne fondly remembers the room his father gave him twenty years earlier for his own use, high atop the family mansion: "About a small room, my *studiolo*. When my father commissioned the builders in 1529, they constructed two small rooms, one atop the other, near the great room. I took possession of the higher of the two. My father had a window and a door with lock installed. I brought up a small table, a chair, and a wall table and installed my *studiolo*: books, drawers, paper, writing desk, and so forth, and whatever I managed to accumulate I carried up there. I also made myself an altar and placed on it whatever people were willing to give me. I kept the room locked, so that no one could enter except my cousin and schoolmate Christian Hersbach, who was always at my house. This was where I spent most of my time. When I came home from school, I went up there to read and write; I took up painting, for my cousin was a good painter and helped me a great deal. And my father was very pleased to see me settled there and helped me to fix up the room, which kept me from hanging about the streets. He always kept this little room for my use, even when I was at Emmerich; and when I came back, I found everything just as I had left it."

Medieval men and women, acutely aware of living in an impoverished world in which every object had value, seem to have been fascinated by household furnishings. Writers did not disdain to celebrate the *oustillemens d'ostel* in verse more often than in prose, and in the vulgar tongue more often than in Latin. It was not enough that a house should be well constructed; it also needed to be "well equipped." Of all the objects mentioned, the bed occurs most often and most prominently. According to Guillaume Coquillart, the bed figures among the modest possessions of even the "poor and miserable" man who owns nothing but "a bed, a table, a bench, a pot, a salt-cellar, five or six glasses, and a pot for cooking peas."

The Bed

The *povre filleresse* in the *Ménagier de Paris* was similarly equipped. Manuals of conversation intended to help the English learn French and vice versa reflect a similar state of mind:

> Ores vous convient avoir lits
> lyts de plummes;
> pour les povres suz gesir,
> lyts de bourre;
> sarge, tapites,
> kieultes pyntes
> pour les lits couvrir;
> couvertoyrs ainsi;
> bankers qui sont beaulx;
> dessoubs le lit ung calys,
> estrein dedens.

> Now muste ye have bedde:
> beddes of fetheris;
> for the poure to lye on,
> beddes of flockes;
> sarges, tapytes,
> quilted painted
> for the beddes to covere;
> coverlettes also;
> bankers that ben fayr;
> under the bedde a chalon,
> strawe therin.

Eustache Deschamps's ballad for newlyweds begins with the bed and its accoutrements: "For your household, new housekeepers, you will need cots, cushions, beds, and flocking."

In 1539 Gilles Corrozet, in his *Blasons domestiques*, enthusiastically celebrates the bed just after his celebration of the bedroom and before remarks devoted to chairs, benches, tables, dressers, chests, and stools. The terms in which he speaks of the bed reflect its almost mythical value: not only is it "delicate and soft" and the "jewel of the bedroom," it is also, all erotic connotations aside, the "bed of honor," the chaste and modest witness to holy wedlock. The bed was almost the only item of furniture ever bequeathed to a loyal servant, a needy relative, or a hospital. And in Quercy in the late fifteenth century the nuptial bed was regularly included as part of a girl's dowry; its value was put at 8 to 10 gold écus. Like clothing, beds could be purchased secondhand. Indeed, the profession of secondhand bed dealer, exercised by both men and women, was often associated with that of ragpicker.

Foreign travelers like Beatis showed no little appreciation for the beds they found in French inns, though they were even more enthusiastic about the German bed (that lice-free marvel) and even the Flemish bed. As early as the thirteenth century literary texts praise the *soefs lits*, feather beds, then fashionable in France.

As the texts just cited suggest, the "complete bed," represented in numerous works of art, comprised three elements: the wooden bedframe; the bed proper; and the various fabrics that were placed on or hung about the bed to enable a person to sleep safe from prying eyes and disturbing light and breezes.

The principal term for the bedframe was a word still in use today, *châlit*, but the words *couche* and *couchette* were also used. Usually of oak, though sometimes of pine or fir, the châlit was generally equipped with a bottom board (called a *lectum de tabulis* in certain Latin texts). Apparently this type of bedstead was called a *châlit bordé* to distinguish it from the *châlit cordé* (*lectum cordegii, lectum cordelhium*) found in the Hôtel-Dieu at Paris, the Dominican convent at Poissy, and the castle at Angers in the time of King René. The latter contained a base of web or ropes not unlike a modern hammock; the bed was strung by a straw- or ropemaker and periodically retightened. We also find beds that were both *bordé* and *cordé*.

Bedframes were high enough above the floor to permit cots to be stored underneath; these were pulled out when

Graduel of Saint-Dié, late 15th century. Nativity. Large bed with platform. Note the tub, bucket, cradle, and stool—simple but well-made furniture. (Library of Saint-Dié, ms 74.)

needed. "A small cot underneath the bed" is mentioned in an inventory of the house of Hugues Aubert of Rouen, an associate of Jacques Coeur (1453). Some cots were equipped with wheels, for ease in moving them about: "*chariolle, couchette roullonee, charliz roulerez, couchette rouleresse, couchette basse a roulletz, qu'on boute dessous les lits.*" Other bedframes could be disassembled or folded up (perhaps by means of hinges); these were useful in the field during wartime. Certain bedsteads, but not all, were equipped with pillars, columns, or risers, in other words, a wood scaffolding with iron rods to hold the bed canopy, a major innovation of the thirteenth century, from which developed the ornamental bed as well as the so-called *lit de justice*, a royal throne capped by a dais.

Bedframes were often so high that steps, made of wood and possibly covered with cloth, were needed to climb into bed. An inventory of Ménitré, King René's country manor, mentions that the king's chamber contained "two long wooden trunks, with two locks each, used as steps, and another stepladder in the *venelle* of the aforementioned bed." The

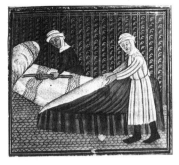

How beds were made in the 14th century. The miniature is supposed to illustrate Guillaume de Digulleville's *Pèlerinage de vie humaine*: "The woman with the stick remade / the bed with white sheets / and her companion with the *gambeson* [a padded garment] sang such a song." (Paris, Saint Genevieve Library, ms 1130.)

terms *venelle* and *ruelle* were used as early as the fourteenth century to refer to the space between the bed and the wall.

Straw (*estrain, fuerre*) was piled in or on the bedframe to form bedding, sometimes called a *chutrin*. On top of the straw was sometimes (but not always) a proper mattress, generally called a *coute, couette,* or *coetis*. Made of twill from Caen, Lunel, or Brittany, of a fabric called *souille,* or of fustian, wool, or even silk sometimes lined with a slip, the mattress was stuffed with straw waste (*poussiere, balosse*), oats, wool flocking, or, best of all, feathers or down. In addition to the wool *matheras,* the cotton *matelas* is often mentioned, particularly in southern France.

Every bed had one or more cushions or a bolster (*traversier, traverslit*); one or more pillows, often filled with down; a couple of sheets (*linceuls*) of variable quality (made of linen, hemp, cotton, or coarse fabric); a fabric bedspread, possibly lined with common or valuable fur; and a down comforter, called a *coustepointe* or *lodier*.

The bed curtains and canopy could be arranged in a variety of ways—as a tent, "pavilion," net, half canopy, or full canopy. In the fifteenth century more than in the fourteenth, many beds were equipped with canopy, *dossiel* or headboard, and three *custodes* or curtains hung from iron rods. Twill, serge, silk, woven tapestries, and fur-lined cloth were all used.

There was in fact a hierarchy of beds. Size was one distinguishing feature: widths ranged from 1 to 3 *lés* (a standard width of cloth), with covers and sheets generally ½ lé wider than the bed. Other features included the kind of mattress, the number and quality of sheets and blankets, and the presence of a pillow in addition to cushions and bolster. The bedframe was also important: some beds had none, others just a rudimentary wooden frame, while still others were meticulously carved pieces of furniture. Finally, some beds had a canopy and curtains, while others, to judge by the evidence of account books, inventories, and miniatures, had none. Value estimates accordingly ranged anywhere from a few sous to several dozen livres. In Paris in the late fifteenth century, a bed of 60 sous parisis (3 livres) was considered quite ordinary.

In a class by themselves are the ascetic beds found in monasteries that remained faithful to the spirit of poverty and penitence. These beds had simple frames, no curtains and certainly no sheets, and, instead of a soft, warm, down mattress, either a rudimentary bed of straw or an apparently uncomfortable mattress of *bourre lanissee*. While staying at the

Great Carthusian monastery in 1517, Beatis deplored the fact that he and his master, the cardinal of Aragon, were obliged to sleep "on small beds of straw without sheets and with crude sheepskins for covers." When Louis IX returned from the crusade, he decided to mortify the flesh by giving up his feather bed and sleeping on a thin cotton mattress.

Some monastic beds were beautiful in appearance yet still austere. Christine de Pisan tells us that the nuns in the dormitory at Poissy slept fully dressed, without sheets, and on flocked rather than down mattresses. Nevertheless, their beds were covered by elegant woven spreads: "There were no nightgowns or lingerie and their beds have no frilly down *coutes* but rather *materas* covered with beautiful Arras tapestries, well made, but this is just decoration, for [the mattresses] are hard and filled with flocking."

Patients' beds in the mid-fourteenth century leprosariums and hospitals of the diocese of Paris apparently had neither frame nor curtain, just a mattress, a pillow, a pair of sheets,

Nuns' dormitory. Miniature from a manuscript of the *Chronicles of Hainault*, 15th century. Space is carefully divided into tiny alcoves separated by wooden partitions. (Paris, Bibliothèque Nationale, French 20128.)

Resignation and devotion. Jean Bourdichon's idea of a beggar's bed, late 15th century. Note the tattered draperies, the holes in roof and walls.

and a cover. Other hospitals were more generous, or more judicious, providing two blankets in summer and three in winter.

The miners at Cosne in the Lyonnais employed by Jacques Coeur slept on two types of bed, according to an inventory presented in evidence at Coeur's trial (1453): one had a couette and cushions of feathers, two sheets, and two blankets; the other, a mattress of *balosse* and a single blanket. The estimated value of the first ranged from 20 to 40 sous, that of the second, 10 sous or less. Neither had a wooden bedframe or curtains.

A celebrated miniature by Jean Bourdichon shows a beggar—symbol of poverty—in his bed: tattered sheets, a straw mattress with an openwork frame, a wretched blanket with holes through which the man's legs protrude, one bandaged, the other with a torn sandal. The bishop's cook at Senlis in the late fifteenth century was somewhat better off, with a bed of twill, a feather bolster, a pair of sheets, and a quilt of gray linsey-woolsey (estimated value for the whole lot: 40 sous tournois). In 1403 Colin Doulle of Conches (Normandy), executed for his "demerits," left "a bed, to wit, a flocked mattress and bolster, a worn, old blanket of reddish cloth, and two pairs of coarse sheets." Sold at auction, these items fetched 40 sous tournois.

In 1460 Perrette La Havée, a Parisian *bourgeoise* and wife to the king's barber, slept in a far more imposing bed, seigneurial in inspiration if not in style. The sheets were of linen, the pillows filled with feathers, and the mattress and cushion of Flemish drill. The bed, which measured 6 by 7 feet, was enclosed by a canopy, headboard, and curtains; it was appraised at 8 livres 6 sous 8 deniers parisis. (At the time 4 livres parisis equaled 5 livres tournois; the ratio for sous and deniers was the same.)

One step higher in magnificence, an inventory of contents of the "long chamber" of Thouars Castle, where Louis d'Amboise, viscount of Thouars, died in 1470, reveals a large bedframe with stairs, a mattress, a bolster, a blanket, a quilt, a cover, and a *garniture*; also, a green tapestry canopy, an *entredeux* (headboard cover), and three blue curtains. The adjacent small bed was done in the same fabrics and decorated in the same way; it, too, had a canopy. Under the large bed was yet another "sliding" bed. Five wall tapestries matched those of the bed.

In the later Middle Ages (the earliest known examples date from the thirteenth century) canopy, curtains, headboard,

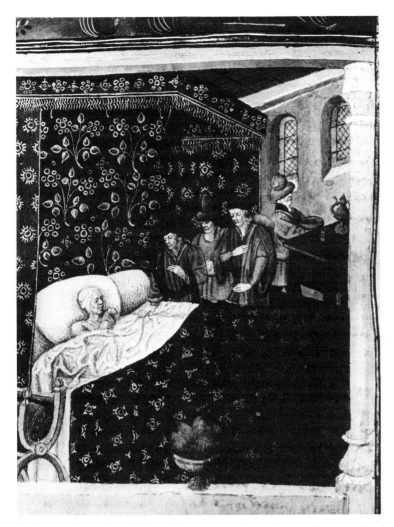

Roman de Tristan, late 15th century. Rich man on his deathbed. Note the sumptuous fabric in the bedspread, headboard, and canopy, and the handsome chair near the head of the bed, to the man's right. (Chantilly, Condé Museum, ms 404.)

bedspread, and wall hangings sometimes formed a matched ensemble called a *chambre*, which could be used when desired or else stored in a trunk or armoire or closet; when the style went out of fashion, the chambre wound up in the attic. Easily carried about, such bedroom decorations were perfectly in tune with the needs of a period when important personages were obliged to move about a great deal.

Some fourteenth- and fifteenth-century bedrooms were remarkable for the luxury of their furnishings and accoutrements. The documents are filled with examples, though I shall mention only the chambre that Catherine of Burgundy brought with her when she married into the Hapsburg dynasty in 1393: "A chambre of blue satin embroidered with the arms of Mademoiselle of Austria, including a full canopy, a headboard, curtains, ten square cushions of the same embroidered with the arms of my lady, and also including a fine bedspread, four tapestries for the walls, a mattress cover, a benchcover, and six wool cushions with arms as above, and three stairs to be placed around the bed, and a blue cloth cover, stuffed and lined with vair."

Such a sumptuous and extensive chambre was an exception, a rare prize, yet one that served as a model, a reference for others. Plain bourgeois interiors soon showed signs of concern for decoration in the form of tapestries, furs on the walls, furniture, and even floor, twill and serge, curtains around bed and windows, cushions, and bench covers. Consider the room in Paris where Maître Pierre Cardonnel, canon of Notre-Dame, died in 1438. The two beds were covered with white bedspreads; the deathbed had a canopy, a headboard, and three cushions of white twill. On the wall were three vermilion tapestries, one with a white deer at the center and dotted with white roses. The effect of this white and red motif must have been striking.

The vast majority of beds, however, lacked even modest curtains and probably had no wooden frames. Wretched straw mattresses were placed directly on the floor or on planks, and covers were of threadbare patchwork, too thin and too few in number to provide much warmth.

The number of beds in a house was a function of its size, the resources of its occupants, and the importance of the household; it could range from one to several dozen. At Cosne the miners who worked for Jacques Coeur lived in several buildings containing some fifty beds in all; unfortunately we do not know how many people shared these beds. In the late fifteenth century Madic Castle contained thirty-one beds and thirty-five cots. When interrogated by Prosecutor Dauvet, Jacques Coeur's *despensier* (bursar) stated that the "great house [at Bourges contained] fifteen or sixteen beds, some of which were quite large, beautiful, and of good quality." In 1525 the estate inventory of Pierre Legendre, treasurer of France, listed some twenty beds, half of them cots, scattered through the rooms of his Paris hôtel in the rue Bourdonnais, with, as a rule, one bed and one cot per room. His country manor at Alincourt contained thirty-odd beds, and the one at Garenne nearly twenty. Thus, Legendre's three main residences—he had others, but they were nearly empty—contained some sev-

French translation of Boccaccio's *Decameron*, 15th century. Ordinary beds. (Paris, Bibliothèque Nationale, French 239.)

enty beds, not counting bedframes without mattresses. In 1542 Thouars Castle, with forty-odd rooms, had nearly as many beds, counting two cradles in the nurse's room and several folding beds.

People did not normally sleep in all rooms of the castle, however. Cellars, storerooms, attics, galleries, and garrets were probably unoccupied. There were seldom any beds in the kitchen, pantry, counting room, or study, and never any in the hall. Beds were found in *chambres* (occasionally even referred to as *chambres a coucher*) and their annexes (wardrobes and retreats), as well as in certain service rooms and above all in the stables, to prevent the horses from being stolen.

It is often said that a single bed in the Middle Ages could accommodate not just a married couple, as one would expect, but also their children (young and not so young); or several brothers and sisters; or servants employed by the same master; or strangers who for one reason or another had to share a room. Soldiers, students, invalids, and paupers often shared beds, as is amply attested by both written and iconographic sources. Large beds that were not just "matrimonial" but "familial" are no myth, as Jeanne de France's book of hours shows. Nevertheless, intimacy of this kind was considered undesirable for reasons of comfort, hygiene, and, above all, morals. In his treatise against lasciviousness, Jean Gerson writes: "Please God that it should be the custom in France for children to sleep alone in small beds, or at worst brothers

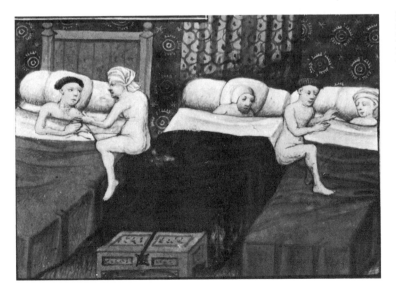

French translation of Boccaccio's *Decameron*. Bedroom. (Paris, Arsenal Library, ms 5070.)

Miniature decorating the manuscript of the *Livre de vie active de maistre Jehan Henry sur le fait des offices d'iceluy hostel Dieu*, 15th century, showing patients' beds in a ward of Paris's Hôtel-Dieu hospital. (Paris, Public Assistance Archives.)

together and sisters or others together, as is the custom in Flanders." Individual beds were the norm in most monasteries and even in some colleges. Hospital personnel were concerned about the problem; at the Hôtel-Dieu in Paris the nurses deplored being forced to sleep "little children, both girls and boys, together in dangerous beds, upon which other patients died of contagious diseases, because there is no order and no private bed for the children, [who must] sleep six, eight, nine, ten, and twelve to a bed, at both head and foot." In other words, sleeping together was often considered a consequence of poverty. Anyone who could afford to sleep alone wished to do so, or at any rate to sleep only with people of their own choosing.

On the other hand, people did not necessarily want to sleep apart from their valet or chamberlain or lady's maid or chambermaid. The servant slept on a cot in the master's own bedroom or in an adjoining wardrobe, or several servants might sleep in a room adjacent to the master's. In Madic Castle, for example, the bedroom next to Madame's was reserved for the *filles de Madame*. And in Rouen Castle, in 1436, "the demoiselles of the captain's wife sleep in the little chamber." Antonio of Beatis notes that in Picardy hostelry rooms contain just one bed for the master and another for his valet, in contrast to Germany, where as many beds as possible are crowded into every room. Commynes recalls in his *Mémoires* that when he was chamberlain to Duke Charles of Burgundy, he sometimes slept in the duke's chamber. The pet (*mignon*) of a king or great lord shared his bedroom on a regular basis. And in the *Ménagier de Paris* the good prud'homme makes this recommendation to his young wife: "If you use chambermaids aged fifteen to twenty, at which age girls are foolish and have not seen much of the world, and if you have them sleep in your wardrobe or chamber, see to it that there is no low portal or window close to the street." The implication is that not all domestics were so favored and that the purpose of having servants sleep close to the master's bedroom was as much to keep an eye on them as to make sure that service was available at a moment's notice.

In works of fiction such as the *Cent nouvelles nouvelles* we find masters living in constant proximity to their private servants. When necessary of course the master could send the servants away, draw the curtains of his bed, and recover his privacy.

Ostentation and Privacy

Contemporary texts like to describe the house as a world unto itself, within which the *chef d'hôtel* enjoys full and uncontested authority. The *Ménagier de Paris* recommends that at the end of the day, when the fires have been banked, all the outside doors be carefully locked and the keys turned over to a trusted individual—Lady Agnes the beguine or Jean the bursar—"so that no one can enter without leave." Alain Chartier attempts to dissuade his readers from becoming courtiers by arguing that nothing is better than living independently in one's own home: "Once your door is closed, no one can enter unless you wish it." And François Villon wrote: "The house is safe but be sure it is shut tight."

Interior space was not homogeneous and undifferentiated, however, particularly in houses above a certain level of comfort. There were various centers of social and private life, of domestic and professional activity. Some areas were heated, others were not (and heated does not mean the same thing as heatable). The kitchen was of course a warm room, as was the master's bedroom; other bedrooms and the hall were generally heated. Monasteries had calfectories. In Germany some rooms were kept heated all day long in wintertime, as we learn from a passage in the *Livre de la description des pays* by Gilles le Bouvier, known as the Berry Herald (mid-fifteenth century): "For the cold that comes to Germany in the winter they have stoves that heat in such a way that they are warm

Heures de Louis de Laval, late 15th century. A couple sits on a bench by a fireplace in the intimacy of their bedroom or hall. (Paris, Bibliothèque Nationale, Latin 920.)

in their rooms, and in winter craftsmen do their work and keep their wives and children there and it takes very little wood to heat them. And nobles and soldiers and other idle people likewise play, sing, drink, and eat and pass the time, for they have no fireplaces."

Le Bouvier's remark suggests that common practice in France was quite different: houses had a fair number of fireplaces, which were not kept going all the time but lighted when someone came in from the wet and the cold; household members were not obliged to remain gathered around the stove. Nevertheless, stoves were not unknown, at least in eastern France (Provence, Savoy, and the County of Burgundy). In the fifteenth century stoves were deliberately introduced into other regions, for example, in the mines owned by Jacques Coeur and in some of the castles of King René, who had German specialists install them.

Rooms that were seldom heated include the workroom, counting room, study, and chapel. When Georges de La Trémoille planned the construction of an oratory for private prayer in his castle at Rochefort-sur-Loire, he specified a "small footwarmer" as a final luxurious touch for this entirely wainscoted room. Portable braziers, also used, were carried from room to room as needed. They were called *speyrogadoria* in Provence and *fouiers* or *fouieres* in northern France (where they were made of iron or brass).

People continued to distinguish between hall and chamber, but change was in the air. Despite the size and ornate decoration of the hall, there was a tendency to convert it into a sort of antechamber or waiting room. Once again Alain Chartier will serve as our guide: "The hall of a great prince ordinarily stinks with and is heated by the breath of the people; the bailiff taps their heads with his rod. Some are booted in with a kick, while others try to hold out" until the prince's private door finally opens.

One solution was to divide the hall into a common hall and a great hall or a lower hall (used as a waiting room) and an upper hall (for receptions). More commonly, however, the chamber was divided into a bedchamber and an official chamber (called a *chambre de parement* or *chambre à parer*). In the latter stood the official bed, majestic but unoccupied. The young wife in one of the *Cent nouvelles nouvelles* (Hundred New Novellas) first entered the great hall of her husband's hôtel, then moved on to the "*chambre à parer*, decorated with beautiful tapestry" and heated with a "fine, roaring fire,"

A noble family as seen by Jean Bourdichon, late 15th century. Calm, comfort, and luxury in clothing, furniture, plates, and pitchers (on sideboard).

in which she found a "beautiful covered table" set with a "fine lunch" and a "handsome buffet well equipped with tableware."

The official chamber served mixed functions. Though public, it also belonged to the intimate heart of the household. Since not just anyone was admitted, there was no risk in displaying one's wealth, fine silver, and rich tapestries. In the late Middle Ages it was necessary to appear magnificent as well as powerful; hence people kept horses for show, swords for show, fabrics for show, and sideboards for show.

Finally, we come to the household's third focus, the master's bedroom, which Gilles Corrozet described as "well lit

Dits et faits mémorables by Valère Maxime, 15th century. Note the bathtub in the bedroom, the woodwork and shutters, and the clean bed. (Paris, Bibliothèque Nationale, French 6185.)

and finely tiled," or, again, "nicely tapestried, clean, carpeted, tiled, matted." Jean de Roye refers to "beautiful rooms, finely carpeted and tiled and filled with beds, tapestries, and other things." And Eustache Deschamps evokes perfect comfort thus: "Warm rooms, with covered walls and floors, locked doors, and windows that do not squeak."

We know from inventories that the chamber was where jewelry, silver, and important papers (accounts, credits and loans, private letters) were kept in chests, dressers, "caskets," and coffers of various sizes, made of oak or cyprus, sometimes with iron fittings but always meticulously closed and locked. Nearby was the study (sometimes called the secret study), the "private counting room," or oratory, and of course the privy chamber (with the inevitable commode) and possibly a steam closet. This was the utmost private space, the place where one went to relax and perhaps to play "chamber games," to take care of body and soul, and to write. In Chartier's words:

> Or veult l'amant faire diz, balades,
> Lettres closes, segrectes ambaxades,
> Et se retrait
> Et s'enferme en chambre et retraict
> Pour escripre plus a l'aise et a traict.

> The lover likes to tell stories, sing,
> write secret letters, perform private
> embassies, and withdraw, and
> closet himself in chamber and privy
> to write more comfortably.

Normally, this private space was shared by a husband and wife. In the residences of the high aristocracy, such as the Hôtel Saint-Pol in Paris, however, a distinction was made between what we may call, with slight anachronism, the lord's apartments and the lady's; each had a separate room and wardrobe.

The Meaning of the Changes

Churches contained a multitude of private chapels, separated by walls of wood or stone and iron grills and equipped with their own furniture and crypt; each chapel was assigned to an individual, a family, or a confraternity. Miniatures depict movable oratories occupied by some important personage in the act of praying, set apart from a retinue of courtiers and servants. Some permanent oratories, made of stone, enabled

Heures de Marie de Bourgogne. A typical oratory in a 15th-century church. The noble lady feels that she is in her own home, with her dog in her lap, her rosary nearby, and her book of hours in her hands. (Vienna, National Library, Cod. 1857.)

the occupant to look down on the altar and other worshipers without being seen and to come and go discreetly (for example, the oratories of Louis XI at Notre-Dame de Cléry and Notre-Dame de Nantilly and in Saumur and that of Jean Bourré at Plessis-Bourré). Of course there were also pews, elbow rests, and prie-dieus; in Flanders men and women were seated separately.

In no particular order, let me list some of the changes that occurred in various cities. In many towns the municipal council met in a special room or building. There were rooms for tennis and jousting and enclosed areas for practicing with bow and arrow, crossbow, and arquebus. There were arsenals for artillery and a tower for the town clock. Some buildings were set aside for exclusive use by members of the university (such as the document room and library at Orleans). There were classrooms for students, as in Saint Paul's School, London, described by Erasmus in the early sixteenth century. Some towns had public libraries (for example, Worcester and Bristol in the fifteenth century). There were rooms for archives, like the Trésor des chartes in the royal palace on the Ile de la Cité in Paris, north of the Sainte Chapelle. Markets had lodges and stalls. Many town authorities sought to contain prostitutes within a particular district, street, or public house. Common baths were kept under surveillance.

Disparate as these indications are, their meaning is clear, especially in the light of similar changes affecting the finest urban hôtels, the most important castles, and the most prestigious palaces. What had once been done more easily outdoors increasingly moved indoors, and areas that had once served many different functions were now replaced by spaces whose functions were rigidly defined.

There was a place for play, another for work, another for justice, still another for individual or collective prayer, another for teaching, and yet another for culture (we await the coming of the theater). Thus, at the very end of the Middle Ages, an ideal of urban space took shape. That ideal was not without parallels to the authorities' vision of the ideal society: more hierarchy, more segregation, stricter regimentation, and closer monitoring of individual behavior.

From the thirteenth to the sixteenth century urban and rural housing slowly improved in quality. Paradoxically, the great upheavals of the late Middle Ages may have been necessary for this improvement to take place. Even though the

Heures de Bretagne, 15th century. Another type of oratory. (Paris, Bibliothèque Nationale, Latin 1159.)

authorities now took a more interventionist attitude and were less willing to allow people to live their own lives in private, the home, in a dialectical reaction, became more of a refuge, a place to retreat and catch one's breath.

Greater individualism? Perhaps. But bear in mind that even during the Renaissance communal housing was still considered the best, whether that of religious communities, schoolchildren, invalids, soldiers, or individuals whose power, prestige, and wealth were reflected first of all in the numbers of people who moved permanently in their orbit.

Knight. 13th century. (Bamberg Cathedral.)

5

The Emergence of the Individual

Georges Duby
Philippe Braunstein

Chartres Cathedral, royal portal, ca. 1145.

Solitude: Eleventh to Thirteenth Century

Georges Duby

PEOPLE crowded together cheek by jowl, living in promiscuity, sometimes in the midst of a mob. In feudal residences there was no room for individual solitude, except perhaps in the moment of death. When people ventured outside the domestic enclosure, they did so in groups. No journey could be made by fewer than two people, and if it happened that they were not related, they bound themselves by rites of brotherhood, creating an artificial family that lasted as long as the journey required. By age seven, at which time young aristocratic males were considered persons of sex, they left the woman's world and embarked upon a life of adventure. Yet throughout their lives they remained surrounded, in the strong sense of the word—whether they were dedicated to the service of God and sent to study with a schoolmaster or joined a group of other young men in aping the gestures of a leader, their new father, whom they followed whenever he left his house to defend his rights by force of arms or force of words or to hunt in his forests. Their apprenticeship over, new knights received their arms as a group, a mob organized as a family. (Generally the lord's son was dubbed along with the sons of the vassals.) From that time forth the young knights were always together, linked in glory and in shame, vouching for and standing as hostage for one another. As a group, accompanied by servants and often by priests, they raced from tourney to tourney, court to court, skirmish to skirmish, displaying their loyalties by showing the colors or shouting the same rallying cry. The devotion of these young comrades enveloped their leader in an indispensable mantle of domestic familiarity, an itinerant household.

Thus, in feudal society, private space was divided, composed of two distinct areas: one fixed, enclosed, attached to the hearth; the other mobile, free to move through public space, yet embodying the same hierarchies and held together by the same controls. Within this mobile cell peace and order were maintained by a power whose mission was to organize a defense against the intrusion of the public authorities, for which purpose an invisible wall, as solid as the enclosure that surrounded the house, was erected against the outside world. This power enveloped and restrained the individuals of the household, subjecting them to a common discipline. Power meant constraint. And if private life meant secrecy, it was a secrecy shared by all members of the household, hence fragile and easily violated. If private life meant independence, it was independence of a collective sort. In the eleventh and twelfth centuries collective privacy did exist. But can we detect any signs of personal privacy within the collective privacy?

Feudal society was so granular in structure, composed of such compact curds, that any individual who attempted to remove himself from the close and omnipresent conviviality, to be alone, to construct his own private enclosure, to cultivate his garden, immediately became an object of either suspicion or admiration, regarded as either a rebel or a hero and in either case considered "foreign"—the antithesis of "private." The person who stood apart, even if his intention was not deliberately to commit evil, was inevitably destined to do so, for his very isolation made him more vulnerable to the Enemy's attacks. No one would run such a risk who was not deviant or possessed or mad; it was commonly believed that solitary wandering was a symptom of insanity. Men and women who traveled the roads without escort were believed to offer themselves up as prey, so it was legitimate to take everything they had. In any case, it was a pious work to place them back in some community, regardless of what they might say, to restore them by force to that clearly ordered and well-managed world where God intended them to be, a world composed of private enclosures and of the public spaces between them, through which people moved only in cortege.

This attitude explains the importance, in real life as well as in the imagination, of the rest of the visible world, which consisted of uncultivated stretches containing neither hearth nor home: marshes, forests, and other dangerous and seductive places that stood outside the law, places of strange encounters where anyone who set foot alone risked finding himself face

to face with savages or elves. Criminals and heretics supposedly sought refuge in these realms of disorder, fearfulness, and
desire, as did those deranged by passion, driven out of their
minds. Tristan carried the guilty Isolde off into the wilderness:
no more bread or salt, only tattered rags and beds of branches.
As soon as the effect of the potion or "poison" that had driven
them mad wore off, however, as soon as their reason was
restored, Isolde commanded Tristan to flee this strange—that
is, isolated—realm and return her to the world of order. For
them, reacculturation meant a return to private life, to the
court, to a gregarious existence.

Yet they returned reinvigorated by their ordeal. To survive the danger, the tribulation of solitude, whether voluntarily or not, was for the strongest individuals, the elect, an
opportunity for improvement. Thus, Godelieve, "devas-
tated," abandoned by her husband, deprived of "company,"
yet by the grace of God able to withstand every temptation,
progressed step by step toward sainthood. The person who
freely chose to do battle with wickedness and who emerged
victorious from the encounter carried off a prize that was
shared with all the members of the family from which he or
she had parted temporarily. Such was the good fortune of the
champion who defeated a single adversary in a duel, in "single
combat" on a closed field of battle; of the sinner purged of
blame by penitential isolation; and of voluntary recluses like
those of Cologne, of whom it was said that "their holy way
of life spread throughout the city the sweetest fragrance of
good reputation." And such was the good fortune of the
heroes of romance, the knights-errant, who stood out from
the common lot not because they were mad but because they
traveled alone. Nevertheless, if escapist literature depicted
these heroes as exempt from the inevitable conviviality, it may
have been because by the twelfth century some people had
begun to find enforced gregariousness too oppressive. In good
society (to the study of which this book is perforce limited),
did people not dream increasingly of escape, even as the progress of civilization slowly but surely freed individuals from
the conviviality of the household?

Signs of growing personal autonomy are increasingly evident in the twelfth century. At this time the pace of economic
change was accelerating and agricultural growth was reviving
highways, markets, and towns; vital ferment (and the appa-

The Desire for Autonomy

Keys, ca. 1340. Excavation at Dracy, Côte-d'Or.

ratus to control it) was transported from the countryside into the cities; money began to play a major role in everyday transactions; and the word "to earn" came into common use. Coffers and purses are mentioned more and more frequently in the documents, and archaeologists sifting through old ruins begin to find the remains of keys. Evidently people felt a greater need than ever before to lock up property that was by its nature movable; they felt a need to save in order to make themselves less dependent on the family. Individual enterprise was tolerated and liberated. The common folk accepted the challenge, rushing to the frontiers where new land was being cleared or setting up shop in suburbs teeming with merchants and artisans, some of whom quickly amassed fortunes. The dominant class was no less eager to acquire wealth. Clerics, as quick to enrich themselves as the common folk, put their administrative expertise at the service of princes and knights who, after dark, sold their tourney trophies for cartloads of hard cash. The new importance of personal initiative and private wealth focused attention on the value of the individual.

Numerous signs attest to the change. Among them were the images by which this society depicted human perfection. Some time between 1125 and 1135, the stonecutters working on the porch of Saint-Lazare in Autun apparently were ordered by those responsible for the iconography to forgo abstraction and give individualized expression to each figure. Ten years later the animation of lips and eyes made the figures on the royal portal at Chartres seem almost alive. Thereafter even the body was liberated from the grip of hieratic stereotypes, and, still later, in the last third of the thirteenth century, a new and decisive step was taken with the advent of portraiture in sculpture, the quest for likeness.

A 15th-century lock. (Paris, Cluny Museum.)

This long-term evolution in the methods of plastic figuration appears to have been perfectly synchronized with changes at other levels of the cultural edifice. Early in the twelfth century the magisterial lecture gave way to the scholastic "dispute": a joust, a duel, a single combat between scholars who clashed like rival champions in a tourney. Even as the faces of the statues were coming to life, a new idea was taking hold among scholars meditating upon Holy Scripture, the explosive idea that salvation was not acquired simply by passive, sheeplike participation in religious rites but was "earned" by an effort of self-transformation. Because sin was now held to reside not in the act but in the intention, in the most intimate recesses of the soul, the new view was an invitation to introspection, to exploration of the conscience. The apparatus of moral governance was shifted inward, to a private space that no longer had anything to do with the community. The penitent cleansed away the taint of sin by contrition, by desire for moral regeneration, and by willingness to transform himself—through reason according to Abelard, through love according to Saint Bernard; both agreed, however, on the need for personal amendment. Interpretable in similar terms were scholastic meditations on marriage, which gradually accredited the notion that wedlock is achieved by mutual consent, hence that the personal commitment of both husband and wife takes precedence over the collective decision of families.

The flourishing of biography in the twelfth century is another symptom. To be sure, Abelard and Guibert of Nogent were imitating ancient models. But their literary works gave stunning confirmation of the autonomy of the individual, who was henceforth just as much the master of his memory as of his personal hoard of cash. The self staked a claim to an identity within the bosom of the group; it insisted upon its right to keep secrets, distinct from the secrets of the collectivity. It is no accident that saints, those heroes of spiritual combat, were frequently celebrated for their ability to hide their intentions and thus circumvent the hostility of their entourage. Lying served to protect a more intimate privacy. Saint Simon, for example, hid his hair shirt from family and servants under his breastplate, and Saint Hildegund concealed her female sex beneath a Cistercian monk's habit.

This evolution coincides with the progressive breakup of the great "families," evidence for which is provided by both written documents and archaeological excavation. It also coincides with the settlement of knights in their own households;

Tomb of Saint Lazarus. Autun, 12th century.

the dissolution of communities of canons, each residing in a private house inside the cathedral cloister; and growing numbers of marriages involving younger sons of the aristocracy. In addition there was increased colonization of areas on the fringes of ancient village lands. At every level of society in the feudal era we note a tendency toward division of the basic cells of private life, which increased in number as they decreased in size. The result, however, was greater prominence for the household, not for the individual. For a long time the individual remained the prisoner of the family. In order to follow the final stages of his liberation, we must concentrate on two narrow sectors of society. Prior to the fourteenth century progress was clearly visible only in monastic society and in knightly games and dreams.

Anchorites

The Rule of Saint Benedict describes itself as a "rule for novices." It recommended the cenobitic life to men deemed not yet strong enough to live as anchorites. But it was understood that there was a higher degree of perfection to be achieved in solitude, that extreme form of flight from the world and the flesh which the monk was exhorted to undertake. The purpose of the rule was to establish conditions conducive to taking the first steps toward that ideal state. In fact, the rule circumscribed not so much space as time, isolating the individual in a material and physical sense so that he would be free to concentrate on himself. The rule of silence, the experience of retirement and seclusion, broke communication between the individual and the group; this was a privation, but it was also a means of spiritual ascension. In actual Benedictine communities the ordeal of silence was attenuated. Living in community, the monks were obliged to communicate, and at Cluny a complex gestural language was developed for the purpose. Furthermore, the rule was waived daily during the meeting in the capitulary and on certain days in the cloister after the hour of sext. In summer it was waived every day after nones and distribution of a collation. Nevertheless, "private" conversations (as the Cluniac customs called them) were prohibited during periods of penitence and Lent. Moreover, the silence of the night was exalted—for Bernard it betokened the highest elevation of soul. Furthermore, a part of the monk's silent time was devoted to individual or "private" reading, yet another exercise in self-absorption and mystical dialogue with Scripture, that is, with God. Finally,

Hermit and knight. Illustration from *Roman de Perceval le Gallois*, 14th century. (Paris, Bibliothèque Nationale, French 12577.)

the Rule of Saint Benedict exhorted monks to engage in brief but frequent and intense periods of private prayer.

As Cluny interpreted the Rule, periods of individual autonomy were abbreviated in order to increase the time devoted to the recitation of psalms, to the collective chant that emphasized the unity of the community. Since the beginning of the eleventh century, however, an alternative to Benedict's Latin conception of the monastic life had been introduced by those familiar with the Christianity of the East, which emphasized solitude and introspection. Christians were called upon to do battle with the devil, not in the security of numbers, but alone, facing the danger head on. From the Italian peninsula the new movement spread throughout the West in the final decades of the eleventh century. A desire to achieve greater perfection in the desert, in isolation, drove Robert de Molesmes to break with the customs of Cluny. He founded a monastery at Cîteaux. The Cistercians proposed to follow the Benedictine rule to the letter. Thus, they remained faithful to the principle of communal life. They sought, however, to distance themselves still further from the tumult of the world and to cloister themselves behind more solid walls. Around every abbey they created a halo of sylvan solitude, which they

Illustration from the *Vie des Pères au désert*, 15th century. (Paris, Arsenal Library, ms 5216.)

defended jealously against all intruders. They insisted that at least the leader of each group of monks carry the quest for individual retirement further still: setting an example for other monks, the Cistercian abbot shut himself up alone in his cell at night, the time of greatest danger. He advanced one step further in his ordeal, for his duty was to keep watch, to man the abbey's lonely outposts.

The Carthusians went further. Not only did they live in the wilderness, among the wild beasts, in the mountains, symbolic of spiritual ascent, but their rule provided that the monks would participate in communal life for very short periods only, just for the time it took to complete various liturgical exercises or festive meals. The rest of the time each monk would remain closeted in silence in his own hut, obliged to pray and work as a true monk should: alone.

Carthusianism represents the least anarchic form of the aspiration to solitude that spread like wildfire in the years following Saint Bruno's conversion. Everywhere hermits withdrew into the wilderness (perhaps more so in western France than elsewhere). Overcoming all obstacles, including doubts on the part of many bishops, the hermitic movement was so successful that it infiltrated even the cenobitic orders. The attitude of Cluny, where doubts about individualism remained strong, is quite revealing. (William of Volpiano denounced it as a form of pride: "Pride is born when someone has said that he will keep himself hidden in secret and will no longer deign to see or visit his brothers.") Nevertheless, in the second quarter of the century Cluny accepted limited experimentation with the anchorite life; the most advanced monks were permitted to spend time in huts in the woods at some distance from the abbey. Abbot Peter the Venerable himself liked to make periodic retreats into the forest. Yet the amount of permissible isolation was carefully apportioned to the strengths of each individual "athlete of redemption," for anxiety about the practice remained. Saint Bernard voices it, though admittedly he is speaking to a person of weaker constitution than a monk, a nun, a woman: "The desert, the shade of the forest, and the solitude of silence offer plentiful opportunities for evil . . . The Tempter approaches in perfect security." And from Elisabeth of Schönau we hear: "Some love solitude less for the hope of a harvest of good works than for the freedom of their own will." Where, indeed, was the line to be drawn between, on the one hand, hermits tempted by independence and, like Adam, victims of pride and, on the other hand, those determined rebels who were called heretics and who also fled into the desert, impelled by hopes of a more direct, personal contact with the Spirit?

In the final third of the twelfth century the hermit played a leading role in stories devised for the amusement of knights, most of them composed in northwestern France. There were two main reasons for this: first, the forest was one of the two primary sites of action in medieval romance, and the hermit's natural place in this period and region was in the woods; second and more important, the chansons and romances were composed as compensation for the frustrations of private life in the feudal era, which so severely cramped individual aspirations. The works depicted in imaginary form that which the young men who formed the most receptive part of their audience had to do without. Literature exalted the individual and celebrated his flourishing in freedom from all constraint—in particular, from religious constraint. Alone and unsupervised, the hermit represented a tolerant form of Christianity, a religion freed from the straitjacket of ritual. And freedom, too, from domestic promiscuity: the knight-errant traveled alone, led solely by his desires.

Knights-Errant

Hence this literature teaches us first of all about that which it denies and proposes to hide from view: it shows in negative form the power of the gregarious life to stifle and repress. At the same time it heightened the need for intimacy and helped to satisfy that need by indicating cracks in the wall through which the individual might escape, following the example of the heroes of fiction. Romantic literature could not have captivated an audience had it cut itself off from reality completely; the ideal that it nourished must not have been totally inaccessible. There can be no doubt that courtly society, like monastic society, placed increasing value on individual experience and provided the means for it to flourish.

The literature of chivalry fulfilled a pedagogical function: it called upon the knight to outdo himself, to overcome trial after tribulation along the way to perfection. Like Cistercian and Carthusian mysticism, it invited the individual to test himself, step by step, in silence. The exemplary figure that literature placed at center stage was that of the knight on the march, alone in the wilderness, surrounded by dangers and face to face with the disquieting presence of the woman or fairy. So far from the scrutiny of others, however, who was

The forest and the court. An illustration from *Lancelot*, 1274. (Paris, Bibliothèque Nationale, French 342.)

in a position to judge him, who could appreciate his value and award his prize? The action of romance therefore takes place in two different settings, one solitary, the other crowded with people: the forest and the court. The literature to which I refer is rightly named *courtly* literature. It has a predilection for sylvan settings, but these are depicted as the obverse of the real world, a countervalue. In reality, the instruction of which the romances were one instrument was carried out in the courts. The knight who wished to advance in the eyes of his master had to outdo his rivals. Knights lived in private communities as regimented as the monks of Cluny; for younger sons who had no hope of inheritance, distinction was everything, the basis of all social action. What the literature of escape evokes with its images of the forest is the series of selection procedures by which some knights distinguished themselves from others. Like the saintly hero to whom contemporary iconography was just beginning to give individualized features, the knightly hero separated himself from the mass of other knights and affirmed his valor through individual exploit. He exhibited his unique prowess in public victory and alone reaped the reward—it, too, unique.

The knight's prowess was not only with arms but also in love. And we must look at the latter in order to find the knightly equivalent of the sylvan huts to which certain Cluniac monks of the mid-twelfth century retreated in search of themselves. In a biography of Robert the Pious written early in the eleventh century, the monk Helgaud relates an anecdote about Hugh Capet, who throws his cloak over a couple he finds fornicating between two of his palace's gates. The most private of private acts, sex—scandalous at any time other than the dark of night—must not be seen by anyone; it must be

shrouded in obscurity, dissimulated behind closed doors. Information on this point being extremely rare, I shall take the
somewhat anachronistic liberty of referring to depositions
made to the inquisitor by the lady of Montaillou, Béatrice de
Planissoles. She confesses that, while her first husband was
still alive, she was raped, by daylight but in her bedroom,
behind a partition; that later, after being widowed, she was
attacked in her own hôtel by the majordomo, who awaited
her one day at dusk, hidden beneath her bed, and, when the
lamps were put out, slipped furtively in beside her, whereupon
she cried out, alerting the servants, who "were sleeping
nearby, in other beds in her chamber" (in the dark the crowded
living conditions were clearly no obstacle); and, further, that
after remarrying she surrendered one day to a priest, but in
the cellar, with a maid standing watch; that, widowed again,
she enticed to her home another priest, to whom she gave
herself in the vestibule near the door, this being at night, and
when she repeated the sin by day, she waited until her daughters and servants had gone. Such was the reality of fornication
in these crowded, open houses. Illicit love was perfectly compatible with gregarious familiarity. Only an insane passion like
that of Tristan and Isolde required the lovers to flee into the
wilderness of strangeness and unreason.

What we call courtly love, refined love, was directed
toward the same goal and displayed in the same locales. Yet
it was a society game, played in the midst of a group. Its rules

Prowess of a solitary knight. Illustration from *Artus le Restoré*, 14th century. (Paris, Bibliothèque Nationale, French 761.)

were so closely patterned after the structures of domestic society that the amorous quest can be interpreted as part of the constant testing and selection that went on in every great household. It was as though the master delegated to his wife the power to choose the best, to select one individual from a group whose members all attempted to shine in her eyes. Even more than competition in sports, courtly love spurred the desire for autonomy that burned within the homogeneity of community. This was particularly true because one of the rules of the game of love was discretion. The lovers were obliged to hide themselves, to withdraw from society, not for brief copulation in the manner of the lady of Montaillou but permanently. They lived within an invisible enclosure, where they constructed, in the midst of a crowd of familiars, a more private cell, a refuge for a love constantly threatened by jealous rivals.

Well played, the game of courtly love created intimacy and enforced silence, obliging the lovers to communicate by means of signs, like the monks at Cluny; they made gestures, exchanged glances, wore particular colors and emblems. When Tristan and Isolde regain their reason and ask the hermit Ogrin how to find their way back into society, he advises them first

Cupid and games of love. Ivories, 14th century. (Paris, Cluny Museum.)

to purify themselves through contrition, inner remorse, and personal resolve to resist temptation forever after, and second, once they are back at court, simply to dissimulate: "Pour honte ôter et mal couvrir, on doit un peu par bel mentir" (To remove shame and cover wrong, it is best to lie a little). Among others they must always lie. For those who did not flee into the forest, who played the game on the appropriate stage, silence is the law of love. Andreas Capellanus says as much in his treatise: "He who wishes to keep his love intact for long must see to it *above all* that it is not divulged to anyone and kept hidden from all eyes. For as soon as several people have knowledge of it, it ceases at once to develop naturally and will go into decline." Hence "lovers must not address one another by signs unless they are sure of being safe from any trap."

Amorous games imposed firm structures upon courtly society; lovers were obliged to live in secret solitude, as if there were nothing between them. They hid behind a veil that their enemies were determined to breach. In these refined relations between male and female, in this difficult ordeal of discretion and silence, the first seeds may have been sown, late in the twelfth century, of what would become intimacy in the modern sense.

The Image of the Body. Through the eye, love's arrow penetrates to the heart it was sent to inflame. All passion begins with an exchange of glances; later, at the penultimate stage of love's progress, the beloved might display her nude body to her lover's eyes. In this tentative exploration of the most intimate of feudal privacies we must consider the attitudes of individuals toward their own bodies and the bodies of others.

Those attitudes were governed by the dualist conception upon which every representation of the world was built. No one doubted that each individual was composed of a body and a soul, flesh and spirit. On the one hand, perishable, ephemeral matter subject to decay, to return unto dust, yet called upon to reform its ways with a view to resurrection on Judgment Day; on the other, the immortal. On the one hand, that which is weighed down by the burden of the flesh, by the opacity of carnal substances; on the other, that which aspires to celestial perfection. Accordingly, the body was deemed dangerous, susceptible to temptation. From it, in particular from its nether parts, uncontrollable impulses naturally emanated. Within it appeared concrete manifestations of wickedness and corrup-

The Body

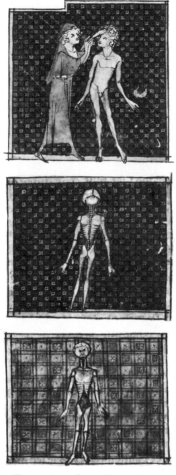

Illustrations from *Cyrurgie de maistre Henri de Mondeville* (Mondeville's treatise on surgery), 14th century. (Paris, Bibliothèque Nationale, French 2030.)

tion: disease and infection, to which every body is susceptible. And to it were applied purgatory punishments to wipe away sin and blame. The body was also a sign, revealing the soul's peculiarities through such features as the color of the hair and complexion of the skin and, in exceptional cases, by the capacity to endure the ordeal of immersion in water or the touch of the red-hot iron. The soul showed through its envelope of flesh, the body being merely its dwelling place, its home, or, rather, its court, its enclosure. The body was the outer layer of a protected zone, restricted as was the domestic space around it. Having proceeded inward through structure upon structure, we come finally to the ultimate privacy.

In investigating contemporary ideas of the body I am indebted to Marie-Christine Pouchelle's important study of Henri de Mondeville's treatise on surgery, written in Paris in the early fourteenth century. The terminology Mondeville uses and the comparisons he makes provide the key to the symbolic system of which the body was a part, a system understood not only by learned scholars but also by the common man, since Mondeville, as a medical practitioner, claims to have incorporated the layman's thoughts and language into his work. It is strikingly apparent that the body was seen as a residence: its interior is called "domestic" and its exterior "sylvan," terms reminiscent of those two scenes of romantic intrigue, the court and the forest.

The body's interior is truly like a court, for the body itself is a house as vast and complex as any monastery or palace, and its interior consists of a hierarchy of spaces: a noble portion, a service portion, and between them a wall—the diaphragm—similar to the wall that separated the workers in feudal society from the others. Below this wall lie the body's nether parts. By nature these must be dominated, subjugated. There, below, the most dangerous rebellions smolder, in the common part of the body, the crude part, the place where all that is superfluous or noxious is eliminated. As in seigneurial residences, this lower section performs a nutritive function; it furnishes food to the organs lodged in the noble space above, the delicate organs associated with the nobler functions of strength and wisdom. In each of the two sections of the body, Mondeville tells us, there is an "oven." The purpose of the lower oven is to cook the nutritive humors, and, rather like a great kitchen fire, it is designed for slow combustion, for simmering soups and other peasant dishes; whereas the upper story contains a roaring fire to light the heart with joy. Here,

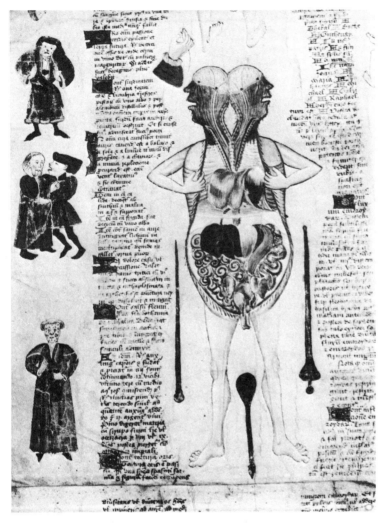

The open body. Illustration from *Art de la médecine et de la chirurgie*, 1412. (Stockholm, Royal Library.)

as in the church in the center of a monastery, matter is made spirit, as the humors are distilled in the upper reaches of the flame where tongues of fire lick the air.

The bodily house is surrounded by an enclosure as unbreachable as the wall around any private dwelling. On earth the body's envelope is the ultimate of enclosures, the most secret and intimate of all; violating it is prohibited by the strictest of taboos. The body is a fortress, a hermitage, but one constantly under threat, besieged, as surrounded by the satanic as was the refuge of the Desert Fathers. Hence it is essential that the body be kept under surveillance, especially those tap-holes through which the Enemy might infiltrate the castle walls. Moralists urged that a guard be mounted over such posterns and windows as the eyes, the mouth, the ears, and the nostrils, portals through which a taste for the world, hence for sin and corruption, might all too easily enter. A vigilant watch must be kept, as at the gates of a monastery.

Woman's body is a mirror image of Adam's body; in particular, the female sex organs are similar in structure to the male, but turned around, introverted, more secret and thus more private but also, like anything hidden, suspect. Woman's body, more susceptible to corruption than man's because less sealed off from the outside world, requires a more vigilant guard, and it is to man that the task of surveillance falls. Woman cannot live without man; she needs to be in a man's power. Anatomically she is destined to remain secluded in a supplementary enclosure, never to leave home without an escort, and then only bundled up in layers of garments more opaque than those of man. Before woman's body a wall is to be erected: the wall of private life. By the nature of her body, she is obliged to live a chaste and retiring life, to keep watch over herself, and to submit to the governance of man from birth until death, because her body is dangerous—both *in* danger and a *source of* danger. Man risks losing his honor because of it, risks being led astray, caught in a trap all the more perilous for being so alluring.

Women. La Chaise-Dieu, Haute-Loire, 14th century.

The Morality of the Body. It is hard to determine what the morality of the body was before the end of the thirteenth century, because art, or at any rate that art which has survived, was not yet firmly realistic and because what was written on the subject conceals nearly everything. The principle was that a person must respect his body because the body is the temple of the soul and will be resurrected on Judgment Day. The body is to be cared for, but prudently, cherished as Saint Paul exhorted men to cherish their wives—cautiously and with suspicion—for the body, like woman, is temptation; it incites desire in oneself and others. The most informative sources suggest a strong tendency to fear the body, to neglect it, and even, in the extremer forms of asceticism, to abandon it to vermin (but the texts are of course colored by the ideology of the Church, the extremist views of professional moralists).

Nevertheless, among the dominant class at least, cleanliness was much prized. In the eleventh and twelfth centuries the Cluniac monasteries and houses of the lay nobility continued to set aside space for baths no less extensive than in the palaces of the early Middle Ages. No formal dinner (that is, no dinner given in the great hall with a large crowd of guests) could begin until ewers had been passed around to the guests for their preprandial ablutions. Water flowed abundantly in the literature of amusement—over the body of the knight-errant, who was always rubbed down, combed, and groomed by his host's daughters whenever he stopped for the night, and over the nude bodies of fairies in fountains and steam-baths. A hot bath was an obligatory prelude to the amorous games described in the fabliaux. Washing one's own body and the bodies of others seems to have been a function specifically ascribed to women, mistresses of water both at home and in the wilderness.

Bathing and grooming were regarded with suspicion by moralists, however, because they unveiled the attractions of the body. Bathing was said to be a prelude to sin, and in the penitential of Burchard of Worms we find a full catalog of the sins that ensued when men and women bathed together. Such suspicions seem to go beyond mere ecclesiastic severity. Lambert of Ardres, the historian of the counts of Guines, describes the young wife of an ancestor of his hero swimming before the eyes of her household in a pond below the castle, but he is careful to indicate that she is wearing a modest white gown. There were twenty-six public baths in Paris in the late thirteenth century, and traces of the strict regulations governing behavior in these places have survived. Such establishments were suspect because they were too public; it was better to wash one's body in the privacy of one's own home. Scrupulous, highly restrictive precautions were taken in the most orderly of all households, the monasteries. At Cluny the custom required the monks to take a full bath twice a year, at the holidays of renewal, Christmas and Easter; but they were exhorted not to uncover their pudenda. The concern with modesty was ubiquitous. Monks were apparently not the only ones who did not undress fully before going to bed. Caught by surprise in their hut of branches, Tristan and Isolde were found innocent of blame because their attire was such that it would have been decent to wear in bed: she in a nightgown, he still wearing his breeches. Did people undress when they made love? The length of time that it takes the husbands of the various Melusinas in all the tales to recognize their wife's true nature makes one doubt it, as does the extreme restraint

Funeral effigy, northern France, 14th century. (Musée d'Arras, Pas-de-Calais.)

of erotic literature in the period. No one but a maniac exhibited his body.

Nevertheless, the body was very carefully attired, the principal aim being to underscore the difference between the sexes. There was, the moralists constantly pointed out, a fundamental obligation to distinguish among "orders," to respect the primordial division between masculine and feminine; hence not to hide the traits specific to one or the other. Accordingly, young dandies who dressed effeminately were violently attacked, and the few women who dared to dress as men provoked disgust. Nevertheless, sexual characteristics were not to be given undue prominence. This concern for moderation and discretion is particularly apparent in regard to the hair. For women the hair was a necessary accoutrement, a natural veil, a sign of inferiority and subjugation. Women were therefore exhorted to take care of their hair, whereas men who paid too much attention to theirs were reviled. But when a woman left her private home and showed herself in public, she was required to refrain from showing her tempting locks, for the hair was invested with a terrible erotic power. Propriety demanded that a woman's hair be gathered and plaited, and any woman who was not a prostitute and no longer a child and who ventured out in public, any married woman who ventured outside her own room into the hall of the house, was further obliged to hide her tresses beneath a wimple.

There is, however, every reason to believe that men and women did not disdain to use their physical charms to enhance their personal power. Consider the amount of space that Henri de Mondeville devotes in his treatise to techniques of beautification. He justifies this in two ways: first, and quite pragmatically, he points out that the physician who knows the artifices of seduction can earn quite a bit of money, for the demand is high; second, and quite revealingly, he thinks it obvious that a person ought to know how to make full use of his physical attractions in order to outstrip competitors and advance in a society in which the individualistic spirit played an increasingly prominent role.

Mondeville wrote early in the fourteenth century, at the culmination of a long period of steady progress. During this period it appears that, as the ideology of contempt for the flesh waned but before the burden of sexual guilt descended

Resurrected souls. Typanum of Bourges Cathedral, 13th century.

upon western Christianity, the body was slowly but surely rehabilitated. I see evidence for this assertion in the changing representations of nudity. Virtually the only instances that have survived belong to the realm of sacred art. Before 1230 sculptors and painters had deliberately accentuated the perversity of the nude, depicting almost no nude figure that was not either in the grip of evil or an incitation to evil. But after that date, for example in the image of the resurrected in the tympanum of Bourges or the figure of Adam in the rood screen of Notre-Dame in Paris or the Cupid at Auxerre, we see nudes that are young, radiant, satisfied, reconciled. What role did humanism, the reawakening awareness of ancient culture, and the new naturalism that had such a profound impact on high culture play in these changes? In any case it is clear that individuals made increasing use of physical beauty in their attempts to win the recognition of their peers.

Adam, 14th century. (Paris, Cluny Museum.)

The same general movement led each individual to pay renewed attention to that which the body-fortress protected for better or worse against the aggressions of Satan: that ill-defined substance, the soul. The care of the soul also became an increasingly individual matter, less subject to the control of the community; religion became more and more a private affair.

At the beginning of the feudal era the "people," the community of the faithful, entrusted their deliverance from evil to delegated representatives. This was first of all the function of the monastery, a community of men more perfect than others because they lived cloistered in the utmost privacy. The monks' task was to pray publicly on behalf of both the living and the dead, depositing in mankind's account the profits of their own purifying penance. In other words, the monastery was the mouth of the people, from which emanated the chants and prayers of all mankind. The prince fulfilled a similar mediating function. His piety ensured his subjects' salvation. If he chanced to sin, the wrath of God immediately fell upon his subjects. As a public person, he too was obliged to pray constantly to God. In the third decade of the twelfth century Galbert of Bruges tells us that Charles the Good, count of Flanders, went every morning from his bed to the Church of Saint Donatian to join his auxiliaries, the canons, in chanting and reading psalms, while the poor, duly registered and certified, lined up to receive a coin from his right hand. The majority of men looked upon such spectacles from afar, watching proxies perform the rites of collective salvation, trusting them to do their office well.

Not everyone was satisfied with this state of affairs, however. As far back as the early eleventh century some men and women were persecuted as heretics because they refused to accept these specialists in prayer as their intercessors, aiming instead to communicate personally with the Holy Spirit and to secure their own salvation through good works. They were prosecuted as a threat to public order and vanquished because they were still just a small minority. At the beginning of the next century others advanced the same claims, but so loudly that the Church, feeling the challenge, reacted by shoring up its structures. It continued to rely on princes, in fact on the host of petty princes that resulted from the fragmentation of the powers of command; it was the responsibility of each prince to oversee the religious activities of every member of his household. But the Church also assigned a much greater role than before to the clergy, to ministers whose role was not to chant in isolation like the monks but to spread the sacraments and the word among the people. But now the people were rounded up in tidy little flocks—parishes—and closely watched. They were divided up, supervised, "encapsulated" as Robert Fossier has observed, and held in close check. Nevertheless, the established Church would never have vanquished heresy had it not also responded to people's expectations by proposing more personal forms of religious practice.

The Church invited ordinary laymen to adopt an attitude toward the sacred not unlike that previously limited exclusively to the clergy. It called upon individuals to take full responsibility for their personal progress toward perfection. The internalization of Christian practices came about very slowly. It began among the "powerful," among those whose official duty was to set an example, which then propagated

Prayer over the psalter and before the image. Illustration from *Heures de Paris*, 1400–1410. (Paris, Bibliothèque Nationale, Latin 1161.)

Giotto, *Saint Francis before the Cross.* (Assisi, Convent of Saint Francis, Upper Church.)

from the upper strata of society to the layers beneath. In the schools, then at the height of intellectual fervor, masters rediscovered techniques of introspection. Meanwhile, the High Church lectured princes and, perhaps even more, princesses and other women who, while enduring the asperity of marriage, turned for solace to spiritual directors. The rich were the first to be invited to read, like monks, the words of prayers from books. The popularity of sacred reading increased steadily in the twelfth century, with a concomitant change from reading aloud along with the officiant at services to more private reading in a low voice, followed by whispered services. In great aristocratic households every master kept among his most private possessions a psalmody or psalter. Men and women learned to use these on their own. The psalter, in part because of its text but especially because of its images, became an instrument of intimate meditation. In the thirteenth century other objects of personal popularity were also in wide use, including those private reliquaries that resemble tiny chapels, some of which were worn about the body. Laymen slowly learned how to enter into mystical communion with the figures depicted on the reliquaries: a saint, the Virgin, Christ. This communion continued in the chapel or church before other, more public images: think of Saint Francis in dialogue with the cross. Such evidence calls for a much more thorough investigation, with careful attention to chronology, for it indicates an expansion of individual devotion, which by the fourteenth century had penetrated to the lowest strata of society. Even in a village as isolated as Montaillou, personal prayer was an ingrained habit—and not just among the marginal individuals suspected of heresy.

The internalization of piety was the result of a process of education carried out primarily by the clergy, aided in the thirteenth century by mendicant friars, who delivered lectures, sermons, and public harangues to sometimes immense audiences. The good seed was there broadcast and allowed to germinate in the soul of each individual. Every man was exhorted to imitate Christ and the saints in the privacy of his soul and, going beyond the mere outward forms of religious practice, to transform his will and his heart from within. This moral appeal succeeded, thanks in part to the use of exempla: simple, edifying stories offered as guides to the individual conscience. One of the largest collections of exempla, composed in the first quarter of the thirteenth century by the Cistercian Caesarius of Heisterbach for the use of preachers, is couched in the form of dialogues: master and disciple meet for private lessons, as every good preacher wished to do with his flock. In all these anecdotes the hero is embarked upon an individual adventure, facing his trials alone and later engaging in dialogue, on the road perhaps but more commonly in a bedroom in the middle of the night, in silent retreat, with a friend or confidant, perhaps with an angel, a ghost, the Virgin, or even the demon tempter. The conversations are always private and concerned with personal choices. Often members of the hero's household figure as bothersome intruders who must be removed from the scene.

In the decades around the year 1200, when the pace of progress was most rapid, religious practice underwent a tremendous upheaval because of the new pastoral concern, which taught a different use of the sacraments. Now the faithful were called upon to consume the bread of life, to place the body of Christ inside their own bodies for an intimate encounter. This practice evoked images that magnified the human person, who became like a tabernacle amid the promiscuity of the household. Even more decisive was the transformation of the act of penance, initially rare and public. After a long period of evolution, dating back to Carolingian times, the Fourth Lateran Council, drawing upon the work of scholars who reflected upon the "intimate" causes of sin, decided in 1215 to make

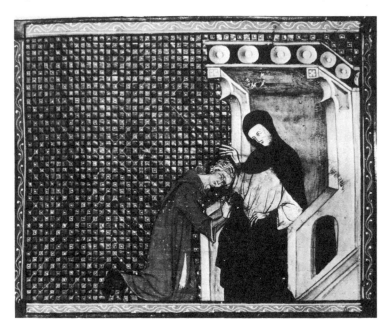

Confession. Illustration from a religious treatise, 14th century. (Chantilly, Condé Museum.)

Jan van Eyck, *Les Très belles heures de Notre-Dame du duc de Berry (Heures de Milan)*. Birth of Saint John the Baptist, 1415–1417. (Turin, Museo Civico d'Arte Antica.)

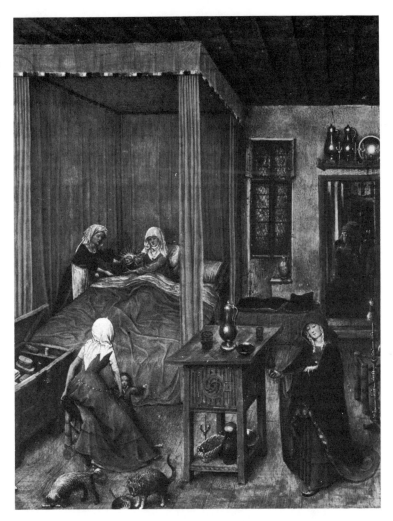

confession private, regular, and compulsory. The decision to make all Christians confess at least once a year was in part a repressive, inquisitorial measure; its purpose was to unearth insubordination and heresy lurking in individual consciences. But can there be a revolution more radical or an effect on attitudes more profound and prolonged than that which followed the change from a ceremony as public as penance had been (a spectacle of exclusion staged in the public square) to a simple private dialogue, as in the exempla, between sinner and priest, or between the soul and God (for oral confession was an inviolable secret, and worthless unless followed by a silent effort of self-correction)?

At Cluny, that citadel of the communal spirit, private confession at least once a week was required by the statutes of Abbot Hugh II some time between 1199 and 1207. Penances became a private affair, a matter of individual prayers recited in a low voice. A few years later the Lateran Council extended a similar obligation to all Christians. As Easter approached, everyone was supposed to prepare for communion by examining his conscience, studying his soul, and practicing the same spiritual exercises that a few pious men had imposed upon themselves early in the twelfth century in order to ferret out any vestige of perverse desires. I am speaking of the authors of the first autobiographies, not only Abelard and Guibert but also the much larger number of monks who corresponded from monastery to monastery, dictating letters that were not intimate but did set two anxious personalities face to face. First introspection, then secret confession and mortification of the flesh: henceforth piety hid behind walls, in private gardens. A slow reversal was finally complete. The decree of 1215 was not immediately put into effect everywhere. But within a century its effects, combined with those of education through sermons and through the casuistry of love and with economic change that liberated the individual by accelerating trade, had begun to change the meaning of the word *private*. A new conception of private life developed imperceptibly in the midst of the gregarious family. From now on privacy meant being oneself among others, in one's own room, at one's window, with one's own property, one's own purse, and one's own faults—recognized and pardoned—as well as one's own dreams, inspirations, and secrets.

Bernhard Strigel, *Portrait of Konrad Rehlinger of Augsburg with His Children*. Placed under the sign of Providence or revealed in the exchange of glances, relations between parents and children are set forth as truthfully in 15th-century painting as in the biographical writing of the period. (Munich, Pinachotek.) See page 563.

Toward Intimacy: The Fourteenth and Fifteenth Centuries

Philippe Braunstein

THE history of space in the process of becoming private, of the phases of retirement and intimacy, is one of feelings, thoughts, and mental images cultivated in secret but fixed in private writing. Compared with the sources of earlier centuries, those of the late medieval period are relatively abundant. Beginning in the thirteenth century, the volume of documents increases markedly, and a fair proportion of private documents has survived. Hence we can feel more confident of entering the private lives of certain individuals whose interest in writing or being painted ensured that some evidence of their identity, manner, and/or voice would be recorded and whose record survived the hazards of the archives.

We must, however, delineate carefully the limits of a risky enterprise. The person who writes about his or her own life, or extends it in fiction, looks inward with an eye no more innocent than that which he casts upon the outside world. But against what standard can we measure the testimony of an individual, or distinguish between the unique testimony and the common experience to which it bears witness?

As private writing, or writing about private life, became more commonplace, profound changes in the attitudes of individuals toward their families and social groups must have occurred. People felt a need to transmit, or at least describe, reactions to events about which earlier generations had been silent. Although we become aware of modifications induced by the habit of writing, the increasing availability of the "mirror" that writing provides, we must not conclude that self-consciousness did not exist or that people previously took no pleasure in private life and had no interest in defending it.

The ability to write was fairly widespread in the late

Middle Ages. The skill was more commonly found in large cities than in rural towns, and laymen shared it with clerics. Writing remained, however, the privilege of a minority of the European population. The written sources tell us about the intimate lives of a relatively small number of people, offering only occasional glimpses of the rest. Evidence from painting, sculpture, and archaeology, however, can help correct and extend our imperfect understanding.

A danger lurks in the temptation to view the final centuries of the Middle Ages as a precursor of "modernity" simply because the people of that age were more garrulous about each other's secrets than were their ancestors. Sensitivity to the voices of the past allows us to be astonished by the freedom of a confidence, the audacity of an expression, the reverie implicit in a text, the love that is evident in lament over the death of a child. Anything that brings us closer to the intimate feelings of people who lived centuries ago tempts us to abolish the distance that stands between us and a lost world. The trap of modernity is to assume that nothing is ever new, that men expressing themselves in private speak the same language across the centuries.

The abundance of sources for the fourteenth and fifteenth centuries requires us to overcome two difficulties: we must not assume a sharp break with earlier times, and we must not treat the period as though it were the beginning of the modern age. Every document used (most of the sources are either Italian or German), every expression uncovered, must be carefully weighed in the light of other, contemporary documents and expressions. Beyond the pleasure of attending to the voice, we must strive to identify the speaker and situate him in his milieu.

THE INVENTION OF SUBJECTIVITY

Social life comprises a series of communities: family, traditional community, professional groups, subjects of a sovereign. The individual is more than a member of so many different groups. Self-consciousness is born when the individual can see himself in perspective, set himself apart from his fellow man; it can lead to a radical questioning of the social order. Those who risked abandoning their position in society, who took to the roads and the forests, lost their social status. The restless wanderers, shady characters, and madmen who fill the pages of the romantic adventures so widely read in the waning Middle Ages were not alone in the forests of disorder, where charcoal burners, outcasts, and hermits avidly seeking another world also roamed.

But self-consciousness, as least as it was expressed in writing, did not often cross the dividing line between the gregarious and the unorganized. Wedded to familiar habits of mind and obligations of society, the late medieval citizen was still quite conscious of the ideology of the common good, according to which the well-being of all represented an advance over the convenience of a few. Was Guicciardini's distinction between a career in public service and an "idle life, devoid of dignity and perfectly private," a mere topos? His

Piccolomini Palace, work of Rossellino. Pienza, Tuscany, 15th century.

Pretorio Palace. Certaldo, Tuscany, late 13th century.

Public pride, private show. The facade of the building bears coats of arms attesting to glorious marriages and perpetuating time. The courtyard, however, is a tranquil place.

contemporary Willibald Pirckheimer of Nuremberg makes a similar remark in his autobiography, where he describes three years following the death of his father, three years spent *privatus* and living only for himself and his friends; after returning to public life he looks upon a statue of himself and execrates those who prefer "private sentiments" to "public utility." For Pirckheimer, to participate in public life is an honor: civic humanism had clearly made its way across the Alps. Individual dignity and self-consciousness were most strikingly manifested in service to the republic. Less pretentious chroniclers such as the Florentine Velluti chose to mention only those personal matters directly associated with official events. Memoir-writers found it difficult to distinguish between public and private. Hans Porner of Brunswick, although he insists that his book is his own and does not speak for the town council, in fact deals only with communal affairs, which overwhelm any personal remarks. The self remained melancholy, unable to do more than stammer; individuals dared to assert themselves only timidly, their model of behavior being that of the good citizen.

The expression of self was also still colored by references to family. The wish to construct palace facades aligned with the street in fifteenth-century Florence has been interpreted as evidence for a break with the family, whose architectural embodiment was the compact block of houses. The need of individuals to assert their independence from their forebears is evident in the glory that attached to success in business or a career and in the exaltation of the *res privata*. Make no mistake, however: the demands of the individual did not end with the affirmation of family in the narrow sense. Behind the family facade people insisted on privacy, as is evident from the way in which rooms were divided among family members; the primary beneficiary was the master of the house, who now enjoyed a private study to which he could retire. This was perhaps the only place where the businessman, paterfamilias, and humanist could be alone.

Work on behalf of a community or "house" honored the individual conscious of his responsibility. Prominent men felt that such activity left little room for private life per se. Anyone tempted to take the necessary time and resources for his own use was held back by fear of being judged selfish or vain by the community; privacy was considered "abject." Outside public life there was no reputation to be made: *Fama non est nisi publica.*

True to their theories, many early modern writers had little to say about private life. A necessarily gregarious existence left little room for the self to flourish naturally. Authors brought up on Cicero and Livy sallied forth armed and helmeted with virtues. We would prefer less labored styles, less rigid attitudes, less self-satisfied writers. Nevertheless, there can be no doubt that the images these public men so carefully sculpted for posterity did in some way reflect their active, public lives and, further, that the model elaborated by a few authors represented an ideal widely shared throughout urban Europe at the end of the Middle Ages.

Must we abandon the cities for rural solitude and simplicity in order to find more intimate forms of self-consciousness? In a fine albeit rhetorical piece of prose, Ulrich von Hutten makes it clear that the private man is no more easily discovered in bucolic surroundings. The humanist conscious of his role in aristocratic and bourgeois society must not look to the country for stimulants to self-fulfillment; solitude impoverishes, and retreat into the "desert," even so benign a desert as the family castle, leads to anxiety. The mind thrives on crowds and excitement:

Donatello, *Marzocco*, 1420. (Florence, Bargello.)

"The country is agitation and noise.

"You talk of the charms of the countryside, of rest, of peace . . . Whether perched on a peak or situated in a plain, the castle was built not for pleasure but for defense, surrounded by moats and trenches, cramped within, burdened with stables for animals large and small, dark buildings for bombards and stores of pitch and sulfur, swollen with stores of armaments and machines of war. Everywhere the disagreeable odor of powder dominates. And the dogs with their filth—what a fine smell that is! And the comings and goings of the knights, among them bandits, brigands, and thieves. Usually the house is wide open, because we do not know who is who and do not take much trouble to find out. We hear the bleating of the sheep, the mooing of the cows, the barking of the dogs, the shouts of men working in the fields, the grinding and clatter of carts and wagons. And near the house, which is close to the woods, we even have the cry of the wolf.

"Every day you must worry about the next, about constant movement, about the calendar of the seasons. You must plow, dress the soil, work on the vines, plant trees, irrigate meadows, harrow, seed, manure, harvest, thresh; the harvest season comes, and then the grape-picking. And if the harvest

Bernhard Strigel, *The Birth of Mary*. (Berlin, Staatliche Museen Preussischer Kulturbesitz.)

Birth scenes enable us to enter the most intimate part of the house, the bedroom, where women attend to the expectant mother.

is bad one year, what astonishing poverty, what astonishing misery, so that one never lacks occasions for emotion, worry, anguish, melancholy, despair, or folly, for wanting to go away, to flee." (Ulrich von Hutten to Willibald Pirckheimer, *Vitae suae rationem exponens,* 1518.)

Without political ambition other than to encourage the powerful to favor scholarship, von Hutten describes himself at the court of the archbishop of Mainz as a man who knows how to find solitude in the midst of tumult. True freedom, the affirmation of his own identity, comes from the private cultivation of reading and writing, which frees him from all public obligations and family burdens. Mystics enjoy the same privilege, but by other means. In the words of J. Mombaer, a Brother of the Common Life, "Whether you are awake or asleep, you are alone even in the midst of others." Von Hutten contrasts this privilege with the hard life of the peasant, who has neither the means nor the time to enjoy the vigorous pleasure of coming to grips with the soul.

FIRST-PERSON SINGULAR

Men did not speak of themselves without good reason; the authority of Proverbs, Aristotle, and Saint Thomas combined to curtail narration in the first person. Some writers have held that truly unfettered autobiography did not exist until the modern age, when, they say, a new mode of self-narration was invented and autobiography finally distinguished itself from history and apologetics. Man, discovering himself at the center of the universe, between two infinities, exulted to find that God had given him the faculty to develop his potential; autobiography proclaimed the individuality of destiny.

Autobiographical narrative did not spring fully armed from the head of the now legitimate individual hero. It emerged gradually from other forms of narrative, which centered on the individual in society. Authors felt an irresistible urge to put in a word for themselves, to indicate their presence at the side of the road when history passed, to remark on events, to place before the eye of God the example of their own tribulations. In other words, egocentric narrative sprang sometimes from the model of Augustinian confession, sometimes from the concern of prudent administrators to remind themselves and their families of the lessons of everyday ex-

perience, and sometimes from the habit of recording memorable events in conveniently accessible form.

Late medieval confessions, journals, and chronicles are sources of information about individual private lives, that is, about people's bodies, perceptions, feelings, and ideas. The insights they contain are sincere insofar as sincerity is possible in memoirs based on memory, in writing that pretends "to paint the individual not in profile but head on."

In painting, the elimination of scenery from portrait art gave us faces painted against a neutral background, lending immortality to individual features for no reason other than to preserve appearances from decay. But even before that, innumerable retables and frescoes contained minor figures more powerful than the saints or magi who formed the ostensible subject of the work; among those minor figures we often find the painter, pretending he was a witness to the very scene he paints. The individual timidly makes his appearance beneath the vaults of universal history, surprised by the echoing sound of his name. The temptation to say more about his minute self comes into conflict with the majesty of the divine, so he withdraws, concealing himself behind third-person narrative or metaphoric discourse. Language served in many ways to

Ambrogio Lorenzetti, *The Effects of Good Government*, "Departure for a Hunt with Falcons" (detail), 1338–1341. Nobles encounter peasants at work. (Siena, Palazzo Pubblico.)

disguise the expression of private feeling. Along with the few examples of genuine self-affirmation, there are innumerable instances of reticence and hesitation, whose context and frequency may be useful for distinguishing between one kind of intimate writing and another. In a work that stands at the crossroads of autobiography and fiction, Emperor Maximilian mentions his pain at the death of his young wife, "for they loved each other a great deal, about which much could be written"—but he chooses not to write it.

The Language of Confession

More than any other narrative form, confession encourages the author to cast himself in the role of protagonist in a spiritual adventure. Beyond Franciscan biography, the models for late medieval confession were Abelard's self-justification, a literary contemplation of disaster, and above all the *Confessions* of Saint Augustine. Whereas Abelard's dramatic confession consisted of a series of discontinuous events, and the serene confession of Adamo di Salimbene attempted to set the sinner's silhouette against the light of Saint Francis, Augustine's autobiography, in which a sudden crystallization of feeling suddenly illuminates the whole of the prior life, inspired several first-rate Italian writers. The most sensitive pages in Dante, Petrarch, and Boccaccio derive from this profound remark of Augustine's: "Memory brings forth not reality itself, which is gone forever, but the words elicited by the representation of reality, which as it disappeared impressed traces upon the mind via the agency of the senses." Beneath the eye of God inner time is the resurrection of past moments, revived by the present. Through his thoughts and writing the new man gives form and meaning to the sinner's hesitant progress; the narrative begins with conversion, just as the created world begins with mankind's salvation.

The organizing power of the Augustinian vision inspired individuals in diverse situations yet fascinated by Augustine's method and moved by feelings of spiritual kinship. Such emotions touched the heart of Petrarch, who shed tears as he read the *Confessions* (*inter legendum fluunt lacrimae*) and, mimicking conversion, identified his pain with Augustine's (*transformatus sum in alterum Augustinum*). Everyone knows how his dialogue with his soul, following a pattern inspired by the confessors' manuals, led him to Mont Ventoux and suggested to him the image of the citadel in which he closeted himself with his master's book.

Paolo Uccello, *Equestrian Statue of Sir John Hawkwood*, ca. 1436. Grandeur and geometry: the condottiere. (Florence, Santa Maria del Fiore.)

Dante begins his poetic autobiography, *Vita nuova*, with a methodological preamble that owes everything to the intellectual atmosphere of private reading: "In one section of the book of my memory is a heading under which I find transcribed the words I intend to use in the present work; and if I do not use them all, I shall at least make a significant summary." The reductive dryness of the analysis makes the remembered experience seem foreordained rather than freely chosen, but through the ordering prism suddenly appears that glorious creature of the spirit, Beatrice transfigured: *la gloriosa donna della mia mente.* Dante does not hesitate to show himself

Taddeo di Bartolo, *The Camerlingo's Scribe* (detail). (Siena, State Archives.)

Giovanni di Paolo, *Saint Jerome Appearing to Saint Augustine,* 1465. Works provoked thought and evoked images. (Berlin, Staatliche Museen Preussischer Kulturbesitz.)

School of Antonio Pollaiuolo.
Reading for work or pleasure.
(Paris, Bibliothèque Nationale.)

Dante, *The Divine Comedy*,
engraving on copper attributed
to Baccio Baldini, after Sandro
Botticelli, 1481. (Paris,
Bibliothèque Nationale.)

in the room where he sought refuge so that he might cry without being heard: *nella mia camera, la ov'io potea lamentarmi senza essere udito.* The intensity of the emotion depends entirely on the alchemy of writing. Writing orders the past and thus keeps the sources of memory alive; it is a liturgy that sustains love, a cult of memory that constitutes and renews the writer's pained consciousness.

Petrarch's work contains autobiographical elements, "scattered fragments of his soul." Literature enables the poet to reassemble the fleeting moments that constitute his elusive self. For that reason he diligently made marginal notes on manuscripts in his possession. In the margins of the *Aeneid*, in a manuscript embellished by miniatures of Simone Martini, Petrarch between 1348 and 1372 entered the names of persons dear to him whom he had lost, thus carrying on a secret correspondence with those of Virgil's heroes cut down in their youth. First to be mentioned is Laura, on the back of the frontispiece, "in the place that comes most often to my attention." To this immortal woman Petrarch dedicates a tender and solemn epigraph, in which the various fragments of an amorous discourse are assembled: "Laura, celebrated for her own virtues and by my poems, which have sung her at leisure, appeared to me for the first time in my earliest adolescence, in the Year of Our Lord 1328, on the sixth day of April, in

the morning, in the church of Santa Clara in Avignon; and in that same city, in the same month of April, on the sixth day of the month, at the same hour of the morning, in the year 1348, she was taken, while I was in Verona, alas, ignorant of what fate had wrought! The sad news reached me at Parma in a letter from my dear Louis on the morning of the tenth day of May 1348. Her body, so pure and so beautiful, was entrusted to the Friars Minor on the very day of her death, toward evening. As for her soul, like that of the African according to Seneca, it returned to heaven whence it came: that is my profound conviction."

Petrarch's assiduous reading of Virgil repeatedly awakened in him the feeling that he had lost everything. In a letter to Philippe de Cabassoles he wrote: "Every day I die" (*quotidie morior*). A man leaves nothing but traces. In the margins of the *Canzoniere*, the only place where he recorded his thoughts daily, Petrarch made notes on his work. He recorded a memory that came to him, after lying forgotten for twenty-five years, during a night of insomnia, and an invitation to dine that delayed his responding to a moment of inspiration. Only God could reconstruct from such notes, such moments, the fabric of a life; but the work is there, with its cries and whispers. Memory and its orchestration, literature and life's raw stuff, are inextricably intertwined. About himself Petrarch left only a postscript, an *Epistle to Posterity*. His voice, transmitted through time, carefully contains his emotion. Despite the distance that he is pleased to establish between the man he was and the writer who will remain, he cannot resist the temptation to describe himself: "Perhaps one of you has heard something about me . . . I was one of your troop, an insignificant man among mortals . . . Though not blessed with a physique of the first order, I enjoyed the advantages of youth: a good complexion, neither brilliant nor pallid, sparkling eyes and an eyesight that remained acute past sixty years of age and then weakened to the point where I was forced, reluctantly, to seek the aid of glasses." This self-portrait suddenly plunges us back into the miseries of private life, which Boccaccio, in his literary portrait of the great man, had attempted to efface by shrouding personal memories in a veil of ancient clichés.

After Petrarch, humanists often referred to, or produced pastiches of, Roman literature. In the fifteenth century the analysis of feeling became noticeably more serene, as writers turned conformist in style and borrowed their moral doctrine from noted authors of the past. First-person narrative contin-

Vittore Carpaccio, *Legend of Saint Ursula.* "Farewell to the Ambassadors" (detail), 1490–1496. (Venice, Accademia.)

ued to be inspired by the Christian preoccupation with spiritual accounting, but little room remained for introspection owing to the new emphasis on philology, conventional description of nature, moderation, and personal glory.

Giovanni Conversini of Ravenna, chancellor to Francesco of Carrara, drew upon Augustinian tradition for the title of his self-examination, *Rationarum vitae,* but his style lacks the anguished accents of a dialogue with the soul. Poggio scoured the pages of the authors of the past ("every day I speak to the dead") in search of virtuous attitudes, but about his own conscience he says nothing. Pier Paolo Vergerio emulates Pliny the Younger in describing a stay in the country. Even Enea Silvio Piccolomini, the future Pope Pius II, whose keen intellect is so often evident in his writing, has left in his *Commentaries* an account of his private life that remains insipid and elusive until he receives the consecration of the tiara. Then, emulating his literary master, Caesar, he begins writing in the third person: Enea Silvio throws over his life the mantle of the papacy. Occasionally, an inflection in his objective style reveals the sound of his authentic voice. He is sarcastic, for example, in describing the maneuvers of the conclave that elected him: "Most of the cardinals gathered near the latrines; there, where discretion and secrecy were most appropriate, they agreed on a way to elect Pope William." He is melancholy when he visits the region where he grew up: "Everywhere the pope encountered obvious signs of his old age." Later, outside Ancona, as he prepares for his life's final act, the impossible crusade, he is resigned: "If this route does not impel the Christians to go to war, we know no other . . . As for ourselves, we know that death lies ahead, and we do not refuse it." In this style there may still be conformity, but it bears the stamp of experience and is based on the imitation of saints and martyrs.

With the *Commentaries* of Pius II we pass imperceptibly to literature of another kind, in which the only link with private life is subjective. We are no longer concerned with those privileged moments that encapsulate the past or with the need to trace the development of a conscience in intimate detail. Here the emphasis is on recording, in chronological order, events notable enough to be saved from oblivion. The elements of personal engagement and personal choice are camouflaged by the apparent objectivity of the narrative.

Memoirs of Action

The purpose of late medieval memoirs and commentaries, as established by such historians as Froissart and Villani, was to examine the past in the light of experience. The narrator's emphases and omissions, enumerations and digressions, sweeping brushstrokes and minute detail, create as it were a negative self-portrait (particularly when the writer's purpose is apologetic).

The Bourgeois of Paris, who kept a journal in difficult times, is an impotent and splenetic observer of events that transcend him. Philippe de Commynes, on the other hand, was not only an intimate of his protagonists, Duke Charles and King Louis, but also an official charged with public and secret missions. His account of his times, his judgments, descriptions, and portraits, are all colored by his feelings and muted by the distance between the man of action and the elderly gentleman enduring a forced retirement. But the author, the private man, appears only fleetingly, and then only if one makes an effort to divine his intentions. As for the personages who occupy the center of the stage, Commynes shows them "in chambers" only when justified by his literary design. We see the fury of the duke of Burgundy at having been deceived, as well as his fearsome melancholy, and we are shown the king of France in his manor and in the agony of death, which Commynes pretends to have witnessed to the final breath.

Piero della Francesca, *Portrait of Sigismondo Malatesta*, 1451. The rigor of the composition raises this portrait of a powerful lord to the level of an archetype. (Paris, Louvre.)

Some authors, bent on recounting their personal experiences in a historical perspective worthy of their ancient models, found themselves unable to walk the narrow line between

Urs Graf the Elder, *Standard Bearer*, 1514. The Swiss artist offers his impression—enthusiastic or sarcastic?—of the violent heroes he had chanced to meet in war. (Museum of Basel.)

public and private. Guicciardini wrote three separate books, one on public life, one on the history of his family, and a third on his own life: the *History of Florence*, the *Family Memoirs*, and the *Souvenirs (Ricordanze)*. But in playing the role of historiographer, he composes a portrait of his father without mentioning that he is the man's son, and when he sets out to "preserve the memory of certain things that belong to me personally," he limits himself to recounting the stages of his distinguished career and to awarding himself a satisfactory grade for having been a good son and husband. Thus, he reduces private life to little more than the reputation of a man noted for having been a good actor on the public stage.

Conversely, other writers sought to defend or explain their behavior in order to justify some public action. Jörg Kazmeier, mayor of Munich during that city's troubles in the late fifteenth century, recounts the events of that time only in order to explain his flight. Arnecke, mayor of Hildesheim in the middle of the fifteenth century, defended himself against accusations of incompetence and prevarication. Götz von Berlichingen, who in his eighties recounted his quarter of a century as a reiter from Switzerland to Hesse, sets out to silence certain persistent slanders at the cost of bending the truth about his role in the Peasants' War. His account begins in childhood, during which his leadership qualities were already in evidence: "I often heard my father, my mother, my brothers and sisters, and the domestics who served them say that I was an extraordinary (*wunderbarlich*) lad." With nothing left to lose, the accused launches a counterattack.

Similarly, Benvenuto Cellini, whose glory was equaled only by his disgrace, responds to his detractors by pointing to the prodigies that accompanied selected episodes in his private and public lives. References to various heroes and villains give the narrative its rhythm and color, from the artist's service with Clement VII to his imprisonment in 1556. There is no dearth of signs to herald the boy's extraordinary fate: an ancestor who founded Florence, biblical grandparents, a salamander found near the baby. A mythological prehistory delivers the hero from the confining limits of his own time. This autobiography of extremes abandons the public domain even as it draws upon its author's established reputation. Adroitly combining narrative and symbolism, it distorts or conceals the reality of the private life.

With Cellini in the mid-sixteenth century we have reached the end of an evolution in the manner of telling others about

Marinus van Reymerswaele, *Tax Collectors.* (Munich, Pinachotek.)

oneself. Fiction, an embroidery upon true or unverifiable facts, was the final product of developments in three areas: spiritual introspection, the contemplation of past experience, and family history.

Family Memory

Laymen who had acquired the habit of writing usually saved private papers and records. Notaries and writers employed on public business, merchants at every level from retail trade to great international firms, and even some artisans formed a group that expanded between the thirteenth and sixteenth centuries to include all the notables in every city in Europe. Nobles were not excluded, nor were women, who in some cases took up writing where their fathers or husbands left off. Writing was associated with a concern that one's property be administered well and that one's heirs inherit a capital consisting not only of real estate but also of spiritual precepts and memoirs.

It was difficult to administer or bequeath such spiritual capital if it was not organized. After 1350 an effort was therefore made to catalog and arrange the material in these family archives, stored in shops, offices, and palace studies: contracts, accounts, lists of births and deaths, remedies and potions, correspondence, family trees. Originally these records were

Marinus van Reymerswaele, *Bankers*. Reports, bookkeeping, accounts: medieval society acquired the habit of recording its activities and keeping accurate accounts. (London, National Gallery.)

kept on note cards, reminders which can often be seen stuck on nails in portraits of merchants and artisans. These gradually gave way to notebooks and ledgers in which debits and credits were recorded. It was some time before a distinction was made between commercial and household accounts, and between household records and personal memoirs.

The most complete commercial and financial records were kept first in the cities of central and northern Italy and then, from the end of the fourteenth century, in the cities of Germany as well. The use of special ledgers for accounting purposes led to the elimination from commercial records of all noncommercial information. This gave rise to so-called secret books, private business journals, *mémoriaux* and *ména-*

gers, livres de raison and books of remembrances, in which information of a private nature was preserved so that it might be passed on. Up to the sixteenth century and beyond, the content of such books varied widely, depending on the family's intellectual level. Their organization was quite haphazard, reflecting their origins as mere collections of daily records and notes. Clauses of a marriage contract might follow a list of children's names, or a medication for horses might be included after a record of their sale.

Mercantile practices are apparent in the summaries drawn from the account books and the large amount of space devoted to inventories (for example, of gowns and jewels given by Lucas Rem of Augsburg to his wife or of relics collected by Nicolas Muffel of Nuremberg), as well as in the practice of striking from the list of children the names of those who died young, which were simply crossed out as though they were bad debts or paid-up accounts.

As late as the fifteenth century, less sophisticated merchants continued to record a variety of irrelevant information in their account books, but such astute businessmen as Giovanni Barbarigo of Venice and Anton Tucher of Nuremberg drew a clear line between business books and private books, even though they continued to record in their domestic accounts various land rents and personal notes and anecdotes. Despite its title, the *libro segreto* of Goro Dati of Florence has nothing in common with the accounts of the Alberti firm and, notwithstanding a melancholy preamble on the passage of time, never rises above notes on personal and family business. The *Zibaldone,* "mixed salad," of the Venetian da Canal contains notes on Mediterranean commercial practices similar to those that might be found in any company office, whereas Giovanni Rucellai of Florence used the same title for a compendium of his experiences in business and politics that included reflections on keeping a household and accounts pertaining to the construction of the facade of Santa Maria Novella and the Brancacci Chapel. In the first quarter of the sixteenth century Lucas Rem of Augsburg attempted to organize his material in sections on his own career, money spent on building, and children, yet he retains the misleading title *Tagebuch,* journal.

Such a variety of information incidental to active, professional lives was recorded in these books that we are able to view from many different angles personal concerns that had to be kept carefully hidden from public sight. The book of

Marinus van Reymerswaele, *Portrait of an Unknown* (detail). Public and private papers became a subject for realistic genre painting in the 15th century. (Paris, Porgès Collection.)

the Valori of Florence bore on its cover the words: "This book must not be shown to anyone."

Of necessity each generation made its own selection. In deciding what to pass on to posterity, merchant writers were guided by two main criteria: utility and dignity. Alone in his *camera privata*, the writer insisted on the inalienable and the exemplary, that is, on decisions that either strengthened or weakened the society or the family, perhaps praising an ancestor or confessing the writer's own errors, and on knowledge essential to the family's well-being, whether it be how to drain the cesspool behind the house or how to keep up the family's network of business contacts and allies.

Consider the livre de raison of Etienne Benoist of Limoges, who for twenty years during the first half of the fifteenth century composed a "family memoir" to pass on to his children. In it he recorded births, marriages, and deaths; contracts (which occupy more than a quarter of the book); and spiritual advice, if one can lump together under this single heading prayers, citations from sacred texts (chosen by the entire family), and an undated "political testament" by an ancestor with the same name as the author, a code of conduct already recopied in the previous generation. The content of this testament is essentially private, political events in the Limousin

Domenico Ghirlandaio, *The Sacrifice of Patriarch Zacharias* (detail), 1486–1490. (Florence, Santa Maria Novella, Tornabuoni Chapel.)

being evoked only insofar as they affect the family. Ultimately the purpose of the book is simply to secure the best possible life for the Benoist family in the years to come.

Among both published and unpublished European chronicles, Florence offers the most numerous as well as the richest source material. Family histories were in vogue because the age of "civic humanism" had a taste for the antique; because bloody family rivalries had marked the city's political history; and because leading citizens were rarely tempted by maritime adventure (which in other places so often led to changes in a family's occupation or interrupted the continuity of family records).

Two of the better known texts illustrate different kinds of family memoir, one stressing personal experience, the other long-term memory. Giovanni Morelli was acutely aware of the antiquity of his family and passionately interested in reconstructing its genealogy. But the purpose of his *Ricordi* is primarily educational: *ammaestrare i nostri figluogli* (to instruct our sons). Morelli presents himself in the third person as the very embodiment of moderation and political conformity, an exemplary merchant, whose success is due to his knowledge. "Of average height and weight . . . he did not like anything wicked, in particular anything that might harm the Commune . . . He always strove to live without complications, never opposing those who governed by word or by deed." His was a morality of moderation and abstemiousness, not to mention tax evasion, so that there is little to savor in his account of his private life except the death of the son, a tragedy for both the father and the lineage, on which note these utilitarian memoirs abruptly end.

Donato Velluti belonged to the generation just prior to Morelli's. His sense of continuity and his historical method derive, perhaps, from his profession as jurist. Looking back on his life and career and on his place in that living organism, the family, he speaks of himself in the first person: "It has seemed to me that I have written things too much in praise of myself . . . I did so not for my glory but in order to recall what happened, thinking that it would be pleasant for my future readers to know the how and the why."

Carefully selecting facts and details, he relates them to the complexities of the contemporary scene and the long history of which they form a part. He describes the gout from which he has suffered since 1347, because the affliction has prevented him from accepting public office. He discusses his marriage

Pieter Brueghel the Elder, *The Payment of the Tithe*. (Paris, Museum of Decorative Arts.)

Vittore Carpaccio, *The Miracle of the Relic of the Cross* (detail), 1494. Members of the Tornabuoni family and the Scuola of Saint John the Baptist have been incorporated into the holy story. (Venice, Accademia.)

for the sake of family continuity. He draws connections between his career and various episodes in Florentine politics. His "domestic chronicle," which had increasingly become a narrative of public events, ends as abruptly as Morelli's "souvenirs," with the death at age twenty-two of his son Lamberto, afflicted by a disease that attacked his genitals.

Self-Narration

The private chronicle naturally emphasized the role of the narrator. Whether or not he was tempted to put himself in the limelight, his voice was the one that would be heard, his interpretation the one that would represent the past. After 1400 memoir-writers no longer shrank from incorporating the nonutilitarian and undignified into their writings. Some authors verged on insouciance and the picaresque: the novel was about to be born. Let us continue to concentrate on Florence, this time in the person of Buonaccorso Pitti. In the first third of the fifteenth century he wrote a chronicle in which the genealogical background and childhood of the author are scarcely mentioned. Instead Pitti set out to write an account of his travels: "Now I will give an account of the journeys I made to different parts of the world after the death of my

father." The work is novel in that, once the obligatory prologue is out of the way, it breaks with the traditional model
of personal narrative. The young author is pleased to offer an
unvarnished account of a love affair, the murder of a mason,
and a vendetta conducted against the background of the
Ciompi uprising. His lively pen is guided not by moral virtue
or family honor or the fatuousness of success but by the
flourishing of the individual self. As the years pass and the
author's travels come to an end, the tale becomes rather leaden
with details of commercial success and public office; the chronicle buries the autobiography beneath the weight of the useful
and proper.

The glimpses of nature in Pitti's journal reveal how far
we have come since the time when merchants first began
keeping brief records. Before life could be seen as a romance,
before men could overcome their reluctance to paint themselves in intimate portraits, they had to feel that they owed
more to their own efforts than to either their origin or divine
protection. Pride in success coupled with dialogue between
past and present contributed powerfully to the development
of the new autobiographical literature. Here, however, the
emphasis differed from that of penitential autobiography,
which exhibited the new man looking back upon the disorder
and absurdity of his past. In the new biography the accent
was on youth: on the earnest, often difficult years of childhood
and training. References to family, politics, and spiritual matters were supported by journals and documents. Like the self-
portrait eternally mirroring the artist's gaze, autobiography,
often composed in life's autumn years, bared the creative en-
ergy of the individual conscious of his destiny.

It is the author's constructive regard, sometimes severe,
more often resigned, that gives flavor to those singular tales
of adventure composed in the late fifteenth and early sixteenth
centuries, primarily in German-speaking areas. The *Bildungs-
roman*, or novel of apprenticeship, was destined to a great
future north of the Alps. For example, Johannes Butzbach,
who eventually became prior of Laach in Eifel, accentuated
the harshness of his unhappy childhood in his *Book of Peregrinations* (1505). He sets the tribulations of the orphan martyr
in counterpoint against his tranquil years of retirement; mysterious are the ways of Providence.

Or consider Matthäus Schwarz of Augsburg, who while
still a child, at the age when the young Dürer painted his first
known self-portrait, conceived the ambition of writing an

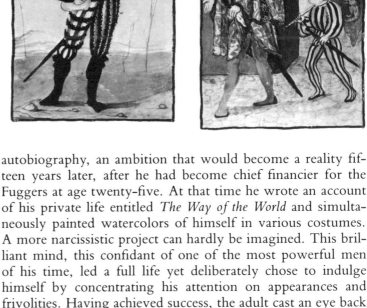

Matthäus Schwarz (1497–1574), *Trachtenbuch*. Three vignettes from among the 137 self-portraits dated and commented on by the author. In 1509, at the age of twelve, Schwarz, who wanted to become a monk at Saint Ulrich in Augsburg, shows himself decorating a private altar in his bedroom. In 1516, aged nineteen, the merchant's son has returned from an educational journey to Italy ostentatiously dressed as a gentleman. In 1547, at age fifty, he wears a sword, collar clasp, and gloves, indicating that he thinks of himself as a prominent citizen; the taffeta (*daphatt*) costume was for a public ceremony in which he must have taken part: the arrival of Emperor Charles V in Augsburg for a meeting of the Reichstag. (Paris, Bibliothèque Nationale.)

autobiography, an ambition that would become a reality fifteen years later, after he had become chief financier for the Fuggers at age twenty-five. At that time he wrote an account of his private life entitled *The Way of the World* and simultaneously painted watercolors of himself in various costumes. A more narcissistic project can hardly be imagined. This brilliant mind, this confidant of one of the most powerful men of his time, led a full life yet deliberately chose to indulge himself by concentrating his attention on appearances and frivolities. Having achieved success, the adult cast an eye back on his childhood. His sentimental and mordant commentary suggests what feelings the men of the Renaissance, after generations of self-absorbed literature, harbored toward their youth.

THE INDIVIDUAL MIRRORED

A Veronese historian conceived the plan of collecting the scattered portraits of 150 identifiable contemporaries of Can Grande della Scala, lord of Verona in the fourteenth century. To take faces of stone and restore their identity: the same immoderate ambition was shared by Michelet—to bring back to life individuals whose actions and passions helped shape the destiny of their society.

Individual portraiture is not practiced by all civilizations in all periods. In the West the revival of portraiture in the middle of the fourteenth century reflected the developing freedom of the individual from social and religious constraints.

And in central and northern Italy portrait art no doubt owed something to the custom of hanging pictures of condemned criminals on the walls in order that the opprobrium of the community might be heaped upon them. Finally, portraiture embodied the respect of families for their ancestors. In Florence (remotely related, perhaps, to Etruscan tradition) likenesses in wax were displayed as devotional objects at Santa Maria Annunziata or preserved in private palaces and brought out for holidays and processions as evidence of the clan's ancient roots and present power.

Royal Portraits

The first individual portraits are so laden with exemplary virtues that it is impossible not to speculate about their truthfulness. It is no accident that the superb knight of Bamberg has been compared with the idealized portrait of Saint Louis. Theoretical visions were embodied in painting, just as images and sensations were encapsulated in written descriptions. Political and religious authorities shrewdly made use of both at a time when hierarchy was embodied in a symbolism of attitude, gesture, and ornament. Even today the forms and colors of Westminster constitute a striking totemic incantation. Charles IV was the first medieval Western sovereign to offer a likeness of himself and his family instead of a portrait of the perfect monarch. (He was also the first emperor to write his own biography, in which he included private events devoid of exemplary value.)

Literary portraits derived from an ancient tradition, which was carried on in the early Middle Ages by narratives retelling the glorious deeds of sovereigns (*res gestae*) and later by chronicles and family histories. The royal portraits of the late Middle Ages, a compromise between conventional representation of the monarchic function and the use of physical details to convey private virtues, are useful for determining when people began to concern themselves with veracity in physical description. Between the twelfth and the sixteenth centuries accurate detail became increasingly important as the rhetoric of kingship lost its celebratory function and adopted the free and easy tone of the chronicler or diplomat.

Emperor Louis the Bavarian (died 1347) was remembered in four eulogies. One simply noted his elegant appearance; the other three added color to the portrait by mentioning that he was slender, solid, well-proportioned, tall, and upright in posture. These details support the judgment of elegance, which

Giovanni Pisano, *Margaret of Brabant, wife of Emperor Henry VII* (d. 1311), fragment of her tomb (1313). An image of the queen but above all a powerful affirmation of her personality. (Genoa, White Palace.)

This miniature, from an illustrated late-15th-century manuscript of Cicero's *Rhetoric*, shows the painter at work. An assistant prepares the colors in small saucers. The patron himself is represented in the canvases that decorate the room. (Ghent, University Library.)

no doubt struck observers even though it was a traditional feature of the princely type. Albertino Mussato's portrait of Louis's predecessor, Henry VII, emphasizes his stature and harmonious proportions. Both descriptions insist on maintaining the proper proportion (*commensurata conformitas*) between parts of the body, a proportion said to be worthy of a statue: in the case of Henry VII it is between the legs and the feet, and in the case of Louis the Bavarian, the shoulders and the neck.

Beyond these general observations, three of the four authors mention the king's hair. Mussato says it was sparse and rather reddish, a detail that would be perfectly plausible were it not contradicted by the other writers and repeated word for word in the portrait of Henry VII mentioned above. His complexion, florid for one author, pink for another, seems to be a figure of rhetoric. The portrait is completed by a few facial details: prominent eyebrows, a strong nose. Mussato adds a few character traits: the king, he says, was enterprising, persevering, courteous, amiable, and gallant. Thus there is agreement about the monarch's overall appearance, disagreement about the details, and on the whole an overabundance of adjectives that casts doubt on the portrait. All that is left is the image of elegance, the memory of a physical presence, summed up in Heinrich Rebdorf's witticism: Why can't a king look like one's image of a king?

For the Scholastics, every visible form revealed the invisible; the created world deciphered itself. The rhythms of architecture, the proportions of the human body, the structure of society—all were in harmony, and the highest expression of that harmony was the person of the monarch. Charged with a divine mission, the royal personage was supposed to conform in appearance, gesture, and voice to the image of his office, an image recognized by all Christians. To know his rank it was enough to set eyes on him. Joan of Arc finds Charles VII in the crowded hall of Chinon. That the king's appearance should be worthy of his office was part of the natural order of things. "Majesty was evident in his face," said Poggio of old Sigismund, entering Rome for his coronation. According to Johannes Grünbeck, Frederick III, whose broad shoulders did not conceal his small size (*statura plus quam mediocri*), had worked since childhood to compose his appearance; all observers were struck by the gravity of his features and by his amiable reserve. His long face, rather squat body, shortness, and timidity were natural defects that Frederick somehow turned to his advantage, proving that a sovereign's behavior could compensate for the graces nature had denied him. More than other men, the king, a public person, constructed his own image.

In describing Emperor Maximilian, the Viennese humanist Cuspinian resorted to the scholastic metaphor of the foursquare king (*statura quadrata, figura quadrata*), built like a church and resplendent with divine majesty. Vitruvius had already established an analogy between the perfection of the human body and that of architecture. Beauty and form (*forma-formosus*) were often linked in scholastic thinking about creation and, later, in the numerological speculations of the geometers

Andrea della Robbia, *Portrait of an Adolescent*, terra-cotta (above). Donatello, *Anonymous Bust*, bronze (below). These may have been members of the Medici family. (Florence, Bargello.)

Peter Parler and his team of sculptors (1375–1385), *Portrait of Emperor Charles IV*, one of twenty-one dynastic statues on the triforium of Saint Guy's Cathedral, Prague.

and artists of the Renaissance. Applied to the person of the prince, this symbolism illuminated both physical and moral qualities. Just as stained glass filtered the divine light and made it radiant, so did the gaze of Maximilian dazzle with its brilliance. Johannes Grünbeck, vanquished by the emperor's sparkling eyes, by his almost sidereal power, thus evoked the charm to which men and women alike succumbed.

An astonishing tale of seduction shows how susceptible the emperor was to the physical qualities of others. With the help of Duke Frederick of Saxony, the young Count von Zimmern used his physical appearance to win from the emperor, in 1497, the restitution of land that had once belonged to his family: "Sire Wernher, who knew how benevolent and loyal the prince-elector was, did himself up in the most elegant possible manner and, since he was a handsome man, well formed in face, body, and figure, he awaited the king's arrival along with the other counts and lords. And after supper, when the princes' dance was over, Sire Wernher put himself forward, and that was all it took for the emperor to notice him several times and to feel from his appearance a particular pleasure; and he asked Duke Frederick, who had done his utmost to remain close to the king, who this person was." Nothing could be denied to beauty.

Nevertheless, some late medieval sovereigns were so common-looking or unattractive that the portraitists refused to make a virtue of their defects and instead heaped criticism upon their heads. The embarrassment of the chroniclers at the sight of ugliness offers proof by contradiction that their more flattering portraits are truthful. Small stature was the primary complaint: "though he was small" (*etsu oarvys statyra*), said Thomas Ebendorfer of Charles IV. After meeting the sovereign, Matteo Villani painted this unflattering portrait: the king, he said, was of mediocre stature, particularly for a German, almost a hunchback, with a neck and face that thrust out ahead of his body. He had black hair, large cheekbones, protruding eyes, and a bald head. The Prague bust confirms the truth of this portrait. On this foreign observer the magic of the royal presence was apparently unavailing, and we hear details of royal behavior that do not sit well with the stereotypes of sovereign majesty: during public audiences the emperor whittled a stick with a knife without once looking at the supplicants who came before him. We sense a reticence to report attitudes that flagrantly flouted the conventions. Ebendorfer, the king's biographer, deplores the fact that the monarch dressed in short clothes, like a pauper (*formam pauperum exprimebat*).

On the whole, the realism of the description is all the more physical when the author cannot sum up the image of royal majesty in a word. The accumulation of accurate detail takes the place of the first impression. Whenever the sense of a perfect harmony (*congruentia*) underlies the palpable reality, whenever the private person is able to assume without apparent effort the public role, then the overall tone of the royal portrait seems truer than its accumulated detail. It satisfies the spirit even if it fails to assuage all curiosity. In literature as well as painting realism was presumably reality without spirit, mere juxtaposition of details without a guiding idea.

What changed toward the end of the Middle Ages was the method of analyzing the real, the tools and the vocabulary: physicians practiced dissection, everyone took frequent confession, private correspondence was in vogue, mirrors were commonplace, oil painting had come into fashion. But multiple viewpoints, virtuosity in imitation, and anatomical accuracy alone were not enough to enable the artist to penetrate to the private individual, any more than squares of colored glass were enough to make a mosaic.

Fifteenth-century Flemish painting is fascinating not simply because of its realistic portrayal of faces and domestic scenes but because it is inspired by an idea, a symbolic vision. The spectator, who stands before the smooth surface of a portrait, is expected to discover its key, to reconstruct the individual portrayed and render up his secret.

Donors and Heroes

Late medieval painting and sculpture allow us to compare sources and verify the accuracy of descriptions. Instinctively, we tend to place greater trust in the painter than in the chronicler. Yet painting was shaped in part by social convention and the intentions of the person commissioning the work. If we use portraits as sources in the history of private life, we must ascertain the limits of their reliability. For the portrait placed the private man in the public eye; it immortalized a pose, usually depicting some prominent personage rather awkwardly decked out in his Sunday best. Late medieval Europe was awash with portraits, not least in churches and family chapels, where pictures of donors and their families threatened to drive out the Madonna and Child and all the saints. Ap-

Sandro Botticelli, *Portrait of Lucrezia Tornabuoni* (Frankfurt, Städtische Galerie.)

The fresco showing the draper at work draws upon the imagery of the trades. The tax collector wanted to leave behind memory of his appearance, his specialized skills, and his happy marriage. The portraits of Lucrezia Tornabuoni and Barent van Orley not only perpetuate fascinating faces but illustrate the virtuosity of Botticelli and Dürer in the representation of character. Painted in profile, with impassive features and striking dress, the wife of the Florentine banker achieves the inaccessible beauty of a goddess. The official painting of the governor of the Netherlands has the earnest grace and urbanity that Dürer believed appropriate to the genre.

Drapers at Work, a fresco from Issogne Castle (Val d'Aosta), 15th century.

parently there was something reassuring about being physically present in sacred surroundings. Chancellor Rolin does not seem surprised to find the Virgin posing in the studio of Saint Luke; he quite properly falls to his knees.

In the meantime, enthusiasm for things ancient led to renewed interest in the sharply chiseled profile, which, from Piero della Francesca to Uccello, emphasized and in some cases idealized the impassive features of the aristocratic hero or his lady. The spirit in which such commissions were executed, the manner adopted to immortalize a face and a name, are matters for a history of forms and fashions and perhaps, in the case of retables, for a social history of representations.

We learn more about individuals by concentrating on changes of two kinds that took place in the fifteenth centuries in the Low Countries as well as in Italy and the cities of the Empire. First, artists began to paint patrons engaged in their professional activities as goldsmiths, moneychangers, businessmen, or geometers. Although the portrait is still carefully staged, the patron's pride in personal success, coupled with the artist's excitement at developing a new genre of painting, combined to create a new illusion of realism. The likeness of a face stands out against a familiar background from which we gain valuable information about the work environment, interior decoration, and shop tools. The theme of intimate space, the room in which the humanist's thoughts take wing

Marinus van Reymerswaele,
The Tax Collector.
(Valenciennes Museum.)

Albrecht Dürer, *Portrait of
Barent van Orley*, 1521.
(Dresden, Gemäldegalerie.)

above inkwell and library, was finally treated for its own sake (using, as pretext, the portrait of Saint Jerome) by Carpaccio, Dürer, and many others.

Some paintings delved even further into the interior, focusing on the family quarters rather than the shop. Study of the portraits of bourgeois notables would no doubt reveal that family pride outweighed professional pride the moment social success was achieved. No longer depicted exclusively on retables, kneeling and ordered by rank, families now formed a tranquil circle in which age, character, and individual aptitudes subtly modifed the harmony that was considered an essential feature of the style. Culminating the evolution of a genre, Konrad Rehlinger of Augsburg commissioned the painter Bernhard Strigel to paint his eight living children and also to show, through an opening in the wall onto a heavenly scene, those siblings who had died young (see illustration facing the start of this section). This is a perfectly abstract scene, nothing less than an embodiment of part of the family tree.

In some paintings family feeling is the main subject, to the point where all trace of ambient decor is eliminated. Francesco Sassetti, an agent of the Medici, had himself painted by Ghirlandaio, without any social affectation in his costume or pose, alone with his son Teodoro II. The child looks up con-

Expressions and Secrets

Two paintings by Domenico Ghirlandaio. Above, *Portrait of Francesco Sassetti and His Son Teodoro.* (New York, Jules S. Bache Collection.) Below, *Portrait of an Elderly Man with His Son.* (Paris, Louvre.)

fidently at his father, who has eyes only for the boy. The pose is as studied as a photographer's portrait might be today. There is no wink of the eye toward the spectator, and we have no way of interfering in the dialogue between father and son. In another portrait the impression of harmony (*congruentia*) between father and son is not disturbed by the realism of the veinous, warty nose, which the feeling transcends. The Franciscan air of bareness must be seen in light of the serene gravity of the will that Sassetti drafted in 1488, two years before his death. It is important to stress that this painting is the product of a commission; the intimist portrait, painted at a time when the Florentine banker was responsible for the diastrous finances of the House of Medici, assumes the character of a manifesto.

The second change that affected European painting in the fifteenth century was the advent of the front or three-quarter view in portraiture, coupled with the elimination of picturesque backgrounds; painting relied instead on sharp contrasts or velvety blacks, as everything superfluous was eliminated from the canvas, leaving only a few signs (a coat of arms or a motto) and a few mute objects (a book, a flower, or a paternoster). The subject stared out at the spectator: think of the incisive gaze in the portrait of a man by Memling that hangs in the Accademia at Venice; or the humble, gentle gaze of Van Eyck's man with a carnation; or the implacable gaze of the condottiere Antonello da Messina; or the almost wild-eyed stare of Oswolt Krel as painted by Dürer. At a time when the *ars moriendi* and *danse macabre* were drawing attention to the body's decay, to its definitive separation from the soul at death, the individual portrait reaped the benefits of a mutation in the painter's technique, which since Van Eyck had conferred previously unparalleled depth and transparency on the painted gaze. The use of oil paint and surface effects made it possible to make the pupil of the eye shine like a mirror, a luminous presence that inhabited the portrait as the soul inhabits the body. When Alberti said that painting was a "transparent window," he was complimenting a mere surface that could somehow reveal depth. Fifteenth-century portraits take us into an imaginary space, an inner space, a vertiginous space born of the encounter between the painter and his model and destined to recreate in every spectator an image of that encounter.

In a climate favorable to enigma, portraits were not innocent; they said more by saying less, adopting the rhetoric

of the unadorned. In the simplest cases an object or two was
enough to reveal the secret: a missal, a pair of embroidered
initials, a letter of exchange. But how can we go beyond "this
small pile of foolish things"? The person who was cannot be
summed up in a snapshot with accessories; the unsaid is no
less important in painting than in literature.

At a somewhat higher level of artifice, concern for personal virtues and personal distinction gave rise to more subtle
and exciting compositions, such as Carpaccio's great portrait
of Francesco Maria della Rovere, duke of Urbino, in which
the hero stands out against a forest of signs. Organized like a
heraldic puzzle, the picture space seems to have sprung fully
armed from the thoughts and nightmares of the sweet-faced
adolescent knight.

Mirrors

A further dimension of mystery was introduced into
painting by the invention of the self-portrait. It is impossible
to count the number of painters who, like master masons
carving the keystone of an arch, succumbed to the temptation
to leave a record of what they looked like. At first they slipped
portraits of themselves into groups of worshipers in their
paintings: Hans Memling stands, a curious onlooker, behind
the retable of Sir John Donne, and Botticelli painted himself
in the proud posture of one of the powerful men of Florence
with whom he spent his time. Later, ceding to the imperious
impulse to paint themselves and forgetting their patrons altogether, some painters produced solitary self-portraits. The
power of the self-portrait over the spectator comes from the
fact that the painter's relation to his own image incorporates
the mirror into the field of transparency; with a gaze and a
few signs the self-portrait creates a novel of self.

Albrecht Dürer painted himself at least eight times. By
the age of fourteen he was already peering intently into his
mirror. His three self-portraits in oil are milestones in the
history of introspection that bridge the divide between the
Middle Ages and the Renaissance. The *Portrait with Holly*,
which hangs in the Louvre, dates from 1493; it was painted
while the artist was working in Basel, engraving the frontispiece to the *Letters* of Saint Jerome. The young man, whose
elbows rest on the base of the frame (Alberti's "transparent
window"), holds in his hand the sprig of holly from which
the work takes its name. The grave look and neutral background focus attention on the symbolic plant and the thoughts

Albrecht Dürer, *Portrait of Oswolt Krel*, 1499. (Munich, Pinachotek.)

Two self-portraits by Albrecht Dürer. Left, *Portrait with Holly*, 1493. (Paris, Louvre.) Right, *Portrait*, 1498. (Madrid, Prado.)

Albrecht Dürer, *Self-Portrait*, 1500. (Munich, Pinachotek.)

it arouses. It is impossible to decide which of two possible interpretations is correct. One holds that Dürer, who would marry the following year (1494), portrayed himself holding a symbol of marital fidelity (*Männestreue*). The other is based on the fact that holly in Greek is *dypsakos*, meaning thirsty, hence that the young man of twenty-two depicted in the painting is "thirsty" for the truth. The legend, which reads *My sach di gat/als es oben schtat* (My affairs stand as the things above), is of no great help in settling the matter.

A major milestone was passed in 1498 with Dürer's second self-portrait in oil, which hangs in the Prado. In Venice the painter had discovered not only light and color but also Mantegna and the ancient style of draftsmanship. He invented the independent landscape and the atmospheric watercolor. And since the *Apocalypse with Figures* he had achieved renown throughout Europe. Without arrogance but certain of his worth, the artist hurled down a challenge to the milieu of artisans and merchants to which he belonged: he proudly insisted that he be granted a status in society worthy of his exalted mission. From Venice in 1506 he wrote his friend

Willibald Pirckheimer: "Here I am somebody; at home I am a parasite" (*Hier bin ich her, daheim ein schmarotzer*). Hence the elegance of the pose, the insolent provocation of the attire, and the Leonardesque *veduta,* which expresses an accord between the secrets of the individual and the mysteries of nature.

The final portrait is striking for its rigorously frontal pose with raised right hand and for its air of mystical fervor. Regardless of whether it was painted in 1500 or 1518, the Munich portrait clearly accentuates the painter's resemblance to the figure of Christ. Does the painting connote an inward spiritual reform, or is it a declaration of the creative power of the artist, which emanates from the creative power of God? In either case Dürer's life henceforth glowed with the light of spirituality, as is evidenced by the fervent character of his painting and intimate writing and by the public testament that accompanied his gift to the city of Nuremberg of his last monumental work, the *Four Apostles.*

By the late Middle Ages it is easier to know people as individuals, whether they are portrayed by others or yield themselves up to our regard. Perhaps there was even a new idea afoot in Europe: an idea of individuality, by which I mean that a few groups of cultivated, high-ranking individuals showed greater awareness than their ancestors of the fragile value of their personal lives.

Making a virtue of what previously would have been considered a want of reserve, they dared to exalt whatever was singular in themselves. To that end, they developed new means of expression, which help us discover who they were. We possess public and, increasingly, private sources of information about urban society in the late Middle Ages with which we can construct snapshots of individuals as they saw themselves or were seen by their contemporaries.

Conjugal love is not surprising, but the invention of the double portrait of the married couple is: on one side husband and wife are shown in grace, with all their attractions intact, and on the other in the horrid putrefaction of death. Realism in physical description is striking for its lack of moral overtones (derived from the tradition of the clinic); it reflects both medical knowledge and a new intimacy in man's relation to his body. One of Dürer's last self-portraits shows him anxiously and without modesty staring at the image of his worn body. Disease justifies this further step toward intimacy.

Candor

Albrecht Dürer, *Self-Portrait,* 1512. Casting aside ornamentation and composition, Dürer pursues his investigation: the intense truthful stare peers out of the somber mirror. (Weimar, Castle Museum.)

THE BODY CLOTHED

In one of Sercambi's novellas we read of a furrier from Lucca who goes to a public bath and removes all his clothing, whereupon he is seized with panic at the idea of losing his identity in the crowd of anonymous bodies. He therefore affixes a straw cross to his right shoulder and clings to it as to a buoy. But the cross comes loose and is grabbed by his neighbor, who says, "Now I am you; begone, you are dead!" The furrier, out of his wits, is convinced that he has died.

Customs and Society

Black humor is a constant of all ages, as is the man without qualities who can be killed by a word. The Tuscan fable reminds us of the tenuousness of a man's professional and social identity, even in a society in which individual success was exalted in every possible way. A man sheds his identity with his clothing because the social man is a man in disguise.

Sercambi was clever in choosing a furrier for his character because the wearing of fur was a mark of distinction. In an ordered society the naked man is considered wild or an outcast by those who wear clothes. Nudity, moreover, brings a man closer to the natural state of the savage, who lurks in dreams and in the forests of desire. At the outer limits of fable we encounter social subversion: society was a fragile thing, resting

Painting on a wedding chest. (Venice, Correr Museum.)

as it did on a consensus embodied in individual appearance. One of the first disciples of Francis of Assisi, Brother Genieve, son of a fabric merchant, caused a scandal when he appeared naked in the square of Viterbo.

The societies of the late Middle Ages remained loyal to the trifunctional schema but made it more complex and less legible. Urban economic growth had created innumerable new social strata between the "workers" and the "magnates." The richest producers were in a position to wield the sword in their own defense and felt closer to the ruling powers than to the subjugated labor force. Ambition and social mobility blurred clear-cut social distinctions. Statutes governing the hierarchy of professions in different cities did not always agree. In fourteenth-century Florence the Arti played a key role in defining political and social status; in Venice they played no role at all. Each city's self-image reflected the peculiarities of its history. Some flexibility was essential to the common good and was both appreciated and exploited by the ruling groups. By the end of the fourteenth century, however, the contours of the dominant classes had become fairly fixed in most self-governing European cities.

Dress was one of the necessary social proprieties. In assemblies and processions each segment of the populace had its own assigned role and place and could be identified by the nature and color of the clothing it wore. Costume therefore became a major issue as economic change found itself impeded by the established political order. In the name of the "common good," regulations attempted to prohibit any manifestation of private arrogance. Innumerable cities passed sumptuary laws in the fourteenth and fifteenth centuries. As long as each individual remained in the place and rank ascribed to him by Providence, the harmony of the body social was not threatened; God, the theory went, had established an intangible order of which costume was merely the expression. So much is clear from the volume published in the mid–sixteenth century along with engravings by Jost Ammann of Augsburg of the clothing worn by people in various professions—a picturesque sociology, based on appearances.

For generations the merchant had been recognized by his bearing, the Venetian senator by his black costume, the Jew by his star, and the prostitute by her yellow dress. A late-fourteenth-century Venetian court document evokes a poor girl held in a hovel who is saved from being condemned to a

Pisanello, *Saint George*. The social man is a man in costume. (London, National Gallery.)

Jost Amman, engravings for *De omnibus artibus*, 1574. A portrait gallery of the various trades, with the shop as setting. The client in the spectacles shop wears clothing appropriate to his age. The maker of cuirasses and other leather goods is dressed in the style of the military men who come to call on him. (Paris, Bibliothèque Nationale.)

life of prostitution because of the screams she lets out when the shameful garb of that trade is handed to her.

For both prostitutes and kings dress was little more than a sign of social function, with some variations. Was private life more than the hidden face of public appearances? Sooner or later the public man set aside his public disguise; his private life was his routine, which we glimpse only by chance. But if the poor man had only a private life, what can his clothing tell us about what it was like, since apart from holidays he wore only work clothes? Outdoor work did not lend itself to intimacy. And as for bed, both the peasant and the bourgeois slept naked.

Fortunately there is another way to look at clothing. Ignoring society's self-image as reflected in its garments, we can look directly at the contents of the wardrobe as revealed by inventories and account books. Princely wardrobes are not very informative. It is sometimes difficult to distinguish between formal and everyday costumes. Here the more common items have undoubtedly disappeared, and the difference between the everyday item and the formal finery had to do less with the quality of the fabric than with the presence or absence of embroidered sleeves, pearled wimples, elaborate hairpieces, and ceremonial cloaks. But the wardrobes of the bourgeoisie and peasantry can tell us a great deal that we were unable to discern in painting or literature. The more or less worn effects of the deceased were lined up in front of the notary and succinctly described: "a pair of old shoes; two hoods, one of them old." An appraising glance quickly revealed which items were still serviceable or could be made to seem so. Private account books record not only a description of the item but also its price. With such information we can evaluate how much was spent on fabric, how much on ornament, and how much on labor, and we can trace the replacement of items as they wore out as well as estimate the proportion of the family budget spent on clothing.

Ethnographers who have studied societies in which sexual characteristics are accentuated and bodies decorated rather than covered teach us that the functional convenience of clothing is not necessarily its primary quality. Among the poor, however, items of protection against the rain and cold occupy a prominent place in fourteenth- and fifteenth-century inventories: hat and hide served their purpose.

Peasant Costume. Estate inventories from across Europe provide a monotonous image of the minimum peasant wardrobe. F. Piponnier has studied inventories from Burgundian villages in the second half of the fourteenth century: the basic items were a tunic, a fur-lined coat, and a hat. When one of these items was missing, it was usually because it went to pay the burial costs. There was little distinction between male and female clothing: the woman's dress was the equivalent of the man's tunic or surcoat. In Tuscany in this same period a woman's wardrobe consisted of two tunics, worn one on top of the other, and a coat. The coat was either a hide turned inside out or a corset lined with rabbit. (The wealthier peasant's coat was lined with cat fur instead of rabbit.) To complete the costume, the peasant wore a fabric hood (and men wore breeches). As for underclothing, men and women wore chemises, and men, long underpants. Undergarments were made of coarse woolen cloth, a fabric of mediocre quality but fairly warm; men's were usually natural colored or beige, women's were blue. Men's hoods were usually blue, women's, red (though sometimes blue or white). Wealth in rural society took the form of extra items of clothing and decoration, which could be obtained from itinerant merchants. (One "irregular"

Heinrich Gross, *Saint Nicholas' Mine at Croix-aux-Mines (Vosges)*, first half of the 16th century. This drawing, last of a series of twenty-five, shows the miners, dressed in work clothes with hoods and leather protectors, being paid for their services. The accountant, the judge, and the overseer stand out from the crowd of workers by their dress, bearing, and armament. (Paris, School of Fine Arts, Masson Collection.)

The Month of July: Departure for a Hunt with Falcon (detail). Fresco of Wenceslaus, 15th century. Plucked from the shadows by the artist is the peasant charged with making preparations for the hunt. (Trent, Good Advice Castle, Eagle Tower.)

kept five hats in her wardrobe.) Archaeological excavations at Rougiers, Dracy, and Brandes have turned up silver belt buckles and aglets, metal purse clasps, and hoods with buttons. Jewelry, apart from a few rings, is rare. Gloves created a sensation: in one fabliau a young peasant uses them as an enticement when he goes courting.

Haves and Have-Nots. Clothing was just as limited in the lower strata of urban society. The most systematic and sophisticated studies of clothing have focused on the slightly better-off segments of the urban population, tracing the sale of fabrics or evaluating the efficacy of sumptuary laws. In 1401 the bourgeois of Bologna were given two days to submit any gowns they possessed to a commission charged with enforcing a law regulating luxury in clothing; 210 garments were seized, and the documents that describe them permit us to judge what was considered excessive. Extreme variety of ornament was no longer tolerated: silver stars; gold fringes and chains; embroidered rays, leaves, and animals; fur collars and sleeves; bright colors that required the use of cochineal or antimony dyes; and pearls and other gemstones were prohibited. In some cases we can estimate separately the value of fabric, labor, and ornament in the price of a garment. For example, in Florence, in 1363, Simone Peruzzi gave his wife a sturdy tunic whose fabric accounted for only 30 percent of its total cost; the silver buttons, vair lining, and gold stripes cost the equivalent of one hundred and forty days of a mason's wages. Equally scandalous, assuming that the same norms apply, was the wedding gown made for a Strozzi daughter in 1447, which cost the equivalent of five hundred days of a skilled laborer's wages; a garland made of two hundred peacock tail feathers, shimmering bits of gold, and pearls, all covered with flowers and gilt leaves, cost 212 livres—one-third of the total. But at the height of their glory the Peruzzi and Strozzi were not subject to such restrictions. After all, the wardrobe of Lady Spinelli, née Gherardini, contained some twenty items valued at 500 florins in 1380, a trifle compared with the 50,000 florins left by her husband when he died—the equivalent of eight to ten years of a mason's labor.

The Economics of Appearance. The figures just cited give some idea of the economic dimensions of a social fact. They measure the distance that separated the planet of the rich, about which we know a little bit, from that of the poor, about which we know even less. The significance of everyday life was different in these two worlds; in one, clothing was a work of art, in the other, an item of utility. Moreover, we cannot write the history of dress without taking account of social change. In Florence a contemporary of Dante would have invested far less in his appearance than his granddaughter would have done. Leaving aside changes in culture and attitude, the Florentine market simply did not offer the same diversity of fabrics and temptations before 1300 as it did after 1400.

Guardianship accounts from Florence from the last third of the thirteenth century reveal that the mother of the family in question dressed in gowns of inexpensive fabric, while the boys wore clothes of better-quality fabric, warm *stanfort* for winter and vermilion serge from Caen for summer. Garments were seldom replaced. In four years the mother bought only three new items—less than two complete sets of clothing.

Similar frugality is revealed in the advice contained in the *Ménagier de Paris* and in the private accounts of Venetian, Franconian, and Hanseatic bourgeois from the fourteenth and fifteenth centuries. In addition to regular outlays, we read of occasional extra expenses such as marriages: the wedding ceremony, gifts, and dowries required investments in fabric, ornament, and jewelry. Lucas Rem of Augsburg carefully recorded in a special section of his *Tagebuch* the price of black cloth from Lindau along with brown velvet and gray satin, all used in his wedding suit, as well as the costs of the rubies, diamond, and sapphire that he gave his wife and the money spent on the reception.

Other expenses were incurred when a son was sent away to college or apprenticeship in a distant city. He needed clothes of good, solid material and comfortable shoes. Nothing wore out more quickly than shoes; the budget of Anton Tucher of Nuremberg from the early sixteenth century shows that new soles were needed every few months as the children grew. The commissioning of a new suit for a child of ten just starting school was an event in the life of a family, and children long remembered having to wear clothes that were too long or too short or no longer in fashion. Recollecting his past, Hans von Weinsberg of Cologne evokes the young man who left his parents' home in 1531 to go to boarding school at Emmerich: "My father had a robe made for me of gray fabric with many folds, white shorts, and high boots, and on my head someone

Vittore Carpaccio, *Portrait of Francesco Maria della Rovere, Duke of Urbino* (detail), 1510. This is the first known Italian portrait of a man standing. This dreamy but determined young man is the nephew of Pope Julius II, whose troops he commanded in Romagna. The duke is surrounded by personal emblems and genealogical signs. The iris and the lily evoke the Virgin, whose name he bears; the leaves of the British oak or robur (*rovere*) that have sprouted behind him underscore his identity and his recapture of the duchy from Cesare Borgia. (Lugano, Thyssen-Bornemisza Collection.)

placed a black hat. That was what I wore as long as I remained at Emmerich, and better clothes would have been of no use to me, since the pupils there sat not on benches but on the floor. In addition, I had a few light summer garments, but eventually they became too small." Looking back, the mature adult approves his father's decision, even if the adolescent at the time gave forth a rather understandable sigh at having to dress in gray. The primary function of clothing was to keep the wearer warm. The history of everyday dress turns on this banality as well as on the careful calculation of costs and the subsequent sighs of pleasure or regret. Public dress is another story, one in which luxury, fashion, taste, and superfluity all play a role.

Dress and Behavior

Whether sumptuous or simply convenient, clothing was an intimate matter, as evidenced by the space devoted to it in the records of expenses and by the way it helped to shape the individual's self-image at the end of the Middle Ages. But we must return to the question of clothing as a sign, for it was more than simply a mark of social rank. Clothing is more than fabric and ornament; it affects behavior, determines it or shows it off. It indicates the stages of life and helps shape the personality. And it underscores the difference between the sexes.

Ostentation. There was little difference in dress between working men and women of the late Middle Ages. At the other extreme, the immobile silhouettes of powerful public figures were shrouded in folds of heavy fabrics lined with precious furs. In between, fashion influenced the choice of fabric and cut. Fashions became more short-lived and tyrannical owing to increased economic mobility and diminished access to privileged castes and circles at court as well as in the city. Styles became increasingly improbable. The structure of the body was revealed or emphasized by padding; the form-fitting curve was combined with folds, blouses, frills, and slashes. Nervous, violent, sophisticated fashion emphasized breasts and other features by exposing or suggesting them. Young clergymen exhibited their muscles and limbs, aiming to look like Saint George or King Arthur's knights rather than priests. It is quite possible that changes in armor, with its articulated surfaces and joints, helped disclose the structure of the male body and contributed to some of the more fantastic refinements in dress.

After the mid-fifteenth century engravings made known throughout Europe the image of the amorous youth who made of the conquest of a lady an enterprise as provocative as a military adventure.

In the presence of these arrogant fops, sure of their charms, whose images survive in portraits from Pisanello to Dürer, young women of good society maintained their reserve. For a long time the ideal woman had been slender, but the late Middle Ages preferred a fuller figure. Nevertheless, female fashion, which loosely followed the evolution of male dress, limited itself to indicating the waistline, more or less daringly baring the shoulders, and either hiding or revealing the hair and a hint of breast. Wimple, hennin, handkerchiefs, and lace stood as delicate and deceptive defenses between the public and the intimate. Seductive as a woman might be, she had best be discreet in her behavior, as recommended by La Tour Landry in his treatise on the education of young girls.

Travel often revealed truths that remained invisible at home. Petrarch, visiting Cologne in 1333, described the disturbing simplicity and freshness of a procession of women engaged in some incomprehensible rite along the banks of the Rhine: "What shapes!" he wrote from Lyons to his friend Cardinal Giovanni Colonna, "What poses! [*Que forma! quis habitus!*] Their heads garlanded with fragrant herbs, their sleeves raised above the elbow, they dipped their white hands and arms into the current, murmuring in their own language a sweet cantilena." Petrarch was surprised by such a harmonious sight "so far from civilization," that is, far from the sophisticated and perverse images current in the freer, more agile society of the Mediterranean. Nevertheless, young Florentines were raised with the same concern for modesty and dignity as their contemporaries in France and the Empire, to judge by the tone of private correspondence or by the homilies of Saint Antonino, archbishop of Florence in the middle of the fifteenth century. Throughout Europe the dress and behavior of married and unmarried women were regulated by a similar sense of propriety.

Sex and Age. Sumptuary laws were directed primarily at ostentatious excess in female clothing, reflecting a deep-rooted misogyny on the part of medieval lawmakers as well as a patriarchal view of relations between the sexes. In 1416 Poggio described a group of young Swiss beauties whom he glimpsed

Albrecht Dürer, *A Peasant and His Wife* (above). Heinrich Aldegrever, *Couple* (below). Two couples from the human comedy: aristocrats and peasants. Although distinguished by their dress, the peasants are hardly wretched. (Paris, Bibliothèque Nationale.)

near Zurich as ripe for marriage. A young girl was a form of capital, and as a matter of sound investment it was best to marry her to a man of settled age, perhaps even a graybeard. Regulations aimed at curtailing the display of luxury and the size of dowries were intended in part to restrain matrimonial competition, the stakes of which risked spiraling out of control.

The married bourgeois buried his bachelor life in his diary, throwing a somber cloak over the follies of his youth; needless to say, he would never tolerate a wife who dressed up or spoke up in private. According to Sassetti, the "perfect merchant" should have a face comely yet grave; he should dress in good taste and study his bearing and gestures. The "perfect courtier," precursor of the seventeenth-century *honnête homme*, composed his behavior with great care; clothing played an important role. As depicted by Baldassare Castiglione, who recorded dialogue in the entourage of Lorenzo the Magnificent, the man of taste combined respect for the proprieties with a carefully calculated elegance. As a means of social discrimination, clothing enabled individuals to appear in a manner befitting their age. Fashion was appropriate to youth, a period of flamboyance between the gray of childhood and the paler colors of maturity and old age.

During the years of youth and apprenticeship clothing

Perugino, *Scenes from the Life of Saint Bernardine* (detail), 1473. Note the contrast between the terrifying men at arms and the tranquil confidence of the handsome young men. (Perugia, National Gallery of Umbria.)

was a means of expressing personal feelings. The use of coded details of dress to indicate tastes, intentions, and desires was hardly an exclusive practice of the Middle Ages; following fashion has always been a way of conforming while at the same time distinguishing oneself from others. But several factors in the late Middle Ages reinforced the individual's need for distinction: the controlling power of the state, which turned free men into subjects; the gradual shutting off of access to institutions, forcing individuals to join private circles; and the continuing favor enjoyed by chivalric romance, which made King Arthur and his peers models for crowned heads from Charles VI to Charles VIII. For wellborn youths the invention of self involved an apprenticeship in ceremony and symbolism: under Charles VI personal fashions born at the court of France served as counterpoint to the increasingly strict rules of etiquette.

Signs and Codes

Groups of companions and allies identifed themselves by means of distinctive insignia, signs of recognition derived from their military, political, and domestic counterparts: coats of arms, heraldic devices, and liveries. The genealogical researches of Tuscan notables were in some cases based on such indices, and the memoir of Georg von Ehingen, a mid-fifteenth-century Franconian knight, describes the patient reconstitution of his family's patrimony from various crosses, coats of arms, and escutcheons scattered across the countryside from the Main to the Danube. In the late Middle Ages signs proliferated as society formed itself into regiments. Rhenish, Hanseatic, and Saxon notables joined "clubs" or *Stuben*; young patricians in Italy joined companies like the Venetian *Calza*, which Carpaccio indicated by its costume; and people everywhere joined confraternities, which marched in procession wearing cowls and carrying candles of many different colors. Even at public games like the *Schembartlaufen* in Nuremberg and the *Palio* in Siena, crowds of people formed images of heraldic figures and performed codified rituals. Orders of lay knights were formed throughout Europe from the second quarter of the fourteenth century on. Members identified themselves by wearing a cross, ribbon, or cloak, indicating that they had freely taken a vow to observe the discipline of the order.

It became customary for princes to distribute uniform items of clothing every year, thereby both demonstrating their

Albrecht Dürer, *Coats of Arms.* (Paris, Bibliothèque Nationale.)

Painted wooden table,
15th century. (Paris,
Cluny Museum.)

generosity and identifying their subjects by a standard set of insignia and colors. Books of uniforms issued by the houses of Saxony and Bavaria in the late fifteenth and early sixteenth century have survived. Dukes were fond of showing off crowds of dependents wearing their insignia; they added new details to their liveries periodically to keep them up to date. The imperial tradition had bourgeois emulators: the House of Fugger distributed uniforms to all its personnel, red for marriages and black for funerals of heads of the firm.

Apprenticeship in Dress. If fashions in dress were a coded system, people had to learn to read the code in order to avoid gaffes and make allusions comprehensible. Two mid-fifteenth-century French texts in which training in the proper way to dress forms an essential part of a youth's education are the work of men of action, familiar with the strategy of signs: Jean de Bueil's *Le Jouvencel* and Antoine de La Sale's *Jehan de Saintré.* The latter describes a thirteen-year-old boy who is aided by a noble lady in inventing his own system of recognition. The atmosphere of the novel is one of education in the ways of courtesy and love, and the young man painstakingly constructs the public expression of his intimate feelings. When asked about his accoutrements by the lady, the boy, Saintré, describes the coat of arms he has forged for himself: "And there is one of black damask inlaid with silver thread, its field filled with green, violet, and gray ostrich feathers in your colors, bordered by white ostrich feathers, and spotted with black feathers and ermine."

Invention could not be totally unfettered, however, against a background so bristling with signs. One needed to acquire the necessary vocabulary and grammar: monograms, embroidered devices (of Charles of Orléans or Marguerite of Burgundy as well as figures of the second rank), heraldic emblems based on flora and fauna and even invented species, and a whole language of color, which combined the traditional symbolism of mystics and scholars with popular beliefs. When Charles VII jousted as the green knight, the court understood the chivalric allusion; Florentines knew since at least the beginning of the thirteenth century that "the man in red" meant the rich man; in placing a crown of roses on his gray head, Matthäus Schwarz may have been dreaming of Lancelot's cap of roses; and Anne of Brittany, when she dressed in black to mourn Charles VIII, was making a political statement, for

Matthäus Schwarz, *Trachtenbuch*. Aged twenty-seven (facing page), the young financial director of the House of Fugger in Augsburg records for posterity a costume that he probably wore for a feast of some sort. (Paris, Bibliothèque Nationale.) In 1549 Schwarz was fifty-two. He had survived a heart attack, and in reviewing the various outfits he had worn since childhood he included this picture (below) of a tired man being carried about in a wagon of his own design.

black was the customary color of mourning in Brittany, whereas in France it was white.

In short, by choosing to appear in a certain way an individual made a statement, which was then subject to interpretation. Some messages were perfectly clear and public; others were assertions of individual freedom in the face of institutional obligations; still others were private, comprehensible to only one other person or to the members of a select group—secrets, puzzles, riddles, laments of a broken heart, or the result of a wager between friends. In his *Trachtenbuch* Matthäus Schwarz depicts himself attending a ball with friends all dressed in the same way, with an hourglass attached to the calf. We shall never know the meaning of this singular gesture.

Fashion, Age, and Memory

Urs Graf, *Feathered Lansquenet*, 1523. The ultimate extravagance: the lansquenet has disappeared behind his plume of feathers. (Museum of Basel.)

Several late medieval and early modern authors drew connections between their personal appearance and events in private or public life. Count von Zimmern recounts his dissatisfaction with his parents, who were insensitive to fashion and forced their adolescent son to dress in long robes when the fashion was for short. The chronicle of Limburg makes adverse comment on the clothes worn by the young in the 1360s. And the household chronicle of Konrad Pellikan of Ruffach records the unfavorable impression made by the outrageous dress of the lansquenets (1480).

The most novel commentary on late medieval and early Renaissance clothing is undoubtedly that in Matthäus Schwarz's *Trachtenbuch*, which consists of vignettes featuring his own costumes, with the author's remarks. He is not concerned with public dress, which, he charges, is nothing but costumes for carnival, but with clothing commissioned by him for various occasions: birthdays, marriages, holidays. Schwarz compares contemporary fashions with those of earlier generations; he was probably the first historian of clothing, with a keen eye for both change and cyclic repetition. He turns a simple catalog of clothing into a veritable chronicle of private life, tracing his own history back to his earliest memories— "as in a fog"—at age four and even beyond, back to his swaddling clothes, his "first clothing" in this world, and his mother's womb ("in which I lay hidden"). We are also shown the indoor dress of the elderly man struck down by a heart attack ("the hand of God") and forced to hobble about the house in a brown greatcoat with cane and bonnet.

All that is missing from this intimate portrait is the naked body, the one thing shared by the invalid in his sickbed, the anxious merchant, the shivering pauper, and the silk-clad prince. So in the middle of the book, and not without humor, Schwarz shows us his own body, "fat as I have become."

Pisanello, *Allegory of Lust.* (Vienna, Albertina.)

THE NAKED BODY

Protection or ornament, clothing was the last wrapping of social life; beyond lay the body's smooth mysteries. Recall the furrier from Lucca in Sercambi's tale who feared losing his identity when he removed his clothes to bathe. Centuries of Christian vigilance and moral prohibitions prevented him from recognizing himself in his naked but opaque body.

Nudity signified withdrawal from social intercourse. Even in the tympanums of cathedrals, both the elect and the damned were clothed. Female nudity as seen by Pisanello was

Stripped Bare

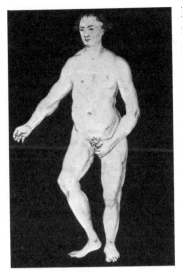

Matthäus Schwarz,
Trachtenbuch. This is one of the
earliest known portraits of a
man posing naked. (Paris,
Bibliothèque Nationale.)

Albrecht Dürer, *Young Woman
Posing Naked*, 1493. (Bayonne,
Bonnat Museum.)

lascivious, unhealthy, wild. In fiction, captive women were forced to disrobe so that the emperor could choose a wife, and naked females were shown participating in scenes of violence by torchlight. Literary representations associated male nudity with madness and savagery. The wolf-child and the deranged knight lost not only memory but also control of their gestures; they cloaked themselves in animal hides. When a savage was brought to the court of Charles VI, people saw the resulting catastrophe as punishment for the infringement of a taboo. In public executions the condemned were stripped of clothing. Pisanello's and Villon's portraits of the hanged and Andrea del Sarto's sketches of the Florentine captains executed in 1530 depict grotesque marionettes in tunics.

Glory and Torture. Undoubtedly these images reflect certain obsessions about the body; in all of them the condemned men are violently, scandalously, degradingly deprived of the reassuring and distinguishing protection of clothing. Other images showed nudity as an invention of Christian culture: Adam in glory and Jesus on the cross represented to the faithful the beginning and end of the history of Creation and Redemption, the splendor of the virgin body and the pain of the martyred one. In the late Middle Ages this spectacle was made flesh: in German the same word, *Fleisch,* referred to both the meat of animals and the flesh of the human body. This ambiguity is evident in the weight of humanity found in northern European painting after 1400, in the triumphant nudity of Adam and Eve and the tortured nudity of the dying Christ. Virtuoso artists infused with a morbid piety delighted in images of dead flesh. From Enguerrand Quarton's *Pietà* to the German *Vesperbilder,* Mantegna's *Dead Christ,* and Holbein's predella in the Basel Museum (in the form of a coffin for a lone cadaver), painters grimly trod the path of salvation.

But the new Adam fulfilled the promise implicit in the glorious body of the first man. In the panels of Van Eyck's *Mystical Lamb,* Adam and Eve are shown for the first time in the history of Western painting with complexion, hair, contours, and creases suggesting that they are creatures of flesh and blood. At Venice, in Rizzo's sculpture, they tremble in their exemplary nudity. Painted or engraved by Dürer, they embody all the elegance that the rediscovery of Antiquity lent to their graceful gestures. These tranquil and noble images domesticated the youthful body and expressed the beauty of a world in which man became the measure of all things.

The first study of a nude posing for a painter is perhaps Dürer's drawing of a standing young woman, dated 1493. She has removed her dress but still wears the slippers which protect her feet from the cold tiles while she poses. This detail of private life gives additional force to a study of a body exposed without pretext or ulterior motive to a gaze that examines it as it might examine a flower or a piece of fruit. Obviously quite a distance has been traveled since the metaphysical Eve of Autun, which has left no trace of its gestation. The young German woman of 1493 is one of many possible fifteenth-century portraits of Eve and cannot be taken for its model.

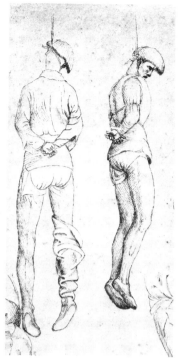

Pisanello, *Hanged Men.* (London, Oppenheimer Collection.)

Domestic altar, 15th century. This retable was small enough to be used in a bedroom. (Paris, Cluny Museum.)

Natural Functions

Although health is a crucial factor in an individual's private life, we must rely on statistics to understand it. The iconographic documentation becomes far richer and more reliable after about 1470, hence it makes sense to analyze portraits from that period statistically to see what can be determined about physical health. On the evidence of painting one would no doubt conclude that urban notables were a well-fed lot, but various details might well reveal complexions and afflictions useful for understanding the physiological history of this social group. At the very least a classification of different temperaments should prove useful, since, according to the *Calendrier des bergers*, character is revealed in the face. The complexion, believed to be the result of various internal decoctions, was such an essential element in medieval perception of a person's identity that fictional heroines simply painted their faces when they wanted to pass unnoticed. Beneath the skin, beyond the complexion, lay the skeleton. Bones too are a clue to health. How big were tombstones and graves, to say nothing of suits of armor, collections of which are scattered

Jörg Breu the Elder, *Inn*. Some guests stuff themselves, others play backgammon, while another warms himself at the tiled fireplace. (Paris, School of Fine Arts.)

all over Europe and do not give the impression that jousters of the Middle Ages were of small size? In recent years systematic exploration of village cemeteries has added to our knowledge of the largest segment of the late medieval population: the peasantry. Peasants, who lacked the leisure to reflect on temperament, no doubt had dark, weathered complexions, just as the literary texts describe them. The few portraits that represent them as persons rather than stereotypes suggest the health and vigor of the model: for instance, the smiling Slovene woman who posed for Dürer or the bearded man with sheepskin cap who was painted by Lucas Cranach the Elder.

Studies of skeletal remains, such as those conducted at Saint-Jean-le-Froid by F. Piponnier and R. Bucaille, have led to exciting new conclusions about the physical constitution, diet, and even blood types of rural populations. Unlike miners who suffered from lead poisoning and skeletal deformations as a result of working conditions (as in the village of Brandes in Oisans), Burgundy peasants show unmistakable signs of good health: well built, they had excellent teeth, and their bones show no signs of chronic disease. The results of such pioneering research cannot be extended automatically to all of Europe. Nevertheless, archaeological findings appear to confirm the veracity of the portrait of the peasant found in the fabliaux or the novellas of Sercambi or in miniatures like those contained in the *Très Riches Heures du duc de Berry*. In the prime of life, peasants had the same innocent, raw vitality that Le Roy Ladurie noted in the population of Montaillou. They ate, drank, and made love with much gusto.

Nourishment. The healthy body was undoubtedly better nourished in the late Middle Ages than in earlier times. The survivors of the Black Plague and their descendants enjoyed improved living conditions, in certain regions at any rate, to judge by such indices as increased grain yield, increased consumption of meat in the cities, and a considerable increase in the consumption of wine and beer from Gascony to the Baltic and central Europe in the thirteenth to sixteenth century. Other signs, such as the real wages paid to construction workers, the meals fed to hospital patients, and the diet of the typical citizen of Arles in the fifteenth century (studied by L. Stouff), give the impression that budgets were less tight than before and that people paid more attention to the nutritional value of food.

Lucas Cranach the Elder,
Portrait of a Peasant. (London,
British Museum.)

Of course this overall impression should not be allowed to obscure the steady stream of vagabonds from fallow farmland to overpopulated cities, the innumerable victims of armed raids and guerrilla warfare, and the lack of resistance of even the best-nourished to epidemic disease. For many people good food remained an intermittent reality, and usually there was little to savor but odors and scents emanating from the kitchens of the rich. People imagined never-never lands in which everything was edible. Rabelaisian feasting belonged to a tradition of celebration in which the entire society shared, but only occasionally. Whether at home or in public inns, eating and drinking were normally done in company: indeed, drinking from a common flagon required a whole ritual of etiquette to determine who would drink first.

Evacuation. Bodily functions other than eating and drinking were treated with greater discretion. Even the relatively abundant documentation for the fourteenth and fifteenth centuries has little to say about evacuation, apart from a few hints contained in texts on medicine and surgery, whose authors, as M.-C. Pouchelle has shown, were regarded by contemporaries as little better than sewer-cleaners and butchers. The surgeon Henri de Mondeville, author of the first French treatise on the body's inner organs and embalmer of Philip the Fair and Louis X (the Headstrong), did examine the body's less noble parts, those situated below the diaphragm where, as the nutritive humors were cooked, waste accumulated before being purged.

Municipal governments in the late Middle Ages faced enormous problems of waste disposal. Commissions of leading citizens and master architects deliberated on the question, which was no more than the public form of a problem faced by every individual and family. For privacy in evacuation every home needed privies, readily accessible outhouses and latrines. Castles and walled cities had public latrines that emptied into moats and ditches. (Such latrines are still extant in the guardroom of Ghent Castle.) In the fifteenth century in the city of Nuremberg, open sewers behind every house ran perpendicular to the river; when waste matter accumulated because the river was low, it had to be carted outside the walls and disposed of. From the records of repairs made to the castles of the dukes of Burgundy and lawsuits in the neighborhood of Sainte-Geneviève in Paris we learn about some of the issues involved in the provision of bathroom facilities. In 1506 Dürer carefully indicated the privies on every floor in a plan he drew of the house he stayed in.

One circumstance in which modesty suffered as a result of enforced promiscuity was the long voyage by galley taken by pilgrims to Jerusalem. Men and women of all orders had no choice but to witness one another in the most intimate postures. The Dominican Felix Faber of Ulm, who traveled to the Holy Land in 1480 and again in 1483, prepared a rather crudely realistic text for the edification of subsequent travelers. After returning to his cell in a Swabian convent, he recounted his adventures and offered some advice:

"As the poet says, 'A ripe turd is an unbearable burden' [*ut dicitur metrice: maturum stercus est importabile pondus*]. A few words on the manner of urinating and shitting on a boat.

"Each pilgrim has near his bed a urinal—a vessel of terracotta, a small bottle—into which he urinates and vomits. But since the quarters are cramped for the number of people, and dark besides, and since there is much coming and going, it is seldom that these vessels are not overturned before dawn. Quite regularly in fact, driven by a pressing urge that obliges him to get up, some clumsy fellow will knock over five or six urinals in passing, giving rise to an intolerable stench.

"In the morning, when the pilgrims get up and their stomachs ask for grace, they climb the bridge and head for the prow, where on either side of the spit privies have been provided. Sometimes as many as thirteen people or more will line up for a turn at the seat, and when someone takes too long it is not embarrassment but irritation that is expressed [*nec est ibi verecundia sed potius iracundia*]. I would compare the wait to that which people must endure when they confess during Lent, when they are forced to stand and become irritated at the interminable confessions and await their turn in a foul mood.

"At night, it is a difficult business to approach the privies owing to the huge number of people lying or sleeping on the decks from one end of the galley to the other. Anyone who wants to go must climb over more than forty people, stepping on them as he goes; with every step he risks kicking a fellow passenger or falling on top of a sleeping body. If he bumps into someone along the way, insults fly. Those without fear or vertigo can climb up to the prow along the ship's gunwales, pushing themselves along from rope to rope, which I often did despite the risk and the danger. By climbing out the hatches to the oars, one can slide along in a sitting position from oar to oar, but this is not for the faint of heart, for straddling the oars is dangerous, and even the sailors do not like it.

"But the difficulties become really serious in bad weather, when the privies are constantly inundated by waves and the oars are shipped and laid across the benches. To go to the seat in the middle of a storm is thus to risk being completely soaked, so that many passengers remove their clothing and go stark naked. But in this, modesty [*verecundia*] suffers greatly, which only stirs the shameful [*verecunda*] parts even more. Those who do not wish to be seen this way go squat in other places, which they soil, causing tempers to flare and fights to break out, discrediting even honorable people. Some even fill their vessels near their beds, which is disgusting and poisons the neighbors and can be tolerated only in invalids, who cannot be blamed: a few words are not enough to recount what I was forced to endure on account of a sick bedmate.

"The pilgrim must be careful not to hold back on account of false modesty and not relieve the stomach; to do so is most harmful to the traveler. At sea it is easy to become constipated. Here is good advice for the pilgrim: go to the privies three or four times every day, even when there is no natural urge, in order to promote evacuation by discreet efforts; and do not lose hope if nothing comes on the third or fourth try. Go often, loosen your belt, untie all the knots of your clothes over chest and stomach, and evacuation will occur even if your intestines are filled with stones. This advice was given me by an old sailor once when I had been terribly constipated for several days. At sea, moreover, it is not safe to use pills or suppositories [*pilulas aut suppositoria accipere*], because to purge oneself too much can cause worse trouble than constipation."

This text, based on personal experience, marks an important step in the description of intimate bodily functions. With wordplay, irreverent comparison, and reasoned analysis of specimen cases worthy of a *Kriegsspiel*, the robustly healthy Friar Felix, a man with an obvious zest for the pen, has left a well-turned essay on a delicate subject. Incidentally, his mention of suppositories is worth noting, as is the teaching of hygienic practices by word of mouth, in this case from man to man. The author even excuses man's uncontrollable response to the sight of other men's sexual parts. Three centuries earlier, Guibert of Nogent had written that such responses revealed wicked thoughts, but Felix knows better: sight sets in motion a complex physiological mechanism—all bodily responses stem from the mind.

"Felix conjunctio!" (happy coupling) the *Carmina burana* exclaims. From the record of physical desire inscribed on parchment by the monks of Ottobeuren to the love songs of the Renaissance runs a tradition of physical pleasure that flourished in the late Middle Ages, less reserved than in preceding centuries. But how closely did the song resemble the act?

Though private by nature, sexual intercourse, the act upon which every family was founded, was surrounded by a series of public rituals. Newlyweds climbed into bed before the eyes of family and friends and the next day exhibited the sheets as proof that the marriage had been consummated. Yet the bride was not exposed to public view, nor was the act of possession or the pleasure it aroused. The sexual act, first or last, legitimate or furtive, demanded darkness and privacy. Propriety required that texts concerning powerful personages avoid mention of anything that might resemble the prelimi-

Making Love

Michelangelo, *The Abduction of Ganymede.* (Paris, Bibliothèque Nationale.)

The Fables of Bidpai, 15th century. (Chantilly, Condé Museum.)

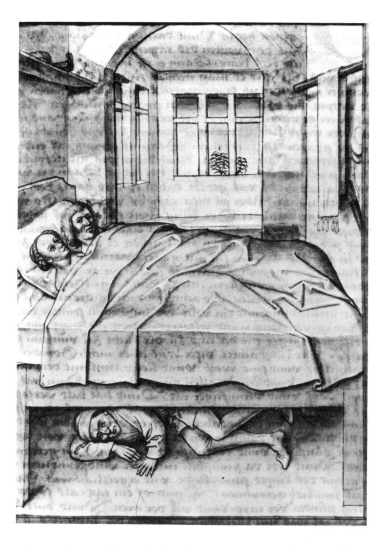

naries to physical love. A few images have survived: of King Louis the Bavarian, for example, alone in his palace but for the necessary servants and wholly preoccupied with the preparations for receiving into his bed his second wife, Marguerite of Holland, with whom he was very much taken.

As for intercourse itself, the only permissible images were monstrous or fabulous. We see demons possess their victim, who seems to have strayed into a bestiary. Leda is vexed by her swan, Ganymede oddly troubled by Michelangelo's eagle. Between demonology and fable lies the common act of lovemaking, which we are never shown.

With some imagination, however, we can reconstruct what sexual behavior must have been like from conversations between lovers, descriptions of various gestures, laws, and trials in which aberrations were named, judged, and condemned. But can we really reconstruct normal sex from special cases and general rules? Saint Antonino of Florence urged mothers to bring their daughters to church, where in his sermons he lectured them about unnatural practices that they might otherwise unwittingly perform as married women; we are struck not only by the astonishing public discussion of sodomy but also by the apparent prevalence of the practice. But did the saintly archbishop launch his public appeal after hearing just a few disturbing confessions or because so many of his flock made similar revelations that he became alarmed?

In depositions made under oath, like those that have revealed so much about the parishioners of Montaillou and their curate, the sexual act is treated as an elementary need of men, who one way or another find themselves a partner. Violence often plays a part; the castellan of Montaillou resorts to it out of desire for the curate's cousin. Sometimes the situation is reversed. The vicar Barthélemy Amilhac reports the following conversation: "She said to me, 'Come see me tonight,' to which I responded, 'What do you want?' And she said to me, 'I love you. I want to sleep with you.' And I said, 'All right.'" *Sancta simplicitas.* In Montaillou pleasure guaranteed the innocence of an affair, especially when an ambitious young man lusted after an "ill-wed" woman, that is, a woman married to a much older man. This was a favorite theme of literature in the *langue d'oc*, a good example of which is the thirteenth-century romance *Flamenca*.

The same breathless haste is evident in court documents, in which we read of violence done to helpless bodies and pleasure wrested by force. All too often, however, the partners are not equals: decent women are misled; little boys and girls fall victim to madmen. One day in 1412, while their tutor tarried over a chess game in a Venetian tavern a minute from their home, the two sons of Amado di Amadi, a wealthy silk merchant, were lured into the back room of their father's shop and raped. Severely punished in adults, homosexuality may not have been an exclusively urban phenomenon, as Jacques Fournier apparently believed when he carried out his investigation of Cathars in southern France; it seems to have flourished in all social classes but among youths of a particular age. Indiscriminate sharing of beds had inevitable consequences:

Arnaud de Verniolles, who figures in the events of Montaillou, was initiated at Pamiers at age twelve by a roommate. The custom of segregating boys between the ages of ten and fifteen probably suffices to explain the frequency of more or less serious sexual play among male companions. About the behavior of young girls we have even less information than about boys. Misogynist writers were suspicious of the gynaeceum: "Women speak in an ugly way among themselves," wrote Jean Dupin in 1340. And the *Roman de la Rose* shows young damsels bathing together. In aristocratic painting of the early sixteenth century we see female friends dressing and exchanging quite sensual caresses with all the immodesty of goddesses.

Care of the Body

The body was freer in the late Middle Ages than it had been previously, in representation if not in real life; it was also the object of more attentive care. Various strands of knowledge and sensibility converged in a practical morality, whose purpose was to maintain the body's mechanism in the best possible condition. To be sure, new forms of devotion that developed in the fourteenth century borrowed from the ascetic tradition the need to put the body in its place. Extreme holiness implies neglect of mortal flesh, and the penitential movement trained flagellants in the mortification and humiliation of the body.

Nevertheless, the majority of the faithful were exhorted to imitate Christ, who was not a hermit, after all, but a man of the people. Saint Antonino and Geilber von Kaisersberg railed not against the body but against the excess of attention to the body that distracted people from the essential life of the spirit. In this respect their preaching did not contradict the New Aristotle, who sought to understand bodily functions better in order to help individuals achieve equilibrium: medicine and morality, together and inseparable, promoted the idea of moderation. This was the central concept of Konrad von Megenberg's great treatise, *Das Buch der Natur* (1349), which recommended a life of the flesh perfectly compatible with a spiritual inwardness. Diet, exercise, fresh air, frequent baths: *mens sana in corpore sano*. The preachers had nothing against the physical exploits of knights in tournament, which took nothing away from the spiritual achievements of the athletes of Christ, in principle all the faithful. Saint George and Saint Michael were fervently admired throughout Europe in the late Middle Ages.

Recipes for Living. People copied recipes for healthy living into family record books between accounts and prayers or bound them together in pamphlets. These compendiums of knowledge and experience contained some pompous and obscure nonsense along with traditional remedies and homely medications juxtaposed with the teachings of academic physicians employed by princes and municipalities. In the fifteenth century, for example, advice on childrearing was widely available. A 1495 treatise by Dr. Bartholomeus Metlinger of Augsburg contained lengthy discussions of breast-feeding and weaning, teething, cradles, fresh air, diet, and the child's first steps.

There was also plenty of advice about prophylactic measures such as fumigation, amber necklaces, and Venetian treacle, which was supposed to cure anything. Signs of preventive vigilance are apparent everywhere in the fourteenth and fifteenth centuries. For travelers, precautions against foreign climes were advisable to reduce the risk of infectious germs or sudden attacks of pestilence. Treatises prepared for Venetian ambassadors described conditions on the roads of central Europe and the precautions to be taken while riding or stopping at inns.

Princes and collectors like the Nuremberg physician Hartmann Schedel amassed collections of medical treatises in which ancient science was combined with other sources of knowledge: information about precious stones, anatomy, the stars, the pharmacopoeia, and various propitiatory potions. For the human body was a vast subject, involving matters ranging from alembication to the zodiac. Various formulas were said to protect against sudden illness when used as directed. Someone in the entourage of Emperor Maximilian compiled an anthology of formulas *contra pestilenciam*, supposed to prevent disease: "No instance is known of death by poisoning or serious attack by pestilence among those who have drunk this *aqua vita* every morning and night. Whoever adopts this habit will eliminate any poison that might attack him." People actively sought immunity from disease.

Illness Lurks Abroad. But the enemy was formidable, and while the doctors analyzed the symptoms, contagion did its work. When a person was stricken, it was essential that he rally his strength in order to put his worldly affairs in order and prevent the demon from gaining a victory. Private life ended in a public battle in which supernatural forces played a prominent role. Codicils to wills were taken down in feverish haste, and final letters were written to close relatives if death came far from home. Even the most robust died quickly; there was nothing to be done. Accounts of the final moments, while the body still sustains the life of the spirit, are particularly moving. A few examples will help us to imagine the deaths of private individuals.

In 1478 a pestilence overtook Venice. Heinrich von den Chaldenherbergen, an important northern merchant, realized that he was done for. Bedridden in a room in the Fondaco, the German section of the city, he summoned his business associates for help in bringing order to his complex affairs, which had changed considerably since he drafted a will in Rome in 1476. We have the following account:

"I, Heinrich Kufuss of Antwerp, attest upon my soul and conscience that Heinrich von den Chaldenherbergen, agent of Sir Andolph von Burg, asked me to come to his room. I went and saw that he was very ill. And said Heinrich asked me to go to the Soranzo Bank and have a bill drawn to the credit of Sire Piero Grimani, which I did in his name. I further told him that he ought to confess and prepare his will and continue to live as a Christian, and that he would not on that account die more quickly. And he answered that it would indeed be

Benedetto San Moro, *The Romance of Troy and Other Stories*. Venetian manuscript, 15th century. Physician administering treatment. (Venice, Marcienne Library.)

good for him to do so and that he wanted to do it. And I answered him and said: 'When you were in Rome around two years ago, to my knowledge you made a will and dispositions,' and I said to him: 'Do you want the will that you made in Rome to stand?' And I said: 'Who are your executors?' And he answered that there was indeed a will, but for the rest he was no longer sure."

That same year a noble lady, Anna von Zimmern, fell ill, collapsed, wrote her will, and died:

"While she was holding a bunch of grapes in her hand without paying particular attention, a tiny yellow worm, similar to a small earthworm, emerged from the fruit, climbed up her little finger—the one called the 'gold finger'—of her left hand, rolled itself up, and attached itself to the skin. When she noticed it, she called Sixt von Hausen to remove the worm from her finger. But shortly thereafter she felt ill, left the table, and was carried to bed by the young women and others of the company. On her orders someone was sent in all haste to Zurich, not more than a German mile away, to find a doctor.

"Whereupon she hastily set about writing her son, Sire Johann Wernher, and his wife a missive, the content of which was as follows: 'My maternal affection and my fondest regards, dearest son and daughter: A tiny worm that came from a bunch of grapes has contaminated one of my fingers, and my condition has worsened to the point where I am now bedridden, quite ill, and very weak, just barely able to write to make this request. Dearest children, do not fail to send a messenger without delay to let me know how my beloved children are doing, the little ones, for I miss you all terribly, both them and you. But do not be alarmed, and above all give me news of the little ones. Done at Baden, on the night of the Nativity of Our Lady 1478.'

"I cannot prevent myself from inserting here a second letter, the content of which was as follows: 'Dearest son, my condition has worsened to the point where I no longer have much hope but to commend myself to Almighty God. I am now prisoner of His will, and He will treat me according to His divine wish. All the sacraments were performed in a Christian manner in great haste prior to this night, for I do not know how things will stand with me tomorrow. Therefore do not abandon your occupations, but send me immediately my letter of indulgence, so that I may have it with me.

John Ardenne of Nawark,
De arte phisicali et de cirurgia.
English manuscript, 1412.
A sick woman. (Stockholm,
Royal Library.)

Do me this favor, and as long as I am alive and after my death show me all the affection of which you are capable. Dearest son, the letter of indulgence is in the armoire, the keys to which are in the drawer. Dictated on the day of the Nativity of Our Lady, in the year 1478.' But before this letter reached Mösskirch, she was dead."

In one of two surviving fragments of his diary for 1503, Dürer recounts the suffering and death first of his father, then of his mother. Awakened too late to help his father, who broke out in a terrible sweat before expiring, the artist recalled his mother's terrible agony: "She experienced a cruel death, and I saw that she was staring at something frightful to behold. She yielded up her soul in great pain." Her agony prefigured Dürer's own, as his body failed him. He was well aware that his disease was incurable, for in the painting of himself naked, he points to a spot on his failing body, and the inscription reads: "That is where I hurt" (*Do ist mir weh*).

If the final agony is always a lonely battle, the public personage owed it to himself and to those around him to set an example of impassive dignity. Margaret of Austria wrote to her dear nephew Emperor Charles V the following letter, which places a seal upon her life as though it were an official act:

"Malines, the last day of November, 1530.
"To Charles V.
"My Lord,
"The hour has come when I can no longer write you in my own hand, for I feel so ill that I believe I have but a short time left to live. Tranquil in my thoughts and resolved to accept whatever God gives me, without pain other than that of being deprived of your presence, of not seeing you or being able to speak to you before my demise, I feel that I must make up for the words I cannot speak with this letter, which I fear will be the last you will receive from me.

"I have made you my residuary legatee, and I leave you your Estates, which during your absence I not only preserved as they were when you entrusted them to me prior to your departure but also augmented considerably; I return to you dominion over them in such wise that I believe I have deserved not only your satisfaction, My Lord, but also the gratitude of your subjects and the reward of Heaven. Above all things, peace is what I recommend to you, and I beg you, My Lord, in the name of the love that you shall bestow upon this poor body, to keep also the memory of my soul. I commend to your grace my poor servants and maids, and address you a final salutation, begging God that he may offer you, My Lord, happiness and long life.

"Your very devoted Aunt Margaret"

Youth was exalted for its very vulnerability. Giuliano de' Medici's blond good looks rallied the citizens of Florence in the festival glorifying the city's renewal. Old age, Petrarch explained in a letter to Guido Sette, was the physical equivalent of a shipwreck, unworthy of much attention. Geiler von Kaisersberg ridiculed from the pulpit the wrinkled old woman of Strasbourg who went for a facelift (*ausputzen*) and emerged uglier than ever. There was a suitable age for beautifying oneself; youth, with nothing to restore, could be forgiven for wanting to flaunt its natural qualities, as long as it remained within reason. Cosmetic care was believed to have therapeutic virtues, and chapters on the maintenance of beauty adorn the most austere medical treatises.

Purification

Parasites. Cleanliness was important, but before the body could be cleaned it had to be rid of parasites. To remove lice, a person turned to the people he or she loved. In Montaillou the chore was performed in the sunlight, on rooftops or doorsteps, by wives and mistresses. Pierre Clergue chatted with Béatrice de Planissoles as she combed him for lice. Or consider once more that extraordinary microcosm, the galley of pilgrims. Friar Felix Faber is, as usual, most informative. Parasites, he says, will flourish unless one takes precautions. "On a boat, too many people travel without a change of clothing; they live in sweat and foul odors, in which vermin thrive, not only in clothing but also in beards and hair. Therefore the pilgrim must not be lax; he must cleanse himself daily. A person who has not a single louse right now can have thousands an hour from now if he has the slightest contact with an infested pilgrim or sailor. Take care of the beard and hair every day, for if the lice proliferate you will be obliged to shave your beard and thus lose your dignity, for it is scandalous not to wear a beard at sea. On the other hand, it is pointless to keep a long head of hair, as do some nobles unwilling to make the sacrifice. I have seen them so covered with lice that they gave them to all their friends and troubled all their neigh-

Sebastian Brant, *Stultifera navis Parisiis* (Ship of Fools), 1498. A man turns to the woman he loves to remove his lice. (Paris, Bibliothèque Nationale.)

Jost Amman, 1574. (Paris, Bibliothèque Nationale.)

M. Albir, *Tractatus de pestilentia*, 15th century. In the 16th century the barber and the master of the baths numbered among health professionals. The barber washed his clients' heads, cut their hair and beard, and prepared plasters and dressings. The master of the bath applied bleeding cups, massaged his patients, and treated their sprains. A century earlier the boundary between the two professions was even less clearly defined. Pleasure, grooming, and health care were intertwined. (Prague, National Library of the University.)

bors. A pilgrim should not be ashamed to ask others to scour his beard for lice."

Filth, which carried with it epidemic disease, somehow had to be eliminated; on this point common sense and the general interest were in accord. Caring for the body not only preserved health but was also a pleasure. Heroes and heroines with fine hair and white or rosy complexions spent a good deal of time on their toilettes. Men and women of the late Middle Ages washed and had themselves massaged more frequently than their offspring, or so it seems, to judge by the abundance of sources dealing with the beautification and care of the body.

Johannes de Cuba, *Hortus sanitatis*, 1491. (Paris, Bibliothèque Nationale.)

Beautification. For men beauty care was limited to athletic exertions followed by ablutions and massage; the comb and scissors served head and beard according to the canons of fashion, which, to judge by surviving portraits, changed as often as fashions in clothing. These attentions, coupled with various lotions for the body, were all that virility would tolerate. Ovid, who remained the fifteenth century's arbiter of elegance, had long ago pointed out that men's bodies do not require much attention; the curled dandies of Venice and Florence, Bruges and Paris, carried things too far. Women took greater pains to make themselves seductive. Since Hippocrates insisted that a good physician should be able to answer any question about the body, treatises on surgery included various methods of beautification, including cosmetics, depilatories, breast creams, hair dyes, and even pommades compounded of ground glass, astringents, and dyes that enabled a woman to simulate virginity.

Thus, far from the world of sturdy peasant women depicted in the *Très riches heures*, from the spinners and spoolers of the fabric-making towns, from the Vosges mines of Heinrich Gross and the Bohemian mines of Mathias Illuminator, where women were employed as washers and sorters—far from such places an artificial ideal of womanhood took shape in spite of criticism from the Church. This ideal was embodied in the pale complexion and plucked eyebrows of Agnès Sorel as she dared to pose, bare-breasted, for a portrait of the Virgin with Child, or, later, at the time of the Peasants' War, in the astonishing doll-like girl painted by Baldung Grien, pasty white beneath her large black hat.

Long hair connoted mourning, and in a mood of black

melancholy Charles the Bold allowed his nails to grow unchecked. Normally, however, people sought to restrain and curtail nature's exuberance. A construct of culture, a woman had to be smooth in order to be agreeable. Medical treatises explained that hair was the condensation of crude vapors and that excess feminine moisture which did not flow naturally was transformed into moss that should be trimmed. To remove hair women used strips of fabric dipped in pitch or destroyed hair follicles with hot needles; powerful depilatories were also used. In a mystery play critical of Parisian debauchery, Mary Magdalene has the following dialogue with her faithful servant Pasiphaë:

> Here are rich ointments to keep your skin
>   beautiful and fresh.
> "Do I shine enough as I am?" the beauty responds
>   after a second or two.
> More brilliant than a picture.

Pisanello, *Young Man Undressing*. (Paris, Louvre, Rothschild Collection.)

Bathing. Clean, smooth, brilliant skin was the result of repeated baths and much diligent care, capped by the application of creams. By the late Middle Ages monastic moralists had ceased to warn about the dangers of bathing. Bathing and steaming were so widespread at all levels of society that it no longer seemed appropriate to question the practice of washing the body frequently from head to toe. As we saw, the Dominican Felix Faber enthusiastically approved of bodily cleanliness and stressed the importance of regular changes of body linen. In the minds of many people frequent washing may have assumed the same spiritual value as frequent confession.

There were two ways of bathing: in bathtub or steam room, alone or with others. Baths at home were prepared in the bedroom, near the fire which was used to heat the water. Providing a bath for one's guests was one of the first duties of hospitality. When Lord Barnabà Visconti in Petro Azario's tale keeps the promises he has made, incognito, to the peasant who helps him find his way, he offers him first a hot bath and then the most sumptuous bed the poor wretch has ever laid eyes on.

The wealthy bourgeois typically disrobed and bathed at home, in private. In the home of Anton Tucher of Nuremberg (ca. 1500), the master of the house undressed in a small room off his bedroom, where a tub was placed next to a brass cauldron on a tiled floor covered with wooden latticework.

G. D. Platzi, *The Witch*, 16th century. Whatever the theme of this painting may be, the mirror, basins, fountain, and flowers strewn about the floor suggest that this young woman in sandals had plenty of time to attend to her body. (Museum of Leipzig.)

Fragrant herbs were allowed to steep in the bath water. Galen recommended strewing rose petals over the bather: "So many were heaped upon mê," recounts the hero of an Austrian courtly epic composed in the late thirteenth century by Ulrich von Lichtenstein, "that it was impossible to see the bath water."

In the country bathing was no less common than in the city, to judge by the fabliaux. Either inside the house or out, the bather crouched in a tub of hot water underneath a cover of taut fabric that kept in the steam. Sometimes two or more people bathed together in rituals of hospitality or sociability:

Woman in a Tub. (Paris, Bibliothèque Nationale.)

for example, the bath after the grape harvest, or the baths that bride and groom took separately on the eve of the wedding, he with the friends of his youth, she with hers.

Both rural and urban areas contained public baths, sometimes administered by the community. Some were for therapeutic purposes as well as washing; the ancient tradition of bathing in hot springs survived in places noted for their healing virtues. In the fifteenth century thermal cures became fashionable, for example, at Bad Teinach in the Black Forest, where the *Wildbad* (or wild bath, meaning natural spring) attracted Duke William of Saxony accompanied by his physician in 1476, or at Hall in the Tyrol, where Ambassador Agostino Patrizi, on his way to Ratisbon in 1471, paused to describe the sophisticated installations.

Watery pleasures were widely shared in the late Middle Ages. North of the Alps the steam bath had long been in wide use. *De ornatu*, an Italian treatise on female beauty care, indicates that the *stuphis*, the steam bath, is a German invention (*sic faciunt mulieres ultramontanee*). The sauna, one of the earliest descriptions of which is found in the writings of the geographer and diplomat Ibrahim ben Yacub, who visited Saxony and Bohemia in 973, was very common in Slavic and Germanic regions. In most villages the steam bath operated several days a week; its location was marked by a sign depicting a bundle of leafy branches.

A late-thirteenth-century epic poem attributed to Siegrid Helbling describes with a wealth of detail all the phases of a steam bath shared by a knight, his valet, and various others. No sooner had the master of the bath sounded his trumpet than people flocked in, barefoot and beltless, carrying chemises or robes folded over their arms. They lay down on wooden benches in thick mists of steam that rose from heated stones upon which water was sprinkled regularly; the back, arms, and legs were kneaded by masseuses, and sweat was made to flow by flagellating the skin with branches. The body was rubbed with ashes and soap. Then a barber trimmed the hair and beard. Finally, the bathers donned their robes and went to rest in an adjoining room.

This description accords well with the illustrations in the Bible of King Wenceslaus of Bohemia and in the *Shepherds' Calendar* for 1491. The bath and steam room were places of relaxation, where people went not only to cleanse their bodies but also to talk, rest, and amuse themselves. What better place for amorous encounters of every kind? Some baths had such bad reputations that it was generally considered disreputable to work in a bathhouse or as a masseuse. The erotic connotations of water color the descriptions of furtive encounters at the baths of Bourbon-l'Archambault in *Flamenca*, an Occitanian poem of guilty love. The immodest and the innocent met in the baths; bathers were scrutinized, judged, desired, seduced. The exchanges of glances that must have taken place are not hard to imagine. We can go even further in our quest for the intimate with the help of a text that gives a contemporary view of bathhouse behavior. The fresh eyes of a foreigner, in this case Poggio visiting Switzerland, correct our preconceptions.

Bathing for Pleasure and Salvation. In 1414 Pope John XXIII took with him to the Council of Constance in the capacity of apostolic secretary the fashionable writer Poggio, friend of the leading Florentine humanists and well-known collector of ancient manuscripts. But when his patron Baldassare Cossa was suddenly deposed, Poggio found himself without a job. Thereupon he traveled as an idle spectator to the baths at Baden, not far from Zurich, where he was surprised by what he saw:

Piero of Eboli, *Baths of the Pouzzoles*, 14th century. (Paris, Bibliothèque Nationale.)

"Baden—the name means 'baths' in German—is a rather flourishing city, situated in a valley dominated by very high mountains close to a great, fast-running river that joins the Rhine six thousand paces from town. Not far from the city, four stadia away, is a superb bathing establishment, built along the river's bank. Around an enormous central square stand magnificent buildings capable of receiving large crowds of people. Inside each of these buildings are baths, to which only certain people are admitted. Some of these baths are public, others private; there are some thirty in all.

"Two of the baths are public, accessible from either side of the central square; these are for the common folk, men, women, youths, and maidens of no particular quality, the dregs of the populace, who come here in large numbers.

"In these pools a sort of stockade has been constructed even though these people are at peace; it separates the men from the women. It is truly laughable to see decrepit old women bathing alongside young beauties, entering the water stark naked while men look on, staring at their natural parts and their buttocks. I often laughed at picturesque spectacles of this sort, contrasting them with floral games, and in my

Johannes Stumpf, *Schweizer Chronik*, 1586. Different ways of bathing: in a large tub with several other people over supper; in the famous baths at Baden, near Zurich, where young and old, men and women, sick and healthy all swim together in the public pool, as spectators look on; and in a swimming hole in the country—the natural form of the thermal cure (*wildbad*). (Paris, Bibliothèque Nationale.)

heart of hearts I admired the innocence of these people, who do not fix their eyes on such details and who think and speak no evil.

"Baths in private homes are quite stylish and also shared by men and women. Simple grills separate the sexes, and in them numerous windows have been cut so that people can drink and converse together and look at one another and even touch, as is the custom. Above the pools are galleries where the men sit, watching and conversing. For everyone is allowed to go to other people's baths, to contemplate, chat, gamble, and unburden the mind, and they stay while the women enter and leave the water, their full nakedness exposed to everyone's view. No guard observes who enters, no gate prevents one from entering, and there is no hint of lewdness. In most cases men and women use the same entrance, and the men encounter half-naked women while the women encounter naked men. Men wear a sort of bathing suit at most, while women wear tunics which are open on top or along the side and do not cover the neck, the breasts, the arms, or the shoulders. People often take meals in the water, for which they pay with their entry token; tables are set on the water, and onlookers often share meals with the bathers . . .

"As for myself, I watched from the gallery, devouring with my eyes the customs, habits, amenities, and freedom, not to say licentiousness of this way of life. It is truly astonishing to see the innocence, the truth, with which they live. Husbands watched as their wives were touched by strangers and did not take offense, did not even pay attention, interpreting everything in the best light. Even the most delicate things become easy thanks to their customs. They could easily have accommodated themselves to Plato's *Politics*, sharing everything in common, for without knowing his theories they instinctively number among his supporters. In some baths the males mingle directly with women to whom they are related by blood or close in other ways. Every day they go to bathe three or four times, spending the greater part of the day singing, drinking, and dancing. They sing in the water, in fact, to the sound of the cithara, crouching down slightly. And it is charming to see young girls, already ripe for marriage, in the fullness of their nubile forms, their faces striking with nobility, standing and moving like goddesses. As they sing, their garments form a floating train on the surface of the waters, so that they might easily be mistaken for wingèd Venuses."

Later, describing games held in a large, tree-filled field along the river, in particular javelin-throwing and a dance display, Poggio has this to say: "Truly I believe that the first man was born in these places, these places that the Jews call Eden; for it is indeed that, the garden of delights. If pleasure can make life happy, I do not see that anything is lacking here for achieving consummate perfection."

Could the body be both exposed and pure? As if in a daydream, the man of culture, the man of the world, loses all his bearings—literary, national, moral. His sense of propriety is profoundly upset by this joyous spectacle in which old and young, male and female, mingle indiscriminately. The decrepit old woman does not hide her withered figure yet occasions no hilarity. Nearly naked youths look at one another, yet their eyes are not inflamed with desire. The dividing line between good and evil has mysteriously disappeared; bodies touch and women hide neither necks nor breasts nor shoulders (*neque . . . neque . . . neque*). It is Poggio who undresses them with his eyes, Poggio who has lascivious thoughts. The scene breathes simplicity and sanity; impropriety exists only in the lexicon of the humanist. He has only to disrobe himself, to bathe his spirit in the fountain of youth. Is he afraid of exposing himself? Fine talk is his profession. Can an intellectual sit beside ladies at the bath without seeking to dazzle them?

Konrad Kyeser, *Bellifortis*, Göttingen manuscript, 1405. A hot bath, designed by a celebrated inventor of machinery. Here there are two bathing rooms, one for men, the other for women. The water is heated in the large spherical object visible in the picture. (Paris, Bibliothèque Nationale.)

But he knows no German. Never mind; he transforms himself into a voyeur before this harmonious community of flesh, joyous and desireless because it wants for nothing. But he is pained by the feeling that he is an outsider to this spectacle of satisfaction.

Poggio's uneasiness is further compounded by the fact that this garden of pleasures, this Eden, is north of the Alps. Plato's City seems to have come to life in a new social contract, in harmony, without violence or jealousy: there are no guards at the gates, no jealous husbands as in Italy. Yet Zurich lies beyond the northern frontier of Poggio's civilization. He is body and soul a child of the Mediterranean. For him the north is a place from which to retrieve ancient manuscripts, which he brings back by the cartload from places like Cluny, Cologne, and Saint-Gall: some were totally unknown in his native

Das Mittelalterliche Hausbuch, a late-15th-century manuscript. In this pen-and-ink drawing all the ingredients of pleasure are assembled around the intimate bath: music, wine, and an animal-filled garden in which couples can walk. (Collection of the princes of Waldburg-Wolfegg.)

Italy, including thirteen new discourses by Cicero, Quintilian's *Institutio Oratoria*, and all of Lucretius. Ancient culture was his true fatherland, and what could an afflicting glimpse of a hyperborean paradise weigh against it? Poggio's brief moment of wonderment may have been the result of a momentary interruption of his career. In any case, he soon got control of himself, enigmatically ending the episode of the joyous bathers, an anticipation of the Renaissance, of Michelangelo's muscular Virgin attended by athletic young men and of unclad merrymaking from Primaticcio to Cranach.

The body in its bath had other connotations in the late Middle Ages. Renaissance meant not only felicity in the world but also progress in the spirit, not only a fountain of youth but also a fountain of eternal life. Illuminated by the pleasure of the senses, the body also inspired spiritual reform. The water of salvation was the inspiration for the Strasbourg poet Thomas Murner's *Badenfahrt* (Cleansing Journey) (1514), an allegory of conversion in which Christ borrows the trumpet of a bathhouse attendant:

> Thereupon God, taking pity on us
> Began to teach us
> How we ought to bathe,
> Wash, and purify ourselves, abandoning our shame
> To the strength and might of His holy name.
> This he did so publicly
> That the whole world saw him.
> No one could truthfully say
> Or complain
> Of not having known
> How to bathe and purify himself,
> How to purify himself anew in God,
> How to rise like a new Adam,
> Reborn in baptism.
> For God gives us in His grace
> The power to overcome original sin.
> This He did so openly
> That the whole world saw Him.
> It was God himself who called us to the bath at the sound
> of His trumpet.

The poem was illustrated by admirable woodcuts representing commonplace scenes at the bath, as if the divine word grew out of the simplest gestures. The life of the body and the life of the spirit were perfectly congruent, the former providing concrete illustration of the latter. Conversion was

no exotic quest, no pilgrimage to the ends of the earth, but a routine practice in which the senses showed the way. Every time a person performed some specific act, he knew that Christ had come that much closer. Accept the invitation to bathe, shed your vices, rid yourself of your sins, reawaken your ardor to do good, and give thanks to the bathhouse attendant.

Thomas Murner, *Die Badenfahrt*, 1514. Three moments in the life of a Christian. (Paris, Bibliothèque Nationale.)

The Bath of the Soul

die badecur	thermal cure	purification
in das bad laden	invitation to bathe	revelation
sich selbst unrein erkennen	recognize one's uncleanness	confession
sich abziehen	disrobe	shed one's vices
vor Gott nackent stehen	appear naked before God	shame
die füs weschen	wash the feet	humility
den leib reiben	rub the body	make confession
die haut kratzen	scrape the skin	penitence
in bad lecken	flagellate oneself with branches	reawaken ardor
der badmantel	the bathrobe	shroud
das ölbad	the oil bath	baptism and extreme unction
das täglich bad	the daily bath	mass
das wildbad	the thermal bath	conversion prior to death
dem bader dancken	thank the bathhouse attendant	thanksgiving

Sacred love, profane love: body and water are symbol and receptacle of the spirit. What is humanism if not the desire to reconcile appearance with the innermost being?

SENSATIONS AND FEELINGS

In studying the intimate we must depend on means of expression. Though nothing would seem more constant than man's perceptual faculties, our ability to record sensation does change with time, hence so does our picture of ways of living, feeling, and thinking. In order to gauge the inner life of the past, or at any rate the difficulty of grasping what it was like, we must emphasize its differences with the present.

Sight

More than smell or taste, sight has implicitly been recognized as the sense most indispensable to the historical record. To measure space in order to use it, man used what he saw closest to hand, namely, the parts of his body: the palm, the armspan, the foot. Even such measures as the league and the bolt have a direct relation to man's body, to man as sower, maker, soldier. Beyond the familiar field of vision—wheat cut high with the reaper, the edge of the forest, the stockade, the moat, and the wall—stretched spaces difficult for man to master: deserts, mountains, swamps. Since defects of vision were not commonly corrected by eyeglasses, it is hardly surprising

The Harvest, fresco of Venceslas, 15th century. (Trent, Good Advice Castle, Eagle Tower.)

Albrecht Altdorfer, *Landscape.*
An elegant simulation of
reality. (Munich, Pinachotek.)

that the panoramic landscape does not appear in descriptive
literature until quite late, and then only symbolically. Man's
nearsightedness accorded quite well with the priority given to
symbolic representation; it also led to a lasting discordance
between realism in the plastic arts and realistic description in
writing.

Consider space. Illustrated Christian primers gave wide
currency to signs whose wealth of meaning was accessible to
all; no logical organization of space was assumed. With the
aid of imagination and memory, most of the faithful could
make sense of the elements of a painted or sculpted scene.
Starting in the fourteenth century, however, another type of
figurative representation took hold; it became possible to suggest the movement of figures in space, as perspective created
new symbolic forms. What we tend to regard as an evolution
toward realism in the late Middle Ages was in fact an elegant

Albrecht Dürer, *Fortified Castle.* This watercolor was painted in the Trentino, in 1495, during the artist's first visit to Italy. (Paris, Louvre.)

simulation of reality, which satisfied a clientele for whom wealth lay in objects and whose thought was invested in the space that joined objects together. The truly devout felt a continued attachment to tangible images, whose symbolic power was reinforced by contemplation. This was the crux of the Renaissance debate over the sacred and the profane image, which turned on physical and cultural characteristics of perception.

The vocabulary of color, like that of measurement, relied in large part on intimate metaphors. To judge by heraldry, fashion, and interior painting, the fifteenth century's sense of color seems at first sight to have been similar to our own. But color had symbolic as well as aesthetic value, which added to the charm of works whose intentions, today hidden, were obvious to the artist's contemporaries. Also worth noting is the disparity between the apparent realism of fourteenth- and fifteenth-century painting and sculpture and the poverty of the descriptive vocabulary in literary works from the same period.

When Froissart, while residing at the court of Gaston Phébus, count of Foix, described the countryside of Ariège, he spoke of "agreeable" hillsides and "clear" rivers; the chronicler's concern was to depict not the picturesque or the natural but the power and wealth of his host. By contrast, when he describes Queen Isabeau of Bavaria's entry into Paris, he pauses with the royal cortege before each station of honor, and his quill brims with red, blue, and gold. But the colors are mentioned only as symbols of the homage paid by the Parisian bourgeoisie to the monarchy.

We could scour the late medieval historical literature for a very long time indeed without encountering any description comparable to Dürer's Alpine watercolors, the first landscapes in the history of Western art without utilitarian or allegorical significance. Conventional symbolism is displaced by lived reality only in a few emotional essays in which nature serves as a setting for a remembered adventure of some kind: the dark waters of the fountain of Vaucluse seen at night exert a troubling fascination on Petrarch; Charles IV fails to lose himself and his army in the isolated and wild woods of Cadore; and the monk Felix Faber nearly dies in the Sinai Desert, tempted by its measureless wastes.

All we have, then, are a few nocturnal scenes, a few incidents distressing enough to merit a brief sketch. There is nothing that can compare with the travel diaries of the nineteenth century. Even pilgrims to the Near East, those most alert to the impressions of the exotic, upon arriving—in some cases in tears—at biblical sites so often visited in imagination, confine themselves to assuring their readers of the veracity of the information available to them before they left home. Not that they were insensitive to the local color; they simply lacked the vocabulary necessary to describe it. Of the five senses, sight may not be the most sensitive.

The same tourists' accounts linger over the gardens of the Holy Land, which Europeans saw as gardens of earthly delight, antechambers of paradise. The birds' songs, the sound of fountains, and the fragrances of the plants enchanted the knights, bourgeois, and clerics who came to sample the delights of the Orient. Even in Europe, the walled garden offered a feast of the senses to powerful personages, lovers, and so-

The Other Senses

Master E.S., *Garden of Love with Chess Players*, 15th century. (Paris, Bibliothèque Nationale.)

phisticates, a pleasure comparable to that of polyphonic music or the mélange of bitter and sweet tastes at the dinner table. The less fortunate had their pleasures too: spices of many varieties, cut flowers, birds in cages. In a world less antiseptic and uniform than our own, the senses of smell, hearing, and taste must have played an essential role in the definition of pleasure both in reality and in the imagination. Descriptions and paintings of felicity rely more on harmonious sounds and subtle fragrances than on seraphic visions to connote a state of grace. When the mystic Margaretha Ebner describes her ineffable rapture, the presence of God in the choir of her church is indicated by gentle breezes and a wonderful fragrance.

Conversely, unbearable odors define the limits of civilization and give grounds for xenophobia. Stench was indelibly associated with certain professions and certain parts of cities; whole segments of the population were made pariahs by their smell. The monk Felix Faber, who suffered from having to mingle indiscriminately with sailors and other pilgrims aboard the galley to the Holy Land, claims that Muslims and Jews can be distinguished by their odor in the baths at Gaza; Christians, he says, do not smell as bad. Italians commonly accused Germans, whatever their status, of carrying the evil odors of the Empire wherever they went. Campano, a humanist sent on a mission to the Reichstag at Ratisbon in 1471, speaks of a persistent, fetid odor; he says that when the foreign visitor returns home he must wash himself five, six, or even seven times to get rid of it. Allowing for polemical exaggeration, it is quite possible that different diets did yield a variety of odors, which defined cultural frontiers. André Siegfried's "geography of odors" was not the frivolous invention of an otherwise serious economist.

To a monk accustomed to the silence of his convent, it is not surprising that the cacophony of shipboard sounds should have seemed intolerable. Felix Faber gave careful consideration to each unpleasantness of the pilgrim's voyage, and noise was one of them. Violent natural sounds accompanied events of evil augur, such as the death of a tyrant or the coming of the devil. According to the Florentine historian Goro Dati, on the night Gian Galeazzo Visconti died, a hurricane and water-spouts indicated that his soul had descended to Hell. In accounts of descents into the pit of Saint Patrick, supposed to be a mouth of Hell in the middle of the Irish landscape, we are told that the valiant knights who ventured into the bowels of the earth had to endure lashing winds, abominable cries, and a devilish din so loud that "all the rivers of the world could not have made more noise."

Thus, the external world affected all the senses. It was a world in which ghosts hovered around every living soul, in which red and blue angels flanked Madonna and Child in Fouquet's painting, and in which the deserts themselves were infested with demons in search of prey.

Confronting reality, the individual needed to master his emotions. Educators, chansons de geste, and "mirrors of princes" prescribed what was appropriate for public display and what should be expressed only in private.

The Expression of Sentiments

Modesty forbade immoderate discussion of happiness or grief. Louis of Diesbach notes that when his wife was dying, he sent the servants away so that he could undress and watch over the body alone. Anne of Brittany, upon learning at eleven o'clock at night of the death at Amboise of Charles VIII, withdrew into her private apartments and refused all company. The next day, she received the condolences of Cardinal Briçonnet, made no answer, and remained by herself for almost twenty-four hours. Obviously we cannot say to what degree she was occupied by grief and to what degree by political

Mathis Grünewald, *The Retable of Issenheim* (detail), 1511–1516. Mary Magdalene in extreme distress. (Colmar, Unterlinden Museum.)

calculation, but she clearly felt a need to be alone with herself and perhaps with her God.

Some fathers recorded their devastation upon the death of a son. Lucas Rem of Augsburg described in his diary the appearance of children he lost at an early age. One black-eyed boy lay ill for twenty weeks before expiring, "the saddest thing I ever saw in my life." Giovanni Conversini of Ravenna maintained that pride "prevents me from showing the pain that is in my heart." More prolix and very moving are the words of Giovanni di Pagolo Morelli of Florence, who wrote about the death of his son Alberto, adding: "Months have passed since his death, but neither I nor his mother can forget him. His image is constantly before our eyes, reminding us of all his ways and habits, his words and his gestures. We see him day and night, lunching, dining, inside the house and out, sleeping and awake, in our villa or in Florence. Whatever we do, it is like a knife that tears into our hearts . . . For more than a year I have not been able to enter his room, for no reason other than my extreme grief."

ALONE

Retreat

Retreat and voluntary seclusion were practiced not only in Carthusian monasteries but also by ordinary citizens, who when they wanted to be alone repaired to their "thinking rooms." Montaigne's "back-shop" belonged to a tradition of private rooms used by late-medieval poets, humanists, and divines. Ghirlandaio and Dürer painted Saint Jerome engaged in solitary, intimate pursuits in a room specially adapted for work and meditation in the manner of the Italian *studiolo*. The Italian custom was soon adopted north of the Alps. The word *studiolo* was even used to denote the locked game room in which Conrad von Weinsberg of Cologne transported his treasures and presided as priest over an altar of fortune.

According to the *Vita nuova*, Dante closeted himself in his private room so that he could shed tears without being seen. Petrarch became so involved in Saint Augustine's tribulations that he cried, struck his forehead, and wrung his hands as he read the *Confessions* in his private chamber; naturally he was not keen to have witnesses to his emotion. Spiritual retreat was aided by the silence of an out-of-the-way place. The constitution of the Brothers of the Common Life, the canons of Windesheim, recommended "abandoning the world in order to turn one's heart with greater intensity toward God."

Retreat referred to both a place of solitude and a desire to renounce the world. Unlike Datini, the Prato merchant who hesitated to accede to the demands of wife and friends that he turn his thoughts to his soul, the "perfect merchant" envisioned by Benedetto Cortugli in his treatise on practical morality closed his account books and retired to his country house, where he spent the remainder of his life preparing for salvation.

In the spiritual sense *retreat* referred to an ascensional movement culminating in an intimate and symbolic place of

Albrecht Dürer, *Saint Jerome*, 1514. (Paris, Bibliothèque Nationale.)

Domenico Ghirlandaio, *Saint Jerome in His Study*, 1480. (Florence, Ognissanti.)

These paintings of Saint Jerome give a detailed picture of a scholar's study and items of Christian iconography (more clearly depicted by Dürer): the lion, the hat, and the crucifix. Ghirlandaio's learned doctor interrupts his work of translating the Bible to stare at the painter and the indiscreet spectators who peer over his shoulder. Some commentators on Dürer's painting have put forward a cosmogonic interpretation: the dog is Sirius, the lion Leo, and the tendrils the Little Bear, suggesting that Jerome is meditating upon heaven's infinite vault.

Albrecht Dürer, *Saint Anthony Reading*, 1519. Penitential silence in the heart of the city. (Paris, Bibliothèque Nationale.)

elevation. Climbing to the summit of Mont Ventoux, Petrarch was struck by the exemplary nature of the ascent, which enabled him to contemplate the panorama of his past while drawing nearer to the essence of life. Ludolph von Sudheim wrote: "By ascending through the airs, man changes truly." Retreat was a "fortress of silence," from which man eliminated everything else in order to receive Jesus Christ. Among the many definitions of the soul given in the *Sermons* of Meister Eckhart, one of the most striking envisions the soul as a fortified castle: "So high above the world and so mighty, this little castle is impregnable to all but the gaze of the Almighty. And because He is One and Simple, He enters in His oneness what I am calling the fortress of the soul."

In the ultimate retreat man did not go to an ideal room but turned inward, delved within himself. To ascend inwardly, to shut out the world, was to create, in the words of the mystic Mechtilde of Magdeburg, an "intimate silence of the soul." With such a retreat, "whether awake or asleep, seated, eating, or drinking, one can be alone even in the midst of others, alone with Christ" (J. Mombaer).

Surely this higher form of retreat was not within reach of everyone in the fifteenth century or any other time. Charles of Orleans, who possessed a vast philosophical and theological library, was given to melancholy musings in his "thinking room"; yet he never took the fateful step of embarking on inward exploration. But many fourteenth- and fifteenth-century authors did set an example of introspection, even if limited to testamentary formulas. They looked to the future with sincere and fervent anxiety. Indications of this can be seen in the revival of ascetic orders, the success of devotional confraternities, in some of the more spectacular aspects of the Mendicants' preaching, and above all in innumerable manifestations of personal piety.

Such dispositions of mind obviously were fortified by training in self-control. Discipline began in the schools, where pupils were taught to remain silent, for silence was considered as important a part of education as the alphabet. In recounting his childhood memories, one early-sixteenth-century Franconian goldsmith brackets together *stille sitzen* (sitting quietly) and *buchstabieren* (learning the letters of the alphabet). If silence makes room for the operation of memory (trained by visual techniques and implicit in habits of recapitulation), it can actually shape the structure of thought.

The Discipline of Memory

Examples abound of the power and precision of memory in the Middle Ages, when a scarcity of books made imagery, particularly religious imagery, a crucial reference. This was true not only in cultivated circles, where the memory was sharpened by long training, but also among the common people, as is shown by court testimony. The most personal aspects of private life drew on memories that combined the fruits of study and experience with the oral traditions of the social group.

Family memory seems not to have exceeded three generations; beyond that span of time, the histories of great personages were obliged to rely on archives, traditions, and legends. Yet individual memory is capable of bringing to life with astonishing vividness the events and even words of a good quarter of a century. Petrarch, in the daily record of his work that goes by the name *Rerum vulgarium fragmenta*, noted: "on Friday, 19 May 1368, unable to sleep, I suddenly sat bolt upright, for there came to me a memory of something that happened more than twenty-five years earlier." Even more remarkable is the testimony of Béatrice de Planissoles, chatelaine of Montaillou, before the inquisitor, in which she mentions an event that took place twenty-six years earlier, or the poor Douai worker who, after the death of the powerful and much-feared fabric merchant Jehan Boinebroke, is able to recall the businessman's mocking words to his mother, uttered thirty years before.

The World of the Mind

A trained memory was a necessity in a society in which writing remained the prerogative of an elite blessed with power and/or knowledge. From the early fourteenth century on, printing techniques made it possible to give wide currency to images, often accompanied by text, which served as aids to memory. Pictures aided people in the chore of memorization, and the Church was quick to avail itself of this useful educational tool.

Devotional Methods. In cherished books Petrarch made marginal notations to jog his memory and remind him of his suffering and tears. Such notes typify a common medieval habit of mind. For example, a page printed in Italy in the

Hugo van der Goes, *The Death of Mary*. Emotion is contained and focused by gestures and meditation. In the foreground are the two customary objects of medieval piety, a book of hours and a rosary. (Berlin, Staatliche Museen Preussischer Kulturbesitz.)

fourteenth century shows the Virgin, after the Ascension, meditating upon the mysteries of the salvation she has just experienced. Around the doleful Virgin the artist has recapitulated the episodes of the story in chronological order, using signs reminiscent of ideograms or rebuses, accompanied by brief captions: the manger is indicated by an ass and an ox; the garden of Gethsemane, by a sword and a lance among the trees; the Ascension, by two footprints on a hill. Worshipers meditated on the life of Christ, emulating Mary, who "kept all these words, pondering them in her heart," remembering in the order indicated by the graphic notes certain well-known episodes of the New Testament and thereby evoking pious sentiments.

Intimate feelings were further stimulated by the intoxicating monotone of murmured prayers and confessions, the "voice of the soul" recommended by the Lateran Council of 1214, as well as by the various forms of repetition that numbered among the most ancient of religious practices. (The string of pearls, ancestor of the rosary, is attested as early as the fourth century.) The recital of a *Pater Noster* after ten *Ave Marias* was the early-fifteenth-century invention of a Carthusian monk at Cologne and marked a stage in the complex process that established a close connection between the Ave Maria and the fifteen mysteries of salvation. Condensed formulas, *clausulae*, concentrated meditation within a circle of pearls rather than allowing the mind to wander, perhaps to stray. The pious of the late Middle Ages kept strict account of their prayers, and if the mechanical nature of the procedure has often been ridiculed, its ascetic intent has just as often been overlooked. Such methods were not mere ritualistic excess, comparable to the practice of ordering thousands of masses in one's will. When a person counted off the 5,500 wounds of Christ or the 1,000 bloody steps along the way to Calvary, he or she was in fact reexperiencing the measureless time of suffering and penetrating the mysteries of the Passion.

Just as late medieval chroniclers often associated personal feelings with specific places, so the mendicant orders emphasized in their religious teachings such mediating objects as the rosary (popularized by the success throughout Europe of a confraternity established in Cologne in 1474); relics (of which private collections proliferated at times to an incredible degree); pious images (which one contemplated in private); and written prayers (which people carried with them as they went about their daily business). In this connection, the archaeolog-

Master of Westphalia, *The Mass of Saint Gregory*, ca. 1473. The Passion is symbolized by objects of meditation. (Soest, Church of Saint Mary in the Fields.)

ical discoveries made beneath the woodwork in the choir of Wienhausen, a Cistercian church in the state of Luneburg, enlighten us about private devotional practices in the late thirteenth century. Along with pins, knives, and glasses with wood or leather frames, investigators have found beneath the canons' stalls pictures that must have fallen from missals or clothing, colored engravings on wood, paper embossed in lead molds, and small packets of bone and pieces of silk that suggest the use of hidden relics. To this class of objects belonged the schematic crucifixion drawn with pen and ink that Dürer carried on his person and that had no pretensions to being a work of art.

What signs and images were most often reproduced? In the late Middle Ages representations of or allusions to Christ's humanity and suffering were more common than images of His divine royalty. Christ's suffering was evoked by symbols such as the whip and the torches of the Mount of Olives. In a society very much aware of heraldic arms and devices, His five wounds served as the mystical escutcheon of the Son of Man. Amid objects at once commonplace and holy, such as clubs, nails, sponge, and ladder, the faithful contemplated Christ's gaping wound, which stood out like a mandorla.

The "immense appetite for the divine," to which both Lucien Febvre and Emmanuel Le Roy Ladurie have called attention, is summed up rather starkly by one writer: "They loved Christ bleeding." Physical realism was essential to the Imitation of Christ. Imitation did not mean vaguely emulating an ideal model of behavior. For the most fervent Christians, whether gathered in pious confraternities or confined to private spiritual exercises, it meant reliving each episode of the Passion in a manner most trying to body and spirit. For the devout Christian the Passion should be "kept constantly in mind" (*frequenter in mente*, in the words of G. Groote). He should prepare himself "by pious effusions" (*per pias affectiones*, according to the chapter on mass in the constitution of the Brothers of the Christian Life). Or he should contemplate the Passion "slowly and with tears" (according to Saint Bonaventure's treatise on the instruction of novices).

Bonaventure gives the following advice: "Contemplate the drops of blood, the blows in the face, the persistence of the whip, the crown of thorns, the derision and spitting, the hammering of the nails into the palms and the feet, the raising of the cross, the twisted face, the discolored mouth, the bitterness of the sponge, the head hanging with all its weight,

Bicci di Lorenzo, *Annunciation*, a major theme of late medieval painting. (Paris, Louvre.)

the atrocious death." The worshiper is exhorted to note every detail of the torture, to scrutinize as if in slow motion the signs and effects of the execution, and to relive in thought and in the flesh the abject agony inflicted upon the Savior of the world.

Trained in the use of such mnemonic and emotive techniques, contemporaries who looked at fifteenth-century religious works saw more than just superb painting. For example, Roger van der Weyden's *Deposition from the Cross*, painted for the constables of Louvain, who placed the canvas on the altar of their confraternity, focuses on a particular moment in the Passion, indicated by the attitudes of the figures. This sumptuously painted episode contains the same two signs found in the humble printed sheets used by more private worshipers: Christ's pallid corpse and the swooning Virgin. An even more subtle example is Giovanni Bellini's *Madonna* in the Accademia at Venice, in which the adoring Virgin is fully aware of the destiny of her child, whose arm hangs stiffly as if in death. These examples show that the altar image and the image of private piety were not necessarily different species, that the

Sano di Pietro, *The Annunciation to the Shepherds* (detail), 15th century. Seeing is believing, or believing is seeing? (Siena, Pinacoteca.)

liturgical and the intimate were not necessarily opposed. The greatest inwardness was not incompatible with public display of piety.

Prayer. According to the mystical theology of Chancellor Jean Gerson, "everything is prayer" when the humblest of believers, the simplest of spirits (*etiamsi sit muliercula vel ydiota*), practices the most exalted spirituality without thinking about it. Whatever the Christian sees becomes material for his prayers. Rooted in constant humility, personal devotion means readiness to receive the Holy Spirit. Prayer, Gerson writes, is "the chain that allows the ship to approach the coast without bringing the coast to the ship." Meditation led to contemplation. Judging by the thousands of handwritten prayers of all kinds preserved in archives across Europe, some of them touching in their spontaneity, it would seem that the habit of

Retable from Everborn Abbey, 15th century. Private devotion led to commissions for works of art. Research has been done on the importance of workshops in Flanders and Brabant in the market for pious objects in 15th-century Europe. Painted and sculpted retables were produced in great numbers. (Paris, Cluny Museum.)

prayer, that is, of intimate conversation with a superior being, profoundly influenced the most secret aspects of private life in the fourteenth and fifteenth centuries.

As with holy images, there was no sharp contrast between official, liturgical prayer and personal, intimate prayer. Nevertheless, in addition to the great psalms and well-known prayers attributed to various Church Fathers and reproduced in innumerable handwritten and printed copies, vast numbers of prayers were offered up in all the circumstances of daily life, written down, and collected in anthologies. Many of these prayers were to Mary. There were fashions in prayer, and from generation to generation and region to region we see different intercessors being invoked with identical words. Nevertheless, the prayers that have survived—written for holidays, weekdays, moments of decision, or in thanksgiving after a time of tribulation—often give vent to spontaneous personal feelings. We find prayers not only in the "books of hours," consulted every day, and anthologies of manuscripts, in which prayers are found next to recipes and formulas, but also in parchment scrolls, sewn into clothing, and locked in tiny boxes—evidence of the prophylactic powers ascribed to these material tokens of man's links to an invisible world.

Ecstasy. Meditation was not clearly differentiated from prayer. Both were means of access to a reality vaster, higher, and more luminous than that of this world: the world of spirit offered glimpses of the world of spirits by way of visions. Mysticism, even if it was nothing more than an extreme manifestation of the spiritual, enjoyed such resounding success in the late Middle Ages that it ceased to be a marginal phenomenon. If we define mysticism as the annihilation of self in order to make room for God on earth, we often read of mystical encounters with the other world in autobiographical and other accounts of revelations vouchsafed to individuals favored with experiences of the ineffable. In her dialogues with Christ, Margaretha Ebner claims to have received many responses, "impossible to transcribe according to the truth of this world, for the more abundant grace is, the less possible it is to express in thought."

In thirteenth-century German the term *kunst* (art) was used to denote such ecstatic experiences, which suggests that they were considered an art, a matter of technique and preparedness, rather than a state. They have since been subjected

Virgin with Child, early 14th century. (Orvieto, Museum of the Opera del Duomo.)

to psychological, psychoanalytic, and clinical scrutiny, which has called attention to the somatic manifestations of these spiritual events. But no reductive interpretation of the inner upheavals described by the mystics can detract from the pure and painful reality of a love which they understood to be divine.

Margaretha Ebner was a nun at Medingen who died in 1351, after long years of suffering. Her visions were accompanied by hypersensitivity and paralysis. In her hypersensitive state she heard music, saw luminous shapes, and stammered in an unknown language: "When I began my *Pater*, my heart was seized by grace and I knew not where it carried me. Sometimes, incapable of prayer, I remained in the grip of a divine joy from matins until Prime. Sometimes a path opened before my eyes and speech (*Rede*) came to me. And sometimes I was uplifted to the point where I was no longer in contact with the earth."

Her paralysis was brought on originally by descriptions of Christ's suffering and later by the mere mention of Jesus' name. At shorter and shorter intervals she lost all use of her limbs and her tongue, falling into a cataleptic state that she called *swige*, silence. In her case we glimpse one of the extreme forms of religious devotion, described with admirable persistence by a subject eager to note the progress of the flames that devoured her. In all the literature of the emotions and love written by medieval women, we owe the moments of freest expression and most surprising revelation to an intense desire to record such all-consuming mystical episodes.

For example, Christ frequently appeared to late-fourteenth-century nuns. "Who is your father," they would ask upon seeing a child in the cloister. "*Pater noster!*" the child would answer and then disappear. At Adelshausen one nun moaned day and night for years, inconsolable because she could no longer see the divine child. The more fortunate Umiliana dei Cerchi cherished her memories of the visit of the *bambino*. A violent Agnes of Montepulciano refused to return to the Virgin the baby that had been entrusted to her for an hour; from her experience she retained a small cross, which the child had worn around its neck. Women lavished devoted attention on wood or plaster images of the Virgin and dreamed of giving birth to Christ; such identification stemmed from religious instruction based on immersion in Bible stories. Familiarity with holy images shaped the imagination and transformed the frustrations of young nuns. In her room Margaretha Ebner kept a cradle in which she rocked a Baby Jesus who refused to sleep so that she would take him in her arms.

Christ appeared even more frequently in the role of divine bridegroom. Adele of Brisach spoke of a "union with God that culminated in a kiss." Christina Ebner pressed herself against the body of Christ as tightly "as the seal presses against the wax." Adele Langmann saw Christ enter her cell and give her a piece of flesh to eat: "This is my body." Margaretha Ebner saw Jesus reach down from the cross to embrace her; she lay on his bosom like the apostle John and took nourishment from him. Such ardent scenes are a far cry from Raphael's or Perugino's elegant and chaste paintings of Saint Catherine's mystical marriage, done for a public that would not have tolerated more disturbing images.

The origins of such mystical visions did not go unquestioned. Margaretha Ebner was well aware that the devil commonly appeared as an angel of light: "Suddenly," she writes, "everything in me turned dark, to the point where I came to doubt, and against my will to believe." It took renewal of her physical suffering to restore her certainty of salvation. For Robert of Uzès, doubt was impossible; at dawn, however, he experienced an attack of melancholy: "Satan wanted to deceive me by appearing to me in the form of Our Lord Jesus Christ." The rarefied atmosphere in which the mystics moved gave palpable presence to the divine and enabled them to detect intimate signs that confirmed the veracity of their visions.

Tilman Riemenschneider (1460-1531), *Christ*. (Heidelberg, Windsheim Triptych.)

Seeing the Invisible

Other people, some famous, some anonymous, have left a record of their intermittent ability to see the invisible in a variety of forms: in somber or luminous dreams, nightmares, enigmatic encounters, and brief contacts with phantoms and ghosts.

Some visions derive from the ancient tradition of prophetic dreams; their literary or political character saps their value as evidence of intimate feelings. Nevertheless, they are full of information about how people conceived of spirits. The future emperor Charles IV, awakened in the middle of the night in his tent near Parma by an angel of God, was in no doubt about the identity of the envoy, whom he addressed as "lord" (*Herr*). With this spirit he flew over great distances, hanging by his hair; he awoke physically exhausted.

According to a pious legend recorded in the family chronicle, Count von Zimmern took part in a fantastic scene. Lost in a forest, the count sees a silent human figure loom up before his eyes, sent to him for the purpose of making a revelation. "Since he spoke of God, the count agreed to ride along behind him." He then sees an enchanted castle whose inhabitants silently mime an endless feast—a bravura passage in the literature of enchantment. But then the scene dissolves and the figure disappears, and amid sulfurous odors and loud cries the count is shown a vision of Hell. Frightened by the sight of his uncle being subjected to eternal punishment, he decides to found an expiatory chapel on the spot; his friends hardly

The Triumph of Death (detail), 15th century. A world replete with dreams and visions. (Palermo, Sclafani Palace.)

recognize him, for "his hair and beard have turned so white."

A tale from the autobiography of Burkard Zink of Augsburg describes a similar fright, but it is even more unusual because it serves no moral or literary purpose. After following two horsemen whom he does not know through a Hungarian forest, the author suddenly finds himself alone at dusk, threatened by boars before a mournful castle. He calls upon God for help, whereupon the castle vanishes and a path appears, enabling him to escape from danger: "I saw then that I had been deceived and that I had followed two phantoms on my ride through the forest . . . When I begged God and made the sign of the cross, all illusion vanished before my very eyes."

The Enemy made his appearance even in the most closely guarded places, as evidenced by an unusual anecdote in Charles IV's account of his youth. An evil spirit made its presence known by throwing a wine goblet on the floor, after which the sound of footsteps could be heard. At dawn the glass was found where the spirit had thrown it. The story belongs to the genre of unexplained terrors. The devil, never named, revealed his presence in a sudden blush or a panicked beating of the heart.

Diffuse anxiety, which occasionally turned to fear, was the basis of the medieval devil's dual image. Those who had not met him were unrealistically precise about his appearance, whereas those whom he afflicted were troubled by the ambiguity of his presence. When we examine accounts of his intervention in daily life, we find that whenever the demon is recognized (which is to say, after he has disappeared), his appearance is quite commonplace and the physical alterations (such as premature aging, lethargy, and hysteria) caused by his presence are quite real. There can be no doubt that a subjective experience of the presence of evil did exist; but, as has often been observed, the most frightening demons are those within.

The True and the Real. Surrounded by celestial and infernal presences, called upon until the moment of final agony to choose between the armies of good and evil that besieged the deathbed, late medieval men and women confronted the invisible with open eyes. From the learned cleric to the illiterate peasant, who shared nothing except their anxiety; from the noble warrior to the village laborer, who succumbed with equal ease to cackling Death's embrace; the men and women of the late Middle Ages lived in a world still filled with spirits. Even the finest spectacles could not clarify the dividing line between the true and the real.

Armande Rives of Montaillou was convinced, on the basis of experience, that "souls have flesh, bones, and all their limbs." A few generations later, George the Hungarian, a knight, asked the angel showing him Purgatory whether the saints he saw there had bodies. The invisible itself was rooted in the corporeal, and the community of the dead and of spirits prolonged its earthly existence by at times mingling with the living. One day all the elect would be reunited in the immutable glory of their Father's house, the spiritual *domus* of Heaven, in which the hierarchical structure of human societies was reproduced.

But as early as the fourteenth century a new age was dawning, as individuals began to feel the need to perpetuate their image and memory in this world. In the cities of the West a great movement began, which pushed back the limits of the known world and the pillars of Heaven. Around the figure of man an intangible, geometrical space was created, as tears, credulity, and amazement were abandoned to the humble.

Let us cast a final glance upon a most palpable pile of objects: documents and pictures, letters and chronicles, images humble and sublime, well-thumbed books of hours, notarized records cut short by death, shreds of clothing—fragile, uncertain traces, left without commentary. No final interpretation, no irrefutable, definitive conclusion emerges. The search for the remains of intimacy is far from complete.

Bibliography

Credits

Index

Bibliography

Acta Sanctorum, ed. Paul Peters. Brussels: Royal Academy of Belgium, 1961. Margaret of Cortona, pp. 298–357; Agnes of Montepulciano, pp. 792–812; Catherine of Siena, pp. 851ff.

Alberti, Leon Battista. *I Libri della famiglia,* ed. Ruggero Romano and Alberto Tenenti. Turin, 1969.

——*De re aedificatoria,* trans. Cosimo Bartoli. Florence, 1550.

Antonino of Florence. *Opera a ben vivere.* Biblioteca dei santi, vol. 11. Milan, 1926.

Appuhn, H. "Das private Andachtsbild im Mittelalter am Hande der Funde des Klosters Wienhausen," *Leben in der Stadt des Spätmittelalters.* Vienna, 1977, pp. 159–169.

Augé, Marc, ed. *Les Domaines de la parenté.* Paris: Maspero, 1975.

Aurell i Cardona, M. "La détérioration du statut de la femme aristocratique en Provence (Xè–XIIIè siècles)," *Le Moyen Age* 91 (1985): 5–32.

Balestracci, D., and G. Piccinni. *Siena nel Trecento, assetto urbano e strutture edilizie.* Florence, 1977.

Barbaros, Francesco. "De re uxoria liber," in E. Garin, ed., *Prosatori latini del Quattrocento, La Letterature italiana, storia e testi.* Milan and Naples, 1952, XIII, 101–137.

Bardet, J.-P., Pierre Chaunu, G. Désert, P. Gouhier, and H. Neveux. *Le Bâtiment. Enquête d'histoire économique, XIVe–XIXe siècle, I: Maison rurales et urbaines dans la France traditionnelle.* Paris and The Hague: Mouton, 1971.

Barthélemy, Dominique. *Les Deux âges de la seigneurie banale. Coucy (milieu XIe–milieu XIIIe siècle).* Paris: Publications de la Sorbonne, 1984.

Baudrillart, Henri. *Histoire du luxe public et privé de l'Antiquité à nos jours.* Paris, 1880.

"Bauernhaus," *Lexikon des Mittelalters,* vol. I. Munich, 1980.

Baumgartner, Emil. *L'Arbre et le Pain, essai sur la Queste de Saint Graal.* Paris: SEDES, 1981.

Belgrano, Luigi Tommaso. *Vita privata dei Genovesi.* Genoa, 1875; repr. Rome, 1970.

Bellomo, Manlio. *Profili della famiglia italiana nell'età dei comuni,* 2nd ed. Catania, 1975.

Bernardino of Siena. *Le Prediche volgari,* ed. Piero Bargellini. Milan and Rome, 1936.

Beyer-Fröhlich, Marianne. *Die Entwicklung der deutschen Selbstzeugnisse.* Munich, 1930.

Bezzola, R. "Les neveux," *Mélanges Frappier.* Geneva: Droz, 1970.

Bloch, Marc. *La Société féodale,* 2nd ed. Paris: Albin Michel, 1968. In English: *Feudal Society,* trans. L. A. Manyon. Chicago: University of Chicago Press, 1961.

Boccaccio. *Decameron,* in *La Letteratura italiana.* Milan, 1950–1954, VIII, 3–764.

——*L'Elegia di Madonna Fiammetta,* in *La Letteratura italiana.* Milan, 1950–1954, VIII, 1060–1217.

Bonassie, Pierre. *La Catalogne du milieu du Xe à la fin du XIe siècle. Croissance et mutation d'une société,* 2 vols. Toulouse: Université de Toulouse-Le Mirail, 1975.

Bossuat, Robert. *Manuel bibliographique de la littérature française du Moyen Age.* Paris: Librairie d'Argences, 1960.

Boüard, M. de. *Manuel d'archéologie.* Paris: SEDES, 1976.

——"De l'*aula* au donjon. Les fouilles de la motte de la Chapelle à Doué-la-Fontaine (Xe–XIe)," *Archéologie médiévale* 3 (1973): 5–110.

——"La salle dite de l'Echiquier, au château de Caen," *Medieval Archeology* 9 (1965): 64–81.

Bouchard, Constance R. "Consanguinity and Noble Marriages in the Tenth and Eleventh Centuries," *Speculum* 56 (1981): 268–287.

Bourdieu, Pierre. *Le sens pratique.* Paris, 1980. In English: *Outline of a Theory of Practice.* Cambridge and New York: Cambridge University Press, 1977.

Brucker, Gene A. *Renaissance Florence.* New York: Wiley, 1969.

Buchner, E. *Das deutsche Bildnis der Spätgotik und der frühen Dürerzeit.* Berlin, 1953.

Caggese, R., ed. *Statuti della Reppublica fiorentina. I: Capitano del popolo, 1322–1325; II: Podesta, 1325.* Florence, 1910–1921.

Callebaut, D. "Le Château des comtes à Gand," *Château-Gaillard* 11 (1983): 45–54.

Chapelot, J., and Robert Fossier. *Le Village et la Maison au Moyen Age.* Paris: Hachette, 1979.

Cherubini, G. *Signori, Contadini, Borghesi, Ricerche*

sulla società italiana del Basso Medioevo. Florence, 1974.

Chevalier, B. *Les Bonnes Villes de France du XIVe au XVIe siècle.* Paris: Aubier-Montaigne, 1982.

Cognasso, Fransesco. *L'Italia nel Rinascimento, Società e Costume, I, Vita privata.* Turin: UTET, 1965.

Cohen, Kathleen R. *Metamorphosis of a Death Symbol: The Transi Tomb in the Late Middle Ages and the Renaissance.* Berkeley and Los Angeles: University of California Press, 1974.

Colardelle, M. "L'habitat médiéval immergé de Colletière à Charavines. Premier bilan des fouilles," *Archéologie médiévale* 10 (1980): 167–203.

Comba, Rinaldo, Gabriella Piccinni, and Giuliano Pinto, eds. *Strutture familiari, epidemie, migrazioni nell'Italia medievale.* Naples, 1984.

Contamine, Phillipe, ed. *La France de la fin du XVe siècle.* Paris: Editions du CNRS, 1985.

————*La Guerre au Moyen Age,* 2nd ed. Paris: PUF, 1986. In English: *War in the Middle Ages,* Oxford: Basil Blackwell, 1984.

————*La Vie quotidienne pendant la guerre de Cent Ans, France et Angleterre, XIVe siècle,* 2nd ed. Paris: Hachette, 1978.

Daffis-Felicelli, C. "Le 'Popolo San Lorenzo,' un quartier florentin au XIVe siècle (structures, patrimoines, société), 1318–1378," unpub. diss. University of Aix-Marseille, 1983.

Dallari, U. "Lo statuto suntuario bolognese del 1401 e il registro delle vesti bollate," *Atti e Memorie della R. deputazione di storia patria per le provincie di Romagna,* series 3, 4 (1889): 1–44.

Davidsohn, Robert. *Storia di Firenze,* 8 vols. Florence, 1956–1968.

Dauvillier, Jean. *Le Mariage dans le droit classique de l'Eglise, depuis le décret de Gratian (1140) jusqu'à la mort de Clément V (1314).* Paris, 1933.

Debord, A. "Fouille du *castrum* d'Andone à Ville-Joubert (Charente)," *Château-Gaillard* 7 (1975): 35–48.

————"Motte castrale et habitat chevaleresque," *Mélanges d'archéologie et d'histoire médiévales en l'honneur du doyen M. de Boüard (Mémoires et documents publiés par la Société de l'Ecole des chartes, XXVII).* Geneva and Paris, 1982, pp. 83–90.

Decaës, J. "La motte d'Olivet à Grimbosq (Calvados), résidence seigneuriale du XIe siècle," *Archéologie médiévale* 9 (1979): 167ff.

Delort, Robert. *La Vie au Moyen Age.* Paris: Seuil, 1982. In English: *Life in the Middle Ages,* trans. Robert Allen. New York: Universe Books, 1982.

————*Le Moyen Age. Histoire illustrée de la vie quotidienne.* Paris: Seuil, 1983.

Demians d'Archimbaud, Gabrielle. *Les Fouilles de Rougiers (Var).* Paris: Centre Nationale de Recherche Scientifique, 1982.

Le Diable au Moyen Age, Sénéfiance series, 6. Aix-en-Provence: CUERMA, 1979.

Dinzelbacher, P. *Vision und Visionsliteratur im Mittelalter.* Stuttgart, 1981.

Dominici, Giovanni. *Regola del governo di cura familiare,* ed. D. Salvi. Florence, 1860.

Dragonetti, R. "Pygmalion ou les pièges de la fiction dans le *Roman de la Rose,*" *Mélanges Bezzola.* Berne: Francke, 1978.

Duby, Georges. *Le Chevalier, la Femme, et le Prêtre.* Paris: Hachette, 1981. In English: *The Knight, the Lady and the Priest: The Making of Modern Marriage in Medieval France,* trans. Barbara Bray. New York: Pantheon, 1983.

————*Guillaume le Maréchal ou le Meilleur Chevalier du monde.* Paris: Fayard, 1984. In English: *William Marshal: The Flower of Chivalry,* trans. Richard Howard. New York: Pantheon, 1986.

————*Hommes et Structures du Moyen Age.* Paris: Mouton, 1973.

————*Saint Bernard, L'art cistercien.* Paris: AMG, 1976.

————*La Société aux XIe et XIIe siècles dans la région mâconnaise,* 2nd ed. Paris: Mouton, 1971.

————and J. Le Goff, eds. *Famille et Parenté dans l'Occident médiéval.* Paris and Rome: Ecole Française de Rome, 1978.

Eames, P. *Furniture in England, France and the Netherlands from the Twelfth to the Fifteenth Century.* London, 1977.

Eisenbart, Lisellotte Constanze. *Kleiderordnungen der deutschen Städte zwischen 1350 und 1700.* Göttingen: Musterschmidt, 1962.

Erickson, Carolly. *The Medieval Vision. Essays in History and Perception.* Oxford, 1976.

Etudes sur la sensibilité au Moyen Age. Proceedings of the 102nd Congrès national des sociétés savantes (Limoges, 1977). Paris, 1980.

"La Femme dans les civilisations des Xe–XIIIe siècles," Proceedings of the Poitiers colloquium, 23–25 September 1976, *Cahiers de civilisations médiévale* 20 (1977): 93–263.

Fink, A. M. and K. V. *Schwarzsch Trachtenbücher.* Berlin, 1963.

Folena, Gianfranco, ed. *Molti e Facezie del Piovano Arlotto.* Milan and Naples, 1953.

"Les Fortifications de terre en Europe occidentale du Xe au XIIe siècle," Colloquium at Caen, 2–5 October 1980, *Archéologie médiévale* 11 (1981): 5–123.

Fossier, Robert. *Enfance de l'Europe,* 2 vols. Paris: Presses Universitaires de France, 1982.

———*La Terre et les hommes en Picardie jusqu'à la fin du XIIIe siècle,* 2 vols. Paris and Louvain: Nauwelaerts, 1968.

Fournier, G. *Le Château dans la France médiévale.* Paris: Aubier Montaigne, 1978.

Francesco di Barberino. *Reggimento e Costumi di donna,* ed. G. E. Sansone. Turin, 1957.

Frati, L. *La Vita privata di Bologna.* Bologna, 1900.

Frey, Dagobert. *Kunstwissenschaftliche Grundfragen,* 1946; repr. Darmstadt, 1972.

Fünf hundert Jahre Rosenkranz: Kunst und Frömmigkeit im Spätmittelalter. Cologne, 1976.

Gaudemet, Jean. *Eglise et société en Occident au Moyen Age.* London: Variorum reprints, 1984.

Génicot, Léopold. *Les Généalogies (Typologie des sources du Moyen Age occidental. 15).* Turnhout: Brepols, 1972.

———*La Noblesse dans l'Occident médiéval.* London: Variorum reprints, 1982.

Giordano da Pisa. *Prediche del beato fra G. da Rivalto dell'ordine de' predicatori, recitate in Firenze dal MCCCII al MCCCVI,* ed. D. Moreni, 2 vols. Florence, 1831.

Giovanni. *Il Pecorone.* Ravenna, 1974.

Gmelin, H. "Personendarstellungen bei den florentinischen Geschitsschreibern der Renaissance," *Beiträge zur Kulturgeschichte des Mittelalters und der Renaissance* 31, 1927; repr. 1973.

Goldthwaite, R. "The Florentine Palace as Domestic Architure," *American Historical Review* 77 (1972): 977–1012.

Gonon, Marguerite. *La Vie familiale en Forez au XIVe siècle et son vocabulaire d'après les testaments.* Lyons: University of Lyons, 1961.

Goody, Jack. *The Development of the Family and Marriage in Europe.* Cambridge and New York: Cambridge University Press, 1983.

Grisward, J. H. *Archéologie de l'épopée médiévale.* Paris: Payot, 1981.

Guerreau-Jalabert, A. "Sur les structures de parenté dans l'Europe médiévale," *Annales ESC* 36 (1981): 1029–1049.

Guglielminetti, Marziano. *Memoria e Scrittura. L'Autobiografia da Dante a Cellini.* Milan: Einaudi, 1977.

Guillaume, J., ed. *La Maison de ville.* Paris, 1984.

Hasenohr, G. "La vie quotidienne de la femme vue par l'Eglise: l'enseignement des 'journées chrétiennes' de la fin du Moyen Age," Proceedings of the Krems Congress, 2–5 October 1984, *Frau und spätmittelalterlicher Alltag.*

Heers, Jacques. *Le Clan familial au Moyen Age.* Paris:

Presses Universitaires de France, 1974.

———*Esclaves et Domestiques au Moyen Age dans le monde méditerranéen.* Paris: Fayard, 1981.

Héliot, P. "Sur les résidences princières bâties en France du Xe au XIIe siècle," *Le Moyen Age,* ser. 4, 10 (1955): 27–61, 291ff.

———"Les origines du donjon résidentiel et les donjons-palais romans de France et d'Angleterre," *Cahiers de civilisation médiévale* 17 (1974): 217–234.

———"Nouvelles remarques sur les palais épiscopaux et princiers de l'époque romane en France," *Francia* 4 (1976): 139ff.

Héritier, F. *L'Exercice de la parenté.* Paris: Seuil, 1981.

Herlihy, David. *Medieval Households.* Cambridge, Mass.: Harvard University Press, 1985.

———and Christine Klapisch-Zuber. *The Tuscans and Their Families: A Study of the Florentine Catasto to 1427.* New Haven: Yale University Press, 1984.

Hervier, D. *Une Famille parisienne à l'aube de la Renaissance. Pierre le Gendre et son inventaire après décès. Etude historique et méthodologique.* Paris: Champion, 1977.

Heyne, M. *Fünf Bücher deutscher Hausaltertümer, III. Körperflege und Kleidung.* Leipzig, 1903.

Hinz, B. "Das Ehepaarbildnis. Seine Geschichte vom 15. bis zum 17. Jahrhundert," unpub. diss. Münster, 1969.

Imhof, Arthur Erwin. *Der Mensch und sein Körper von der Antike bis Heute.* Munich, 1983.

Kent, Francis W. *Household and Lineage in Renaissance Florence: The Family Life of the Capponi, Ginori, and Rucellai.* Princeton: Princeton University Press, 1978.

Kriegk, Georg Ludwig. *Deutsches Bürgertum im Mittelalter.* Frankfurt-am-Main: Rütten & Löning, 1868–1871.

Laurioux, B. "De l'usage des épices dans l'alimentation médiévale," *Médiévales* 5, November 1983.

Le Goff, Jacques. *La Civilisation de l'Occident médiéval,* 2nd ed. Paris: Arthaud, 1972.

———"Mélusine maternelle et défricheuse," *Pour un autre Moyen Age,* Paris, 1977, pp. 307–331. In English: "Melusina: Mother and Pioneer," *Time, Work, and Culture in the Middle Ages,* trans. Arthur Goldhammer. Chicago: University of Chicago, Press, 1980.

Leguay, Jean-Pierre. *La Rue au Moyen Age.* Rennes: Ouest-France, 1984.

Lehoux, F. *Le Cadre de vie des médecins parisiens aux XVIe et XVIIe siècles.* Paris: Picard, 1976.

Lenzi, M. L. *Donne e Madonne, l'educazione femminile nel primo Rinascimento italiano.* Turin, 1982.

LeRoy Ladurie, Emmanuel. *Montaillou, village occitan, de 1294 à 1324.* Paris: Gallimard, 1982. In English: *Montaillou: The Promised Land of Error,* trans. Barbara Bray. New York: George Braziller, 1978.

Le Lettere di Margherita Datini a Francesco di Marco (1384–1410), ed. Valeria Rosati. Prato, 1977.

Lévi-Strauss, Claude. *Les Structures élémentaires de la parenté,* 2nd ed. Paris: Mouton-De Gruyter, 1967. In English: *The Elementary Structures of Kinship,* trans. James Harle Bell and John Richard von Sturmer, ed. Rodney Needham. Boston: Beacon Press, 1969.

Lorcin, M.-T. "Le corps a ses raisons dans les fabliaux: corps féminin, corps masculin, corps de vilain," *Le Moyen Age,* 3–4, 1984.

Lorren, C. "La demeure seigneuriale de Rubercy (milieu XIIe–début XIIIe)," *Château-Gaillard 7* (1977): 185–192.

Marchello-Nizia, Charles. "L'historien et son prologue: forme littéraire et stratégies discursives," in D. Poirion, ed., *La Chronique et l'Histoire au Moyen Age.* Paris: Presses universitaires de Paris-Sorbonne, 1984.

———"Le roman du Châtelain de Coucy et de la Dame de Fayel," *Perspectives médiévales* 3 (1977).

———"La rhétorique des songes et le songe comme rhétorique dans la littérature française médiévale," *Proceedings of the Colloquium "Dreams of the Middle Ages,"* Rome, October 1983.

———"Entre l'histoire et la poétique, le 'songe politique,'" *Revue des sciences humaines, Moyen Age flamboyant,* 1981–1983.

Mazzei, Lapo. *Lettere di un notaro a un mercante del secolo XIV, con altre lettere e documenti,* ed. Cesare Guasti, 2 vols. Florence, 1880.

Mazzi, M. S., and S. Raveggi. *Gli Uomini e le Cose nelle campagne fiorentine del Quattrocento.* Florence, 1983.

Ménard, Phillipe. *Les Fabliaux. Contes à rire du Moyen Age.* Paris: Presses Universitaires de France, 1983.

Misch, Georg. *Geschichte der Autobiographie.* Frankfurt-am-Main, 1949–1955. In English: *A History of Autobiography in Antiquity,* trans. E. W. Dickes. London: Routledge & Paul, 1950.

Molin, Jean-Baptiste, and Protais Mutembé. *Le Rituel du mariage en France du XIIe au XVIe siècle.* Paris: Beauchesne, 1974.

Molmenti, Pompeo Gherardo. *La Storia di Venezia nella vita privata, I: La Grandezza.* Bergamo, 1905.

Monfrin, J. "Joinville et la prise de Damiette," *Académie des inscriptions et belles lettres,* minutes of 1976 meetings. Paris: Klincksieck, 1976.

Morelli, G. di P. *Ricordi,* ed. Vittorio Branca. Florence, 1956.

Mortet, Victor. *Recueil de textes relatifs à l'histoire de l'architecture et à la condition des architectes en France au Moyen Age.* Paris: Picard, 1911.

Le Moyen Age, volume in *Dictionnaire des lettres françaises.* Paris: Fayard, 1964.

Murner, Thomas. *Die Badefahrt, mit Erläuterungen über das altdeutsche Badwesen,* ed. Ernst Mart. Strasburg: J. H. E. Heitz, 1887.

Musset, Lucien. "L'aristocratie normande au XIe siècle," in P. Contamine, ed., *La Noblesse au Moyen Age.* Paris: Presses Universitaires de France, 1976.

Palmieri, Matteo. *Della vita civile.* Bologna, 1944.

Paolino Minorita. *Del reggimento della casa.* Perugia, 1860.

Paolo da Certaldo. *Libro di buoni costumi,* ed. Alfredo Schiaffini. Florence, 1945.

Paradiso degli Alberti, ritrovi e ragionamenti del 1389, romanza di Giovanni da Prato, ed. A. Wesselofsky. Bologna, 1867.

Pastoureau, M. "Et puis vint le bleu," *Europe, Le Moyen Age maintenant,* October 1983.

Payen, Jean-Charles. *Littérature française, le Moyen Age,* vol. 1. Paris: Arthaud, 1970.

Perosa, Alessandro. *Giovanni Rucellai e il suo zibaldone. I: Il Zibaldone quaresimale.* London: Warburg Institute, 1960.

"Per una storia delle dimore rurale," Proceedings of the Cuneo Colloquium, 8–9 December 1979, *Archeologia Medievale 7* (1980).

Perret, M. ". . . A la fin de sa vie ne fuz-je mie" (Joinville), *Revue des sciences humaines, Moyen Age flamboyant,* 1981–1983.

Pesez, J.-M. "Une maison villageoise au XIVe siècle: les structures," *Rotterdam Papers 2* (1975): 139–150.

———and F. Piponnier. "Les maisons fortes bourguignonnes," *Château-Gaillard 5* (1972): 143–164.

Piponnier, François. "Une maison villageoise au XIVe siècle: le mobilier," *Rotterdam Papers 2* (1975): 151–170.

Platina, Bartholomaeus. *L'Ottimo Cittadino,* ed. F. Battaglia. Bologna, 1940.

Poirion, Daniel. *Le Poète et le Prince. L'Evolution du lyrisme courtois de Guillaume de Machaut à Charles d'Orléans.* Paris: Presses Universitaires de France, 1965.

———"Le temps perdu et retrouvé . . . au XVe siècle," *Revue des sciences humaines, Moyen Age flamboyant,* 1981–1983.

Poirion, R. *Littérature française, le Moyen Age,* vol. 2. Paris: Arthaud, 1970.

Poly, Jean-Pierre, and E. Bournazel. *La Mutation*

féodale. Paris: Presses Universitaires de France, 1980.

Post, P. "Die französisch-niederländische Männertracht 1350–1475," unpub. diss. Halle, 1910.

Pouchelle, Marie-Christine. *Corps et Chirurgie à l'apogée du Moyen Age*. Paris: Flammarion, 1983.

Power, Eileen. *Medieval Women*, ed. M. M. Postan. Cambridge: Cambridge University Press, 1975.

La Prière au Moyen Age. Sénéfiance series, 10. Aix-en-Provence: CUERMA, 1981.

Quenedey, R. *L'Habitation rouennaise. Etudes d'histoire, de géographie et d'archéologie urbaines*. Rouen, 1926.

Ritter, Raymond. *Châteaux, donjons et places fortes. L'architecture militaire française*. Paris, 1953.

Roux, S. *La Maison dans l'histoire*. Paris: Albin Michel, 1976.

Sacchetti, Franco. *Il Trecentonovelle*, ed. Vincenzo Pernicone. Florence, 1946.

Salernitano, Masuccio. *Il Novellino*, ed. Alfredo Mauro. Bari, 1940.

Scheffler, W. "Die Porträts der deutschen Kaiser und Könige im späteren Mittelalter (1292–1519)," *Repertorium für Kunstwissenschaft*, 33, 1910.

Schiaparelli, A. *La Casa fiorentina e i suoi arredi nei secoli XIV e XV*. Florence: Sansoni, 1908.

Schultz, Alwin. *Deutsches Leben im 14. und 15. Jahrhundert*. Vienna: F. Tempsky, 1892.

Sercambi, Giovanni. *Novelle*, ed. Giovanni Sinicropi. Bari: Laterza, 1972.

Statuta communis Parmae, ab anno 1266 ad annum circiter 1304. Parma, 1867.

Strozzi, A. Macinghi. *Lettere di una gentildonna fiorentina del secolo XV ai figliuoli esuli*, ed. Cesare Guasti. Florence, 1877.

Suckale, R. "Uberlegungen zur Zeichenhaftigkeit mittelalterlicher Andachtsbilder," *Städelsches Jahrbuch* 6 (1977): 177–200.

Tamassia, N. *La Famiglia italiana nei secoli Decimoquinto e Decimosesto*. Milan, Palermo, and Naples, 1910; repr. Rome, 1971.

Toubert Pierre. *Les Structures du Latium médiéval*, 2 vols, Paris and Rome: Ecole Française de Rome, 1974.

———"La théorie du mariage chez les moralistes carolingiens," *Settimane di studio del Centro italiano di studi sull'alto medioevo*, XXIV, 1976: il matrimonio nella società altomedievale*. Spoleto, 1977, pp. 233–285.

Valous, Guy de. *Le Monachisme clunisien des origines au XVe siècle*, 2 vols. Paris: Picard, 1935.

Van de Walle, A. "Le château des comtes de Flandre à Gand: quelques problèmes archéologiques," *Château-Gaillard* 1 (1962): 163–169.

Vauchez, André. *La Spiritualité du Moyen Age occidental*. Paris: Presses Universitaires de France, 1975.

Velluti, D. *La Cronica domestica scrittatura il 1367 e il 1370, a cura di S. Del Limgo e G. Volpe*. Florence, 1914.

Vercauteren, F. "Une parentèle dans la France du Nord au XIe et XIIe siècle," *Le Moyen Age*, ser. 4, 19 (1963): 223–245.

Verde, A. *Lo Studio fiorentino (1473–1503), ricerche e documenti, III, 2. Studenti "fanciulli a scuola," 1480*. Pistoia, 1977.

Vogt, K. *Italienische Berichte aus dem spämittelalterlichen Deutschland, von Francesco Petrarca zu Andrea de' Franceschi (1333–1492)*, Kiler Historische Studien, 17. 1973.

Vogt, M. "Beiträge zur Geschichte der Visionenliteratur im Mittelalter," *Palaestra*, 146, 1924.

Waas, A. *Der Mensch im deutschen Mittelalter*. Cologne, 1964.

Warlop, Ernest. *The Flemish Nobility before 1300*. Courtrai: G. Desmet-Huysman, 1975.

Wood, Margaret. *The English Mediaeval House*. London: Phoenix House, 1965.

Zdekauer, Lodovico. *La Vita privata dei Senesi nel Dugento*. Siena: L. Lazzeri, 1896.

Zink, M. "Musique et subjectivité. Le passage de la chanson d'amour à la poésie personnelle au XIIIe siècle," *Cahiers de civilisation médiévale*, July–December 1982.

———*La Subjectivité littéraire autour du siècle de Saint Louis*. Paris: Presses Universitaires de France, 1985.

Zoepf, Ludwig. "Die Mystikerin Margaretha Ebner (1291–1351)," *Beiträge zur Kulturgeschichte des Mittelalters und der Renaissance*, 16. Leipzig and Berlin: Teubner, 1914.

Zoli, Andrea, ed. *Statuto del secolo XIII del commune di Ravenna*. Ravenna, 1904.

Credits

The sites and objects illustrated in this book (on the pages noted) are found in various locations, as follows: Abbey of Fontevraud, 46ab, 100; Accademia, Florence, 292; Accademia, Venice, 175, 187, 188, 194, 265, 290–291, 306–307, 546, 554; Accademia Carrara, Bergamo, 182a; Albertina, Vienna, 581; Antinori Palace, Florence, 177a; Archives of the Drôme, Valence, 31, 75, 426abc; Archives of Meurthe-et-Moselle, 151; Archives of the Nord, 150; Archives of Poitiers, 479; Arsenal Library, Paris, vi–vii, 108, 333a, 337, 372, 436, 438, 442, 443, 446, 464a, 468, 497, 516; Atger Museum, Montpellier, 423; Autun Library, 125; Auxterre Library, 90; Bamberg Cathedral, 506; Barberini Palace, Rome, 166; Bargello, Florence, 191ab, 539, 559; Dominique Barthélemy archives, 410b; Bayerische Staatsbibliothek, Munich, 333b; Bayeux Museum, 64–65; Bergues Library, 391a; Besançon Library, 80a; Bibliothèque Nationale, 36, 61, 86, 89, 103, 126b, 129, 152, 156, 202, 205, 213, 214, 243, 251, 260, 295, 314, 317, 318, 321, 322, 325, 327, 329, 330, 332, 345, 347, 348, 349, 351, 354, 361, 365, 366, 367, 369, 371, 374, 379, 380, 382, 383, 384, 385, 386, 391b, 392, 393, 394, 428, 429, 433, 434, 439, 464b, 472, 473, 474, 475, 480, 482, 493, 494, 496, 500, 504, 515, 518, 519, 522, 529, 544ab, 556, 570, 575, 577, 578b, 579, 582a, 589, 597, 598a, 599, 602, 603, 604ab, 605, 606, 607, 609, 614, 617a, 618; Bibliothèque Sainte-Geneviève, Paris, 52b, 69, 135; Biccherna Register, State Archives, Siena, 171; Bonnat Museum, Bayonne, 582b; Boulogne Library, facing p. 1, 32, 52a; Bourges Cathedral, 527a; British Library, London, 252; British Museum, London, 239, 586; Buoux, Vaucluse, 67ab; Caen Castle, 59; Cambrai Library, 47a, 335; Capodimonte Museum, Naples, 270; Castle Museum, Weimar, 567; Castel Sant'Angelo, Rome, 183; Center for Advanced Study of Medieval Civilization, Poitiers, 102; Chapel San Nicola, Tolentino, 305; Chartres Cathedral, 508; Château-Gaillard, Eure, 409; A. Chatelain, 400, 403, 406, 419; Charavines, Isère, 66, 73; Chevreuse, Yvelines, 406; Church of Aulnay, Charente-Maritime, 76; Church of the Carmine, Florence, 192a; Church of Saint-Donat, Drôme, 70; Church of Saint Mary in the Fields, Soest, 621; Church of Saint Priest, Volvic, 102; Cistercian Abbey, Santa Cruz, Spain, 43; Cluny Museum, Paris, 323, 415, 512b, 520, 527b, 578a, 583b, 624; Collegiate Church, San Gimignano, 267; Condé Museum, Chantilly, 140, 144, 341, 362, 381, 387, 495, 531, 590; Conques Abbey, 37; Phillipe Contamine archives, 484; Convent of Saint Francis, Assisi, 277, 530; Correr Museum, Venice, 298, 568; La Couvertoirade, Aveyron, 424; Davanzati Palace, Florence, 182b, 190, 192b, 195, 197, 203, 234, 241, 303; Dijon Library, 116, 131, 146abc, 324; Douai Library, 51; Doué-la-Fontaine, Maine-et-Loire, 398, 399, 401, 407; Dracy, Côte-d'Or, 512a; Georges Duby archives, 40; Ducal Palace, Mantua, 159; Duomo, Prato, 230, 266, 285, 304; Ecole des Beaux-Arts, Paris, 342; Escorial Library, Madrid, 81, 418; Ferrande Tower, Pernes-les-Fontaines, 2; Fountains Abbey, Yorkshire, 46c; Gemäldegalerie, Dresden, 286a, 563b; General Library, Liège, 364; Ghent, Flanders, 410; Giandonati Palace, Florence, 173; Gondi Palace, Florence, 177c, 181; Good Advice Castle, Trent, 572, 610; Göttingen Library, 119; Guinette Tower, Etampes, Essonne, 422; Houdan, Yvelines, 403; Issogne Castle, Val d'Aosta, 562b; Jena University Library, 114; Laboratory of Medieval Mediterranian Archeology, Aix-en-Provence, 57, 67ab, 414; Langeais, Indre-et-Loire, 402; Laon Library, 91, 130; Library of Carcassonne, 334; Library of Saint-Dié, 491; Library of Saint-Omer, 53; Loches, Indre-et-Loire, 419; Louvre, Paris, 222ab, 223, 283, 289a, 547, 564, 566a, 600 (Rothschild Collection), 612, 622; Marcienne Library, Venice, 594; Medici-Riccardi Palace, Florence, 176a, 227; Pierpont Morgan Library, New York, 34, 459; Munich Library, 82, 132, 137, 147; Municipal Library, Avignon, 476; Mussées d'Arles, 74; Museo Civico d'Arte Antica, Turin, 532; Museum of the Augustinians, Toulouse, 72, 78; Museum of Basel, 548, 580; Museum of Decorative Arts, Paris, 553; Museum of Leipzig, 601; Museum of the Opera del Duomo, Siena, 221b, 231, 626; National Archives, Paris, 435, 486; National Gallery, London, 253, 550, 569; National Gallery of Umbria, Perugia, 576; National Library, Vienna, 310, 312, 368, 375, 503; National Library of the University, Prague, 598b; Ognissanti, Florence, 617b; Oise Archives, 445; Oppenheimer Collection, London, 583a; Orléans Library, 80b; Palazzo Pubblico, Siena, 168, 169, 193, 242, 541; Petit Palais, Avignon, 246; Petit Palais, Paris, 431, 437, 467; Piazza Postierla, Siena, 174; Piccolomini Palace,

Pienza, Tuscany, 537; Pinachotek, Munich, 534, 549, 565, 566c, 611; Pinacoteca, Siena, 162, 623; Poblet Abbey, Spain, 45; Porgès Collection, Paris, 551; Prado, Madrid, 566b; Pretoria Palace, Certaldo, Tuscany, 538; Public Assistance Archives, Paris, 498; Restormel, Cornwall, 396; Rheims Library, 83; Rochester, Kent, 405; Royal Albert I Library, Brussels, 47b, 55, 79; Royal Library, Stockholm, 328, 523, 596; Rucellai Palace, Florence, 176b; Saint Guy's Cathedral, Prague, 560; Sainte-Geneviève Library, Paris, 492; Sainte-Richarde Church, Andlau, 149; San Gimignano Town Hall, 215, 232; San Martino dei Buonuomini, Florence, 284; San Matteo Hospital, Florence, 268; Sant'Agostino, Siena, 172, 185, 271, 280; Santa Croce, Florence, 186; Santa Maria del Fiore, 542; Santa Maria Novella, Florence, 218, 299, 309, 552; Santa Trinità, Sassetti Chapel, Florence, 160, 279; Schifanoia Palace, 287; School of Fine Arts, Paris, 571, 584; Sclafani Palace, Palermo, 628; Scrovegni Chapel, Padua, 273, 274, 275, 308; Scuola di San Giorgio degli Schiavoni, Venice, 179, 217, 286b; Soussey, Côte-d'Or, 412; Staatkunstinstitut, Frankfurt-on-Main, 196; Staatliche Museen Preussischer Kulturbesitz, Berlin, 184, 216, 221a, 248, 249, 540, 543b, 620; State Archives, Siena, 171, 250, 543; State & University Library, Göttingen, 118; Stifsbibliothek, Saint Gall, 39; Strozzi Palace, Florence, 177b, 180; Thyssen-Boinemisza Collection, Lugano, 573; Tomb of Saint Lazarus, Autun, 513; Trivulziana Library, Milan, 289b; Troyes Library, 44, 48, 49, 50, 54; Turin National Library, 326, 338; Uffizi, Florence, 164, 257, 269; University Library, Ghent, 558; Unterlinden Museum, Colmar, 616; Valenciennes Museum, 563a; Vatican Museum, Rome, 206; Vicar's Palace, Pescia, 235; Vienna Archives, 478; Villy-le-Moutier, Côte-d'Or, 413; White Palace, Genoa, 557; Windsheim Triptych, Heidelberg, 627.

Photographs were supplied by the following agencies and individuals: Aerofilms, London, 394; R. Agache, 42, 58; J. P. Anders, 184, 216, 221a, 248, 249, 540, 543b, 620; Anderson-Viollet, 257, 268, 569; Bildarchiv Foto, Marburg, 76, 82, 114, 132, 137, 147; Bulloz, 64–65, 368, 434, 467, 486, 571, 589, 616; CAHMGI, Grenoble, 66, 70, 73; CNMH/SPADEM, 46b (J. Feuillie), 52a (J. Feuillie), 53, 86, 100, 149 (Lefevre-Pontalis), 402, 508; CRAM, Caen, 59, 398, 399, 401, 407; K. J. Conant, 40; G. Dagli Orti, 91, 130, 159, 162, 168, 169, 171, 193, 242, 250, 305, 326, 330, 338, 341, 362, 381, 418, 423, 523, 537, 538, 539, 541, 543b, 554, 559ab, 565, 566ab,

572, 576, 594, 596, 598c, 610, 623, 626; EHESS, 455, 456, 512; F. Garnier, facing p. 1, 32, 52, 69, 135, 140, 144, 492, 495, 531; Giraudon, 222, 298, 312, 321, 323, 333a, 337, 342, 375, Alinari-Giraudon, 172, 174, 176a, 178, 180, 182b, 185, 186, 187, 189, 191ab, 215, 218, 229, 232, 266, 271, 285, 286, 291, 530, 542, 562a, 563b, 617b, Anderson-Giraudon, 2, 166, 175, 177bc, 179, 181, 182a, 183, 188, 194, 217, 221b, 227, 231, 239, 253, 265, 267, 270, 273, 274, 275, 277, 280, 287, 292, 304, 306–307, 308, 546, 552, 554, 586, 628, Bridgeman-Giraudon, 252, 601, Brogi-Giraudon, 176ab, Bruckmann-Giraudon, 534, 550, 621, CFL, 347, 375, 387, 461b, 494, 498, 501, 506, 520ab, 524, 526, 527, 549, 551, 562b, 563a, 564ab, 568, 581, 583a, 584, 611, 612, Hanfstaengl-Giraudon, 550, Lauros-Giraudon, 582b, 627; R. Goguey, Dijon, 413; M. Langrognet, 173, 189, 190, 192b, 195, 197, 200, 234, 235, 303; MAS, Barcelona, 81; A. Maulny, 479; J. M. Pesez & F. Piponnier, 414; Rapho/J. M. Charles, 409; E. Renno, 567; Réunion des Musées nationaux, Paris, 222b, 223, 246, 283, 289a, 323, 412, 512b, 547, 578a, 583, 622, 624; Roger-Viollet, 309, 461a, 462, 566c, 600; J. Roubier, 37, 46c, 405, 410a, 513, 527a; G. Saint-Yrieix, 412; Scala, Florence, 160, 161, 164, 192a, 203, 206, 230, 241, 269, 279, 284, 286b; Seuil Archives, 424, 435, 472, 473, 474, 475, 482, 486, 544a, 557, 560, 604ab, 605, 606, 607, 609; Studio M. Delcroix, 335; J. Vigne, 391, 491; YAN, 72, 78, 440; Zodiaque, 43, 45, 46c, 483.

Credits for color plates, in order of appearance are: Condé Museum, Chantilly, Giraudon; Escorial Library, Madrid, G. Dagli Orti; Escorial Library, Madrid, Giraudon; Escorial Library, Madrid, G. Dagli Orti; Chapel of the Annunciation, Duomo, Prato, Scala; Ducal Palace, Mantua, G. Dagli Orti; Baptistry of Saint John, Urbino, G. Dagli Orti; National Gallery of Umbria, G. Dagli Orti; Condé Museum, Chantilly, G. Dagli Orti; Condé Museum, Chantilly, Giraudon; Conde Museum, Chantilly, G. Dagli Orti; British Museum, London, Edimédia © Archives Snark; San Nicola Chapel, Tolentino, G. Dagli Orti; Fine Arts Museum, Strasbourg, G. Dagli Orti; San Carlos Museum, Mexico City, G. Dagli Orti; National Gallery of Umbria, Perugia, G. Dagli Orti.

The authors and editors wish to express their gratitude to Michel de Boüard, Michel Fixot, and Jean-Marie Pesez, who generously provided invaluable documents.

Index